by Andrew Barbour

The complete guide, thoroughly up-to-date

Packed with details that will make your trip

The must-see sights, off and on the beaten path

What to see, what to skip

Mix-and-match vacation itineraries

City strolls, countryside adventures

Smart lodging and dining options

Essential local do's and taboos

Transportation tips, distances and directions

Key contacts, savvy travel tips

When to go, what to pack

Clear, accurate, easy-to-use maps

Books to read, videos to watch, background essays

Fodor's Travel Publications, Inc.
New York • Toronto • London • Sydney • Auckland
www.fodors.com/

Fodor's South Africa

EDITOR: Stephen Wolf

Editorial Contributors: Rob Andrews, Robert Blake, David Brown, Karen Cure, Sue Derwent, Sylvia Gill, Caroline Haberfeld, Phyllis Hands, Anto Howard, Bronwyn Howard, Christina Knight, Pat Kossuth, Carol Lazar, David Low, Michael McKeown, June Muchemenyi, Louise Orlando, Beverley Bernstone Pender, Tony Pinchuck, Myrna Robins, Heidi Sarna, Helayne Schiff, M.T. Schwartzman (Gold Guide editor), Dinah A. Spritzer, Raymond Travers, Kate Turkington

Editorial Production: Linda K. Schmidt

Maps: David Lindroth, *cartographer*; Steven Amsterdam, *map editor*

Design: Fabrizio La Rocca, *creative director*; Guido Caroti, *associate art director*; Jolie Novak, *photo editor*

Production/Manufacturing: Rebecca Zeiler

Cover Photograph: Peter Guttman

Copyright

Special Sales

CONTENTS

Maps

ON THE ROAD WITH FODOR'S

WE'RE ALWAYS THRILLED to get letters from readers, especially one like this:

It took us an hour to decide what book to buy and we now know we picked the best one. Your book was wonderful, easy to follow, very accurate, and good on pointing out eating places, informal as well as formal. When we saw other people using your book, we would look at each other and smile.

Our editors and writers are deeply committed to making every Fodor's guide "the best one"—not only accurate but always charming, brimming with sound recommendations and solid ideas, right on the mark in describing restaurants and hotels, and full of fascinating facts that make you view what you've traveled to see in a rich new light.

About Our Writers

Our success in achieving our goals—and in helping to make your trip the best of all possible vacations—is a credit to the hard work of our extraordinary writers.

Andrew Barbour took the scenic route back to his native South Africa, driving a battered 1960 Land Rover from London to Cape Town with his wife. On their one-year trek, they braved malaria, amoebic dysentery, and a bizarre bovine disease while stopping frequently to retrieve parts of their car that had fallen off. The trip was a sabbatical for Andrew after having worked at Fodor's since 1989, when he joined the company as an editor, tackling books that covered all corners of the earth.

Phyllis Hands, retired principal of the Cape Wine Academy, is one of South Africa's foremost wine experts. A delightful raconteur and much loved figure in the Winelands, she is the author of *South African Wine,* an encyclopedic study of wine making in South Africa. Phyllis recently launched her own wine consulting business.

Bronwyn Howard, who wrote our new Swaziland chapter, is a freelance journalist and marketing consultant, writing articles about nearly anything connected with the great outdoors. Having lived and worked in Johannesburg for most of her life, Bronwyn, like many city dwellers with a yen for the outdoors, likes nothing better than to don a pair of hiking boots and head for the hills whenever she has some spare time.

Carol Lazar, Travel Editor of South Africa's *Saturday Star* and the *Sunday Independent,* is one of the country's top travel writers. Author, humor columnist, and travel writer, she has appeared on TV and radio.

Zimbabwean **Michael McKeown,** after working in various parts of Africa, began his writing career in Greece, which provided the impetus for a book on Crete and its people. He is now a regional editor for the quarterly *Impressions of Africa.* As a freelance writer he specializes in history, wildlife, and conservation issues. He wrote the bulk of our new Zimbabwe chapter.

June Muchemenyi is News Editor for the monthly *Africa Travel News,* based in Harare, and writes on tourism issues in Southern Africa. She contributed the introduction and the Harare section of our new Zimbabwe chapter.

Born and educated in South Africa, **Tony Pinchuck** left his home turf for London in 1979 after completing a degree in African politics. Over the last decade he has undertaken several comprehensive expeditions back to Southern Africa, which have resulted in his writing two guidebooks and numerous pieces for European publications.

Myrna Robins, who writes for the *Cape Argus* newspaper, has repeatedly been voted South Africa's best food writer. Author of several cookbooks on the Cape's vibrant cuisine, including *Cape Flavour— A Guide to Historic Restaurants of the Cape,* she lives in the shadow of Table Mountain and spends her weekends in the exquisite hamlet of MacGregor, in the Riviersonderend Mountains.

South African born and bred journalist **Raymond Travers** lives in Nelspruit, the capital of Mpumalanga. He has written for South African Airway's in-flight magazine and now has a beat for the *Lowvelder,* a Nelspruit paper that covers the Lowveld area around Kruger National Park. When he's not sitting behind the keyboard, you'll find him flying planes, taking in the Kruger Park, or enjoying a few cold ones at a neighborhood pub.

Kate Turkington, who has been travelling since age four, is a South African journalist and broadcaster. She is Managing Editor of *Marung* and *Flamingo,* the in-flight magazines for Air Botswana and Air Namibia. She has waltzed at dawn with a Chinese dance instructor in a Beijing Square, fallen over an Emperor penguin in Antarctica, stood at the bottom of a rainbow in Ireland, been winched over a raging river 9,000 ft up in the Andes in Peru, and heard the stars sing in the Kalahari Desert. Kate wrote the new Botswana chapter for this edition.

Many, many thanks go to Diane Ebzery of African Portfolio, who arranged and sponsored the editorial reconnaissance trip that led to the addition of Swaziland, Zimbabwe, and Botswana to this second edition of our *South Africa* guide; Jean Hawtayne and Liz Rawlins of Satour in Pretoria, who assisted with the South African leg of the trip; and South African Airways, Air Zimbabwe, and Zimbabwe Express for their kind sponsorship of the trip. Thanks also to Sylvia Gill, a freelance writer and public relations expert who is a font of knowledge about South Africa's rapidly changing tourism scene.

New This Year

We couldn't be happier to announce that our team of writers has added three entire countries to our book this year: the tiny kingdom of Swaziland on the Mozambique border and the friendly, fascinating, and wildlife-rich countries of Zimbabwe and Botswana. This is part of a long range plan to cover all of Southern Africa in our next edition, when we will add Namibia, Zambia, and Mozambique.

We're also proud to announce that the American Society of Travel Agents has endorsed Fodor's as its guidebook of choice. ASTA is the world's largest and most influential travel trade association, operating in more than 170 countries, with 27,000 members pledged to adhere to a strict code of ethics reflecting the Society's motto, "Integrity in Travel." ASTA shares Fodor's devotion to providing smart, honest travel information and advice to travelers, and we've long recommended that our readers consult ASTA member agents for the experience and professionalism they bring to the table.

On the Web, check out Fodor's site (www.fodors.com/) for information on major destinations around the world and travel-savvy interactive features. The Web site also lists the 85-plus radio stations nationwide that carry *Fodor's Travel Show,* a live call-in program that airs every weekend. Tune in to hear guests discuss their wonderful adventures—or call in to get answers for your most pressing travel questions.

How to Use This Book

Organization

Up front is the **Gold Guide,** an easy-to-use section divided alphabetically by topic. Under each listing you'll find tips and information that will help you accomplish what you need to in Southern Africa. You'll also find addresses and telephone numbers of organizations and companies that offer destination-related services and detailed information and publications.

The first chapter in the guide, Destination: South Africa helps get you in the mood for your trip. New and Noteworthy cues you in on trends and happenings, What's Where gets you oriented, Pleasures and Pastimes describes the activities and sights that really make Southern Africa unique, Fodor's Choice showcases our top picks, and Festivals and Seasonal Events alerts you to special events you'll want to seek out.

Chapters in *Fodor's South Africa* are arranged in the way that most travelers move around the country and the region from there. Each city chapter begins with an Exploring section subdivided by neighborhood; each subsection recommends a walking or driving tour and lists sights in alphabetical order. Each regional chapter is divided by geographical area; within each area, towns are covered in logical geographical order, and attractive stretches of road and minor points of interest between them are indicated by the designation *En Route.* Throughout, Off the Beaten Path sights appear after the places from which they are most easily accessible. And within town sections, all restaurants and lodgings are grouped together.

To help you decide what to visit in the time you have, all chapters begin with recommended itineraries; you can mix and match those from several chapters to create a complete vacation. The A-to-Z section that ends all chapters covers getting there and getting around. It also provides helpful contacts and resources.

At the end of the book you'll find Portraits, wonderful essays about seeing wildlife, about personal and political issues in South Africa, and about Zimbabwe's history, followed by suggestions for any pre-trip research you want to do, from recommended reading to movies on tape with South Africa as a backdrop.

Icons and Symbols

★ Our special recommendations
✕ Restaurant
🏠 Lodging establishment
✕🏠 Lodging establishment whose restaurant warrants a special trip
🐤 Good for kids (rubber duckie)
☞ Sends you to another section of the guide for more information
✉ Address
☎ Telephone number
🕐 Opening and closing times
💲 Admission prices (those we give apply to adults; substantially reduced fees are almost always available for children, students, and senior citizens)

Numbers in white and black circles that appear on the maps, in the margins, and within the tours correspond to one another.

Dining and Lodging

The restaurants and lodgings we list are the cream of the crop in each price range. Price categories within South Africa are as follows (in Swaziland, Zimbabwe, and Botswana, price charts appear in the Pleasures and Pastimes sections of the chapters):

For restaurants:

CHART 1

CATEGORY	COST*
$$$$	over R80
$$$	R60–R80
$$	R40–R60
$	under R40

*Rates are per person, excluding drinks and service.

For hotels:

CHART 2

CATEGORY	(A) COST* CHAPTERS 2, 4, 5, & 7	(B) COST* CHAPTERS 3 & 6
$$$$	over R600	over R750
$$$	R400–R600	R500–R750
$$	R250–R400	R250–R500
$	under R250	under R250

*Rates are for a double room, including VAT and Tourism Promotion Levies. The cost may also include breakfast and dinner.

Hotel Facilities

We always list the facilities that are available—but we don't specify whether they cost extra: When pricing accommodations, always ask what's included. In addition, assume that all rooms have private baths unless otherwise noted.

Restaurant Reservations and Dress Codes

Reservations are always a good idea; we note only when they're essential or when they are not accepted. Book as far ahead as you can, and reconfirm when you get to town. Unless otherwise noted, the restaurants listed are open daily for lunch and dinner. We mention dress only when men are required to wear a jacket or a jacket and tie. Look for an overview of local habits in the Gold Guide.

Credit Cards

The following abbreviations are used: **AE**, American Express; **DC**, Diners Club; **MC**, MasterCard; and **V**, Visa.

Don't Forget to Write

You can use this book in the confidence that all prices and opening times are based on information supplied to us at press time; Fodor's cannot accept responsibility for any errors. Time inevitably brings changes, so always confirm information when it matters—especially if you're making a detour to visit a specific place. In addition, when making reservations be sure to mention if you have a disability or are traveling with children, if you prefer a private bath or a certain type of bed, or if you have specific dietary needs or other concerns.

Were the restaurants we recommended as described? Did our hotel picks exceed your expectations? Did you find a museum we recommended a waste of time? If you have complaints, we'll look into them and revise our entries when the facts warrant it. If you've discovered a special place that we haven't included, we'll pass the information along to our correspondents and have them check it out. So send us your feedback, positive *and* negative: email us at editors@fodors.com (specifying the name of the book on the subject line) or write the South Africa editor at Fodor's, 201 East 50th Street, New York, New York 10022. Have a wonderful trip!

Karen Cure
Editorial Director

Southern Africa

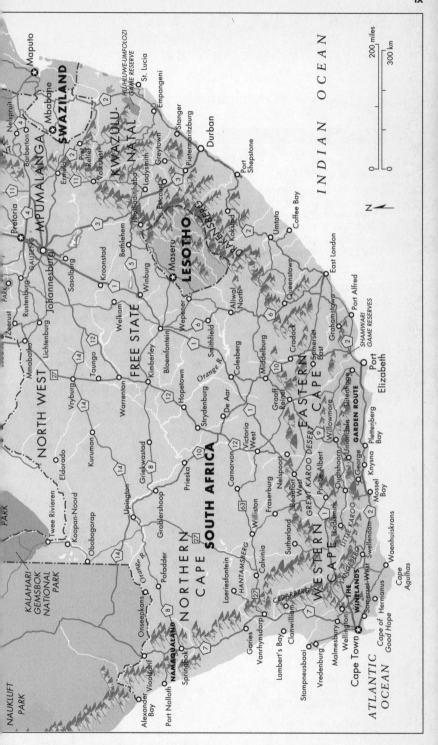

SMART TRAVEL TIPS A TO Z

Basic Information on Traveling in South Africa, Savvy Tips to Make Your Trip a Breeze, and Companies and Organizations to Contact

A

AIR TRAVEL

TO SOUTH AFRICA

South Africa's major airports are Johannesburg, Cape Town, and, to a lesser extent, Durban. Flying time from Miami to Cape Town is 14 hours; from New York, the flight takes 15 hours. The return from Johannesburg will take 18 hours if it stops at Isla do Sal for refuelling. The London–Johannesburg flight lasts about 12 hours.

South African Airways flies nonstop from New York (JFK) to Johannesburg and from Miami to Cape Town. Other carriers from the United States connect through Europe or Africa and have cheaper fares. The options from Europe include most European national airlines.

TO ZIMBABWE AND BOTSWANA

To get to Zimbabwe and Botswana from the United States, you must connect through Johannesburg (on South African Airways) or a European city (on Air Zimbabwe or a European carrier). Air Zimbabwe flies from London and Frankfurt nonstop to Harare. British Air, Air France, KLM, and Lufthansa fly from European cities to Harare. Air Botswana has two weekly flights from London to Gaborone; otherwise, connect into Botswana through Johannesburg or Harare.

The international gateways to Zimbabwe are Harare (the capital) and Victoria Falls. In Botswana, the cities are Gaborone (the capital), Maun (near the Okavango Delta), and Kasane (near Chobe National Park).

MAJOR AIRLINE OR LOW-COST CARRIER?

Most people choose a flight based on price. Yet there are other issues to consider. Major airlines offer the greatest number of departures; smaller airlines—including regional, low-cost and no-frill airlines—usually have a more limited number of flights daily. Major airlines have frequent-flyer partners, which allow you to credit mileage earned on one airline to your account with another. Low-cost airlines offer a definite price advantage and fewer restrictions, such as advance-purchase requirements. Safety-wise, low-cost carriers as a group have a good history, but **check the safety record before booking** any low-cost carrier; call the Federal Aviation Administration's Consumer Hotline (☞ Airline Complaints, *below*).

➤ FROM THE UNITED STATES: **Air Zimbabwe** (☎ 212/980–8010). **Alitalia** (☎ 800/223–5730). **Egypt Air** (☎ 212/315–0900). **South African Airways** (☎ 800/722–9675).

➤ FROM THE U.K.: **Air Zimbabwe** (☎ 0171/491–3783). **Botswana Air** (☎ 0171/757–2737). **British Airways** (☎ 0181/897–4000). **South African Airways** (☎ 0171/312–5000).

➤ WITHIN SOUTH AFRICA: Four major domestic airlines serve the country's nine principal airports (numbers are for Johannesburg offices): **British Airways operating as Comair** (☎ 011/921–0222). **Metavia Airlines** (☎ 011/394—3780). **South African Airways** and its commuter airline, **SA Airlink,** (☎ 011/356–1111). **Sun Air** (☎ 011/397–2244).

➤ WITHIN ZIMBABWE: **Air Zimbabwe** (☎ 14/575–111). **Zimbabwe Express** (☎ 14/705–266 or 14/705–923).

➤ WITHIN BOTSWANA: **Air Botswana** (Gaborone: ☎ 351–921).

GET THE LOWEST FARE

The least-expensive airfares to South Africa are priced for round-trip travel. Major airlines usually require that you **book far in advance** and stay no more than 30 to get the lowest fares. Ask about "ultrasaver" fares, which are the cheapest; they must be booked 90 days in advance and are nonrefundable. A little more expensive are "supersaver" fares, which require only a 30-day advance purchase. Remember that penalties for refunds or scheduling changes are stiffer for international tickets, usually about $150. International flights are also sensitive to the season: **plan to fly in the off season** for the cheapest fares. If your destination or home city has more than one gateway, **compare prices to and from different airports.** Also price flights scheduled for off-peak hours, which may be significantly less expensive.

To save money on flights from the United Kingdom and back, **look into an APEX or Super-PEX ticket.** APEX tickets must be booked in advance and have certain restrictions. Super-PEX tickets can be purchased at the airport on the day of departure— subject to availability.

DON'T STOP UNLESS YOU MUST

When you book, **look for nonstop flights** and **remember that "direct" flights stop at least once.** International flights on a country's flag carrier are almost always nonstop; U.S. airlines often fly direct. Try to **avoid connecting flights,** which require a change of plane. Two airlines may jointly operate a connecting flight, so ask if your airline operates every segment—you may find that your preferred carrier flies you only part of the way.

USE AN AGENT

Travel agents, especially those who specialize in finding the lowest fares (☞ Discounts & Deals, *below*), can be especially helpful when booking a plane ticket. When you're quoted a price, **ask your agent if the price is likely to get any lower.** Good agents know the seasonal fluctuations of airfares and can usually anticipate a sale or fare war. However, waiting can be risky: The fare could go *up* as seats become scarce, and you may wait so long that your preferred flight sells out. A wait-and-see strategy works best if your plans are flexible, but if you must arrive and depart on certain dates, don't delay.

CHECK WITH CONSOLIDATORS

Consolidators buy tickets for scheduled flights at reduced rates from the airlines then sell them at prices that beat the best fare available directly from the airlines, usually without advance restrictions. Sometimes you can even get your money back if you need to return the ticket. Carefully read the fine print detailing penalties for changes and cancellations, and **confirm your consolidator reservation with the airline.**

➤ CONSOLIDATORS: **United States Air Consolidators Association** (✉ 925 L St., Suite 220, Sacramento, CA 95814, ☎ 916/441–4166, ℻ 916/441–3520).

TRAVEL PASSES

South African Airways' **African Explorer** pass allows you to travel within the country, between 4 and 8 legs, at a discount. Itineraries must be specified in advance, and the pass must be purchased in conjunction with an international ticket. You can however change the travel days on your itinerary without penalty, provided seats are available. The pass is valid for one month's travel.

Airlines routinely overbook planes, knowing that not everyone with a ticket will show up, but sometimes everyone does. When that happens, airlines ask for volunteers to give up their seats. In return these volunteers usually get a certificate for a free flight and are rebooked on the next flight out. If there are not enough volunteers the airline must choose who will be denied boarding. The first to get bumped are passengers who checked in late and those flying on discounted tickets, **so get to the gate and check in as early as possible,** especially during peak periods.

Always **bring a photo ID to the airport.** You may be asked to show it before you are allowed to check in.

ENJOY THE FLIGHT

For better service, **fly smaller or regional carriers,** which often have higher passenger-satisfaction ratings. Sometimes you'll find leather seats, more legroom, and better food.

For more legroom, **request an emergency-aisle seat**; don't however, sit in the row in front of the emergency aisle or in front of a bulkhead, where seats may not recline.

THE GOLD GUIDE / SMART TRAVEL TIPS

If you don't like airline food, **ask for special meals when booking.** These can be vegetarian, low-cholesterol, or kosher, for example.

Some international carriers still allow smoking on their flights, so **contact your carrier regarding its smoking policy** if the issue is important to you.

COMPLAIN IF NECESSARY

If your baggage goes astray or your flight goes awry, complain right away. Most carriers require that you file a claim immediately.

➤ AIRLINE COMPLAINTS: U.S. Department of Transportation **Aviation Consumer Protection Division** (✉ C-75, Room 4107, Washington, DC 20590, ☎ 202/366–2220). **Federal Aviation Administration (FAA) Consumer Hotline** (☎ 800/322–7873).

AIRPORTS

➤ AIRPORT INFORMATION: For listings of major airline numbers within South Africa, Zimbabwe, and Botswana, *see* the A to Z sections *in* Chapters 2, 9, and 10, respectively.

Johannesburg International Airport (☎ 011/975–9963) lies 19 km (12 mi) from the city. Most international flights arrive and depart at this airport. The airport has a tourist information desk, a VAT refund office, and a computerized accommodation service. Several international flights departing from Cape Town are also routed via Johannesburg.

Harare International Airport (☎ 14/575–528) is 15 km (9 mi) south of the city center.

Botswana's **Sir Seretse Khama Airport** (☎ 314–518) is 15 km (9 mi) north of Gaborone.

B

BUS TRAVEL

Greyhound and **Translux Express** operate extensive bus networks that serve all major cities in the South Africa. In the Cape provinces, **Intercape Mainliner** offers the most comprehensive service. For information on bus travel in Zimbabwe and Botswana *see* the A to Z sections *in* Chapters 9 and 10.

➤ BUS COMPANIES: **Greyhound** (Johannesburg office, ☎ 011/333–3671 or 839–3037). **Intercape Mainliner** (Cape Town office, ☎ 021/386–4400). **Translux Express** (Johannesburg office, ☎ 011/774–3333)

PASSES

Translux Express sells a variety of Lux Passes that allow pass holders to travel anywhere on the Translux route network within a predetermined number of days.

C

CAMERAS, CAMCORDERS, & COMPUTERS

Always **keep your film, tape, or computer disks out of the sun.** Carry an extra supply of batteries, and **be prepared to turn on your camera, camcorder, or laptop** to prove to security personnel that the device is real. Always **ask for hand inspection of film,** which becomes clouded after successive exposure to airport X-ray machines, and **keep videotapes and computer disks away from metal detectors.**

➤ PHOTO HELP: **Kodak Information Center** (☎ 800/242–2424). *Kodak Guide to Shooting Great Travel Pictures,* available in bookstores or from Fodor's Travel Publications (☎ 800/533–6478; $16.50 plus $4 shipping).

CUSTOMS

Before departing, **register your foreign-made camera or laptop with U.S. Customs** (☞ Customs & Duties, *below*). If your equipment is U.S.-made, call the consulate of the country you'll be visiting to find out whether the device should be registered with local customs upon arrival.

CAR RENTAL

Rates in South Africa begin at $20 per day and 20¢ per kilometer (about 30¢ per mile) for an economy car. You must rent for a minimum of three days to qualify for a free 200-km daily allowance. Rates for rentals of 3 to 7 days range from $40 to $60 a day, including 14% Value Added Tax (VAT). For car rental information in Zimbabwe and Botswana *see* the A to Z sections *in* Chapters 9 and 10.

➤ MAJOR AGENCIES: **Avis** (☎ 800/331–1084, 800/879–2847 in Canada). **Budget** (☎ 800/527–0700, 0800/181181 in the U.K.). **Hertz,** known as **Imperial Car Hire** in South Africa (☎ 800/654–3001, 800/263–0600 in Canada, 0345/555–888 in the U.K.).

CUT COSTS

To get the best deal, **book through a travel agent who is willing to shop around.**

Also **ask your travel agent about a company's customer-service record.** How has it responded to late plane arrivals and vehicle mishaps? Are there often lines at the rental counter, and, if you're traveling during a holiday period, does a confirmed reservation guarantee you a car?

Be sure to **look into wholesalers,** companies that do not own fleets but rent in bulk from those that do and often offer better rates than traditional car-rental operations. Prices are best during off-peak periods. Rentals booked through wholesalers must be paid for before you leave the United States.

➤ RENTAL WHOLESALERS: **Auto Europe** (☎ 207/842–2000 or 800/223–5555, FAX 800/235–6321). The **Kemwel Group** (☎ 914/835–5555 or 800/678–0678, FAX 914/835–5126).

NEED INSURANCE?

When driving a rented car you are generally responsible for any damage to or loss of the vehicle. You also are liable for any property damage or personal injury that you may cause while driving. Before you rent, **see what coverage you already have** under the terms of your personal auto-insurance policy and credit cards.

BEWARE SURCHARGES

Before you pick up a car in one city and leave it in another, **ask about drop-off charges or one-way service fees,** which can be substantial. Note, too, that some rental agencies charge extra if you return the car before the time specified on your contract. To avoid a hefty refueling fee, **fill the tank just before you turn in the car,** but be aware that gas stations near the rental outlet may overcharge.

MEET THE REQUIREMENTS

To rent a car, you must be over 25 years old and have a minimum of five years' driving experience. In South Africa your own driver's license is acceptable. An International Driver's Permit is a good idea; it's available from the American or Canadian automobile association, or, in the United Kingdom, from the Automobile Association or Royal Automobile Club.

CHILDREN & TRAVEL

Be sure to plan ahead and **involve your youngsters** as you outline your trip. When packing, include things to keep them busy en route. On sightseeing days try to schedule activities of special interest to your children. If you are renting a car don't forget to **arrange for a car seat** when you reserve.

LODGING

Many of South Africa's luxury lodges and private game reserves do not accept children under 10 or 12 without prior arrangement, and many other hotels require children to eat dinner at a separate, earlier seating.

➤ BEST CHOICES: **Southern Sun** (☎ 011/482–3500), the giant hotel group that operates Southern Sun and **Holiday Inn** properties throughout the country, and **Karos Hotels** (☎ 011/484–1641), allow children under 18 to stay free when accompanied by a parent.

FLYING

As a general rule, infants under two not occupying a seat fly at greatly reduced fares and occasionally for free. If your children are two or older **ask about children's airfares.**

In general the adult baggage allowance applies to children paying half or more of the adult fare. When booking, **ask about carry-on allowances for those traveling with infants.** In general, for babies charged 10% of the adult fare you are allowed one carry-on bag and a collapsible stroller, which may have to be checked; you may be limited to less if the flight is full.

According to the FAA it's a good idea to use safety seats aloft for children weighing less than 40 pounds. Airlines, however, can set their own policies: U.S. carriers allow FAA-approved models but usually require that you buy a ticket, even if your child would otherwise ride free, since the seats must be strapped into regu-

THE GOLD GUIDE / SMART TRAVEL TIPS

lar seats. Airline rules vary regarding their use, so it's important to **check your airline's policy about using safety seats during takeoff and landing.** Safety seats cannot obstruct any of the other passengers in the row, so get an appropriate seat assignment as early as possible.

When making your reservation, **request children's meals or a free-standing bassinet** if you need them; the latter are available only to those seated at the bulkhead, where there's enough legroom. Remember, however, that bulkhead seats may not have their own overhead bins, and there's no storage space in front of you—a major inconvenience.

GROUP TRAVEL

If you're planning to take your kids on a tour, look for companies that specialize in family travel.

➤ FAMILY-FRIENDLY TOUR OPERATORS: **Rascals in Paradise** (✉ 650 5th St., Suite 505, San Francisco, CA 94107, ☎ 415/978–9800 or 800/872–7225, FAX 415/442–0289).

CONSUMER PROTECTION

Whenever possible, **pay with a major credit card** so you can cancel payment if there's a problem, provided that you can provide documentation. This is a good practice whether you're buying travel arrangements before your trip or shopping at your destination.

If you're doing business with a particular company for the first time, **contact your local Better Business Bureau and the attorney general's offices** in your state and the company's home state, as well. Have any complaints been filed?

Finally, if you're buying a package or tour, always **consider travel insurance** that includes default coverage (☞ Insurance, *above*).

➤ LOCAL BBBs: **Council of Better Business Bureaus** (✉ 4200 Wilson Blvd., Suite 800, Arlington, VA 22203, ☎ 703/276–0100, FAX 703/525–8277).

CUSTOMS & DUTIES

When shopping, **keep receipts** for all of your purchases. Upon reentering the country, **be ready to show cus-**

toms officials what you've bought. If you feel a duty is incorrect, appeal the assessment. If you object to the way your clearance was handled, get the inspector's badge number. In either case, first ask to see a supervisor, then write to the port director at the address listed on your receipt. Send a copy of the receipt and other appropriate documentation. If you still don't get satisfaction you can take your case to customs headquarters in Washington.

ENTERING SOUTH AFRICA

Visitors over 18 years of age may bring in duty-free gifts and souvenirs to the total value of R500 (about $140), plus 400 cigarettes, 50 cigars, 250 grams of tobacco, 2 liters of wine, 1 liter of other alcoholic beverages, 50 milliliters of perfume, and 250 milliliters of toilet water.

ENTERING THE U.S.

You may bring home $400 worth of foreign goods duty-free if you've been out of the country for at least 48 hours and haven't already used the $400 allowance or any part of it in the past 30 days.

Travelers 21 and older may bring back 1 liter of alcohol duty-free. In addition, regardless of your age, you are allowed 200 cigarettes and 100 non-Cuban cigars. (At press time a federal rule restricting tobacco access to persons 18 years and older did not apply to importation.) Antiques, which the U.S. Customs Service defines as objects more than 100 years old, enter duty-free, as do original works of art done entirely by hand, including paintings, drawings, and sculptures.

You may also send packages home duty-free: up to $200 worth of goods for personal use, with a limit of one parcel per addressee per day (and no alcohol or tobacco products or perfume worth more than $5); label the package PERSONAL USE, and attach a list of its contents and their retail value. Do not label the package UNSOLICITED GIFT, or your duty-free exemption will drop to $100. Mailed items do not affect your duty-free allowance on your return.

➤ INFORMATION: **U.S. Customs Service** (Inquiries, ✉ Box 7407, Washington, DC 20044, ☎ 202/927–6724; complaints, Office of Regulations and Rulings, 1301 Constitution Ave. NW, Washington, DC 20229; registration of equipment, ✉ Resource Management, 1301 Constitution Ave. NW, Washington, DC 20229, ☎ 202/927–0540).

ENTERING CANADA

If you've been out of Canada for at least seven days you may bring in C$500 worth of goods duty-free. If you've been away for fewer than seven days but more than 48 hours, the duty-free allowance drops to C$200; if your trip lasts 24–48 hours, the allowance is C$50. You may not pool allowances with family members. Goods claimed under the C$500 exemption may follow you by mail; those claimed under the lesser exemptions must accompany you.

Alcohol and tobacco products may be included in the seven-day and 48-hour exemptions but not in the 24-hour exemption. If you meet the age requirements of the province or territory through which you reenter Canada you may bring in, duty-free, 1.14 liters (40 imperial ounces) of wine or liquor *or* 24 12-ounce cans or bottles of beer or ale. If you are 16 or older you may bring in, duty-free, 200 cigarettes and 50 cigars; these items must accompany you.

You may send an unlimited number of gifts worth up to C$60 each duty-free to Canada. Label the package UNSOLICITED GIFT—VALUE UNDER $60. Alcohol and tobacco are excluded.

➤ INFORMATION: **Revenue Canada** (✉ 2265 St. Laurent Blvd. S, Ottawa, Ontario K1G 4K3, ☎ 613/993–0534, 800/461–9999 in Canada).

ENTERING THE U.K.

From countries outside the EU, including South Africa, you may import, duty-free, 200 cigarettes or 50 cigars; 1 liter of spirits or 2 liters of fortified or sparkling wine or liqueurs; 2 liters of still table wine; 60 milliliters of perfume; 250 milliliters of toilet water; plus £136 worth of other goods, including gifts and souvenirs.

➤ INFORMATION: **HM Customs and Excise** (✉ Dorset House, Stamford St., London SE1 9NG, ☎ 0171/202–4227).

D

DINING

Dress in most restaurants tends to be casual, but draw the line at wearing shorts and a halter top to dinner at any restaurant away from the beach. Very expensive restaurants and old-fashioned hotel restaurants (where colonial traditions die hard) may require a jacket and tie. ☞ Pleasures & Pastimes *in* Chapter 1.

DISABILITIES & ACCESSIBILITY

ACCESS IN SOUTH AFRICA

South Africa is slowly adding facilities for travelers with disabilities, but standards vary widely from place to place. Many of the large chains now offer one or more rooms in their hotels specially adapted for travelers with disabilities. Zimbabwe and Botswana have very few facilities for travelers with disabilities.

TIPS AND HINTS

When discussing accessibility with an operator or reservationist, **ask hard questions.** Are there any stairs, inside *or* out? Are there grab bars next to the toilet *and* in the shower/tub? How wide is the doorway to the room? To the bathroom? For the most extensive facilities meeting the latest legal specifications, **opt for newer accommodations,** which are more likely to have been designed with access in mind. Older buildings or ships may offer more limited facilities. Be sure to **discuss your needs before booking.**

➤ COMPLAINTS: **Disability Rights Section** (✉ U.S. Department of Justice, Box 66738, Washington, DC 20035–6738, ☎ 202/514–0301 or 800/514–0301, FAX 202/307–1198, TTY 202/514–

–0383 or 800/514–0383) for general complaints. **Aviation Consumer Protection Division** (☞ Air Travel, *above*) for airline-related problems. **Civil Rights Office** (✉ U.S. Department of Transportation, Departmental Office of Civil Rights, S-30, 400 7th St. SW, Room 10215, Washington, DC 20590, ☎ 202/366–4648) for problems with surface transportation.

TRAVEL AGENCIES & TOUR OPERATORS

The Americans with Disabilities Act requires that travel firms serve the needs of all travelers. That said, you should note that some agencies and operators specialize in making travel arrangements for individuals and groups with disabilities.

➤ TRAVELERS WITH MOBILITY PROBLEMS: **Access Adventures** (⊠ 206 Chestnut Ridge Rd., Rochester, NY 14624, ☎ 716/889–9096), run by a former physical-rehabilitation counselor. **Accessible Journeys** (⊠ 35 W. Sellers Ave., Ridley Park, PA 19078, ☎ 610/521–0339 or 800/846–4537, FAX 610/521–6959), for escorted tours exclusively for travelers with mobility impairments. **Flying Wheels Travel** (⊠ 143 W. Bridge St., Box 382, Owatonna, MN 55060, ☎ 507/451–5005 or 800/535–6790, FAX 507/451–1685), a travel agency specializing in European cruises and tours. **Hinsdale Travel Service** (⊠ 201 E. Ogden Ave., Suite 100, Hinsdale, IL 60521, ☎ 630/325–1335), a travel agency that benefits from the advice of wheelchair traveler Janice Perkins. **Wheelchair Journeys** (⊠ 16979 Redmond Way, Redmond, WA 98052, ☎ 425/885–2210 or 800/313–4751), for general travel arrangements.

DISCOUNTS & DEALS

Be a smart shopper and **compare all your options before making a choice.** A plane ticket bought with a promotional coupon may not be cheaper than the least expensive fare from a discount ticket agency. For high-price travel purchases, such as packages or tours, keep in mind that what you get is just as important as what you save. Just because something is cheap doesn't mean it's a bargain.

LOOK IN YOUR WALLET

When you use your credit card to make travel purchases you may get free travel-accident insurance, collision-damage insurance, and medical or legal assistance, depending on the card and the bank that issued it. American Express, MasterCard, and Visa provide one or more of these services, so **get a copy of your credit card's travel-benefits policy.** If you are a member of the American Automobile Association (AAA) or an oil-

company-sponsored road-assistance plan, always **ask hotel or car-rental reservationists about auto-club discounts.** Some clubs offer additional discounts on tours, cruises, or admission to attractions. And don't forget that auto-club membership entitles you to free maps and trip-planning services.

DIAL FOR DOLLARS

To save money, **look into "1-800" discount reservations services,** which use their buying power to get a better price on hotels, airline tickets, even car rentals. When booking a room, always **call the hotel's local toll-free number** (if one is available) rather than the central reservations number—you'll often get a better price. Always ask about special packages or corporate rates.

When shopping for the best deal on hotels and car rentals **look for guaranteed exchange rates,** which protect you against a falling dollar. With your rate locked in you won't pay more even if the price goes up in the local currency.

➤ AIRLINE TICKETS: ☎ 800/FLY–4–LESS.

➤ HOTEL ROOMS: **Steigenberger Reservation Service** (☎ 800/223–5652).

SAVE ON COMBOS

Packages and guided tours can both save you money, but don't confuse the two. When you buy a package your travel remains independent, just as though you had planned and booked the trip yourself. Fly/drive packages, which combine airfare and car rental, are often a good deal.

JOIN A CLUB?

Many companies sell discounts in the form of travel clubs and coupon books, but these cost money. You must use participating advertisers to get a deal, and only after you recoup the initial membership cost or book price do you begin to save. If you plan to use the club or coupons frequently you may save considerably. Before signing up, find out what discounts you get for free.

➤ DISCOUNT CLUBS: **Entertainment Travel Editions** (⊠ 2125 Butterfield Rd., Troy, MI 48084, ☎ 800/445–

4137; $23–$48, depending on destination). **Great American Traveler** (✉ Box 27965, Salt Lake City, UT 84127, ☎ 800/548–2812; $49.95 per year). **Moment's Notice Discount Travel Club** (✉ 7301 New Utrecht Ave., Brooklyn, NY 11204, ☎ 718/234–6295; $25 per year, single or family). **Privilege Card International** (✉ 237 E. Front St., Youngstown, OH 44503, ☎ 330/746–5211 or 800/236–9732; $74.95 per year). **Sears's Mature Outlook** (✉ Box 9390, Des Moines, IA 50306, ☎ 800/336–6330; $14.95 per year). **Travelers Advantage** (✉ CUC Travel Service, 3033 S. Parker Rd., Suite 1000, Aurora, CO 80014, ☎ 800/548–1116 or 800/648–4037; $49 per year, single or family). **Worldwide Discount Travel Club** (✉ 1674 Meridian Ave., Miami Beach, FL 33139, ☎ 305/534–2082; $50 per year family, $40 single).

DRIVING

Southern Africans drive on the left. For pedestrians, that means that you should look right before crossing the street. The country has a superb network of multilane roads and highways, some of which charge a toll. The speed limit on major highways is 120 kph (75 mph), but many drivers far exceed that. In fact, South Africans tend to be aggressive and reckless, thinking nothing of tailgating at high speeds and passing on blind rises. During national holidays, the body count from highway collisions is staggering. The problem is compounded by widespread drunk driving, even though the legal blood-alcohol limit is 0.08. Local minibus taxis pose another threat, swerving in and out of traffic without warning to pick up customers. For obvious reasons, the wearing of seat belts is required by law.

South African roads have wide shoulders, separated from the main lanes by a yellow line. Slow traffic is expected to pull onto this shoulder to allow faster traffic to pass, but be sure that the shoulder ahead is not obstructed by cyclists, pedestrians, or a stopped vehicle. If a slower vehicle pulls onto the shoulder to allow you past, it's common courtesy to flash your hazard lights a couple of times in thanks. In built-up areas road shoulders are occasionally marked by red lines. This is a strict "no–stopping" zone.

In very remote areas only the main road might be paved, while most secondary roads are of high-quality gravel. Traffic is often light in these areas, so be sure to carry a spare, a jack, a tire iron, and extra water.

Huge 24-hour service stations are positioned at regular intervals along all major highways. Self-service stations do not exist, so an attendant will pump the gas, check the oil and water, and wash the windows. In return, tip him or her R2–R3. South Africa now has a choice of unleaded or leaded gasoline, and many vehicles operate on diesel—be sure you get the right fuel. Some South African-manufactured automobiles still need special engine modifications to enable them to run on unleaded fuel — check when booking a hired car as to what fuel to use. Petrol is measured in liters, and expect to pay the equivalent of US$2–US$2.50 a gallon, about twice what you would pay in the States.

Many cities, most notably Johannesburg, now use mini traffic circles in lieu of four-way stops. These are extremely dangerous, since many drivers don't bother to stop. Theoretically, the first vehicle to the circle has right-of-way; otherwise, yield to the right. In practice, keep your wits about you at all times.

In South African parlance, traffic lights are known as "robots." And for Americans and Canadians, don't forget: Drive left, and look right.

In Zimbabwe and Botswana, major highways typically have two lanes only. Smaller roads often consist of one paved lane with wide dirt shoulders. When cars approach, drivers move the left side of their cars or trucks onto the dirt, each keeping the right (driver's) side on the pavement.

AUTO CLUBS

The **Automobile Association of South Africa** extends privileges to members of the American Automobile Association in the United States and the Automobile Association in Britain. Contact a local office in your home country for more information.

➤ Auto Clubs: **Automobile Association of South Africa** (✉ A.A. House, 479 De Korte St., Braamfontein, Johannesburg 2017, ☎ 011/358–7788). In the United States, **American Automobile Association** (☎ 800/564–6222). In the U.K., **Automobile Association** (AA, ☎ 0990/500–600), **Royal Automobile Club** (RAC, membership ☎ 0990/722–722; insurance 0345/121–345).

E
ELECTRICITY

To use your U.S.-purchased electric-powered equipment, **bring a converter and adapter.** The electrical current in 220 volts, 50 cycles alternating current (AC); wall outlets take plugs with three round prongs.

If your appliances are dual-voltage, you'll need only an adapter. Don't use 110-volt outlets, marked FOR SHAVERS ONLY, for high-wattage appliances such as blow-dryers. Most laptops operate equally well on 110 and 220 volts and so require only an adapter.

EMERGENCIES

South Africa's national emergency number for the police is 10111; and for an ambulance it is 999. Consult the front page of the local telephone directories for other emergency numbers.

In **Zimbabwe,** dial 994 (ambulance), 993 (fire) and 995 (police). In **Botswana,** dial 997 (ambulance), 998 (fire), and 999 (police).

G
GAY & LESBIAN TRAVEL

➤ Gay- and Lesbian-Friendly Travel Agencies: **Advance Damron** (✉ 1 Greenway Plaza, Suite 800, Houston, TX 77046, ☎ 713/850–1140 or 800/695–0880, FAX 713/888–1010). **Club Travel** (✉ 8739 Santa Monica Blvd., West Hollywood, CA 90069, ☎ 310/358–2200 or 800/429–8747, FAX 310/358–2222). **Islanders/Kennedy Travel** (✉ 183 W. 10th St., New York, NY 10014, ☎ 212/242–3222 or 800/988–1181, FAX 212/929–8530). **Now Voyager** (✉ 4406 18th St., San Francisco, CA 94114, ☎ 415/626–1169 or 800/255–6951, FAX 415/626–8626). **Yellowbrick Road** (✉ 1500 W. Balmoral Ave., Chicago, IL 60640, ☎ 773/561–1800 or 800/642–2488, FAX 773/561–4497). **Skylink Women's Travel** (✉ 3577 Moorland Ave., Santa Rosa, CA 95407, ☎ 707/585–8355 or 800/225–5759, FAX 707/584–5637), serving lesbian travelers.

H
HEALTH

STAYING WELL

Unless signs indicate otherwise, you can drink the water and eat all fresh produce in Southern Africa. The major problem facing travelers is malaria, which occurs in the prime game-viewing areas of the Eastern and Northern Transvaal, in northern KwaZulu-Natal, and throughout Zimbabwe and Botswana. All travelers heading into these regions should take antimalarial drugs. Chloroquine and paludrine are widely prescribed together, but there is evidence of resistance to these drugs. A more effective measure is Lariam (mefloquine), although this can cause side effects. **See your doctor at least one month before your departure.**

The best way to prevent malaria is to avoid being bitten by mosquitos in the first place. After sunset, wear long-sleeve pants and shirts, apply repellent (100% DEET is good, if toxic), and use mosquito nets for sleeping if they're provided. Upon returning home, if you experience flulike systems, including fever, painful eyes, backache, and severe headache, be sure to tell your doctor immediately that you have been in a malarial zone.

Many lakes and streams, particularly in the eastern half of the country, are infected with bilharzia (schistosomiasis), a parasite carried by a small freshwater snail. The fluke enters through the skin of swimmers or waders, attaches itself to the intestines or bladder, and lays eggs. Symptoms of this treatable condition include blood-tinged urine, general malaise, and abdominal pain. Avoid wading in still waters or in areas close to reeds. Fast-moving water is considered safe.

During the rainy season, ticks are often prevalent in stock farming and game areas. If you intend walking or hiking in these areas, use a suitable insect repellent or wear long trousers.

Always scrub down well after your activities to remove any ticks. Microscopic 'pepper ticks' can cause tick bite fever. If you develop a violent, unremitting headache 6–10 days after discovering tick bites, see a doctor. The fever usually breaks after about 10–12 days. Symptoms may be mild or severe, depending on the patient.

Zimbabwe also has tse-tse flies in the Middle Zambezi Valley. The risk of contracting sleeping sickness is not great, but if you do the disease can be fatal, and it can move very fast. Again, if upon your return from southern Africa you feel flu symptoms, consult your doctor immediately and mention that you have been in a tse-tse fly area in Zimbabwe.

South Africa has no national health system, so check your existing health plan to see whether you're covered while abroad and supplement it if necessary. South African doctors are generally excellent. The equipment and training in private clinics rival the best in the world, but public hospitals tend to suffer from overcrowding and underfunding.

➤ HEALTH WARNINGS: **National Centers for Disease Control** (✉ CDC, National Center for Infectious Diseases, Division of Quarantine, Traveler's Health Section, 1600 Clifton Rd., M/S E-03, Atlanta, GA 30333, ☎ 404/332–4559, FAX 404/332–4565).

SHOTS AND MEDICATIONS

Aside from malaria tablets (☞ *above*), travelers entering South Africa within six days of leaving a country infected with yellow fever require a yellow fever vaccination certificate. The South African travel clinics are now also recommending that you be vaccinated against Hepatitis A and B, particularly if you intend traveling to more isolated areas.

MEDICAL PLANS

No one plans to get sick while traveling, but it happens, so **consider signing up with a medical-assistance company.** Members get doctor referrals, emergency evacuation or repatriation, 24-hour telephone hot lines for medical consultation, cash for emergencies, and other personal and legal assistance. Coverage varies by plan, so **review the benefits carefully.**

➤ MEDICAL-ASSISTANCE COMPANIES: **International SOS Assistance** (✉ Box 11568, Philadelphia, PA 19116, ☎ 215/244–1500 or 800/523–8930; ✉ 1255 University St., Suite 420, Montréal, Québec H3B 3B6, ☎ 514/874–7674 or 800/363–0263; ✉ 7 Old Lodge Pl., St. Margarets, Twickenham TW1 1RQ, England, ☎ 0181/744–0033). **MEDEX Assistance Corporation** (✉ Box 5375, Timonium, MD 21094-5375, ☎ 410/453–6300 or 800/537–2029). **Traveler's Emergency Network** (✉ 3100 Tower Blvd., Suite 1000B, Durham, NC 27707, ☎ 919/490–6055 or 800/275–4836, FAX 919/493–8262). **TravMed** (✉ Box 5375, Timonium, MD 21094, ☎ 410/453–6380 or 800/732–5309). **Worldwide Assistance Services** (✉ 1133 15th St. NW, Suite 400, Washington, DC 20005, ☎ 202/331–1609 or 800/821–2828, FAX 202/828–5896).

I

INSURANCE

Travel insurance is the best way to **protect yourself against financial loss.** The most useful policies are trip-cancellation-and-interruption, default, medical, and comprehensive insurance.

Without insurance you will lose all or most of your money if you cancel your trip, regardless of the reason. It's essential that you **buy trip-cancellation-and-interruption insurance,** particularly if your airline ticket, cruise, or package tour is nonrefundable and cannot be changed. When considering how much coverage you need, look for a policy that will cover the cost of your trip plus the nondiscounted price of a one-way airline ticket, should you need to return home early. Also **consider default or bankruptcy insurance,** which protects you against a supplier's failure to deliver.

Medicare generally does not cover health-care costs outside the United States, nor do many privately issued policies. If your own policy does not cover you outside the United States, **consider buying supplemental medical coverage.** Remember that travel health insurance is different from a medical-assistance plan (☞ Health, *above*).

Citizens of the U.K. can buy an annual travel-insurance policy valid for most vacations during the year in which it's purchased. If you are pregnant or have a preexisting medical condition, make sure you're covered.

If you have purchased an expensive vacation, particularly one that involves travel abroad, comprehensive insurance is a must. **Look for comprehensive policies that include trip-delay insurance,** which will protect you in the event that weather problems cause you to miss your flight, tour, or cruise. A few insurers sell waivers for preexisting medical conditions. Companies that offer both features include Access America, Carefree Travel, Travel Insured International, and Travel Guard (☞ *below*).

Always **buy travel insurance directly from the insurance company**; if you buy it from a travel agency or tour operator that goes out of business you probably will not be covered for the agency or operator's default, a major risk. Before you make any purchase, **review your existing health and home-owner's policies** to find out whether they cover expenses incurred while traveling.

➤ TRAVEL INSURERS: In the United States, **Access America** (✉ 6600 W. Broad St., Richmond, VA 23230, ☎ 804/285–3300 or 800/284–8300), **Carefree Travel Insurance** (✉ Box 9366, 100 Garden City Plaza, Garden City, NY 11530, ☎ 516/294–0220 or 800/323–3149), **Near Travel Services** (✉ Box 1339, Calumet City, IL 60409, ☎ 708/868–6700 or 800/654–6700), **Travel Guard International** (✉ 1145 Clark St., Stevens Point, WI 54481, ☎ 715/345–0505 or 800/826–1300), **Travel Insured International** (✉ Box 280568, East Hartford, CT 06128–0568, ☎ 860/528–7663 or 800/243–3174), **Travelex Insurance Services** (✉ 11717 Burt St., Suite 202, Omaha, NE 68154-1500, ☎ 402/445–8637 or 800/228–9792, FAX 800/867–9531), **Wallach & Company** (✉ 107 W. Federal St., Box 480, Middleburg, VA 20118, ☎ 540/687–3166 or 800/237–6615). In Canada, **Mutual of Omaha** (✉ Travel Division, 500 University Ave., Toronto, Ontario M5G 1V8, ☎ 416/598–4083, 800/

268–8825 in Canada). In the U.K., **Association of British Insurers** (✉ 51 Gresham St., London EC2V 7HQ, ☎ 0171/600–3333).

L

LANGUAGE

South Africa has a mind-numbing 11 official languages: English, Afrikaans, Ndebele, Northern Sotho, Southern Sotho, Swati, Tsonga, Tswana, Venda, Xhosa, and Zulu. Happily for visitors, English is the widely spoken, unofficial lingua franca, although road signs and other important markers often alternate between English and Afrikaans (South-African Dutch).

South African English is heavily influenced by Afrikaans and, to a lesser extent, by some of the African languages. First-time visitors may have trouble understanding the South African accent, which lengthens certain vowels, clips others short, and swallows still others. Listed below are some of the words, both English and Afrikaans, that you should know. For a list of culinary terms, *see* Dining in Pleasures & Pastimes *in* Chapter 1.

Bakkie: pickup truck

Bottle store: liquor store

Dagga: marijuana

Jol: a party

Howzit?: How are you?

Izit?: Really?

Just now: soon or recently

Lekker: nice

Oke: fellow, chap

Robot: traffic light

Shame: how cute or what a pity

Shebeen: township bar

Sis: gross, disgusting

Takkie: sneaker

Toyi-toyi: to dance in protest

Veld: countryside

Voetsak!: go away, get lost

Zimbabwe's official languages are Shona, Ndebele, and very widely-spoken English. Nambia is also spoken in Matabeleland. **Botswana**'s mother tongue is Setswana, but

English is the official language. Sekalanga is also spoken in eastern parts of the country.

LODGING

The South African Tourism Board (Satour) operates a grading system rating the quality of a hotel. A one-star rating suggests the bare essentials, while a hotel with a five-star rating (the highest) can be assumed to meet high international standards. Bear in mind, though, that stars relate to the level of facilities provided (e.g., TV, heated towel rack, room service, etc.), not the quality of the hotel. In a second, more subjective rating system, Satour awards silver plaques to those few hotels that offer an extraordinary level of service.

Most hotel rooms come with en suite bathrooms, and you can usually choose between rooms with twin or double beds. A full English breakfast is often included in the rate, particularly in more traditional hotels. In the luxury lodges of the Transvaal Escarpment, the rate usually covers the cost of dinner, bed, and breakfast, while in game lodges the rate includes everything but alcohol.

APARTMENT AND VILLA RENTALS

If you want a home base that's roomy enough for a family and comes with cooking facilities, **consider a furnished rental.** These can save you money, however some rentals are luxury properties, economical only when your party is large. Home-exchange directories list rentals (often second homes owned by prospective house swappers), and some services search for a house or apartment for you (even a castle if that's your fancy) and handle the paperwork. Some send an illustrated catalog; others send photographs only of specific properties, sometimes at a charge. Up-front registration fees may apply.

➤ RENTAL AGENTS: **Property Rentals International** (✉ 1008 Mansfield Crossing Rd., Richmond, VA 23236, ☎ 804/378–6054 or 800/220–3332, FAX 804/379–2073).

FARM STAYS

Contact **Farm and Country Holiday** (✉ 8 Erin Rd., Rondebosch, Cape Town 7700 [mailing address: Box 266, Newlands 7725], ☎ 021/689–8400, FAX 021/685–1974).

GAME LODGES

Safariplan/Wild African Ventures (✉ 673 E. California Blvd., Pasadena, CA 91106, ☎ 800/358–8530) and **Sites of Africa** (✉ Box 781329, Sandton 2146, South Africa, ☎ 011/883–4345), also known as Game Lodge Reservations, act as central reservations and information clearinghouses for a large number of game lodges throughout southern Africa.

HOME EXCHANGES

If you would like to exchange your home for someone else's, **join a home-exchange organization,** which will send you its updated listings of available exchanges for a year and will include your own listing in at least one of them. Making the arrangements is up to you.

➤ EXCHANGE CLUBS: **HomeLink International** (✉ Box 650, Key West, FL 33041, ☎ 305/294–7766 or 800/638–3841, FAX 305/294–1148) charges $83 per year.

HOTELS

Since the 1994 elections, such major international chains as **Hyatt International** (☎ 800/228–9000) have begun constructing hotels around the country. At press time, however, the hotel scene was still dominated by South African conglomerates, most notably the **Southern Sun Group** (Johannesburg office, ☎ 011/482–3500), which runs **Southern Sun Hotels, Southern Sun Resorts,** and **Holiday Inn Hotels** and manages the budget French hotel chain **Formule 1** (Johannesburg office, ☎ 011/440–1001).

Other major South African chains are **Karos Hotels** (Johannesburg office, ☎ 011/484–1641) and **Protea Hotels** (Johannesburg office, ☎ 0800/11–9000 toll-free).

The **Leading Hotels of South Africa** (Johannesburg office, ☎ 011/884–3583) is a loose association of the country's most exclusive hotels and lodges.

Portfolio of Places (Johannesburg office, ☎ 011/880–3414, FAX 011/788–4802) publishes *The Country Places Collection,* a widely respected list of South Africa's best small country hotels and lodges, as well as select city hotels. Portfolio also publishes a similar guide to bed-and-breakfasts.

M
MAIL

The South African mail service is increasingly unreliable. Mail can take weeks to arrive, and money and other valuables are frequently stolen from letters and packages. You can buy stamps only at post offices, open weekdays 8:30–4:30 and Saturdays 8–12. Stamps for local use marked "standardised post" may be purchased from newsagents in booklets of 10 stamps. Federal Express and several other express-mail companies offer more reliable service as do the new Fast Mail and Speed Courier Services.

Mail service in Zimbabwe and Botswana is more reliable than in South Africa, but it is rather slow. Because of their size, neither country has postal codes.

RECEIVING MAIL

The central post office in each city has a poste restante desk that will hold mail for you. Be sure the post office's mail code and your name are prominently displayed on all letters. Most hotels also accept faxes and express-mail deliveries addressed to their guests. A better place to receive mail is American Express offices; for a list of offices worldwide, write for the Traveler's Companion from **American Express** (⊠ Box 678, Canal St. Station, New York, NY 10013).

MONEY

Prices quoted throughout the book are in rand, Zimbabwe dollars, and Botswana's pula. Many game lodges quote prices in U.S. dollars; in Zimbabwe this is because the US$ is more stable than the Z$. Other Zimbabwe hotels might also charge US$.

The unit of currency in South Africa is the rand (R), with 100 cents (¢) equaling R1. Bills come in R10, R20, R50, R100, and R200 denominations, which are differentiated by color. Coins are minted in R5, R2, R1, 50¢, 20¢, 10¢, 5¢, 2¢, and 1¢ denominations.

Zimbabwe's currency is the dollar. There are $2, $5, $10, $20, and $50 bills; coins come in 1¢, 5¢, 10¢, 20¢, 50¢, and $1 denominations.

Botswana's unit of currency is the pula, which is broken down into 100 thebe. There are P1, P2, P5, P10, P20, and P50 bills, and 1t, 2t, 5t, 10t, 25, 50t, and P1 coins.

ATMS

Before leaving home, **make sure that your credit cards have been programmed for ATM use in South Africa** (most South African ATMs take five-digit PIN numbers). Note that Discover is accepted mostly in the United States. Local bank cards often do not work overseas or may access only your checking account; **ask your bank about a MasterCard/Cirrus or Visa debit card,** which works like a bank card but can be used at any ATM displaying a MasterCard/Cirrus or Visa logo. These cards, too, may tap only your checking account; check with your bank about their policy.

➤ ATM Locations: **Cirrus** (☎ 800/424–7787). A list of **Plus** locations is available at your local bank.

COSTS

Because of inflation in South Africa and the fluctuations of the Zimbabwe dollar, it's difficult to give exact prices. It's safe to say, though, that the region—excluding Botswana, which is rather expensive—is an extremely cheap destination for foreign visitors. With the weakness of the rand against major foreign currencies, visitors will find the cost of meals, hotels, and entertainment considerably lower than at home.

A fabulous bottle of South African wine costs about $10, and a meal at a prestigious restaurant won't set you back more than $30 per person. Double rooms in the country's finest hotels may cost $250 a night but $100 is more than enough to secure high-quality lodging in most cities. Hotel rates are at their highest during peak season, November through March, when you can expect to pay anywhere from 50% to 90% more than in the off-season.

Not everything in South Africa is cheap. Expect to pay international rates and more to stay in one of the exclusive private game lodges in the

Eastern Transvaal. Mala Mala, the most glamorous lodge in the country, charges $1,000 per couple per night. Flights to South Africa and within the country itself are also extremely expensive.

The following are sample costs in **South Africa** (in U.S.$) at press time: cup of coffee 50¢–75¢; bottle of beer in a bar 75¢–$1; ¼ roasted chicken with salad and drink at a fast-food restaurant $3–$4; room-service sandwich in a hotel $4–$7; a 2-km (1¼-mi) taxi ride $3.

The following are sample costs (very favorable at the existing exchange rate) in **Zimbabwe** at press time: cup of coffee 30¢; bottle of beer in a bar 55¢; average cost of lunch in cities $3.50; room-service sandwich in a hotel $2.50; a 2-km (1¼-mi) taxi ride 80¢.

The following are sample costs in **Botswana** at press time: cup of coffee $2; bottle of beer in a bar $2.75; average cost of lunch in cities $11; room-service sandwich in a hotel $8; a 2-km (1¼-mi) taxi ride $5.50.

CURRENCY EXCHANGE

At press time, **coversion rates** for Southern Africa were as follows: **South Africa** R4.9 to the U.S. dollar; **Zimbabwe**'s very high Z$18.75 to the US$ makes it the region's most affordable country; **Botswana** P3.5 to the U.S. dollar is not such a bargain.

For the most favorable rates, **change money at banks.** Although fees charged for ATM transactions may be higher abroad than at home, Cirrus and Plus exchange rates are excellent, because they are based on wholesale rates offered only by major banks. You won't do as well at exchange booths in airports or rail and bus stations, in hotels, in restaurants, or in stores, although you may find their hours more convenient. To avoid lines at airport exchange booths, **get a small amount of local currency before you leave home.** Rennies Travel Foreign Exchange outlets cash Thomas Cook travelers cheques and charge no commission.

For safety's sake, keep all foreign-exchange receipts until you leave South Africa. South Africa has restrictions on how much money its citizens can take out of the country, so you may need the receipts as proof when changing any unspent rand back into your own currency. You must also have a permit from the **South African Reserve Bank** (⌧ Box 427, Pretoria 0001, ☎ 012/313–3911) to take more than R500 out of the country.

➤ EXCHANGE SERVICES: **International Currency Express** (☎ 888/842–0880 on the East Coast or 888/278–6628 on the West Coast for telephone orders). **Thomas Cook Currency Services** (☎ 800/287–7362 for telephone orders and retail locations).

TRAVELER'S CHECKS

Whether or not to buy traveler's checks depends on where you are headed. **Take cash if your trip includes rural areas** and small towns, traveler's checks to cities. If your checks are lost or stolen, they can usually be replaced within 24 hours. To ensure a speedy refund, buy your checks yourself (don't ask someone else to make the purchase). When making a claim for stolen or lost checks, the person who bought the checks should make the call.

P

PACKING FOR SOUTHERN AFRICA

In Southern Africa, it's possible to experience muggy heat, bone-chilling cold, torrential thunderstorms, and scorching African sun all within a couple days. The secret is to pack lightweight clothes that you can wear in layers, and at least one sweater. If you're coming in winter or going game viewing at a private lodge, take along a warm jacket, too. It can get mighty cold sitting in an open Land Rover at night.

South Africans tend to dress casually, donning shorts and T-shirts as soon as the weather turns pleasant. People dress much as they do in the United States: Businessmen still wear suits, and if a couple is going out to a fancy restaurant, they tend to get dolled up. By contrast, life in Zimbabwe and Botswana is decidedly more casual. You are unlikely to see suits, except on city hotel staff and government officials, and only high-end city hotel restaurants will present you with the opportunity to dress up.

In summer, lightweight cottons are ideal, but highveld (South Africa's high interior plateau) evenings can be cool. Highveld winters are famous for frosty early mornings and nights, but afternoon temperatures often top 60°F or 70°F.

It's easy to get fried in the strong African sun, especially in mile-high Johannesburg where the temperature can be deceptively cool. Pack plenty of sunscreen, sunglasses, and a hat. An umbrella comes in handy during those late-afternoon thunderstorms.

If you're heading into the bush, consider packing binoculars, a strong insect repellent like 100% DEET, and sturdy pants that can stand up to the wicked thorns that protect much of the foliage. Avoid black, white, or garish clothing that will make you more visible to animals (and insects, which tend to mistake you for a buffalo if you wear black)—medium tones will make you blend in most. And leave behind perfumes, which mask the smell of the bush and also attract insects. Lightweight hiking books are a good idea if you plan to set out on any of South Africa's great trails; otherwise, a sturdy pair of walking shoes should suffice.

Bring an extra pair of eyeglasses or contact lenses in your carry-on luggage, and if you have a health problem, **pack enough medication** to last the entire trip or have your doctor write you a prescription using the drug's generic name, because brand names vary from country to country. It's important that you **don't put prescription drugs or valuables in luggage to be checked**: it might go astray. To avoid problems with customs officials, carry medications in the original packaging. Also, don't forget the addresses of offices that handle refunds of lost traveler's checks.

LUGGAGE

In general, you are entitled to check two bags on flights within the United States and on international flights leaving the United States. A third piece may be brought on board, but it must fit easily under the seat in front of you or in the overhead compartment.

If you are flying between two foreign destinations, note that baggage allowances may be determined not by piece but by weight—generally 88 pounds (40 kilograms) in first class, 66 pounds (30 kilograms) in business class, and 44 pounds (20 kilograms) in economy. If your flight between two cities abroad *connects* with your transatlantic or transpacific flight, the piece method still applies.

Airline liability for baggage is limited to $1,250 per person on flights within the United States. On international flights it amounts to $9.07 per pound or $20 per kilogram for checked baggage (roughly $640 per 70-pound bag) and $400 per passenger for unchecked baggage. Insurance for losses exceeding these amounts can be bought from the airline at check-in for about $10 per $1,000 of coverage; note that this coverage excludes a rather extensive list of items, which is shown on your airline ticket.

Before departure, **itemize your bags' contents** and their worth, and label the bags with your name, address, and phone number. (If you use your home address, cover it so that potential thieves can't see it readily.) Inside each bag, **pack a copy of your itinerary.** At check-in, **make sure that each bag is correctly tagged** with the destination airport's three-letter code. If your bags arrive damaged or fail to arrive at all, file a written report with the airline before leaving the airport.

PASSPORTS & VISAS

Once your travel plans are confirmed, **check the expiration date of your passport.** It's also a good idea to **make photocopies of the data page**; leave one copy with someone at home and keep another with you, separated from your passport. If you lose your passport, promptly call the nearest embassy or consulate and the local police; having a copy of the data page can speed replacement.

U.S. CITIZENS

All U.S. citizens, even infants, need only a valid passport to enter Southern Africa for stays of up to 90 days.

➤ INFORMATION: **Office of Passport Services** (☎ 202/647–0518).

CANADIANS

You need only a valid passport to enter South Africa for stays of up to 90 days.

➤ INFORMATION: **Passport Office** (☎ 819/994–3500 or 800/567–6868).

U.K. CITIZENS

Citizens of the United Kingdom need only a valid passport to enter Southern Africa for stays of up to 90 days.

➤ INFORMATION: **London Passport Office** (☎ 0990/21010) for fees and documentation requirements and to request an emergency passport.

S

SAFETY

Crime is a major problem in South Africa, particularly in large cities, and all visitors should take precautions to protect themselves. Do not walk alone at night, and exercise caution even during the day. Avoid wearing flashy jewelry (even costume jewelry), and don't invite attention by wearing an expensive camera around your neck. If you are toting a handbag, wear the strap across your body; even better, wear a money belt, preferably hidden from view, under your clothing.

Carjacking is another problem, with armed bandits often forcing drivers out of their vehicles at traffic lights, in driveways, or by faking an accident. Keep your car doors locked at all times, and leave enough space between you and the vehicle in front so you can pull into another lane if necessary. If you are confronted by an armed assailant, do not resist. Due to the number of sophisticated antihijacking and vehicle tracking devices being used, carjackers may try to force you off the road, so as to steal the car with the engine running. Alternatively, you may be forced to accompany them for some time, showing them where the hidden emergency switches are. If this happens, don't panic, scream or otherwise draw attention to yourself. Follow their instructions very carefully, do not attempt to try and remove your valuables or other items from the car and you've a far better chance of emerging from the experience unscathed.

Make sure that you know exactly where you're going. Purchase a good map and obtain comprehensive directions. Taking the wrong exit off a highway into a township could lead you straight to disaster. Many cities are ringed by 'no-go' areas. Establish from your hotel or the locals as to which areas to avoid.

African "taxi" ranks are often the site of random shootings and knifings, sparked off by continual "taxi wars" as rival associations literally attempt to kill off the competition. If you blunder inadvertently into one of these, get out of the area as soon as possible. Peak hours are usually the time when trouble starts.

Never, ever visit a township or squatter camp on your own. Unemployment is rife, leading to unemployed, armed bandits roaming the streets. If you wish to see a township, there are reputable companies who run excellent tours and know which areas to avoid. Rather book yourself on one of these.

The countryside is much safer, but bandits do pose a problem in certain areas, most notably along the Wild Coast and in the Transkei, previously a quasi-independent homeland.

In Zimbabwe and Botswana, crime is much less of a problem. The worst thing likely to happen is being pickpocketed in cities or at airports. Usual common sense precautions are therefore advised.

SENIOR-CITIZEN TRAVEL

Senior citizens, known as "pensioners" in South Africa, often receive substantial discounts on admission prices and tickets. Many establishments, however, require a South African pensioner's card, not available to foreign travelers. It doesn't hurt to ask for a discount, though.

To qualify for age-related discounts, **mention your senior-citizen status up front** when booking hotel reservations (not when checking out) and before you're seated in restaurants (not when paying the bill). Note that discounts may be limited to certain menus, days, or hours. When renting a car, **ask about promotional car-rental discounts,** which can be cheaper than senior-citizen rates.

➤ ADVENTURE TRAVEL: **Overseas Adventure Travel** (✉ Grand Circle Corp., 625 Mt. Auburn St., Cambridge, MA 02138, ☎ 617/876–0533 or 800/221–0814, FAX 617/876–0455).

➤ EDUCATIONAL TRAVEL PROGRAMS: **Elderhostel** (✉ 75 Federal St., 3rd floor, Boston, MA 02110, ☎ 617/426–8056). **Interhostel** (✉ University of New Hampshire, 6 Garrison Ave., Durham, NH 03824, ☎ 603/862–1147 or 800/733–9753, FAX 603/862–1113). **Folkways Institute** (✉ 14600 Southeast Aldridge Rd., Portland, OR 97236-6518, ☎ 503/658–6600, FAX 503/658–8672).

SHOPPING

Be very picky about what you buy in South Africa. Imported clothes are expensive, and the local versions tend to be shoddily made. Traditional arts and crafts—whether they're made in South Africa or other African countries—are better buys. Keep an eye out for Zulu baskets, Ndebele beaded aprons, Zimbabwean printed fabrics, Kuba cloth from Zaire, fetishes and masks from West Africa, and Mali mud cloth and wedding blankets. Be wary of cheap imitations: "ebony" carvings often achieve their black luster through the use of shoe polish. Real ebony is heavy, and you can't scratch the black off.

By and large, you'll find that South Africa has more Pan-African crafts and artifacts than you will find in Zimbabwe or Botswana. If you see a hand-painted Ghanese barbershop sign that you like in Cape Town or Johannesburg, for example, don't expect to find any others in Harare or Gaborone.

WINE

Many wineries will mail your wine purchases to your home. Wine dispatched to the United States and Canada is usually sent as an "unsolicited gift" at the buyer's risk. It's not strictly legal, and if customs stops the shipment they will either make you pay customs duties or confiscate it outright. Some wine shippers in South Africa report no problems mailing wines to the United States and Canada; others report a high failure rate.

➤ SHIPPERS: **Steven Rom** (✉ Checkers Galleria Centre, 76 Regent Rd., Sea Point, South Africa, ☎ 021/439–6043, FAX 021/434–0401).

➤ IMPORTERS: If you don't want to take the risk, contact one of the companies in the United States and Canada that import a wide range of Cape wines: **Cape Venture Co.** (☎ 203/329–6663), **South African Wine Club** (☎ 800/504–9463), or **Maisons Marques & Domaines U.S.A.** (☎ 510/286–2010); and in Canada, **Remy Canada Inc.** (☎ 416/485–3633) or **Peter Mielzynski Agencies Ltd.** (☎ 905/820–8180).

STUDENTS

To save money, **look into deals available through student-oriented travel agencies.** To qualify you'll need a bona fide student ID card. Members of international student groups are also eligible.

➤ STUDENT IDS AND SERVICES: **Council on International Educational Exchange** (✉ CIEE, 205 E. 42nd St., 14th floor, New York, NY 10017, ☎ 212/822–2600 or 888/268–6245, FAX 212/822–2699), for mail orders only, in the United States. **Travel Cuts** (✉ 187 College St., Toronto, Ontario M5T 1P7, ☎ 416/979–2406 or 800/667–2887) in Canada.

➤ HOSTELING: **Hostelling International—American Youth Hostels** (✉ 733 15th St. NW, Suite 840, Washington, DC 20005, ☎ 202/783–6161, FAX 202/783–6171). **Hostelling International—Canada** (✉ 400-205 Catherine St., Ottawa, Ontario K2P 1C3, ☎ 613/237–7884, FAX 613/237–7868). **Youth Hostel Association of England and Wales** (✉ Trevelyan House, 8 St. Stephen's Hill, St. Albans, Hertfordshire AL1 2DY, ☎ 01727/855215 or 01727/845047, FAX 01727/844126). Membership in the U.S., $25; in Canada, C$26.75; in the U.K., 9.30).

➤ STUDENT TOURS: **Contiki Holidays** (✉ 300 Plaza Alicante, Suite 900, Garden Grove, CA 92840, ☎ 714/740–0808 or 800/266–8454, FAX 714/740–2034).

T

TAXES

HOTEL

South African hotels that participate in Satour's grading system add a Tourism Promotion Levy of R1.70–R5.70 per room to the bill, depending on the establishment's star rating.

VALUE-ADDED TAX (VAT)

In South Africa, the VAT, currently a whopping 14%, is included in the price of most goods and services, including hotel accommodations and food. **To get a VAT refund,** foreign visitors must present their receipts (minimum of R250) at the airport, and be carrying any purchased items with them or in their luggage. You must fill out Form VAT 255, available at the airport VAT refund office. **Whatever you buy, make sure that your receipt is an original tax invoice, containing the vendor's name and address, VAT registration number, and the words "tax invoice."** Refunds are given in the form of a check, which can be cashed immediately at an airport bank. If you have packed your purchases in luggage that you intend to check, be sure you visit the VAT refund desk before you go through check-in procedures. For items in your carry-on baggage, visit the refund desk in the departures hall.

TELEPHONES

The country code for South Africa is 27; for Swaziland, 268; for Zimbabwe, 263; for Botswana, 267. When dialing from abroad, drop the initial 0 from local South African area codes and the initial 1 from Zimbabwean area codes. Swaziland and Botswana have no area codes.

In South Africa a three-minute local call costs 75¢. Calls are significantly cheaper between 19h00 and 07h00 (weekdays) and over weekends and public holidays. South Africa has two types of pay phones: coin-operated phones that accept a variety of denominations and card-operated phones. Available in R10, R20, R50, and R100 denominations, phone cards are incredibly useful, saving you the hassle of juggling handfuls of coins. In addition, a digital meter tells you how much credit remains while you're talking. Telephone cards are available in news shops and tobacconists, but you can buy them for slightly less at offices of Telkom, the national telephone company.

South African phone numbers are not standardized, so don't be surprised to find some telephone numbers with fewer digits than others. Some remote farms and lodges still use a central exchange. This is slowly changing; some of the numbers in this book may already be out of date, in which case call directory assistance at 1023 (local) or 1025 (national). You do not need to dial the area code when making a local call.

Zimbabwe's phone system isn't 100% reliable, especially during the rainy season (November–February), when phone lines can go out for days at a time. If you're having trouble getting through, just keep dialing (after three tries you might just connect).

LONG-DISTANCE

Using AT&T, MCI, and Sprint long-distance services makes calling home relatively convenient, but you may find the local access number blocked in many hotel rooms. First ask the hotel operator to connect you. If the hotel operator balks, ask for an international operator, or dial the international operator yourself. One way to improve your odds of getting connected to your long-distance carrier is to travel with more than one company's calling card (a hotel may block Sprint, for example, but not MCI). If all else fails, call your phone company collect in the United States or call from a pay phone in the hotel lobby. **In Swaziland, there are no access agreements to allow you to use U.S. long distance services.** Thus you will not be able to make calls using your U.S. calling card from Botswana or Swaziland.

➤ ACCESS CODES: **AT&T USADirect:** from **South Africa** (☎ 0800/99–0123) and from **Zimbabwe** (☎ 110–899). **MCI Call USA:** from **South Africa** (☎ 0800/990–011) only. **Sprint Express:** from **South Africa** (☎ 0800/990-001) and from **Botswana** (☎ 0800/180–280).

TIME

Southern Africa is two hours ahead of Greenwich Mean Time. That makes it seven hours ahead of North American eastern standard time (six ahead of eastern daylight time).

TIPPING

Tipping is an integral part of South African life, and tips are expected for services that you might take for granted at home. Most notable among these is when you fill up with gas; there are no self-service stations,

THE GOLD GUIDE / SMART TRAVEL TIPS

and you should tip the attendant R2–R3. In restaurants, the size of the tip should depend on the quality of service, but 10% is standard, unless, of course, a service charge has already been added to the bill. Give the same percentage to bartenders, taxi drivers, and hairdressers. Hotel porters should receive R1.50–R2 per bag.

Tipping is less common in Zimbabwe and Botswana, but it is always appreciated. Loose change or 10% is appropriate. *See* Big Game Adventures *in* Chapter 11 for advice on tipping guides, game rangers, and trackers throughout Southern Africa.

TOUR OPERATORS

Buying a prepackaged tour or independent vacation can make your trip to Southern Africa less expensive and more hassle-free. Because everything is prearranged, you'll spend less time arranging what could be a huge planning.

Operators that handle several hundred thousand travelers per year can use their purchasing power to give you a good price. Their high volume may also indicate financial stability. But some small companies provide more personalized service; because they tend to specialize, they may also be more knowledgeable about a given area. Also, companies that have offices both where you are coming from and where you are going might have someone in place to help you if you run into difficulties on your trip.

A GOOD DEAL?

The more your package or tour includes, the better you can predict the ultimate cost of your vacation. Make sure you know exactly what is covered, and **beware of hidden costs.** Are taxes, tips, and service charges included? Transfers and baggage handling? Entertainment and excursions? These can add up.

If the package or tour you are considering is priced lower than in your wildest dreams, **be skeptical.** Also, **make sure your travel agent knows the accommodations** and other services. Ask about the hotel's location, room size, beds, and whether it has a pool, room service, or programs for children, if you care about these. Has

your agent been there in person or sent others you can contact?

BUYER BEWARE

Each year consumers are stranded or lose their money when tour operators—even very large ones with excellent reputations—go out of business. So **check out the operator.** Find out how long the company has been in business, and ask several agents about its reputation. **Don't book unless the firm has a consumer-protection program.**

Members of the National Tour Association and United States Tour Operators Association are required to set aside funds to cover your payments and travel arrangements in case the company defaults. Nonmembers may carry insurance instead. Look for the details, and for the name of an underwriter with a solid reputation, in the operator's brochure. Note: When it comes to tour operators, **don't trust escrow accounts.** Although the Department of Transportation watches over charter-flight operators, no regulatory body prevents tour operators from raiding the till. You may want to protect yourself by buying travel insurance that includes a tour-operator default provision. For more information, *see* Consumer Protection, *above*.

It's also a good idea to choose a company that participates in the American Society of Travel Agent's Tour Operator Program (TOP). This gives you a forum if there are any disputes between you and your tour operator; ASTA will act as mediator.

➤ TOUR-OPERATOR RECOMMENDATIONS: **American Society of Travel Agents** (☞ Travel Agencies, *below*). **National Tour Association** (✉ NTA, 546 E. Main St., Lexington, KY 40508, ☎ 606/226–4444 or 800/755–8687). **United States Tour Operators Association** (✉ USTOA, 342 Madison Ave., Suite 1522, New York, NY 10173, ☎ 212/599–6599, FAX 212/599–6744).

USING AN AGENT

Travel agents can be excellent resources. In fact, large operators accept bookings made only through travel agents. But it's a good idea to **collect brochures from several agen-**

cies, because some agents' suggestions may be influenced by relationships with tour and package firms that reward them for volume sales. If you have a special interest, **find an agent with expertise in that area**; ASTA (☞ Travel Agencies, *below*) has a database of specialists worldwide. Do some homework on your own, too: Local tourism boards can provide information about lesser-known and small-niche operators, some of which may sell only direct.

SINGLE TRAVELERS

Prices for packages and tours are usually quoted per person, based on two sharing a room. If traveling solo, you may be required to pay the full double-occupancy rate. Some operators eliminate this surcharge if you agree to be matched with a roommate of the same sex, even if one is not found by departure time.

GROUP TOURS

Among companies that sell tours to Southern Africa, the following are nationally known, have a proven reputation, and offer plenty of options. The classifications used below represent different price categories, and you'll probably encounter these terms when talking to a travel agent or tour operator. The key difference is usually in accommodations, which run from budget to better, and better-yet to best.

➤ SUPER-DELUXE: **Abercrombie & Kent** (✉ 1520 Kensington Rd., Oak Brook, IL 60521-2141, ☎ 630/954-2944 or 800/323-7308, 𝔽𝔸𝕏 630/954-3324). **Big Five Tours & Expeditions** (✉ 819 S. Federal Hwy., Suite 103, Stewart, FL 34994, ☎ 800/244-3483, 𝔽𝔸𝕏 561/287-5990). **Travcoa** (✉ Box 2630, 2350 S.E. Bristol St., Newport Beach, CA 92660, ☎ 714/476-2800 or 800/992-2003, 𝔽𝔸𝕏 714/476-2538).

➤ FIRST-CLASS: **African Travel** (✉ 1100 E. Broadway, Glendale, CA 91205, ☎ 800/421—8907, 𝔽𝔸𝕏 818/507-5802). **Born Free Safaris** (✉ 12504 Riverside Dr., North Hollywood, CA 91607, ☎ 800/372-3274, 𝔽𝔸𝕏 818/753—1460). **Bushtracks** (✉ Box 4163, Menlo Park, CA 94026, ☎ 650/326-8689, 𝔽𝔸𝕏 650/463-0925). **Design Travel & Tours** (✉ Box 528, Glen Ellyn, IL 60137, ☎ 800/543-

7164, 𝔽𝔸𝕏 630/942-9049). **Discover Tours** (✉ 6776 Magnolia Ave., Riverside, CA 92506, ☎ 800/545-8653, 𝔽𝔸𝕏 909/684—7281). **Luxury Adventure Safaris** (✉ 4635 Via Vistosa, Santa Barbara, CA 93110, ☎ 800/733-1789, 𝔽𝔸𝕏 805/964-8285). **Mountain Travel-Sobek** (✉ 6420 Fairmount Ave., El Cerrito, CA 94530, ☎ 510/527-8100 or 800/227-2384, 𝔽𝔸𝕏 510/525-7710). **S. A. Adventures Inc.** (✉ 6075 Roswell Rd., Suite 304, Atlanta, GA 30328, ☎ 800/999-7180, 𝔽𝔸𝕏 404/851-9816). **Safari Consultants Ltd.** (✉ 16 N. 1st Ave., St. Charles, IL 60174, ☎ 800/762-4027, 𝔽𝔸𝕏 630/513-0209). **Safaricenter** (✉ 3201 N. Sepulveda Blvd., Manhattan Beach, CA 90266, ☎ 800/223-6046, 𝔽𝔸𝕏 310/546-3188). **SITA World Travel** (✉ 8125 San Fernando Rd., Sun Valley, CA 91352, ☎ 800/421-5643, 𝔽𝔸𝕏 818/767-4346). **Sue's Safaris** (✉ Box 2171, Rancho Palos Verdes, CA 90274-8171, ☎ 800/541-2011, 𝔽𝔸𝕏 310/544-1502). **United Touring Company** (✉ 1 Bala Plaza, Suite 414, Bala Cynwyd, PA 19004-1401, ☎ 800/223-6486, 𝔽𝔸𝕏 610/617-3312). **Wildland Adventures** (✉ 3516 N.E. 155th St., Seattle, WA 98155, ☎ 800/345—4453, 𝔽𝔸𝕏 206/363—6615). **Wildlife Safari** (✉ 346 Rheem Blvd., Moraga, CA 94556, ☎ 800/221-8118, 𝔽𝔸𝕏 510/376-5059).

PACKAGES

Like group tours, independent vacation packages are available from major tour operators and airlines. The companies listed below offer vacation packages in a broad price range.

➤ GAME VIEWING: **Abercrombie & Kent** (☞ Groups, *above*). **African Travel** (☞ Groups, *above*). **African Portfolio** (✉ 225 East 79th St., New York, NY 10021, ☎ 800/700-3677, 𝔽𝔸𝕏 212/737-6930; ✉ 160 Enterprise Rd., Highlands, Harare, Zimbabwe, ☎ 14/481-117, 𝔽𝔸𝕏 14/495-704). **Africa Tours** (✉ 875 Ave. of the Americas, Suite 2108, New York, NY 10001, ☎ 800/235-3692, 𝔽𝔸𝕏 212/563—4459). **Baobab Safari Company** (✉ 210 Post St., Suite 911, San Francisco, CA 94108, ☎ 800/835-3692, 415/391-5788, 𝔽𝔸𝕏 415/391-3752). **Big Five Tours & Expeditions** (☞ Groups, *above*). **Born Free Safaris** (☞ Groups, *above*). **Wildlife Safari** (☞ Groups, *above*).

THEME TRIPS

➤ Customized Safari Packages: **Luxury Adventure Safaris** (☞ Groups, *above*). **Born Free Safaris** (☞ Groups, *above*). **Design Travel & Tours** (☞ Groups, *above*). **S. A. Adventures Inc.** (☞ Groups, *above*). **Safaricenter** (☞ Groups, *above*). **Safari Consulants Ltd.** (☞ Groups, *above*). **SITA World Travel** (☞ Groups, *above*). **Sue's Safaris** (☞ Groups, *above*). **United Touring Company** (☞ Groups, *above*). **Wild African Ventures** (✉ 745 S. Marengo Ave., Pasadena, CA 91106, ☎ 800/358–8530, FAX 626/792—8055). **Wildland Adventures** (☞ Groups, *above*).

➤ Bird-Watching: **Lawson's Tours** (✉ Box 507, Nelspruit 1200, Mpumalanga, ☎ 013/755—2147 or 013/755–2108, FAX 013/755–1793), led by famed ornithologist Peter Lawson, is the premier bird-watching tour company in South Africa. Lawson is knowledgeable and passionate about birds, both of which he communicates to his guests. Lawson also conducts photographic and general wildlife tours.

➤ Golf: **ITC Golf Tours** (✉ 4134 Atlantic Ave., Suite 205, Long Beach, CA 90807, ☎ 800/257–4981, FAX 562/424–6683).

➤ Learning: **American Museum of Natural History's "Discovery Tours"** (✉ 79th St. and Central Park West, New York, NY 10024, ☎ 212/769–5700 or 800/462–8687).

➤ Senior Travel: **Grand Circle Travel** (✉ 347 Congress St., Boston, MA 02210, ☎ 800/221–2610, FAX 617/346—6700).

TRAIN TRAVEL

A trip aboard the famous **Blue Train** (✉ Box 2671, Joubert Park 2044, ☎ 011/773–7584/7585, FAX 011/773–8151) has long been one of the highlights of any trip to South Africa. Since its inception in 1923, the Blue Train's 24-hour passage between Cape Town and Johannesburg through the Karoo Desert has served as a standard for luxury and shameless pampering. The Blue Train has been re-vamped and standards have improved after dropping slightly in recent years. Rooms are now air-conditioned and have button-operated blinds and curtains, radios, and a service bell for ordering

drinks or having ironing done. The comfortably furnished lounge car offers refreshments and drinks throughout the day and is a good place to meet fellow-travelers. Food in the well-appointed dining car, where you can now expect silver cutlery and the crispest linen, has also improved. Men are required to wear a jacket and tie to dinner. On the Pretoria–Cape Town route, guests are treated to champagne when the train stops in Kimberley and taken by coach on a tour of the historic diamond-mining town.

In addition to its regular run between Cape Town and Johannesburg, the Blue Train occasionally goes to the game-rich Eastern Transvaal and journeys farther to view the splendors of Victoria Falls in Zimbabwe. All meals and alcohol are included in the ticket price (which averages R5,100–R5,400 for a one-way fare).

A new competitor that is earning rave reviews at the expense of the Blue Train is romantic **Rovos Rail** (✉ Box 2837, Pretoria 0001, ☎ 012/323–6052, FAX 012/323–0843), 12 beautifully restored Edwardian-era carriages drawn by a steam engine. The luxury train carries a maximum of 46 passengers, attended by 16 staff members, including two gourmet chefs. In addition to two-day Cape Town–Johannesburg runs ($1,066–$1,500 per person), Rovos Rail offers a variety of trips ranging from a four-day jaunt to the Eastern Transvaal to a 12-day rail safari to Dar es Salaam in Tanzania, stopping at Victoria Falls on the way. Trips are coupled with excursions, such as a game drive in a private reserve in the lowveld (low-lying subtropical area in the Eastern Transvaal). The ticket covers everything, including alcohol and meals.

Mainline Passenger Services (✉ Box 2671, Joubert Park 2044, ☎ 011/773–2944), part of the South African rail network known as **Spoornet**, operates an extensive system of passenger trains connecting most major cities. Departures are usually limited to one per day, although trains covering minor routes leave less frequently. Distances are vast, so many journeys require overnight travel. Traveling first class is your best bet, and it doesn't cost significantly more than second class. You must reserve tickets in advance for first- and second-class accommodation, whereas third-class tickets require no advance booking. You can book up to three months in advance with travel agents, reservations offices in major cities, and at railway stations.

TRAVEL AGENCIES

A good travel agent puts your needs first. Look for an agency that has been in business at least five years, emphasizes customer service, and has someone on staff who specializes in your destination. In addition, **make sure the agency belongs to the American Society of Travel Agents** (ASTA). If your travel agency is also acting as your tour operator, *see* Buyer Beware in Tour Operators, *above*).

➤ LOCAL AGENT REFERRALS: American Society of Travel Agents (ASTA, ☎ 800/965–2782 24-hr hot line, FAX 703/684–8319). Alliance of Canadian Travel Associations (✉ Suite 201, 1729 Bank St., Ottawa, Ontario K1V 7Z5, ☎ 613/521–0474, FAX 613/521–0805). Association of British Travel Agents (✉ 55–57 Newman St., London W1P 4AH, ☎ 0171/637–2444, FAX 0171/637–0713).

TRAVEL GEAR

Travel catalogs specialize in useful items, such as compact alarm clocks and travel irons, that can **save space when packing.** They also offer dual-voltage appliances, currency converters, and foreign-language phrase books.

➤ MAIL-ORDER CATALOGS: **Magellan's** (☎ 800/962–4943, FAX 805/568–5406). **Orvis Travel** (☎ 800/541–3541, FAX 540/343–7053). **Travel-Smith** (☎ 800/950–1600, FAX 800/950–1656).

U

U.S. GOVERNMENT

The U.S. government can be an excellent source of inexpensive travel information. When planning your trip, **find out what government materials are available.**

AdvisoriesU.S. Department of State (✉ Overseas Citizens Services Office, Room 4811 N.S., Washington, DC 20520); enclose a SASE. Interactive hot line (☎ 202/647–5225, FAX 202/647–3000). Computer bulletin board (☎ 301/946–4400).

➤ PAMPHLETS: **Consumer Information Center** (✉ Consumer Information Catalogue, Pueblo, CO 81009, ☎ 719/948–3334) for a free catalog that includes travel titles.

VISITOR INFORMATION

SOUTH AFRICA

For information about traveling to and within South Africa before you go, contact the nearest office of the **South African Tourism Board** (Satour).

➤ SOUTH AFRICAN GOVERNMENT TOURIST OFFICES: U.S.: (✉ 500 5th Ave., Suite 2040, New York, NY 10110, ☎ 800/822–5368, FAX 212/764—1980; 9841 Airport Blvd., Suite 1524, Los Angeles, CA 90045, ☎ 800/782–9772, FAX 310/641—5812). **Canada:** (✉ 4117 Lawrence Ave. E, Suite 2, Scarborough, Ontario, M1E 2S2, ☎ 416/283–0563, FAX 416/283—5465). **U.K.:** (✉ Nos. 5–6 Alt Grove, Wimbledon SW19 4DZ, ☎ 0181/944–8080, FAX 0181/944—6705).

ZIMBABWE

➤ ZIMBABWE TOURISM OFFICE: **U.S.:** (✉ 1270 Ave. of the Americas, Suite 2315, New York, NY 10020, ☎ 212/332–1090, FAX 212/332–1093). **Canada:** (✉ Zimbabwe High Commission, 332 Somerset St., West Ottawa, Ontario K2P 0J9, ☎ 613/237–4388, FAX 613/563–8269). **U.K.:** (✉ Zimbabwe Tourism Office, 429 Strand, London, WC2R 05A, ☎ 171/240–6169, FAX 171/379–1167).

BOTSWANA

➤ BOTSWANA EMBASSY: **U.S. and Canada:** (✉ Suite 7M, 3400 International Dr. NW, Washington, DC 20008, ☎ 202/244–4990). **U.K.:** (✉ 6 Stratford Pl., London W1N 9AE, ☎ 171/499–0031).

W

WHEN TO GO

Southern Africa being in the Southern Hemisphere, its seasons are reversed—it's summer down there during the North American and European winter.

Peak tourist season is November through March, when hotel prices rise dramatically and making a reservation can be difficult. The situation is exacerbated during major school holidays—especially December 1–

January 15, the South African equivalent of summer vacation—when South African families take to the roads in droves. Schools also have two weeks' vacation around Easter and a month in July.

In terms of weather, the best time to visit Cape Town is from November through March. Keep in mind, however, that the shoulder months of October and April can be fabulous and uncrowded. Cape winters (May–August) are cold, windy, and rainy.

Much of the rest of the country receives its rain in the hot summer months. As a result, peak season for other travel is arguably the worst season for game viewing in Mpumalanga—animals are harder to spot in dense foliage, and the abundance of water all around means that they don't need to stick around water holes, where they are easier to see. The best time for seeing animals is during the dry winter season (June–August), when trees have no leaves and the game gathers around the few remaining water sources. Prices are lower at this time of year, but it can be very cold. A happy compromise may be spring and autumn (October and April), the shoulder months.

Johannesburg and the highveld enjoy glorious summers, with hot, sunny days broken by afternoon thunderstorms. Winter nights are frosty; days are generally mild and sunny. More recently, Johannesburg winters have become colder, sometimes with rain, sleet and even a little snow. If you're visiting the country during winter, bring wool sweaters and heavier outer layers. The Eastern Cape has similarly been experiencing cold winters, sometimes getting snow.

KwaZulu-Natal is warm year-round, but summers are steamy and hot, and August sees high winds buffet the coastline. The water along the KwaZulu-Natal coast is warmest in February, but it seldom dips below 65°F at any time of year.

Southern Africa has a 7 to 8-year drought and flood cycle, and in recent years the country has been subject to heavy, unseasonal rains. Pack good rain-gear wherever you go, and remember to bring layers for the colder rainy days.

The following are average daily maximum and minimum temperatures for some major cities in South Africa. For information on seasonal temperatures in Zimbabwe and Botswana, *see* the When to Tour sections of Exploring Zimbabwe and Exploring Botswana at the beginning of Chapters 9 and 10.

Climate in South Africa

CAPE TOWN

Jan.	79F	26C	May	68F	20C	Sept.	66F	19C
	61	16		48	9		48	9
Feb.	81F	27C	June	64F	18C	Oct.	70F	21C
	61	16		46	8		52	11
Mar.	77F	25C	July	64F	18C	Nov.	75F	24C
	57	14		45	7		55	13
Apr.	73F	23C	Aug.	64F	18C	Dec.	77F	25C
	54	12		46	8		59	15

DURBAN

Jan.	82F	28C	May	77F	25C	Sept.	73F	23C
	70	21		57	14		59	15
Feb.	82F	28C	June	73F	23C	Oct.	75F	24C
	70	21		52	11		63	17
Mar.	82F	28C	July	73F	23C	Nov.	77F	25C
	68	20		52	11		64	18
Apr.	79F	26C	Aug.	73F	23C	Dec.	81F	27C
	63	17		55	13		68	20

JOHANNESBURG

Jan.	79F	26C	May	66F	19C	Sept.	73F	23C
	59	15		45	7		50	10
Feb.	77F	25C	June	61	16C	Oct.	75F	24C
	57	14		39	4		52	11
Mar.	75F	24C	July	63F	17C	Nov.	75F	24C
	55	13		39	4		55	13
Apr.	70F	21C	Aug.	66F	19C	Dec.	77F	25C
	50	10		43	6		57	14

SKUKUZA (KRUGER NATIONAL PARK)

Jan.	91F	33C	May	82F	28C	Sept.	84F	29C
	70	21		50	10		55	13
Feb.	90F	32C	June	79F	26C	Oct.	86F	30C
	68	20		43	6		61	16
Mar.	88F	31C	July	79F	26C	Nov.	88F	31C
	66	19		43	6		64	18
Apr.	84F	29C	Aug.	81F	27C	Dec.	90F	32C
	59	15		48	9		68	20

➤ FORECASTS: **Weather Channel Connection** (☎ 900/932–8437), 95¢ per minute from a Touch-Tone phone.

1 Destination: South Africa

THE RAINBOW NATION, AND ITS NEIGHBORS

MY FAMILY first came to South Africa from England over a half century ago. Earlier, Nigeria had been home for seven years. And as cliché as it might sound, once Africa gets into your blood, it's hard to deny her pull. Now it was South Africa's sunshine and opportunities that beckoned.

We were immigrants, equipped only with an old car, lots of enthusiasm, and three young children—"Not enough," the white Afrikaner Immigration official growled after we landed at Cape Town. "We need more white children". Undaunted, we set off north through the Karoo Desert for Egoli—Johannesburg, City of Gold—blissfully ignorant about the complex, and to our great fortune stunningly, beautiful country that we would settle in.

Today, in spite of South Africa's current problem with violence, we still wouldn't choose to live anywhere else. There's no room for Old World boredom or complacency when you live in a country where people debate in 11 different official languages—Archbishop Desmond Tutu calls us "The Rainbow Nation" for our racial diversity—and which has the world's newest and most liberal democratic constitution. It is difficult to imagine a country more vibrant and alive than this.

The whole world knows of our infamous past. Our groundbreaking Truth and Reconciliation Commission is ensuring that we don't forget it. So much heartbreak, trauma, truth, and lies were revealed almost daily at its 1997 public hearings. Amazingly, there's little bitterness or racial conflict—a lead set by Nelson Mandela, arguably the world's most respected leader.

Brits and Boers still rant and rave at one another—the legacy of the turn-of-the-century Anglo-Boer Wars—but usually only at international rugby and cricket matches, when the Lions and the Springboks prepare to do latter-day battle. And of course, from time to time, South Africa's great warriors, the Zulus, fueled by ancient tribal animosities, will have a bloody feud. That's all part of the heady racial mix, a mix that isn't hidden by hypocrisy or embedded in warm, fuzzy euphemisms. In this country, race is discussed openly and up-front in the media, in schools and universities, in the home, and wherever people are gathered together.

This doesn't mean that blacks, whites, and people of mixed descent live side by side on every street and block. If you go to the more up-market suburbs of Johannesburg or Cape Town, you might see a few of the new black elite at a party, movie house, or trendy restaurant, but most blacks still live in townships like Soweto, in low-cost housing, in the rural areas, or in squatter camps. As the schools become (by law) more and more racially integrated, this situation is bound to change. Change *is* the keynote of the new South Africa, and the depth of change required will likely take new generations to fully realize.

In a strange way, politics are also bringing people together: There is a high level of disappointment about the ANC government's failure to meet its election promises. A vaunted policy for equal education for all has not materialized—many black schools in townships are overcrowded and barely functioning, levels of teacher commitment are at an all-time low, and millions of pupils do not even have textbooks.

Universal housing is another chimera. Apart from a scattering of showcase projects, the government has had little impact on the notoriously poor delivery of South Africa's mass housing program. It might prove true that old voting habits will put the same people back in office at the next election, but complaining about the government is a great unifying force. Whatever our race or background, we all have our collective go at politicians riding the gravy train.

Aa a foreigner in South Africa, you'll meet with tremendous hospitality. A friend of mine from Boston, visiting the Kimberley Mine Museum, ended up spending a few days in this historic city with a local schoolmaster and his family. Talk, talk, talk to everyone you can—South Africans love to talk about their country. Next to Ireland, I can't think of a place where people are so keen and ready to discuss their country, warts and all, with such honesty and enthusiasm.

When you cross the borders of South Africa into Swaziland, Zimbabwe, or Botswana, leave some of your first-world expectations at home—that's part of what Africa is all about—and you'll have a whale of a time. The tiny monarchy of Swaziland, bounded by Mozambique and South Africa's Gauteng Province, is a land of green rolling mountains, grey rocks, swirling mists, meandering streams, and a thoroughly laid-back atmosphere. The country is ruled by the young British-educated King Mswati III. His father, King Sobhuza, ruled for 60 years—he was, in his day, the longest-reigning monarch in the world—and sired over 100 children. Swaziland has a unique charm, compounded not only of its rural, peaceful landscapes, but also its sometimes bizarre mix of old and new. A journalist interviewed the King's *sangoma* (spiritual advisor and medicine man) a few years ago. She was surprised to find, after she had crawled through the low entrance of his round thatched hut, past his sacred, ritualistic regalia and divining bones, an Apple Macintosh propped against the far mud wall. For a glimpse of the real, nontourist Africa, don't miss the Umhlanga (Reed Dance), held in spring, late September, or early August, at the Royal Village near the capital city, Mbabane, when hundreds of Swazi maidens dance for their king.

Since gaining independence from Britain in 1980, Zimbabwe has come of its own economically, in spite of occasional difficulties, and has done remarkably well in areas of conservation and wildlife management. Along with its variety of landscapes—from the rocky hills in the south to the Zambezi River system on the northern border with Zambia—you'll find southern Africa's best wilderness guides here.

Zimbabwe—southern Africans call it "Zim"—is known first and foremost for its wonder of the world, Victoria Falls. That is both good and bad, because the genuinely amazing falls and the white-water rafting below them are well worth the attention,

but the tourism scene that has grown up around them isn't pretty. The rest of the country, happily, is far more cheerful, easygoing, and down-to-earth and less expensive. Wildlife in Hwange National Park, around Lake Kariba, and in the glorious Mana Pools area below Lake Kariba in the middle Zambezi River valley is superb. And for a glimpse into Africa's past, the stone citadel of Great Zimbabwe—the largest ancient structure south of the Sahara—is what remains of the heart of a vast trading empire. For a taste of local culture, don't miss a visit to a traditional village—these are not reconstructions for tourists but the real thing—in a communal lands area.

Independent since 1966 and renowned for its friendly inhabitants, Botswana is generally recognized as Africa's most stable democracy. Although it's landlocked, this scenically diverse country about the size of France or Texas has some of the most amazing terrain in the world—the great Kalahari Desert, the moonscapes of the biggest salt pans on earth, the Makgadikgadi Pans, the mighty Chobe River with its huge elephant populations, the pristine wetland perfection of the Okavango Delta, the game-rich Moremi Reserve, and the Linyanti-Kwando areas. Botswana is still the Africa of the old travel maps, explorers' tales, and uncharted wildernesses. Largely undiscovered by travelers, it is a dream destination teeming with animals and birds. Get there quickly before it becomes de rigueur on too many people's itineraries.

—By Kate Turkington

NEW AND NOTEWORTHY

South Africa's tourist industry is booming. New hotels continue to mushroom, including a Hilton in Sandton, one of Johannesburg's poshest suburbs; the Commodore Hotel on Cape Town's waterfront—all rooms have views of Table Mountain or the harbor—and the elegant Cape Grace. Durban's gracious old lady, the Edward, has had a classy facelift which has more than restored her former glory. And the growing number of charming and well-run bed and breakfasts dish out homegrown hospitality in houses that range from modest to magnificent.

Local culture has been chosen as the South African Tourist Board's theme for the next three years, focusing on the idea of country being the Rainbow Nation, made up of a diversity of cultures each offering their own art, music, and cuisine.

Many Capetonians thanked their lucky stars when the Mother City *didn't* win the 2004 Olympic bid—the city is growing fast enough as it is, they grumble—particularly the Waterfront, with new hotels, restaurants, speciality shops, and pubs opening almost daily. But the country's s top tourist attraction is still classy and relatively safe. Don't miss out on the fabulous new Table Mountain Cableway—its revolving cars give you a breathtaking 180° view of the Mother City.

South Africans (for whom sport is the national religion) are over the moon that their teams are chewing up the opposition internationally and at home—particularly the cricket team and the Springbok World Cup Rugby champions. Bafana Bafana, the national soccer team, is everybody's favorite—an unthinkable situation pre-apartheid days, when soccer was mainly a black townships game.

Now that the post-apartheid glow has subsided, politics are like politics world-wide—everybody moans about the present government. Lester Venter's recent best-selling book, *When Mandela Goes,* underlines the general anxiety about what happens post-Mandela. Winnie Midikizela–Mandela, in the wake of her grilling at the 1997 Truth and Reconciliation Commission—and her poised denial of all accusations of wrongdoing on her part—removed her name from subsequent elections for lack of support.

Because of the weak rand and the fluctuating Zimbabwe dollar, Southern Africa is one of the best travel bargains in the world. And the quality of service and lodgings makes the value even higher.

In 1998, Kruger National Park celebrates its centenary and is still a must on any visitor's itinerary.

On a somber note, political and personal violence in South Africa continues, especially around major cities and in the KwaZulu-Natal province. Common sense precautions and advance planning will significantly reduce the likelihood of encountering difficulties. *See* the Safety section of the Gold Guide for detailed information about staying safe while in South Africa.

WHAT'S WHERE

Johannesburg

A mile high, South Africa's largest city sprawls across the highveld plateau, its soaring skyscrapers giving way to endless suburbs. Johannesburg is built—literally and figuratively—on gold, and the relentless pursuit of wealth has imbued it with a pulsing energy. Much of the anti-apartheid struggle was played out in the dusty black townships ringing the city, and a tour of Soweto and the city center will give you a feel for the new South Africa. Johannesburg itself is an unlovely city, with few attractions to hold you long. Arrange a trip down a gold mine, and then take yourself north to Pretoria, the genteel capital of South Africa, or to Sun City, a glittering fantasyland of casinos, golf, water rides, and big-game adventure.

Mpumalanga and Kruger National Park

Classic Africa—the Africa of heat, thorn trees, and big game—unfolds before you in the Mpumalanga, a wild and beautiful province abutting Mozambique. The great allure here is game-watching, either in famed Kruger National Park or in an exclusive private reserve. But the province has much more to offer than animals. The Drakensberg ("Dragon Mountains" in Afrikaans) split the province in two, dividing the subtropical lowveld from the high interior plateau. Tucked away in these mountains of mists, forests, waterfalls, and panoramic views lie some of South Africa's most luxurious hotels and lodges, as well as beautiful hikes and historic gold-rush towns.

Cape Town and the Peninsula

Capetonians tend to look with pity upon those who don't have the good fortune to live in their Eden. Their attitude is understandable—Cape Town is indeed one of the world's fairest cities. Backed by Table Mountain, the city presides over a coastline of unsurpassed beauty: of mountains cascading into the sea, miles of beaches, and 17th-century wineries snoozing under giant oaks. Modern South Africa was born here, and the city is filled with historic reminders of its three centuries as the sea link between Europe and the East.

The Western Cape

This diverse region serves as the weekend playground for Capetonians. The jewel of the province is the Winelands, a stunning collection of jagged mountains, vine-covered slopes, and centuries-old Cape Dutch estates that produce some of the world's finest wine. Farther afield, the Overberg is a quiet region of farms and beach resorts that ends at Cape Agulhas, the southernmost tip of Africa. The long, lonely coastline is a marvel of nature—rocky mountains dropping sheer to the sea, pristine beaches, and towering dunes. The west coast and Namaqualand is a desolate landscape dotted with tiny fishing villages and isolated diamond mines. Every spring the semi-desert region's wildflower explosion is a nonpareil sight. Inland, the pretty towns of the Cedarberg ("Cedar Mountains") and Hantam Plateau make great bases for long hikes and drives.

The Garden Route and Little Karoo

The Garden Route is a beautiful 208-km (130-mi) stretch of coast that takes its name from the region's year-round riot of vegetation. Here, you'll find some of South Africa's most inspiring scenery: forest-cloaked mountains, myriad rivers and streams, and golden beaches backed by thick, indigenous bush. You'll also find Plettenberg Bay, South Africa's glitziest beach resort, and Knysna, a charming town built around an oyster-rich lagoon. The Little Karoo, separated from the coast by a range of mountains, is a semi-arid region famous for its ostrich farms, turn-of-the-century "feather palaces," and the Cango Caves, one of the world's most impressive networks of underground caverns.

Durban and KwaZulu-Natal

Steamy heat, the heady aroma of spices, and a polyglot of English, Indian, and Zulu give the bustling port city of Durban a tropical feel. Some of the country's most popular bathing beaches extend north and south of the city; inland you can tour the battlefields where Boer, Briton, and Zulu struggled for control of the country. The Drakensberg are a breathtaking sanctuary of soaring beauty, crisp air, and some of the country's best hiking. In the far north, Hluhluwe-Umfolozi and several private reserves have wildlife rivaling that of Mpumalanga.

Swaziland

From the rolling hills in the northwest to the purple Lubombo Mountains in the east, Swaziland has the look of an African paradise, where you can explore craft markets, ride horses through Ezulwini Valley, and raft the mighty Usutu River.

Zimbabwe

If you arrive in Zimbabwe from South Africa, with its mix of peoples and races, you'll notice straight away that this is black Africa. In Zimbabwe's cities life moves more slowly. And of course there are the country's landscapes and wildlife: from hippos snorting in the Zambezi River to elfin klipspringer antelope bounding around the granite hills of Matobo National Park. In between are the ancient stone ruins of Great Zimbabwe, more national parks, and the world's best white-water rafting.

Botswana

Botswana itself is a natural wonder. Its variety of terrains, from vast salt pans to the waterways of the Okavango Delta to the Kalahari Desert, have diversity seldom found in such a small area. And with so little industry, you may have never seen stars as bright as this. The Kalahari Bushmen say that you can hear the stars sing— listen.

PLEASURES & PASTIMES

Beaches

South Africa has some of the finest beaches on earth—literally hundreds of miles of golden sands, often without a soul on them. The surf is big, and dangerous undertows and side washes are common.

Beaches in major cities have lifeguards, and helicopters periodically patrol the coastline. Cape Town and the entire Western Cape have glorious beaches, but the water is extremely cold year-round, and wind can be a problem. The water is warmer along the Garden Route, with the best swimming at Plettenberg Bay. Around Durban and the resorts of KwaZulu-Natal, the water is ideal for swimming, but keep an eye out for the stinging Portuguese man-of-war (bluebottle), particularly when the wind is coming from the east. All major resort beaches in KwaZulu-Natal are protected by shark nets. For truly deserted beaches and warm water, head to Rocktail Bay Lodge in the far north of KwaZulu-Natal.

Big Game Adventures

Southern Africa may not have the vast herds of East Africa, but it has far more species of animals, and it is thankfully free of the minivan lineups around animals that happen in Kenya's national parks. In fact, nowhere on the continent do wild animals enjoy better protection than in southern Africa, and nowhere do you have a better chance of seeing Africa's big game—elephant, black and white rhino, lion, buffalo, cheetah, leopard, and hippopotamus. The antelopes and smaller animals—giraffe, zebra, kudu, sable, springbok, waterbuck, impala, warthog, and predators like hyena, wild dog, bat-eared fox, and jackal—are no less fascinating than the larger animals. The experience of tracking game in a Land Rover or of walking in the wild with an armed ranger will fill you with awe for the elemental magic of the African bush. Binoculars are a must, and bring a zoom-lens for your camera if you have one.

Bird-Watching

South Africa itself ranks as one of the finest bird-watching destinations on the planet. Kruger National Park alone has recorded more than 500 different bird species, many of breathtaking beauty. Birds in Zimbabwe and Botswana are spectacular as well. Look for sacred ibis, a variety of eagles and falcons and vultures, red-and-yellow billed hornbills, numerous egrets and storks, and the favorite lilac-breasted roller, to name a few. The best time for bird-watching is October–April, when migrants are in residence.

Canoeing and White-Water Rafting

The world's most incredible white-water rafting is on the Zambezi River, through the gorges below Victoria Falls. It's an adventure you won't soon forget, and no prior experience is necessary. A great canoe trek, from 3 to 7 days long, is on the Zambezi below Lake Kariba, where the water meanders between Zimbabwe and Zambia, afloat with hippos and crocs under the distant Zambezi Escarpment.

Cricket

White South Africans are crazy about it—during international matches, you'll often find crowds gathered in front of the windows of electronics stores watching the action. These international competitions, known as test matches, are played against teams from England and former colonies like India, the West Indies, and Australia. A one-day test match is as riveting as anything baseball can produce. The longer five-day test matches involve subtle nuances of strategy that will confound—and probably bore—anyone not born to the game. South Africa's provinces also compete against each other in the annual Castle Cup. A major push is under way to introduce cricket into black communities, but it remains an essentially white sport.

Dining

South Africa won't unseat France anytime soon from its culinary throne. But there are three bright spots that you should keep in mind. The first is the abundance of fresh seafood, from plump Knysna oysters to enormous Mozambiquean prawns to the Cape's magnificent clawless lobsters, known as crayfish. The second is the country's love affair with Indian cuisine, first brought to South Africa by Indian laborers in the 19th century. Samosas and curries appear on almost every menu, and Durban's bunny chow is a fast-food curry-filled loaf of bread. Third, Cape Malay represents South Africa's own cuisine, a centuries-old blend of recipes brought by early Dutch settlers and slaves transported from the Dutch East Indies. Most evident in the Cape, the cuisine is characterized by mild, slightly sweet curries and the use of aromatic spices.

Here is a brief glossary of South African cooking terms:

Biltong. An integral part of South African life, biltong is air-dried meat, made of everything from beef to kudu. Unlike jerky, it's not smoked. Strips of meat are dipped in vinegar, rolled in salt and spices, and hung up to dry. You can buy it in strips or ready-cut into bite-size chunks.

Bobotie. A classic Cape Malay dish consisting of delicately spiced ground beef or lamb topped with a savory custard.

Boerewors. Afrikaans for farmer's sausage (pronounced *boor*-ah-vorse), this coarse, flavorful sausage has a distinctive spiciness. It's a standard feature at *braais*.

Braai. Short for *braaivleis* (grill meat), braais are the South African equivalent of a barbecue—and a way of life. South Africans consume enormous amounts of meat, and a braai invariably consists of more than a hamburger thrown on the grill. Expect lamb chops, boerewors (☞ *above*), chicken, steak, and beer, beer, beer. Sports stadiums even have special beer-and-braai areas where fans can cook up a storm, and some national parks offer visitors the use of free gas grills.

Bredie. Bredie is a slow-cooked stew, made with everything from meat to water lilies.

Line fish. This is the generic restaurant term for fish caught with a pole, as opposed to a net, and the assumption is that quality is better as a result. Kingklip is one very common and tasty linefish.

Pap. Also known as *putu,* pap (pronounced "puhp") is a maize-meal porridge that is a staple for many black South Africans. At braais, you may find it served as an accompaniment to boerewors, topped with stewed tomato and onion.

Peri-Peri. Based on the searing hot piri-piri chile, peri-peri sauce was introduced by Portuguese immigrants from neighboring Mozambique. There are as many recipes as there are uses for this tasty condiment and marinade. Some recipes are tomato-based while others use garlic, olive oil, and brandy. Either way, peri-peri brings out the best in grilled prawns and chicken.

Potjiekos. Another type of stew (pronounced *poy*-key-koss), simmered in a three-legged wrought-iron cooking pot. Visitors to private game lodges are likely to sample impala potjiekos at least once during their stay.

Sadza. In Zimbabwe, this is the staple corn mash served with stew and vegetables.

Sosaties. In this South African version of a kebab, chunks of meat are marinated in Cape Malay spices and grilled.

Fishing

South Africans are among the most avid anglers in the world. During peak holidays, the long coastline is lined with surf-casters trying for everything from cob to stumpnose, rock cod, shad, blacktail, and moonfish. Trout-fishing in the Natal Midlands and Mpumalanga Drakensberg is also a major draw. In the Okavango Delta and all along the Zambezi River in Zimbabwe you can experience a thrill of a lifetime—tiger fishing. Aptly named, the tiger fish is an incredibly strong fighter, with jaws like a bear trap. They make bass look like blue-gills.

Flora

South Africa's floral wealth is astounding. Many small parks in South Africa support more plant species than the entire British Isles. Nowhere is this blessing of nature more evident than in the Cape, home to the smallest and richest of the world's six floral kingdoms. More than 8,500 species of plants grow in the province, of which 5,000 are endemic. Much of the Cape vegetation consists of *fynbos* (pronounced *feign*-boss), hardy, thin-leaved plants ideally suited to the Cape environment. Proteas, including the magnificent king protea, are examples of fynbos.

Golf

The success of local heroes like Gary Player, David Frost, and Ernie Els confirms that golf in South Africa has a fervid following. The country has dozens of championship-quality courses, many designed by Gary Player himself. The stretch of coastline extending south from Durban has gone as far as to christen itself "The Golf Coast." You can play on almost any course in the country, and greens fees are low compared with those in the United States. Don't expect golf carts—a caddy carries your clubs—and the pace of play tends to be faster than it is stateside.

Hiking

Hiking is a major activity in South Africa, and you'll find trails almost everywhere you go. Perhaps the most exciting hikes are the wilderness trails conducted by rangers in Kruger National Park and Hluhluwe-Umfolozi, where hikers sleep out in the bush and spend the day tracking animals, learning about the ecology, and becoming familiar with the ways of the wild. The country's most famous route is the Otter Trail, a five-day hike that runs through pristine wilderness along the coast of the Garden Route. More traditional hikes, ranging in length from a couple of hours to a week, wend through the scenic splendors of the Drakensberg, the Cedarberg in the Cape, or Blyde River Canyon in Mpumalanga.

Hiking is less an opportunity in Zimbabwe and Botswana—unless you have an armed guide with you—because the national parks are filled with predators and dangerous animals like buffalo, rhinoceros, hippopotamus, and elephant. One exception to this is Matobo National Park, where you can climb around on the rocks at leisure, while the animals are in a separate reserve bordering the park.

Rugby

Although long associated with white Afrikaners, rugby became a unifying force in South Africa during the 1995 Rugby World Cup, when South Africa's "Springboks" beat the New Zealand "All Blacks" in the final, sparking a nationwide celebration among all races. Except for standouts like Chester Williams, rugby is still a largely white sport, and inspires a devotion bordering on religion. In addition to a series of international matches staged each year, the rugby calendar is notable for the Currie Cup, played to decide the best provincial team in the country. In 1995, the "Banana Boys" of KwaZulu-Natal took the trophy.

Surfing

In the cult movie *Endless Summer,* globetrotting surfers discovered the perfect wave at Cape St. Francis, near Port Elizabeth. South Africa *is* one of the major surfing countries in the world, with South Africans figuring prominently on the professional circuit. Durban is probably the center of wave mania, hosting a series of international competitions each year; other great surfing spots include Port Elizabeth and Plettenberg Bay. The beaches around Cape Town and up the West Coast (Elands Bay, particularly) are famous, too, although you need a wetsuit to survive the cold water.

Wine and Beer

Forgotten during the years of international sanctions, South African wines are only now getting the recognition they deserve. Visitors to South Africa will be delighted by the quality and range of wines available, including Pinotage, a uniquely South African blend of pinot noir and cinsault grapes (cinsault is known in South Africa as hermitage). Equally appealing are the low, low prices: Expect to pay no more than $10 for a superior bottle of wine. Generally speaking, South African reds tend to be a shade less refined than the whites, although some winemakers are recognizing this and making softer cabernets that drink better when young. Among the whites, sauvignon blanc and riesling are very well made. Some of the best results are in the country's ports.

South Africans are big beer drinkers, too—almost in the same league as Australians. South African Breweries (SAB) has a virtual monopoly on beer, and you're likely to drink a fair share of either Castle or Lion lager, pleasant, slightly hoppy beers. Just remember that South African beer has a high, 5% alcohol content.

FODOR'S CHOICE

Special Moments

South Africa

⭐ **A sunset picnic atop Table Mountain, Cape Town.** Pack a bottle of chilled Cape wine, and good bread and cheese, and take the cable car to the summit, where views stretch forever and sunset never quits. Warning: This is *extremely* romantic.

⭐ **Walking in wildflowers in spring, Namaqualand.** "The Garden of the Gods" is an apt epithet for the annual wildflower spectacular, when the drab desert hillsides explode in a rainbow of colors.

⭐ **Watching whales at Hermanus.** From July to November, whales make their annual procession up the coast of South Africa. From the cliff-top walkways of Hermanus, you look straight down on these graceful behemoths.

⭐ **Hiking at Cathedral Peak, Drakensberg.** The awe-inspiring beauty of the mountains around Cathedral Peak makes it a hiker's dream, with dozens of walks and trails that tackle the surrounding peaks or disappear into hidden gorges and valleys. Take a cooling dip in a mountain stream, search for ancient Bushman paintings, or just drink in the unbelievable views.

⭐ **Wine-tasting and lunch at Vergelegen, Somerset West.** After 300 years, this lovely wine estate is more gracious than ever, encouraging visitors to dally in the formal gardens, relax under the ancient camphor trees, savor the estate wines, and lunch on a veranda overlooking manicured lawns and rose gardens.

⭐ **A game drive in Sabi Sand Game Reserve.** Few things in life are more thrilling than trailing a pride of lions through the bush in an open Land Rover. And nowhere are you more likely to see this spectacle than in Sabi Sands, the country's foremost private game reserve.

⭐ **Sundowners amid the towering dunes at Waenhuiskrans.** Hop on board a Land Rover for a memorable trip through a giant dune field, stopping on the crest of a powdery dune for sundowners overlooking the Indian Ocean.

Zimbabwe

⭐ **Great Zimbabwe National Monument.** The stone ruins of this once-great citadel bring to mind the pre-European might of Africa, a continent of powerful kingdoms and trade routes that stretched across this vast continent.

⭐ **Twilight on the Zambezi River, Mana Pools.** If the quiet water lazing past and the Zambian mountains across the river weren't enough, you might have a band of elphants lope by your camp to get to the river for an evening drink.

⭐ **White-water rafting on the Zambezi River, below Victoria Falls.** A white-water trip down one of Africa's great rivers is a nonstop roller-coaster ride of thrills and spills, with the added grandeur and drama of the surrounding landscape.

Botswana

⭐ **Messing about in a mokoro.** Glide silently with your solitary, skillful poler through the crystal clear waters of the Okavango Delta. It will be a moment of peace that will return to you long after you've left the Delta and Africa behind.

⭐ **Sunset on the Chobe river.** Take to the water—in a canoe, a motorboat, or open-sided cruise boat—to view the great elephant and buffalo herds silhouetted against flaming pink, red, and orange skies as they come down to drink. Sunsets are spectacular on this broad, beautiful, quintessentially African river.

Dining
South Africa

⭐ **Bosman's, Paarl.** Superb Continental cuisine and peerless service make dinner at this elegant Winelands restaurant in the famous Grand Roche Hotel an affair to remember. $$$$

⭐ **Buitenverwachting, Cape Town.** A gorgeous, historic winery provides the backdrop for the best food in the Cape, a mouthwatering blend of Continental savoir faire and the freshest Cape ingredients. Simply not to be missed. $$$$

⭐ **Cybele Forest Lodge, Kiepersol.** Traditional five-course dinners, prepared with flair and skill, make a trip to this cozy sanctuary in the hills well worthwhile. $$$$

⭐ **Linger Longer, Johannesburg.** When goose-liver pâté sets you on cloud nine before you even reach main courses of crisped duckling or boned loin of lamb with garlic and mustard, this is, without a doubt, Johannesburg's finest. $$$$

⭐ **Royal Grill, Durban.** This lovely restaurant is a standard-bearer of culture in Durban, a reminder of a grander, more gracious age. Delicate Continental cuisine complements its turn-of-the-century elegance. $$$$

⭐ **Artists' Café, Sabie.** Eccentric, uneven, but ever delightful, this Italian spot hides in an old railway station in the mountain mists of Mpumalanga. $$

⭐ **Muisbosskerm, Lambert's Bay.** Traditional Afrikaner food and alfresco dining on the beach are the draws of this West Coast favorite, where you watch seafood being cooked on open fires and in huge black pots. It's rustic, beautiful, and a lot of fun. $$

Lodging

South Africa

★ **Mount Nelson, Cape Town.** The grande old dame of Cape Town, this historic hotel has been the place to see and be seen in Cape Town for nearly a century. $$$$

★ **Palace of the Lost City, Sun City.** For sheer, unadulterated extravagance, you can't beat this fantastic and fantastical hotel, built to resemble an ancient African palace. No expense has been spared, and the results are breathtaking. $$$$

★ **The Plettenberg, Plettenberg Bay.** Jaw-dropping views of the sea and the sweep of the bay are the main draws of this tasteful hotel in the heart of South Africa's premier beach resort. It's a great place to drop anchor a while. $$$$

★ **Arniston Hotel, Waenhuiskrans.** In a remote Cape Malay fishing village on a coastline of towering dunes and crystal water, this is one of South Africa's great beach retreats. $$$

★ **Simunye Pioneer Settlement, Melmoth.** Nowhere do you come closer to traditional Zulu culture than at this remote luxury lodge. Horses carry you in, and there's no electricity, but it's an unforgettable, magical experience—a rare opportunity to meet South African blacks one-on-one. $$$

Private Game Lodges

South Africa

★ **Londolozi Tree Camp, Sabi Sands.** This small lodge does almost everything right, from rooms of unmatched elegance to superb cuisine and game viewing. A class act all the way. $$$$

★ **Phinda Forest Lodge, Zululand.** Hidden in the green world of a sand forest, this elegant lodge uses glass instead of walls to make you feel like you're living outside. The effect is startling and magnificent, as is the animal watching and range of activities. $$

★ **Tanda Tula, Timbavati.** You sleep under canvas, but luxury is the name of the game at this super bush camp. Enjoy en suite bathrooms, comfy beds, and tasteful furnishings while listening to lions roar outside your tent. $$

★ **Nottens Bush Camp, Sabi Sands.** Hurricane lanterns, rustic cabins, and down-home hospitality give you a real taste of life in the bush. Don't come for the game, but the sheer thrill of being in Africa. $

★ **Rocktail Bay Lodge, Maputaland.** With miles of empty beaches, giant turtles, dune forests-nothing but nature as far as the eye can see—this tiny lodge is one of the most special places in the country. $

Zimbabwe

★ **Matetsi Game Lodges, near Victoria Falls.** The last word on safari style in Zimbabwe, the near-perfection of Matetsi's two lodges—one on a dry river bed, the other on the banks of the Zambezi—are matched by service both in the bush and in camp. $$$$

★ **Ruckomechi Camp, Mana Pools.** The Zambezi River coursing by on one side, fertile terraces reaching back to thick woodlands, and the country's finest wildlife make time spent at Ruckomechi an African idyll. $$$$

Botswana

★ **Camp Okavango, Okavango Delta.** In the heart of one of the world's most beautiful and pristine wilderness areas, this tented camp is the epitome of charm, elegance, and grace. You may or may not see the biggest game here—but that's not what it's all about. You're here for tranquility, beauty, and an unparalleled water wilderness experience. $$$$

★ **Jack's Camp, Makgadikgadi Pans.** At the only desert camp in the harshly mesmerizing Kalahari, venture into the impenetrable Makgadikgadi salt pans on four-wheel-drive quad bikes, search for Stone Age implements where no man may have set foot for eons, and sleep out under the desert stars. $$$$

★ **Kwando Camp, Chobe area.** The Kwando wildlife experience captures the essence of Botswana—ancient, immense, and unspoiled. With only two camps of six tents apiece, you are guaranteed exclusivity and privacy as you watch wall-to-wall big game in a half-million acres of uncharted wilderness. $$$$

FESTIVALS AND SEASONAL EVENTS

South Africa's top seasonal events are listed below. Contact the South African Tourism Board (Satour) or provincial tourist organizations for exact dates and further information.

SUMMER

➤ EARLY JAN.: The 17-day **Cape Coon Carnival** celebrates the New Year in grand style, as thousands of coloreds (the South African term for people of mixed Malay, Black, and/or European descent) dressed in bright costumes take to the streets of Cape Town to sing and dance.

AUTUMN

➤ APR.: The **Two Oceans Marathon** draws 8,000 runners for perhaps the most scenic race in the world, a grueling 56-km (35-mi) course that circumnavigates part of the Cape Peninsula, including the dizzying heights of Chapman's Peak Drive.

WINTER

➤ JUNE: The **Comrades Marathon** is an agonizing, 80-km (50-mi) double marathon and South Africa's most famous sporting event. The race, run between Pietermaritzburg and Durban, wends through the glorious scenery of the Valley of a Thousand Hills.

➤ JUNE–JULY: The **sardine run** occurs every year, when huge shoals of these small fish migrate up the south coast of KwaZulu-Natal. Men, women, and children race into the water, using whatever's at hand-buckets, nets, even clothing-to capture the slippery fish.

➤ JULY: The **Durban July** is the country's biggest horse race and fashion love-fest, where women race-goers compete to wear the most outrageous, glamorous attire.

➤ JULY: The **Durban Tattoo**, a 17-year tradition, is a military pageant filled with music, color, pomp, and ceremony.

➤ JULY: The **Gunston 500 Surfing Championships** in Durban draw the world's best to compete in the South African leg of the international surfing circuit.

➤ JULY: The **National Arts Festival** in Grahamstown is the country's most famous celebration of the arts, a wild and wacky 10-day extravaganza showcasing the best of South African theater, film, dance, music, and art.

SPRING

➤ AUG.–SEPT.: The **wild-flowers of Namaqualand and the West Coast** are one of nature's great spectacles, with bright spring blooms emerging in their millions from the seemingly barren semidesert. Several of the region's towns hold major flower festivals.

➤ AUG.–NOV.: The annual **whale migration** along the Western Cape coast of the Overberg brings southern right whales, humpback whales, and Bryde's whales close to shore, giving even landlubbers a great view of these graceful leviathans.

➤ OCT.: Purple **jacaranda blossoms** blanket the pleasant captial city of Pretoria, whose quiet streets are lined with these elegant trees.

2 Johannesburg

Vast in size and in human ambition, Johannesburg is built on gold, and the relentless pursuit of wealth has imbued it with a pulsing energy. Much of the country's antiapartheid struggle was played out in the dusty black townships ringing the city, and a tour of Soweto and the city center will give you a feel for the new South Africa. Arrange a trip down a gold mine, then take yourself north to Pretoria, the genteel capital of South Africa, or to Sun City, a glittering fantasyland of casinos, golf, water rides, and big game adventure.

JOHANNESBURG IS THE LARGEST CITY in sub-Saharan Africa—a modern, bustling metropolis that powers the country's economy. Home to more than 6 million people, it sprawls across the featureless plains of the mile-high highveld, spawning endless suburbs that threaten even Pretoria, more than 30 miles distant. It feels like Los Angeles in the veld, and most visitors leave almost as quickly as they arrive.

By Andrew Barbour

Updated by Bronwyn Howard

Jo'burg, as it is known, owes its existence to vast underground riches. Although substantial deposits were recorded as early as 1881, gold was officially discovered here in 1886 by an Australian, George Harrison, who stumbled upon a surface deposit while prospecting on the Witwatersrand (White Water Ridge). Unknown to him, he was standing atop the world's richest gold reef, and his discovery sparked a gold rush unrivaled in history. Gold remains the lifeblood of Johannesburg, and the mines that ring the city now delve more than 2 miles into the earth to extract the precious yellow metal.

It's difficult to overstate the impact of these goldfields on the development of Johannesburg and modern South Africa. In 1899, Britain engineered a war with the Boer Republics just to get its hands on them, and the entire cultural and political fabric of black South Africa has been colored by gold. During the course of the last century, British and Irish fortune hunters, many of whom became wealthy mining magnates and settled in today's Parktown suburb, together with millions of blacks from South Africa, Mozambique, Zimbabwe, and Botswana, made the long journey to I'Goli (a Zulu name meaning "the place of gold") to work in the mines. Forced to live in all-male hostels far from their families, the black mineworkers developed a distinct mine culture that they took with them when they returned to their villages. Go to a wedding in a remote corner of Zululand, and you'll notice that traditional dancers keep their arms and legs close to their bodies, a dance style that developed from necessity in mining hostels' narrow, overcrowded corridors. Today, this has evolved into the stamping, rhythmic "gumboot dancing."

More than anything else, gold has brought about the urbanization—and politicization—of the black population. People follow money, and Johannesburg became a magnet for hundreds of thousands of unemployed rural blacks. By the start of World War II, huge squatter camps—the precursors of townships like Soweto (an abbreviation for "southwestern townships")—had sprouted on the periphery of the city. By the 1960s, township poverty and overcrowding had become the kindling onto which South Africa's hated apartheid legislation poured petrol. In June 1976, police fired on Soweto students protesting the use of Afrikaans in schools, and the townships burst into flame. More than 1,000 people lost their lives in the year of rioting that followed. Ten years later the townships were ungovernable, and the country began its slow movement toward civil war.

Now, under South Africa's first democratic government, the word is out throughout Africa, and blacks continue to pour into the city. And like the first miners who rushed to stake their claims here, they have gold fever. Everyone, it seems, is out to make a buck. The sad truth, however, is that there's not enough to go around as the masses continue to flood in, with overcrowding and so-called squatter camps being the unfortunate result. Nevertheless, the city thrives on an invisible energy, an explosive combination of need, greed, and ambition. It's no surprise that Johannesburg moves faster than any city on the continent.

Very little of the city's past—white or black—has survived this single-minded pursuit of money. Johannesburg builds constantly, paving over the unsightly cracks of history. Even the old mine tailings, the very symbols of the city's raison d'être, are rapidly disappearing. New methods for extracting gold have made it profitable to reprocess these familiar yellow mountains. From a traditional traveler's perspective, Johannesburg is a bust, which is why most visitors spend a night here after their flight and then head straight to more scenic locales.

It would be a mistake to pass through Johannesburg, though, and not tour Soweto or see different aspects of the city, for they provide glimpses of the country's future. Downtown, amid the concrete canyons of the country's financial heart, a new South Africa is emerging, one previously hidden in the townships: the sidewalks are suddenly alive with vendors hawking vegetables, young women ladling out *pap* (maize meal) and sauce, and herbalists dispensing *muthi* (traditional medicine). It's black, it's different, and it's here to stay.

Although sidewalk markets are bustling, "white flight" has knocked the city center into an economic tailspin. Most businesses have now relocated to the affluent northern suburbs, most notably Sandton; it's difficult to find even a decent coffee stand in downtown Johannesburg these days. The trend bears an uncanny resemblance to the collapse of America's inner cities. The major rap against the city center is violent crime, and there *is* a good chance of being mugged, or worse. Do what you have to—travel in a group, hire a bodyguard, or just don't carry any valuables—but at least take a look downtown. If you restrict yourself to the affluent northern suburbs, you might as well have booked a flight to New Jersey.

Indeed, the northern suburbs look as if they belong anywhere *but* Africa. Shopping malls go out of their way to make customers feel like they're in Florence or Paris. Most disturbing of all, however, is the pervasive sense of fear. Appalled by the surge in crime, many whites live behind great walls, protected by 24-hour security services and sophisticated defense systems. Although many of the blacks you're likely to see in the suburbs are gardeners or uniformed maids, increasing job opportunities and affluence have resulted in a gradual migration from the black ghettos of the townships to middle-class suburbs, so it is no longer unusual for whites and blacks to be neighbors or to see blacks driving luxury cars.

If the city beyond the gates seems fraught with danger, life within the suburban *laager* is good. Johannesburg's glorious climate seldom disappoints, and many whites structure their days around the pool and the *braai* (barbecue). It's a typically suburban lifestyle, forgettable in its ordinariness and enviable for its sense of contentment. To someone passing through, however, it's a closed world of limited interest. If you do decide to spend time in the city, you're better off focusing on the events and revolutions that have kept South Africa on the front page of newspapers for decades: take a tour through Soweto or the city center, descend into a gold mine, or head for the wild beauty of the Magaliesberg. After that, take off for somewhere else more beautiful.

Less than an hour north of Johannesburg lies Pretoria, the country's pleasant capital. Though it was once a bastion of hard-line Afrikanerdom, the town now has a refreshing cosmopolitan breeze blowing through the streets. In addition to several historic buildings, Pretoria is most famous for its jacaranda trees, whose purple blossoms blanket the city in September and October. Like Johannesburg, Pretoria lies in the tiny province of Gauteng (*how*-teng), a conurbation on the highveld, 6,000 ft above sea level. You have to travel 90 minutes beyond the borders of Gauteng to reach Sun City, an entertainment and gambling resort set amid the arid beauty of North West Province. You'll find Las Vegas-style hotels, championship golf courses, and water rides, as well as the Pilanesberg National Park, the third-largest national park in South Africa.

If you travel northwest of Johannesburg and Pretoria, you'll reach the wonderful outdoor playground of the Magaliesberg hills, where the countryside is bisected by spectacular, deep gorges. The area is home to baboons, monkeys, small antelope, and a wide variety of birds. For the wild at heart who want to get away from city limits, the Magaliesberg is definitely the place to go. You can take a hike or explore the area's numerous *kloofs* (gorges) and rock faces; visit delightful roadside stalls; admire the scenic vistas across Hartebeesport Dam; and explore country pubs or tea gardens.

Caution: For information on personal safety, *see* the Gold Guide.

Pleasures and Pastimes

Arts and Crafts
Partly as a result of a recession, Johannesburg has spawned several delightful arts and crafts markets. Most are open on weekends, and you can pick up some good bargains. Try the Rooftop Market at Rosebank Mall on Sundays when crowds meander past bright pottery, leather goods, bonsai, and clothing, alongside tables of homemade breads, cheeses, cakes, and *biltong* (jerky). Or head into the countryside on Johannesburg's northwestern side on the first weekend of every month, when the region's creative talent hosts the wonderful Crocodile River Ramble. Drive down farm roads to visit the galleries and studios of artists, sculptors, potters, woodworkers, and others.

Dining
Unlike Cape Town, Johannesburg has no cuisine of its own. What it does have is an array of first-class restaurants serving cuisine from all over the world, including some of the country's finest French and Italian eateries. Some restaurants prepare South African favorites. Surprisingly, seafood in Jo'burg restaurants is often better than what you find down at the coast. Most restaurants lie in the northern suburbs and are accessible only by car. For less expensive food, the area has its share of pizzerias, steak houses, and fast-food chains. The wonderful weather allows ample opportunities to enjoy sidewalk cafés in Rosebank, Melville, and Sandton Square. For a description of South African culinary terms, *see* Pleasures & Pastimes *in* Chapter 1. For price ranges, *see* Chart 1 *in* On the Road with Fodor's.

Hiking
Out of town, the Melville Koppies, near the suburb of Northcliff, has good places to walk—which are enhanced by the company of a member of the botanical society on the third weekend of every month. Hikers and climbers revel in the Magaliesberg region, a magnificent geologic fault that runs northwest of Johannesburg between Rustenburg and Pretoria. Most resorts here have a network of walking trails; you can also explore several exquisite kloofs with the local hiking and mountain clubs.

Lodging
When choosing a hotel in Johannesburg, your most important consideration should be location. The city center remains the financial and business heart of the metropolis, and its streets give visitors a taste of the emerging new South Africa. But this area is also the most danger-

ous part of the city, so you should exercise caution during the day and *never* walk the streets after dark when everything closes. Hotels in the northern suburbs tend to be a great deal safer, with easy access to shopping malls, movie houses, and restaurants. Rosebank and Sandton are rapidly developing into major commercial centers. For price ranges, *see* Chart 2 (A) *in* On the Road with Fodor's.

EXPLORING JOHANNESBURG

The word Johannesburg is often used to describe a vast area encompassing the entire Witwatersrand. The city is extremely spread out, and although the major centers tend to be laid out on an easy gridwork of streets, suburban areas often consist of roads running at odd angles. Get yourself a good street map if you want to become fully acquainted with as many areas of Johannesburg as possible.

Downtown Johannesburg's high crime rate deters inner-city investment. Many of the finer shops and restaurants have closed, their owners migrating northward. A brief walking tour will nevertheless help you get acquainted with the city—and the country's odd First World–Third World mix in the city center, where the two often exist cheek-by-jowl. You'll find more evidence of this juxtaposition when you head south to Newtown and the Oriental Plaza, an eclectic mélange of history and people, in which race matters little in the struggle to adapt to a rapidly changing South Africa.

In the northern suburbs, you'll find fantastic chrome-and-glass shopping malls encompassing luxury goods and pleasant restaurants in underground courts. You can go to movies and shop long after dark here—and your car will probably still be in the parking lot when you're ready to leave. In chic districts like Rosebank and Melville, the mood alternates between sleepy suburbia and trendy vitality.

Though Johannesburg is rarely associated with the great outdoors, it has its share of pleasant parks and nature reserves hugging the outskirts of the city. In the outer areas it's possible to envision how the inland plateau must have appeared to the first settlers in the region. Beyond this, encircled by cities, platinum mines, and the old Bophuthatswana homeland, lies the Magaliesberg region. Still largely unspoiled, it is a haven from the busy city for many—a place where it's still possible to see wildlife up close.

Pretoria, the Jacaranda City, is generally warmer and more wholesome than its up-country cousin. Leafy avenues crisscross peaceful suburbs, and much of its cultural heritage remains intact, preserved in museums and national monuments. It's altogether quieter, gentler, and more gracious than Johannesburg.

Great Itineraries
You won't need a great deal of time to explore the area. If you don't intend going beyond city limits, two days is probably sufficient. If you want to look at areas beyond Johannesburg, such as the Magaliesberg or Sun City, allow yourself at least five days.

Johannesburg sprawls, and sights can be some distance from one another. Buses are not reliable and many places you'll be visiting don't have taxi ranks, so it's a good idea to rent a car. Try to arm yourself with a detailed map of the city beforehand. Automobile Association maps and those published by Map Studio are generally excellent. They are available at most bookstores.

The three tours that follow these itineraries combine driving and walking. You may want to create your own tour by choosing a few sights from all three.

Numbers in the text correspond to numbers in the margin and on the Johannesburg map.

IF YOU HAVE 2 DAYS

Begin your first day in downtown Johannesburg at **Top of Africa,** at the top of the Carlton Centre, for a thorough overview of the city. Explore downtown Johannesburg on foot, taking in sights such as the City Hall and Johannesburg Library. (The city center can be dangerous— keep your wits about you at all times and avoid carrying cameras and looking like a tourist.) Continue northwest into Braamfontein and see the **Gold-Mining Statue** at the top end of Rissik Street. It's a longish but relatively pleasant walk through Braamfontein to the University of the Witwatersrand's **Senate House.** Hidden inside, you'll find the **Gertrude Posel Gallery.**

You may also wish to head south to visit the fabulous **Museum Afrika** and the **Market Theatre Complex,** both of which will probably keep you busy for a few hours. If you've built up an appetite after sightseeing you can stop for a bite at one of the pubs or small restaurants in the complex. Further down Bree Street, toward Fordsburg, you'll find the **Oriental Plaza,** Johannesburg's little India.

If you feel you've seen enough of Johannesburg, spend your second day in the leafy city of **Pretoria.** Start off at the **Voortrekker Monument and Museum** on the city outskirts. It's fairly easy to reach inner-city sights as they're a lot closer together. Depending on your schedule, visit either **Melrose House** or **Paul Kruger House Museum.** If you are keen to see the works of one of the country's greatest painters, head to the **Pierneef Museum,** or if wildlife sounds better, take in the **Transvaal Museum.** Also consider driving northward to the splendid **National Zoological Gardens.** You'll probably want to spend what remains of the day here. Or head toward Arcadia to see the beautiful **Union Buildings** from which you'll have a bird's-eye view of the city. If you missed Pierneef, drive down the hill to the **Pretoria Art Museum.**

IF YOU HAVE 4 DAYS

On your first day, visit the sights of downtown Johannesburg described *above.* Spend your second day exploring the northern suburbs or the northwest section of Johannesburg. You'll need a car. A good way to see the colonial houses on the **Parktown-Westcliff Ridge** is to reserve a tour. Allow two to three hours for the tour. Afterward, travel north via Jan Smuts Avenue to the **Johannesburg Zoo** and **National Museum of Military History.** Then head to trendy **Melville** to explore interesting shops and enjoy a cup of coffee or an outdoor meal on Seventh Street. As an alternative, go to the suburbs of **Rosebank** or **Sandton** and spend time shopping at the Rosebank Mall or Sandton City, where you'll also find good eateries.

If you want to head beyond the city limits, make your way northwest to the **Kromdraai Conservancy.** Explore Wonder Cave, view game at Rhino Park, or fish at Rainbow Trout Farm. If it's the first weekend of the month, you can visit a few art galleries or pottery studios on the **Crocodile River Arts & Crafts Ramble.**

Here you have a choice: to spend the third and fourth days in the **Magaliesberg** and **Pretoria** or to go to the glitzy **Sun City** and **Pilanesberg Game Reserve** (for the latter option, skip to the seven-day itinerary, *below*).

It's a 90-minute drive from the northern suburbs to the sleepy town of **Magaliesberg.** Nearby is the Mount Grace Country House Hotel, where you can spend the night away from the city and get a jump on exploring the Magaliesberg the next day. From the Mount Grace, travel down the R24 until you reach the junction onto the R560 to **Hekpoort.** You'll drive through undulating countryside filled with fruit and flower farms. The spectacular cliffs of the **Magaliesberg range** will be on your left. After a hike, continue on to the **Hartebeesport Dam,** the resort town of **Hartebeesport,** and the **Hartebeesport Cable Way,** from which you'll have a marvelous view of the surrounding area. Take the R511 back to Johannesburg.

Spend the fourth day exploring Pretoria—this will probably take the whole day, if you follow the itinerary for the second day described *in* If You Have 2 Days, *above.* Allow an hour each way for the drive between Johannesburg and Pretoria. Avoid traveling during the rush hours (7 AM–8:30 AM and 4 PM–5:30 PM).

IF YOU HAVE 7 DAYS

For the first four days, follow the itinerary outlined *above.* On the fifth day, get off to an early start on the way to the **Rustenburg Nature Reserve.** Spend a few hours here, enjoying either the self-guided walk or the automobile trail.

Then head to fantasyland: **Sun City.** Spend the rest of the day exploring the complex—don't forget to take in the fabulous Lost City. Play the slots or, if you prefer the outdoors, enjoy the water rides and manmade beach at the Waterworld playground. You can attend a rock concert, enjoy a round of golf, and stay overnight in one of Sun City's impressive hotels.

On your last two days, take the short drive from Sun City east (toward Rustenburg) to the **Pilanesberg Game Reserve.** You should probably plan to spend a day or two exploring the park, which is situated within an ancient volcanic crater. The hides (blinds for observing wildlife) are well worth going to; bird-watching is generally excellent. In addition, look out for the Big Five—lion, elephant, rhino, buffalo, and leopard. The park also has ranger-led night drives.

Return to Johannesburg or continue on to other destinations in South Africa on the afternoon of day 7.

Central Johannesburg

A Good Tour

Begin by driving to Yeoville's **Rockey Street** ①, where you'll witness a polyglot of cultures. To get here, take the Harrow Road exit from the southbound M1. The exit becomes Houghton Drive. Take the third road left onto St. Andrew Street and the first right on Golf Street. Then cross Louis Botha Avenue and drive south down Harrow Road. Turn left after four blocks onto Raleigh Street, which in turn becomes Rockey Street. This is a one-way street going east. Plenty of street parking is available.

After you've finished exploring Rockey Street, head west to downtown Johannesburg, some 10 minutes' drive away. Perhaps the best way to see this area is on foot. Traffic congestion and one-way streets can make it difficult to sightsee by car, particularly if you're not familiar with the area. Park somewhere central (such as at the Carlton Centre) and walk from there.

To get into town from Rockey Street, turn left onto De La Rey Street. Drive one block north and turn left on one-way Hunter Street. After

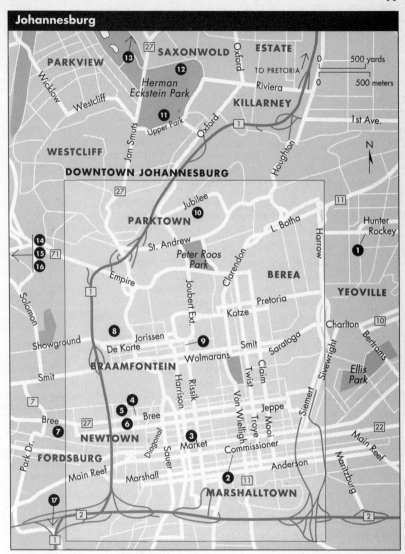

Johannesburg

City Hall, **3**

Gertrude Posel
Gallery, **8**

Gold Mining
Statue, **9**

Gold Reef City, **17**

Johannesburg
Botanical Gardens
and Emmarentia
Dam, **16**

Johannesburg
Zoo, **11**

Market Theatre
Complex, **4**

Melville, **14**

Melville Koppies, **15**

Museum Afrika, **5**

Oriental Plaza, **7**

Parktown, **10**

Rockey Street, **1**

Rosebank , **13**

SA Breweries
Museum, **6**

South African
National Museum of
Military History, **12**

Top of Africa, **2**

four blocks the road becomes a two-way street. Three blocks later, turn right on Grafton Street and drive four blocks north to Louis Botha Avenue and turn left. Keep in the right-hand lane. Follow the road until you reach Empire Road, turn right, and continue to Jan Smuts Avenue. Turn left onto Jan Smuts and go up the hill into Braamfontein. This road becomes Simmonds Street shortly after you cross the Queen Elizabeth Bridge over the railway line.

You are now in Johannesburg's downtown district. Due to the one-way streets, you'll need to turn left onto Market Street (six blocks south of the bridge). Proceed for seven blocks and turn right onto Kruis Street. As you cross Commissioner Street one block later, look out for signs to the Carlton Centre's underground parking (entrance on the left-hand side of the road). Park your car.

Elevators will take you into the Carlton Centre itself. At the top of the complex is the observation deck, **Top of Africa** ②, which will give you a good view of the city from above. Leave the building by the Commissioner Street entrance.

Walk down Commissioner Street in a westerly direction for six blocks until you reach Harrison Street. Turn right onto Harrison Street. After one block, cross Market Street. The grandiose 1913 **City Hall** ③ is on your right. At the end of the block, at President Street, turn right and go up the steps. The Hall is often open and you may be able to see the graceful interior. When you're finished, stay on President Street, cross Harrison, and continue westward for one block to reach the Florentine palace-inspired City Library built in 1935 and Library Gardens on Simmonds Street. This is across the road on your left. Alternatively, you can cross Harrison Street from City Hall and walk through the park—with the Cenotaph, a war memorial, in the center—to reach Simmonds Street. You will see ugly emerald green stalls on the left side of the park. These were part of an ill-fated project, known as the Civic Spine, conceived to draw people back into the city center. This was notably unsuccessful—the hawkers for whom the stalls were intended seemed to prefer to continue cluttering the rest of Johannesburg's streets. The City Library will be directly in front of you in this case.

From here, turn right onto President Street and walk east for four blocks, to Eloff Street. Most of Eloff Street is reserved for buses only. You'll see **African hawkers** selling wares ranging from offbeat clothing to fresh produce—an intriguing contrast to the relatively stylish shops behind them. At the corner of Eloff and President Streets, a clothing store marks the elegant **Markham's Building** (1886), one of the few Victorian buildings to miss the demolition squads. Turn right (south) and head back down Eloff Street toward Commissioner Street. En route, look out for another building so spared, the Colosseum (at Commissioner and Eloff Streets), which was built in 1933 and was once a theater. It, too, was wrested from the hands of developers but not totally saved—the historic shell houses a cosmetics store. Next door is His Majesty's, another former theater that was rebuilt in 1934; it has now been converted into offices. At this point, turn left along Commissioner Street for three blocks to get back to the Carlton Centre.

Exit the Carlton Centre parking lot by car onto Kruis Street. Turn right at the exit and drive north along Kruis Street for one block to reach Commissioner Street. Turn left on Commissioner Street (heading west). After going four blocks, turn right onto Rissik Street. Continue north along Rissik Street for five blocks until you reach Jeppe Street. The fountain in the center of the street (between Market and President Street) was also part of the ill-fated Civic Spine project. The historic building on the right at one time housed the Rissik Street Post Office. Turn left onto Jeppe Street. Travel six blocks in a westerly direction. Turn right onto Becker Street and cross Bree Street after one block to arrive at the **Market Theatre Complex** ④. Park in the enormous lot near the Flea Market. Cross Bree Street to **Museum Afrika** ⑤. Next to the museum are numerous pubs and restaurants where you might take a break after all your sightseeing. Walk east along Bree Street for one block to Wolhuter Street to arrive at the **SA Breweries Museum** ⑥.

Next, take a drive west along Jeppe Street (a one-way street going west at this point). After passing under the highway, the road will merge with Bree Street and become a two-way road. After three blocks, look out for the **Oriental Plaza** ⑦ on your left. Park in the large car park.

TIMING

This tour can easily fill up an entire day. The walk through the downtown will take one to two hours, depending on how long you want to take at the sights along the way. Allow yourself three hours to visit the Market Theatre Complex and at least one to see the Oriental Plaza. You should also allow extra time for traffic congestion and delays, particularly if you catch rush hour.

Sights to See

❸ **City Hall.** This Victorian survivor, now a theater, is lovely to look at inside and outside. Statues and wood-framed windows overlook the park in Harrison Street. The main entrance is on Pritchard Street. Inside, you'll find high, pressed ceilings and old-fashioned theater boxes. Look in the pages of *The Star* newspaper to find out what's scheduled here; a classical music concert is the best way to fully appreciate the hall's wonderful acoustics. Phone ahead first to arrange to see the interior as the hall is closed to casual visitors when in use for certain functions. Ask the caretaker or supervisor to show you around.☒ *Harrison and President Sts. Entrance opposite Loveday St.,* ☎ *011/836–4671.* ☜ *Free.* ☉ *Daily 7* AM*–midnight.*

❹ **Market Theatre Complex.** You'll find an interesting collection of alternative shops, theaters, galleries, bars, and coffee houses here. ☒ *Bree and Wolhuter Sts., Newtown.*

❺ **Museum Afrika.** This is the first major museum to attempt to give credit to the blacks' contributions to the development of the city. An excellent exhibit traces the impact of gold on the lives of the black population, from the miners forced to live in male-only hostels to the burgeoning townships with their squatter camps, *shebeens* (bars), and vibrant jazz. Another exhibit covers the fight for democracy and the events leading to the elections that gave Nelson Mandela the presidency. The museum also has a first-rate display of ancient San (Bushmen) rock art. Upstairs, the Bensusan Museum examines the art and technology of cameras with fun hands-on exhibits. ☒ *121 Bree St., Newtown,* ☎ *011/833–5636.* ☜ *R2.* ☉ *Tues.–Sun. 9–5.*

❼ **Oriental Plaza.** With its heady smell of spices and incense, this enormous mall (really a series of undercover and open-air bazaars) will take you straight to India. Mingle with multiracial crowds as you explore small shops and colorful stalls selling everything from Indian spices and foods to fabric and curtains. It's a great place to pick up bargains, particularly on fabric, but watch out for flaws as the Plaza specializes in "seconds." ☒ *Bree and High Sts., Fordsburg.* ☉ *Mon.–Sat. 9–5.*

❶ **Rockey Street.** The street is a slice of New York's East Village in Africa. Hard-rock clubs and ethnic eateries rub shoulders with tattoo parlors, secondhand bookshops, lingerie and leather stores, and boutiques selling African beads. Out on the street, white youths with pink mohawks and nose rings hang out with blacks dressed in the latest fashions. Say what you will, but it's one of the few places where black and white mix easily in the city.

❻ **SA Breweries Museum.** This unique museum is dedicated to a great South African favorite—beer! (And South African Breweries is the country's major brewery.) You'll find out all about the history of beer brewing in South Africa and the process of beer making here. Afterward, enjoy a complimentary beer in a delightful country-style pub. ⊠ *President and Bezuidenhout Sts. (entrance on Becker St.), Newtown,* ☎ *011/836–4900.* ⊘ *Tues.—Sat. 10–6.*

❼ **Top of Africa.** Carlton Centre may not be the World Trade Center—the building is only 50 stories high—but it does have Top of Africa, a 360-degree view of the city, including its trademark mine dumps, which are fast disappearing as new methods of extracting gold remaining in the sand have been discovered. Note the absence of high-rise buildings to the south: the warren of mining tunnels has made the ground too unstable to support skyscrapers. The building has an attractive bar and restaurant, which serves drinks and light meals. ⊠ *Carlton Centre, Main St.,* ☎ *011/331–6608.* ☞ *R7.50.* ⊘ *Daily 9–7.*

Northern Suburbs

A Good Tour

We recommend you start this tour in the south and head northward. Take the M1 south to Braamfontein, leaving the highway at Jan Smuts Avenue. Cross Empire Road and drive up the hill. The main sight here is the **Gertrude Posel Gallery** ⑧, situated in Senate House, Wits University. Because of the one-way streets, getting there is not very straightforward. It's best if you drive under an ornate pedestrian bridge (Wits University is on your right) at Stiemens Street and turn right at the second intersection thereafter, onto De Korte Street, going west. After three blocks, turn right on Eendracht Street. After one block, turn right onto Jorissen Street, a one-way street going east. Senate House is about halfway down the block. It is clearly marked. Ample street parking is available in the vicinity. Inside, the gallery is not well marked and is difficult to locate. Ask the person on duty at the information desk for directions.

Afterward, continue driving down Jorissen Street and turn right onto Biccard Street after four blocks. After three blocks, turn left onto Smit Street. Travel two blocks and take the slipway left onto Rissik Street. Keep to the center of Rissik Street which is a one-way street going north. As Rissik becomes Loveday Street, you will see the **Gold Mining Statue** ⑨ on your right. Traffic coming up from the city center can be fast and furious. Park nearby and walk back to the statue to take a closer look if you wish. Parking is available at the Civic Centre across the road on the left (as you come up Rissik/Loveday Street).

Those interested in historic buildings will want to walk through **Parktown** ⑩; contact the Parktown-Westcliff Heritage Trust (☞ Sights to See, *below*) for full details and addresses of historic houses, churches, and schools and information about building tours. To get to Parktown, keep to the second lane from the left on Loveday Street to get onto Hoofd Street. As Hoofd curves to the left, it becomes Joubert Street Extension. Follow the road down the hill and reach the traffic lights at Empire Road. Cross Empire Road and continue up the hill. The road is now called Victoria Street. Continue along Victoria Street and cross three sets of traffic lights. At the third set, continue straight on and cross the bridge over the highway. The road will curve sharply left. Take the first turn to the right, onto Rockridge Road, and park on Rockridge Road, which is close to all of Parktown's historic houses.

Afterward, relax at **Johannesburg Zoo** ⑪ or Zoo Lake. The **South African National Museum of Military History** ⑫ is nearby. To reach the zoo, drive north along Jan Smuts Avenue from central Johannesburg. (If you're going from Parktown, travel west along Rockridge Road. This becomes Eton Road. In turn, this intersects with Jan Smuts Avenue. Turn right onto Jan Smuts Avenue.) Continue north for some distance. As you reach Forest Town, turn right onto Upper Park Drive and follow signs to zoo parking. Parking for the South African Museum of Military History is further on Upper Park Drive, after the road has become Erlswold Way. Look for signs to the museum; parking is available near the War Memorial. Afterward, you might consider relaxing at tranquil Zoo Lake. To get there from the War Memorial, turn left as you leave the parking area onto Erlswold Way. Continue on Erlswold Way, and take the next road right onto Westwold Drive. Then take the first left (after a short distance) onto Prince of Wales Terrace. Off-street parking is available on the left-hand side of the road.

If you're interested in shopping or outdoor dining, head for **Rosebank** ⑬; the easiest way to get there is along Jan Smuts Avenue either from the zoo or the center of town. If you're going after your visit to Zoo Lake, continue on Prince of Wales Terrace until you reach Avonwold Road. Turn right onto Avonwold Road and continue for three blocks until you reach Jan Smuts Avenue. Turn left onto Jan Smuts Avenue and head north. After seven blocks, you will reach the Seventh Avenue–Tyrwhitt Road intersection; turn right onto Tyrwhitt Road. After three blocks, turn right onto Bath Street (a one-way street going south). Toward the end of the first block is Rosebank Mall on your left-hand side, where you can park safely undercover.

TIMING

This is a very long tour, so we suggest you decide in advance what interests you in particular and stay with that. Braamfontein and the Gertrude Posel Gallery should take no more than 30 minutes to see. However, if you plan to visit Parktown, you should allow at least a morning. If you're doing a guided walk, ask how long this is likely to take. Alternatively, tell the guide how much time you want to spend beforehand. It will take about four hours to see all of the sights around the zoo. As for Rosebank, remember that shops generally close at 5, although some stay open a little later. Cafés and restaurants remain open fairly late.

Sights to See

⑧ **Gertrude Posel Gallery.** Don't let the mediocre exhibitions upstairs put you off—go downstairs to see the first-rate Standard Bank Collection of African Art. Much of the work, particularly the beadwork, comes from southern Africa. There are also masks, headrests, pots, drums, and initiation statues from West Africa, as well as Kuba cloth from Zaire. ⊠ *Campus level, Senate House, University of Witwatersrand, Jorissen St.,* ☎ *011/716–3632.* ⚏ *Free.* ☉ *Tues.–Fri. 10–4.*

⑨ **Gold Mining Statue.** One of the most famous symbols of the city, the statue depicts three men—two black and one white—drilling a rock face. It's a beautifully balanced sculpture that captures the physical effort of mining for gold deep underground. The bronze statue, by sculptor David McGregor, was a gift from the Transvaal and Orange Free State Chambers of Mines. ⊠ *Rissik and De Korte Sts., Braamfontein.*

⑪ **Johannesburg Zoo.** This park is a pleasant but unremarkable place that can be swamped with schoolchildren during the week. If you're in Jo-

hannesburg on the first Sunday of the month, you might like to see—
or even participate in—the monthly Walk for Wildlife, a fund-raising
walk around the zoo. ⊠ *Upper Park Rd., Forest Town,* ☎ *011/646–
2000.* ⊠ *R10. (Walk for Wildlife, R12 to walk and R10 to watch.)* ☉
Daily 8:30–5:30.

⑩ Parktown. A superb way to introduce yourself to the colonial history
of early Johannesburg is to stroll through this suburb perched on the
Braamfontein Ridge. The city's early mining magnates, such as the Op-
penheimers and the Cullinans, settled here and commissioned renowned
architects—most notably, Sir Herbert Baker—to build their magnificent houses, many of which are national monuments. In many cases,
interiors have been converted to modern uses but exteriors remain pristine. The Parktown-Westcliff Heritage Trust fought to preserve these
old mansions, many of which were almost demolished to make way
for the ubiquitous office blocks that cover much of southern Parktown.

Perhaps the cream of the suburb's architectural treasures is **Northwards**
on Rockdale Avenue, designed by Sir Herbert Baker, one of South Africa's
premier architects during the late 1800s. For many years, it was the
home of socialite Jose Dale Lace, whose ghost is still said to grace Northwards's Mistral's Gallery. What is now Wits Business School on St.
David's Place is the mansion **Outeniqua**, built in 1906 for the managing director of Ohlssons Breweries. Across the road is a house known
as **Eikenlaan**, built in 1903 for James Goch, a professional photogra-
pher and the first to use flash photography in South Africa. In June
1985, the home was turned into Mike's Kitchen Steakhouse.

Contact the **Parktown-Westcliff Heritage Trust** (☎ 011/482–3349,
mornings only) to arrange a guided tour of the area. If you're going
to be in town on a Thursday morning, book the weekly tours of Northwards. During May, the Trust hosts a Heritage Weekend offering "topless bus" and walking tours, accompanied by informative guides.

⑬ Rosebank. This suburb linking Parktown and Sandton is attractive, but
it lacks the old-world charm of places such as Melville. Street vendors
clutter the sidewalks selling curios ranging from African animals to malachite jewelry. The large shopping malls here have lots of chrome and
glass; shops are interspersed with several restaurants. Rosebank Mall
(☞ *Shopping, below*) is home to a large cinema complex specializing
in art movies from around the world. You can, however, find quiet
squares away from the constant hive of activity. On sunny highveld
days (of which there are many), you can dine al fresco at one of Rosebank's numerous sidewalk cafés that serve a variety of food.

⑫ South African National Museum of Military History. This excellent exhibition hall examines South Africa's role in the major wars of the 20th
century, with an emphasis on World War II. On display are Hurricane
and Messerschmidt fighters, various tanks of English and American
manufacture, and a wide array of artillery. Among the most interesting exhibits are the modern armaments South Africa used in its war
against the Cuban-backed Angolan army during the 1980s, including
highly advanced artillery, French-built Mirage fighters, and Russian tanks
stolen by the South Africans from a ship en route to Angola. More recent exhibits include the national military art collection, memorabilia
from the Anti-Conscription Campaign, and an exhibit on the history
of Mkhontwo-Izizwe or MK (the African National Congress's military
arm), from inception until their incorporation into the South African
National Defence Force. Some displays have become run-down but the
museum is worth a visit. ⊠ *20 Erlswold Way,* ☎ *011/646–5513.* ⊠
R5. ☉ *Daily 9–4:30.*

Northwestern Johannesburg

A Good Drive

Consider driving to **Melville** ⑭ if you want to browse quaint shops and dine outdoors. The easiest way to reach this area from the northern suburbs is to take the N1 highway south. Take the DF Malan Drive exit and turn left onto DF Malan Drive. Pass through the suburbs of Northcliff, Franklin Roosevelt Park, and Montgomery Park. DF Malan Drive becomes Main Street as it reaches Melville. Three blocks after this, turn left onto 9th Avenue and, after two blocks, right on 4th Street, where you'll find stores, coffee shops, and outdoor cafés.

Continue on to the **Melville Koppies** ⑮ (assuming you're there when it's open). Backtrack on DF Malan Drive and turn right on Judith Road. The entrance to the koppies is on the right. Most people park on the sidewalk in the vicinity.

Next, to proceed to the **Johannesburg Botanical Gardens and Emmarentia Dam** ⑯, head back to DF Malan Drive and turn right. Take the next right turn onto Thomas Bowler Avenue. Continue down Thomas Bowler Avenue for four blocks. Turn right on Olifants Road. The entrance to the Botanical Gardens and Emmarentia Dam are about halfway down the block on your right. If you cross the dam wall, you will have gone too far. There is ample, free parking near the entrance to the gardens.

TIMING

Allow at least a morning to see both Melville and the Johannesburg Botanical Gardens and Emmarentia Dam. If you have more time, you might want to spend a morning in Melville and the afternoon at Emmarentia Dam. Remember to allow sufficient time for driving (Melville is about 30 minutes from Sandton and Rosebank and 20 minutes from central Johannesburg). Allow yourself at least 3–4 hours to see Melville Koppies.

Sights to See

⑯ **Johannesburg Botanical Gardens and Emmarentia Dam.** This gigantic parkland is a wonderful haven amid the bustle of a big city and a fine place to walk. You may relax on benches beneath weeping willows surrounding the dammed pond or wander across to the rose and herb gardens, filled with arbors, statues, fountains, and ponds. If you're here on a Saturday or Sunday, expect to bump into several bridal parties. ⊠ *Olifants Rd., Emmarentia,* ☎ *011/782–7064.* ☞ *Free.* ☉ *Daily from sunrise to sunset.*

⑭ **Melville.** This trendy suburb essentially grew around the South African Broadcasting Company (SABC) in nearby Auckland Park. It was once an average middle-class enclave until several well-known South African television and radio personalities migrated to the area, turning it into one of the hippest places in the northern suburbs. Seventh Street has a number of pleasant shops and coffee houses with sidewalk seating. Although you may not find anything uniquely African here, you'll see how suburban white South Africa entertains itself, particularly over weekends when coffee houses are filled and shop and boutique owners do a brisk trade. If you're here on the second Saturday of the month, take in the atmosphere of the Melville Mardi Gras, when the streets are closed to traffic and buskers entertain the crowds.

⑮ **Melville Koppies.** This small nature reserve is across Judith Road on the northern side of the Johannesburg Botanical Gardens. You can enjoy guided ecology walks with volunteer guides, many of whom are members of the local botanical society; they will introduce you to the rich

diversity of highveld flora found here. There is also an archaeological
site dating back to the Iron Age. Bird-watching is excellent here; expect to see many varieties of grassland and highveld birds as well as
species found in the area's suburban gardens. ✉ *Judith Rd. and DF
Malan Dr., Melville,* ☎ *011/888–4831.* ✇ *Free.* ☉ *Sept.–May, 1st and
3rd Sun. of each month 3–6; 2nd Sun. of each month 9–noon.*

SOUTH OF TOWN

🕻 **Gold Reef City.** Fifteen kilometers (9 mi) south of downtown is the most
popular tourist attraction in the city. Go figure. The place is a rinky-
dink theme park that transforms a bona fide part of Johannesburg's
gold-mining history into banal kiddie rides and trite entertainments.
Tucked away amid all the dross are some original 19th-century mining cottages and a couple of interesting museums, but it's all difficult
to take seriously. The only redeeming aspects of a visit are going down
an old gold mine, seeing molten gold being poured, and watching a
gumboot dance, a riveting hostel dance developed by black miners. ✉
Northern Pkwy., off N1, Ormonde, ☎ *011/496–1600.* ✇ *R24 (R28
on weekends and public holidays) including all rides and shows, mine
tour R24 extra.* ☉ *Tues.–Sun. 9:30–5. Dancing at 11:30 and 3; mine
tours every 30 mins 10–5.*

Around Johannesburg

Crocodile River Arts & Crafts Ramble. Local artists, potters, sculptors,
and other craftspeople host this weekend. Their studios and galleries,
in a delightful country setting northwest of Johannesburg, are open to
the public on the first weekend of every month. You may purchase crafts,
clothing, and knitted garments; enjoy light meals or picnic outdoors;
and watch an artist at work. ✉ *Follow DF Malan Dr. in a westerly direction, toward Swartkops, Muldersdrift, and Kromdraai. Signboards,
painted white and bearing a green crocodile, will direct you to the studios. Maps are obtainable along the route or from Johannesburg Publicity Association,* ☎ *011/659–2915.*

Cullinan Diamond Mine. Forty-eight kilometers (30 mi) east of Pretoria is this fully operational mine three times the size of the famous hole
at Kimberley. The 3,106-carat Cullinan diamond was unearthed here
in 1905, a giant crystal that was later cut into several smaller stones
including the Star of Africa. Machinery extracts 12 tons of kimberlite
and 6,000 carats of diamonds each day. About 80% of these are for
industrial use, but the rest are high-grade gems. On the mine's one daily
tour you'll see the big hole, watch a 12-minute video, pass through a
typical mine security check, view replicas of the most famous diamonds,
and travel through a mock-up of an underground tunnel. ✉ *Premier
Diamond Tours, 95 Oak Ave., Cullinan,* ☎ *012/134–0081.* ✇ *R22.*
☉ *Tours weekdays at 10:30 and 2; Sat. at 10:30; Sun. at 2. Reserve in
advance. No children under 10.*

Kromdraai Conservancy. This wonderful and apparently little-known
area is just a 45-minute drive from the northwestern suburb of Northcliff. Begin at the fabulous **Wonder Cave** (☎ 011/957–0106), where
the profusion of stalactites and stalagmites rivals the famous Cango
Caves in the Cape. Go on to try your hand at fly fishing at **Rainbow
Trout Farm** (☎ 011/957–0008) where you can buy the fish you've caught
(or others, if you haven't). Rods and tackle may be rented for an additional fee. You can spot most of the Big Five at nearby **Rhino Park**
(☎ 011/957–0109), where ostrich peck at your windows in the vain
hopes of being fed, herds of wildebeest and antelope dot the plains,
and rhinos slumber in thorn tree thickets. Don't miss the lion enclosure but be warned—the animals tend to be very frisky! If you're there

on the first weekend of the month (Crocodile River Ramble weekend), pop in at **Iris Ridge Farm** (☎ 011/957–0205) to enjoy tea and scones. At other times, phone the farm beforehand to arrange to see an 1875 gold mine, one of the earliest on the Reef. The proprietor will probably regale you with details of its history, making this a very interesting visit. ⊠ *Off the R47 to Tarlton.* ⌨ *R15–R20.*

Lippizaner Centre. Midway between Johannesburg and Pretoria, this complex is home to white Lippizaner stallions, a distinguished breed of horses with a centuries-old lineage. The horses are trained in the classic Spanish riding style, and during their weekly shows perform a complex ballet of exercises to the strains of Verdi, Mozart, and Handel. ⊠ *Dahlia Rd., Kyalami,* ☎ *011/702–2103.* ⌨ *R35.* ☉ *Performances Sun. at 11. Closed mid-Oct.–mid-Nov.*

Witwatersrand Botanical Gardens. In the relatively open countryside on the extreme western edge of Johannesburg, you'll find these gardens, which comprise vast expanses of lawn fringed with trees. You can cross the Hennops River as it meanders through the grounds and admire indigenous cycads and aloes. You will also observe resident black eagles soaring, sometimes above a waterfall; you may walk above the waterfall for a bird's-eye view of the eagles' nesting sites. If you're hungry, take a light meal at the kiosk or enjoy a more formal lunch or dinner at The Garden Restaurant. If you're here on a Sunday afternoon, arrange to take a picnic lunch and enjoy the bimonthly evening concerts (May–August), hosted by the National Symphony Orchestra, the Welsh Men's Choir, and South Africa's top classical music talent. ⊠ *Malcolm Rd., Poortview, Roodepoort,* ☎ *011/958–1750.* ⌨ *R5.*

DINING

Downtown

$$$ ✕ **Gramadoelas at the Market Theatre.** A cosmopolitan clientele of diplo-
★ mats, playwrights, and actors frequents this attractive restaurant that specializes in traditional South African cuisine. The decor is a fascinating jumble of Africana, including huge Cape Dutch canvases and rustic oil lamps. Initially focused on Cape Malay dishes, the restaurant has widened its scope to include traditional African dishes like *mopani* worms, stewed dried caterpillars served with *periperi* (Portuguese chili sauce). If a starter of worms makes you wriggle, opt for *snoek sambal* with *moskonfyt,* a smoked fish pâté served with a syrup made from the residue of wine-pressed grapes. Main courses include traditional *bobotie* (spiced minced lamb with a custard topping), *sosaties* (curried kebabs), and *tomato bredie* (tomato-based stew). For dessert, don't miss Cape *melktert* (spiced custard tart) or delicious *malva* pudding, made with apricot jam and vinegar topped with cream and sugar. ⊠ *Market Theatre, Wolhuter St., Newtown,* ☎ *011/838–6960. AE, DC, MC, V. Closed Sun.*

$ ✕ **Chon Hing.** Tucked away in a side street and looking a little world-weary, this Chinese restaurant is still one of the best-kept secrets of the cognoscenti. No cloths mask the Formica tabletops, and the chairs are upholstered in red plastic, but in a place like this it's the food that keeps people coming back again and again. You can order one of the set menus, but you're better off selecting dishes from the two pages at the back of the menu. Good choices are beef flank served with noodles or rice, prawns stuffed with minced chicken, and calamari in black bean sauce. For a real treat, order steamed rock cod. ⊠ *26 Alexander St., at John Vorster Sq., Ferreirastown,* ☎ *011/83–3206. AE, DC, MC, V. BYOB.*

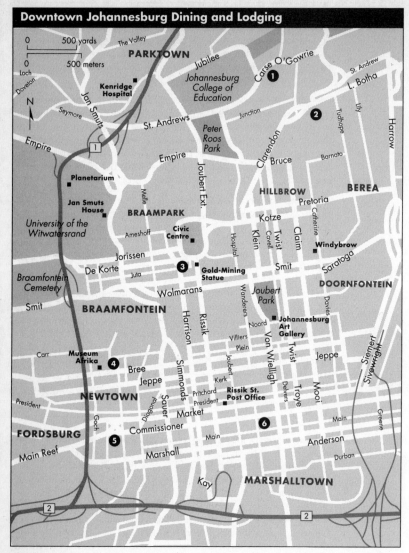

Downtown Johannesburg Dining and Lodging

Dining
Chon Hing, **5**
Gramadoelas at the
Market Theatre, **4**

Lodging
The Carlton, **6**
Hotel Formule 1, **2**
The Parktonian, **3**
Sunnyside Park
Hotel, **1**

Northern Suburbs

$$$$ ✕ **Daruma.** Long regarded as *the* Japanese restaurant in town, Daruma continues to draw crowds despite its high prices. You can sit at the sushi bar or opt for the small Shogun-Noma room, divided into private dining areas by wood-and-paper screens. The menu covers the full range of Japanese cuisine, from sashimi to *soba* (buckwheat) noodles. You can also order various set menus. The ingredients are absolutely fresh and the presentation superb. ⊠ *Corlett Dr. and Atholl Oaklands Rd., Melrose North,* ☎ *011/880–2548. Reservations required. AE, DC, MC, V. Closed Mon. No lunch Sun.*

$$$$ ✕ **Linger Longer.** Ever since the annual "Top Ten" restaurant awards
★ were initiated a decade ago, this restaurant has stood among the top three. Set in the spacious grounds of a former home in Wierda Valley, it has an air of gracious elegance. Some rooms have a Wedgwood-like quality—deep green walls with pale trim and striped curtains—whereas others glow in salmon pink. A goose-liver pâté appetizer is one of the dishes that made Linger Longer famous. Excellent main courses include crisped duckling in ginger and lemongrass sauce, and boned loin of lamb with garlic, parsley, and coarse-grain mustard. Among the imaginative desserts, crêpes filled with warm cream cheese, vanilla, and brandied raisins are particularly good. ⊠ *58 Wierda Rd., Wierda Valley,* ☎ *011/ 884–0465. AE, DC, MC, V. Closed Sun. No lunch Sat.*

$$$$ ✕ **Ma Cuisine.** Because chef-patron Jorn Pless shapes a *table d'hôte* around what he buys fresh at the market each day, you don't know what you're going to eat in this French restaurant until you sit down— and even then you have no choices. If that smacks of culinary roulette, rest assured that almost everyone comes out a winner. Most diners find that they haven't tasted anything as exquisite as Pless's well-balanced meals in years, and he is never short of people willing to place their gastronomic enjoyment in his hands—among them Queen Elizabeth II. Lunch is a three-course affair, dinner a full-blown five courses, including a starter, fish, sorbet, main course, and dessert. You can watch the chefs at work in the glassed-in kitchen. ⊠ *40 7th Ave., Parktown North,* ☎ *011/880–1946. Jacket and tie. Reservations required. AE, DC, MC, V. Closed Sun. and Mon.*

$$$$ ✕ **Pescador Restaurant.** Tucked away in a suburban shopping center, this Portuguese restaurant serves some of the best seafood in Gauteng. Diners come from far and wide for butterflied queen prawns marinated in a beer, garlic, and chili sauce, then grilled. The combination platter of succulent, tender calamari and juicy prawns is another favorite. Don't forget to ask about the line fish specials, especially if it's the season for musselcracker or "74," two of South Africa's tastiest fish. The atmosphere is relaxed and friendly, and the decor has a distinctly Portuguese flavor, with murals of villages and fishing bric-a-brac on the walls and old sails on the ceiling. ⊠ *Grayston Centre, Grayston Dr., Sandown,* ☎ *011/884–4429. AE, DC, MC, V. No lunch Sat.*

$$$ ✕ **Ciro at the Ritz.** Elegant Ciro occupies a quaint old house in Parktown North. Sit inside under the lovely pressed-tin ceiling or opt for the adjoining conservatory, with hanging plants and a large skylight. Ciro's forte is imaginative dishes based on French-Italian provincial cuisine, including such appetizers as duck livers with mango on a potato galette served with an orange-port sauce. For a main course, veal scallops are panfried either with fresh porcini mushrooms gratinéed with brie or with a nut crust topped with sliced avocado and served with a mint-cucumber yogurt sauce. One worthy dessert is cherry cheesecake mille-feuille, made with layers of phyllo pastry, ricotta cheese, and mascarpone, served with a fruit coulis. ⊠ *17 3rd St., Parktown Nor
011/880–2470. AE, DC, MC, V. Closed Sun. No lunch Sat.*

Northern Suburbs Dining and Lodging

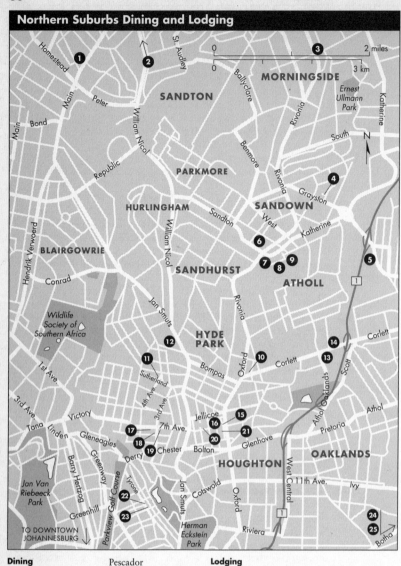

Dining

Armadillo, **17**

Ciro at the Ritz, **18**

Daruma, **13**

Franco's Pizzeria & Trattoria, **23**

Ile de France, **1**

Leipoldt's, **3**

Linger Longer, **8**

Ma Cuisine, **19**

O Fado, **12**

Osteria Tre Nonni, **11**

Paros Taverna, **15**

Pescador Restaurant, **4**

Plaka Taverna, **10**

Red Chamber Mandarin Restaurant, **21**

Shamiyana, **14**

Turtle Creek Winery, **9**

Widgeons Bistro, **22**

Lodging

Holiday Inn Garden Court–Sandton, **7**

Holiday Inn Johannesburg International, **25**

Hotel Formule 1, **5, 24**

Karos Indaba, **2**

Park Hyatt Hotel, **16**

Rosebank Hotel, **20**

Sandton Sun & Towers, **6**

$$$ ✕ **Ile de France.** Chef-owner Marc Guebert is the only member in Africa
★ of the *Maîtres Cuisiniers de France,* that illustrious group of chefs that
includes the likes of Roger Vergé, Pierre Troisgros, and Paul Bocuse.
Each member specializes in a particular culinary realm, and Guebert
champions soufflés. In fact, to visit his restaurant and not eat his souf-
flé Grand Marnier is considered something of a gastronomic gaffe. For
starters, try grilled goose liver served with a Madeira sauce, or fried
calves' brains in black butter and capers. His quenelles, flavored with
smoked salmon and coated with chardonnay sauce, are light as clouds.
More down to earth is a superb rack of lamb. For a gastronomic treat,
try the *menu dégustation,* a six-course tasting menu that costs about
R110. ⊠ *26 Cramerview Centre, 227 Main Rd., Bryanston,* ☎ *011/
706–2837. AE, DC, MC, V. No lunch Sat.*

$$$ ✕ **O Fado.** Floor-length check tablecloths and hand-painted crockery
elevate this Mozambique-Portuguese restaurant above the level of a
neighborhood *tasca.* Solid choices include *caldo verde,* a potato-based
kale soup with a slice of *chouriço* sausage; grilled sardines with roasted
peppers, sliced onions, and boiled potato; and *bacalhau a bras,* shred-
ded salt cod mixed with fried potatoes, egg, and onions, and gar-
nished with tomato and olives. The restaurant is also renowned for its
prawns (the seafood platter is enough for two), and grilled chicken
periperi is a safe bet. For a dessert with a difference, try the avocado-
and-gin ice-cream cake. ⊠ *Hutton Ct., 291 Jan Smuts Ave., Hyde Park,*
☎ *011/880–4410. AE, DC, MC, V. Closed Sun. No lunch Sat.*

$$$ ✕ **Osteria Tre Nonni.** Paintings and yellowed photographs of aged grand-
fathers peer down from the whitewashed walls of this North Italian restau-
rant in Craighall. Prices are high, but the place is always abuzz with elegant
Italian families tucking into *paglia e fieno alle noci* (green and white home-
made spaghetti with nuts, onions, brandy, and cream), sole baked in foil
with porcini and truffles, and delicious *filetto al pepe verde* (beef fillet
with whiskey, cream, and green Madagascar peppercorns). Carpaccio
is a magnificent starter. ⊠ *9 Grafton Ave., Craighall,* ☎ *011/327–0095.
Reservations required. DC, MC, V. Closed Sun. and Mon.*

$$$ ✕ **Paros Taverna.** This Greek restaurant is hidden at the top of a flight
of stairs in the Rosebank Mall, where, on warm summer nights, you
can sit outside on the sheltered terrace and sip a bottle of retsina while
dipping into bowls of *tzadziki* (yogurt and garlic), *taramousalata* (fish-
roe dip), and puréed eggplant. By far the best dish on the menu is *kalamarakia,* incredibly tender squid grilled in olive oil, garlic, and lemon.
A couple of orders of kalamarakia and a mixed platter of nine *mezede*
(appetizers or side dishes) can easily feed four. For dessert don't miss
homemade halvah ice cream. ⊠ *Rosebank Blvd., Oxford Rd., Rosebank,* ☎ *011/788–6211. AE, DC, MC, V. Closed Mon.*

$$ ✕ **Armadillo.** Tables spill out onto the sidewalk at this trendy restau-
rant in Parktown North, which serves a small but tasty menu of
Mediterranean fare. It's a great place to graze, because the size of the
dishes falls somewhere between that of an hors d'oeuvre and a main
course. You can choose from seven pizzas—the best comes topped with
tangy Italian sausage. Other recommendations are *prego* salad, spicy
strips of fillet sautéed and served atop mixed greens and grilled egg-
plant slices; and tender, succulent calamari, served in a skillet in its own
juices. Brown-bread ice cream makes for a tasty dessert. ⊠ *3rd and
7th Aves., Parktown North,* ☎ *011/447–5462. AE, DC, MC, V.*

$$ ✕ **Leipoldt's.** Named after the writer who first celebrated the national
cuisine, this restaurant focuses on traditional South African fare, much
of which traces its origins to the Cape Malay community. More than
60 dishes are served buffet-style, and you can try as many as you'd like.
Typical offerings are tomato bredie, sosaties, bobotie, and *boerewors*
(a coarse farmer's sausage). For dessert, try syrupy *koeksisters* (a super-

sweet doughnut) or melktert. Faded historic photographs and animal heads on the walls provide South African ambience. ✉ *Pavillion Shopping Centre, Rivonia Rd. and Kelvin Dr., Morningside,* ☎ *011/804–4321. AE, DC, MC, V. Closed Sun. No lunch Sat.*

$$ ✕ Shamiyana. This Punjabi restaurant has a strong reputation among local curry aficionados and visiting North Indians. Soft Indian music, red walls, and a tented ceiling create an authentic Indian feeling. Select from a wide array of tandoori, kebab, biryani, and vegetarian dishes. One favorite is chicken *makhanwala,* a mildly spicy dish of boneless chicken cubes cooked with cashew nuts and cream in tomato sauce. To cool down afterward, try one of the many flavors of ice cream. Prices appear reasonable, but side dishes, bread, and rice are extra. ✉ *71 Corlett Dr., Birnham,* ☎ *011/786–8810. AE, DC, MC, V.*

$$ ✕ Turtle Creek Winery. Scion of the illustrious Linger Longer, this brash young progeny has inherited some of the wit and wisdom of its parent, if not its elegance and high prices. Young sophisticates hang out here, sipping South Africa's best wines (available by the glass), helping themselves to tapas, and dining on focaccia topped with roast lamb and olives. Tables spill out of the high-ceilinged bar onto an oak-shaded patio, which quickly fills with an after-work crowd. Try fresh baked trout wrapped in vine leaves and stuffed with anchovies, tomato, and garlic, or cassoulet of lamb with white beans, smoked sausage, baby onions, and feta. The steak-and-kidney and chicken-thyme-and-mushroom pies are famous, too. Pass up dessert for platter of cheeses and a glass of port. ✉ *58 Wierda Rd. W, Wierda Valley, Sandton,* ☎ *011/884–0466. AE, DC, MC, V. No dinner Sun.*

$$ ✕ Widgeons Bistro. Dark green walls and plaid tablecloths lend old-world charm to this intimate Parkview restaurant. The menu is eclectic, with flavors of Italy, colonial Africa, and the Far East. Spaghetti *con aglio e oglio,* accented with a smattering of chilis, is the tastiest in town. Penne *ai Communisti,* made with onions, smoked salmon, and a splash of vodka is also very good. Otherwise, try the seafood platter, cooked with coconut milk, periperi, brandy, wine, and lots of coriander. The restaurant is licensed, but feel free to bring your own bottle. ✉ *60 Tyrone Ave., Parkview,* ☎ *011/486–2053. AE, DC, MC, V. Closed Sun. No lunch Mon.*

$ ✕ Franco's Pizzeria & Trattoria. Dark wood paneling, red-check tablecloths, and soft Italian music give this spot a welcoming appeal. Chef-owner Franco Forleo comes from Brindisi and specializes in southern Italian cuisine. The menu includes 14 pizzas and a range of pasta dishes, but habitués usually choose one of the specials, such as *capelli al salmone e caviale* (angel-hair pasta with smoked salmon and caviar), or seasonal *frutti di mare* like butterfish, yellowtail, and kabeljou. Remember to bring your own wine—and that this is one of the few restaurants open for lunch on Saturday. ✉ *Parkview Centre, 54 Tyrone Ave.,* ☎ *011/646–5449. AE, DC, MC, V. BYOB. Closed Mon.*

$ ✕ Plaka Taverna. Greek music floats above the buzz of conversation, a gyro spit turns slowly near the door, and a refrigerated case displays an array of mezede. Most people sit on the roofed terrace or at the few street-side tables. Start with a couple of ouzos and share a platter of gyro meat, feta, olives, cucumber, and tomato. Follow that with a platter of meze, a Greek salad, and a carafe of wine, and your bill will still be less than R40 per person. If you're really hungry, choose the spit-roasted lamb or grilled marinated chicken. ✉ *3a Corlett Dr., Illovo,* ☎ *011/788–8777. AE, DC, MC, V. Closed Mon.*

$ ✕ Red Chamber Mandarin Restaurant. This is where the Chinese community gathers on Sunday morning for its traditional dim sum or *yum char* (tea and snacks). During the rest of the week, chefs from Taiwan,

Hong Kong, Beijing, and Guangzhou turn out some of the best Chinese food in the city, drawing a loyal following of wealthy Chinese locals. There are more than 100 dishes on the menu, but feel free to make special requests; some of the best dishes aren't listed. Highlights include cubes of eggplant and chili cooked and served in a sizzling wok, and steamed shrimp dumplings. ⊠ *Rosebank Mews, Rosebank,* ☎ *011/ 788–5536. AE, DC, MC, V. Closed Tues.*

LODGING

Downtown

$$$ **Carlton.** Since 1972 this hotel has set the standard for luxury accommodation and service in Johannesburg. It also charges hundreds
★ of rand less than the Sandton Sun. The hotel occupies a skyscraper in the heart of the city center, making it an ideal choice for businesspeople. The lobby sets the tone for the hotel with its rich burgundy tones, marbled floors, wood paneling, and beautiful Asian art. Individually decorated suites are magnificent: huge and incredibly opulent. Don't even consider walking in the streets after dark. ⊠ *Main St. at Kruis St. (mailing address: Box 7709, Johannesburg 2000),* ☎ *011/331–8911,* FAX *011/331–3555. 169 rooms. 2 restaurants, 2 bars, room service, pool, health center. AE, DC, MC, V.*

$$$ **Parktonian.** Close to the Rotunda transport center, the major theaters, and just a three-minute drive from the central business district, this Braamfontein property offers the best value in the city—even if its neighborhood isn't safe to walk in at night. The guest rooms are all suites, by far the largest of any city hotel. All have a separate living room and bedroom, minibar, cable TV, and veranda. You can enter the hotel directly from a secure parking garage. ⊠ *120 De Korte St., Braamfontein (mailing address: Box 32278, Braamfontein 2017),* ☎ *011/403–5740,* FAX *011/403–2401. 308 rooms. 2 restaurants, bar, room service, pool, health center. AE, DC, MC, V.*

$$$ **Sunnyside Park Hotel.** Just minutes by car from the city center, this Parktown hotel is one of the few in the city with a history. Built in 1895 as a mansion for a mining engineer, it later served as the residence of Lord Milner, eventual governor of the Transvaal. New sections have been added to the original mansion, but wood paneling and old prints help recapture something of the hotel's illustrious past. Rooms are pleasant, done in autumnal tones with bird prints and wicker furniture. Request a front-facing room overlooking the gardens. Service is not one of the hotel's strong points: rooms may not be ready by mid-afternoon and the front-desk staff could be more helpful. The surrounding area is generally safe during the day, but it's not advisable to wander out at night. ⊠ *2 York Rd., Parktown (mailing address: Box 31256, Braamfontein 2017),* ☎ *011/643–7226,* FAX *011/642–0019. 96 rooms. Restaurant, 2 bars, room service, pool. AE, DC, MC, V.*

$ **Hotel Formule 1.** This budget French chain has five identical hotels around Johannesburg and one near the airport, each built from prefabricated parts and assembled as though from a giant Lego set. The hotels are designed to overcome the worst failings in human nature, with wall-mounted TVs and beds. All rooms have a toilet and shower cubicle. You're not quite sure whether you're in prison or the 21st century. That said, you won't find clean accommodations any cheaper. ⊠ *1 Maree St., Bramley Park, Sandton,* ☎ *011/887–5555,* FAX *011/887– 3732;* ⊠ *1 Mitchell St., Berea,* ☎ *011/484–5551,* FAX *011/484–5705;* ⊠ *Herman and Kruis Sts., Isando,* ☎ *011/392–1453,* FAX *011/974–3845. AE, DC, MC, V.*

Northern Suburbs

$$$$ ⊞ **Park Hyatt Hotel.** If you like lots of black, gold, and glass decor, this one's for you. Enormous picture windows afford stunning views over the northern suburbs. The black-and-gold theme extends to the rooms, which are the last word in luxury with televisions, minibars, wardrobe safes, 24-hour room and laundry service, complimentary magazines, a choice of smoking and no-smoking accommodations, and twin, queen, or king-size beds. Should you book one of the Regency Club suites, you'll be entitled to complimentary sundowner cocktails at 6 PM—not to mention even more glorious views. Local art lines the walls in discreetly-lit passageways, and there's an ultramodern restaurant and wine bar, a luxurious health club, and a solar-heated pool on the roof. The hotel has an airport greeting service and makes arrangements for baby-sitting and car rental. ⊠ *Oxford Rd. and Bierman Ave., Rosebank (mailing address: Box 1536, Saxonwold, 2132),* ☎ *011/280–1234,* FAX *011/280–1238. 244 rooms. Restaurant, café, bar, room service, pool, health club, laundry service. AE, DC, MC, V.*

$$$$ ⊞ **Sandton Sun & Towers.** This five-star hotel in Sandton adjoins one
  ★ of the largest and most exclusive malls in the country, and it's close to the burgeoning collection of businesses that have fled to the northern suburbs. The Sun and Sun Towers are two nominally separate hotels, linked by a walkway and sharing facilities. Both occupy high-rises with commanding views of the northern suburbs and the highveld. The focal point of each hotel is a central atrium soaring the height of the building. Guest rooms are small but superbly laid out, with understated lighting and elegant decorative touches. There is little to recommend one hotel over the other, although the Towers is smaller and farther removed from the bustle of Sandton Mall. The Towers also has two floors of executive suites, with their own bar, breakfast room, and full-time staff. ⊠ *5th and Alice Sts. (mailing address: Box 784902, Sandhurst 2196),* ☎ *011/780–5000,* FAX *011/780–5002. 565 rooms. 4 restaurants, 2 bars, room service, 2 pools, beauty salon, health club.*

$$$ ⊞ **Holiday Inn Johannesburg International.** A few hundred yards from the airport, this Holiday Inn stands head and shoulders above the other airport hotels—which for the bossy service isn't saying much. Most guests spend one night here either at the beginning or end of their trip, even though there's nothing to do outside the hotel. There is a coffee bar in the foyer. Shuttle buses run to the airport every 15 minutes. If you're coming by car, the easiest way to reach the hotel is to drive through the airport and follow the signs marked AIR FREIGHT. ⊠ *Off R24, Kempton Park (mailing address: Box 388, Kempton Park 1620),* ☎ *011/ 975–1121,* FAX *011/975–5846. 365 rooms. Restaurant, bar, room service, pool. AE, DC, MC, V.*

$$$ ⊞ **Karos Indaba.** Indaba is an African word for meeting place, and an apt name for one of the major conference venues in Johannesburg, capable of hosting several major functions simultaneously in a wide variety of board rooms, auditoriums, and ballrooms. The property is huge, covering more than 30 acres on the outskirts of Johannesburg, about 30 minutes by car from both the airport and the city center. The hotel itself is very attractive, with a thatched roof lending rustic African charm to an otherwise business-oriented establishment. Rooms in the older thatched section are comfortable but a bit dark. Rooms in the newer Ninth Block are lighter, done in attractive greens and rusts, and feature their own verandas and minibars, as well as separate bath and shower. Sunday brunch under the jacarandas on the hotel's terrace is a local favorite. ⊠ *Hartebeespoort Dam Rd., Witkoppen (mailing address: Box 67129, Bryanston 2021),* ☎ *Central reservations, 011/*

643–8052, FAX *011/643–4343; hotel, 011/465–1400. 210 rooms. Restaurant, bar, pool, sauna, tennis court, health club, squash.*

$$$ 🏨 **Rosebank Hotel.** Ideally situated 15 minutes by car from the city center and minutes on foot from the shops, cinemas, and restaurants of Rosebank's malls, the Rosebank is another favorite among businesspeople who appreciate low-key atmosphere and efficient service. The lounge and reception area are newly renovated. Rooms are attractively decorated with prints and dark wood furniture and paneling. The newer north wing retains the style of the old building. There is also an airport shuttle service (by request) and the hotel has an arrangement with Imperial Car Hire. Parking is available at around R14.25 per day. For walkers, this is a much better choice than the Sunnyside or the Parktonian: the streets of Rosebank are among the safest and most interesting in Johannesburg. ✉ *Tyrwhitt and Sturdee Aves., Rosebank (mailing address: Box 52025, Saxonwold 2132),* ☎ *011/447–2700,* FAX *011/447–3276. 318 rooms. 3 restaurants, 2 bars, room service, pool, beauty salon, exercise room. AE, DC, MC, V.*

$$ 🏨 **Holiday Inn Garden Court–Sandton.** This no-frills hotel was knocked together in record time for the 1995 Rugby World Cup. If it has a prefabricated feel, it's also ideally located, catercorner from the Sandton City mall. These days, it caters mainly to businesspeople staying for a few days. Rooms are small and functional, but clean, each with twin and double beds, air-conditioning, TV, and tea- and coffee-makers. ✉ *Katherine St. and Rivonia Rd. (mailing address: Box 783394, Sandton 2196),* ☎ *011/884–5660,* FAX *011/783–2004. 157 rooms. Restaurant, bar, pool. AE, DC, MC, V.*

NIGHTLIFE AND THE ARTS

The best place to find out what's going on in Johannesburg is in the Tonight section of the *The Star,* Johannesburg's major daily. Another great source of information is the weekly *Mail & Guardian.* Make your bookings through **Computicket** (☎ 011/445–8445 for information, ☎ 011/445–8000 for credit card purchases), which has outlets throughout the city, including most major malls.

The Arts

Classical Music

The **National Symphony Orchestra** (☎ 011/714–4501 for information; ☎ 011/445–8000 for tickets) stages concerts in Linder Auditorium (✉ Johannesburg College of Education, St. Andrews Rd., Parktown) and occasionally at City Hall (✉ President and Simmonds Sts., Johannesburg Central). Concerts generally start at 8 PM, and you can attend preconcert talks at 7:15 PM. Other events include musical fireworks concerts, picnic concerts at Johannesburg Zoo, a Christmas Concert, and Songs of Praise, a festival of Easter music and hymns. If you're visiting the city in September, consider making a reservation for the incredibly popular Johannesburg Pops concerts, held in one of the city's enormous parks. Concerts showcase contemporary music, played in classical style. Picnic baskets are sold (order when making a reservation) and each evening ends with a fireworks display.

Theater

The beautiful **Alhambra Theatre** complex (✉ Sivewright Ave. and Beit St., Doornfontein, ☎ 011/402–6174 for information; ☎ 011/402–7726 for tickets) is made up of three theaters: the Alhambra, the Rex Garner, and the Richard Haines. The complex presents primarily mainstream productions, like West End and Broadway material.

The **Civic Theatre** (⊠ Loveday St., Braamfontein, ☎ 011/403–3408 for information; box office, ☎ 011/339–4609 day or ☎ 011/403–3411 evening) is Johannesburg's principal cultural venue. Housed in a slick, modern complex, the Civic has one enormous theater and three smaller stages. Many productions have a South African focus—works by such famous local talents as Pieter-Dirk Uys and Paul Slabolepszy.

The **Market Theatre** (⊠ Bree and Wolhuter Sts., ☎ 011/832–1641) occupies an old Indian produce market that dates back to the early 1900s. Now completely refurbished, the three-theater complex has a wealth of character and includes a great bar and restaurant and an art gallery with changing exhibits. Theater productions encompass everything from plays by Athol Fugard to imported West End comedies. The theater occasionally features ethnic African music. Experimental plays get the litmus test of audience approval at the Market Theatre Laboratory, across Bree Street.

Nightlife

Multiracial Hillbrow used to be the city's nightlife center, but the neighborhood has become a crime-ridden, no-go zone full of hookers, massage parlors, and porno houses. In its place, **Rosebank** has emerged as the hot new spot, and you'll find clubs, bars, and coffee shops scattered through the neighborhood, particularly along Oxford Road. **Rockey Street** in Yeoville also has a happening nightlife scene, with clubs and bars offering everything from jazz to grunge. Unfortunately, the street is also a popular hangout for drug dealers and addicts. Many white residents of the northern suburbs, concerned about personal safety, head to the modern **Randburg Waterfront** (⊠ Republic Rd., Randburg), a gimmicky, mall-like development of almost a hundred restaurants, bars, and clubs clustered around an artificial lake.

Bars and Pubs

The **Guildhall Executive Bar and Restaurant** (⊠ Meischkes Bldg., Market St., ☎ 011/836–5560), in the city center, is the oldest bar in Johannesburg. Walk through swinging doors into a paneled room rich with wood and smoke. **Players** (⊠ Bolton Rd. and Bath Ave., Rosebank, ☎ 011/442–9313), a cavernous bar, may be the biggest meat market in the city, particularly on Friday in summer when an after-work crowd jams its outdoor veranda. **The Yard of Ale** (⊠ Market Theatre complex, Bree St., ☎ 011/836–6611), in the city center, is a great, no-nonsense bar with an outdoor veranda. It's a good place to quaff a few brews before heading to Kippies (☞ *below*) or after working up a sweat at the Saturday flea market.

Live Music

House of Tandoor (⊠ 26 Rockey St., Yeoville, ☎ 011/487–1569) has some of the best live jazz and blues in town, either in the Back Bar or the Blues Kitchen. **Kippies** (⊠ Market Theatre complex, off Bree St., Newtown, ☎ 011/834–3743) is the city's premier jazz venue, featuring traditional and township South African jazz. It also serves light meals. **Picasso Bistro** (⊠ Old Mutual Sq., 169 Oxford Rd., Rosebank, ☎ 011/788–1213) is a sophisticated wine bar and coffee house. Open late, it's *the* place to see and be seen. **Rattlesnake Route 552 Roadside Diner** (⊠ Mutual Village, Rivonia Blvd., Rivonia, ☎ 011/803–9406) bills itself as a '60s dining experience, but when the partyers start singing and dancing on the tables, no one really cares.

Nightclubs

Jagger's (⊠ Mutual Sq., Rosebank, ☎ 011/788–1718), underneath the Tivoli Pizza Restaurant, is a popular techno-pop dance club. **Kryp-**

ton (✉ Constantia Centre, Tyrwhitt Ave., Rosebank, ☎ 011/788–4708) is a techno club, with dancers grooving wall-to-wall to an urgent, unending beat.

OUTDOOR ACTIVITIES AND SPORTS

Participant Sports

Golf

Johannesburg's finest golf courses are open to foreign visitors, although weekend play tends to be restricted to members only. Expect to pay R70–R100 for a round. The century-old **Royal Johannesburg Golf Club** (✉ Fairway Ave., Linksfield North, ☎ 011/640–3022) has two courses: the East Course is the more famous of the two, and has hosted the South African Open seven times. The **Wanderers Golf Club** (✉ Rudd Rd., Illovo, ☎ 011/447–3311), permanent host of the South African P.G.A. Championship, is a tough course, well bunkered and with plenty of water on the early holes; it demands exacting iron shots to its small greens. **Glendower Club** (✉ Marais Rd., Bedfordview, ☎ 011/453–1013) lies in a nature reserve. The recent addition of more water hazards and extra length makes this one of the most challenging courses in the country. You can rent clubs at Royal Johannesburg and at **Roger Manning Golf Shop** (✉ Huddle Park Golf Course, adjoining Royal Johannesburg, Linksfield North, ☎ 011/640–3065).

Spectator Sports

Cricket

The **Wanderers' Club** (✉ 21 North St., Illovo, ☎ 011/788–5010) is the country's premier cricket ground, and the site of many of the international contests between South Africa and touring sides from England and its former colonies.

Rugby

South Africa's showcase rugby stadium is **Ellis Park** (✉ Staib St., Doornfontein, ☎ 011/402–8644), where the Springboks beat New Zealand's All Blacks to win the 1995 World Cup. It's a magnificent stadium, capable of seating nearly 65,000 people. It's home to the Transvaal rugby team, which competes against other provincial sides in the annual Bankfin Currie Cup competition.

SHOPPING

Johannesburg is the best place in the country to buy quality African art, whether it's tribal fetishes from Central Africa or oil paintings by early white settlers. Dozens of galleries and curio shops are scattered throughout the city, often selling the same goods at widely different prices. Newtown Market Africa, which you should consider seeing before making purchases elsewhere, has the best prices (☞ Markets, *below*).

And if you thought America had a thing for malls, wait until you see Jo'burg's northern suburbs. Blink and another mall has gone up. Even more astonishing is how exclusive they are, lined with chichi shops selling the latest from Italy, France, and the States—at twice the price you would pay at home. Most malls also have department stores like Edgars and Woolworth's, as well as cinemas and restaurants.

Malls

The major mall in Johannesburg is **Sandton City** (✉ Sandton Dr. and Rivonia Rd.), with hundreds of stores and a confusing layout that guarantees you'll get lost for days. The wing of shops leading from the mall to the Sandton Sun Hotel has some worthwhile African art galleries. Adjoining Sandton City is **Sandton Square** (⊠ 5th St.), built to resemble an Italian palazzo, complete with expensive Italian shops, bakeries, and restaurants. Closer to the city, **Hyde Park Mall** (⊠ Jan Smuts Ave., Hyde Park, ☎ 011/325–4340) is the city's most upscale shopping center, where fashion victims come to sip cappuccino and browse in Exclusive Books, a branch of the country's best chain of book stores. Rosebank is a happening suburb focused on a conglomeration of five shopping centers (⊠ Cradock St., between Biermann Ave. and Baker St.). The great plus about **Rosebank Mall** (⊠ Between Bath and Cradock Aves.) and the surrounding area is that you can actually walk and sit outside—something of a novelty in security-conscious Johannesburg. This is the place to come for casual al fresco lunches at one of the area's many cafés and restaurants. More recently however, the area has seen the introduction of extensive hawking along the pavements—here you can shop for curios including artifacts fashioned from coat-hanger wire, clay pots decorated Ndebele style, ubiquitous guinea fowls, soapstone carvings, and malachite jewelry. Downtown, adjoining the Carlton Hotel, the **Carlton Centre** (⊠ Commissioner and von Weilligh Sts.) is home to 200 stores.

Markets

Newtown Market Africa, a flea market held every Saturday in front of the Market Theatre, is the best place in town for African art and curios at low, low prices. Vendors from Cameroon, Nigeria, and Zaire come here to sell masks, fetishes, traditional wood pillows, Kuba raffia cloth, and Mali blankets. Bargain hard and you should be able to get vendors to knock a third off the price. ⊠ *Wolhuter St., between Bree and Jeppe Sts.* ⊘ *Sat. 9–4.*

Rosebank's Rooftop Fleamarket features a lot of locally made crafts, kitsch, bread, cheese, biltong, and mass-produced African curios. Frequently, African musicians, dancers, and buskers entertain the roving Sunday crowds. ⊠ *Rosebank Mall, 50 Bath Ave., Rosebank,* ☎ *B&B Markets, 011/442–4488.* ⊘ *Sun. 9–5.*

Specialty Stores

AFRICAN ART

Abyssinia Art Gallery, in the Market Theatre complex, has an excellent collection of masks, glass beads, Ethiopian silver crosses, carvings, and spears from various African tribes. Prices are decent. ⊠ *Shop 8, Market Theatre complex, Wolhuter and Bree Sts., Newtown,* ☎ *011/834–2301.* ⊘ *Mon.–Sat. 9–5.*

Everard Read Gallery is one of the largest privately owned galleries in the world. It acts as agent for several important South African artists, as well as a number of international contemporary artists. The gallery specializes in wildlife paintings and sculpture. ⊠ *6 Jellicoe Ave., Rosebank,* ☎ *011/788–4805.* ⊘ *Mon.–Sat. 9–6.*

Kim Sacks Gallery, in a lovely old home, has one of the finest collections of authentic African art in Johannesburg. Displayed throughout its sunny rooms are Zairian raffia cloth, Mali mud cloth, Zulu telephone-wire baskets, and an excellent collection of original masks and carvings from across the continent. Unusual wood sculptures, ceramics, and prints by outstanding South African artists are also for sale. Pieces are labeled by country and tribe of origin; when possible, they are also dated. Prices are high. ⊠ *Frances St. and Cavendish Rd., Bellevue,* ☎ *011/648–6107.* ⊘ *Weekdays 9–5; Sat. 10–3. Phone for details of evening opening hours.*

Master Weavers sells locally woven rugs and tapestries, most done in muted colors and depicting people or scenes from nature. Prices are high. ⊠ *Shop G76, Fourways Mall, William Nicol, Fourways,* ☎ *011/ 465–6425.* ⊙ *Mon.–Sat. 9–5, Sun. 10–2.*

Rural Craft has a good collection of Xhosa and Ndebele beadwork, including wedding aprons and jewelry. The shop also sells fabrics made by rural Ndebele, Xhosa, and Zulu women. ⊠ *Shop 42E, Mutual Gardens, 31 Tyrwhitt Ave., Rosebank,* ☎ *011/880–9651.* ⊙ *Weekdays 8:30– 4:30, Sat. 8:30–2:30.*

Soweto Art Gallery, tucked away in three small rooms in a shabby downtown office block, is a no-nonsense shop where the paintings are mostly unframed or stacked against the wall. Elegant it's not, but the gallery features the works of some very talented African artists from townships all over the Johannesburg area. The subject matter is pure Africa, culled from the ghettos of the townships and brought to life in vibrant canvasses. Oils, linocuts, and sculpture are represented. ⊠ *34 Harrison St., Suite 34, 2nd floor, Johannesburg,* ☎ *011/836–0252.* ⊙ *Weekdays 8–6, Sat. 8–1.*

Totem Gallery specializes in artifacts from West and Central Africa, including Kuba cloth from Zaire, Dogon doors from Mali, glass beads, masks from Burkina Faso, and hand-painted barbershop signs. Some pieces come with detailed descriptions of their history. Prices are high. ⊠ *Sandton City,* ☎ *011/884–6300.* ⊙ *Mon.–Sat. 9–5;* ⊠ *Rosebank,* ☎ *011/447–1409.* ⊙ *Weekdays 9–5, Sat. 9–4.*

BOOKS

Exclusive Books (⊠ Sandton City, ☎ 011/883–1010; ⊠ Hyde Park Mall, ☎ 011/325–4298) is the best chain of bookstores in the country, with a great selection of African literature, history, travel, and culture.

Facts & Fiction (⊠ Rosebank Mall, ☎ 011/447–3028; ⊠ Sandton Square, ☎ 011/784–5416) allows you to not only browse the bookshelves but also the Internet at the Internet Café. The store has a good variety of CD-ROMs, as well as a coffee bar where you can enjoy tasty cakes while you flip through magazines and newspapers.

GOLD

Krugerrands, with images of President Kruger and a springbok on either side, are among the most famous gold coins minted today. They lost some of their luster during the apartheid years, when they were banned internationally. Krugerrands are sold individually or in sets containing coins of one ounce, ½ ounce, ¼ ounce, and ⅒ ounce of pure gold. You can buy Krugerrands through most city banks, but several branches of First National Bank sell them over the counter. The most convenient branches are in Sandton City, Carlton Centre, and Rosebank.

SIDE TRIPS FROM JOHANNESBURG

The Magaliesberg

The Magaliesberg is a range of hills stretching 120 km (74 mi) between Pretoria and the town of Rustenburg, about a 90-minute drive northwest of Johannesburg. The Boer War once raged here and the remains of British blockhouses can still be seen. However, the region is most remarkable for its natural beauty. Grassy slopes cleft by ochre buttresses, streams adorned with ferns, waterfalls plunging into pools, and superb rock formations contribute to the Magaliesberg's unique beauty. You can get surprisingly close to wildlife on foot: you can view mountain reedbuck, klipspringers, baboon troupes, or vervet monkeys and search for rock hyrax (*dassie*) among the stones. Activities in the area focus on the outdoors—you can go hiking, swim in crystal streams, or take a picnic lunch to one of the natural hideaways.

The Magaliesberg is very popular with locals, and the main areas and attractions get extremely crowded on weekends. Advance booking for weekends is advisable—many places limit numbers of visitors.

Hiking in the Magaliesberg can be extremely hot and dry and is not recommended in midsummer. Use a daypack or small rucksack, carry an ample water supply, and use adequate sun protection. Remember to take your own lunch and wear sturdy footwear. A raincoat, swimsuit, and small towel may come in handy in summer.

Much of the Magaliesburg is privately owned, although a protected nature area near the summit remains undeveloped by law. Don't go wandering around unless you're in a resort—you may be trespassing. (Some landowners are not averse to shooting at trespassers.)

Exploring

For driving directions to the Magaliesberg, *see* Arriving and Departing, *below.* From the R560 and R27, the Magaliesberg's northern aspect is magnificent. Small farms have pink peach blossoms in spring and yellow sunflowers in autumn. **Olifantsnek** is a rock formation that bears an uncanny likeness to an elephant, for which it is named. Slightly beyond is Olifantsnek Dam.

Hartebeesport Dam is beautifully situated on R560 at the foot of the Magaliesberg's spectacular slopes; the area is popular with fishing and watersports enthusiasts. The **Cableway** on the eastern side of the dam is the best way to view the surrounding countryside from on high— and local paragliders floating alongside the cliffs. The dam site was a location for the film version of *Tigers Don't Cry* by popular South African author, Wilbur Smith. *Cableway:* ☎ *01211/30–706.* ✉ *R14 roundtrip.* ☉ *Weekdays 9–3:30, weekends 9–5.*

If you walk or drive across the **Dam Wall,** you get a bird's-eye view of the whole thing—particularly spectacular after heavy rains when the sluice gates are open.

The resort town of **Hartebeesport** is a tropical oasis where bougainvillea cascades everywhere in summer. Explore the craft shops and dine al fresco as you watch the world go by.

As you continue westward, you'll find numerous delightful **tea gardens—** and a country pub or two. Many are run by Afrikaaners who've escaped the rat race. The food is generally satisfying; however, expect service to be laid back. A few establishments have small curio shops selling basketware, African masks, walking sticks (*kieries*), and semiprecious stones.

Tranquil **Rustenburg Nature Reserve** lies at the western edge of the range. At the visitor's center, you may find out about the area's geology, fauna, and flora. Be sure to take a walk on Peglerae Interpretive Trail, a 5-km (3-mi) walk-by-numbers with rare plants and unusual rocks. Afterward, enjoy a picnic lunch at a picnic site. A self-guided auto trail is also available. ✉ *Box 511, Rustenburg, 0300.* ☎ *0142/31–050.* ✉ *R5. Small charge for the Peglerae Trail guidebook.*

Western Cane Trading is *the* place to go if you simply can't resist enormous pots of tea accompanied by homemade cakes (R20–R30) in a beautiful garden filled with roses and birds. Off the shady veranda is a pleasant shop, filled with country delights ranging from bath salts and homemade candles to cane furniture and teddy bears. ✉ *Turn off the R24 onto the R509 to Koster and travel approximately 7 km (4 mi) up the road (take the Vlakfontein turnoff),* ☎ *0142/77–1361.*

Lodging

$$$ 🏨 **Mount Grace's Country House Hotel.** This peaceful country hotel near the town of Magaliesberg has accommodations in delightful thatched buildings at differing heights, which have glorious views of the mountain. The Mountain Village is the most luxurious lodging, with sunken baths, heated towel rails, a minibar, and endless views of the area. If you're looking for more privacy, you might prefer to stay at Grace Village, which is a little more secluded and further down the mountain. The most reasonable lodging is the Thatchstone Village. Country-style decor—thatch, wood, and wicker—creates a delightful ambience in the hotel, and the food is wholesome country fare. 🏨 *On the R24 to Hekpoort, near the town of Magaliesberg (mailing address: Box 251 Magaliesberg, 2805),* ☎ *011/880–1675, 0142/77–1350, or 0142/77–1202,* FAX *011/880–3282. 65 rooms. 2 restaurants, bar, pool, bowling, croquet, hiking, fishing, library. AE, DC, MC, V.*

Magaliesberg A to Z

ARRIVING AND DEPARTING

From Sandton, take the N1 south toward Roodepoort and get off at the 4th Avenue/Fairlands exit. At the bottom of the exit, turn right onto 4th Avenue toward the suburb of Constantia Kloof. Proceed under the highway bridge and turn right at the second set of traffic lights, onto the M47/R47 to Tarlton. After crossing the R28 from Krugersdorp, the R47 becomes the N17. Continue to the T-junction and turn right, toward Hekpoort. You are now on the R563. Keep to the right-hand lane as the left-hand lane peels off soon afterward. The road will wind a little, and you'll have beautiful views of the Magaliesberg. After you have passed a Boer War blockhouse high on a hill on the right-hand side, look for the "Bekker Schools" sign at the bottom of the hill, and turn left onto this road. At another T-junction, turn right toward Rustenburg, onto the R560. Shortly after passing Hartebeespost Dam on your right, you will reach another T-junction. Turn left onto the R27, again going toward Rustenburg.

Another route is the R24, which approaches the Magaliesberg from Krugersdorp, passes the town of Magaliesberg, and joins the R560. The Johannesburg branch of the Automobile Association has an excellent map of the Magaliesberg showing major routes and resorts.

HIKING

The **Johannesburg Hiking Club** (☎ 011/465–9888; weekdays 8:30–noon) hikes the Magaliesberg and surrounding areas every Sunday.

The **Mountain Club of South Africa (Southern Transvaal Section)** has regular hiking and climbing meets. For events in the area, call the club's main office in Cape Town (☎ 021/45–3412.

HOT-AIR BALLOONING

For a special experience, sail high above the Magaliesberg in a hot-air balloon with **Bill Harrop's Original Balloon Safaris** (☎ 011/705–3201, FAX 011/705–3203) and enjoy a champagne breakfast afterward.

VISITOR INFORMATION

The **tourist information office** (⊠ On R24, ☎ 0142/77–1733) for the area is on the main road through Magaliesberg town (on the southern side of town if you're driving from Krugersdorp).

Pretoria

Pretoria is overshadowed by Johannesburg, 48 km (30 mi) to the south, and few people outside South Africa know it as the country's capital. It's a pleasant city, with historic buildings and a city center that is easily explored on foot. Pretoria is famous for its jacaranda trees, and the best time to visit is in spring (September and October), when the city is blanketed with their purple blossoms. Founded in 1855, the city was named after Andries Pretorius, the hero of the Battle of Blood River (☞ *below and* Chapter 7), and it has remained a bastion of Afrikaner culture. With the triumph of the Nationalist Party in 1948, it also became the seat of Afrikaner power, and the city developed a reputation for hard-line Afrikaner insularity. Much of that has changed in recent years, and President Nelson Mandela now occupies the lovely Union Buildings overlooking the city. International acceptance of the new South Africa has also seen an influx of foreign embassies and personnel, bringing a refreshing cosmopolitanism to Pretoria. As a result, many of the country's finest restaurants are here.

A Good Tour
Numbers in the text correspond to numbers in the margin and on the Pretoria map.

If you're coming from Johannesburg, your first stop should be the **Voortrekker Monument and Museum** ⑱. To get there, take the Fountains/Voortrekkerhoogte exit from the R28. At the traffic lights at the bottom of the exit, turn left toward Voortrekkerhoogte. Turn right at the next set of traffic lights. The entrance gates to the monument are on the right-hand side of the road, shortly after the traffic lights. Brown information signs will in any event direct you to the monument from the highway. Return to the highway (R28) and drive north into the city. The R28 becomes Potgieter Street going into Pretoria central. (This is a one-way street going north). Turn right on Kerk Street. The **Kruger House Museum** ⑲ is on your left. Street parking is available. Walk four blocks east down Kerk to **Church Square** ⑳. Walk one block north from Church Square on Paul Kruger Street and turn right into Vermeulen Street to reach the **Pierneef Museum** ㉑.

Head back to Kerk Street and collect your car. Drive one block east to Schubart Street (a one-way street going south) and turn right onto Schubart Street. Drive four blocks south until you reach Visagie Street. Turn left on Visagie Street and drive two blocks. You will now be on the north side of the **Transvaal Museum** ㉒, the best natural science museum in the country. Across Paul Kruger Street from the museum stands **City Hall** ㉓. Walk south down Paul Kruger Street for two block and turn left on Jacob Maré Street to reach **Melrose House** ㉔. Cross the street to view the beautiful **Burgers Park** ㉕.

Continue down Jacob Maré Street and turn left on Van der Walt Street at the corner. Walk three blocks to Skinner Street. At the corner of Skinner Street, you'll pass the brick **Staats Model School** ㉖. Continue north along Van der Walt Street for two blocks until you reach Pretorius Street and **J. G. Strijdom Square** ㉗, named for one of South Africa's prime ministers. To the right of the square is the awe-inspiring State Theatre and Opera House. Walk west on Pretorius Street for two blocks to reach Paul Kruger Street once more. Walk south down Paul Kruger Street for three blocks to reach the Transvaal Museum, where you will have parked your car.

Drive south on Paul Kruger Street to Jacob Maré Street, turn left and pass Burgers Park on your left. Take the next road right, turning north on the one-way Van der Walt Street. Continue for 12 blocks until you reach the one-way DR Savage Drive and turn left. Drive three blocks and turn right on Bosman Street, and after a block, turn left on Boom Street. Another 1½ blocks will take you to the entrance to the **National Zoological Gardens** ㉘ on your left. To continue on to

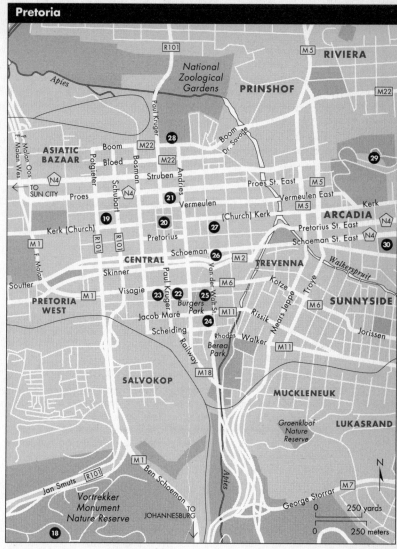

Pretoria

the **Union Buildings** ㉙, continue driving west on Boom Street and turn left onto Hamilton Street. At Edmond Street turn left, and the Union Buildings will be on the left. This road becomes a wide throughway with ample parking. In the valley directly below the Union Buildings lies the **Pretoria Art Museum** ㉚. To reach this, drive south down Hamilton Street once you've had your fill of the Union Buildings. Drive five blocks to reach the one-way Schoeman Street and turn left. Drive two long blocks to reach Wessels Street. The Pretoria Art Museum is on the corner.

To get back to the R28 and the N1S to Johannesburg, head south down Wessels Street for one block to reach Park Street, turn right, drive for one block, then turn left on Leyds Street. After three blocks, turn left onto Church Street. Continue for seven blocks, then turn left on Andries Street. After four blocks, turn left onto Visagie Street, going west. After three blocks, turn left on Schubart Street and follow the signs back to Johannesburg. Going back to Johannesburg, the R28 becomes the N1S. Follow the signs to the N1S if you don't want to end up in Krugersdorp.

TIMING

It will take about 30 minutes to travel from Johannesburg to Pretoria on the N1. As you near Pretoria, the N1 branches. Take the R28 to enter the city center. If you want to see everything, we suggest you schedule an entire day in Pretoria. The walk alone will probably take a morning. You might want to drive to Kruger House and then continue north to see the Union Buildings. Arrange to take a picnic lunch as the gardens are a lovely place for a picnic.

Sights to See

㉕ **Burgers Park.** This lovely parkland lies across the road from Melrose House. Note the gates, which are all that remain of yet another Victorian mansion that lost out to the developers. Heady scents will lead you to fragrant rose gardens and flower beds filled with indigenous plants. At the center of the park, another converted Victorian house now contains a delightful restaurant. ✉ *Jacob Maré St., between Van der Walt and Andries Sts.* ✉ *Free.*

㉒ **Church Square.** A statue of President Kruger by Anton van Wouw dominates the pleasant square, which is flanked by some of Pretoria's most historic buildings: the Old Raadsaal (Town Hall), built in early Italian Renaissance style; the Palace of Justice, which was used as a military hospital during the Boer War; and the modern Provincial Administration Building. President Kruger arranged for the construction of many of these buildings.✉ *Surrounded by Paul Kruger St. (north–south) and Church St. (east–west).*

㉓ **City Hall.** An imposing structure that borrows freely from classical architecture, the building has a tympanum on the front by Coert Steynberg, one of South Africa's most famous sculptors—it symbolizes the growth and development of Pretoria. Statues of Andries Pretorius, the hero of the Battle of Blood River, and his son Marthinus, the city's founder, stand in the square fronting City Hall. ✉ *Paul Kruger St. (opposite Transvaal Museum, at the end of the gardens),* ☎ *012/326–5012.* ☉ *Weekdays 8–3.*

㉗ **J. G. Strijdom Square.** The square is dominated by a huge bust of former Prime Minister Strijdom. Despite the fervid anticommunist stance of the old Nationalist government, the square's monumental architecture bears a striking resemblance to that of former Soviet states; J. G. Strijdom's head could just as easily be Lenin's. ✉ *Church and Van der Walt Sts., next to the State Theatre.*

⑲ Kruger House Museum. This was once the residence of Paul Kruger, who served as president of the South African Republic between 1883 and 1902 and is one of the most revered figures in South African history. The home, still fully furnished, is humble and somber, befitting this deeply religious leader. Exhibits in the adjoining museum trace Kruger's career, culminating in his exile by the British and eventual death in Switzerland in 1904. Of particular interest are the expressions of support that Kruger received from all over the world, including the United States, when Britain instigated the Boer War (1899–1902). Across the road is the Dutch Reformed Church (now a national monument) where Mrs. Kruger was buried. ⊠ *Kerk St. at Potgieter St.,* ☎ *012/326–9172.* ⌑ *R5.* ☉ *Weekdays 8:30–4, weekends 9–4.*

㉔ Melrose House. Built in 1886, this opulent structure is one of the most beautiful Victorian homes in the country, with marble columns, mosaic floors, and lovely stained-glass windows. The house is furnished in period style. Its dining room is where the 1902 Treaty of Vereeniging was signed, ending the Boer War. ⊠ *275 Jacob Maré St.,* ☎ *012/322–2805.* ⌑ *R2.* ☉ *Tues.–Sat. 10–5, Thurs. until 8, Sun. noon–5.*

㉘ National Zoological Gardens. Pretoria's zoo is considered one of the world's best, with an enormous collection of animals from almost every continent. The animal enclosures here are much larger than those of most zoos, but a cage is still a cage. A cable car (R6.50) transports visitors high above the zoo to a hilltop lookout. ⊠ *Boom St.,* ☎ *012/328–3265.* ⌑ *R16 (includes admission to aquarium and snake park).* ☉ *Daily 8–5:30.*

㉑ Pierneef Museum. In a turn-of-the-century house, the museum displays works by Jacob Pierneef (1886–1957), one of South Africa's finest painters. Remarkable for his great range of styles, he is most famous for his unique, almost abstract renderings of South African landscapes. ⊠ *Vermeulen St., between Andries and Paul Kruger Sts.,* ☎ *012/323–1419.* ⌑ *Free.* ☉ *Weekdays 8:30–4.*

㉚ Pretoria Art Museum. This unimpressive gallery space houses a very impressive collection of South African art. Much of the collection consists of works by famous white artists, including Pierneef, van Wouw, Irma Stern, and Hugo Naudé, but more and more black artists are now receiving recognition—look for works by Ephraim Ngatane (1938–71), an early exponent of township art. The museum also stages changing exhibitions. ⊠ *Schoeman and Wessels Sts.,* ☎ *012/344–1807.* ⌑ *R2.* ☉ *Tues.–Sat. 10–5, Wed. until 8, Sun. noon–5.*

㉖ Staats Model School. The building stands as a fine example of a school from late 19th-century Transvaal Republic days. During the Boer War it served as a prison for British officers. It was from here that Winston Churchill made his famous escape after Boers captured him near Ladysmith. Appropriately, the school now houses an education department. It is not open to the public. ⊠ *Skinner and Van der Walt Sts.*

㉒ Transvaal Museum. The extensive collection of land and marine animals from around the world, with an emphasis on African wildlife, is worth the visit. The museum also features the Austin Roberts Bird Collection, a comprehensive display of southern African birds. Much of the museum is laid out with students in mind, and exhibit descriptions are exceptionally informative. Of particular interest are the Genesis exhibits, tracing the evolution of life on earth, and the geology section, with displays of weird and wonderful rocks and minerals. This is a great place to bring kids. *Note:* The museum is currently being extended— you may find certain halls and exhibits closed due to renovations. ⊠ *Paul Kruger St., across from City Hall,* ☎ *012/322–7632.* ⌑ *R5 (donation only during renovations).* ☉ *Mon.–Sat. 9–5, Sun. 11–5.*

㉙ Union Buildings. Designed by Sir Herbert Baker, this impressive red sandstone complex is home to the administrative branch of government and now serves as the headquarters of President Nelson Mandela. The complex incorporates a hodgepodge of styles—a Spanish-tile roof, wood shutters inspired by Cape Dutch architecture, and Greek columns—that somehow works beautifully. Formal gardens step down the hillside in terraces, dotted with war memorials and statues of former prime ministers. The view of the city from here is superb. ⊠ *Access off Kerk or Edmond Sts. Not open to the public.*

⑱ Voortrekker Monument and Museum. This unabashed tribute to the ideals at the heart of apartheid doesn't have a place in the new South Africa, but for the moment it remains, as much a part of Pretoria's landmarks as the sprawling edifice of UNISA (the University of South Africa, a correspondence university) as you enter the city from the south. Completed in 1949, the monument honors the Voortrekkers, Boer families who rejected British rule in the Cape and in 1835–38 trekked into the hinterland to found their own nation. The Hall of Heroes traces in its frieze the momentous events of their Great Trek, culminating in the Battle of Blood River (December 16, 1838), when a small force of Boers defeated the Zulu army without losing a single life (☞ Chapter 7). The Voortrekkers considered this victory a confirmation of their special relationship with God. Each year, at precisely noon on the anniversary of the battle, a ray of sunlight strikes the cenotaph engraved with the words "We for thee, South Africa." An adjoining museum displays scenes and artifacts of daily Voortrekker life, as well as the Voortrekker Tapestries, 15 pictorial weavings that trace the historical high points of the Great Trek. Even if you don't appreciate all the symbolism, the sheer grandeur of the monolith is worth seeing. ⊠ *Off M7. Follow brown signs off R28,* ☎ *012/323–0682.* 🎫 *Monument R5, museum R5.* ⊙ *Daily 9–4:45.*

Dining

$$$$ ✕ **Chagalls at Toulouse.** At the end of their meal, a contingent of visiting French chefs gave this restaurant a standing ovation. The food is *that* good. Chef Eric Springer has worked in the kitchens of some of Paris's most famous restaurants, and his haute cuisine *Française* is considered the finest in South Africa. The menu changes twice a year and invariably creates a stir. Start with such appetizers as creamed cauliflower with crumbed Irish salmon, or lobster and potato charlotte in caviar and salmon-egg butter. Main courses include lightly roasted breast of wild duck served with warm potato salad and confit of duckling leg, and marinated fillet of kudu antelope dressed with apple and nuts. The restaurant's setting, in a country lodge on the outskirts of Pretoria, is lovely. ⊠ *Fountains Valley, Pretoria,* ☎ *012/341–7511. Jacket and tie. AE, DC, MC, V. Closed Sun. No lunch Sat.*

$$$ ✕ **La Madeleine.** Noted for its classic and creative French cuisine, this
★　　restaurant ranks among the country's top ten. The wine list, too, has won a slew of awards. The menu changes daily, depending on what's available at the market. Expect as a starter a salad with langoustine in a parcel of phyllo pastry served on a swirl of gazpacho. A typical main course might be two quails, boned and cooked in puff pastry and served with marsala sauce. Desserts include such heavenly treats as honey ice cream with chocolate mousse cake and crème brûlée. ⊠ *258 Esselen St., Sunnyside, Pretoria,* ☎ *012/446–076. Reservations required. AE, DC, MC, V. Closed Sun. and Mon. No lunch Sat.*

$$$ ✕ **La Perla.** This grand Continental restaurant is a favorite haunt of ambassadors and ministers. The interior, with wood-paneled walls and tables separated by etched-glass panels, is ideal for private, power lunches. The menu includes a selection of standard European dishes like pan-fried quail with fresh herbs, *piccata Milanese,* and saddle of game. Starters include a half-dozen snails and prawns on a skewer. Meticulous preparation and service make up for any lack of innovation in the menu. The wine list is also outstanding. ⊠ *211 Skinner St., Pretoria,* ☎ *012/322–2759. Reservations required. AE, DC, MC, V. Closed Sun. No lunch Sat.*

$$ ✕ **Brasserie de Paris.** This delightful French oasis occupies an unassuming building in suburban Hatfield. In typical Parisian style, café tables adorn the outside veranda. Appetizers include frogs' legs Provençal and delicious pâté *en croute* (in a crust). For a main course, choose between ox tongue in white wine sauce with gherkins and mustard, and duck leg cooked slowly with veal stock and red wine, served with a shallot sauce. Fish is also on the menu, including skate wings. ⊠ *525 Duncan St., Hatfield,* ☎ *012/342–5057. AE, DC, MC, V. Closed Sun. No lunch Sat.*

The Arts
CLASSICAL MUSIC

The **Transvaal Philharmonic** plays in the State Theatre (⊠ Church St., ☎ 012/322–1665).

THEATER

The **State Theatre Pretoria** (⊠ Church St., ☎ 012/322–1665) is home to the Performing Arts Council Transvaal (PACT), a state-funded group that supports a wide range of theater, as well as ballet and opera companies. To fully appreciate this grand theater, book a guided tour, which includes the backstage areas. (You can make a tour reservation one week in advance.)

Spectator Sports
The place to see cricket (in summer) and rugby (in winter) in Pretoria is at the gigantic **Loftus Versveld Stadium** (⊠ Kirkness St., Sunnyside, Pretoria, ☎ 012/433–4011). When you go to a rugby match here, it's almost more interesting to watch the spectators—the local team, Northern Province, are known as the Blue Bulls and spectators arrive wearing blue hats adorned with mock blue horns. The heckling from the stands is an education in itself. If you want to take a more serious interest in the game, take along a pair of binoculars or you won't see anything further than about fifteen rows from the field.

Pretoria A to Z
ARRIVING AND DEPARTING

By Bus. Translux (☎ 012/315–2333) and **Greyhound** (☎ 012/828–4040) buses run regularly between Pretoria (⊠ Pretoria Station, corner of Paul Kruger and Scheiding Sts.) and Johannesburg's Rotunda on their way to destinations around the country.

By Car. The quickest way to reach Pretoria from Johannesburg is via the **N1 Highway,** which turns into the R28 as it nears the city. Outside rush hour, the 30-mile drive takes no more than half an hour.

EMBASSIES AND CONSULATES

Australian High Commission. ⊠ *292 Orient St., Arcadia, Pretoria,* ☎ *012/342–3740.*

Canadian High Commission. ⊠ *1103 Arcadia St., Hatfield, Pretoria,* ☎ *012/422–3000.*

British High Commission. ⊠ *255 Hill St., Arcadia, Pretoria,* ☎ *012/ 433–121.*

U.S. Embassy. ⊠ *877 Pretorius St., Arcadia, Pretoria,* ☎ *012/342–1048.*

Pretoria Tourist Information Centre. ⊠ *Sammy Marks Centre, Vermeulen St.,* ☎ *012/308–7694 or 308–7980.*

The **National Parks Board** handles accommodation reservations for all national parks and can furnish information. ⊠ *643 Leyds St., Muckleneuk (mailing address: Box 787, Pretoria 0001),* ☎ *012/343–1991,* FAX *012/343–0905.*

Pilanesberg National Park

Abutting Sun City, the 150,000-acre Pilanesberg National Park rises from the arid parchment of the North West Province. Like Tanzania's Ngorongoro Conservation Area, Pilanesberg is centered around the caldera of an extinct volcano dating back some 100 million years. It lacks the drama and mind-numbing scale of Ngorongoro, but it's lovely nevertheless—rings of concentric mountains converge on a central lake filled with crocodiles and hippos. Open grassland, rocky crags, and densely forested gorges provide ideal habitats for a wide range of plains and woodland game, including the rare brown hyena, sable, and gemsbok.

With the introduction of lion in 1993, Pilanesberg National Park can now boast the Big Five. The lions are just the latest scene in a modern-day remake of that biblical hit Noah's Ark. Since 1979, more than 6,000 animals have been relocated to the park, including some elephants that spent most of their lives in the United States. Today, it's hard to believe that the park, reclaimed from farmland, was ever anything but wild. The lion and elephant populations are still low for an area this size, but the park should reach its full carrying capacity within five years. The park is a bird-watcher's paradise, with a vast range of grassland species, water birds, and birds of prey.

Most tourists combine a trip to the Pilanesberg with a visit to Sun City next door. Safari companies based in Sun City can show you the park on game drives, but many people opt to drive themselves. As beautiful as the park is, however, it's no substitute for a trip to the Mpumalanga and Kruger National Park. Its major pluses are its proximity to Sun City and Johannesburg, just 90 minutes away—and the fact that it's malaria-free.

Lodging

Unless you stay at Manyane, the park's government-run rest camp, be prepared to drop a lot of cash at game lodges that fail to deliver an authentic bush experience. The major exception is Tshukudu (*below,* where you'll still drop a lot of cash), a luxury safari lodge that offers a superb Mpumalanga-style game experience. You can also visit the park from Sun City (☞ *below*) on game drives.

For price ranges, *see* Chart 2 (A) *in* On the Road with Fodor's.

$$$$ ⌖ **Bakubung.** Abutting the national park, this lodge sits at the head of a long valley with terrific views of pristine bushveld. The lodge takes its name, meaning "People of the Hippo," from a hippo pool that forms the lodge's central attraction, and it's not unusual to have hippos grazing 100 ft from the terrace restaurant. Despite this, the lodge never really succeeds in creating a bush feel, perhaps because it's such a big convention and family destination. Its brick buildings also feel vaguely institutional. Nevertheless, the guest rooms, particularly the executive studios, are very pleasant, thanks to light pine furniture, colorful African bedspreads, and super views of the valley. Ask for an upstairs room if you want a thatch ceiling. The lodge conducts game drives (at extra cost) in open-air vehicles, and guests can accompany rangers on guided walks. A shuttle bus (R20 return) runs every 1–2 hours to Sun City, 10 km (6 mi) away. ⊠ *Pilanesberg Nat. Park (mailing address: Box 294, Sun City 0316),* ☎ *01465/2–1861,* ℻ *01465/2–1621. 76 rooms, 50 chalets. Restaurant, bar, café, pool, tennis, game drives. Breakfast and dinner included. AE, DC, MC, V.*

$$$$ ⛫ **Kwa Maritane.** You won't hear too many complaints about this lodge's setting, in a bowl of rocky hills on the edge of the national park. Unfortunately, the hotel fails to take advantage of its greatest asset: many of the hotel buildings look inward onto swimming pools and lawns. And, as at Bakubung, the bustle of convention-goers and children tends to drown out the mesmerizing sound of the bush. The big exception is the resort's terrific blind, overlooking a water hole and connected to the lodge via a tunnel. Guest rooms, with high thatched ceilings and large glass doors that open onto a veranda, are comfortable, if generic. Prints of African game offer some reminder of the lodge's setting, but the overall effect is too little too late. Guests can pay to go on day or night game drives in open-air vehicles, or on guided walks with an armed ranger. A free shuttle runs regularly to Sun City; the return trip costs around R4.⊠ *Pilanesberg Nat. Park (mailing address: Box 39, Sun City, 0316),* ☎ *01465/2–1820,* ℻ *01465/2–1147. 155 rooms. Restaurant, bar, 2 pools, tennis, miniature golf, sauna, animal blind, game drives. Breakfast and dinner included. AE, DC, MC, V.*

$ ⛫ **Manyane.** The cheapest lodging in the Sun City area, the park's main rest camp lies in thinly wooded savanna east of the Pilanesberg's volcanic ridges. Modeled after Kruger's modern rest camps, Manyane is short on charm but long on functional efficiency and cleanliness. Thatch roofing helps soften the harsh lines of bare tile floors and ugly brick. Guests can choose either a two-, four-, or six-bed chalet, all with fully equipped kitchens and bathrooms. An à la carte restaurant is open for all three meals. Among the camp's greatest attractions are the enormous walk–in aviaries, housing many of the region's more spectacular bird species. You can go inside and get really close to brilliantly colored carmine bee-eaters, plum-colored starlings, violet-eared waxbills, crimson-breasted shrikes, and others. It's a great place to snap superb bird photographs—without needing an enormous telephoto lens. Short, self-guided nature trails from the chalets are available. You won't see anything large, however, but a short interpretative trail gives interesting background to the geology and flora of the park and leads to a small water hole. ⊠ *Pilanesberg Nat. Park,* ☎ *01465/55–351. Reservations: Box 937, Lonehill 2062,* ☎ *011/465–5423 or 011/465-5437,* ℻ *011/465–1228. 60 chalets with bath. Restaurant, bar, pool, miniature golf, playground. AE, DC, MC, V.*

$$$$ ⛫ **Tshukudu Game Lodge.** Few private lodges can match the beauty of this tiny luxury lodge inside Pilanesberg. Built into the side of a steep, rocky hill, Tshukudu overlooks open grassland and a large water hole where elephants come to bathe. If you watch long enough, you'll probably see most of the Big Five from your veranda. Winding stone stairways lead up the hill to lovely, thoughtfully set thatched chalets with private balconies, wicker furniture, bold African materials, and black-slate floors. Fireplaces, minibars, and mosquito nets are standard, and sunken bathtubs command spectacular views of the water hole. It's a long 132-step climb to the main lodge on the summit, making this an impractical choice for the elderly or those with disabilities. At night, you can use a spotlight to illuminate game at the water hole below. **Game Experience:** Tshukudu lies in the middle of the 135,850-acre Pilanesberg National Park, and as a result must share the park roads with other visitors. The biggest drawback is a park regulation banning off-road driving, which means rangers can't follow animals into the bush. Under these circumstances, you're unlikely to see a hunt or a kill. Your chances of seeing the Big Five will be virtually guaranteed, however, if the proposed plan to put radio-collars on animals is adopted. By just following the signal, rangers will be able to track down any animal they choose. You'd get to see all the game, but gone would be the adventure and suspense of tracking, and you might as well go to a zoo. Instead, learn the names of Pilanesberg trees and grasses or follow the spoor of wild animals on walks with knowledgeable field guides. ⊠ *Box 6805, Rustenburg, 0300,* ☎ FAX *01465/21–620. 12–16 guests. Bar, pool. No children under 12. No private vehicles allowed. Transfer from Bakubang in a safari vehicle. AE, DC, MC, V.*

Pilanesberg A to Z

ARRIVING AND DEPARTING

For information about getting to and from the park, *see* Sun City, *below.*

GUIDED TOURS

Pilanesberg Safaris (☎ 01465/5–6135) conducts 2½-hour game drives in open-air vehicles. Game drives leave early in the morning, in the afternoon, and at night, when rangers illuminate nocturnal animals with a powerful spotlight. Rangers are in radio contact with other vehicles in the field, allowing them to coordinate the search for game. The company also offers 3½-hour bush walks, led by an armed ranger who focuses on the small details of the bush, ranging from the medicinal uses of various trees to the identification of animal spoor. If you prefer to see the big picture, go up in a hot-air balloon (☎ 01465/2–1561); a four-hour flight costs about R1,200 per person. The company operates from Sun City and the park's Manyane rest camp.

RESERVATIONS AND FEES

Entry to the park costs R13. The park gates are open September–March 5:30 AM–7 PM and April–August 6 AM–6:30 PM. Direct all inquiries to Pilanesberg National Park(⊠ Box 6651, Rustenburg 0300, ☎ 01465/ 5–5351).

Sun City

Sun City is a huge entertainment and resort complex in the middle of dry bushveld, 177 km (110 mi) northwest of Johannesburg. It's the dream child of Sol Kerzner, the South African entrepreneur who first saw the possibilities of a casino in the rocky wilds of the Pilanesberg mountains (which, being in Bophuthatswana, was exempt from South Africa's then strict antigambling laws). Now, nearly two decades later, Sun City comprises four hotels, two casinos, major amphitheaters, and a host of outdoor attractions. The complex is split into two parts: the original Sun City and the Lost City, a new project anchored by the magnificent Palace Hotel.

Comparisons with Las Vegas are inappropriate. Sun City is a resort, not a city, although it does rely on the same entertainments: gambling, slot machines, topless revues, and big-time extravaganzas. Sun City stages enormous rock concerts, major boxing bouts, the annual Sun City Golf Challenge, and the occasional Miss World Pageant. It also displays that familiar Vegas sense (or lack) of taste—the Palace being a notable exception—doling out the kind of ersatz glitter and glare that appeals to a shiny polyester crowd. Whatever your feelings about the complex, you have to admire Kerzner's creativity when you see the Lost City, where painted wild animals march across the ceilings, imitation star-spangled skies glitter even by day, lush jungles decorate the halls, and stone lions and elephants keep watch over it all.

The resort burst onto the international scene in the apartheid era, when a few American and British music stars broke the cultural boycott to play Sun City. Back then, it was part of Bophuthatswana, one of the nominally independent homelands designed to give blacks a semblance of self-government. Today, Bophuthatswana has been reabsorbed into South Africa as part of the new North West Province.

Sun City's genuine appeal lies not in the slots but in the remarkable Palace Hotel and the nearby Pilanesberg National Park (☞ *above*). The national park, the third largest in the country, offers a chance to see the Big Five (lion, leopard, elephant, rhino, and buffalo) and is malaria-free to boot. You can either drive yourself through the park or join guided tours in open-air Land Rovers; all of the safari companies will pick you up at your hotel.

Sun City also has a full round of outdoor sports and activities, including two Gary Player-designed golf courses and a manmade lake where visitors can waterski, parasail, and sailboard. The latest addition is Valley of the Waves, a giant pool that creates perfect waves for bodysurfing onto a manmade beach. For the adventurous, there's the heart-stopping Temple of Courage, a water chute designed to hurtle you down a 300-ft rock face at speeds of up to 35 km (21 mi) per hour.

Lodging

Accommodations in Sun City are very expensive, and only the Palace can justify its rates. You may opt to stay instead in the nearby rest camps and private lodges of the Pilanesberg National Park (☞ *above*).

CATEGORY	COST*
$$$$	over R900
$$$	R700–R900
$$	R500–R700
$	under R500

All prices are for a standard double room, including VAT and any Tourism Promotion Levies.

$$$$ ☆ **Palace of the Lost City.** Even if you never go near Sun City, consider
★ staying at this soaring, magnificent complex. It's the most spectacular hotel in the country, and has become an attraction in its own right. Given the tackiness of Sun City, you would think any hotel based on the concept of a lost African palace would suffer from theme-park syndrome. Nothing could be further from the truth. Sculpted cranes and leaping kudu appear to take flight from the hotel towers, elephants guard triumphal stairways and bridges, and graceful reminders of Africa strike you at every turn. No expense has been spared—the hotel cost R800 million—and the attention to detail is mind-boggling. All rooms have hand-carved doors and furnishings; the jungle paintings on the ceiling of the lobby's rotunda took 5,000 hours to complete; and the hand-laid mosaic floor is made up of 300,000 separate tiles. Guest rooms, done in rich earth tones, blend African motifs with delicate Eastern touches. Carved wooden screens open into an elegant bathroom with separate bath and shower, and a huge wood armoire hides a safe, TV, and minibar. If you really want to splurge, choose one of the grand suites (at more than R11,000 per night). The hotel's two restaurants serve some of the finest cuisine in the country. ✉ *Box 308, Sun City 0316,* ☎ *01465/7–3121,* 𝔽𝔸𝕏 *01465/7–3101. 338 rooms. 2 restaurants, 2 bars, room service, pool. AE, DC, MC, V.*

$$$ ☆ **The Cascades.** The lavish use of mirrors, brass, and black marble in the lobby sets the tone for this sophisticated high-rise hotel, only yards from the Lost City's massive entertainment center. Rooms have an understated African elegance, decorated in soothing rust colors highlighted with bold blues and yellows. All overlook the Gary Player golf course, the gardens, and an artificial waterfall. For the best views, request a room on an upper floor. ⊠ *Box 7, Sun City,* ☎ *01465/2–1000,* FAX *01465/7–3447. 243 rooms. 2 restaurants, 2 bars, room service, pool. AE, DC, MC, V.*

$$ 🏨 **Sun City Hotel.** This is the original Sun City property, and it still houses the gaming casino, banks of slot machines, and the topless extravaganza. If gambling and nonstop action are your scene, this will appeal to you, but most people find its tackiness overwhelming. The main room is decked out like a Tarzan jungle, with palms and manmade waterfalls, rope walkways, and rain forest and bamboo murals. The sound of rushing water drowns out the jangle of the slots somewhat, but nothing can conceal the glitter of this lurid spectacle. Thankfully, the rooms are a big improvement. Cream and white decor predominates, and the furniture is inspired by elegant, old Cape designs. ⊠ *Box 2, Sun City,* ☎ *01465/2–1000,* FAX *01465/7–4210. 340 rooms. 4 restaurants, 2 bars, room service, pool, casino. AE, DC, MC, V.*

$ 🏨 **The Cabanas.** After the bells and whistles of the Sun City Hotel, this budget option comes as a peaceful surprise. Paths thread through pleasant gardens to the rooms, in small apartment blocks overlooking a manmade lake. They are clean and cheerful, with tile floors, bright bedspreads, and sliding glass doors that open onto the lawns. All have TV, tea- and coffee-makers, and air-conditioning. The hotel's proximity to Waterworld, a playground, and a petting zoo makes it popular with families. ⊠ *Box 3, Sun City,* ☎ *01465/2–1000,* FAX *01465/71–4227. 380 rooms. 2 restaurants, 2 bars, pool. AE, DC, MC, V.*

Sun City A to Z

ARRIVING AND DEPARTING

By Bus. Impala Rand Tours (☎ 011/974–6561) operates a daily bus service to Sun City from Johannesburg's Rotunda (⊠ Leyds and Loveday Sts., Braamfontein). The bus leaves at 9 and returns at 8. A same-day return ticket costs R75, and a one-way fare costs R60. The buses also leave from the airport and the Sandton Sun Hotel. Additional buses depart from the airport and Rotunda on Friday and Saturday afternoons. If you really want to party the night away, take the Saturday afternoon bus from the Rotunda—this only leaves Sun City at 1 AM on Sunday morning. Discount vouchers for the area are included if you take the bus.

By Car. Plan about 1½–2 hours to drive the 177 km (110 mi) to Sun City from Johannesburg. The best route is up the N1 to Pretoria, then west by way of the N4.

By Plane. Sun Air (☎ 011/397–2244 in Jo'burg, 01465/2–1359 in Sun City) has daily service (except Saturday) to Sun City from Johannesburg, and thrice-weekly flights from Durban and Cape Town.

JOHANNESBURG A TO Z

Arriving and Departing

By Bus

All **inter-city buses** depart from the Rotunda (⊠ Leyds and Loveday Sts., Braamfontein), the city's principal transport hub. **Greyhound** (☎ 011/333–3671 or 839–3037) and **Translux** (☎ 011/774–3333) operate extensive routes around the country. **Intercape Mainliner** (☎ 011/333–5213) runs to Cape Town; both **Golden Wheels** (☎ 011/773–4552) and **Roadshow Intercity** (☎ 082/449–9037) have economy fares to Durban.

By Car

Major rental agencies with offices in either the city or in Sandton include **Avis** (✉ Carlton Hotel, Main St., Johannesburg Central, ☎ 011/331–6050), **Budget** (✉ Holiday Inn Crowne Plaza, corner of Rivonia Rd. and Grayston Dr., Sandton, ☎ 011/883–5730), **Europcar** (✉ 196 Oxford Manor, Oxford Rd., Illovo, ☎ 011/447–6573), and **Imperial** (✉ Sandton Sun, corner of 5th and Alice Sts., Sandhurst, ☎ 011/883–4352; ✉ Juta St., behind the Parktonian, Braamfontein, ☎ 011/339–3762).

By Plane

Johannesburg International Airport (☎ 011/975–9963) formerly known as Jan Smuts, lies 19 km (12 mi) from the city. Most international flights depart from this airport. **Major airlines** serving Johannesburg include **Air Namibia** (☎ 011/442–4461), **Air Zimbabwe** (☎ 011/331–1541), **Alitalia** (☎ 011/880–9254), **British Airways** (☎ 011/441–8600), **KLM Royal Dutch Airlines** (☎ 011/881–9696), **Lufthansa** (☎ 011/484–4711), **Qantas** (☎ 0w111/884–5300), **Singapore Airlines** (☎ 011/880–8566), **South African Airways** (☎ 011/356–1111), **Swissair** (☎ 011/484–1980), and **Virgin Atlantic Airlines** (☎ 011/886–7270).

In addition to South African Airways, the **major domestic carriers** serving Johannesburg are British Airways, operating as **Comair** (☎ 011/921–0222), **S.A. Airlink** (☎ 011/973–2941), and **Sun Air** (☎ 011/397–2244).

The airport has a tourist information desk, a VAT refund office, and a computerized accommodation service.

BETWEEN THE AIRPORT AND JOHANNESBURG

Impala Rand Tours (☎ 011/974–6561) runs buses between the airport and the Rotunda (✉ Leyds and Loveday Sts., Braamfontein), near the city center. Buses make the 30-minute trip every half hour, and charge R30. **Magic Bus** (☎ 011/884–3957) operates a minibus airport service every half hour that calls at the Holiday Inn Crowne Plaza (Sandton), the Balalaika, and the Sandton Sun & Towers. The trip costs R40 and takes 35–50 minutes. Magic Bus also offers door-to-door pickup anywhere in the city for R120; two or more passengers pay R65 each.

Rental-car companies with offices at the airport include **Avis** (☎ 011/394–5433), **Budget Rent-a-Car** (☎ 011/394–2905), **Europcar Car Hire** (☎ 011/394–8832), **Imperial** (☎ 011/394–4020), and **Tempest Car Hire** (☎ 011/394–7309).

Taxis are available from the ranks outside the terminals. Licensed taxis must have a working meter. Expect to pay about R80–R120 for a trip to the city center or to Sandton.

By Train

Johannesburg's **train station** is opposite the Rotunda (✉ Leyds St. at Loveday St.) in Braamfontein. The famous, luxurious *Blue Train,* which makes regular runs to Cape Town as well as the Lowveld and Victoria Falls (☞ Rail Travel *in* the Gold Guide), departs from here, as do **Mainline Passenger Services** (☎ 011/773–2944) trains to cities around the country. Trains to other major cities include the *TransKaroo* to Cape Town, the *Komati* to Nelspruit in Mpumalnga, and the *TransNatal* to Durban. Many of these national services have overnight trips and are extremely comfortable, offering good value for the money. You should probably skip the dining car because the food is not terribly appetizing—rather , opt for the light meals and snacks.

Getting Around

Most visitors need concern themselves only with the city center and the northern suburbs. The city center is laid out in a grid, making it easy to get around, but it's not advisable to tour the area on foot except in groups. Jan Smuts Avenue runs north from the city center right through the major suburbs of Parktown, Rosebank, Dunkeld, Hyde Park, Craighall, and Randburg. The William Nicol Highway splits off this avenue and runs toward Sandton, the emerging new city center. An easier way to get from the city center to Sandton is up the M1 which splits to become the N1 South, leading toward Roodepoort and the southern suburbs, or the N1 North, leading toward Pretoria and Pietersburg.

By Taxi

Don't expect to rush out into the street and hail a taxi. There are taxi ranks at the airport, the train station, and the Rotunda, but as a rule you must phone for a cab. Taxis should be licensed and have a working meter. Three of the most **reliable companies** are City Taxi (☎ 011/336–5213), **Maxi Taxi** (☎ 011/648–1212), and **Rose Taxis** (☎ 011/725–3333 or 011/725–1111). Ask the taxi company how long it will take the taxi to get to you—many taxis are radioed while on call and the time to get to your area may vary considerably, depending on whether there is a taxi in the vicinity already. The meter starts at R2 and clicks over at a rate of R3.20 per km. Expect to pay about R120 to the airport from town and about R60 to the city center from Sandton. Charge for waiting time is about R36 per hour.

Contacts and Resources

Embassies and Consulates

Pretoria is the capital of South Africa, and most embassies are located there (☞ Pretoria A to Z, *above*). Some countries also maintain consulates in Johannesburg.

U.K. Consulate. ✉ *19th floor, Sanlam Centre, Jeppe and Von Wielligh Sts., Johannesburg,* ☎ *011/333–2624.*

U.S. Consulate. ✉ *11th floor, Kine Centre, Market and Kruis Sts., Johannesburg,* ☎ *011/331–1681.*

Emergencies

Ambulance (☎ 999). **Police** (☎ 10111).

In the event of a **medical emergency,** you're advised to seek help at one of the city's private hospitals. Among the most reputable are **Milpark Hospital** (✉ Guild Rd., Parktown, ☎ 011/480–5600), **Rosebank Clinic** (✉ 14 Sturdee Ave., Rosebank, ☎ 011/788–1980), and **Sandton Medi-Clinic** (✉ Main St. and Peter Pl., Lyme Park, ☎ 011/709–2000).

Guided Tours

DIAMOND TOURS

Mynhardts conducts 45-minute tours of its diamond-cutting operation, beginning with a 10-minute video on the history of diamonds. You are then taken to the cutting and polishing factory, where you'll learn how to evaluate a stone. You can also purchase diamonds if you wish. (For information on a tour of a working diamond mine, *see* General-Interest Tours, *below, and* Off the Beaten Path, *above.*) ✉ *240 Commissioner St., Johannesburg Central,* ☎ *011/334–8897.* ▧ *Tours are free, by appointment only.* ⊙ *Weekdays 8:30–4:30.*

For **city tours,** call **Springbok Atlas** (☎ 011/493–3780) and **Jimmy's Face to Face Tours** (☎ 011/331–6209). They both have two- to three-hour tours of the city that may include visits to the Johannesburg Stock Exchange, the observation deck of the Carlton Centre, the diamond-cutting works, and some of the city's more interesting parks and suburbs. Other tours explore Pretoria; Cullinan, a working diamond mine; Sun City; and the Pilanesberg National Park.

GOLD-MINE TOURS
The **Chamber of Mines** (✉ 5 Hollard St., Johannesburg Central, ☎ 011/498–7204) conducts weekly tours of a working gold mine These interesting and worthwhile tours include a trip down a mine shaft and a demonstration of molten gold being poured. The tours, which take place on Wednesday and Thursday, leave Johannesburg very early in the morning and return only about 4 PM. Lunch is included; reservations are essential (cash only).

TOWNSHIP TOURS
Jimmy's Face to Face Tours (☎ 011/331–6209) has the best tours of the townships. The three-hour Soweto tour takes you in minibuses through the largest black city in Africa. The tour looks past the headlines to show visitors how urban blacks live from day to day. Jimmy's Johannesburg Night Tour features an authentic local meal, a theater production, and some township jazz.

Travel Agencies
American Express Travel Service. ✉ *Braampark, 33 Hoofd St., Braamfontein, Johannesburg,* ☎ *011/359–0111;* ✉ *Upper Mall, Hyde Park* ☎ *011/325–4317,* FAX *011/325–4936.* ☉ *Weekdays 8:30–5, Sat. 9–12:30.*

Rennies Travel is the representative of Thomas Cook in South Africa and has its own tours through southern Africa, known as *Options,* which enable you to tailor-make your itinerary. ✉ *Shop L14, Sandton City Shopping Centre, Rivonia Road, Sandton,* ☎ *011/883–8521,* FAX *011/883–1242;* ✉ *Shop L20A, Eastgate Shopping Centre, Bradford Road, Bedfordview,* ☎ *011/616–1241* FAX *011/616–3001;* ✉ *Surrey House, 35 Rissik St., Johannesburg,* ☎ *011/492–1990.* ☉ *Weekdays 8:30–4.*

Visitor Information
Johannesburg Publicity Association sells a useful brochure, "Gauteng—The Gateway Province of South Africa," which details most of the city's sights and attractions. The association also has brochures on attractions, tours, and lodging. ✉ *North State Bldg., Kruis and Market Sts.,* ☎ *011/336–9461.*

3 Mpumalanga and Kruger National Park

Archetypal Africa—open country full of big game and primal wilderness—unfolds before you in Mpumalanga. Its most obvious allure is game-watching in and around Kruger National Park. But don't miss out on the majestic Drakensberg—mountains of mists, forests, waterfalls, and panoramic views around which you'll find some of South Africa's most luxurious hotels and lodges, as well as historic gold-rush towns and fantastic hiking and fishing.

MPUMALANGA SPREADS EAST from Johannesburg to the border of Mozambique. In many ways it's South Africa's wildest and most exciting province. The 1,120-km (700-mi) Drakensberg Ranges—which originate in KwaZulu-Natal—cut the province in two, dividing the high, interior plateau from a low-lying subtropical belt that stretches to the Indian Ocean. The Lowveld—where Kruger National Park alone covers a 320-km (200-mi) swath of wilderness—is classic Africa, with as much heat, dust, untamed bush, humidity, and big game as you can take in.

Larger than Israel or Wales, Kruger National Park encompasses some of the most stunning and diverse terrain on the continent, from crocodile-infested rivers to rocky mountains and thick thornscrub. And roaming this classic slice of Africa are animals in numbers large enough to make a conservationist squeal with delight: 1,500 lions, 7,500 elephants, 1,300 white rhinos and 30,000 buffalo, to list but a few. With credentials like these, it's no surprise that Kruger provides the country's best and most fulfilling game experience.

The Drakensberg Escarpment rises to the west of Kruger and provides a stark contrast to the Lowveld: It's a mountainous area of trout streams and waterfalls, endless views, and giant plantations of pine and eucalyptus. Lower down, the forests give way to banana, mango, and papaya groves. People come to the Escarpment to hike, unwind, soak up its beauty, and get away from the heat of the Lowveld. Some of South Africa's most interesting and historical events took place here—conflicts between Boer settlers and local Pedi people and later the British, the Pilgrim's Rest gold strike of 1873, and the stuff of bush lore—which only adds to Mpumalanga's appeal. Touring the area by car is easy and rewarding—here, unlike in the Natal Drakensberg, you can reach many of the best lookouts without stepping far from your car.

A major gold strike in Pilgrim's Rest in 1873 sparked a gold rush every bit as raucous and wild as those in California and the Klondike. And legend has it that you can still find a few old-time prospectors panning for gold in the area. Miners from all over the world descended on these mountains to try their luck in the many rivers and streams. Although the safest route to the goldfields was the 800-km (500-mi) road from Port Natal (now Durban), many opted for a 270-km (170-mi) shortcut from Lourenço Marques (now Maputo), in Mozambique—through the wilds of the Lowveld, where malaria, yellow fever, lions, and crocodiles exacted a dreadful toll.

Those early gold-mining days have been immortalized in *Jock of the Bushveld,* a classic of South African literature. Jock was a Staffordshire terrier whose master, Sir Percy Fitzpatrick, worked as a transport rider during the gold rush. After a stint at the Barberton *Herald* (now Nelspruit's *Louvelder*) as a staff reporter, Sir Percy entertained his children with tales of Jock's exploits as they logged their miles in Mpumalanga, braving leopards, baboons, and all manner of dangers. Rudyard Kipling—who wandered this wilderness as a reporter covering the first Anglo-Boer War in the early 1880s—encouraged Fitzpatrick to write down the stories. One hundred years later Jock is still a household name in South Africa. You'll see dozens of Jock-of-the-Bushveld markers all over Mpumalanga, seemingly wherever he cocked his leg.

Although some of the "*bundu*-bashing" (bushwhacking) and gold-rush atmosphere still exists here, depending on where you go, the rough-and-ready days of the pioneering Lowveld are rapidly disappearing. If you dig deep, you can still find traces of the last of the big-game hunters and pioneers of the Lowveld—which can make for entertaining conversation at the tap. More and more, however, luxury guest lodges prove to be the modern-day gold rush. People from around the globe come to indulge in the lodges' elegant five-course dinners and obscene English breakfasts in a variety of stunning locales.

Warning: The Lowveld area, which stretches from Malelane (East of Nelspruit) to Komatipoort on the Mozambique border and up throughout Kruger National Park, is a malarial zone, in which you are advised to take antimalarial drugs.

Pleasures and Pastimes

Big Game Adventures

There is nothing quite like tracking lions on foot—with an armed ranger leading the way, of course—or having an elephant mock-charge to within six yards of your Land Rover. The slow-motion gallop of a giraffe, the cocky trot of a hyena, and the worlds-within-worlds of the smaller creatures of the bush—such as the banded mongoose or the Cape pangolin—are all Mpumalanga musts. If you don't stay in one of the area's private game lodges, be sure to go out with a park ranger on one of the wilderness trails to get your feet on the ground in the wilds of South Africa.

Dining

As Mpumalanga continues to get more and more tourist traffic, the region's culinary scene keeps getting better and better—both in higher-end restaurants and in attractive cafés. A number of private game lodges on the fringe of Kruger National Park likewise serve fairly sophisticated fare, which can add romance to a couple of nights in the bush.

For a description of South African culinary terms, *see* Pleasures and Pastimes *in* Chapter 1. For price ranges, *see* Chart 1 *in* On the Road with Fodor's.

Lodging

The quality of service and accommodation in Mpumalanga and Kruger is very high by South African standards. Even when you're paying premium rates, though, don't be surprised to see dogs, cats, pet monkeys, and birds breaking into the dining room. Almost every Escarpment lodge has its contingent of free-roaming pets, so if you're allergic or dislike animals, do some research before you reserve. At the same time, some lodges display an almost monastic respect for peace and quiet, even eliminating TVs and radios from the rooms. So if you find yourself whispering in the bar, just order another round of martinis.

Luxury lodges are not for everyone, and you can choose from several other options, including regular hotels. If you're watching your pennies, consider a self-catering cottage and driving to one of the lodges for its five-course dinner—usually a good value.

One benefit of staying on the Escarpment is that it allows you to sleep in the cool, malaria-free uplands and descend into the sweltering Lowveld only for game-viewing drives. Most of the lodges in this chapter are no more than an hour by car from Kruger National Park and the exclusive game lodges of the Sabi Sands. Organized tours can take you for day or night drives and bring you back in time for supper and bed.

At most guest lodges on the Escarpment, prices include a five-course dinner and a full English breakfast. Vegetarians should call ahead to make special arrangements. Some lodges and hotels have special rates, particularly midweek. And many do not accomodate children under

12—inquire when you make reservations if you have children. For price ranges, *see* Chart 2 (B) *in* On the Road with Fodor's.

In Kruger the decision is whether to stay in a national park rest camp or a private game lodge. And that decision might have everything to do with your budget: Where rest camps can cost R300 per night for a couple (lodging only), private lodges cost between R750 and R2,700 per person per night (room, board, and activities included). That said, for the price, the intimacy and expertise of private lodges and their staff often make for the experience of a lifetime. The Private Game Reserves and Lodges section at the end of this chapter has its own price chart.

For a complete rundown on Southern African wildlife-viewing, *see* Big Game Adventures *in* Chapter 11.

Exploring Mpumalanga and Kruger National Park

Great Itineraries

Mpumalanga has a wealth of activities, from poking around cultural villages to hiking on mountain trails, looking into local history, taking in panoramic views, and driving and tramping around game reserves. If you have only a couple of days in the area, split them between the mountain scenery of the Escarpment and wildlife-viewing in the Lowveld. If you have more time, you could complete a tour of the Drakensberg Escarpment area in two days, but you're better off budgeting three or more if you plan to linger anywhere. To take in parts of Kruger National Park or one of the private game lodges—which is simply a must—add another three days or more. The best way to get around Mapumalanga is by car, either from Johannesburg or after flying into Nelspruit. Don't forget that Swaziland (☞ Chapter 8), is under two hours southeast of Nelspruit. If you plan to go to Swaziland, the town of Barberton makes a pleasant stopover on the way south.

Numbers in the text correspond to numbers in the margin and on the Mpumalanga map.

IF YOU HAVE 3 DAYS

Fly into the regional capital of Nelspruit, then rent a car and drive to ⛫ **Pilgrim's Rest** ⑦ or ⛫ **Graskop** ⑧ for lunch, followed by an afternoon taking in views of the Escarpment's edge at the **Pinnacle** ⑨, **God's Window** ⑩, and one of the spectacular local waterfalls. If you feel like going on a longer-range afternoon drive, head up to spectacular Blyde Canyon Nature Reserve for a look at the **Three Rondawels** ⑭ rock formations. The next morning make your way down to the Lowveld to Kruger National Park or one of the private lodges listed at the end of this chapter. Whether you opt for the national park or a private reserve, be sure to get in a day or night bush drive *and* a bush walk with an armed ranger. These complementary activities will give you the broadest experience of wildlife. If animals are actually your prime reason to come to Mpumalanga, you could decide to spend all three days in the park or at a private reserve. If you plan to spend the rest of your vacation in civilization, a minimum of three days in the bush is advisable.

IF YOU HAVE 5 DAYS

With five days, the biggest decision will be how much time to spend wildlife-watching and how much to explore the Escarpment and its historic towns. If you are planning to see game in Zimbabwe or Botswana, take three days on the mountains and two in and around Kruger National Park. Start off on a drive from Johannesburg to ⛫ **Dullstroom** ①, which is known for its restaurants and lodges, and for superb trout fishing. If you don't spend the night, have lunch and continue through **Lydenburg** ② where the **Gustav Klingbiel Nature Reserve** has

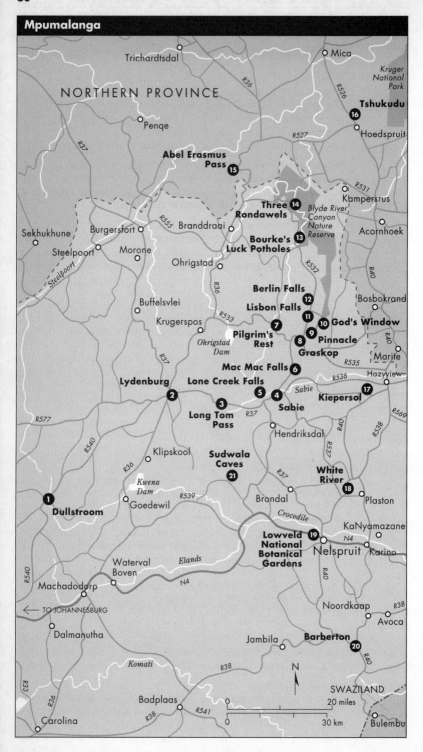

Mpumalanga

an interesting archaeology museum. Beautiful **Long Tom Pass** ③ will take you toward ⌨ **Sabie** ④, which is a good town in which to overnight. The next day, head to ⌨ **Pilgrim's Rest** ⑦ to take in a little local history at the town's museums or through **Graskop** ⑧ to see some of the Escarpment's most scenic vistas. If you are going to spend three days in the bush, head down to Kruger or a private lodge to make it there in time for dinner and a night game drive. Otherwise, spend the night in Pilgrim's Rest or Graskop and start out early the next morning for **Blyde River Canyon Nature Reserve** and its hiking trails and Escarpment scenery.

An alternative route out of Johannesburg would take you straight to the **Lowveld National Botanical Gardens** ⑲ outside of Nelspruit. From there, continue to ⌨ **White River** ⑱, taking a day trip, perhaps, to **Barberton** ⑳, an early gold-rush town with interesting period houses and nearby outdoor activities. You could then approach Kruger National Park from the south.

IF YOU HAVE 7 TO 10 DAYS

The best way to structure a longer stay in Mpumalanga is to set aside four or more days in the bush—half at Kruger and half in a private lodge, perhaps. Then split the rest of your time between the Escarpment and the Lowveld. If you're planning to continue to Swaziland, leave Barberton for last, as it's a short hop from the Swazi border.

When to Tour Mpumalanga and Kruger National Park

Where you stay on the **Escarpment** may well dictate the kind of weather you get. High up, around Pilgrim's Rest, Graskop, and Sabie, the weather can be chilly, even in summer. At these elevations fog and mist can also be a hazard during the summer, especially while driving. On the other hand, summer in the Lowveld, is downright steamy.

Kruger National Park is hellishly hot in summer (December–March), with afternoon rain a good possibility. The bush is green, the animals sleek and glossy, and the bird life prolific, but you won't see as many animals. Dense foliage makes finding them harder, and they don't need watering holes and rivers, where they're easy to spot as they come to drink. Winter is great for game-viewing, on the other hand, as trees are bare and animals congregate around the few available water sources. With cooler weather, you might even see lions and leopards hunting by day. Lodges drop their rates as much as 30%–40% off of peak season highs. The drawbacks are cold weather, bare trees and bush, and animals looking thin and out of condition.

Shoulder seasons are a happy compromise. October and November weather is pleasant, trees are blossoming, and migrant birds are arriving—even better, antelope herds begin to drop their young. April temperatures are also fine, many migrant birds are still around, and the annual rutting season has begun, when males compete for the right to mate with females.

There are various annual festivals worth seeing as well. Komatipoort hosts an agricultural and prawn festival in April in which you can take part in a *bok-drol-spoeg*—in Afrikaans, literally "buck-dropping-spit"—competition, in which local lads see who can spit gazelle pellets the farthest. Sabie has its annual Forest Festival in April, when you can see lumberjacks cutting up logs in a matter of seconds. In Northern Province, Hoedspruit hosts an annual Wild Festival on a mid-April weekend, where you can taste all kinds of game meat and *biltong* (much loved local jerky).

Nelspruit hosts the Lowveld Agricultural Show in August, if you're interested in a look at South African farm life. In September there is a fly-fishing competition in whichever town hosts it for the year: such as Dullstrom, Lydenburg, or Machadodorp. Dates for these festivals vary from year to year; SATOUR and local publicity associations will have specific dates.

MPUMALANGA

Next to Cape Town and the Winelands, Mpumalanga should be highest on your South African itinerary. Nowhere else in the country can you spend one day seeing spectacular wildlife, the next climbing or gazing over the Escarpment, and a third poking around some of the country's most historic towns—spending a minimum amount of time in the car getting from place to place.

Dullstroom

❶ *2½ hrs east of Johannesburg on the N4, turn off for Belfast and follow the R540 out of town for 35 km (22 mi).*

The tiny hamlet of Dullstroom sits amid rolling, grass-covered mountains and sparkling streams. At 6,600 ft, it's one of the coldest towns in South Africa, and sweaters and roaring fires are common comforts even in midsummer. Dullstroom is the trout-fishing capital of Mpumalanga. The fish were introduced into the streams of the Transvaal Drakensberg at the turn of the century, and trout-fishing is now the third-largest moneymaker in the region, after timber and tourism. There is very good dining and lodging in town.

Dining and Lodging

$$ ✕ **Die Tonteldoos.** This small bistro is a popular stop for breakfast, lunch, or dinner (until 8:30 PM) on your way to or from the Lowveld. Owner Brian Whitehorn's menu is heavily influenced by French cuisine, with many sauces based on rich reductions. Highly recommended are the steak fillet topped with camembert and red wine sauce, and any of the game pies. For something lighter, try *spanikopita* (spinach and feta cheese wrapped in phyllo dough) or a silky trout terrine accompanied by sage and olive bread. Garden salads and open sandwiches on chunky whole-wheat bread are popular snacks. ⊠ *R540, Dullstroom,* ☎ *01325/4–0115. Reservations essential weekends. AE, DC, MC, V.*

$$$$ ✕🏠 **Walkersons.** No other Mpumalanga lodges offer such genuine luxury—like the wealth of antiques and works of art found in the public areas—and few have a setting on a 1,500-acre farm of grass-covered hills laced with trout streams. The main lodge, built of stone and thatch, overlooks a small dam. Inside, such disparate items as Persian rugs, French tapestries, and 19th-century English oils come together beautifully. All rooms face the lake and have sponge-painted walls, mosquito nets, and fireplaces. Two-thirds of the farm has been made into a nature reserve populated with wildlife like wildebeest, springbok, blesbok, and zebra. There are several walking trails to follow through the reserve, or you can take a two-hour game drive in an open Land Rover. The lodge's five-course dinner is flawlessly presented. A meal might begin with Roquefort mousse with figs or smoked trout in phyllo baskets. Following a soup of brandied butternut squash and nutmeg, expect as a main course of something like beef fillet with green pepper sauce and rosemary potatoes. ⊠ *Off R540, 13 km (8 mi) north of Dullstroom (mailing address: Box 185, Dullstroom 1110),* ☎ *01325/4–0246,* 🆋 *01325/4–0260. 15 rooms with bath. Restaurant,* *bar, pool, hot tub, trout fishing, game drives. Breakfast and dinner in-cluded. AE, DC, MC, V.*

$$$ ✕⌂ **Critchley Hackle Lodge.** Foreign travelers often use this country lodge midway between Johannesburg and Kruger Park as a one-night stopover on their way to the Lowveld, but for South Africans it's more of a week-end getaway, with its lovely antiques and crackling fireplaces. Rooms in stone and brick cottages arranged around a trout pond all have their own fireplaces. Wooden chests, floral curtains, and rough brick walls contribute to their warm rusticity. An unfortunate drawback is traffic noise from the nearby R540. The dining room exudes a formality that works well for dinner but can seem heavy at other meals. The standard-for-lodge-fare five-course dinner is not altogether memorable, with its emphasis on roasts. Light lunches are served on the patio. ✉ *Off R540 (mailing address: Box 141, Dullstroom 1110),* ☎ *01325/40145,* FAX *01325/40262. 19 rooms. Restaurant, bar, indoor pool, sauna, tennis, trout fishing. Breakfast and dinner included. AE, DC, MC, V.*

$$ ✕⌂ **Dullstroom Inn.** In an old trading store that dates from 1910—which is still famous for its pub—the inn has rooms that are small but attractively done in colonial style, with floral patterns and old-fashioned iron bed-steads. No rooms have a phone or TV. If you're not staying at the inn, it's still worth stopping at the wood-paneled pub, with its roaring fire and excellent selection of draft lagers and bitters. The extensive pub menu features such staples as steak-and-kidney pie, ploughman's lunch, and oxtail. Try the guinea fowl casserole and sticky toffee pudding. ✉ *Teding van Berkhout and Oranje Nassau Sts. (mailing address: Box 44, Dullstroom 1110),* ☎ *01325/4–0071,* FAX *01325/4–0278. 11 rooms with bath. Restaurant, pub. Breakfast included. AE, DC, MC, V.*

Lydenburg

❷ *58 km (36 mi) northeast of Dullstroom on the R540.*

In an open plain between the Drakensberg and Steenkampsberg moun-tains, Lydenburg was founded in 1849 after the early Boer settlers (Voortrekkers) were forced to abandon their original settlement at Andries-Ohrigstad, where many of them died from malaria. Shaken by those years of death and misery, the survivors gave the new town the name Lydenburg, which means "town of suffering." Ironically, Ly-denburg prospered so well that in 1857 its citizens seceded from the Transvaal during the incessant bickering that marked relations among Voortrekker factions. "De Republiek Lydenburg en Zuid-Afrika," as the new country was known, remained independent for three years be-fore rejoining the Transvaal.

The 5,400-acre **Gustav Klingbiel Nature Reserve,** about 3 km (1½ mi) east of town along the R37, is made up of mountain grassland popu-lated by eland, kudu, blue wildebeest, leopard, and other animals. Four hiking trails meander through the park, ranging from the 5-km (3-mi) Pedi Route to the two-day, 19-km (12-mi) Ribbok Route.

The excellent **Lydenburg Museum** is also within the reserve. The mu-seum traces human development in the region from the Early Stone Age (1½ million–150,000 years ago) to the present. Exhibits display tools and artifacts from each period. The most important archaeological find in the area has been the Lydenburg Heads, seven clay heads dat-ing back to AD 490, during the early Iron Age. The heads are thought to have been used in initiation ceremonies, either as masks or icons. The pieces on display are reproductions of the originals, now in the South African Museum in Cape Town. ✉ *R37, 2½km (1 mi) east of Lydenburg,* ☎ *01323/2121.* ✉ *R7 per vehicle.* ☉ *Daily 8–4.*

❸ Spectacular as **Long Tom Pass** is, this mountain pass is more famous for its historical associations than its scenic beauty. For it was here, from September 8 to 11, 1900, that one of the last pitched battles of the Boer War (1899–1902) was fought. Lydenburg had fallen easily to the British on September 7, but the retreating Boers reformed on the heights above town and began shelling the British with their two remaining Creusot siege guns. Known as Long Toms because of their long barrels and range, these guns could hurl a 90-pound shell a distance of nearly 9½ km (6 mi). The guns were a tremendous headache for the British, who could not match their range. The Boers, struggling to get these monsters up the pass, can hardly have felt any more kindly toward them—at least 16 oxen were required to pull each gun. It took the British two days to winkle the Boers out of their positions on the pass and drive them over the steep wall of the Escarpment. Even then, the Boers managed to set up a gun position on the other side of the valley to shell the British as they maneuvered down the Staircase, a series of switchbacks zigzagging down the pass. You can still see shell holes in the Staircase. From the Klingbiel Nature Reserve, follow the R37 as it begins its winding ascent toward the pass.

Sabie

❹ *30 km (19 mi) east of Lydenburg.*

As you descend Long Tom Pass, the town of Sabie comes into view far below, in a bowl formed by the surrounding mountains. It is by far the most pleasant and enjoyable town in the region, with plenty of restaurants, shops, and bars. It makes a great base for exploring.

Gold was first discovered in appreciable amounts in Mpumalanga around present-day Sabie. On November 6, 1872, a prospector named Tom McLachlan located deposits of gold in a creek on the farm known as Hendriksdal, now a small hamlet about 16 km (10 mi) from Sabie. Sabie itself owes its origins to an altogether luckier strike. In 1895, Henry Glynn, a local farmer, hosted a picnic at the Klein Sabie Falls. Loosened up by a few drinks, his guests started taking potshots at empty bottles arrayed on a rock ledge. The flying bullets chipped shards of rock off the cliff face, revealing traces of gold beneath. Fifty-five years later, when mining operations closed down, more than 1 million ounces of gold had been taken from the Klein Sabie Falls.

Today, timber has replaced gold as the community's livelihood. The town sits in the heart of the world's largest manmade forest: more than 1,154,000 acres of exotic pine and eucalyptus. The first forests were planted in 1876 to provide the area's mines with posts and supports. Today, much of the timber is still used to prop up shafts in the Gauteng diamond mines.

As its name suggests, the town's **Market Square** was the commercial hub of Sabie in its early days. On the square, pleasant gardens surround **St. Peter's Anglican Church.** The solid stone building was designed by famed architect Sir Herbert Baker and built by Italians in 1913. Just outside the First National Bank you can still see the old **hitching rail** (1911), where travelers would tether their horses. Also in the square is a **Jock of the Bushveld marker,** said to commemorate Jock and Sir Percy Fitzgerald's arrival in Sabie in 1885.

❺ **Lone Creek Falls** is the prettiest and most peaceful of three local waterfalls. An easy, paved walkway leads to the falls, which plunge 225 ft from the center of a high, broad rock face framed by vines and creepers. The path crosses the river on a wooden bridge and loops through the forest back to the parking lot. If you're feeling energetic, follow the steep steps leading up to the top of the falls. Leave town on Main Road and turn left onto Old Lydenburg Road. This 6½-km (4-mi) dead-end road leads to three of the region's principal waterfalls—Bridal Veil Falls, Horseshoe Falls, and, the last stop along the road, Lone Creek Falls, which is the most accessible of the three to the elderly and those with disabilities.

❻ Another local cataract, **Mac Mac Falls,** is arguably the most famous of all in Mpumalanga. Set in an amphitheatre of towering cliffs, the water plunges 215 ft into a pool, and rainbows play in the billowing spray. The falls owe their interesting name to President Thomas Burger, who, while visiting the nearby gold diggings at Geelhoutboom in 1873, noticed that many of the miners' names began with "Mac," revealing their Scottish background. He promptly dubbed the area Mac Mac.

Unfortunately, you can view the falls only from an observation point surrounded by thick wire fencing, which destroys much of the atmosphere. On top of that, the fence is in poor condition, and the litter lying around it is dismaying. But if you are passing here on the way from Sabie to Graskop or Pilgrim's Rest, you might want to stop nonetheless. There is also a number of curio peddlers here; they are among the cheapest in the area.

Dining and Lodging

$$ ✕ **Artists' Cafe.** Housed in a former railway station in Hendriksdal that doubles as an art gallery, this delightful Tuscan-inspired restaurant has rough whitewashed walls and corrugated-tin roofing that provide a simple backdrop for Coptic crosses, African masks, and colorful tapestries. Dave Tod and his daughter Brenda serve up tasty dishes like bruschetta with mushrooms and pecorino cheese, Greek salads, a beef cacciatore, even roast duck with orange sauce. ✉ *Hendriksdal, off R37, 16 km (10 mi) from Sabie,* ☎ *013/764–2309. MC, V.*

$$ ✕ **Hill Watering.** Tucked away in a suburban home in Sabie, this guest-lodge-cum-restaurant is the domain of the artistic Jonathan Montague-Fitt. His presentation of pecan-encrusted chicken supreme or fillet teriyaki with angel hair noodles and Japanese crudités is inspired. Starters include such delights as trout and scallion roulade with horseradish mousseline, or Stilton soup with sesame croutons. Souf-flés, both sweet and savory, rise to astonishing heights, while the chocolate and hazelnut mille feuille never fails to please. ✉ *50 Marula St., Anderson, Sabie,* ☎ *013/764–1421. Reservations essential. AE, DC, MC, V. No lunch.*

$$$ 🚃 **Shunters' Express.** If you don't get a chance to take Rovos Rail or the Blue Train across South Africa, come here instead for a stationary journey back in railroad history. This restaurant and hotel is in the old government coaches of the White Train. Rooms are in sleeping cars—some of which have been increased in size for comfort—from which there are views of a picturesque lake, set among mountains and forests. The hosts occasionally take guests out on the water before dinner. The original galley is still used as a kitchen, and the bar and dining cars are also as they once were. It's not surprising, then, that food is also of the period: Expect things like well-prepared roasts and spare ribs basted in port. The station platform also serves as an al fresco dining area. Horseback riding is another option, and with groups rides can be arranged to end up at a local cave where impressive barbecues are set out. To get here, take the R537 from Sabie and turn left at the Shunter's Express sign. ✉ *White River Rd. (half-way between Sabie and White River),* ☎ *013/751–3319. 14 rooms. Restaurant, bar. Dinner reservations essential. AE, DC, MC, V.*

$ ▣ **Percy's Place.** This tiny hotel in the center of Sabie is the best value in the entire Mpumalanga. Rooms are individually decorated in a bright country style, and have tea- and coffeemakers and overhead fans. Breakfast is not included, but several cafés are within easy walking distance. Guests check in next door at the Zeederberg Coachhouse. ⊠ *Ford and 10th Sts., Sabie 1260,* ☎ *013/764–2630. 5 rooms with bath. MC. V.*

Pilgrim's Rest

❼   *16 km (10 mi) north of Sabie on R533.*

Pilgrim's Rest is a delightful, albeit touristy, reminder of gold rush days. It was the first proper gold-mining town in South Africa, centered around the richest gold strike in Mpumalanga. Alec "Wheelbarrow" Patterson, a taciturn Scot who had struck out on his own to escape the hordes of new miners at Mac Mac, discovered gold here in September of 1873. Mining operations ceased only in 1972, and since then the entire town has been declared a national monument. Many of the old corrugated-iron houses have been beautifully restored and now serve as museums, hotels, gift shops, and restaurants. It's definitely worth a visit, even for just a few hours.

Those corrugated-iron houses that you see today date from the more staid years after 1900 when Pilgrim's Rest had become a company town. During the mad years of 1873–1875, when most of the alluvial gold was panned by individual prospectors, Pilgrim's Rest consisted of nothing more than a collection of tents and mud huts. Rumors about the richness of the strike quickly carried around the world, and miners drifted in from California, Australia, and Europe. By January 1874, more than 1,500 diggers were working Pilgrim's Creek. Only a few struck it rich; the rest spent their earnings in local canteens until their claims played out and they drifted off.

Your first stop should be the **Information Centre** in the center of town, where you buy tickets to the various museums. Start your walking tour at the top end of town at **St. Mary's Anglican Church.** Built in 1884, the iron-roof stone building replaced the original makeshift wattle-and-daub structure. It really must have been an uphill battle for the early ministers to lure miners from the town's 18 canteens. After a back-breaking week spent on the sluices, Holy Communion just didn't pack the punch of a belt of Cape brandy or Squareface gin.

The tiny **Pilgrim's and Sabie News Printing Museum** is full or displays of antique printing presses and old photos. The building, constructed in the late 19th century as a residence, later served as the offices of the weekly Pilgrim's and Sabie News. The first newspaper in Pilgrim's Rest was the Gold News, published in 1874 and notable for its libelous gossip. The editor, an Irishman by the name of Phelan, felt obliged to keep a pair of loaded pistols on his desk. The printing museum is up Main Street from St. Mary's church. ⊠ *Main St., uptown, no phone.* ▣ *R1.50. Tickets available from information center.* ☉ *Daily 9–1, 1:30–4.*

NEED A BREAK?	If you do nothing else in Pilgrim's Rest, stop for a drink at the **Royal Hotel** bar (⊠ Main St., uptown, ☎ 013/768–1100). The building first served as a chapel at a girls' school in Cape Town. It was dismantled in 1870, shipped to Lourenço Marques (now Maputo), then carried by ox wagon to Pilgrim's Rest, where it ministered a different kind of spirit to thirsty miners. The bar retains much of its gold rush atmosphere, with wood-panel walls, an antique cash register, and a wonderful old bar counter. If you're hungry, you can order fish-and-chips or steak and eggs.

The **House Museum,** across and up the street from the Royal Hotel, re-creates the way of life of a middle-class family in the early part of this century, was built in 1913 of corrugated iron and wood. The house is typical of buildings erected at the time throughout the area. ⊠ *Main St., uptown, no phone.* ☎ *R1.50. Tickets available at information center.* ⊙ *Daily 9–1, 1:30–4:30.*

The **Pilgrim's Rest Cemetery** sits high on the hill above Main Street. The fascinating inscriptions on the tombstones evoke the dangers and hardship of life in Mpumalanga a century ago. That of Fred Sanders, for example, tells how he was "shot in a skirmish on the 27th August, 1878, aged 24." Tellingly, most of the dead were in their 20s and 30s, and it's amazing how many hailed from Wales, Scotland, and England. The cemetery owes its improbable setting to the Robber's Grave, the only grave that lies in a north-south direction. It contains the body of a thief who was banished from Pilgrim's Rest for stealing gold from a tent; the man foolishly returned and was shot dead. He was buried where he fell and the area around his grave became the town's unofficial cemetery. To get here, follow the steep path that starts next to the picnic area, near the post office.

In 1930, 16 general dealers lined the streets of Pilgrim's Rest. By 1950, mine production had taken a nose-dive and most of the businesses had shut down. The **Dredzen Shop and House Museum** re-creates the look of a general dealer during those lean years. The attached residence focuses on life in Pilgrim's Rest in the years immediately following World War II. After you come down the hill from the cemetary, turn left on Main Street to get to the museum. ⊠ *Main St., uptown, no phone.* ☎ *R1.50. Tickets available at information center.* ⊙ *Daily 9–1, 1:30–4:30.*

You can also tour **Alanglade,** the beautiful home of TGME's mine manager, set in a forested grove a mile north of town. The huge house was built in 1916 for Richard Barry and his family and is furnished with pieces dating from 1900 to 1930. Look carefully at the largest pieces, and you will see that they are actually segmented, so they could be taken apart and carried on ox wagons. ⊠ *Vaalhoek Rd., off R533, no phone.* ☎ *R2. Tickets available at information center.* ⊙ *Tours Mon.–Sat. at 10:30 and 2.*

At the **Diggings Museum,** in the creek where the alluvial gold was originally panned, you'll find displays of a water-driven stamp battery and some of the tents and wattle-and-daub huts typical of the early gold-rush years. The tour lasts about an hour, and is more enjoyable than actually informative. The retired prospector who conducts the tours enlivens the proceedings with yarns about the old days. You'll also see a display of gold-panning and get to poke around in some of the old diggings. The museum is about a mile south of Pilgrim's Rest on R533. ⊠ *R533, no phone.* ☎ *R1.50. Tickets available at information center.* ⊙ *Tours daily at 10, 11, noon, 2, and 3.*

Dining and Lodging

$ ✕ **Vine Restaurant and Pub.** In a former trading store dating from 1910, the Vine uses antique sideboards, sepia photos, and country-style wood furniture to capture a gold rush–era feeling. The food is straightforward and hearty. Try traditional South African *bobotie* (a curried ground-mutton pie), *potjiekos* (stew), or oxtail and *samp* (corn porridge). Or order a meat pie or toasted sandwich. The pub in the back is charmless—you're better off drinking at the Church Bar at the Royal Hotel (☞ *below*). ⊠ *Main St., downtown Pilgrim's Rest,* ☎ *013/768–1080. AE, DC, V.*

$$$ 🏨 **Royal Hotel.** Established in 1873, this hotel dates back to the very beginning of the gold rush in Pilgrim's Rest—you'll see its corrugated-iron facade in sepia photos displayed around town. Rooms are small and tucked away behind the street, but it's worth staying here to get into the spirit of the town. Reproduction four-poster beds, wood ceiling fans, and marble-and-oak washstands in the rooms help recapture the original Victorian look. None has a TV or phone. The Royal also owns several other Victorian buildings around town, including the 14-room Pilgrims and a variety of smaller cottages. Unless you want to take an entire cottage for yourself, opt for the main hotel. ⊠ *Main St., in upper town (mailing address: Box 59, Pilgrim's Rest 1290),* ☎ *013/768–1100,* 🖷 *013/768–1188. 42 rooms with bath. Restaurant, bar. Breakfast included. AE, DC, MC, V.*

$ 🏨 **District 6 Miners' Cottages.** On a hill above Pilgrim's Rest, these self-catering cottages are the best value in town. The cottages are all miners' homes dating back to 1920, and they're delightful. From their verandas there are spectacular views of the town and surrounding mountains. The interiors are furnished with period reproductions, complete with wood floors, brass bedsteads, and claw-footed tubs. Each cottage consists of a small living room, two double bedrooms, a fully equipped kitchen and pantry, and a bathroom. You can walk to the two restaurants in town in five minutes. If you arrive after hours, pick up keys from Royal Hotel. ⊠ *District 6, Pilgrim's Rest,* ☎ *013/768–1211. 7 cottages with bath and kitchen. No credit cards.*

Hiking

The 1,225-acre **Mount Sheba Nature Reserve** contains one of the last stands of indigenous forest in the Transvaal Drakensberg. Fourteen trails of varying difficulty run through the reserve, each taking from 1½ to 2½ hours. Some walks lead to waterfalls hidden in the bush or to pools where you can swim. A map is available from the reception desk at the Mount Sheba Hotel.

Graskop

❽ *20 km (13 mi) southeast of Pilgrim's Rest.*

In the 1850s, the farm Graskop—so named because of the vast tracts of grassveld and singular lack of trees in the area—was owned by Abel Erasmus, who afterwards became the local magistrate. The little town was declared a township in 1914 and in 1918 the first school was built. Graskop considers itself the "Window on the Lowveld," and several nearby lookouts do have stunning views over the edge of the Escarpment. Even if the town itself is largely forgettable, it does make a good base for exploring. The nearby Blyde River Canyon is spectacular; farther afield, you can get in a day of game viewing farther north beyond Abel Erasmus Pass at Tshukudu.

❾ The **Pinnacle** is a 100-ft-high quartzite "needle" that rose dramatically out of the surrounding fern-clad ravine countless millennia ago. Beneath and to the right of the viewing platform, there is a plateau which you can see only from the topmost of eight waterfalls: the watercourse drops down some 1,475 ft in a series of alternating falls and cascades. From Graskop, take the R532 north and turn right after 2½ km (1½ mi) onto the R534, marked "God's Window". Continue 1½ km (1 mi) and look for a parking area on the right.

❿ Part of the Blyde River Canyon Nature Reserve, **God's Window** is the most famous of the Lowveld lookouts. As such it is geared for tourists, with toilet facilities, paved parking areas, curio vendors, and marked walking trails. The altitude here is 5,700 ft, just a little lower than Johannesburg. But you still feel as though you're standing on top of the world, because the Escarpment drops away almost vertically to the Lowveld. Paved walking trails lead to various lookouts. The God's Window lookout has a view back along the Escarpment framed between towering cliffs. For a broader panorama, follow the paved track up through the rain forest to a small, unfenced area that offers sweeping views of the entire Lowveld. On sunny days carry water—it's a 10-minute climb. From the Pinnacle, turn right onto R534, pass two overlooks, and after 4½ km (2¾ mi) turn into the parking area on the right.

⑪ Set in a bowl between hills, **Lisbon Falls** cascade 120 ft onto rocks below, hurling a lovely spray over a deep pool. You can hike down to the pool on a path from the parking area. From God's Window, turn right onto the R534 and continue 6 km (4 mi). At the T-junction with R532, turn left (towards Graskop); after 1 km turn right onto the road marked Lisbon Falls.

⑫ A small stream, Waterfall Spruit, runs through a broad expanse of grassland to **Berlin Falls.** The cascade itself is a thin stream that drops 150 ft into a deep-green pool surrounded by tall pines. Berlin Falls is a little over a mile north of Lisbon Falls off of the R532.

Dining and Lodging

$ ✕ **Harrie's Pancake Bar.** Harrie's was the original pancake bar in the area, and it's still the best. (Tour groups know this, too, so you might have to stand in line on weekends.) If the weather's fine, take a seat on the veranda overlooking the street. Otherwise, warm yourself by the fire inside and listen to classical music while mulling over the selection of pancakes and infusion coffees. Pancakes in South Africa are a thicker version of crepes, stuffed with either dessert fillings or savories like ground beef, Dutch bacon, ratatouille, or spinach and feta. Harrie's is open December–April, daily 10–6, and May–November, daily 9–4:30. ⊠ *Louis Trichardt Ave. and Kerk St.,* ☎ *013/767–1273. AE, MC, V.*

$$ ⌾ **Graskop Hotel.** Aside from self-catering establishments, this is the only decent option in Graskop proper. And in fact it's rather attractive. The public areas are decorated with an interesting collection of African art. Zulu baskets brighten long corridors, avant-garde metal ostriches flank the foyer, and Swazi pots and sculpture dot the lounge. Rooms are light and airy, with white walls, green wicker furniture, and lots of blond wood. Unfortunately, the walls are too thin to keep out noise from neighboring rooms. ⊠ *Main St. (mailing address: Box 568, Graskop 1270),* ☎ ⠋⠁⠭ *013/767–1244. 24 rooms, 18 with bath, and 15 family cottages. 2 restaurants, bar, pool. Breakfast included. AE, DC, MC, V.*

$$ ⌾ **Lisbon Hideaway.** In a peaceful meadow overlooking a small stream,
★ this self-catering establishment makes a great base from which to explore the Escarpment. Graskop, several waterfalls, and the magnificent viewpoints of God's Window are minutes away. Accommodation is either in wood cabins or an old, stone miner's cottage that sleeps four. The wood cabins are modern and comfortable, done in wicker and floral patterns. Each cabin sleeps a maximum of six, with two bedrooms, a living/dining room, and a fully equipped kitchen. Don't let the self-catering set-up put you off. Talkative owner Phillip Flischman runs the Spar supermarket in Sabie and will stock the kitchen for you on request. ⊠ *Lisbon Falls Rd. off R532, 10 km (6 mi) from Graskop (mailing address: Box 43, Graskop 1270),* ☎ *013/767–1851. 3 chalets and 1 cottage, all with bath. MC.*

Blyde River Canyon Nature Reserve

60 km (38 mi) northeast of Graskop

Heading north from Graskop, after passing Lisbon and Berlin Falls, the dense plantations of gum and pine fall behind, and the road runs through magnificent grass-covered peaks. Once inside the nature reserve, turn off for **Bourke's Luck Potholes.** Named after a gold prospector, the potholes are a series of bizarre holes carved into the rock in the gorge where the Treur and Blyde Rivers converge. The holes were dug over the eons by the abrasion of pebbles suspended in the swirling water. Here, as well, is the headquarters for the **Blyde River Canyon Nature Reserve,** one of South Africa's scenic highlights. The canyon begins here and winds northward for nearly 30 km (19 mi). Several long canyon trails start from here (☞ Hiking, *below*), and an interesting nature center explains the geology and ecology of the canyon. The canyon proper begins is some 27 km (19 mi) north of Berlin Falls. ✉ *R532,* ☎ *01315/8–1215.* ⊡ *R2.50.* ☯ *Reserve: daily 7–5. Visitor center: daily 7:30–4.*

Continuing north from Bourke's Luck Potholes, you get occasional glimpses of the magnificent canyon and the distant cliffs of the Escarpment. Nowhere, however, is the view better than from the **Three Rondawels** (Drie Rondawels), 14 km (9 mi) from the potholes. This is one of the most spectacular vistas in South Africa—you'll find it in almost every travel brochure. The Blyde River, hemmed in by towering buttresses of red rock, snakes through the bottom of the canyon. The Three Rondawels are rock formations that rise up from the canyon floor and bear a vague similarity to the round, thatched African dwellings known as rondawels.

Before Europeans moved into the area, of course, the indigenous local people named the Three Rondawels: "The Chief and His Three Wives." The flat-topped peak to the right is *Mapjaneng*—The Chief—named in honor of a Mapulana chief named Maripe Mashile, who routed invading Swazi at the battle *Moholoholo,* which means "the very great one." The three wives, descending order from right to left are named *Maseroto, Mogoladikwe,* and *Magabolle.*

The descent down the Escarpment through **Abel Erasmus Pass** is breathtaking. (From the Three Rondawels, take the R532 to a T-junction and turn right onto the R36.) The **J.G. Strijdom Tunnel,** burrowing through the mountainside, serves as the gateway to the Lowveld. As you emerge from the dark mouth of the tunnel, the Lowveld spreads out below you, and the views of both it and the mountains are stunning.

Once on the flat plains of the Lowveld, the road cuts east through plantations of mango and citrus. Keep an eye out for a lovely example of a baobab tree, on the right-hand side next to a fruit stand. These weird and wonderful trees don't grow much farther south than this.

Hiking

The **Blyde River Canyon Trail** is a 56-km (35-mi) hike that runs from God's Window right along the edge of the Escarpment to the Sybrand van Niekerk resort. The mountain scenery is spectacular, making it one of the most popular trails in the country. Several shorter trails explore the canyon from trailheads at Bourke's Luck Potholes. The number of hikers on these trails is controlled, so it's essential to reserve far in advance. To do so, contact the Blyde River Canyon Nature Reserve office (☎ 01315/8–1215).

Hoedspruit

63 km (39 mi) northeast of Graskop.

Hoedspruit itself is a nondescript place, little more than a supply depot for the surrounding farms. This is diehard Afrikaner country, and it's not unusual to see men packing pistols on their hips.

16 From Hoedspruit, turn left onto R40 and drive 4 km (2½ mi) to **Tshukudu.** This 12,350-acre game farm bills itself as a safari lodge, but it's more like an animal park. Go somewhere else for a two- or three-night big-game adventure, but stop here for a day visit, which includes lunch, a game drive (including a stop at a lion pen), and a bush walk. The highlight of the day is the chance to meet some of the farm's orphaned animals, many of them completely tame. Don't be surprised if you're ambushed by a tame lion, nudged by a wildebeest, or accompanied by two baby elephants on your bush walk. Advance reservations are essential. ✉ *R40, north of Hoedspruit,* ☎ *01528/3–2476.* 🖃 *R50 (includes lunch, game drive, and walk). By appointment only.*

Kiepersol

17 *28 km (17½ mi) east of Sabie.*

This one-road town used to be a trading station. Bananas were grown nearby. There's little here beyond its church and hotel.

Dining and Lodging

$$$$ ✕🏨 **Blue Mountain Lodge.** A member of Small Luxury Hotels of the World, this exclusive retreat elicits either fervent support or scorn— there is little room in between. The emphasis here is on creating a fantasy getaway for jaded city-dwellers. The owners, Valma and Kobus Botha, both worked in the film industry, and their lodge has a setlike quality. Artificial moss adds instant age to stonework, and sponge-painting creates an illusion of fading murals on palace walls (it looks terrific if you're in a romantic mood, fake if you're feeling cynical). Compared with similarly priced rooms at Cybele (☞ *below*), the eight Victorian suites are huge, impeccably maintained, and a better value. Each of them follows a theme, ranging from English country to American Colonial, and all have fireplaces, verandas, and minibars, but no TVs. The best is the Out of Africa Suite, done all in white, with billowing mosquito netting, white bedspreads, lots of wood, and a clawfoot bathtub in the center of the room. Avoid the less-expensive Quadrant suites, however. Set in a cobbled courtyard reminiscent of Old Europe, they feel too sharp and angular, a flaw not helped by gaudy stripes painted on the walls. Meals are a refreshing departure from the traditional offerings of other lodges. The cuisine is lighter, with a nouvelle California style that pairs sweet and savory, Western and Asian tastes. Look for dishes like a quenelle of lobster and mussels on a bed of roasted peppers, papaya salad with peanut sauce, or cabeljou (a local sea fish) with litchi sauce. Presentation and service are superb. ✉ *Off R514, 10 km (6 mi) from Kiepersol (mailing address: Box 101, Kiepersol 1241),* ☎ 𝖥𝖠𝖷 *013/737–8446. 13 rooms with bath. Restaurant, bar, pool, bass fishing. Breakfast and dinner included. AE, DC, MC, V.*

$$$$ ✕🏨 **Cybele Forest Lodge.** Cybele started the whole concept of the coun-
★ try lodge in Mpumalanga, and to a large extent it still sets the pace, as its awards suggest. It is Cybele's service that separates it from its competitors, and that's essentially what you pay for. The staff has achieved a fine mix of professionalism and friendliness, and they go out of their way to make you feel special. The English-country decor of the main lodge complements the service. The two living rooms, warmed by fires and cluttered with attractive bric-a-brac and books, have a reassuring,

lived-in feel. Once you leave the warmth of the public rooms, though, much of Cybele's magic is lost, and if you were to judge the lodge solely on its guest rooms you would likely be disappointed. The cottage and studio rooms are small and undistinguished. The larger Garden and Courtyard suites, decorated in English-country style, are comfortable but show signs of wear. The magnificent Paddock Suites, however, with thatched roofs and spectacular views over the forested hills, have their own garden and swimming pool and a private outdoor shower hidden in the foliage—sort of a Blue Lagoon scene for the over-40 crowd. Cybele built much of its reputation on the quality of its food, and it certainly keeps customers coming back. The traditional five-course dinner melds classic French and traditional English country cooking. A light mushroom broth might be followed by risotto with ratatouille, then a choice of rack of lamb or trout fillets with a light lemon-cream sauce. For dessert, a rich gâteau with chocolate sauce would be typical. ⊠ *Off R40 between Hazyview and White River (mailing address: Box 346, White River 1240),* ☎ *013/764–1823,* ⎈ *013/764–1810. 12 rooms with bath. Restaurant, bar, pool, horseback riding, trout fishing. Breakfast and dinner included. AE, DC, MC, V.*

$$ ⊞ **Carrigans Country Estate.** Modeled after old gold-rush homes in Barberton and Pilgrim's Rest, the cottages at this lovely bed-and-breakfast have wraparound verandas that overlook the distant hills of the Drakensberg. Each two-bedroom cottage is decorated in period style, complete with a fireplace, mosquito netting, and a claw-foot bathtub. All cottages have fully equipped kitchens, their own living and dining rooms, and two bathrooms. The nearest grocery store is 5 km (3 mi) away, but if you don't care to cook, the owner's wife will prepare a supper hamper (R50 per person) of gazpacho, smoked trout, roast chicken, and dessert. Even better, Cybele's wonderful food is just a five-minute drive away. ⊠ *Off R40, between Hazyview and White River (mailing address: Box 19, Kiepersol 1241),* ☎ *013/764–1713,* ⎈ *013/764–3451. 4 cottages. Pool. Breakfast included. AE, DC, MC, V.*

White River

⑱ *35 km (22 mi) south east of Sabie*

The R40 runs south through Lowveld thornscrub, with the distant barrier of the Escarpment visible on the right. It passes through the service town of Hazyview before continuing on to White River, a pleasant farm town with several interesting arts and crafts shops.

Dining and Lodging

$$$ ✕ **A...Makietie.** Dishes such as local fish basted with a spicy garlic sauce—chef Jason van Loggerenburg loves his garlic—or tandoori chicken salad populate the interesting international menu here. If you're feeling like something basic, try the bargain barbecue chicken and chips. ⊠ *Alie van Bergen St. (just off Kruger Park St.),* ☎ *013/750–1161. AE, DC, MC, V.*

$$ ✕ **Bagdad Café.** Snappy service, eclectic-rustic atmosphere—such as local township art and masks—and very tasty food make this one of the finest eateries in the Lowveld. Chef-owner Alison Crossley and partner Steve will also chat with you if you've got questions about the menu. A tuna salad with a seafood sauce makes a good starter, and look for main dishes like smoked trout with a walnut and lemon sauce. ⊠ *Hazyview Rd., (R40, just outside of White River),* ☎ *013/751–1777. AE, DC, MC, V.*

$$$$ ✕🏠 **Highgrove House.** On a hillside overlooking avocado and banana orchards, this former farmhouse is considered one of the very best lodges in the country. Rooms are in white cottages scattered about the lovely gardens, and each has a veranda, sitting area, and fireplace. The decor, both in the main lodge and the cottages, has colonial overtones, with plenty of gathered curtains and floral upholstery. The lodge bears distinct similarities to Cybele in Kiepersol (☞ *above*), but lacks that lodge's easygoing atmosphere. Here, you don't feel quite at liberty to lie on the couches or throw your leg over the side of an armchair. Perhaps for that very reason, the lodge is immaculate. Highgrove serves an excellent five-course Anglo-French dinner. A typical meal might be a melange of Knysna oysters, quail eggs, and caviar with a sour-cream dressing followed by slivers of guinea fowl and foie gras with a port and cranberry sauce. One heavenly dessert is tartelettes of fresh figs and almonds. Weather permitting, lunch and breakfast are served in the gazebo by the pool. Nonguests must reserve ahead for meals. ✉ *R40, between Hazyview and White River (mailing address: Box 46, Kiepersol 1241),* ☎ *013/764–1844,* 🖷 *013764–1855. 8 suites. Restaurant, bar, pool. Breakfast and dinner included. AE, DC, MC, V.*

$$$ ✕🏠 **Huala Lakeside Lodge.** This attractive lodge sits on a forested promontory, surrounded on three sides by a large dam. All rooms have water views, and the majority of activities involve swimming or boating on the lake. Guest rooms, in sandy yellow cottages, have a warm, comfortable feel, thanks to overhead beams, ivory stucco walls, and matching floral bedspreads and curtains. If you can, book the Malachite Suite, in a lovely cottage set apart from the main buildings, with a four-poster bed and its own swimming pool. The lodge's five-course dinner, served in an elegant, candlelit room, is ambitious but inconsistent. Lamb with figs might stand out, whereas trout in cream sauce proves bland and uninspired. Breakfast and light lunches are served on the veranda under large umbrellas, overlooking the pool and lake. ✉ *Off R40, between Hazyview and White River (mailing address: Box 1382, White River 1240),* ☎ 🖷 *013/764–1893. 21 rooms with bath. Restaurant, bar, room service, pool, waterskiing. Breakfast and dinner included. AE, DC, MC, V.*

$$$ ✕🏠 **Kirby Country Lodge.** This is one of those relaxed places where you can kick back and not worry about appearances. If the rooms aren't as fancy as those at some of the lodges, they're not as expensive either. The fact that 70% of its guests are repeat or referral visitors is an indication that the lodge is doing something right. Owners Geoff and Debbie March personally welcome you to their thatched, white-brick farmhouse set in pleasant gardens shaded by enormous trees. Much of the furniture in the guest rooms is antique, either hand-me-downs from the March family or unearthed in attics. Rooms have phones, but no air-conditioning or fans. Debbie prepares most of the food, with an emphasis on Continental cuisine. Look for chilled soups and smoked trout in summer, as well as roasts and fillets. Debbie's winter specialty of oxtail falls gently off the bone. For dessert, expect crème brûlée, chocolate mousse, or a traditional bread-and-butter pudding. Lunch is for residents only, and nonguests must book for dinner. ✉ *Off R538, between White River and Plaston (mailing address: Box 138, Plaston 1244),* ☎ *013/751–2645. 8 rooms with bath. Restaurant, bar, pool. Breakfast and dinner included.*

Nelspruit

19 kilometers (12 miles) southwest of White River on the R40.

Although it serves as the capital of the Eastern Transvaal, Nelspruit **⑲** has little to offer other than the **Lowveld National Botanical Gardens.**

Set on the banks of the Crocodile River, these gardens display over 500 plant species indigenous to the valley, including a spectacular collection of cycads and ferns. Several trails wind through the gardens, one leading to a pleasant waterfall. ⊠ *2 mi outside Nelspruit on White River Rd.,* ☏ *01311/55–1988.* ◫ *R3.50.* ◷ *Daily Oct.-Apr. 8–6, May-Sept. 8–5:15.*

Barberton

 50 km (31 mi) south of Nelspruit on the R40

The history of the southern Lowveld and Middleveld—between the southern boundary of Kruger National Park, the Swaziland border, and the village of Badplaas to the west—begins in the hills and valleys of the region, where Bushman rock-paintings, archaeological ruins, wagon trails, and early gold diggings are all easily accessible. Routes to the Lowveld via Badplaas and Barberton pass through beautiful mountain scenery on quiet country roads. Stop at one of the roadside fruit stalls that's sprung up in the area for a taste of local produce.

The Barber family and its significant gold discoveries in the 1880s named this historical town, among the oldest in the area. It was the seat of South Africa's first stock exchange. Yet two years after gold was discovered, Barberton was all but deserted by prospectors who moved to the Witwatersrand, where Johannesburg's mining continues to this day. Barberton is now a thriving agricultural center and a tourist haven with a number of memorials linked to its pioneering days. The town has a number of hiking trails following the paths of early miners. And the requisite statue of Jock of the Bushveld stands proudly in the center of the town, along with a statuesque town hall and the Garden of Remembrance, which marks the fallen soldiers of the South African War.

Barberton makes for an easy day-trip from Sabie or a stopover on the way to Swaziland. When you get into town, look for the **Market Square**'s information bureau and the **Victorian Tea Garden** for a cup of tea.

The **Barberton Museum**'s best exhibits cover gold mine culture and history. Some of that culture has to do with colorful gold-rush characters like infamous Cockney Liz, a Phoenix Hotel (☞ *below*) barmaid and prostitute. ⊠ *Town Square, Pilgrim St.,* ☏ *013/712–2121.* ◫ *Free.* ◷ *Daily 9–4.*

For a look at the lifestyle of a turn-of-the-century upper-middle-class Barberton family, the **Belhaven House Museum** looks much as it did after it was built in 1904. The late-Victorian/early-Edwardian furnishings seem a world apart from the rowdy gold-rush side of town. ⊠ *Town Square, Lee St.,* ◫ *Free.* ◷ *Weekdays 9–5.*

Baker and general dealer James Stopforth built the original wood-and-iron house and outbuildings (stable, woodwork shed, and outside bedroom) of **Stopforth House** in 1886. It was rebuilt in 1892, and the Stopforth family occupied it until 1983. This is another place to look into Barberton's past. ⊠ *18 Bowness St.* ◫ *Free.* ◷ *Mon.–Sat. 9–4:30.*

For a brief period in the 1880s and '90s, Barberton's **De Kaap Stock Exchange** was a mainstay of the region's economy. It served as the district's first gold exchange, but the gold reef in the area wasn't deep enough to sustain profitable long-term mining. The exchange's facade has been preserved as a National Monument since 1965. ⊠ *Pilgrim St.* ◫ *Free.*

The **Fortuna Mine Hiking Trail,** in the southern part of Barberton, is nestled in the foothills of Lone Tree Hill, one of the better known peaks of the Makonja Range. The 2-km (1¼-mi) trail passes through an area populated by some 80 trees species. A little over ¼ km, the trail reaches an old mining tunnel, which was driven through the rocky hillside in the early 1900s for the transport of gold-bearing ore to the Fortuna Mine. Insufficient quantities of gold were found for the mining operation, but the rock formations here are estimated at 400 million years old, which puts dates them as the oldest sedimentary rock formations yet found on earth. Allow 1½ hours for the hike.

Mpumalanga A to Z

Arriving and Departing

BY BUS

Greyhound (☎ 013/752–5134) runs daily between Johannesburg and Nelspruit (Joshua Doore Centre). The trip takes five hours.

BY CAR

It takes less than four hours to drive the 350 km (220 mi) from Johannesburg to Nelspruit, capital of Mpumalanga and a major gateway to the region. The best route is north from Joburg on the N1 to Pretoria, then east on the N4.

BY PLANE

Nelspruit Airport (☎ 013/741–3192) is a one-hour hop from Johannesburg, about half that from other points in Mpumalanga. It is served by **Metavia** (☎ 013/741–3141) and **S.A. Airlink** (☎ 013/752–5257).

BY TRAIN

Spoornet's Komati train (☎ 011/773–2944) travels between Johannesburg and Nelspruit via Pretoria daily. The trip takes about 12 hours. The luxury *Blue Train* (☞ Rail Travel *in* the Gold Guide) also makes occasional runs from Pretoria to Nelspruit; Rovos Rail (☞ Train Travel *in* the Gold Guide), the Edwardian-era competitor of the Blue Train, travels from Pretoria to Komatipoort, just outside Kruger National Park. Most passengers combine a journey on Rovos Rail with a package trip to a game reserve or one of the exclusive lodges on the Escarpment.

Getting Around

BY CAR

Renting a car is the only option if you really want to explore Mpumalanga.

BY MINIBUS

Public bus service is limited or nonexistent in Mpumalanga. If you don't have your own car, you're dependent on one of the tour companies to get around the Escarpment and into the game reserves (☞ Guided Tours, *below*). Many of these companies also operate shuttle services that transfer guests between the various lodges and to the airport. It's usually possible to hire these chauffeured minibuses on an hourly or daily rate.

Contacts and Resources

CAR RENTAL

Avis (☎ 013/741–1087), **Budget** (☎ 013/741–3871), and **Imperial** (☎ 013/741–3210) all have offices at Nelspruit Airport. **Avis** (☎ 013/741–1087) also has a desk at Skukuza Airport, in Kruger National Park. If you're planning to drive from Johannesburg, *see* Johannesburg A to Z *in* Chapter 2.

EMERGENCIES

In case of an emergency, contact the police at 10111. In the event of a serious medical emergency, contact MRI (☎ 013/751–3930) or Life Crisis (☎ 013/751–3739) both companies offer emergency helicopter services.

The best-equipped hospitals in the Lowveld are in Nelspruit: **Nelspruit Private Hospital** (☎ 013/759–0613) and **Rob Ferreira Hospital** (☎ 013/741–3031).

Flight Seeing. National Airways Corporation offers all types of helicopter charters, including lodge hopping. Deserving special mention is the Misty Mountain experience where the guest is taken on a helicopter journey from one waterfall and site to another, stopping off at the Pinnacle, near Graskop, for a picnic breakfast. ☎ 013/741–4838.

Orientation. All tour operators offer a package of trips that cover the major sights of the Escarpment, as well as game-viewing trips into Kruger National Park and private reserves. The most reputable operators in the area are Dragonfly Safaris (✉ Box 1042, White River 1240, ☎ 013/750–1060, Welcome Tours (✉ Box 997, Johannesburg 2000, ☎ 011/442–8905, ℻ 011/442–8865) and Lowveld Environmental Services Box 5747 Nelspruit 1200, ☎ 013/744–7063.

Nelspruit Publicity Association. ✉ *Shop 5, Promenade Centre, corner of Paul Kruger and Louis Trichardt Sts.,* ☎ *013/755–1988,* ℻ *013/755–1350.* ⊘ *Weekdays 8–5, Sat. 9–1.*

Pilgrim's Rest Information Centre. ✉ *Main St.,* ☎ *013/768–1211.* ⊘ *Daily 9–12:45, 1:15–4:30.*

Sondela, the SATOUR office in Sabie, provides information on the area and hires out mountain bikes. ✉ *Main St., Sabie,* ☎ *013/764–3492.* ⊘ *Mon.–Sat. 8–5, Sun. 9–1.*

Barberton Information Bureau. ✉ *Market Sq.,* ☎ *013/712–5156.* ⊘ *Weekdays 8–5, Sat. 9–1.*

KRUGER NATIONAL PARK

Kruger lies in the hot, malarial fug of the Lowveld, a subtropical section of Mpumalanga and Northern Province that abuts Mozambique. The park cuts a swath 80 km (50 mi) wide and 320 km (200 mi) long from Zimbabwe and the Limpopo River in the north to the Crocodile River in the south. Along the way, it crosses 14 different ecozones, each supporting a great variety of plants, birds, and animals.

The southern and central sections of the park are where you will see the most game. Riverine forests, thorny thickets, and large grassy plains studded with knobthorn and marula trees are typical of this region and make ideal habitats for a variety of animals, including black and white rhino (once on the verge of extinction), leopard, and giraffe. The most consistently rewarding drive in the park is along the road paralleling the Sabie River from Skukuza to Lower Sabie.

As you head north to Olifants and Letaba, you enter major elephant country, although you're likely to spot any number of other animals as well, including lion and cheetah. North of Letaba, however, the landscape becomes a monotonous blur of mopane, nutrient-poor land that supports only stunted mopane trees, which even the animals avoid. Some species, most notably tsessebe and roan antelope, thrive up here nevertheless. If you have a week in Kruger, it's worth driving north to check it out. With less than that, you should stick to the southern and central sections of the park.

Summer in Kruger can be stinking hot—temperatures of 100°F are common—and many northern European visitors become simpering pud-

Kruger National Park

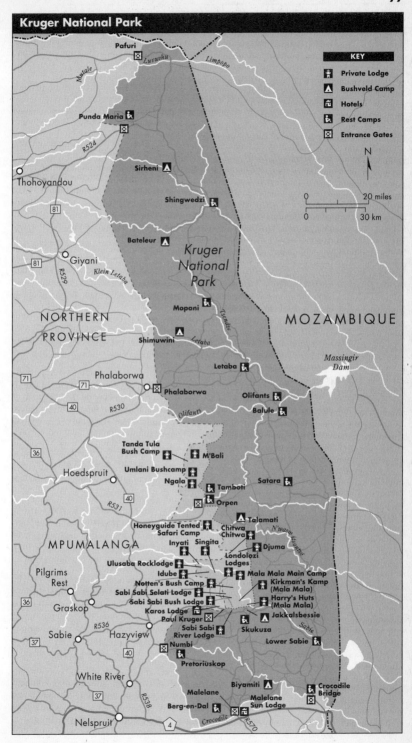

KEY

Private Lodge

Bushveld Camp

Hotels

Rest Camps

Entrance Gates

N

0   20 miles

0   30 km

Pafuri

Luvuchu

Limpopo

Matale

Punda Maria

R524

Sirheni

Thohoyandou

Shingwedzi

81

Bateleur

Giyani

Kruger
National
Park

81

R529

Klein Letaba

Mopani

Tsendze

MOZAMBIQUE

NORTHERN

PROVINCE

Shimuwini

Letaba

71

Phalaborwa

Letaba

Massingir
Dam

71   R530

Phalaborwa

Olifants

40

Balule

Olifants

36

Tanda Tula
Bush Camp

M'Bali

Hoedspruit

Umlani Bushcamp

Ngala   Tamboti

Satara

R531   Orpen

Talamati

Honeyguide Tented
Safari Camp   Chitwa
Chitwa

MPUMALANGA

Inyati   Singita   Djuma

Londolozi
Lodges

Pilgrims
Rest

Ulusaba Rocklodge

Idube   Mala Mala Main Camp

Notten's Bush Camp   Kirkman's Kamp
(Mala Mala)

36   Sabi Sabi Selati Lodge

Graskop   Sabi Sabi Bush Lodge   Harry's Huts
(Mala Mala)

Karos Lodge
Paul Kruger   Jakkalsbessie

R536   Sabi Sabi
River Lodge   Skukuza

Sabie

37   Hazyview   Numbi   Lower Sabie

40

Pretoriuskop

White River

Biyamiti

37   Malelane   Crocodile
Bridge

Berg-en-Dal   Malelane
Sun Lodge

R538

R570

Nelspruit   Crocodile

4

dles of discontent. If you feel the heat, come at another time or stay in the cool uplands of the Mpumalanga Drakensberg (☞ Chapter 3) and visit Kruger just for game drives. Whatever you do, *avoid the park during school vacations*. During the July and Christmas holidays, Kruger looks more like summer camp than a game reserve. Reservations are hard to obtain (book a year in advance), and hour-long traffic jams at game-sightings are not uncommon.

Park Activities

See Kruger A to Z, *below,* for information about reservations and fees.

Bush Drives

First-time visitors sometimes feel a little lost driving themselves through the park: they don't know what to look for, and they can't identify the animals they do find. An affordable solution is to hire a game ranger to show you the park and its animals. The rest camps at Berg-en-Dal, Letaba, and Skukuza all offer ranger-led bush drives in open-air Land Rovers (minimum of two people). Not only can rangers explain the finer points of what you're seeing, but they can also take you into areas off-limits to the public. They may even take you on short walks through the bush, something else you can't do on your own. Day excursions cost R94 per person, less than renting a car for a day. Book drives at least a week in advance.

Night Drives

★ Even if you tour the park by yourself during the day, be sure to go on a ranger-led night drive, when the park is closed to regular visitors. Passengers sit in large, open-air vehicles, and use powerful spotlights to pick out animals, including a number of nocturnal creatures you would never see otherwise, including bush babies, servals, civets, and, if you're really lucky, aardvarks. Night is also the time when hyenas, lions, and leopards hunt. The major rest camps offer these drives, with the notable exception of Lower Sabie and Olifants. The three- to four-hour trip leaves the rest camps half an hour before the gates close. Night drives cost about R55 per person, and again it's advisable to reserve a few days in advance.

Wilderness Trails

★ Spend a few days hiking through the wilds of Africa and you'll probably never be satisfied driving around a game reserve again. On foot, you gain an affinity for the animals and the bush that's impossible in the confines of a car. Kruger has seven wilderness trails, each of which can accommodate eight people. Led by an armed ranger, you'll spend the day walking through the bush, returning each day to the same trail camp. These trails are not get-fit hikes but slow meanders, the point being to learn about your surroundings: the medicinal purposes of trees, the role of dung beetles in the ecology, even how to recognize animals by their spoor. In general, you can't get as close to animals on foot as you can in a vehicle. You *will* see animals, though, and many hikers can recount face-to-face encounters with everything from rhino to elephant and lion. It's a heart-pumping thrill you won't soon forget. Hikes last three nights and two days (starting on Sundays and Wednesdays), and you should be prepared to walk as much as 19 km (12 mi) a day. No one under 12 or over 60 is allowed. Hikers sleep in rustic, two-bed huts and share a reed-wall bathroom with flush toilets and showers. Meals are simple bush fare, including stews and barbecues; you must provide your own booze and soft drinks. These trails are incredibly popular—try to reserve 13 months in advance, when bookings open. The cost is R935 per person per trail.

Bushman Trail. Situated in the southwestern corner of the park, this trail takes its name from the San rock paintings and sites found in the area. The trail camp lies in a secluded valley dominated by granite hills and cliffs. Game sightings frequently include white rhino, elephant, and buffalo. Check in at Berg-en-Dal.

Metsimetsi Trail. The permanent water of the nearby N'waswitsontso River makes this one of the best trails for winter game-viewing. Midway between Skukuza and Satara, the trail camp hunkers in the lee of a mountain in an area of gorges, cliffs, and rolling savanna. Check in at Skukuza.

Napi Trail. Sightings of white rhino are common on this trail, which runs through mixed bushveld between Pretoriuskop and Skukuza. Other frequent sightings include black rhino, cheetah, leopard, elephant, and wild dog. The trail camp hides in dense riverine forest at the confluence of the Napi and Mbyamiti rivers. Check in at Pretoriuskop.

Nyalaland Trail. They don't come much more remote than this trail camp, in pristine wilderness in the far north of the park. Bird-watching is the big thrill in this land of huge baobabs and fever trees. The camp lies on the bank of the Madzaringwe Spruit, near the Luvuvhu River. You're almost sure to see hippo, crocodiles, nyala, and elephant. Check in at Punda Maria.

Olifants Trail. East of Olifants rest camp, this trail camp commands a great view of the Olifants River and affords regular sightings of elephant, lion, buffalo, and hippo. The landscape varies from riverine forest to the rocky foothills of the Lebombo Mountains. Check in at Olifants.

Sweni Trail. East of Satara, this trail camp overlooks the Sweni Spruit and savanna dotted with marula and knobthorn trees. The area attracts large herds of zebra, wildebeest, and buffalo—with their attendant predators, lion and spotted hyena. Check in at Satara.

Wolhuter Trail. If you want to come face-to-face with a white rhino, choose this trail midway between Berg-en-Dal and Pretoriuskop. The undulating bushveld, interspersed with rocky *kopjes* (hills), is ideal habitat for these tremendous prehistoric beasts, but you're also likely to see elephant, buffalo, and lion. Check in at Berg-en-Dal.

National Parks Lodging

Unless you stay in a hotel outside Kruger, you are dependent on park-administered rest camps. Accommodations at these camps are usually in free-standing chalets or thatched rondawels, round huts modeled after traditional African dwellings. All rooms have air-conditioning, refrigerators, and *braais* (barbecues), and most come with kitchenettes and bathrooms en suite (attached). You may as well face up to the fact that you're going to miss an episode or two of *ER*—there's no TV in the park, and to call a friend for the latest scoop you'll have to use the public phones near the main buildings.

All of the major rest camps operate restaurants and cafeterias. Less popular camps in the north have à la carte restaurants that serve pretty decent fare, including game steaks. Restaurants in the other camps all offer set-menu meals. Without exception, the food bears the overcooked, underseasoned imprimatur of a government institution—a wildebeest on the hoof looks good next to this stuff. Dinner is a traditional four-course affair of soup, fish, a roast of some kind, and dessert, served buffet-style. Lunch is similar but mercifully smaller. To add insult to gastric injury, prices are high: about R35 for lunch and R40 for dinner. A marginally better option is to order something from the cafeteria, which serves up reasonably priced burgers, hot dogs, curry, bacon and egg, and a variety of toasted sandwiches.

With choices like these, it's not surprising the majority of South African visitors cook their own food. Indeed, braaiing is a time-honored tradition in Kruger, as intrinsic to a park visit as a barbecue is to Americans on the Fourth of July. Even the rest areas dotted through the park have free gas grills for visitors who wish to cook their breakfast after an early morning game drive. If you are going to do your own cooking, try to reserve a rondawel equipped not only with a kitchenette but also a full complement of kitchen utensils.

Almost every rest camp has a shop offering a limited selection of groceries, charcoal, curios, and books. Don't waltz into these places looking for a sprig of mint for your Thai beef salad. They sell only the bare essentials, including canned foods, milk, bread, a selection of frozen meats, and beer and wine. If you do find fresh vegetables, they're likely to be potatoes and onions. Consider buying a cooler and stocking up at a grocery store outside the park instead.

It's necessary to book a year in advance if you want a room during peak seasons (December–January and July). Reservations must be made directly with the **National Parks Board.** ⊠ *Box 787, Pretoria 0001,* ☎ *012/343–1991,* FAX *012/343–0905.*

Rest Camps
For a couple staying in an en suite rondawel expect to pay R230–R300 per night. Costs increase for additional beds. A site to pitch your own tent costs R40 for up to two people throughout the park.

$–$$ 🛏 **Balule.** On the bank of the Olifants River, this rustic camp differs radically from the others and will appeal to those who want to experience the true feel of the bush. There are no shops or restaurants, and there's no electricity—only lanterns. Accommodations are in basic, three-bed huts with no windows (vents only) and shared bathroom facilities. Cooking is done in a communal kitchen. Visitors must check in at Olifants (☞ *below*), 11 km (7 mi) away. *No facilities.*

$–$$ 🛏 **Berg-en-Dal.** Built in 1984, this rest camp lies at the southern tip of the park, in a basin surrounded by rocky hills. Berg-en-Dal is known for its white rhino, leopard, and wild dog, but it lacks the tremendous game density of some of the camps farther north. A small dam runs by one side of the perimeter fence, offering good game-viewing, including a close look at cruising crocodiles. Berg-en-Dal itself is one of the more attractive camps, drawing great benefit from its thoughtful landscaping, which has (unusually for Kruger) left so much of the indigenous vegetation intact. The strategic positioning of accommodations among bushes and trees affords more seclusion than any of the older camps. Berg-en-Dal has two types of accommodations: three-bed chalets and family cottages that sleep six in two bedrooms. All huts come with fully equipped kitchens, including pots, pans, and cutlery. The units with the best views of the surrounding bush are numbers 26 (family cottage), 25, 27, and 30–39. *Restaurant, cafeteria, pool, shop, gas station, laundromat, bush drives, night drives.*

$–$$ 🛏 **Crocodile Bridge.** In the southeastern corner of the park, this small rest camp doubles as an entrance gate and makes a convenient stopover for visitors who arrive too late to reach another camp. Although the Crocodile River provides the scenic backdrop for the camp, any sense of being in the wild is quickly shattered by views of power lines and farms on its south side. The road leading from the camp to Lower Sabie is well known for its sightings of general game as well as buffalo, rhino, cheetah, and lion. A hippo pool lies just 5 km (3 mi) away. Accommodations are in two- or three-bed huts with fully equipped kitchenettes and bathrooms en suite. *Shop, gas station, laundromat.*

$–$$ ⊞ **Letaba.** Overlooking the frequently dry Letaba River, this lovely camp sits in the middle of elephant country in the central section of the park. Excellent game-viewing sites in the area are the Engelhardt and Mingerhout dams. The camp itself has a real bush feel: All the huts are thatched, and the grounds are overgrown with apple leaf trees, acacias, mopane, and lala palms. The restaurant and snack bar, with attractive outdoor seating, look out over the broad, sandy river bed. Even if you aren't staying at Letaba, stop in for the superb exhibit on elephants at the Environmental Education Centre. The display examines the social and physical characteristics of the huge animals, from their development in the womb to their death from starvation as a result of tooth loss. Letaba is also home to a collection of the greatest tusks found in the park. Accommodations are in large cottages and two-, three-, and four-bed rondawels, some without bathrooms and kitchenettes. Cooking utensils are not provided. Unfortunately, dense local foliage means that few rooms have views. Units C17–C30 and D32–D37 offer the best outlooks. Attractive alternatives are the large, East African-style safari tents furnished with four beds, tables and chairs, a refrigerator, and a fan. The campground, on the fence perimeter, offers lots of shade. *Restaurant, cafeteria, shop, car repair workshop, gas station, laundromat, bush drives, night drives.*

$–$$ ⊞ **Lower Sabie.** This is one of the most popular camps in Kruger for good reason: it commands tremendous views over a broad sweep of the Sabie River, and sits in one of the best game-viewing areas of the park (along with Skukuza and Satara). The camp is well known for white rhino, lion, and cheetah, and elephant and buffalo frequently come down to the river to drink. The vegetation around the camp consists mainly of grassland savanna interspersed with marula trees and knobthorn, and there are plenty of watering holes within a few minutes' drive. Lower Sabie is small compared with minitowns like Skukuza, and you get a pretty good feel for the surrounding bush. Accommodations are in five-bed cottages and one-, two-, three-, and five-bed huts, some of which lack kitchens and bathrooms. Cooking utensils are also not provided. The huts with the best views of the river are numbers 3–24 and 73–96. *Restaurant, cafeteria, shop, gas station, laundromat.*

$–$$ ⊞ **Mopani.** Built in the lee of a rocky kopje overlooking a dam, this huge settlement is the newest and most attractive of Kruger's rest camps. The dam and the camp are an oasis for both animals and people amid the numbing monotony of the mopane shrubveld in the northern section of the park. You will probably see more game from the rest camp than you will in hours of sweaty driving through the surrounding country. Constructed of rough stone, wood, and thatch, the camp merges well into the thick vegetation. Shaded wood walkways connect the public areas, all of which overlook the dam—the view from the open-air bar is outstanding. The restaurant is à la carte (you must reserve before 6) and the food far superior to the buffet-style swill served at other rest camps. The cottages, too, are better equipped and much larger than their counterparts elsewhere in Kruger. Units with kitchenettes come with a full complement of crockery, cutlery, and cooking utensils, and six-bed family cottages are nothing less than fully furnished houses. Among the two-bed huts with views of Pioneer Dam are numbers 4, 7, 9–12, 47, 49, 51, 52, 54, 101, and 102. The family cottages with the best views are numbers 5, 43, 45, 48, and 53. *Restaurant, cafeteria, bar, shop, pool, gas station, laundromat, night drives.*

$–$$ ☒ **Olifants.** In the central section of the park, Olifants has the best setting of all the Kruger camps. It sits high atop cliffs on a rocky ridge, with panoramic views over the distant hills and the Olifants River below. A lovely, thatch-sheltered terrace allows visitors to sit for hours with a pair of binoculars and pick out the animals below. Lions often make kills in the river valley, and elephant, buffalo, giraffe, kudu, and other game come down to drink and bathe. If you have to give up your first-born to secure one of the thatched rondawels overlooking the valley (numbers 1–12), do so. It's worth reserving these rondawels for at least two nights (book a year in advance) so you can hang out on the veranda and watch Africa unfold below—you won't be disappointed. Olifants offers a lot more than a good view, however. It's a charming old camp, graced with wonderful indigenous trees like sycamores and knobbly figs, mopane, and sausage trees. Accommodations are in two- and three-bed thatched rondawels, some with fully equipped kitchens. The camp has two drawbacks: no night drives and no swimming pool. *Restaurant, cafeteria, shop, laundromat, gas station.*

$–$$ ☒ **Orpen.** Little needs to be said about this tiny rest camp, which lies just yards from Orpen Gate, in the central section of the park. The only reason to stay here is if you arrive at the gate too late to make it to another camp before the roads are closed. None of the two-bedroom units has a bathroom or cooking facilities. The rooms, arranged in a rough semicircle around a large lawn, look out toward the perimeter fence, about 150 ft away. *Shop, gas station.*

$–$$ ☒ **Pretoriuskop.** This large rest camp, conveniently close to the Numbi Gate in the southwest corner of the park, makes a good overnight stop for new arrivals. The landscape here consists of rocky kopjes and steep ridges that provide an ideal habitat for mountain reedbuck and klipspringers. The area's sourveld vegetation also attracts browsers like giraffe and kudu, as well as white rhino, lion, and wild dog. Like several other Kruger camps, Pretoriuskop is laid out so guests see less of the surrounding bush than of their neighbors grilling *boerewors* (coarse farmer's sausages) and chops. Accommodations are in typical thatched rondawels and cottages, some of which lack bathrooms and kitchens. The campground enjoys some shade, but sites lack privacy. *Restaurant, cafeteria, shop, laundromat, pool, gas station, night drives.*

$–$$ ☒ **Punda Maria.** Few foreign tourists make it to this camp in the far northern end of the park, near Zimbabwe. This is a shame, for in many ways it offers the best bush experience of any of the major rest camps. It's a small enclave, with whitewashed, thatched cottages arranged in terraces on a hill. The camp lies in the sandveld, a botanically rich area notable for its unique plant life and birds. An interesting nature trail winds through the settlement. Two-bed huts all come with bathrooms en suite, and many have fully equipped kitchenettes. *Restaurant, shop, gas station.*

$–$$ ☒ **Satara.** Second in size only to Skukuza, this camp sits in the middle of the hot plains between Olifants and Lower Sabie, in the central section of Kruger. The knobthorn veld surrounding the camp provides the best grazing in the park and attracts large concentrations of game, which in turn attract plenty of lion. Just standing at the perimeter fence, you often see giraffe, zebra, waterbuck, and other antelope. Keep an eye out, too, for rare sable, black rhino, and eland. Despite its size, Satara has far more appeal than Skukuza, possibly because it offers more privacy—the huts aren't all piled on top of one another—and possibly because of the tremendous birdlife that flies in from the bush. The restaurant and snack bar are very pleasant, with shady seating overlooking the lawns and the bush beyond. Accommodations are in large cottages and two- or three-bed thatched rondawels, some with kitchenettes (no cooking utensils). The rondawels, arranged in large circles, face inward onto a central, parklike space. The only huts with good views of the bush are numbers G161–G179. The best of the lot is G167, close to the fence. Campsites are secluded, with an excellent view of the bush, although none of the sites enjoys much shade. *Restaurant, cafeteria, shop, laundromat, car repair workshop, gas station, night drives.*

$–$$ ☒ **Shingwedzi.** This camp lies in the northern section of the park, amid the blistering plains of mopane shrubveld. The camp benefits enormously from the riverine growth associated with the Shingwedzi River and Kanniedood Dam. As a result, you will probably find more game right around the camp than anywhere else in the region. Among the species that thrive in the harsh mopane environment are elephant, roan antelope, Sharpe's grysbok, and tsessebe. The use of thatch and unworked tree trunks as roof supports gives the camp a rugged, pioneer feel. Both the restaurant (à la carte) and outdoor cafeteria have views over the Shingwedzi River. Accommodations are of two types, A and B. Choose A. These whitewashed units have steeply pitched thatch roofs that accommodate an additional two-bed loft; some also have fully equipped kitchenettes. The B units, painted a dull beige, are built of brick and roofed with unsightly tile; only one has a bathroom and none has a kitchenette. It's anyone's guess why all of the huts face each other across a mopane grove, ignoring the lovely views of the bush beyond the perimeter fence. The campground is large but barren, with almost no shade. *Restaurant, cafeteria, shop, gas station, pool, laundromat, night drives.*

$–$$ ☒ **Skukuza.** This is by far the largest camp in Kruger, and serves as the park's headquarters. It's large enough to pass for a small town, and as a result it has completely lost all bush feel. At times you wonder if you're in a game reserve at all. Skukuza is popular for good reason, though. It's easily accessible by both air and road, and it lies in a region of thorn thicket that supports a high density of game, including lion, cheetah, and hyena. The camp itself sits on a bank of the crocodile-infested Sabie River, with good views of thick reeds and grazing waterbuck. A museum and education center offer an interesting look at the history and ecology of the park. Accommodations are in two- or three-bed rondawels and four-bed cottages. Some rondawels lack kitchens, but all have refrigerators. The rondawels with the best riverfront views are numbers 88–92. Guests also have the option of staying in permanent tents of the sort used on luxury East African safaris. Sited on a concrete platform, each tent comes with two or four beds, a cupboard, refrigerator, and fan. *2 restaurants, cafeteria, grocery, library, car repair workshop, gas station, police, bank, post office, car rental, bush drives, night drives.*

$–$$ ☒ **Tamboti.** Kruger's first tented camp, and also its newest, has a name with the romantic ring of a traditional East African safari, but because of its lack of facilities—which would test even a Spartan—it actually bears more of a resemblance to a Boy Scouts' outing. Its position on the banks of the frequently dry Timbavati River is superb, among apple leaf trees, sycamore figs, and jackalberries. From your tent, it isn't uncommon to see elephants just beyond the barely visible electrified fence digging in the river bed for moisture, which is why you need to book well ahead to get a place. Each of the walk-in tents has its own deck overlooking the river, but the ones to make a beeline for are numbers 21 and 22, which enjoy the deep shade of large riverine trees—something to value highly in the midsummer sweat. All kitchen, washing, and toilet facilities are in two shared central blocks, and you have to bring all your own cooking and eating utensils. *No facilities.*

Bushveld Camps

If you're prepared to cook for yourself, Kruger's bushveld camps are infinitely more attractive than the major rest camps. They're small and intimate—you can't get lost the way you can at Skukuza—and access is restricted to residents only. As a result, you experience more of the bush and less of fellow tourists. These camps do not have restaurants, gas pumps, or grocery stores, but all huts have fully equipped kitchens. The only drawback is that most of the cottages are intended for four or more people. Because of the four-bed minimum requirement, most bushveld camps cost from R525–R760 per night. The handful of one-bedroom cottages at Biyamiti, Shimuwini, Sirheni, and Talamati go for R295 and understandably get snapped up fast.

$$$ ⬚ **Bateleur.** Hidden in the northern reaches of the park, this is one of the most remote destinations in Kruger. Shaded by tall trees, the camp overlooks the dry watercourse of the Mashokwe Spruit. A raised platform provides an excellent vantage point from which to view game coming to drink from rainy season pools, and two nearby dams draw a variety of animals. The camp accommodates a total of 34 people in seven family cottages. Each thatched cottage has two bathrooms, a fully equipped kitchenette, and veranda. *Bush drives, night drives.*

$$$ ⬚ **Jakkalsbessie.** You couldn't ask for a better game-viewing location, along the Sabie River near Skukuza. The game density here is among the highest in southern Africa. The only drawback is the noise from aircraft landing at Skukuza airport. Eight family cottages can house a maximum of 32 visitors. Each of the thatched cottages features two bedrooms, two bathrooms, a fully equipped kitchen, and a veranda. An added bonus is the camp's proximity to the big grocery store at Skukuza. *No facilities.*

$$–$$$ ⬚ **Biyamiti.** Close to the park gate at Crocodile Bridge, this large camp overlooks the normally dry sands of the Mbyamiti River. The vegetation consists of mixed combretum woodland, which attracts healthy populations of kudu, impala, and elephant, as well as lion and black and white rhino. The camp consists of 15 thatched cottages, which can accommodate 70 people. All cottages have large verandas and fully equipped kitchens. *Night drives.*

$$–$$$ ⬚ **Shimuwini.** Bird-lovers descend in droves on this isolated camp, set on a lovely dam on the Letaba River. Towering jackalberry and sycamore figs offer welcome shade, as well as refuge to a host of local and migratory birds. Away from the river, the riverine forest quickly gives way to mopane—bushwillow woodland, not typically known for supporting large amounts of game. Even so, roan and sable move through the area, and in the peak of summer elephants arrive to browse on the mopane. The camp can house 71 guests in one-, two-, and three-bedroom cottages, all with verandas and kitchens. *Bush drives, night drives.*

$$–$$$ ⬚ **Sirheni.** Another major bird-watching camp, Sirheni sits on the edge of Sirheni Dam, in the far north of the park. A rewarding drive for birders and game-spotters alike runs along the Mphongolo River, but the area can't rival the game density of the Sabie and Crocodile river basins farther south. A maximum of 80 guests can stay in the camp's one- and two-bedroom cottages, all with their own verandas and fully equipped kitchens. *Bush drives, night drives.*

$$–$$$ ⬚ **Talamati.** On the banks of the normally dry N'waswitsontso River in Kruger's central section, this tranquil camp offers one of the best game-viewing experiences in the park. Grassy plains and mixed woodlands provide an ideal habitat for herds of impala, zebra, and wildebeest, as well as lion, cheetah, and elephant. Two hides (blinds) give guests a chance to watch birds and game from the camp itself. The camp can house 80 people in four- and six-bed cottages, all fully equipped. *Bush drives, night drives.*

Near Kruger National Park

$$$$ 🏨 **Malelane Sun Lodge.** This pleasant hotel offers a level of luxury that cannot be matched by rest camps inside the park. If you're prepared to pay the entrance fee to Kruger Park every day, you can have the best of Kruger and a comfortable base, too. The hotel sits just yards from the park's Malelane Gate, overlooking the Crocodile River. The focal point is a creatively sculpted swimming pool, edged with manicured lawns and served by a thatched bar area. Rooms, done in subtle greens and lit by faux miners' lanterns, are more attractive than those at Karos (☞ *above*), but the hotel lacks the bush feel that Karos captures so well. Its main advantage is its proximity to Swaziland and the casino there. ⊠ *Off N4 toward Malelane Gate (mailing address: Box 392, Malelane 1320),* ☎ *013/790–3304,* ℻ *013/790–3303. 102 rooms. Restaurant, 2 bars, room service, pool, 9-hole golf course, tennis, squash. Breakfast included. AE, DC, MC, V.*

$$–$$$$ 🏨 **Karos Lodge.** Like Malelane Lodge, this attractive hotel next to the
★   Paul Kruger Gate offers visitors a luxury alternative to the bare-bones accommodation of Kruger's rest camps. The hotel has two major advantages over its main competitor: guests have quick access to the south-central portion of the park, where game-viewing is best; and the hotel *feels* likes it's in the wilds of Africa, whereas Malelane Lodge could be anywhere. Dinner is served in a traditional *boma,* a traditional reed enclosure around a blazing campfire; rangers lead guided walks through the surrounding bush; and guests can even sleep overnight in a tree house. The rooms are connected by a raised wood walkway that passes through thick indigenous forest. Rooms have Spanish-tile floors and standard hotel furniture, as well as air-conditioning, cable TVs, and minibars. ⊠ *R536, next to Paul Kruger Gate (mailing address: Box 54, Skukuza, 1350),* ☎ *013/735–5671,* ℻ *013/735–5676. 96 doubles. 2 restaurants, 4 bars, room service, pool, tennis. Breakfast included. AE, DC, MC, V.*

Kruger A to Z

Arriving and Departing

For information about bus, train, and plane transport to Nelspruit, 50 km (31 mi) from Kruger's Numbi Gate and 64 km (40 mi) from Malelane Gate, *see* Mpumalanga A to Z *in* Chapter 3.

BY CAR

From Johannesburg, drive north on the N1 to Pretoria and then head east on the N4 to Nelspruit, where you can choose which of the park's entrances to use. The Malelane and Numbi gates, closest to Nelspruit, are about four hours from Johannesburg.

BY PLANE

Two airlines fly into the park or to nearby airports. **British Airways/Comair** (☎ 013/735–5644) has three flights daily between Johannesburg and Skukuza, the park headquarters and the largest rest camp in the park. One of these goes via Hoedspruit, a small service town close to Kruger's Orpen Gate that is also convenient for some of the private game lodges on the west side of the national park. All passengers landing at Skukuza must pay a R55 entrance fee to the park. **S.A. Airlink** (☎ 01524/8–5823) sends at least one flight a day from Johannesburg to Phalaborwa, a mining town on the edge of the park's central section.

Getting Around

BY CAR

Avis (☎ 013/735–5651) is the only car rental agency with an office at Skukuza, inside the park. If you have five or more people in your group, consider hiring a minibus. Not only do you get your own window, but you also sit much higher than in a regular car—a big plus when you're searching for game hidden in dense bush. **Avis** (☎ 01524/5169), **Budget**(☎ 01524/85404), and **Imperial** (☎ 01524/2376) have rental desks at Phalaborwa airport.

Depending on the month, rest camp gates close between 5:30 and 6:30 at night and open again between 4:30 and 6:30 in the morning. The driver of any vehicle caught on the roads between these hours is liable to a fine or prosecution.

Reservations and Fees

Admission to the park is R20 per vehicle, plus R10 for each visitor, whether you're staying overnight or longer. Reservations for all accommodations, bush drives, and wilderness trails must be made through the **National Parks Board** (⊠ Box 787, Pretoria 0001, ☎ 012/343–1991, FAX 012/343–0905).

Safari Operators

British Airways/Comair (⊠ Box 7015, Bonaero Park 1622, ☎ 011/921–0209, FAX 011/973–3913) is the biggest safari company in Kruger. Visitors can choose from a variety of tour packages ranging from quickie overnight jaunts to five-day extravaganzas that also take in the scenic splendors of the Mpumalanga Escarpment (☞ Chapter 3). Visitors fly into Skukuza on one of British Airways/Comair's regularly scheduled flights, tour the park in minibuses, and sleep in rest camps, usually Skukuza. Tour leaders are knowledgeable about the park's ecosystems, and usually know where to find animals you would probably miss on your own. British Airways/Comair and **S.A. Airlink** (⊠ Box 7529, Bonaero Park 1622, ☎ 011/394–2430, FAX 011/394–2649) also put together fly-drive packages from Johannesburg. Other operators offering **minibus tours** of Kruger Park are **Mfafa** (⊠ Box 3334, Nelspruit 1200, ☎ FAX 013/737–8398), **Springbok Atlas** (⊠ Box 10902, Johannesburg 2000, ☎ 011/493–3780, FAX 011/493–3770), and **Welcome Tours** (⊠ Box 2191, Parklands 2121, ☎ 011/328–8050, FAX 011/442–8865).

PRIVATE GAME RESERVES AND LODGES

CATEGORY	COST*
$$$$	over R2,200
$$$	R1,700–R2,200
$$	R1,000–R1,700
$	under R1,000

All prices are per person sharing a double room, including all meals, bush walks, and game drives.

Mpumalanga is the heart of South Africa's big-game country, where you'll find the country's most famous private lodges and some of the best wildlife-viewing in the world. All lodges reviewed below lie in game reserves adjoining the immense Kruger National Park (☞ *above*). In the last couple of years, most of the veterinary fences separating Kruger from these reserves have been dismantled, allowing game to roam freely back and forth.

The most famous and exclusive of these parks is the **Sabi Sand Game Reserve.** Collectively owned and managed, the 153,000-acre reserve is home to dozens of private lodges, including Mala Mala and Londolozi. The Sabi Sand fully deserves its exalted reputation, boasting perhaps the highest game density of any private reserve in southern Africa. North of the Sabi Sand lies the 59,000-acre **Manyeleti Game Reserve.** During the apartheid era, this park was reserved for blacks, who were not allowed into the country's major national reserves. It remains a public park today, although a couple of lodges have won private concessions. The **Timbavati Game Reserve,** also collectively owned and managed, lies north of the Manyeleti. The 185,000-acre Timbavati is renowned for its rare white lions, the product of a recessive gene that surfaces occasionally. Game-viewing is good up here, but it can't rival Sabi Sand, largely owing to a wide belt of mopane shrubveld, an unproductive habitat that supports little besides elephants, roan antelope, and tsessebe. Generally speaking, the Timbavati has plenty of lions and more elephant breeding herds than Sabi Sand, but it lacks a large rhino population.

All lodges will arrange pickups from the airports at Skukuza, Nelspruit, Phalaborwa or Hoedspruit. Some have their own private private airstrips and can arrange for you to fly in by light aircraft. For information about arriving in Mpumalanga, *see* Mpumalanga A to Z, *above.*

Lodges covered below are marked on the Kruger National Park map.

Sabi Sand Game Reserve

Chitwa Chitwa

Game Experience: Hunting was allowed on a neighboring farm until 1991, when it was completely banned in the area. Although the animals were once understandably skittish, they have become used to humans and vehicles. This is now excellent game-viewing terrain, and most guests see the Big Five within two to three days. Chitwa Chitwa puts a maximum of two vehicles in the field, and has traversing rights over 7,400 acres.

$ Chitwa Chitwa is a small camp in the isolated northern reaches of Sabi Sand Game Reserve. Run by a married couple, Charl and Maria Brink, this camp has a youthful spirit and places much emphasis on style. In fact, Chitwa Chitwa's whole operation resembles a beer commercial filled with beautiful people. The lodge overlooks a small dam where animals frequently come to drink. The main public area consists of a large, thatched A-frame dominated by an impressive bar. Although it has no view, the room feels very open and has comfortable couches and rattan chairs. African art and animal skulls give it an authentic bush air. The guest rooms are huge and elegant. Earth-color walls provide the backdrop for original African art, and mosquito nets, cotton linen, and ceiling fans help complete the ethnic-chic decor. Two luxury suites have their own private terraces and fireplace. ✉ *Reservations: Box 784052, Sandton 2146,* ☎ *011/883–1354 or 011/784–8131,* FAX *011/783–1858; or* ☎ *013/735–5357 (lodge). 22 guests. Bar, pool, private airstrip. AE, DC, MC, V.*

Djuma

Game Experience: Djuma has a common boundary with Kruger and access to the third-largest concession in the Sabi Sand, making its game-viewing first-class. With three vehicles in the field, it manages to show the Big Five to 70% of guests in an average stay. Pass up one morning drive in favor of a long bush walk with Jurie. You'll learn far more from him in three hours than in a month of game drives with another ranger. Djuma has traversing rights over 22,000 acres.

$$ Djuma abuts Chitwa Chitwa in the northeast corner of the Sabi Sand Game Reserve and uses the same entrance gate as its neighbor. The hosts are a husband-and-wife team, Jurie and Pippa Moolman, who are young, interesting, and passionate about their work. Jurie has a B.S. in ecology and his one-hour bush walks are by far the most informative of any in Sabi Sand. Don't come to this tiny camp for the Big Five, however. Djuma will appeal instead to visitors who are on their second or third African trip, and who really want to experience life in the bush. You'll find none of the formality that prevails at larger lodges, and the Moolmans welcome you into their extended family. Jurie and Pippa eat all their meals with you and sit together around the fire with chef Bertwell, trackers Morris and Able, and rangers Dixon and Campbell. Two friendly bull terriers roam the camp; at press time, Jurie and Pippa were raising an orphaned baby warthog. Accommodations are in thatched rondawels that have only the bare essentials. Fluorescent lights cast an ugly glow, and the wall between the bathroom and the bedroom doesn't go all the way to the ceiling. There are overhead fans but no air-conditioning. ⊠ *Reservations: Box 338, Hluvukani 1363,* ☎ *011/ 789–2722,* FAX *011/789–5160; or* ☎ *013/735–5118,* FAX *013/735–5070 (lodge). 14 guests. Bar, pool, private airstrip. AE, DC, MC, V.*

Idube

Game Experience: Nearly 70% of guests who stay 2–3 nights go away with memories of elephant, lion, leopard, buffalo, and rhino. The reason is simple: the lodge is part of a consortium of six adjoining lodges that pool their land and cooperate via radio in finding the big game. During a game drive, as many as 14 vehicles might be combing 24,700 acres, and it's almost inevitable that they will find the animals. Of the six lodges, though, Idube's rangers probably put the least emphasis on the Big Five, preferring to give guests quality sightings of a couple of these animals rather than showing just the tail end of all five.

$$ Tucked away in the Sabi Sand Game Reserve, this small lodge sits in a grassy clearing overlooking a dry stream and a water hole. Idube prides itself on its personal attention and relaxed atmosphere, and it gets a lot of repeat business as a result. Guests eat together at long tables, and the informal atmosphere generated by the staff makes this potentially awkward experience easy and fun. The public rooms make effective use of thatch, wood, and African art to create a bush ambience. The guest rooms, however, are a disappointment, built of institutional brick with tile roofs and floors. They're very large, though, and huge sliding doors give guests a good view of the surrounding bush. ⊠ *Box 2617, Northcliff 2115,* ☎ *011/888–3713,* FAX *011/888–2181. 18 guests. Bar, pool, private airstrip. AE, DC, MC, V.*

Inyati

Game Experience: Inyati is part of the same consortium of six lodges as Idube and Ulusaba, and can rely on the eyes of rangers in as many as 14 vehicles to find animals. The lodge puts more emphasis on the Big Five than Idube, and guests will probably find these animals within two hours. Many of the rangers here are black and extremely knowledgeable about the bush. George, the senior ranger, is one of the finest in Sabi Sand. The lodge also offers trips on the Sand River on a large floating pontoon powered by a silent bass motor.

$$ Set on a hillside in Sabi Sand, this lovely lodge presides over a broad sweep of lawns running down to the Sand River and a hippo pool. Life here unfolds on the thatched veranda, where guests use binoculars to scan the bush-covered hills for lion and other game. A wooden viewing deck, set under large trees by the river, offers an even better vantage point from which to see animals coming to drink.

Inyati delivers the animals and much, much more. The service is among the best of all the lodges, a welcome mix of professionalism and friendliness. A glass of champagne might materialize after a game drive, or a bottle of sherry may accompany sautéed mushrooms at lunch. The food at Inyati is excellent, head and shoulders above that at comparably priced lodges. Surprisingly, the guest rooms are nothing fancy: simple thatched cottages with rustic log furniture and Africa-inspired materials and curios. They all have air-conditioning, and rooms 1–3 and 6–9 have good river views. ⊠ *Box 38838, Booysens 2016,* ☏ *011/ 880–5950,* ℻ *011/788–2406. 20 guests. Bar, pool, gym, private airstrip. AE, DC, MC, V.*

Londolozi

Game Experience: Londolozi's rangers make a major effort to find the Big Five, but they do a good job of showing guests other animals, too. The lodge is particularly famous for its leopards, and was the first to habituate these shy animals to the presence of vehicles. Although rangers don't require formal qualifications, they undergo a rigorous two- to three-month training program and can explain animal behavior in layman's terms. They stay with sightings longer than those of most lodges, and will position their Land Rover so guests can take the best possible photos. The game density in this part of the reserve is excellent, thanks in no small part to the 19 km (12 mi) of Sand River that meander through the property. Londolozi puts a maximum of nine vehicles into the field, a tiny number when you consider they have traversing rights over 37,000 acres.

In the heart of Sabi Sand Game Reserve, Londolozi offers a better bush experience than its more famous and expensive neighbor, Mala Mala. The service is outstanding, and the quality of the accommodations and food superior. Londolozi is part of the Conservation Corporation, one of the most highly regarded wildlife companies on the continent. All waste is recycled or composted, none of the rooms uses air-conditioning, and rangers show enormous respect for the land. Londolozi comprises three camps, all within a few hundred yards of each other on a bank of the Sand River. ⊠ *Private Bag X27, Benmore 2010,* ☏ *011/784– 7077,* ℻ *011/784–7667. AE, DC, MC, V.*

$$$$ **Bush Camp.** A step down from Tree Camp (☞ *below*), this lodge employs many of the same decorative devices as its upscale neighbor but lacks its charm. The stone and thatch structure lies in a forest of ebony and boerbean and commands impressive views of the river. Dark beams, wicker furniture, and African art set the tone for the main lounge, which opens onto a broad deck supported on stilts above the riverbank. Rooms, in stone cottages hidden in the forest, differ little from those at Tree Camp. *16 guests. Bar, pool, private airstrip.*

$$$$ **Tree Camp.** Shaded by thick riverine forest, this magnificent lodge is
★ Londolozi's top-of-the-line camp. The lodge is built into the riverbank, and makes clever use of the natural rock and indigenous forest. The main living area consists of a huge, thatched A-frame with a wooden deck on stilts jutting out over the river. Guest rooms, in thatched chalets, are an exquisite blend of modern luxury and *Out of Africa* chic: track lighting captures the glow of burnished Rhodesian teak; mosquito nets drape languidly over snow-white beds; and old railway sleepers, skillfully crafted into furniture and window frames, add to the rich textures of the room. From the wraparound deck, you look out onto a world of cool green forest. *12 guests. Bar, pool, private airstrip.*

$$$ **Main Camp.** The largest of the three camps, Main Camp accommodates guests in chalets. The lodge is an enormous, thatched A-frame that extends out onto a broad wood deck above the riverbank. Fireplaces, comfy armchairs, and bookcases filled with wildlife literature give the room a warm, lived-in feel. Rising from below the deck, an enormous jackalberry tree provides cooling shade. Chalet rooms are smaller than in the satellite camps, but they are lovely nevertheless. Sliding glass doors lead onto a private deck overlooking the forest and river. Inside, rosewood chests and headboards, mosquito nets, and hessian mats work their bush magic. *20 guests. Bar, pool, private airstrip.*

Mala Mala

Game Experience: Mala Mala started the whole frenzy about the Big Five, and it still places a huge emphasis on delivering buffalo, leopard, lion, elephant, and rhino. They even give out Big Five certificates—something of a formality since the vast majority of guests see the Big Five within two days. Thankfully, the rangers don't make you feel like you're taking an animal inventory, and they stop for as long as you like at other animals, too. Mala Mala has been operating for 30 years as a photo safari lodge, and much of the game is now completely habituated to the presence of the lodge's Land Rovers, allowing them extremely close. The biggest advantage Mala Mala has over its competition, however, is its size: 54,300 acres, a full third of the Sabi Sand Game Reserve, including a 32-km (20-mi) boundary with the Kruger National Park. A maximum of 16 vehicles traverse the land at any one time. Another major bonus is the lodge's 53 km (33 mi) of river frontage, which attracts animals to the sweet grasses that grow on the banks. The dense riverine forest is an ideal habitat for leopards and birds.

Mala Mala enjoys a reputation as the best safari lodge in Africa. Its name carries a real cachet in jet-set circles, and international celebrities, politicians, and industry tycoons flock here. It's also the most expensive lodge in the country and intends to stay that way, catering to a clientele that equates stratospheric prices with quality. Without question, Mala Mala does offer a superb experience, but after many years the competition has caught up. Today, Mala Mala's guest rooms can't hold a candle to the glorious mix of bush and luxury offered by Londolozi's Tree Camp or Singita, and its food is no better than that of a half-dozen other lodges in Mpumalanga. Mala Mala's rangers are legendary—strapping young men with BS degrees who mix charm with a comprehensive knowledge of the bush and its animals. Your ranger is more than your guide to the game—he is your host and valet, hovering by your elbow to fetch you drinks, pool towels, whatever. He may eat his meals with you, and it almost comes as a surprise when he doesn't follow you into the bedroom at the end of the day. Some visitors may find the constant attention irritating. Mala Mala operates three camps, ranging from the ultraexpensive Main Camp to the budget Harry's Huts, which was up for sale at press time. ⊠ *Box 2575, Randburg 2125,* ☏ *011/789–2677,* 𝖥𝖠𝖷 *011/886–4382. AE, DC, MC, V.*

$$$$ **Main Camp.** For first-time visitors to Africa, this large camp overlooking the Sand River offers a very gentle introduction to the bush. The magnificently appointed guest rooms, in a mix of rondawels and larger suites, could be in any luxury hotel in the world. Each room has two bathrooms to make it easier for couples to prepare for early morning game drives, and such amenities as hair dryers, air-conditioning, and telephones. Beige wall-to-wall carpeting adds to its generic hotel feel. Fortunately, the main public area is steeped in African lore. Drawing on the camp's history as a hunting lodge, the lounge displays a host of animal skins and heads, old hunting spears, and antique rifles. Massive elephant tusks frame a huge fireplace, and African sculptures and reference books dot the tables. *50 guests. Bar, pool, private airstrip.*

$$ **Harry's Huts.** This is Mala Mala's budget lodge, competitively priced with most of the other lodges in Sabi Sand. The huge advantage of staying here is that you get the Mala Mala game experience at a fraction of the cost of Main Camp, which explains why it's almost always full. But that could all change—at press time the "for sale" signs were up for the lodge and its accompanying 3,700 acres of land. Tucked away in thick riverine forest, the lodge faces the Sand River across a lawn dominated by a huge marula topped by a strangler fig. But it isn't going to win any aesthetic awards. The rectangular cottages, painted in geometric Ndebele style, are roofed with a wavy composite material more often found on prefabricated huts and hideous '60s architecture. The rooms are small, rustic, and very simple. The main public areas are also plain, furnished in wicker. Lunch and breakfast are served on the veranda overlooking the river; dinner is in the boma. *16 guests. Bar, pool, private airstrip.*

$$ Kirkman's Kamp. This lodge is an absolute delight, with far more
★ charm—at a much lower price—than Main Camp. At its core stands a 1920s farmstead, a relic of the days when this area was a cattle ranch. With its corrugated-iron roof and deep verandas, it has a strong colonial feel that will appeal to Britons and those who've watched *Out of Africa* more than twice. The theme of the camp is Harry Kirkman, the manager of the cattle farm and one of the first game rangers at Kruger National Park. The main room, with high wood ceilings and creaking overhead fans, is lined with trophy heads, old maps of the Transvaal, sepia photos of Kirkman's hunting experiences, and antique rifles. It all spirits you back to another age, and the atmosphere is magical. The farmstead and guest rooms overlook a broad sweep of lawn leading down to the Sand River. The rooms, constructed in recent years, continue the colonial theme, with claw-foot tubs in the bathrooms, white wood-slat ceilings, old photos, and French doors opening onto a small veranda. *20 guests. Bar, pool, private airstrip.*

Notten's Bush Camp

Game Experience: Notten's has traversal rights over 4,900 acres but only one Land Rover, so the chances of finding the Big Five are slim. When you do find leopard, lion, or rhino, though, you don't have to share the sighting with a horde of other vehicles. A wise strategy for first-time visitors is to get your big-game fix at a large lodge and then come here to unwind and get a feel for the bush. The ranger is informative and fun, and provides a wealth of information about everything from trees to insects and birds.

$ You probably won't see the Big Five at this delightful little camp, but you may have the bush experience of your life. This means it's not ideal for a first trip to Africa unless you're combining it with other camps that can deliver game sightings. Sandwiched between Mala Mala, Londolozi, and Sabi Sabi, Notten's family-run operation is the antithesis of the animal treasure hunts conducted by its more famous neighbors. Owners Gilly and Bambi Notten personally tend to their guests, and a stay at their camp is like visiting good friends who happen to live in the bush. It's a measure of their success that 70% of their guests are return visitors. The lodge sleeps 10 people in simple cottages lit only by paraffin lamps and candles. At night, flickering torches line the walkways and a hurricane lantern on your veranda guides you back to your room.

After the evening game drive, guests meet for drinks in the boma and then dine together under the stars. The atmosphere is more like that of a dinner party than a commercial lodge, and Gilly Notten regales her guests with hilarious tales about life in the bush. Breakfast and tea are served in an open-sided shelter overlooking a grassy plain and a pan where animals come to drink. A lounge area is furnished with comfy chairs, bookshelves filled with wildlife literature, and a refrigerator where guests help themselves to drinks. The bush camp operates an honor bar—just help yourself and settle your account when you leave (you're welcome to bring your own booze, too). For weekends and major holidays, you need to make reservations about 6 months in advance; at other times, two months is usually sufficient. ✉ *Box 622 Hazyview 1242,* ☎ *013/735–5105,* ℻ *013/735–5970. 10 guests. Honor bar, pool. No credit cards.*

Sabi Sabi

Game Experience: Sabi Sabi normally puts around 12 vehicles (16 at peak times) onto its 12,300 acres, an area one-fourth the size of Mala Mala. This translates into plentiful game sightings, and it's almost certain that you will see the Big Five in two or three days. Rangers undergo a three-month training and standards here are high with keen attention paid to the interests of guests, whether they be birds, trees, or any other aspect of the local environment. Sabi Sabi's major advantage over its competitors is its 10 km (6 mi) of Sabie River frontage. Sweet grasses and dense riverine forest attract large numbers of general game, as well as birds, hippos, leopards, and crocodiles.

At the southern end of Sabi Sand Game Reserve, Sabi Sabi is the largest, and among the most expensive, private safari operations in Mpumalanga. Bush and River lodges, the more capacious of its three camps, have large public spaces that make them more like hotels than any other in the Mpumalanga private reserves. On the other hand, the exclusive Selati Lodge, which takes only 14 people, has an intimate, "old-Africa" atmosphere. What draws guests to Sabi Sabi in such large numbers is its setting along the Sabie River—the only perennial water source in Sabi Sand—and the sheer density of game supported by its highly varied habitats. That's not to say Sabi Sabi is simply about bagging the Big Five. Although you do stand an excellent chance of seeing them, there's a strong emphasis here on ecology; guests are encouraged to broaden their experience to become aware of the birds, smaller animals and myriad sounds and smells of the bush. ✉ Box 52665, Saxonwold 2132, ☎ 011/483–3939, ℻ 011/483–3799. AE, DC, MC, V.

$$$$ **Selati Lodge.** Formerly a private hunting lodge, Selati is the most intimate and most stylish of the Sabi Sabi accommodations, limited to just seven chalets. A turn-of-the-century atmosphere is created by the use of train memorabilia that recalls the now-defunct Selati railroad that once passed this way. There's no electricity and the lodge flickers at night under the light of the original shunters' oil lamps; in one thatched chalet old leather suitcases serve as a table, while in another an antique sewing machine has a new lease of life as a vanity table. Deep colored wood, cream fabrics, and mosquito nets draped over large double beds hark back to the traditional East African safari. As you'd expect with this level of luxury, each cottage is en suite but also has the added extra of its own outdoor shower. *14 guests. Bar, pool, private airstrip.*

$$$ **Bush Lodge.** This large lodge overlooks a water hole and the dry course of the Msuthlu River. The reception area leads back through attractive open courtyards to a thatched, open-sided dining area, an airy bar, and a lounge where residents can watch nature videos. Public rooms are tastefully decorated with African art and artifacts, animal skulls, and African prints. A viewing deck offers magnificent views of game at the water hole, as does the pool. Chalets, all thatched, are connected by walkways that wend through manicured lawns and beneath enormous shade trees. The five thatched suites are lovely, decorated with wicker and pretty African-print bedspreads and upholstery. Each suite has a deck overlooking the dry river course, as well as air-conditioning. Suites 20 and 21 have the best views of the water hole. *54 guests. Bar, pool, private airstrip.*

$$$ **River Lodge.** Shaded by giant jackalberry trees, this attractive lodge is smaller and more relaxed than Bush Lodge. It's popular among birders, who spend hours peering into the thick riverine forest that surrounds the camp. The lodge looks onto a dry riverbed, beyond which lies the perennial Sabie River. Guest rooms are spread out along the river. Otherwise, amenities are very similar to those at Bush Lodge. *48 guests. Bar, pool, private airstrip.*

Singita

★ **Game Experience:** At press time, Singita provided an almost identical game-viewing experience to Londolozi (☞ *above*), as its rangers were trained by Conservation Corporation and its two Land Rovers traversed the same 37,000 acres. The rangers from both lodges relay game-sightings to one another via radio.

$$$$ This is undoubtedly the most luxurious lodge in Sabi Sand Game Reserve. In its decor, atmosphere, and modus operandi, it bears a striking resemblance to Londolozi, probably because the same Conservation Corporation managed and promoted the property up to mid-1997 and at press time was still responsible for reservations. For unfettered extravagance, though, Singita leaves Londolozi far behind. Overlooking the Sand River, the lodge has eight guest cottages and six luxury suites that are each bigger than a small house. Cottages feature double-sided fireplaces, separate living rooms, enormous verandas—even an outside shower in case your inner Tarzan feels confined in the cavernous one in the bathroom. Mosquito nets, railway-sleeper furniture, masks, beads, and animal skulls round out the African decor. The six luxury suites are fronted by walls of glass opening onto an expansive teak deck with a private sunken pool that affords magnificent views of the Sand River. Rooms are lavishly furnished with a combination of antique and contemporary African pieces. In keeping with the uncompromising luxury, all accommodations have air-conditioning.

The main lodge consists of a giant, thatched A-frame and a large deck raised on stilts overlooking the river. An enormous fireplace, topped by a stuffed buffalo head, dominates the room, and zebra skins, skulls, and trophy horns complete the safari theme. At dinner, fine glass and china foster a colonial formality that works surprisingly well. ✉ *Private Bag X27, Benmore 2010,* ☎ *011/784–7077,* ℻ *011/784–7667. 24 guests. Bar, pools, private airstrip. AE, DC, MC, V.*

Ulusaba Rocklodge

Game Experience: Ulusaba belongs to the same consortium of six game lodges as Inyati and Idube (☞ *above*), so the quality of its game-viewing is superb and guests are likely to see the Big Five in 2–3 days. The most reliable way to achieve this is on one of their game drives accompanied by a ranger and tracker. If you're less goal-oriented, a walking safari with an armed guide won't deliver the same quantity of animals, but will certainly provide a more intimate experience of the wild.

$$$ Perched atop a rocky hill in Sabi Sand Game Reserve, this magnificent aerie has all the makings of the finest game lodge on the continent. The lodge is literally built into the side of a cliff, 600 ft above a water hole and the bushveld plains. The road leading up to the lodge is so steep that guests must be driven up in four-wheel-drive vehicles, and the view from the top is mind-blowing. A maze of stone walkways and steps gives the lodge a fortresslike feel, and log railings are all that prevent guests from doing a swan dive over the cliffs. In the inky blackness of an African night, Ulusaba seems to hover over the veld like a spacecraft.

The rooms provide some of the finest accommodation you will find in a game lodge. Huge windows have panoramic views of the bush, and high thatch ceilings, white stucco walls, and natural wicker create a light, airy effect. All rooms are air-conditioned. The three public areas—the pool deck, restaurant, and bar—are ingeniously built into a cliff face, and buffet meals are eaten at three long tables each in the friendly company of a ranger. The atmosphere is congenial and informal: it's the kind of place where your ranger will happily sit up till late in the bar gabbing, if that's what you want. ✉ *Box 239, Lonehill 2062,*

☎ *011/465–6646,* FAX *011/465–6649. 22 guests. Bar, pool, private airstrip. AE, DC, MC, V.*

Manyeleti Game Reserve

Honeyguide Tented Safari Camp

Game Experience: The Manyeleti Game Reserve is a public park but it's amazingly underused, and you will see very few other vehicles. The park's grassy plains and mixed woodland attract good herds of general game and their attendant predators. Honeyguide's competent rangers have all completed training courses or worked in other lodges. You can either opt for traditional game-viewing in open-air vehicles at the main camp or book into Outpost Camp where all safaris are on foot, during which you track animals accompanied by a ranger. You'll probably see fewer animals than from a vehicle, but you'll come back with a much better feel for the bush. Honeyguide has exclusive rights over 12,300 acres, but its two vehicles can also traverse almost the entire reserve.

This tented camp offers the best value of all the Mpumalanga lodges, especially if you stay at their budget Outpost Camp, which specializes in highly regarded foot safaris. The camp brilliantly achieves the delicate balance of combining professional service with a casual atmosphere—a welcome relief if the stuffy overattentiveness of some of the more upscale lodges isn't to your taste. Both the main camp and the rustic bush camp lie in the 59,280-acre Manyeleti Game Reserve adjoining Kruger National Park. ⊠ *Box 781959, Sandton 2146,* ☎ *011/880–3912,* FAX *011/447–4326. MC, V.*

$ **Main Camp.** Honeyguide was one of the first lodges to use the luxury
★ East African-style safari tents that have since become so popular. But to call these comfortable canvas homes tents is really an insult, because they have everything a more conventional room does while giving guests the true feel of camping in the wild. Each tent is large enough to accommodate two beds, a cupboard, clothing shelves, and battery-operated lights. A bathroom en suite, accessed through the back zip of the tent, provides complete privacy, as well as hot showers. Four of the 12 tents are larger and a little more expensive than the others and have baths as well. A shaded wood deck extends from the front of the tent and overlooks a dry riverbed and thick riverine forest. Despite its economy price tag, the camp has some true luxury touches: tea or coffee served in your tent at dawn, and a fully stocked bar on each vehicle for sundowner cocktails. *24 guests. Bar, pool, private airstrip.*

$ **Outpost Camp.** Representing a growing trend among the Mpumalanga private game reserves, this intimate and thoroughly rustic camp is light years away from the large formal lodges of Sabi Sand. Don't expect smartly decked-out waiters, ethnic-chic decor, or pampering. But for a raw experience of the bush, you'll find this camp and its rock-bottom price tag hard to beat. Four two-bed tents have showers and toilets en suite that are open to the African sky, and meals are cooked by a chef over an open fire. If you've switched off your cell phone and want to leave civilization behind, the real joy here is that there are no vehicles—all your game outings are done on foot. *8 guests. Bar, private airstrip.*

Timbavati Game Reserve

M'Bali

Game Experience: Rhino are scarce in this part of the Timbavati, so it's unlikely you will find all of the Big Five. However, most guests do see elephant and lion, and frequently buffalo. M'Bali places a stronger emphasis on walking and the bush experience than do most lodges, and

f a game drive at least
elephant almost every
ed and knowledgeable
ame drives, the lodge
t rangers coordinate
dge, Motswari. They
4,600 acres.

f the Timbavati Game
enjoys the best view
w the lodge daily in
to the Mpumalanga
e to the guest tents,
ss the image of some
ded to re-create the
uito nets shroud the
s, a closet, and elec-
nt from the sun and
hroom, underneath
airs. At night, after
herous. Elderly vis-
cottage instead. ⊠
011/463–1992. 18

tertaining, well-in-
ecifically tell them
focus on the Big
mous territory of
em. In general, the
alo than the Sabi
tah. Ngala's main
major ecozones—
, and riverine for-
ls. Unfortunately,
opane belt, which
o reach the other
mopane and then
an hour. For the
ing than those of-

Timbavati Game
a offers the same
above). The main
at are refreshing
dges. Track light-
ant counterpoint
ouble-sided fire-
ounge filled with
Dinner at Ngala
nclosed boma or
and silver place
cottages, set in
ach with its own
arpeting, thatch,
rivate Bag X27,
E, DC, MC, V.

Tanda Tula Bus

★ **Game Experience:**
Big Five, and you're
day stay. The cam
acres, but two vehi
help finding game
phant, lion, and wil
are well trained an

$$ This luxury tented
than almost any ot
like it's coming fro
in East African saf
leaving you staring
effect is magical a
ventional room. C
by far the most lu
their own wood d
Each tent is beauti
from colorful Afr
and dresser. An os
ern touch. A larg
lounge, where bre
Tanda Tula's bush
with the moon re
1380, ☎ FAX 015
Western Cape, ☎
pool. AE, DC, M

Umlani Bush

Game Experienc
an armed ranger
morning. Anima
to get up close a
thrill of seeing b
than compensate
ecology. In the e
drive. Umlani's
cooperates with
Nevertheless, yo

$ Snoozing under
camp offers visi
The focus here
big game, and a
huts made from
tain. The bed
each room has
open to the sky
add to the bush
your videocam
feel like you're
relaxed. ⊠ *Bo*
012/329-6441

they encourage guests to do a long walk instead of a game drive at least once during their stay. In winter, guests encounter elephant almost every day on these walks. The rangers are all highly qualified and knowledgeable about the animals and the area's ecosystem. On game drives, the lodge puts a maximum of two vehicles into the field, but rangers coordinate game-sightings with three vehicles from a sister lodge, Motswari. They have traversing rights over an enormous area of 34,600 acres.

$$ This beautiful tented camp lies at the northern tip of the Timbavati Game Reserve. Built on a hillside overlooking a dam, it enjoys the best view of any tented camp—elephants come to bathe below the lodge daily in winter, and on a clear day you can see all the way to the Mpumalanga Escarpment. Sand pathways run down the hillside to the guest tents, on raised wood platforms supported by stilts. Dismiss the image of some poky little tent in a campsite. These are huge, intended to re-create the spirit of the old East African hunting safaris. Mosquito nets shroud the beds, and each tent is equipped with bedside tables, a closet, and electric lights. An A-frame thatch shelter shields the tent from the sun and rain. The only drawback is the location of the bathroom, underneath the wood deck and reached by way of very steep stairs. At night, after the electricity is turned off, these stairs become treacherous. Elderly visitors should ask to stay in the lodge's single stone cottage instead. ⊠ *Box 67865, Bryanston 2021,* ☎ *011/463–1990,* ⅲ *011/463–1992. 18 guests. Bar, pool, private airstrip. AE, DC, MC, V.*

Ngala

Game Experience: Ngala's rangers are first-class: entertaining, well-informed, and attentive to guests' needs. Unless you specifically tell them you want to concentrate on birds or trees, they do focus on the Big Five. And with eight vehicles traversing an enormous territory of 35,800 acres, you'll have a good chance of seeing them. In general, the Timbavati sees bigger herds of elephant and buffalo than the Sabi Sand, but it's not as good for leopard, rhino, and cheetah. Ngala's main advantage over Sabi Sand is its proximity to four major ecozones—mopane shrubveld, marula combretum, acacia scrub, and riverine forest—that provide habitats for a wide range of animals. Unfortunately, Ngala sits at the northern end of the property in the mopane belt, which is unproductive and barren for much of the year. To reach the other ecozones, you must drive 30 minutes through the mopane and then 30 minutes back, shortening your game-viewing by an hour. For the same reason, bush walks from camp are less interesting than those offered in Sabi Sand.

$$$ This exclusive lodge lies in mopane shrubveld in the Timbavati Game Reserve. Part of the Conservation Corporation, Ngala offers the same level of professionalism and service as Londolozi (☞ *above*). The main lodge has a Mediterranean style and sophistication that are refreshing after the hunting-lodge decor espoused by so many lodges. Track lighting and dark-slate flooring and tables provide an elegant counterpoint to high thatched ceilings and African art. A massive, double-sided fireplace dominates the lodge, opening on one side onto a lounge filled with comfy sofas and chairs and on the other a dining room. Dinner at Ngala is more formal than at most lodges, served in a reed-enclosed boma or in a tree-filled courtyard lit by lanterns; crystal glasses and silver place settings enhance the sophisticated atmosphere. Guest cottages, set in mopane shrubveld with no views, contain two rooms, each with its own thatched veranda. Rooms make extensive use of hemp carpeting, thatch, and dark beams to create an appealing warmth. ⊠ *Private Bag X27, Benmore 2010,* ☎ *011/784–7077,* ⅲ *011/784–7667. AE, DC, MC, V.*

Tanda Tula Bush Camp

★ **Game Experience:** Tanda Tula does not place a strong emphasis on the Big Five, and you're unlikely to see all these animals in a two- or three-day stay. The camp operates only two vehicles on an area of 14,800 acres, but two vehicles from other lodges sometimes provide additional help finding game. This part of the Mpumalanga is known for its elephant, lion, and wild dog, but rhino are scarce. Tanda Tula's game rangers are well trained and extremely attentive to the desires of their guests.

$$ This luxury tented camp in the Timbavati brings you closer to the bush than almost any other lodge. When lions roar nearby, the noise sounds like it's coming from under the bed. The reason is simple: guests sleep in East African safari-style tents with huge window flaps that roll up, leaving you staring at the bush largely through mosquito netting. The effect is magical and much more rewarding than sleeping in a conventional room. Of the tented camps in Mpumalanga, Tanda Tula is by far the most luxurious. Its 12 tents, all with bathrooms en suite and their own wood decks, overlook the dry bed of the Nhlaralumi River. Each tent is beautifully decorated with wicker chairs, bedspreads made from colorful African materials, and elegant side tables, a cupboard, and dresser. An oscillating fan and electric lights add a convenient modern touch. A large, open-sided thatched shelter serves as the main lounge, where breakfast and lunch are served. Of particular note are Tanda Tula's bush braais, held in the dry bed of the Nhlaralumi River with the moon reflecting off the bright sand. ⊠ *Box 151, Hoedspruit 1380,* ☏ 𝕱𝕬𝕏 *01528/3–2435. Reservations: Box 32, Constantia 7848, Western Cape,* ☏ *021/794–6500,* 𝕱𝕬𝕏 *021/794–7605. 24 guests. Bar, pool. AE, DC, MC, V.*

Umlani Bushcamp

Game Experience: Umlani places a strong emphasis on bush walks, and an armed ranger usually leads guests on a two- to three-hour walk each morning. Animals run from humans who are on foot, so don't expect to get up close and personal with an elephant. However, the visceral thrill of seeing big game while on foot, even from 150 ft away, more than compensates—plus you learn a tremendous amount about bushveld ecology. In the evening, a ranger takes guests on a conventional game drive. Umlani's sole vehicle has traversal rights over 24,700 acres and cooperates with Tanda Tula and another lodge in the search for game. Nevertheless, you would be lucky to see all of the Big Five during a stay.

$ Snoozing under enormous shade trees in the Timbavati, this superb bush camp offers visitors a very different experience from the other lodges. The focus here is on a bush experience, as opposed to the search for big game, and accommodations are accordingly rustic. Guests sleep in huts made from reeds and thatch, and the door is a simple reed curtain. The bed—you do get one—is protected by a mosquito net, and each room has its own bathroom and shower en suite, exhilaratingly open to the sky. There's no electricity here, but the kerosene lanterns add to the bush ambience. Despite this, there are facilities to charge your videocamera battery. It's not everyone's cup of tea, but you really feel like you're out in the African wilds, and the atmosphere is fun and relaxed. ⊠ *Box 26350, Arcadia, Pretoria 0007,* ☏ *012/329–3765,* 𝕱𝕬𝕏 *012/329–6441. 10 guests. Bar, pool. AE, DC, MC, V.*

4 Cape Town and the Peninsula

Backed by the familiar shape of Table Mountain, Cape Town presides over a coastline of unsurpassed beauty: of mountains edging the sea, miles of beaches, and 18th-century wineries napping under giant oaks. Modern South Africa was born here, and the city is filled with reminders of its historic role in overseas trade between Europe and the East. Today Cape Town is home to the country's best museums, restaurants, and hotels.

IF YOU VISIT ONLY ONE PLACE in South Africa, make it Cape Town. Sheltered beneath the familiar shape of Table Mountain, this historic city is instantly recognizable, and few cities in the world possess its beauty and style.

A stroll through the lovely city center reveals Cape Town's three centuries as the sea link between Europe and the East. Elegant Cape Dutch buildings, with their whitewashed gables, abut imposing monuments to Britain's imperial legacy. In the Moslem quarter, the call to prayer echoes from minarets while the sweet tang of Malay curry wafts through the cobbled streets. And everywhere, whether you're eating outdoors at one of the country's best restaurants or sipping wine atop Table Mountain, you sense—correctly—that this is South Africa's most urbane, civilized city.

As impressive as all this is, though, what you will ultimately recall about Cape Town is the sheer grandeur of its setting—Table Mountain rising above the city bowl, the sweep of the bay, and mountains cascading into the sea. You will likely spend more time marveling at the views than anything else.

The city lies at the northern end of the Cape peninsula, a 15-km (25-mi) tail of mountains that hangs down from the tip of Africa, ending at the Cape of Good Hope. Drive 15 minutes in any direction and you will lose yourself in a stunning landscape of 18th-century Cape Dutch manors, historic wineries, and white-sand beaches backed by sheer mountains. Francis Drake wasn't exaggerating when he called the peninsula "the fairest Cape we saw in the whole circumference of the earth," and he would have little cause to change his opinion today. You could spend a week exploring just the city and peninsula, and a lifetime discovering the nearby wonders of the Western Cape (☞ Chapter 5), including the Winelands, one of the great highlights of a trip to South Africa.

Capetonians know they have it good and look with condescending sympathy on those with the misfortune to live elsewhere. On weekends they hike, sail, and bike in their African Eden. At night they congregate at the city's fine restaurants, fortified with the Cape wine that plays such an integral role in the city's life. Laid-back Cape Town has none of the frenetic energy of hard-nosed Johannesburg. Maybe that's because Cape Town doesn't need to unearth its treasures—the beauty of the place is right in front of you as soon as you roll out of bed.

In this respect the city is often likened to San Francisco, but Cape Town has what San Francisco can never have—history and the mountain. Table Mountain is key to Cape Town's identity. It dominates the city in a way that's difficult to comprehend until you visit. In the afternoon, when creeping fingers of cloud spill over the mountain and reach toward the city, the whole town seems to shiver and hold its breath. Depending upon which side of the mountain you live on, it even dictates when the sun will rise and set.

Indeed, the city owes its very existence to the mountain. The freshwater streams running off its slopes were what first prompted early explorers to anchor here. In 1652 Jan van Riebeeck and 90 Dutch settlers established a revictualing station for ships of the Dutch East India Company (VOC) on the long voyage east. The settlement represented the first European toehold in southern Africa, and Cape Town is still sometimes called the Mother City.

Those first Dutch settlers soon ventured into the interior to establish their own farms, and 140 years later the settlement supported a population of 20,000 whites as well as 25,000 slaves brought from distant lands like Java, Madagascar, and Guinea. Its position on the strategic cusp of Africa, however, meant that the colony never enjoyed any real stability. The British, entangled in a global dogfight with Napoléon, occupied the Cape twice, first in 1795 and then permanently in 1806. With them they brought additional slaves from Ceylon, India, and the Philippines. Destroyed or assimilated in this colonial expansion were the indigenous Khoikhoi (Hottentots), who once herded their cattle here and foraged along the coast.

For visitors used to hearing about South Africa's problems in black and white, Cape Town will come as a surprise—the city is black, white, and colored. Today more than 1 million coloreds—the term used to describe people of mixed race, of Khoikhoi or slave descent—live in the city and give it a distinct spice.

Perhaps the greatest celebration of this colored culture is the annual Coon Carnival, when thousands of wild celebrants take to the streets in vibrant costumes to sing *moppies* (vaudeville-style songs), accompanied by banjos, drums, and whistles. The carnival is the most visible reminder of a way of life that saw its finest flowering in District Six, a predominantly colored neighborhood on the fringes of the city center whose destruction was a tragic result of apartheid in Cape Town. District Six was a living festival of music and soul, a vibrant community bound by poverty, hope, and sheer joie de vivre. In 1966 the Nationalist government invoked the Group Areas Act, rezoned District Six a whites-only area, and razed it. The scars of that event still run deep. A new museum seeks to recapture the mood of the lost community, and a move is afoot to build low-cost housing in the area.

Other legacies of apartheid fester. Each year for decades, thousands of blacks have streamed to the Cape in search of work, food, and a better life. They end up in the squatter camps of Crossroads and Khayelitsha, names that once flickered across TV screens around the globe. Many visitors never see this side of South Africa, but if you make the one-hour trip to the Winelands along the N2, you can't miss the pitiful shacks built on shifting dunes as far as the eye can see. After the First-World luxury of the city center, the sight is sobering. A tour of these areas offers a glimpse of the old South Africa—and the enormous challenges facing the new one.

Pleasures and Pastimes

Beaches

All year-round, the Cape's beaches on both the Atlantic and Indian oceans are truly legendary and with good reason. They stretch endlessly and you can walk for miles without seeing a fast-food outlet or cool-drink stand. But you will see seagulls, dolphins, penguins, and whales (in season). Forget swimming on the Atlantic side—even a dip-in will freeze your toes. The heat plus the scent of coconut-oiled beauties make for a heady atmosphere. The "in" crowd flocks to Clifton, a must for sunbathers. Although Camps Bay, Llandudno, and Sandy Bay have their attractions, if it's swimming and surfing you're into, take yourself to the warmer waters of Muizenberg, Sunrise Beach, Fish Hoek, and Simonstown. Windsurfers congregate at Milnerton and Blouberg, where several world championships are held and there's great sailing, surfing, wind, and views. The False Bay ocean is warm and the surfing waves are great.

Don't miss Boulders or Miller's Point for snorkeling among great rocks in secluded coves and pools.

History

Wherever you are, there's history in the air. Take a cultural tour of the townships and Bo-Kaap and District Six to see communities that are blossoming as they emerge from the yoke of apartheid. Try to get onto a Robben Island tour that lands you on the island so that you can see for yourself how Nelson Mandela and those thousands imprisoned for so-called political offenses lived for nearly three decades under the old regime. Cape Town's small, so walking tours are easy and you can pack in a lot in just a few hours.

Markets

Cape Town has the best markets in the country—informal, creative, artistic, with a good selection of the usual tatty or really splendid African curios. The Waterfront markets are tremendous, and serious goody hunters might strike gold at the Greenpoint open-air market on a Saturday. Greenmarket Square's terrific: Look out for rubber-tire sandals, to be found only in Cape Town. The Rondesbosch Park craft market on the first Saturday of the month has unusual items, as has the Constantia market, held on summer weekends. Markets are an intriguing alternative way to shop, and you can pick up amazing local things. The locals are friendly and enjoy talking about everything from the lousy traffic in Cape Town to whether or not Parliament should remain here.

Picnics

Cape Town is the ultimate picnic land. Pack a basket and head off to Zeekoeivlei or Rondevlei for bird-watching, or to Chart Farm to pick roses. Or you can picnic on one of the farmsteads in Constantia, the Tokai forests, Silvermine, or the Constantia mountain. Capetonians love evening beach picnics on long summer days: Choose Clifton, Camps Bay, or Hout Bay and watch the pink sun turn crimson before it slips below the horizon.

Walking and Hiking

Cape Town is a walker's paradise. The downtown area is fascinating, and the nearby country walks are a joy. Climb up Table Mountain, meander through Kirstenbosch Botanical Gardens, stroll along the beaches, or walk through nature reserves such as Cape Point and Koeberg. The latter is past Blouberg near the great Atlantis sand dunes (where you can practice sand skiing if you're interested), and here you'll find blesbok and bat-eared foxes and spectacular dune scenery. For serious hikers there are mountain trails galore. If you're into climbing, go with the Mountain Club. Cape Town's wilderness areas really are wild, so you should always have a guide. It's safer.

EXPLORING CAPE TOWN

Cape Town is surprisingly small. The center of the city is known as the City Bowl, cradled between the sea and a semicircle of mountains, including Table Mountain. An orderly street grid and the constant view of Table Mountain make it almost impossible to get lost. Major arteries running toward the mountain from the sea are Adderley, Loop, and Long streets; among the major cross streets are Strand, Longmarket, and Wale. The heart of the historic city—where you'll find many of the museums and major buildings—is Government Avenue, a pedestrian mall at the top of Adderley Street. St. George's Mall, another major pedestrian thoroughfare, runs the length of commercial Cape Town.

Once you leave the City Bowl, orienting yourself becomes trickier. As you face Table Mountain from the city, the distinctive mountain on your left is Devil's Peak; on the right are Signal Hill and Lion's Head. Signal Hill takes its name from a gun fired there every day at noon. If you look carefully you will see that Signal Hill forms the body of a reclining lion, while the maned Lion's Head looks south past Table Mountain. On the other side of Signal Hill and Lion's Head lie the Atlantic communities of Sea Point, Clifton, and Camps Bay. Heading the other way, around Devil's Peak, you come to Cape Town's exclusive southern suburbs—Rondebosch, Newlands, Claremont, and Constantia. The happening Waterfront lies north of the City Bowl on the other side of the horrendous freeways that separate the docks from downtown.

The Cape peninsula extends 40 km (25 mi) below the city, culminating at Cape Point in the Cape of Good Hope Nature Reserve. A spine of mountains runs down the center of the peninsula, crowding most of the towns and roads onto a narrow shelf next to the sea. The east side of the peninsula is washed by the waters of False Bay. Here, connected by a coastal road, lie the resort towns of Muizenberg, St. James, Kalk Bay, and Fish Hoek, as well as the naval base at historic Simon's Town. The western shores of the peninsula are wilder and emptier, pounded by huge Atlantic swells. In addition to the tiny hamlets of Scarborough, Kommetjie, and Noordhoek, you'll find the fishing port of Hout Bay and the dizzying heights of Chapman's Peak, one of the most awe-inspiring drives in the region.

Great Itineraries

IF YOU HAVE 2 DAYS

Do an early morning city walk to see the sights or take in a half-day city tour. You will see Parliament, the Gardens, the Castle, City Hall, the Nico Malan, and other historical highlights.

For lunch, go to the V & A Waterfront and eat at one of the outside restaurants if the weather's good, inside if it's not. Visit the various Waterfront attractions, including the Aquarium (a must), the *Victoria Museum Ship,* and the SAS *Somerset.* Go to the Robben Island Museum at Quay Five and book a ticket for Robben Island for the following day. Take the Penny Ferry across the harbor and keep your eyes open for frolicking seals. Then go to the IMAX Theatre to see a show. If you don't dine at the Green Dolphin and listen to terrific jazz, then move away from the Waterfront and go uptown.

Perhaps have dinner in one of the Cape's many excellent restaurants and then go to the theater, ballet, or opera at the Nico Malan, or at the Baxter. Alternatively, take in a movie and then go to an African jazz club.

Early next morning be at the V & A Waterfront in good time to take your Robben Island tour, which should last about three hours. On your return, go straight to the Lower Cableway and ride to the summit of Table Mountain. Have lunch in the restaurant and hike one of the trails (walks last about an hour).

When you come down from the mountain, drive to Camps Bay and dine at one of a beach-view restaurant. Then kick off your shoes and walk on the beach.

To round out the evening you might want to take in a show at the Playhouse Theatre in Camps Bay.

IF YOU HAVE 5 OR MORE DAYS

Spend the first day or two exploring Cape Town. There's a lot to see. Pop into museums and galleries, visit Bo-Kaap and wander around this old Cape Malay area with its cobblestone streets and quaint buildings. On the afternoon of the second day, browse the Waterfront. Plan ahead to visit Robben Island, as ferry seats can be booked a day or two in advance.

On the morning of Day 3, explore Robben Island and, on your return, lunch at the Waterfront. In the afternoon you might visit the Castle, have high tea at the Mount Nelson hotel and dinner at one of the stunning restaurants in the Kloof Nek area. There's also plenty of good jazz in this part of the world.

On Day 4, drive out to Constantia and the Winelands. Visit the estates, enjoy the countryside, do a little winetasting, have lunch, then in the afternoon drive over Constantia Neck to Hout Bay. Go to the harbor and take an early afternoon cruise to Seal Island. Or take the booze cruise to Clifton and enjoy the spectacular sight of the beaches, and the Twelve Apostle Mountains with Table Mountain in the background. Perhaps have dinner on this side of the mountain, at Greenpoint, Sea Point, or Camps Bay.

Day 5 is penguin day. You simply have to take the trek—it's a fairly long drive—and wend your way along the False Bay coast to Boulders, where you'll find the penguins in profusion. This is one of the few sites in the world where these comical little creatures live and breed. Then go on a little farther for a seafood lunch at Millers Point. In the afternoon, grab your map and follow the road to the Cape Point reserve, and, of course, Cape Point. If you can make your way through the tourist buses, you can climb to the peak of the point, or take the shuttle train. It looks as if this is where the Indian and Atlantic oceans meet, but of course it's not. No matter, it's a romantic tip of Africa.

If you still have a few days, drive up the West Coast to Langebaan and into the interior to Darling, where Pieter Dirk Uys, South Africa's most beloved and wicked satirical actor, has a theater and restaurant, Evita's Peron, in the converted Darling railway station.

Also visit Stellenbosch, cradle of the Afrikaner nation, Franschoek, and Paarl, with its sparkling pearl-like rock. There are farm stalls, wine estates, and markets galore along these country roads.

Table Mountain

Along with Victoria Falls (☞ Chapter 8), Table Mountain is one of southern Africa's most beautiful and impressive natural wonders. The views from its summit can reduce you to speechless awe. The mountain rises more than 3,500 feet above the city, its flat top visible to sailors 65 km (40 mi) out to sea. In summer, when the southeaster blows, moist air from False Bay funnels over the mountain, condensing in the colder, higher air to form the tablecloth of cloud. Legend attributes this low-lying cloud to a pipe-smoking contest between the Devil and Jan van Hunks, a pirate who settled on Devil's Peak. The Devil lost, and the cloud serves to remind him of his defeat.

The first recorded ascent of Table Mountain was made in 1503 by Portuguese admiral Antonio de Saldanha, who wanted to get a better sense of the topography of the Cape peninsula. He couldn't have asked for a better view. In one direction you look down on today's city, cradled between Lion's Head and Devil's Peak. In another you see the crescent of sand at Camps Bay, sandwiched between the sea and the granite faces of the Twelve Apostles. Farther south the peninsula trails off toward the Cape of Good Hope, its mountains forming a ragged spine between False Bay and the empty vastness of the Atlantic. No matter where you look, you just can't get over how high you feel.

Despite being virtually surrounded by the city, Table Mountain is a remarkably unspoiled wilderness. Most of the Cape peninsula's 2,200 species of flora are found on the mountain, including magnificent examples of Cape Town's wild indigenous flowers, known as fynbos, silver trees, and red and blue disas. The best time to see the mountain in flower is between September and March, although you can be sure to find some flowers whatever the time of year. Long gone are the days when Cape lions, zebras, and hyenas roamed the mountain, but you can still glimpse grysboks (small antelopes), baboons, and rock dassies (hyrax).

Atop the mountain, well-marked trails offering 10- to 40-minute jaunts crisscross the Western Table near the Cableway. Two excellent new walks with spectacular views were opened to coincide with the launch of the new Cableway system in September 1997. Many other trails lead to the other side of Platteklip Gorge and into the mountain's catchment area, where you'll find reservoirs, hidden streams, and more incredible views. Be aware, though, that weather on the mountain can change quickly. Even if you're making only a short visit, take a sweater. If you're planning an extended hike, carry water and plenty of warm clothing.

During the warm summer months Capetonians are fond of taking picnic hampers up the mountain. The best time to do this is after 5: Some say sipping a glass of chilled Cape wine while watching the sun set from Table Mountain is one of life's great joys. Otherwise, you can eat at either of the two restaurants at the top of the mountain. The smaller bistro serves excellent Mediterranean-style meals, with an accent on local specialties. The large self-service restaurant gives you a good choice of South African–style food and includes a dish of the day and favorites such as quiche, Malay curry, and babotie. As you might expect, both restaurants offer a good wine list with local wines predominating. For noshers, there's a convenient fast-food kiosk. The restaurants are open from 8 AM until late (the time of the last cable car varies according to how many visitors there are).

You have only two ways of reaching the top of the mountain: Walk, or take the Cableway.

Riding the Cableway
Cable cars take five minutes to reach the summit. There used to be terrible congestion at the Lower Cable station, but the building of the new Cableway, with four enlarged revolving cars that give a 180° view, has eased things somewhat. You cannot make reservations for the Cableway, and so should arrive as early as possible. In peak season (mid-November–mid-March) you might wait as long as four hours to board. Capetonians enjoy taking the Cableway up the mountain at about 4 to watch the glorious sunset and have a glass of wine. They picnic or eat at one of the restaurants, then, after dinner, take in the view of Cape Town by night. Although keep in mind that the weather changes four times a day, so you might find yourself on top of Table Mountain covered in clouds, without a view. To buy tickets, you must appear in person at the Lower Cableway. In peak season, the Cableway is open from 8 AM until late (the last car might leave the top of the mountain at 1 AM). Winter hours are shorter. Call the Cableway company for a schedule. Several tour operators include a trip up the mountain in their schedules. (☞ Guided Tours *in* Cape Town A to Z, *below*). ⊠ *Tafelberg Rd.,* ☎ *021/24–5148.* ☜ *R55 round-trip, R28 one-way, under 4 free.*

The Lower Cableway lies on the slopes of Table Mountain near its western end. It's a long way from the city on foot, and you're better off traveling by car, taxi, or bus. To get there from the City Bowl, take Buitengracht Street toward the mountain. Once you cross Camp Street, Buitengracht becomes Kloof Nek Road. Follow Kloof Nek Road through the residential neighborhood of Gardens to a traffic circle; turn left on Tafelberg Road and follow signs to the Lower Cableway.

A Golden Arrow bus (the destination placard reads KLOOF NEK) leaves every 30 minutes from OK Bazaars on Adderley Street and stops at the traffic circle on Kloof Nek, about 2 km (1.2 mi) from the Cableway. Transfer there to the Cableway Shuttle, which meets the bus. The whole trip takes 30 minutes and costs R3.

A taxi from the City Bowl to the Lower Cableway costs about R30.

Walking up the Mountain
More than 300 walking trails—some easy, some insanely difficult—wend their way up the mountain. The two most popular set out from the Kirstenbosch National Botanic Gardens (☞ *below*) and from Tafelberg Road (via Platteklip Gorge), the road that leads past the Lower Cableway. Both are strenuous hikes rather than climbs, and the ascent takes two or three hours. Table Mountain can be dangerous if you're not familiar with the terrain. If you don't feel comfortable tackling the mountain alone, contact one of the many services offering guided walks to the top, including the **Cape Town School of Mountaineering** (021/61–9673), **Guided Ascents in Africa (GAIA)** (021/448–2697 or 082/494–9635), **Walk to the Top** (021/438–7206), and **The Leading Edge** (021/797–3366 or 803/309–1554). Guided tours take two to seven hours; expect to pay R50–R300 per person, which includes descent by cable car.

The City Bowl

Numbers in the text correspond to numbers in the margin and on the Cape Town map.

A Good Walk
Begin your walk at **Captour's Tourist Rendezvous Travel Centre** ①. At no time during the walk will you be more than 15 minutes from this starting point. Head up Adderley Street toward the **Golden Acre** ② shopping center. Turn left on Darling Street and head toward the **Castle of Good Hope** ⑤ and the **Grand Parade** ③. Just across the way is the beautiful former **City Hall** ④. Retrace your steps toward Adderley Street, turning left one block before you get there onto Parliament Street, to reach the austere **Groote Kerk** ⑥. The Groote Kerk faces Church Square, now a parking lot, where churchgoers used to unharness their oxen. On the skinny traffic island in the middle of Spin Street is a concrete plaque marking the **Slave Tree** ⑦. A brass plaque commemorating the slave tree and a cross section of the tree itself are on display in the **South African Cultural Museum** ⑧, next door on Adderley Street. Next door stand the **Houses of Parliament** ⑨. Walk around the back of the parliament buildings and head up Government Avenue, a wide and attractive squirrel-filled, tree-lined walkway that leads past many of the country's most important institutions and museums. The huge white building on your right is the **South African Library** ⑩, the oldest in the country. Continue up Government Avenue into the loveliest part of the city, a swath of greenery crisscrossed by promenades. It's a great place to sit on a bench and watch the world go by. At the center of this green lung is the **Company's Gardens** ⑪. Continue along Government Avenue, and walk past Parliament to the **Tuynhuys** ⑫. The **South African National Gallery** ⑬ stands farther up Government Avenue.

On parallel Queen Victoria Street you'll come across the **South African Museum** ⑭. The temple in front of the South African Museum is the **Delville Wood Monument** ⑮. Directly across Government Avenue from the South African Museum is the **Jewish Museum** ⑯ and next door the imposing **Great Synagogue** ⑰, South Africa's mother synagogue. Continue up Government Avenue to **Bertram House** ⑱. Head back down Government Avenue and cut across the front of the South African Museum to **Queen Victoria Street** ⑲. For something completely different, head down Bloem to **Long Street** ⑳. Turn left on Wale Street and walk four blocks to the **Bo-Kaap** ㉑. Near the corner of Wale and Rose stands the **Bo-Kaap Museum** ㉒. Retrace your steps down Wale Street to **St. George's Cathedral** ㉓. Across Wale is the entrance to **St. George's Mall** ㉔. From there, turn left onto **Church Street** ㉕. Head down Burg Street to reach **Greenmarket Square** ㉖, the center of the city since 1710. The **Old Town House** ㉗ faces the square. Work your way back to Long Street and walk toward the sea. When you reach Strand Street, turn right to reach the **Koopmans–De Wet House** ㉘.

Sights to See

Adderley Street. Originally named Heerengracht after a canal that ran the length of the avenue, this street has always been Cape Town's principal thoroughfare. It was once the favored address of the city's leading families, and its oak-shaded sidewalks served as a promenade for those who wanted to see and be seen. By the mid-19th century the oaks had all been chopped down and the canal covered, as Adderley Street became the main commercial street. By 1908 it had become such a busy thoroughfare that the city fathers paved it with wooden blocks in an attempt to dampen the noise of countless wagons, carts, and hooves.

⑱ **Bertram House.** Built around 1840, this is the only surviving Georgian brick town house in Cape Town. Once a common sight in the city, these boxlike, two-story houses were a response by the English community to Cape Dutch architecture. The projecting front porch was intended to shield the house from the worst effects of the frequent southeasters. The collection of furniture, silver, jewelry, and Chinese porcelain recaptures the look and feel of an early 19th-century home. The guide available at the entrance describes the entire collection. ⊠ *Government Ave. and Orange St.,* ☎ *021/24–9381.* ⊠ *R1.* ☉ *Tues.–Sat. 9:30–4:30.*

NEED A BREAK? Government Avenue ends opposite the famous gateway to the **Mount Nelson** hotel, complete with two pith-helmeted gatekeepers (⊠ 76 Orange St., ☎ 021/23–1000), which was erected in 1924 to welcome the Prince of Wales on his visit to the Cape. The "Nellie" remains Cape Town's most fashionable, expensive, and genteel social venue. More importantly, it serves the city's best high tea, although the new Table Bay Hotel at the V&A Waterfront also provides a memorable version. Both hotels provide a pastry selection to tempt the most jaded palate.

★ ㉑ **Bo-Kaap.** In the late 17th and early 18th centuries, this district was the historic home of the city's Muslim population brought from the East as slaves. Today, the area remains strongly Muslim, and it's fascinating to wander the narrow cobbled lanes past mosques and colorful, flat-roofed houses. Many of the homes combine elements of Cape Dutch and British architecture, and altogether they represent the largest collection of pre-1840 architecture in South Africa. The Bo-Kaap is also known as the Malay quarter, despite the fact that its inhabitants originated from all over the East, including the Indonesian archipelago, India, and Madagascar.

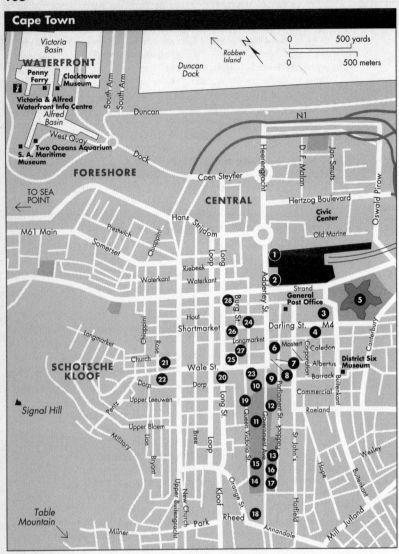

Cape Town

㉒ **Bo-Kaap Museum.** Built in the 18th century, this museum was originally the home of Abu Bakr Effendi, a well-known member of the Muslim community. The house has been furnished to recreate the lifestyle of a typical Malay family in the 19th century. Since the exhibits aren't labeled, you might do better to visit the museum as part of a guided tour of the Malay quarter (☞ Guided Tours *in* Cape Town A to Z, *below*). ✉ *71 Wale St.,* ☎ *021/24–3846.* 🎫 *R1.* ☉ *Tues.–Sat. 9:30–4:30.*

❶ **Captour's Tourist Rendezvous Travel Centre.** Here you can pick up information on most of the major monuments and buildings associated with the settlement of Cape Town. (☞ Contacts and Resources *in* Cape Town A to Z, *below*.)

★ **❺** **Castle of Good Hope.** Despite its name, the castle isn't one of those fairy-tale fantasies you find perched on a cliff above the Rhine. It is a squat fortress that hunkers into the ground as if to avoid shell fire. Built between 1665 and 1676 by the Dutch East India Company (VOC) to replace an earthen fort constructed by Jan van Riebeeck in 1652, it is the oldest building in the country. Its pentagonal plan, with a diamond-shape bastion at each corner, is typical of the Old Netherlands defense system adopted in the early 17th century. The design was intended to allow covering fire to be provided for every portion of the castle. As added protection, the whole fortification was surrounded by a moat, with the sea nearly washing up against its walls. The castle served as both the VOC headquarters and the official governor's residence and still houses the regional headquarters of the National Defence Force.

Tours of the castle—the only way to get inside—cover the ramparts, magazine, dungeons, and torture chamber. It can be torture just listening to the tour guides, some of whom will bore you to distraction. Fortunately, you can explore the excellent William Fehr Collection on your own. Housed in the governor's residence, the collection consists of antiques, artifacts, and paintings of early Cape Town and South African history. Conservationists should go upstairs to see John Thomas Baine's *The Greatest Hunt in Africa,* celebrating a "hunt" in honor of Prince Alfred when nearly 30,000 animals were driven together and slaughtered. ✉ *Buitenkant St.,* ☎ *021/469–1249 or 021/469–1250,* 🎫 *R7.50.* ☉ *Daily; public tours at 10, noon, 2, and 3.*

㉕ **Church Street.** The center of Cape Town's art and antiques business, the section between Burg and Long streets is now a pedestrian mall as well, filled with art galleries, antiques dealers, and small cafés. On Friday this is the site of an antiques and flea market.

❹ **City Hall.** The old seat of local administration is home to the Cape Town Philharmonic Orchestra (which also holds performances at the Nico Malan State Theatre) and the City Library (☞ Nightlife and the Arts, *below*).

★ **⓫** **Company's Gardens.** These are all that remains of a 43-acre garden laid out by Jan van Riebeeck in April 1652 to supply fresh vegetables to ships on their way to the Dutch East Indies. By 1700, free burghers were cultivating plenty of crops on their own land, and in time the VOC vegetable patch was transformed into a botanic garden. It remains a delightful haven in the city center, graced by fountains, exotic trees, rose gardens, aviaries, and a pleasant outdoor café. At the bottom of the gardens, close to Government Avenue, look for an **old well** that used to provide water for the town's residents and the garden. The old water pump, engraved with the maker's name and the date 1842, has been overtaken by an oak tree and now juts out of the tree's trunk some 6 feet above the ground. A huge **statue of Cecil Rhodes** looms over the path that runs through the center of the gardens. He points to the north, and an inscription reads "Your hinterland is there," a reference to Rhodes's dream of extending the British Empire from the Cape to Cairo.

⑮ Delville Wood Monument. The monument honors South Africans who died in the fight for Delville Wood during the great Somme offensive of 1916. Of the 121 officers and 3,032 men who participated in the three-day engagement, only five officers and 750 men survived unhurt. Facing the memorial is a **statue of Brigadier-General Lukin,** who commanded the South African Infantry Brigade during World War I.

③ Grand Parade. Once a military parade ground, this is now just a bleak parking lot. A statue of Edward VII serves as a parking attendant. It was here, upon his release on February 11, 1990, after 27 years in prison, that Nelson Mandela addressed an adoring crowd of more than 100,000 supporters. A dull flea market is held here on Wednesday and Saturday mornings.

② Golden Acre. Until earlier in the century, this part of the city was all at sea—literally. The land was reclaimed as part of a program to expand the docks. If you look at old paintings of the city, you will see that originally waves lapped at the very walls of the Castle (☞ *above*), now more than half a mile from the ocean. At the bottom of the escalator leading from the railway station into the Golden Acre is a solid black line that marks the approximate position of the shoreline in 1693.

⑰ Great Synagogue. Built in 1903 in the baroque style, this synagogue has notable twin towers and a dome. The building is kept locked for security, but ask in the offices at the back of the building to be let in. Services are held twice daily. ⊠ *84 Hatfield St.,* ☎ *021/45–1405.*

★ ㉖ Greenmarket Square. For more than a century, this cobbled square served as a forum for public announcements, including the 1834 declaration abolishing slavery. In the 19th century, the square became a vegetable market as well as a popular watering hole—the city's hardest boozers used to drink themselves comatose at the nearby Old Thatched Tavern and London Hotel. Today, the square is a fun open-air market, with vendors selling a wide selection of clothing and sandals, as well as African jewelry, art, and fabrics. For present buying, it's virtually unbeatable.

⑥ Groote Kerk (Great Church). One of the most famous churches in South Africa, Groote Kerk was built in 1841 on the site of an earlier Dutch Reformed church dating from 1704. The adjoining clock tower is all that remains of that earlier building. Among the building's interesting features are the enclosed pews, each with its own door. Prominent families would buy their own pews—and lock the doors—so they wouldn't have to pray with the great unwashed. The enormous pulpit is the work of the famous sculptor Anton Anreith and carpenter Jan Jacob Graaff. The lions supporting it are carved from local stinkwood; the upper portion is Burmese teak. The organ, with nearly 6,000 pipes, is the largest in the Southern Hemisphere. Approximately 200 people are buried beneath the Batavian soapstone floor, including eight governors. There are free guided tours on request. ⊠ *43 Adderley St., but enter on Church Sq.,* ☎ *021/461–7044.* ☞ *Free.* ☉ *Weekdays 10–2.*

⑨ Houses of Parliament. You can tour the houses during the Easter and winter recesses or attend debates when parliament is in session. Foreigners wishing to watch a debate must bring passports and reserve a space in the gallery, either by visiting Room 12 or calling ahead. The current buildings were constructed in 1885 by Charles Freeman, but they have been expanded many times. Paintings of former speakers of the house adorn the chambers. Free tours are given daily at 9, 10, 11, noon, and 1. ⊠ *Parliament St.,* ☎ *021/403–2460.* ☞ *Free.*

16 **Jewish Museum.** Housed in the first synagogue in South Africa (1863), the museum profiles through photographs, books, art works, and artifacts, Jewish communities around the Cape as well as Jewish history in South Africa. Many of South Africa's Jews came here from Lithuania. Today, some 20,000 Jews live in Cape Town. In the apartheid years, when South Africa's future hung in the balance, their numbers declined noticeably. Many emigrated to the United States, Canada, and Australia. Jews have experienced little discrimination in South Africa, either under the apartheid Nationalist regime or the new ANC government. ⊠ *84 Hatfield St.,* ☎ *021/45–1546.* ☞ *Free.* ⊙ *Tues. and Thurs. 1:30–5, Sun. 10:30–noon.*

28 **Koopmans–De Wet House.** Now a museum, this lovely 18th-century home is a haven of peace in the city center. The structure you see today dates largely from the period 1771–93. It is notable for its neoclassical facade, which has been variously attributed to Anton Anreith and Louis Thibault. The house enjoyed its heyday under Maria de Wet (1834–1906), a Cape Town socialite who entertained most of the major figures in Cape society, including Boer presidents and British governors. The furnishings date to the early 19th century, when the house belonged to Maria's grandmother. The collection includes a stunning selection of antiques, carpets, paintings, and porcelain. Buy or borrow the excellent guide to the museum, which describes every item in the collection. ⊠ *35 Strand St.,* ☎ *021/24–2473.* ☞ *R3.* ⊙ *Tues.–Sat. 9:30–4:30.*

NEED A
BREAK?

The **Martin Melck House** (⊠ 96 Strand St., ☎ 021/419–6533), three blocks from Koopmans–De Wet House, is a beautiful 18th-century building that served as the parsonage for an adjoining Lutheran church. It's home to **A Table at Colin's,** a delightful spot to pause over an elegant lunch under white fabric umbrellas in the brick courtyard shaded by trees and pink bougainvillea. An exhibition space upstairs displays modern works for sale by South African artists.

20 **Long Street.** The section of Long between Orange and Wale streets is lined with magnificently restored Georgian and Victorian buildings. Wrought-iron balconies and fancy curlicues on these colorful houses create an impression reminiscent of the French Quarter in New Orleans. During the '60s, Long Street did a good imitation of the Big Easy, including a host of bars, prostitutes, and sleazy hotels. Today, antiques dealers, secondhand bookstores (Clarke's is a must, with a fantastic collection of Afrikaaner books old and new), pawn shops, and funky and vintage clothing outlets make it the best browsing street in the city. There's also a good selection of backpackers' lodges. At the mountain end is Long Street Baths, an indoor swimming pool and old Turkish hamam.

27 **Old Town House.** For 150 years this was the most important civic building in Cape Town. Built in 1755 as a guardhouse, it also saw duty as a meeting place for the burgher senate, a police station, and from 1840 to 1905 as Cape Town's city hall. The building is a beautiful example of urban Cape Dutch architecture, with thick whitewashed walls, green-and-white shutters, and small-paned windows. Today the former city hall is home to the Michaelis Collection, an extensive selection of brooding Dutch landscape paintings, as well as changing exhibits. ⊠ *Greenmarket Sq.,* ☎ *021/24–6367.* ☞ *Free.* ⊙ *Feb.–Dec., daily 10–5.*

19 **Queen Victoria Street.** The famous old street is lined with some of the city's most stately buildings, which house the national archives, the Land

Bank, the state attorney's office, the supreme court, and the City and Civil Service Club.

❼ Slave Tree. Slaves were auctioned under the tree that once stood here. A cross section of the enormous Canadian pine is displayed at the ☞ South African Cultural Museum. Slavery began in the Cape Colony in 1658, when free burghers petitioned the government for farmhands. The first group of 400 slaves arrived from Guinea, Angola, Batavia (modern Java), and Madagascar. During the first British occupation of the Cape (1795–1803), 17,000 slaves were brought from India, Ceylon, and the Philippines, swelling the total slave population to 30,000. Slavery was abolished by the British in 1834, an act that fueled one of South Africa's great historical events, the Great Trek, when thousands of outraged Afrikaaners set off in their covered wagons to establish a new state in the hinterland.

★ ❽ South African Cultural Museum. Ironically the museum started out as a slave lodge, built in 1679 by the Dutch East India Company. Today the museum is a great place to come for an overview of South Africa's early settler history. Displays detailing the settlement and colonization of the Cape are superb; letters, coins, paintings, clothes, and furniture bring the period almost palpably to life. The museum also has minor collections of Roman, Greek, Egyptian, and Asian antiquities, as well as displays of antique silver, musical instruments, glass, ceramics, weapons, and coins. From 1815 to 1914 the building housed the supreme court. Guided tours are available on request. ⊠ *Adderley and Wale Sts.,* ☎ *021/4618280.* ☜ *R5.* ☉ *Mon.–Sat. 9:30–4:30.*

❿ South African Library. The National Reference Library, as it is also known, owes its existence to Lord Charles Somerset, governor of the Cape Colony, who in 1818 imposed a wine tax to fund the creation of a library that would "place the means of knowledge within the reach of the youth of this remote corner of the Globe." In 1860 the library moved into its current home, a neoclassical building modeled after the Fitzwilliam Museum in Cambridge, England. The library has an extensive collection of Africana, including the works of many 18th- and 19th-century explorers. ⊠ *Botanical Gardens,* ☎ *021/24–6320.* ☜ *Free.* ☉ *Weekdays 9–6, Sat. 9–1.*

⓮ South African Museum. This is a natural history museum that may well disappoint nature lovers. Its exhibits are mediocre and concentrate primarily on sea mammals. Far more interesting is the section on African peoples and cultures. A Bushmen diorama traces the history and way of life of the San (Bushmen) and includes examples of their rock paintings and tools. Similar exhibits examine the Khoikhoi (called Hottentots by the Dutch), Nguni, and Sotho peoples. As South Africa struggles to come to grips with its apartheid past, there is some debate about why these San and black cultural exhibits are included in a museum devoted to the study of animals, whereas white and Asian cultures are celebrated at the South African Cultural Museum. It's a very good question. The adjoining planetarium stages a variety of shows throughout the week. ⊠ *25 QueenVictoria St.,* ☎ *021/24–3330,* ℻ *021/24–6716.* ☜ *Museum R2, planetarium R5.* ☉ *Museum daily 10–5. Planetarium shows Tues.–Fri. at 1; Sat. at noon, 1, and 2:30; Sun. at 2 and 3:30.*

★ ⓭ South African National Gallery. Don't miss this art gallery. The museum houses a decent collection of 19th- and 20th-century European and British artworks, but it's most interesting for its South African works, many of which reflect the country's traumatic history. Look for Willie Bester's *Challenges Facing the New South Africa,* done in wood and mixed media. The director is known for her innovative, brave, and sometimes controversial exhibitions. The museum café serves salads, sandwiches, pastas, and cakes. Free guided tours are given on Wednesday at 1 and Saturday at 3. ⊠ *Government Ave., Gardens,* ☎ *021/45–1628.* ⊡ *Free.* ⊙ *Tues.–Sun. 10–5.*

㉓ St. George's Cathedral. The cathedral was once the religious seat of one of the most recognizable faces—and voices—in the fight against apartheid, Archbishop Desmond Tutu. In his position as the first black archbishop of Cape Town, the bishop vociferously denounced apartheid and relentlessly pressed for a democratic government. Today Tutu continues to be a voice of moderation and tolerance and heads the Truth and Reconciliation Council, which while addressing crimes committed in the apartheid era, strives for peaceful reconciliation. The present Anglican cathedral was designed by Sir Herbert Baker in the Gothic Revival style; construction began in 1901, using sandstone from Table Mountain. The structure contains the largest stained-glass window in the country, some beautiful examples of late-Victorian stained glass, and a 1,000-year-old Coptic cross. ⊠ *Wale St.,* ☎ *no phone.* ⊡ *Free.* ⊙ *Daily 8–5. Services weekdays at 7:15 and 1:15; Sat. at 8 AM; Sun. at 7, 8, 9:15, and 11 AM.*

㉔ St. George's Mall. This promenade stretches almost all the way to the Foreshore. Shops and cafés line the mall, and street vendors hawk everything from T-shirts to African arts and crafts. Daily, buskers and dancers gather to entertain the crowds.

⑫ Tuynhuys (Town House). Parts of the Tuynhuys date to the late 17th and early 18th centuries. The building contains the offices of the state president and is not open to the public.

The Victoria & Alfred Waterfront

Capetonians are almost unanimous in their praise of the Victoria & Alfred Waterfront, a six-year project undertaken to breathe new life into a historical part of the city docks. Today the Waterfront is Cape Town's most vibrant and exciting attraction, the focus of the city's nightlife and entertainment scene. Hundreds of shops, cinemas, restaurants, and bars share quarters in restored warehouses and dock buildings, all connected by pedestrian plazas, promenades, and canals. It's clean, it's safe, and it's car-free. Two of Cape Town's five-star hotels opened here last year, and there's a new marina and thriving up-market residential developments. Although there's been talk of a floating resort, that's all it is, still talk.

A Good Walk

It makes sense to begin your walk at the **Victoria & Alfred Waterfront Information Centre.** From the Information Centre (which you must visit before you do anything else, to get the latest news on this constantly changing part of the city), walk down Dock Road to the long, narrow stone shed that once housed the **Rocket Life-Saving Apparatus.** Next door is **Mitchell's Waterfront Brewery.** The heady smell of malt emanating from Mitchell's will be enough to send anyone with a thirst into the adjoining **Ferryman's Tavern.** Facing Ferryman's Tavern is the **AGFA Amphitheatre.** From the amphitheater, walk over to Quay 5 (in front of Tequila Cantina) and the **Victoria Basin,** embarkation point for many tours of the harbor and **Robben Island.** Walk back past the red Fisherman's Choice restaurant to Market Square and the mustard-colored **Union-Castle House.** Walk past the National Sea Rescue Institute (NSRI) shed and around the bottom of Alfred Mall to the end of the pier and the **Victoria Museum Ship.** Next to the Victoria is the **Penny Ferry.** Back on North Quay, follow the cut past the Alfred Mall to the

S.A.S. *Somerset.* The ship is part of the **South African Maritime Museum.** Head back to the Information Centre. From there, cross Dock Road and climb the stairs to Portswood Ridge, where there are several late-19th-century buildings once used by the harbor administration. Many have been converted into office space. At the top of the stairs stands the brick **Time Ball Tower.** Next to the tower is the original **Harbour Master's Residence.** Take the stairs back down to Dock Road and turn right to reach the new **aquarium.**

Sights to See

AGFA Amphitheatre. This popular outdoor performance space mounts shows almost daily, ranging from concerts by the Cape Town Philharmonic Orchestra to gigs by jazz and rock bands. Check with the ☞ **Information Centre** for the schedule of events. The amphitheater stands on the site where, in 1860, the teenage Prince Alfred inaugurated the construction of a breakwater to protect shipping in the harbor. Table Bay was never an ideal natural harbor. In winter, devastating northwesterly winds pounded ships caught in the exposed waters. Between 1647 and 1870 more than 190 ships went down in Table Bay. Since the breakwater was built, only 40 ships have foundered here.

★ **Aquarium.** The Two Oceans Aquarium is thought to be one of the finest in the world. Stunning displays show the marine life of the warm Indian Ocean and the cold Atlantic Ocean. The diversity of marine life and the sophistication of the displays are what make it so unique. Displays are imaginative, comprehensive, and extremely well labelled. The vast, glass-enclosed, five-story kelp forest is breathtaking. Keep your eyes on the great man-eating sharks as well as the other colorful inhabitants of the oceans. This is one of the most exciting places to visit at the Waterfront. ✉ *Dock Road, Waterfront,* ☎ *021/418–3823.* ⊙ *Daily 9:30–6.* ☞ *R27.*

Ferryman's Tavern. With the heady smell of malt emanating from ☞ Mitchell's Brewery adjoining the pub, you won't have to wait long for a nice cool one. Constructed in 1877 of bluestone and Table Mountain sandstone, this is one of the oldest buildings in the harbor. Before 1912 the temperance movement in Cape Town had managed to force a ban on the sale of alcohol within the docks. As a result, a host of pubs sprang up just outside the dock gates, particularly along Dock Road. ✉ *Market Plaza,* ☎ *021/419–7748.*

Harbour Master's Residence. Built in 1860, in front there is a beautiful, century-old dragon tree, a native of the Canary Islands. The resin of this tree species, known as "dragon's blood," was used in Europe to treat dysentery.

Mitchell's Waterfront Brewery. One of a handful of microbreweries in South Africa. The brewery produces four beers: Foresters Draught lager, Bosuns Bitter, Ravenstout, and Ferryman's Ale. Weekdays at noon the brewery offers tours, which include beer-tasting and a look at the fermentation tanks. ✉ *Dock Rd.,* ☎ *021/419–5074.* ☞ *Tour R20.*

Penny Ferry. This rowboat service carries passengers across the cut, the narrow entrance to the Albert Basin. The Penny Ferry was started in 1871 to row harbor employees across the cut to the South Quay, where Bertie's Landing, a popular bar and restaurant, now stands. The service was extended to the public in 1880 and the fare set at a penny. It now costs R1. Keep an eye out for **Cape fur seals,** which like to hang out in the water and on the wooden docks surrounding Bertie's Landing.

★ **Robben Island.** This notorious prison in Table Bay held apartheid South Africa's most famous opponents, including Nelson Mandela,

Robert Sobukwe, and Walter Sisulu. The island, whose name means seal in Dutch, has served as a prison since the 17th century, first for lepers, paupers, and mental patients, and later for political prisoners of the British, including the Xhosa chief Nxele in 1820. In 1982 Nelson Mandela was transferred from Robben Island to a prison on the mainland; he was released on February 11, 1990. If you do nothing else in Cape Town, take a guided tour of Robben Island: It is an integral part of South Africa's history.

Tours of the island are organized by the Robben Island Museum, and visitors are taken around the island and the prison by guides who were themselves political prisoners in the past. There are three tours daily (at 9:30, 11:15 and 1:15) departing from the V & A Waterfront at Sealink. You can book for the same day or buy tickets for the following few days. The boat crossing, depending on the vessel, takes 30 to 45 minutes. The island tour itself lasts for two hours, during which time you walk through the prison and see the cell in which Mandela was imprisoned as well as the quarry where the South African president pounded rocks for so many years. During peak season, tours are crowded and, as numbers are limited, it's advisable to go with the tour company. The Robben Island Museum (☎ 021/419–1300) advises visitors to be at the departure point at least an hour before the time of departure. Tickets are R80 (free for children under 4). On special days, for example Heritage Day, extra tours are scheduled. The tour offered by the Robben Island Museum is the only one that actually visits the island: several operators advertise Robben Island tours and just take visitors on a boat trip *around* the island. ☞ Guided Tours *in* Cape Town A to Z, *below.*

Rocket Life-Saving Apparatus. In the days before helicopters and rescue craft, this gear was used to rescue seamen from the many ships that foundered in Table Bay. The procedure was very basic: A rocket attached to a long rope was fired out to a sinking ship, and seamen were winched ashore along the rope. The apparatus was last used—unsuccessfully—just 30 years ago.

S.A.S. Somerset. The Somerset is the only surviving boom-defense vessel in the world. During World War II, harbors were protected against enemy submarines and divers by booms, essentially metal mesh curtains drawn across the harbor entrance. The *Somerset* (then named the H.M.S. *Barcross*) controlled the boom across Saldanha Bay, north of Cape Town. You can explore the entire ship, including the bridge and the engine room. The ship is part of the South African Maritime Museum (☞ *below*).

South African Maritime Museum. The museum provides a look at ships and the history of Table Bay, including a model of Cape Town harbor as it appeared in 1886. In the model workshop you can watch modelers build scale replicas of famous ships. ⊠ *Dock Rd.,* ☎ *021/419–2505.* ⊟ *R2 (includes entrance to S.A.S. Somerset).* ☉ *Daily 10–5.*

Time Ball Tower. The tower was built in 1894, before the advent of modern navigational equipment, when ships' crews needed to know the exact time to help them calculate longitude. Navigators set their clocks by the time ball, which fell every day at noon, much like the ball that marks the stroke of midnight in New York's Times Square on New Year's Eve.

Union-Castle House. Designed in 1919 by Sir Herbert Baker, the house was headquarters for the famous Union-Castle shipping line. Before World War II many English-speaking South Africans looked upon England as "home," even if they had never been there. The emotional link between the two countries was symbolized most strongly by the mail steamers, carrying both mail and passengers, that sailed weekly between South Africa and England. In 1977, amid much pomp and ceremony, the last Union-Castle mail ship, the *Windsor Castle*, made its final passage to England. Even today, older South Africans like to wax lyrical about the joys of a voyage on one of those steamers. Union-Castle House is now home to several banks and small businesses. Inside Standard Bank you can still see the iron rings in the ceiling from which mail bags were hung. ⊠ *Quay 4.*

Victoria & Alfred Waterfront Information Centre. The center, opposite the V & A Hotel, has the lowdown on everything happening in the area, including upcoming events and shows. Here you can arrange walking tours of the Waterfront and book reservations for the Table Mountain Cableway (☞ *above*). A scale model shows what the Waterfront will look like when it's finished. ⊠ *Pierhead,* ☎ *021/418–2369,* FAX *021/21–2565.* ☉ *Weekdays 9:30–5, weekends 9:30–6.*

Victoria Basin. The Basin was constructed between 1870 and 1905 to accommodate the huge increase in shipping following the discovery of diamonds at Kimberley and gold on the Witwatersrand. Across the basin is the South Arm, used as a debarkation point for British troops, horses, and material during the Boer War (1899–1902). Much of the fodder for the British horses was shipped in from Argentina and catastrophically infested with rats and fleas. As a result, bubonic plague broke out in Cape Town in February 1901, creating wholesale panic in the city. African dockworkers, suspected of harboring the disease, were forbidden to leave the city and ultimately confined to specific quarters. During the epidemic, 766 people contracted the plague; 371 died.

Victoria Museum Ship. The vessel is a replica of an 18th-century Royal Navy frigate, complete with cannons and creaking spars. The ship contains an interesting collection of treasures salvaged from the many wrecks that litter the coastlines of South Africa and other countries. Among the retrieved artifacts are George IV sovereigns, pieces of eight from Mexico, rusted cannons, and portholes from the *Lusitania*. Most of the exhibits come from 18th- and 19th-century wrecks. ⊠ *Pierhead,* ☎ *021/25–4127.* 🖾 *R6.* ☉ *Daily 9–6.*

The Peninsula

This driving tour takes you south from Cape Town on a loop of the peninsula, heading through the scenic southern suburbs before running down the False Bay coast to Cape Point. It's a magnificent drive back to the city along the wild Atlantic coast. Plan a full day to travel the entire loop, more if you want to stop along the way.

Numbers in the text correspond to numbers in the margin and on the Cape Peninsula map.

A Good Drive

Take the N2 or De Waal Drive (M3) out of the city center. The two highways merge near Groote Schuur Hospital. They split again soon after—follow the M3 toward Muizenberg and the southern suburbs. After 1 km (½ mi) you pass **Mostert's Mill** ㉙, one of two remaining windmills in the Cape. Continue on the M3 for another kilometer (½ mi) to the exit marked with a sign to the **Rhodes Memorial** ㉚. Return to the M3 and head south toward Muizenberg. After 1½ km (1 mi), exit right onto Rhodes Avenue (M63). This road winds through huge groves of pine and eucalyptus to the **Kirstenbosch National Botanic Gardens** ㉛, one of the most beautiful spots in the Cape. Turn right as you leave the Botanic Gardens. When you reach a T junction, turn right again and begin the winding climb to the pass at Constantia Nek. From the traffic circle at the top you can either cut over the mountains and down into Hout Bay (☞ *below*) or turn left onto the M41 (the sign reads WYNBERG AND GROOT CONSTANTIA) and begin the snaking descent into Constantia and **Groot Constantia** ㉜. Leaving Groot Constantia, turn right on Main Road then right again onto Ladies Mile Extension (a sign points you to Muizenberg and Bergvliet). Another right at the first traffic light puts you on Spaanschemat River Road, and a final right turn funnels you onto Klein Constantia Road. Follow this to **Buiten-verwachting** ㉝. Turn left out of Buitenverwachting and continue for ½ km (¼ mi) to **Klein Constantia** ㉞. Head back down Klein Constantia Road. Just past the turnoff to Buitenverwachting, turn down Nova Constantia Road, which leads to Spaanschemat River Road. Turn right and continue about 2 km (1 mi) to the junction with Tokai Road. Turn right again at the PORTER SCHOOL sign and drive 1 km (½ mi) to **Tokai Manor** ㉟. Return to the junction and continue straight on Tokai Road, which meets up with the M3. Follow the signs to Muizenberg through various twists and turns until you end up on the M4. After ½ km (¼ mi), Boyes Drive leads off the M4. The M4, or Main Road, on the other hand, takes you into the center of **Muizenberg** ㊱. Emerging from the town center, Main Road runs parallel to the sea. Watch on your right for a small thatched building with rough, whitewashed walls; this is De Post Huys. Continue down the street to Rhodes Cottage Museum. From Muizenberg, Main Road heads down the peninsula, hugging the shore of False Bay. Strung along this coastline are a collection of small towns that long ago merged to form a thin suburban belt between the ocean and the mountains. **Kalk Bay** ㊲, **Fish Hoek** ㊳, and **Simon's Town** ㊴ are all on this stretch. Simon's Town is the last community of any size before you reach Cape Point. From here the road traverses a wild, windswept landscape as beautiful as it is desolate. You can stop at tiny **Boulders Beach** ㊵ to look at the colony of jackass penguins. The mountains, covered with rugged fynbos, descend almost straight into the sea. Don't be surprised to see troops of baboons lounging beside the road as you approach the **Cape of Good Hope Nature Reserve** ㊶. Close the windows of your car and don't attempt to feed the baboons. They are dangerous. Turn left out of the nature reserve onto the M65, drive 8 km (5 mi), then turn left again to continue on the M65 to **Scarborough** ㊷ and **Kommetjie** ㊸. From Kommetjie the M65 leads to a major intersection. Turn left onto the M6 (Hout Bay), go through one set of lights, then turn left again, following the signs to Hout Bay. The road passes through the small community of **Noordhoek** ㊹ before beginning its treacherous climb around **Chapman's Peak Drive** ㊺. From Chapman's Peak you descend into the fishing village of **Hout Bay** ㊻. Stay on the M6 (a sign reads CITY AND LLANDUDNO) when it splits off the M63. After less than a km (½ mi), turn right on Valley Road to the **World of Birds** ㊼. From Hout Bay the M6 climbs past the exclusive community of Llandudno and then runs along the coast to **Camps Bay** ㊽. Follow Victoria Road (M6) out of Camps Bay and turn right at the sign reading KLOOF NEK ROUND HOUSE. This road snakes up the mountain until it reaches a five-way intersection at Kloof Nek. Make a sharp left onto the road leading to **Signal Hill** ㊾. For more great views of the city, return to the Kloof Nek intersection and take **Tafelberg Road** ㊿.

Sights to See

Boyes Drive. If you prefer scenic views to historical sites, Boyes Drive is probably a better option than the main highway. The drive runs high along the mountains, offering panoramic views of False Bay and the Hottentots Holland mountains, before rejoining the M4 at Kalk Bay (☞ *below*).

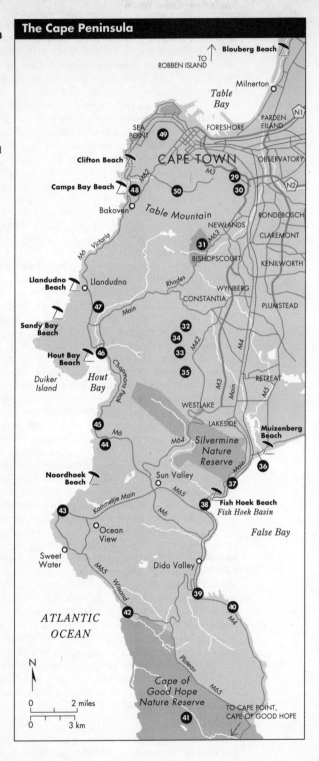

The Cape Peninsula

③③ Buitenverwachting. A gorgeous winery that was also once part of Van der Stel's original Constantia farm, Buitenverwachting means "beyond expectation," and its setting certainly surpasses anything you might have imagined: An oak-lined avenue leads past the Cape Dutch homestead to the thatched modern cellar. Acres of vines spread up hillsides flanked by more towering oaks and the rocky crags of the Constantiaberg.

Buitenverwachting's wine is just as superb as its setting. The largest seller is the often dry Buiten Blanc, an easy-drinking blend of a few varieties. The best red is Christine, which until the 1991 vintage was known as Grand Vin; it's a blend of mostly cabernet sauvignon and 30% merlot. The winery's restaurant (☞ Dining, *below*) is probably the finest in the Cape. ⊠ *Off Klein Constantia Rd.,* ☎ *021/794–5190,* FAX *021/794–1351.* ☑ *Tastings free.* ☉ *Weekdays 9–5, Sat. 9–1.*

NEED A
BREAK?

Buitenverwachting serves great picnic lunches under the oaks on the estate's lawns. It's an idyllic setting and a most civilized way to cap a morning of wine-tasting. Each picnic hamper is packed with a selection of breads, meat, chicken, pâtés, and cheeses. You can buy a bottle of estate wine as an accompaniment to the meal. The picnic costs R25 per person and reservations are essential. ☎ *021/794–1012. Closed Sun.*

④⑧ Camps Bay. This is a popular holiday resort with a long beach and plenty of restaurants and bars. The craggy faces of the Twelve Apostles, huge granite buttresses reaching down to the sea from the mountains behind, loom over the town.

★ **④① Cape of Good Hope Nature Reserve.** The reserve covers some 19,100 acres, including Cape Point and the Cape of Good Hope. Much of the park consists of rolling hills covered with fynbos and laced with miles of walking trails, for which maps are available at the park entrance. It also has beautiful deserted beaches. Eland, baboons, ostrich, and bontebok are among the animals that roam the park. A tarred road runs 14 km (8 mi) to the tip of the peninsula. A turnoff leads to the Cape of Good Hope, a rocky beach at the southwesternmost point on the continent. A plaque marks the spot—otherwise you would never know you're standing on a site of such significance. The opposite is true of Cape Point, a dramatic knife edge of rock that slices into the Atlantic. Looking out to sea from the viewing platform, you feel you're at the tip of Africa, even though that honor officially belongs to Cape Agulhas, about 160 kilometers (100 miles) to the southeast (☞ Chapter 5). From Cape Point the views of False Bay and the Hottentots Holland mountains are breathtaking. The walk up to the viewing platform and the old lighthouse is very steep; a shuttle bus (R2) makes the run every 10 minutes or so. Take an anorak or sweater—the wind can take your breath away. A small shop sells snacks and curios. During peak season, visit Cape Point as early as in the day as you can; otherwise you'll be swamped by horrendous numbers of tourist buses and their occupants. ⊠ *Off the M65 and M4,* ☎ *021/780–1100.* ☑ *R5 per person (R10 minimum).* ☉ *Daily 7–5.*

NEED A
BREAK?

The **Homestead Restaurant,** midway through the Cape of Good Hope Nature Reserve, is a great place to warm up over coffee on a windy day or to drain a beer on the terrace when the weather's fine. The food can be dreadful, so preferably have lunch in Simon's Town or Hout Bay before or afterwards and just enjoy a drink.

★ **④⑤ Chapman's Peak Drive.** A trip around the peninsula exhausts anyone's supply of superlatives, but it's hard to beat the dramatic beauty of the

10-km (6-mi) stretch of road between Noordhoek and Hout Bay, designed by Robert Glenday and built over seven years, ending in 1992. The road literally clings to the mountainside, with a narrow retaining wall separating you from a sheer drop into the sea—528 feet down at its highest. It's dizzyingly beautiful, made more so by the fact that the road constantly ducks and weaves. Follow the signs to Chapman's Peak Drive from Hout Bay on the Atlantic side. If coming from the False Bay side, go past Simon's Town and follow the signs.

Constantia. Backed by the rugged mountains of the Constantiaberg and overlooking the Cape Flats and False Bay, Constantia is an idyllic spot to while away a day—or a week. Vineyards carpet the lower slopes, while plantations of pine predominate higher up. This is very much the domain of the suburban gentry. If you don't have time to visit the Winelands (☞ Chapter 5), Constantia is a must. Here you'll find three excellent estates, Buitenverwachting, Groot Constantia, and Klein Constantia.

De Post Huys (✉ Main Rd., ☎ 021/788–7035). One of the oldest buildings in the country, it was constructed in 1673 as a lookout post and signal station.

➌➑ Fish Hoek. This is one of the most popular resort towns on the False Bay coast, with a smooth, sandy beach that is protected from frequent summer southeasters by Elsies Peak. One of the many Cape windsurfing paradises, it's also one of the best places to see whales during calving season—from approximately August to November, though there have been whale sightings as early as June and as late as January. Until last year Fish Hoek was the only teetotaling town in the country. In 1810 Lord Charles Somerset issued the first grant of Crown land in Fish Hoek on condition that no wine house should ever exist on the property. Somerset was evidently alarmed by the excesses associated with a wine house near Kommetjie, where wagon drivers would become too drunk to deliver their supplies to the Royal Navy at Simon's Town.

★ ➌➋ Groot Constantia. Constantia takes its name from the wine estate founded here in 1685 by Simon van der Stel, one of the first Dutch governors of the Cape. After his death in 1712 the land was subdivided, with the heart of the estate preserved at Groot Constantia. The enormous complex enjoys the status of a national monument and is by far the most commercial and touristy of the wineries. Van der Stel's magnificent homestead, the oldest in the Cape, lies at the center of Groot Constantia. It's built in traditional Cape Dutch style, with thick whitewashed walls, a thatched roof, small-pane windows, and ornate gables. The house is a museum furnished with exquisite period pieces. The old wine cellar sits behind the manor house. Built in 1791, it is most famous for its own ornate gable, designed by sculptor Anton Anreith. The cellar houses a wine museum, with displays of wine-drinking and storage vessels dating to antiquity.

In the 19th century the sweet wines of Groot Constantia were highly regarded in Europe and especially favored by King Louis Philippe and Bismarck. Today Groot Constantia is known for its splendid red wines. The best is the excellent Gouverneurs Reserve, made from mostly cabernet sauvignon grapes with smaller amounts of merlot and cabernet franc. Full of tannin and fruit, this big, robust wine will be at its best in 8 to 10 years. The Pinotage is consistently good, too, reaching its velvety prime in about five years. The estate operates two restaurants: the elegant Jonkershuis (☞ Dining, *below*) and the Tavern, which serves light meals at picnic tables on the lawn. You can also bring your own picnic and relax on the lawns behind the wine cellar. ✉ *Off*

Main Rd., ☎ *021/794–5128.* 🎫 *Museum R2, wine tasting R6, cellar tour R6.* 🕙 *Daily 10–4:30. Cellar tour hourly 10–4.*

NEED A
BREAK?
The **Old Cape Farmstall** (✉ near the entrance to Groot Constantia, ☎ 021/794–2034) is worth a visit and has lovely homemade goodies that make great gifts. The Farm Stall's restaurant (☎ 021/794–2034) serves teas and lunches and champagne breakfasts on Sunday.

Groote Schuur Hospital. Dr. Christian Barnard performed the world's first heart transplant here in 1967. Just off Main Road, you'll see this visible landmark on the slopes of Table Mountain below the scenic De Waal Drive.

46 **Hout Bay.** Cradled in a lovely bay and guarded by a 1,000-foot peak known as the Sentinel, Hout Bay is the center of Cape Town's cray-fishing industry, and the town operates several fish-processing plants. Mariner's Wharf is Hout Bay's salty answer to the Waterfront in Cape Town, a collection of bars and restaurants on the fishing dock. You can also buy fresh fish at a seafood market and take it outside to be grilled. Cruise boats depart from Hout Bay's harbor to view the **seal colony** on Duiker Island (☞ Cape Town A to Z, *below*).

37 **Kalk Bay.** The name of Kalk Bay recalls that seashells were once baked in large kilns near the shore to produce lime (kalk). Today a small harbor shelters the town's weathered fishing fleet. Across the bay lies Seal Island, home to large populations of seals and sea birds. The waters surrounding the island are a breeding area for the great white shark.

★ **31** **Kirstenbosch National Botanic Gardens.** The gardens extend up the eastern slopes of Table Mountain, overlooking the Cape Flats and distant mountains. Walking trails meander through the gardens, and grassy banks are ideal for a picnic or afternoon nap. The plantings are limited to species native to southern Africa. The focus is on fynbos—hardy, thin-leaved plants that proliferate in the Cape. Among these are proteas, including silver trees and king proteas, ericas, and restios (reeds). Another extraordinary feature of the park is a large cycad garden. Those who have difficulty walking can take a comprehensive 45-minute tour (R10) by six-person cart. Concerts are held here on summer Sundays at 5. With Table Mountain as a magnficent backdrop and the gardens all around, you can catch the best of South Africa's entertainment with everything from classical music to township jazz to rock and roll. The outdoor restaurant is popular among Capetonians on weekends and serves super breakfasts. ✉ *Rhodes Ave., Constantia,* ☎ *021/762–1166.* 🎫 *R5.* 🕙 *Apr.–Aug., daily 8–6; Sept.–Mar., daily 8–7.*

34 **Klein Constantia.** *Klein* (rhymes with "stain") means "small" in Afrikaans, and indicates the relative size of this portion of van der Stel's original Constantia estate. The winery has an impressive modern cellar, deliberately unobtrusive so as not to detract from the vine-covered mountain slopes. Its Cape Dutch homestead, visible as you drive in, was built in the late 18th century. This estate also produces wines of superb quality, as awards displayed in the tasting area attest. The excellent Sauvignon Blanc is used as a point of reference by many South African connoisseurs and vintners. Whereas early vintages were particularly opulent, more recent ones have been a little racy upon first release. The closest you'll come to the famous Constantia wine of the 18th century is the Vin de Constance, a sweet wine made from predominantly muscat de Frontignan grapes. The Cabernet Sauvignon is one of the best produced in the Cape—a collector's wine that will develop wonderfully over time. ✉ *Klein Constantia Rd.,* ☎ *021/794–*

5788, FAX *021/794–2464.* ⚏ *Tastings free.* ⊗ *Weekdays 9–5, Sat. 9–1. Cellar tour by appointment.*

㊸ Kommetjie. A quiet fishing village known for its crayfish, Kommetjie is also a popular spot for birders, since this is the roosting area for four species of cormorant, as well as the Arctic tern in winter. A 45-minute walk down Long Beach leads to the wreck of the *Kakapo*, a steamship that ran aground on her maiden voyage in 1900.

㉙ Mostert's Mill. Built in 1796, this thatched wheat mill consists of a tower with a rotating cap to which sails were attached. Mills like this were once common in the area. Inside is the original mechanism, but it's not necessarily worth pulling off the highway to see. ⊠ *Rhodes Dr., Mowbray, no phone.* ⊗ *Daily 9–5.*

㊱ Muizenberg. At the turn of the century this was the premier bathing resort in South Africa, attracting many of the country's wealthy mining magnates. The mansions along Main Road date to this period. Today Muizenberg remains popular among locals, particularly surfers, who prefer the comparatively warm waters of False Bay and its white-sand beach. Long gone, though, are the days when anyone thought of Muizenberg as chic. A drab complex of shops and fast-food outlets, complete with kiddie pools, blights the beachfront, and the views of mountains and sea cannot make up for it. Drive a little way along the coast to Sunrise beach, though, and you'll find one of the world's best beach walks. You can walk for miles along pristine beaches, which makes this spot popular with Capetonians and their hounds.

㊹ Noordhoek. Noordhoek is another popular beach community (☞ Beaches, *below*) with stunning white beaches that stretch forever. The bordering village has become a retreat for the arts-and-crafts community and there are lots of galleries and boutiques selling unusual items.

Rhodes Cottage Museum. Considering the great power wielded by Cecil John Rhodes (1853–1902), one of Britain's great empire-builders, his seaside cottage was surprisingly humble and spare. Yet this is where the man who was instrumental in the development of present-day South Africa chose to spend his last days in 1902, preferring the cool sea air of Muizenberg to the stifling opulence of his home at Groote Schuur. The cottage, including the bedroom where he died, has been completely restored. Other rooms display photos documenting Rhodes's life. His remains are buried in the Matopos Hills in Zimbabwe. ⊠ *246 Main Rd., Muizenberg,* ☎ *021/788–1816.* ⚏ *Free.* ⊗ *Tues.–Sun. 10–1 and 2–5.*

★ ㉚ Rhodes Memorial. Rhodes served as prime minister of the Cape from 1890 to 1896. He made his fortune in the diamond rush at Kimberley, but his greatest dream was to forge a Cape–Cairo railway, a tangible symbol of British dominion in Africa. The classical-style granite memorial sits high on the slopes of Devil's Peak, on part of Rhodes's old estate, Groote Schuur. A mounted rider symbolizing energy faces north toward the continent for which Rhodes felt such passion. A bust of Rhodes dominates the temple—ironically, he's leaning on one hand as if he's about to nod off. This is traditionally one of the premier necking spots for students from the nearby University of Cape Town. ⊠ *Off Rhodes Dr., Rondebosch,* ☎ *021/689–9151.* ⚏ *Free.*

....

NEED A
BREAK?   The **Rhodes Memorial Tea Garden,** tucked under towering pines behind the memorial, is a pleasant spot for tea or a light lunch. Tables on the outdoor terrace have lovely views of the Cape Flats. *Closed Mon.*

....

㊷ Scarborough. The town is a tiny holiday community with one of the best beaches on the peninsula (☞ Beaches, *below*). Scarborough is becoming popular with artists and craftspeople, and you'll find their offerings exhibited at informal galleries. From Scarborough the road hugs the shoreline, snaking between the mountains and the crashing surf. Another beach, which makes Scarborough's pale in comparison, lies about 5 km (3 mi) farther on and is visible from the road. To reach it, turn left at the turnoff to Soetwater, then left again at the bottom of the hill.

★ **㊾ Signal Hill.** Here the road swings around the shoulder of Lion's Head then runs along the flank of Signal Hill. The views of the city below and Table Mountain are superb. The road ends at a parking lot overlooking Sea Point and all of Table Bay.

★ **㊴ Simon's Town.** By far the most interesting of the False Bay communities, the town serves as a base for the South African navy. Men in uniform brush shoulders with anglers and tourists, and residents of the town have preserved and nurtured its proud naval history, which stretches back two centuries. More than 20 buildings on the main street alone date to the mid-19th century. Although the town is named after Simon van der Stel, one of the first Dutch governors of the Cape, most of its history is British. It was here in 1795 that British troops landed before defeating the Dutch at the Battle of Muizenberg, and the town served as a base for the Royal Navy from 1814 to 1957, when the town was handed over to South Africa. The batteries of naval and antiaircraft guns along St. George's Road leading into town are reminders that this is still an active naval station.

Exhibits in the **Simon's Town Museum** trace the town's early history, its development, and its relationship to the British and South African navies. Other displays focus on the Khoikhoi and San, the earliest inhabitants of the area. The museum is in the Old Residency, built in 1777 for the governor of the Dutch East India Company. ⊠ *Court Rd., Simon's Town,* ☎ *021/786–3046.* ☞ *R2.* ☉ *Weekdays 9–4, Sat. 10–1.*

The **South Africa Naval Museum** stands next door. Here you come to appreciate the role of South Africans in the two world wars. Perhaps the most interesting display is a life-size reconstruction of the operations room and control center of a modern submarine. The museum occupies the Mast House and Sail Loft, an 1815 building designed to store ships' masts, some as long as 117 feet. ⊠ *St. George's Rd., Simon's Town,* ☎ *021/787–4686.* ☞ *Free.* ☉ *Daily 10–4.*

St. George's Road leads to Jubilee Square, a dockside plaza that serves as the de facto town center. Next to the dock wall stands a sculpture of **Just Nuisance**, a Great Dane adopted as a mascot by the Royal Navy during World War II. Just Nuisance apparently liked his pint of beer and would accompany sailors on the train into Cape Town. He had the endearing habit of leading drunken sailors—and only sailors—that he found in the city back to the Union Jack Club, where they could sleep it off. The navy went so far as to induct him into the service as an able seaman attached to H.M.S. *Afrikander.* He died at the age of seven in April 1944.

At the southern end of town, just off St. George's Road, stands the **Martello Tower.** Built in 1795, it is the oldest surviving British building in South Africa. This circular tower was modeled after a fort at Cape Mortella in Corsica that caused enormous problems for a British fleet during the Napoleonic Wars. It is not open to the public, but you can get into the base to view the exterior on weekdays from 10 to 3:45.

40 **Boulders Beach.** This series of small coves lies on the outskirts of town among giant boulders. The swimming is fine—no heavy surf or currents—but the beach is most interesting for its resident colony of jackass penguins. You can walk and swim among these waddling birds. This is one of only two mainland colonies in southern Africa. The other is at Betty's Bay in the Overberg (☞ Chapter 5).

Simon's Town is the last community of any size before you reach Cape Point. From here the road traverses a wild landscape as beautiful as it is desolate. The mountains, covered with rugged fynbos, descend almost straight into the sea. Don't be surprised to see troops of baboons lounging beside the road.

50 **Tafelberg Road.** The road crosses the northern side of Table Mountain before ending at Devil's Peak. From the Kloof Nek intersection you can descend to Cape Town directly or return to Camps Bay and follow the coastal road back to the city. This route takes you through the beautiful seaside communities of Clifton (☞ Beaches, *below*) and Bantry Bay and then along the seaside promenade in Sea Point.

35 **Tokai Manor.** Built in 1795, this is one of the finest Cape Dutch homes in the country. Famed architect Louis Michel Thibault designed its facade. The homestead is reputedly haunted by a horseman who died when he tried to ride his horse down the curving front steps during a drunken revel. You can stop for a look, but the house is not open to the public.

47 **World of Birds.** Here you can walk through aviaries housing 450 species of indigenous and exotic birds, including eagles, vultures, penguins, and flamingos. No cage separates you from the birds, so you can photograph even giant raptors from impossibly close quarters. ⊠ *Valley Rd., Hout Bay,* ☎ *021/790–2730,* ℻ *021/790–4839.* 🎫 *R13.* ☉ *Daily 9–6.*

OFF THE BEATEN PATH   **District Six Museum.** Housed in the Buitenkant Methodist Church, this new museum preserves the memory of one of Cape Town's most vibrant multicultural neighborhoods and of the district's destruction in one of the cruelest acts of the apartheid Nationalist government. District Six was proclaimed a so-called "white" area in 1966 and residents, mainly working class blacks and Indians, were evicted from their homes, which were razed to make way for a white suburb. The people were forced to "resettle" in bleak, outlying areas on the Cape Flats and by the seventies, the area was totally obliterated. Because of the controversy, District Six was never developed and today, the ground is still bare—a grim reminder of the past. There are plans to bring former residents back into the area and re-establish the suburb; however, the old swinging District Six can never be recreated. Authors Adam Small and Jansje Wissema wrote of the tragedy in their book *District Six*: "What happened . . . was a breaking of a place, a sundering of thousands of lives." At press time the museum was assembling its collection, but you could still get a feel for life in District Six through photographs and articles donated by ex-residents and their children. One ex-resident has returned District Six's street signs, which he had taken as a memento, keeping them hidden for years out of fear. ⊠ *25a Buitenkant St., Cape Town,* ☎ *021/461–8745.* 🎫 *R3 donation requested.* ☉ *Mon.–Sat. 10–4:30.*

The **Irma Stern Museum** is dedicated to the works and art collection of Stern (1894–1966), one of South Africa's greatest painters. The museum is administered by the University of Cape Town and occupies the Firs, the artist's home for 38 years. She is best known for African studies, particularly her paintings of indigenous people inspired by trips to the Congo and Zanzibar. Her collection of African artifacts, including priceless Congolese stools and carvings, is superb. ✉ *Cecil Rd., Rosebank,* ☎ *021/685–5686.* ✉ *R2.* ☉ *Tues.–Sun. 10–1 and 2–5.*

BEACHES

With panoramic views of mountains tumbling to the ocean, the sandy beaches of the Cape peninsula are stunning and are a major draw for Capetonians. Beautiful as the beaches may be, don't expect a traditional holiday of sun, sand, and splashing in the surf. The water around Cape Town is very, very cold. Beaches on the Atlantic are washed by the Benguela Current flowing up from the Antarctic, and in midsummer the water hovers around 12°C–15°C (55°F–60°F). The water on the False Bay side is usually 5°C (9°F) warmer. All Cape beaches are renowned for their clean, golden powdery sand. Beachcombers will find every kind of beach to suit them from intimate coves to sheltered bays and wild, wide beaches stretching forever. If you are looking for a classic beach holiday, head for the warm Indian Ocean waters of KwaZulu Natal (☞ Chapter 7) or the Garden Route (☞ Chapter 6).

The major factor that affects any day at a Cape beach is wind. In summer, howling southeasters, known as the Doctor, are all too common and will ruin any trip to the exposed beaches of False Bay; during these gales you're better off on Atlantic beaches. The easiest way to tell if the southeaster is blowing is to look at Table Mountain: If it's wearing its shroud of cloud, the Doctor is in.

Every False Bay community has its own beach, but most are not reviewed here. In comparison with Atlantic beaches, most of them are built up and unappealing, sandwiched between the sea and the commuter rail line. Once you travel south on the peninsula past Simon's Bay, beaches become wild and undeveloped, especially in the Cape of Good Hope Nature Reserve. Wherever you go, remember that the surf is dangerous, with powerful waves, strong undertow, and dangerous rip tides. Lifeguards work many of the main beaches, but some areas have rescue service only on weekends and during school holidays.

Atlantic Coast

The beaches below are listed from north to south and are marked on the Cape Peninsula map in the exploring section.

Blouberg. Make the 25-km (16-mi) trip north from the city to the other side of Table Bay and you'll be rewarded with an exceptional (and the most famous) view of Cape Town and Table Mountain. It is divided into two parts: Big Bay, which hosts surfing and sailboarding contests; and Little Bay, better suited to sunbathers and families. It's frequently windy here, which is fine if you want to fly a kite but a nuisance otherwise. Swim in front of the lifeguard club. ✉ *Follow N1 north toward Paarl, and then R27 to Milnerton and Bloubergstrand.*

Clifton. This is where the in crowd comes to see and be seen. Some of the Cape's most desirable houses cling to the slopes above the beach, and tall schooners often anchor in the calm water beyond the breakers. Granite outcroppings divide the beach into four segments, imaginatively known as First, Second, Third, and Fourth beaches. Fourth Beach is popular with families, while the others support a strong social and singles scene. Swimming is reasonably safe here, although the undertow is strong and the water, again, freezing. Lifeguards are on duty. On weekends and in peak season Clifton can be a madhouse, and your chances of finding parking at these times are nil. ✉ *Off Victoria Rd., Clifton. Hout Bay bus from OK Bazaars on Adderley St.*

Camps Bay. Table Mountain and the granite faces of the Twelve Apostles provide the backdrop for this long, sandy beach that slopes gently to the water from a grassy verge. The surf is powerful and there are no lifeguards, but sunbathers can cool off in a tidal pool or under cool outdoor showers. The popular bars and restaurants of Camps Bay lie only yards away across Victoria Road. One drawback is the wind, which can blow hard here. ⊠ *Victoria Rd. Hout Bay bus from OK Bazaars on Adderley St.*

Llandudno. Die-hard fans return to this beach again and again, and who can blame them? Its setting, among giant boulders at the base of a mountain, is glorious, and sunsets here attract their own aficionados. Unfortunately, the surf is very dangerous, as the wreck of the tanker *Romelia* offshore attests. Lifeguards are on duty. If you come by bus, brace yourself for a long walk down (and back up) the mountain from the bus stop on the M6. ⊠ *Llandudno exit off M6 and follow signs. Hout Bay bus from OK Bazaars on Adderley St.*

Sandy Bay. Backed by wild dunes and covered with the Cape's indigenous wild flowers or fynbos, Cape Town's unofficial nudist beach is also one of its prettiest. Sunbathers can hide among rocky coves or frolic on a long stretch of sandy beach. Shy nudists will appreciate its isolation, 20 minutes on foot from the nearest parking area in Llandudno. Wind, however, can be a problem: If you're caught in the buff when the southeaster starts to blow, you're in for a painful sandblasting. Getting here by bus means a very long walk going down and up the mountain. ⊠ *Llandudno exit off M6 and follow signs to Sandy Bay. Hout Bay bus from OK Bazaars on Adderley St.*

Hout Bay. This beach appears to have it all: a knockout view of the mountains, gentle surf, and easy access to the restaurants and bars of Mariner's Wharf. The reality is not quite so stunning, with the town's industrial fishing harbor and its mini-oil slicks and other waste products nearby. ⊠ *Off the M6, Hout Bay. Hout Bay bus from OK Bazaars on Adderley St.*

Noordhoek Beach. This may be the most impressive beach on the peninsula, a vast expanse of white sand stretching 6½ km (4 mi) from the base of Chapman's Peak to Kommetjie. It's also one of the wildest and least populated, backed by a lagoon and nature reserve. Because of the wind, it attracts horseback riders and walkers rather than sunbathers. Lifeguards are on duty during peak season, however. There is no bus service.⊠ *Off M6, Noordhoek.*

False Bay

Muizenberg. Once the fashionable resort of South African high society, this long, sandy beach has lost much of its glamour and now appeals to families and beginner surfers. A tacky pavilion houses a swimming pool, water slides, toilets, changing rooms, and snack shops. The beach is lined with colorful bathing boxes of the type once popular at British resorts. Lifeguards are on duty, and the sea is shallow and reasonably safe. ⊠ *Cape Metro train on Simon's Town line.*

Fish Hoek. Protected by Elsies Peak, this sandy beach attracts retirees, who appreciate the calm, clear water—it may be the safest bathing beach in the Cape. Fish Hoek is also popular with catamaran sailors and sailboarders, who often stage regattas offshore. Jager Walk, a pathway that runs along the rocky coastline, begins at the beach's southern end. ⊠ *Cape Metro train on Simon's Town line.*

DINING

By Myrna
Robins

Cape Town is the culinary capital of South Africa. Nowhere else in the country is the populace so discerning about food, and nowhere else is there such a wide selection of restaurants. Western culinary history here dates back more than 300 years—Cape Town was founded specifically to grow food—and that heritage is reflected in the city's cuisine. A number of restaurants operate in historic town houses and 18th-century wine estates.

Dutch settlers, French Huguenots, and the English have all placed their stamp on the region's cuisine, but no one has had a greater impact than the Malay slaves who were brought here in the late 17th century. It is their influence that gives Cape cuisine its distinctive use of spices. Cape curries tend to be mild compared to their Indian counterparts, and they are generally quite sweet. A good example of classic Cape cuisine is *bobotie*, a semisweet curried mince topped with savory custard.

It can be surprisingly difficult to find first-class seafood in Cape Town, but don't leave without trying crayfish, a clawless rock lobster with succulent tail meat. You'll also find linefish—any of the many game fish hooked in Cape waters by line fishermen, as opposed to school fish, which are netted by trawlers—on menus all over town. Among the best are geelbek, kingklip, kabeljou, snoek, and yellowtail.

Don't expect to see many non–South African wines on restaurant wine lists. The close proximity of Winelands vineyards inspires fierce loyalty in Capetonians (as well as penny-pinching common sense), and they tend to fuss a great deal over which wines to drink with their meal. One great boon of the Cape's wine heritage is that you can bring your own wine into even the most exclusive restaurant, often with no corkage fee. Where fees are charged, they tend to be small (R5–R10).

Many restaurants are crowded in high season, so it's best to book in advance whenever possible. With the exception of the fancier restaurants in hotels—where a jacket is required—the dress code in Cape Town is casual (but not shorts). For a description of South African culinary terms, ☞ Pleasures & Pastimes *in* Chapter 1. For price ranges, ☞ Chart 1 *in* On the Road with Fodor's.

City Bowl

$$$$ ✕ **Atlantic Grill Room.** This flagship restaurant of the recently opened Table Bay hotel (☞ Lodging, *below*) holds a prime position at the city's waterfront development. The room is decorated with updated colonial elegance, and seating on the terrace affords stunning views of working docks against a mountain backdrop. Cosmopolitan executive chef Ian Mancais has introduced menus that combine elements from Asia, Europe, and California. First courses favor seafood, but a densely flavored ragout of chanterelle, fleurette, and cepe mushrooms, finished with olive-truffle dressing and topped with a seed-strewn pastry star makes an excellent vegetarian starter. Seared Karoo peppered lamb is teamed with an eggplant terrine and ratatouille salsa, and wok-fried monkfish is served on a soba noodle cake with wilted bok choy and mustard greens dressed with black bean sauce. Artistically plated desserts offer light, fruity creations and heritage Cape favorites like brandied pudding. The extensive wine list presents a vast choice of the best of the Cape, French champagnes being the only foreign intruders. ⊠ *Table Bay Hotel, Prince Alfred Breakwater, V&A Waterfront,* ☎ *021/406–5688. AE, DC, MC, V.*

Cape Town Dining and Lodging

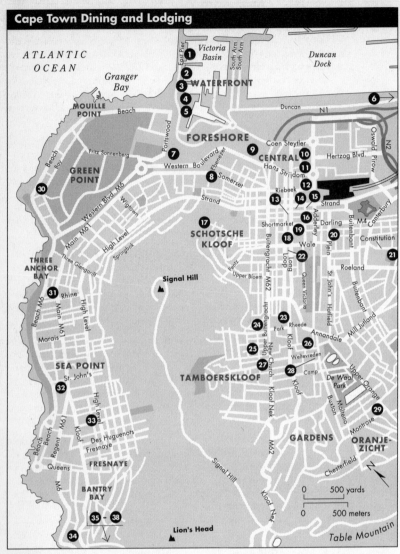

Dining

Atlantic Grill Room, **1**

Blue Danube, **27**

Blues, **35**

Cape Colony, **26**

Floris Smit Huijs, **18**

Jackson's, **32**

Nando's Tasca, **3**

Noon Gun, **17**

Panama Jack's, **6**

Quay West, **4**

Rozenhof, **23**

San Marco, **31**

Squares, **16**

Tokyo, **14**

Wangthai, **11**

Yellow Pepper Deli and Eaterie, **22**

Lodging

Bay Hotel, **35**

Best Western Cape Suites Hotel, **21**

Breakwater Lodge, **7**

Cape Grace, **4**

Cape Sun, **15**

The Capetonian, **10**

City Lodge, **9**

Clarens Manor, **33**

Ellerman House, **34**

Holiday Inn Garden Court–Greenmarket Square, **19**

Holiday Inn Garden Court–St. George's Mall, **12**

Hout Bay Manor Hotel, **36**

La Splendida, **30**

Lady Hamilton Hotel, **28**

Metropole Hotel, **13**

Mijlof Manor Hotel, **24**

Monkey Valley, **37**

Mount Nelson, **26**

Peninsula All Suites Hotel, **32**

Place on the Bay, **38**

Table Bay Hotel, **2**

Townhouse Hotel, **20**

Underberg Guest House, **25**

Victoria & Alfred Hotel, **5**

Victoria Junction, **8**

Villa Belmonte, **29**

$$$$ ✕ **Blue Danube.** Chef-patron Thomas Sinn made his mark during an eight-year stint at a top suburban restaurant: now he gives free rein to his considerable talent on the ground floor of a tall, turn-of-the-century house on the city perimeter. The tastes of his Austrian homeland are apparent in updated classics from Western and Central Europe. Complimentary appetizers precede starter dishes like Tafelspitz gelee (beef simmered in broth then sliced) with spring onions and pumpkin seeds, or saffron soup with mussels and shrimps. A parfait of duck liver is paired, unexpectedly, with cashew nuts, and gravlax is fanned, more traditionally, on dilled cream. Robust main courses include lamb knuckle with pureed potato and onion, and other meat choices of entrecôte, venison, veal, and Hungarian beef goulash. For dessert you might choose gooseberry strudel with hazelnut ice cream, roasted almond parfait on berries and a cream-cheese crepe with sabayon, or a platter of local and imported cheeses. Unhurried, professional service and a carefully selected wine list are hallmarks here. ⊠ *102 New Church St., Tamboerskloof,* ☎ *021/23–3624. AE, DC, MC, V. Closed Sun. No lunch Mon. or Sat.*

$$$$ ✕ **Cape Colony Restaurant.** Tall bay windows, a high domed ceiling, and a giant trompe-l'oeil mural, an inventive evocation of Table Mountain in the days of yore, are a befitting setting in the city's most historic and unashamedly colonial hotel. Fusion cuisine reigns supreme here, the Asian and Mediterranean accents tempered with a touch of Malay. The Asian box, a colorful mélange of seafood and meat, sets the tone for visual treats to come. Deep-fried Cape seafood and vegetables in featherlight batter, topped with an Asian brown sauce, fill abalone shells. Of the pasta dishes, the open lasagna with smoked salmon is inventive and delicious. Kingklip comes with Cape Malay–spice crust, and linefish is teamed with slow-baked tomatoes and caper salsa. Lamb is given Provençal treatment, and beef fillet is partnered with grilled polenta. Visually stunning desserts include star anise–spiked crème brûlée, and traditional malva pudding served with apricot and almond ice cream. A pricey but authoritative wine list offers the best South African vintages supplemented by labels from every major wine-growing country. ⊠ *Orange St., Gardens,* ☎ *021/23–1000. Reservations essential. AE, DC, MC, V.*

$$$ ✕ **Floris Smit Huijs.** This appealing restaurant occupies a restored
★ 18th-century town house in the city center and draws a devoted lunch crowd of office workers and gourmets. The menus reflect Asian, European, and African influences gathered during the extensive travels of owners Steve Moncrieff and Piero Romero. Tastes of southern Africa are offered in first courses like Cape Malay chicken salad with garlic, ginger, and coriander, and Mozambican prawn pâté phyllo-wrapped with a seafood saffron sauce. Seafood and vegetarian pastas are also good. More substantial dishes include venison medallions on a sauce of crème de cassis and blueberry, and pan-fried lamb kidneys with port and French mustard. A small dessert list stars a wicked double-chocolate mousse. The wine list is small but carefully chosen. Street parking is a nightmare at lunch, but there is a garage one block up the hill. ⊠ *55 Church St.,* ☎ *021/23–3414. Reservations essential for lunch in season. AE, DC, MC, V. Closed Sun. and July. No lunch Sat.*

$$$ ✕ **Panama Jack's.** In this raw-timber structure in the heart of the docks, the music is loud, the tables are crowded, and the decor is nonexistent, but nowhere in town will you find bigger crayfish. Choose one from the large, open tanks or stick to less expensive fare like mussels, oysters, calamari, and local fish. The seafood platter for two is huge, but much of it tastes like it was fried earlier. It can be difficult to find this place at night, so you may want to come for lunch if it's your first

visit. ⊠ *Royal Yacht Club basin, off Goliath Rd., Docks,* ☎ *021/47–3992. AE, DC, MC, V. No lunch Sat.*

$$$ ✕ **Quay West.** The restaurant of the Cape Grace hotel (☞ *Lodging, below*) overlooks the bascule bridge gateway to the new international yacht basin at the waterfront. A fresh decor of primrose yellow and white adds to the soothing, unintimidating setting. Starters range from phyllo-wrapped feta and smoked salmon trout on a berry compote to grilled aubergine with tomato, pesto, and ricotta. Main courses include sophisticated pastas and Asian-style salmon (marinated with soy sauce, sesame seed oil, and spices), along with heartier offerings of braised lamb shoulder and layered escalopes of ostrich and chicken. Linefish, lamb chops, and sirloin steak are available from the grill. Dessert can be as simple as fresh and preserved fruits with a duo of sorbets, or as complex as tarte tatin of pear and chèvre with pumpkin ice cream and port syrup. The carefully compiled wine list is well annotated. A shorter lunch menu is less expensive, and breakfast is a bargain. ⊠ *Cape Grace Hotel, West Quay, V&A Waterfront,* ☎ *021/418–0520. AE, DC, MC, V.*

$$$ ✕ **Rozenhof.** Within easy walking distance of the hotels in Gardens,
  ★ this late-18th-century town house offers stylish fare and one of the best wine selections in town. Yellowwood ceilings and brass chandeliers provide historical Cape touches, and works by local artists adorn the walls. The menu is inspired by Asia and the Mediterranean and supplemented with time-honored local dishes. Summer salads make delectable first courses, and the cheese soufflé with herbed mustard cream has become a classic. Cape salmon trout is complemented by Japanese mustard greens, slow roasted tomatoes and a drizzle of wasabi, and the duck comes with grape stuffing and Muscatel sauce. Layers of local Gorgonzola and mascarpone paired with preserved figs and a glass of port make a savory-sweet alternative to contemporary Cape-style and Italian desserts. ⊠ *18 Kloof St.,* ☎ *021/24–1968. AE, DC, MC, V. Closed Sun. No lunch Sat.*

$$ ✕ **Nando's Tasca.** Hemmed in by a plethora of ethnic and fast-food restaurants, this spot in the heart of the waterfront offers authentic tastes of Portugal's robust peasant cuisine. Traditional dishes from the home country and former Portuguese African colonies are lovingly preserved by the large Portuguese community in South Africa: most of them feature on Nando's menu. The restaurant is noisy, cheerful, and informal. The bar-counter, blue wall, tiles, and banners contribute to the atmosphere of a *taberna Portugesa.* When the so-called Doctor—a strong southeaster—prevails, avoid the tables near the door. In balmy weather, sit outside and watch maritime activities against the backdrop of Table Mountain. Portions are generous: Warm Madeira bread with garlic butter makes a good accompaniment to first courses of chicken livers or giblets, *chourico* (spicy Portuguese sausage), or mussels in red wine sauce. Calamari comes in various guises, and there's a good selection of other seafood and of Portuguese beef dishes. If you like your food fiery, order chicken or prawns *peri-peri,* but stipulate that your order be basted with the chili sauce during grilling, so that it soaks into the meat and becomes fiery. Desserts are run-of-the-mill. The wine list includes a few Portuguese labels. ⊠ *154 V&A Waterfront,* ☎ *021/419–3009. AE, DC, MC, V.*

$$ ✕ **Tokyo.** Run by a Japanese father-and-son team, this city-center restaurant is the most affordable of the few Japanese eateries in town. Black trelliswork, lacquered trays, and colorful kimonos create a suitable atmosphere. The sushi bar features fish bought fresh each morning from Cape harbors. Diners can also order *teppanyaki* (meat, seafood, and vegetables grilled on hibachi tables) and tempura. The *bentou* fish box makes a perfect lunchtime sampler. ⊠ *31a Long St.,*

Cape Town, ☎ *021/23–6055. Reservations not accepted. AE, DC, MC, V. Closed Sun. and July. No lunch Sat.*

$$ ✕ **Wangthai.** Thai restaurants are only now catching on in South Africa, and this is one of the best. *Satays,* grilled meat with a spicy peanut dip, make a good starter, as do spring-roll-wrapped prawns. *Tom Seab* is an outstanding aromatic beef broth scented with *galangal,* a type of ginger. Colorful stir-fries combine chicken, pork, or beef with coriander leaves and sweet basil or the fire of roasted chilies. Pungent red and green curries are tempered by coconut milk and mounds of sticky rice. Wangthai's setting in an office block on the foreshore won't win any awards but is convenient to city-center hotels and the Tourist Rendezvous Travel Centre. ✉ *31 Heerengracht St.,* ☎ *021/418–1858. AE, DC, MC, V. No lunch weekends.*

$ ✕ **Noon Gun.** Perched high on Signal Hill in the old Malay Quarter, in the shadow of the cannon whose midday fire alerts Capetonians to check their watches, Noon Gun has unsurpassed views of the city, Table Mountain, and the bay. This former tearoom offers tastes of the best of Cape Malay heritage fare at reasonable prices. Plastic tablecloths, paper napkins, and basic cutlery have not discouraged international reviewers from acclaiming venerable dishes like bobotie and *bredie, dhal* curry and *masala* fish, along with slow-cooked, tamarind-spiked *denningvleis,* a marinated mutton classic. There's the usual accompaniments based on cucumber, tomato, and onion and a more unusual and delectable chili-fired *sambal* of mixed dried fruit. The finales are just as traditional and star *koeksusters,* a syrupy braided doughnut, and *melktert,* a cinnamon-flavored, egg custard–filled puff pastry. Liquor is taboo here, but the iced juices, chunky with fresh fruit, are refreshing. ✉ *273 Longmarket St., Cape Town,* ☎ *021/24–0529. Reservations essential in season. No credit cards. Closed Sun.*

$ ✕ **Squares.** Overlooking St. George's Mall, this fresh, stylish restaurant is a great place for breakfast, lunch, or snacks. A variety of eggs—scrambled and fried—along with toasted croissants with tomato, cheese, and bacon or smoked salmon are offered all day. Seafood choices include grilled linefish and fried calamari with rice and lemon-thyme mayonnaise. Sandwiches, salads, pizza, filled pitas, and pasta are favorites. For an indulgent finale, order the dense chocolate brownie with ice cream and hot chocolate sauce. Squares gets crowded here at lunchtime, so be sure to make a reservation. ✉ *Town Sq., St. George's Mall,* ☎ *021/24–0224. Reservations essential. AE, DC, MC, V. Closed Sun. No dinner.*

$ ✕ **Yellow Pepper Deli and Eaterie.** For good, home-cooked food at bargain prices this popular outlet has few rivals. Diners can order from a chalkboard menu or select what they fancy from dishes displayed behind a glass counter. Sophisticated Greek *mezes* (appetizers) and Mediterranean salads precede hearty dishes like vegetarian lasagna, bobotie, chicken and spinach bake, and peasant sausage casserole. Arrive early to claim a portion of malva pudding, an outstanding version of this traditional Cape baked dessert—fluffy, syrupy, and topped with cream. Try to sit in the high-ceilinged, arty interior: outdoor diners suffer from the noise and fumes of traffic. ✉ *138 Long St.,* ☎ *021/24–9250. AE, DC, MC, V. Closed Sun. No dinner.*

Atlantic Coast

$$$ ✕ **Blues.** Doors open to frame an inviting vista of palms, sand, and azure sea from the balcony of this popular restaurant in Camps Bay. The mood and menu are Californian, the clientele young and sophisticated. Appetizers inspired by Thailand and the Mediterranean are juxtaposed with local smoked salmon trout and West Coast mussels. The pasta is deservedly popular, and the quality of fresh line- and shellfish is virtually guaranteed. Crisp stir-fried vegetables add color to generous portions that are attractively presented. For dessert, try chocolate brownies, sticky toffee pudding with butterscotch sauce, or one of the great American ice cream concoctions. ⊠ *The Promenade, Victoria Rd., Camps Bay*, ☎ *021/438–2040. Reservations essential in season. AE, DC, MC, V.*

$$$ ✕ **Jackson's.** Award-winning chef John Jackson uses Cape ingredients to create the vibrant flavors of Provence, Italy, and the Middle and Far East. A meal could begin with an Asian combination of Nonya crepes and marinated beef satays, then move on to kingklip, a favorite Cape fish, with grilled eggplant and a chili-tomato sauce. Stir-fried chicken and mushrooms in brown-bean sauce join up with Chinese noodles, and veal escalopes are served with spinach and pear puree. Variations on a chocolate theme, and Provençal honey and lavender crepes with ice cream are among the imaginative dessert choices. Standards occasionally slip when Jackson is off duty, but the restaurant offers mostly top-notch dining at moderate prices. He also presides over the adjoining Café Bijou, which has a lighter but equally sophisticated menu. ⊠ *313 Beach Rd., Sea Point*, ☎ *021/439–8888. AE, DC, MC, V. Closed Sun. No lunch.*

$$$ ✕ **San Marco.** Restaurants open and close in Cape Town with alarming speed. This Italian institution in Sea Point is a happy exception, a meeting place for generations of diners since it first opened its doors as a *gelateria*. Come here not for the decor but for consistency and authenticity and for dishes that are cooked only after you order them. Start with superb grilled calamari, then move to homemade pasta or one of the veal dishes—escalopes cooked with sage and white wine are especially good. If one of the less common Cape linefish such as elf (shad) is offered, don't miss it. Finish with a selection of the house's renowned ice creams and sorbets, which are dressed with a splash of liqueur. ⊠ *92 Main Rd., Sea Point*, ☎ *021/439–2758. Reservations essential in season. AE, DC, MC, V. Closed Tues. and 1 month in midwinter. No lunch Mon.–Sat.*

Southern Suburbs

$$$$ ✕ **Au Jardin.** In this corner of the historic Vineyard Hotel in Newlands,
★ complete with fountain and views of Table Mountain, talented French chef Christophe Dehosse and his team imbue classic French cuisine with subtle Cape and Mediterranean accents. Appetizers might include a prawn-and-sweetbread duo with sorrel, roast quail salad with toasted pine nuts and balsamic vinegar, or chèvre baked in tomato, cream, and garlic. Local linefish might be flamed with Pernod, teamed with morels, or served on a ratatouille base, with tapenade. Guinea fowl, rabbit, and lamb are given stellar Gallic treatment. For dessert try caramelized pineapple tart with rum-raisin ice cream. There's also a *ménu dégustation*, and the lighter à la carte menu at lunch is less expensive than the evening selection. The wine list presents the best of the Cape, but there are also French labels for conservative tastes. ⊠ *Vineyard Hotel, Colinton Rd., Claremont*, ☎ *021/683–1520. AE, DC, MC, V. Closed Sun. No lunch Sat. or Mon.*

$$$$ ✕ **Buitenverwachting.** On a historic wine estate in Constantia, this su-
★ perb restaurant is consistently rated among the country's top 10. Window-side tables provide views of the vineyards sloping up toward the mountains. Meticulously prepared dishes are presented with artistic flair and often a surprise element. Imaginative starters include freshwater prawns in coconut-chili nage with green-tea noodles, and quail cutlets filled with foie gras and served with an apple-rosemary tart. Look

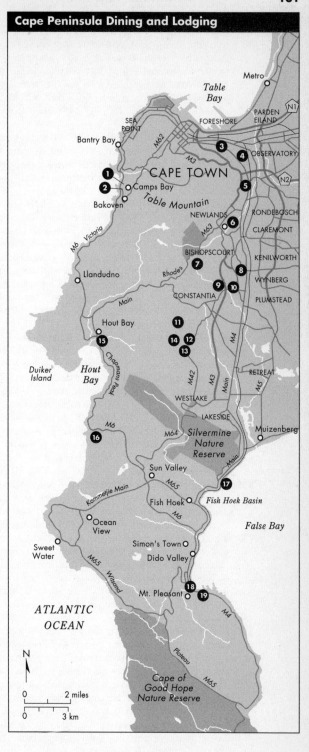

Cape Peninsula Dining and Lodging

for dishes based on local seafood and Karoo lamb and game. Medallions of springbok are teamed with grapes and smoked bacon; ostrich loin comes with gluhwein sauce (hot, spiced red wine that is sweetened) and cinnamon-spiked barley. Many dessert masterpieces use local fruit, among them mango and plum sorbet with fresh berries and an amaretto *samoosa* (filled, light pastry triangle) with apples and caramel ice cream. ⊠ *Klein Constantia Rd., Constantia,* ☎ *021/794–3522. Reservations essential. AE, DC, MC, V. Closed Sun., Mon., and July. No lunch Sat.*

$$$$ ✕ **The Cellars.** Classic table settings and highly professional service complement artfully presented fare in this restaurant in the historic Cellars-Hohenhort Hotel in Constantia. Seasonal menus draw their inspiration from French contemporary and English country-house cuisines, while making full use of the Cape's bounty of seafood, meat, and fresh produce. Summer starters include chilled marinated west-coast mussels and a paupiette of salmon and lobster (thin slices of salmon stuffed with lobster rolled then wrapped in bacon and braised) on a bed of zucchini. For a main course consider tender ostrich fillet or sautéed game fish with olive oil and basil. Caramelized apple tart and ice cream, sparked with a classic Constantia tangerine liqueur, is an excellent dessert. The luncheon menu is lighter and less expensive. A sister restaurant, the Cape Malay Kitchen, presents table d'hote indigenous fare. ⊠ *15 Hohenort Ave., Constantia,* ☎ *021/794–2137. Reservations essential. AE, DC, MC, V.*

$$$ ✕ **Constantia Uitsig.** This restaurant in a restored farmstead attracts a
★   large, loyal following. Reserve a table on the enclosed veranda for tremendous views of the mountains. The menu is a harmonious blend of northern Italian and Provençal cuisines. Tomato tart with basil and fontina sings with Mediterranean flavor, as does the excellent homemade pasta. For something more substantial, try grilled Karoo lamb with Provençal herbs, duck breast with Madagascar green peppercorns, or chef Frank Swainston's butter-tender Florentine tripe braised in tomato-and-vegetable sauce. His version of the perennially popular tiramisu is also recommended. ⊠ *Spaanschemat River Rd., Constantia,* ☎ *021/794–4480. Reservations essential. AE, DC, MC, V. No lunch Mon.*

$$$ ✕ **Emily's Bistro.** In a down-market neighborhood minutes from the city, this unpretentious boîte serves substantial fare with artistic flair. The small menu highlights innovative dishes with Cape Malay accents, as well as updated versions of traditional South African cooking. A warm salad of kerrievis (curried fish), sultanas (golden raisins), and chutney on a red-lentil puree with orange crème-fraîche sauce could precede quails stuffed with wild mushrooms or duck livers and herbs served with black-olive-and-potato rösti. Finish with lemon-and-lavender mascarpone mousse with macerated fruit in red wine syrup. ⊠ *77 Roodebloem Rd., Woodstock,* ☎ *021/448–2366. AE, DC, MC, V. Closed Sun., Mon., and Sept. No lunch Tues. or Sat.*

$$$ ✕ **La Colombe.** The Uitsig farm is home to a comparative newcomer that has quickly attracted devotees of Provençal fare. The walls and woodwork of this small restaurant are painted sunshine yellow and sky blue, and French doors in the dining room open onto a courtyard. The menu is chalked on one blackboard, a limited wine list on another. Youthful chef Franck Dangereux transforms local produce into a menu that sings of his native French province: expect flavorful renderings of *pan bagna* (salad nicoise sandwiched into French bread), mini *pissaladière* (pizza topped with slow-cooked onions, black olives, and anchovies), or *beignets de courgettes* (zucchini fritters) to precede items like pan-fried entrecôte steak with garlic or breast of duck. Cape linefish is given star treatment in delicate lemon butter and studded with diced tomato and cucumber. Desserts range from a trio of fruity sorbets to a crème Catalan caramelisee. Carafes of white and red house wines are a good value. ⊠ *Uitsig Farm, Spaanschemat River Rd., Constantia,* ☎ *021/794–2390. Reservations essential in season. AE, DC, MC, V. Closed Tues.*

$$$ ✗ **Parks.** This restored Victorian villa in Constantia has been jam-packed since it opened three years ago. The reasons are twofold: The elegant decor is convivial, not intimidating, and Michael Olivier's zesty contemporary cuisine strikes the right chord with local and out-of-town patrons. Starters of warm Camembert tartlet with caramelized onions, and deep-fried Cajun potato skins with chili jam and tomato-cilantro salsa are typical of the eclectic menu. Roast duckling with cassis sauce is an Olivier classic, and char-grilled beef fillet is paired with *pommes frîtes* and Madagascar green-peppercorn sauce. For dessert don't pass up a hazelnut-shortbread sandwich filled with praline cream over raspberry coulis. ⊠ *114 Constantia Rd., Constantia,* ☎ *021/797–8202. Reservations essential. AE, DC, MC, V. Closed Sun. No lunch Sat.*

$$ ✗ **Africa Cafe.** Locals and tourists crowd this Observatory restaurant, the country's first to serve indigenous dishes from across the continent. Multicolored cloths and stunning hand-glazed crockery brighten the ocher interior of the old terrace house, complementing an equally vibrant cuisine. Fresh fruit cocktails accompany a communal starter tray of snacks from everywhere: Ethiopia to Zambia, Kenya to Angola. You could easily make a meal of this tasty mélange of patties, dips, puffs, and pastries. The accompanying chili dip is among the best you will taste anywhere. Curried ostrich and Malawi chicken macadamia are favorite main dishes, and vegetarians applaud the Senegalese stuffed papaya. ⊠ *213 Lower Main Rd., Observatory,* ☎ *021/47–9553. AE, DC, MC, V. Closed Sun. No lunch.*

$$ ✗ **Jonkershuis.** This establishment offers classic Cape hospitality in a 19th-century building adjoining the gracious manor house at Groot Constantia, the Cape's oldest wine estate. Fresh linefish and roast loin of lamb keep company on the menu with classic bobotie-spiced beef mince studded with dried fruit and nut slivers and topped with a savory baked custard, and *smoorsnoek,* a popular Cape fish braised with onion, potato, and chili and served with baked sweet potatoes in fresh orange sauce. The traditional chicken pie is made from a recipe handed down through generations of Dutch settlers. If you want to taste all of these dishes, ask for a Cape sampler. Jonkershuis also serves hearty breakfasts and light refreshments. ⊠ *Groot Constantia Estate, Main Rd., Constantia,* ☎ *021/794–6255. Reservations essential in season. AE, DC, MC. No dinner Sun. or Mon.*

False Bay

$$ ✗ **Brass Bell.** Whether diners choose to eat in the main restaurant, the cabin, on the terrace, or in the gazebo, they enjoy views of False Bay, frolicking surfers, and fishing boats heading for the harbor. This cheerful, informal place can get crowded and noisy. There's a choice of two menus—the main restaurant presents a more formal menu, while the other areas share a lighter, more casual menu—both of which offer good value for money. The emphasis is on fish and seafood, but vegetarians and carnivores alike will find sufficient items to please them. The fare is mostly simple fare, but is enlivened by a few Cape traditional dishes. ⊠ *Waterfront, Kalk Bay,* ☎ *021/788–5456. Reservations essential in season. AE, DC, MC, V.*

LODGING

Finding lodging in Cape Town can be an expensive nightmare during high season, December through Easter, when prices rise by as much as 50%. The worst period of all is the South African school holidays, December 15 to January 15, when usually the only hotels with vacancies are in Zaire. If you arrive in Cape Town without a reservation, head for **Captour's Tourist Rendezvous Travel Centre** (☞ Contacts and Resources *in* Cape Town A to Z, *below*), which has a helpful accommodation desk.

Hotels in the city center are a good option if you're here on business or don't want to drive. During the day the historic city center is a vibrant place. At night, though, it's shut up tight; night owls may prefer a hotel amid the nonstop action of the redeveloped waterfront. Hotels and B&Bs in the southern suburbs, especially Constantia, offer unrivaled beauty and tranquillity and make an ideal base if you're exploring the Winelands and the peninsula. You need a car, though, and should plan on 15–30 minutes to get into town. Atlantic Coast hotels provide the closest thing in Cape Town to a beach-holiday atmosphere, in spite of the cold ocean waters.

Keep in mind that international flights from the United States and Europe arrive in the morning and return flights depart in the evening. Since most hotels have an 11 AM checkout, you may have to wait for a room if you've just arrived; if you're leaving, you will be hauled kicking and screaming out of your room hours before your flight. Most hotels will try to accommodate you, but they often have no choice in peak season. Some of the larger hotels have residents-only lounges where you can spend the hours awaiting your flight. Take note that guest house and B&B accommodations in Cape Town have mushroomed and that throughout the city and surrounding suburbs you can find lodgings ranging from the elegant, country-home luxurious to the quaintly rustic.

The most reliable source of good B&B establishments is the **Portfolio of Places** (☎ 011/880–3414, FAX 011/788–4802) brochure. Or contact **Bed & Breakfast** (⊠ 17 Talana Rd., Claremont 7700, ☎ 021/61–6543, FAX 021/683–5159).

If you don't like tiptoeing around someone's house, or you want to save money, consider taking a fully furnished apartment, especially if you're staying two or more weeks. Among the dependable brokers are **Cape Holiday Homes** (⊠ Box 2044, Cape Town 8000, ☎ 021/419–0430) and **Private Places** (⊠ Box 489, Milnerton 7435, ☎ 021/52–1200). Another good choice is **Holiday Booking Services** (⊠ Box 514, Cape Town 8000, ☎ 021/24–3693, FAX 021/24–1907), with more than 500 high-quality, furnished, self-catering apartments on its books.

Harbour View Cottages, Cape Town's first and only guest street with an entire little community of houses to rent, are unusual, trendy, classy, and quite charming and are near the harbor, as the name implies. There are 16 beautifully restored, small, self-catering houses, with daily housekeeping services. ⊠ *Office, 1 Loader St., Cape Town, 8000,* ☎ *021/418–6081,* FAX *021/418–6082. AE, DC, MC, V.*

For price ranges, *see* Chart 2 (A) *in* On the Road with Fodor's. Mailing addresses, if different from the street address, are given in parentheses in the service information at the end of the review.

City Bowl

$$$$ ☐ **Cape Sun.** One of the top hotels in the city center, this 32-story tower dominates the skyline, and is near the Captour office, St. George's Mall, and the Golden Acre shopping center. The lobby, with marble floors, a paneled ceiling, and green-marble pillars, sets the tone for the hotel. Rooms reflect a Cape Dutch influence: they are done in pale yellows and blues and light- and dark-wood paneling and are decorated with Cape Dutch furniture and line drawings of Cape Dutch estates. Guests can opt for a room facing the sea or Table Mountain. Both views are spectacular, but request a room on a high floor—the sea view from lower rooms is partially obstructed by other buildings. ☒ *Strand St. (Box 4532), Cape Town 8000,* ☎ *021/23–8844,* FAX *021/23–8875. 350 rooms with bath. 2 restaurants, bar, room service, sauna, exercise room, travel services. AE, DC, MC, V.*

$$$$ ☐ **Mount Nelson.** This distinctive pink landmark is the grande dame ★ of Cape Town. Since it opened its doors in 1899 to accommodate passengers of the Union-Castle steamships, it has been the focal point of Cape social life. Its guest book reads like a *Who's Who* of South African history, and it's still the favorite locale for Cape Town society functions. Named by *Tatler* and *Harpers & Queen* magazines as one of the best hotels in the world, it retains an old-fashioned charm and gentility that other five-star hotels often lack. High tea is served in the lounge, to piano accompaniment; the Grill Room offers a nightly dinner dance; and the staff almost outnumbers the guests. The hotel stands at the top of Government Avenue, but, surrounded as it is by 7 acres of manicured gardens, it might as well be in the country. For peak season, December–March, it's advisable to book a year in advance. ☒ *76 Orange St., Cape Town 8001,* ☎ *021/23–1000,* FAX *021/24–7472. 226 rooms with bath. 3 restaurants, bar, 2 pools, exercise room, 2 tennis courts, squash. AE, DC, MC, V.*

$$$ ☐ **Best Western Cape Suites Hotel.** This village-style hotel, with low buildings and adjoining individual units, is five minutes from the center of Cape Town, near Parliament, and a 15-minute walk from the waterfront. Comfortably luxurious, each suite has a fully equipped kitchen, a plus if you're traveling as a family. Rooms are spacious and pleasantly furnished. Some rooms have mountain views, and others look into the city. Although it's on a corner site, the hotel is well insulated, so traffic noise is not a major problem, and inner rooms tend to be quieter. If you have a car, you can park it virtually outside your room. A free shuttle takes guests to popular sights within about 13 km (8 mi) of the hotel, for example to the trendy shopping area of Cavendish Square in Claremont and to Clifton beach. ☒ *Constitution and De Villiers Sts. (Box 51085, Waterfront), Cape Town 8002,* ☎ *021/461–0727,* FAX *021/ 462–4389. 126 rooms with bath. 2 restaurants, bar, 2 pools, exercise room, recreation room, free parking. AE, DC, MC, V*

$$$ ☐ **Villa Belmonte.** In a quiet residential neighborhood on the slopes above the city, this small guest house offers privacy and luxury in an attractive Dutch Revival residence. Owners Tabea and Cliff Jacobs have sought to create the feeling of an Italian villa through the use of marbling, molded ceilings, and natural wood floors. Wide verandas command superb views of the city, Table Mountain, and Devil's Peak. Rooms, each with air-conditioning and decorated according to a theme, make effective use of colorful draperies, wicker furniture, and small-pane windows. It's a 20-minute walk to the city center. ☒ *33 Belmont Ave., Oranjezicht 8001,* ☎ *021/462–1576,* FAX *021/462–1579. 8 rooms with bath. Restaurant, bar, room service, pool. No children under 8. AE, DC, MC, V. CP.*

$$ ▥ **The Capetonian.** In the foreshore between the waterfront and the city center, this newly renovated hotel offers a high standard of luxury and elegance at half the price of the Cape Sun. Floral carpets, wood headboards, African artwork, and draperies in rich autumnal colors make the large rooms inviting. Request a room on an upper floor for a good view of the harbor. ⊠ *Pier Pl., Heerengracht (Box 6856), Roggebaai 8012,* ☎ *021/21–1150,* FAX *021/25–2215. 169 rooms with bath. 2 restaurants, bar, room service. AE, DC, MC, V.*

$$ ▥ **Holiday Inn Garden Court–Greenmarket Square.** Facing historic Greenmarket Square, this minimum-service hotel has one of the best locations in the city, especially for those who don't have a car. All rooms were recently refurbished and have cable TV and air-conditioning. Mountain-facing rooms overlooking the square are pleasant, but the dawn chorus of vendors setting up their stalls may drive you to distraction. Parking is a major headache in this part of town. ⊠ *10 Greenmarket Sq. (Box 3775), Cape Town 8000,* ☎ *021/23–2040,* FAX *021/23–3664. 170 rooms with bath. Restaurant, bar. AE, DC, MC, V.*

$$ ▥ **Holiday Inn Garden Court–St. George's Mall.** This no-frills hotel at the bottom of St. George's Mall, seconds from the Captour office and major public transportation, offers competitive rates. Rooms, done in gray and other subdued tones, are comfortable and clean. Plump for one of the twin corner rooms—for just R20 more you'll stay in a larger room with huge windows on two sides, although the view is still only of the street. ⊠ *St. George's Mall (Box 5616), Cape Town 8000,* ☎ *021/419–0808,* FAX *021/419–7010. 136 rooms with bath. Restaurant, bar, room service, indoor pool, sauna, exercise room. AE, DC, MC, V.*

$$ ▥ **Mijlof Manor Hotel.** The Mijlof is a comfortable retreat from the city center (20 minutes away on foot). In a residential neighborhood below Signal Hill, this mid-range hotel is built around a 1710 Tamboerskloof farmhouse, most of which is concealed now by a modern wing. Cape Dutch–style rooms are large and well equipped, but you can probably do better at the nearby Underberg Guest House. The wood-paneled bar is a popular watering hole. ⊠ *2A Milner Rd., Tamboerskloof, Cape Town 8001,* ☎ *021/26–1476,* FAX *021/22–2046. 70 rooms with bath. Restaurant, 2 bars, room service, pool, beauty salon. AE, DC, MC, V.*

$$ ▥ **Townhouse Hotel.** Its proximity to government buildings and its easygoing atmosphere (not to mention extremely competitive rates) make the Townhouse popular with members of parliament. Rooms are bright and have whitewashed rough-brick walls, checked curtains, and dried-flower montages. If you want a view of Table Mountain, request one of the twin-bed rooms. ⊠ *60 Corporation St. (Box 5053), Cape Town 8000,* ☎ *021/45–7050,* FAX *021/45–3891. 104 rooms with bath. Restaurant, bar, room service, health club. AE, DC, MC, V.*

$$ ▥ **Underberg Guest House.** In a restored Victorian farmhouse in Tam-
★ boerskloof, this guest house caters primarily to businesspeople, who appreciate the privacy and location, a 20-minute walk from the city center. The rooms are airy and light, thanks to high ceilings and large windows, and have an elegance seldom found in conventional hotels. Each room has a a TV, minibar, tea- and coffeemaker. ⊠ *Carstens St., Tamboerskloof, Cape Town 8001,* ☎ *021/26–2262,* FAX *021/24–4059. 10 rooms with bath, 1 suite. Bar, dining room. Breakfast included. No children under 12. AE, DC, MC, V.*

$ ▥ **Lady Hamilton Hotel.** You get good value and an excellent location at this hotel on a peaceful residential street in Gardens, 15 minutes on foot from the city center. Rooms are attractive and bright, decorated with blond wood furniture and African-print bedspreads. ⊠ *10 Union St., Gardens, Cape Town 8001,* ☎ *021/23–3888,* FAX *021/23–*

7788. 52 rooms with bath. Restaurant, bar, room service, pool. AE, DC, MC, V.

$ 🏨 **Metropole Hotel.** Celebrating its 100th birthday in 1996, this basic hotel in the center of town is known for its creaky, old-fashioned charm. The lobby, enlivened by delicate floral wallpaper, centers around a teak-paneled elevator, the second-oldest in Cape Town. Unfortunately, standard rooms are dull and nondescript, but the price *is* right. The Mandarin suites, with rosewood paneling and understated Chinese decor, are far more attractive, but for the extra money you may be better off at the Townhouse Hotel. Street noise may be a problem during the day. ✉ *38 Long St. (Box 3086), Cape Town 8000,* ☎ *021/23–6363,* FAX *021/23–6370. 33 rooms with bath. Bar, coffee shop, room service. AE, DC, MC, V. CP.*

Waterfront

$$$$ 🏨 **The Cape Grace.** It's not a surprise that this well-appointed, exclu-
★ sive hotel at the V & A Waterfront became an instant success. Built on a spit of land jutting into a working harbor, the Cape Grace offers views of seals frolicking in the surrounding waters and seagulls soaring above. The large guest rooms have harbor or mountain views. Elegant and understated with both French period decor and a wonderful modern design, it's owned and run by one of the country's leading hotelier families, the Brands. The attention to detail throughout is outstanding, from the antique pieces to the fresh flowers in the rooms. There's a wonderful well-stocked library for browsing, and a superb restaurant overlooking the pool, Quay West, that serves local and international cuisine. Guests have free use of the nearby health club and the hotel's courtesy car for service into the city. Booking well in advance is essential. ✉ *West Quay, V & A Waterfront,Cape Town 8002,* ☎ *021/410–7100,* FAX *021/419–7622. 102 rooms with bath. Restaurant, bar, pool, library. AE, DC, MC, V.*

$$$$ 🏨 **Table Bay Hotel.** This hotel is new, glitzy, and on arguably the best spot, at the tip of the V & A Waterfront. It's the top pick for celebrities—Michael Jackson and Richard Branson stayed here—which, no doubt, gives it a distinct buzz. The decor is sunny and eclectic, with picture windows, marble and mosaic floors, a timber ceiling, and lots of plants. In the lounge, you can browse the selection of international newspapers as you sit fireside, relaxing to live chamber music. The Victorian style rooms, surprisingly, are rather ordinary and have ocean or mountain views. The health spa can give you every kind of treatment and prides itself on being the only sea spa in the country. The hotel is famous for its extraordinary orchid and floral displays. ✉ *Quay 6, V & A Waterfront, Cape Town 8002,* ☎ *021/406–5000,* FAX *021/406–5767. 239 rooms with bath, 15 suites. 3 restaurants, 2 bars, lobby lounge, pool, beauty salon, spa, health club, shops, business services, meeting room. AE, DC, MC, V.*

$$$$ 🏨 **Victoria & Alfred Hotel.** You couldn't find a better location for this upmarket hotel, in a converted warehouse smack in the middle of the waterfront, surrounded by shops, bars, and restaurants. Rooms are huge, furnished in neo–Cape Dutch style, and decorated in muted rust and sea colors. Views from the costlier mountain-facing rooms are spectacular, encompassing not only Table Mountain but the city and docks as well. Waterfront buses leave regularly for the city center, a five-minute ride away. ✉ *Pierhead (Box 50050), Waterfront, Cape Town 8002,* ☎ *021/419–6677,* FAX *021/419–8955. 68 rooms with bath. Restaurant, bar, room service. AE, DC, MC, V.*

$$$$ 🏨 **Victoria Junction.** This is South Africa's first loft hotel and with its spot on Main Road, Greenpoint, adjacent to the waterfront, and its distinctly funky and art deco–style decor, it's popular with those look-

ing for something different. The spacious loft rooms have high ceilings and beds on special platforms, but be warned: You have to be nimble to climb to your large double bed in the upstairs section of the room. The chaise-like furniture in the sitting areas is arty but not all that comfortable unless you enjoy reclining like a Goya model. Although the health-conscious food is disappointing, The Set is a trendy restaurant for business lunches, and the bar always jumps at happy hour. ⊠ *Somerset and Ebenezer Rd., Greenpoint (Box 51234, Waterfront), Cape Town 8002,* ☎ *021/418–1234,* ℻ *021/418–5678. 172 rooms with bath, Restaurant, coffee shop, bar, pool. AE, DC, MC, V*

$$ 🏨 **City Lodge.** Location is everything at this no-frills chain hotel, a five-minute walk from the waterfront and 10 minutes from the city center. Rooms are standard, decorated with ship prints and blond furniture, and all have TVs and tea- and coffeemakers. ⊠ *Dock and Alfred Drives, Waterfront (Box 6025, Roggebaai), Cape Town 8012,* ☎ *021/419–9450,* ℻ *021/419–0460. 164 rooms with bath. Bar, breakfast room, pool. AE, DC, MC, V.*

$ 🏨 **Breakwater Lodge.** You won't find another hotel this close to the waterfront offering rates so low. Next to a 19th-century prison on Portswood Ridge, the Breakwater certainly won't win any awards for charm or coziness. Long, narrow corridors lead to rooms that are tiny and sterile, furnished with the kind of chipboard-and-veneer furniture that you find at do-it-yourself stores. Nevertheless, the rooms are clean and have TVs, phones, and tea- and coffeemakers. Ask for a room with a view of Table Mountain. ⊠ *Portswood Rd., Waterfront, Cape Town 8001,* ☎ *021/406–1911,* ℻ *021/406–1070. 327 rooms, 217 with bath, 110 with shared bath. 2 restaurants, bar. AE, DC, MC, V.*

Atlantic Coast

$$$$ 🏨 **Bay Hotel.** Of the luxury hotels in and around Cape Town, this beach hotel in Camps Bay is the most relaxed and unpretentious. The three-story structure is across the road from a white-sand beach and is backed by the towering cliffs of the Twelve Apostles. From the raised pool deck, guests look out over sea and sand, far from the hurly-burly of Cape Town. Cane furniture, colorful paintings, and attractive peach and sea tones make the rooms bright. Service is excellent, with an emphasis on privacy. Ask for a premier room if you want a sea view. ⊠ *Victoria Rd. (Box 32021), Camps Bay 8040,* ☎ *021/438–4444,* ℻ *021/438–4455. 70 rooms with bath. 4 restaurants, bar, room service, pool, billiards. AE, DC, MC, V.*

$$$$ 🏨 **Ellerman House.** Without a doubt, this is one of the finest (and most
★   expensive) hotels in South Africa. Built in 1912 for shipping magnate Sir John Ellerman, the hotel sits high on a hill in Bantry Bay and enjoys stupendous views of the sea. Broad, terraced lawns fronted by elegant balustrades step down the hillside to a sparkling pool. The drawing and living rooms, decorated in Regency style, are elegant yet not forbiddingly formal. Guest rooms benefit from enormous picture windows, high ceilings, and spacious tile bathrooms. Of particular note is the Africa-theme room, decorated with cane furniture, ostrich-egg lamps, and African sculptures. The hotel accommodates only 14 guests, and a highly trained staff caters to their every whim. In the kitchen, four chefs prepare whatever guests request—there are no menus. All drinks except wine and champagne are included in the rates. ⊠ *180 Kloof Rd., Bantry Bay 8001 (Box 515, Sea Point 8060),* ☎ *021/439–9182,* ℻ *021/434–7257. 11 rooms with bath. Restaurant, bar, room service, pool, sauna, gym. No children under 18. AE, DC, MC, V. CP.*

$$$$ 🏨 **Place on the Bay.** These luxury self-catering apartments are on the beachfront in Camps Bay, within easy walking distance of a host of restaurants and bars. Apartments are tasteful, modern affairs that make extensive use of glass and speckled marble. Many units have good sea views from their balconies. If you really want to have it all, take the magnificent penthouse, which occupies the entire top floor and comes with its own chef, car, chauffeur, and swimming pool. All units have daily maid service. ⊠ *Fairways and Victoria Rds., Camps Bay 8001,* ☎ *021/438–7060,* FAX *021/438–2692. 21 apartments with bath. Restaurant, bar, pool. AE, DC, MC, V. MAP.*

$$$ 🔲 **Clarens Manor.** This astonishing guest house close to Sea Point is the inspiration of Francois Ferreira, the former chef of two South Africana premiers, P.W. Botha and F.W. De Klerk. The house is 90 years old and has decorative original woodwork. The refurbished upstairs rooms are grand in size and decor, and the downstairs lounges and dining room are warm and comfortable. Some of the bedrooms have a wooden deck overlooking the pool and a vista across rooftops to the sea. Francois's culinary skill is recognized by heads of state around the world. His Asian- and French-influenced South African cuisine is lovingly prepared and it is magnificent. Meals here resemble private dinner parties. You'll be treated like a dignitary and ferried around the city and to and from the airport as part of the service. Laundry service is also included in the rate. ⊠ *35 Clarens Rd., Sea Point, Cape Town 8060,* ☎ *021/434–6801,* FAX *021/434–6845. 6 rooms. Dining room, 2 lounges, pool. AE, DC, MC, V.*

$$$ 🔲 **Hout Bay Manor Hotel.** Chapman's Peak provides the backdrop for this charming hotel in Hout Bay, a fishing village 20 minutes from Cape Town. Built in 1871 in Cape Dutch style, the hotel is popular with older travelers, who appreciate its peace and quiet, which are broken only by the sound of the courtyard fountain. Public rooms are attractive, with high ceilings and creaking wood floors. Canopy beds, delicate floral fabrics, and claw-foot tubs create a Victorian feeling at odds with the gray wall-to-wall carpeting. A brick terrace, shaded by oaks and large umbrellas, is an attractive spot for breakfast, drinks, and pub lunches. The beach at Hout Bay and several restaurants are within easy walking distance. ⊠ *Main Rd. (Box 27035), Hout Bay, 7872,* ☎ *021/ 790–4730,* FAX *021/790–4952. 11 rooms with bath. Restaurant, bar, room service. AE, DC, MC, V. CP.*

$$$ 🔲 **La Splendida.** Designed to look like a Miami South Beach Art Deco hotel, this trendy all-suites addition to the Cape Town scene has a great location on Beach Road, Mouille Point. Most of the rooms have stunning views of the sea, while others have an equally nice view looking out to Lion's Head mountain. Well-proportioned rooms are zanily decorated with bright colors and natural fabrics with an overall feeling is light and airy. Cafe Splendide, the outstanding hotel restaurant with interesting eclectic cuisine, is a favorite with local yuppies. The V & A Waterfront is a seven-minute walk. You have a choice of executive or penthouse suites (slightly larger and a bit more expensive), but whichever you choose, you'll be very comfortable. ⊠ *121 Beach Rd., Mouille Point 8001,* ☎ *021/439–5119,* FAX *021/439–5112. 22 suites. Restaurant, lap pool. AE, DC, MC, V.*

$$$ 🔲 **Peninsula All Suites Hotel.** Housed in an attractive 11-story building 100 yards from the ocean, this exclusive Sea Point establishment is ideal for families or groups of friends. Guests can choose from a variety of suites that sleep four to eight people and command incredible views of the sea. The larger suites are the most attractive, full of light and air, thanks to picture windows, sliding doors, wide balconies, and white tile floors. Small studio suites look more like conventional hotel rooms. Each suite has a fully equipped kitchen with microwave oven. The hotel is a time-share property, so booking during the busy December holiday could be a problem. ⊠ *313 Beach Rd., Sea Point 8001 (Box*

768, Sea Point 8060), ☎ *021/439–8888,* FAX *021/439–8886. 110 suites. 2 restaurants, bar, room service, 2 pools, sauna, exercise room. AE, DC, MC, V.*

$$ ⊞ **Monkey Valley.** This secluded, self-catering resort in Noordhoek is
★   one of the best places on the peninsula for families. Built on stilts, each of the thatched log cottages lies amid thick vegetation overlooking a nature reserve and the white sands of Noordhoek Beach. Cottages have two or three bedrooms, fully equipped kitchens, and large balconies. The wood interiors are attractive and rustic, brightened by floral fabrics, country-style furniture, and fireplaces. The resort has its own restaurant, and there is a large grocery store 5 km (3 mi) away. Owner Judy Sole runs an outstanding establishment and is a character in her own right. ⊠ *Mountain Rd. (Box 114), Noordhoek 7985,* ☎ *021/789–1391,* FAX *021/789–1143. 17 cottages. Restaurant, bar, pool, playground. AE, DC, MC, V.*

Southern Suburbs

$$$$ ⊞ **Cellars-Hohenort Country House Hotel.** It's easy to forget the out-
★   side world at this idyllic getaway in Constantia. Set on 9 acres of gardens on the slopes of Table Mountain, this luxury hotel commands spectacular views across Constantia Valley to False Bay. The 18th-century cellars of the Klaasenbosch wine estate and the Hohenort manor house form the heart of the hotel. Guest rooms are large and elegant, furnished in English-country style with brass beds, flowery valances, and reproduction antiques. Rooms in the manor house have the best views of the valley. Although the hotel lacks the historical significance of the Alphen (☞ *below*), it offers a level of luxury and tranquillity that its more famous competitor cannot match. None of the rooms is air-conditioned, however. The brand new Presidental Suite sleeps a family of six. ⊠ *93 Brommersvlei Rd. (Box 270), Constantia 7800,* ☎ *021/ 794–2137,* FAX *021/794–2149. 55 rooms with bath, 1 suite. 2 restaurants, 2 bars, room service, 2 pools, tennis court, beauty salon. No children under 14. AE, DC, MC, V.*

$$$ ⊞ **Alphen Hotel.** If you want a taste of gracious Cape living and his-
★   tory, stay at this elegant Constantia hotel. Built in 1752 in Cape Dutch style, the former manor house is now a national monument and one of the Cape's historical treasures. The owners are descendants of the distinguished Cloete family, which has farmed the land around Constantia since 1657. Cloete paintings and antiques, each with a story to tell, adorn the public rooms. Standard guest rooms, housed in adjoining buildings, are small and don't match the magnificence of the manor house. The hotel has two other drawbacks: no air-conditioning and light traffic noise from the nearby highway. ⊠ *Alphen Dr. (Box 35), Constantia 7848,* ☎ *021/794–5011,* FAX *021/794–5710. 29 rooms with bath. 2 restaurants, bar, room service, pool. AE, DC, MC, V.*

$$$ ⊞ **Auberge Penrose.** Close to the University of Cape Town and the golf courses at Mowbray and Rondebosch, this attractive guest house offers a friendly welcome and attentive service. From the cozy breakfast room, guests enjoy great views of Devil's Peak and the Rhodes Memorial. Rooms are airy and comfortable, with high ceilings, floral draperies, and brass bedsteads. All rooms have telephones, TVs, and minibars. Auberge Penrose sits on a small plot of land close to the road. If you need quiet, you're better off at the Palm House (☞ *below*). ⊠ *9 Rhodes Ave., Cape Town 7700,* ☎ *021/685–7700,* FAX *021/685–7141. 11 rooms with bath. Bar, dining room, pool. AE, DC, MC, V. Breakfast included.*

$$$ ⊞ **Constantia Uitsig.** This 200-acre winery has an enviable setting, backed by the magnificent mountains of the Constantiaberg and overlooking the vineyards of Constantia Valley. Rooms, in whitewashed farm cottages set amid manicured lawns and gardens, are comfortable and inviting. Wicker headboards, timber ceilings, and bright floral patterns add a rustic feeling. The restaurant in the original farmhouse draws diners from all over the Cape. If you value peace and quiet, this is a great place to stay. ⊠ *Spaanschemat River Rd. (Box 32), Constantia 7848,* ☎ *021/794–6500,* ℻ *021/794–7605. 16 rooms with bath. 2 restaurants, 2 pools, room service. AE, DC, MC, V.*

$$–$$$ 🛏 **Palm House.** Towering palms dominate the manicured lawns of this peaceful guest house in suburban Kenilworth, a 15-minute drive from the city. The house is an enormous, stolid affair, built in the early 1920s by a protégé of Sir Herbert Baker and filled with dark-wood paneling, wood staircases, and fireplaces. Guest rooms are large and decorated with bold floral fabrics and reproduction antiques. Upstairs rooms benefit from more air and light. Guests often meet for evening drinks in the drawing room. ⊠ *Oxford St., Wynberg 7800,* ☎ *021/761–5009,* ℻ *021/761–8776. 10 rooms with bath. Restaurant, bar, pool. No children under 10. AE, DC, MC, V. CP.*

$$ 🛏 **The Vineyard.** Set in pleasant gardens in residential Newlands, this comfortable hotel is built around Paradise, the 19th-century weekend home of Lady Anne Barnard, and is popular with English tourists. Unfortunately, not much of the old house is evident in the design of the hotel. Rooms are fairly standard, with wall-to-wall carpeting, pale floral bedspreads, and dried-flower arrangements on the walls. Rooms with a view of Table Mountain are considerably more expensive. The hotel is 10 minutes by car from the city but within walking distance of the Newlands sports arenas and the shops of Cavendish Square. ⊠ *Colinton Rd. (Box 151), Newlands 7725,* ☎ *021/683–3044,* ℻ *021/683–3365. 124 rooms with bath. 2 restaurants, bar, room service, pool, beauty salon, exercise room. AE, DC, MC, V.*

False Bay

$$ 🛏 **British Hotel.** In a stone Victorian building in historic Simon's Town,
★ these self-catering apartments offer the best deal on the peninsula. The four apartments are huge, with fully equipped kitchens, two or three bedrooms, two sitting rooms, and wide Victorian balconies overlooking the harbor. High ceilings, wood floors, and giant windows create a sense of space and elegance. The decor differs from unit to unit but draws much of its inspiration from the turn of the century. Ask for Number 2, a two-bedroom apartment that perfectly balances the old-fashioned and the modern, with claw-foot bathtubs, cane furniture, and sponge-painted walls. ⊠ *St. George's St., Simon's Town (30 Hudson St., Cape Town 8001),* ☎ *021/25–3414,* ℻ *021/790–4930. 4 apartments. AE, DC, MC, V.*

$$ 🛏 **Lord Nelson Inn.** This hotel on the main road in Simon's Town offers comfortable, no-frills accommodation at a good price. Rooms are small, decorated in country style with pine furniture, muted colors, and wall-to-wall carpeting. If you want a harbor view or balcony, request a superior room. ⊠ *58 St. George's St., Simon's Town 7995,* ☎ *021/786–1386,* ℻ *021/786–1009. 10 rooms with bath. 2 restaurants, 2 bars, room service. AE, DC, MC, V. CP.*

NIGHTLIFE AND THE ARTS

Each month Captour publishes *What's On in the Cape,* probably the best roundup of events in the city, including exhibitions, theater, concerts, and nightlife. The entertainment section of the *Weekly Mail & Guardian* newspaper lists the major cultural events in Cape Town, Johannesburg, and Durban; it's informed, opinionated, and up-to-date. *The Argus* newspaper's "Tonight" section gives you a complete daily listing of what's on, plus all the booking numbers. Tickets for almost every cultural and sporting event in the country (including movies) can be purchased at **Computicket** (☎ 021/21–4715), with more than 18 outlets around the city. Two of the most convenient are in the Golden Acre on Adderley Street and at the waterfront. You can also book by phone with Computicket using any major credit card.

The Arts

The **Nico Malan Theatre Centre** (✉ D.F. Malan St., Foreshore, ☎ 021/21–7839), a huge (and particularly unattractive) theater complex on the foreshore, is the hub for performing arts and other cultural activities. Originally controversial—because like many apartheid state-run institutions it was for whites only—today the Nico is popular among all sections of the community as it offers a varied selection of the performing arts. Exciting indigenous Afrocentric productions bring a whole new vista to Cape Town's cultural scene and have help make the Nico a vital part of the city's cultural landscape. Cape Town City Ballet and the Cape Town Philharmonic Orchestra, as well as the city's theater and opera companies, make their homes here. Drama, ballet, and opera productions are held in the Nico's three theaters. Since the election there's been a conscious effort throughout the country to make the performing arts more representative and multicultural. The formerly Eurocentric emphasis has subsided, and today there's a palpable African-arts excitement in the air. Classics are still well represented, as are the latest contemporary worldwide trends. Summer productions of dance, opera, and African jazz also take place at the Oude Libertas Amphitheatre, an open-air venue set among vineyards outside Stellenbosch (☞ The Winelands *in* Chapter 5). During summer, when the weather's good, Cape Town has its own version of Central Park's Shakespeare in the Park at **Maynardville Open-Air Theatre** (✉ Church and Wolfe Sts., ☎ 021/77–8591) in Wynberg. Theatergoers often bring a picnic supper to enjoy before the show.

Classical Music

The **Cape Town Philharmonic Orchestra,** which recently merged with the Cape Town Symphony Orchestra, alternates performing at City Hall and the Nico Malan (☞ *above*) alternately. The **Spier Summer Festival** (☎ 021/434–5423, FAX 021/434–0845), which takes place between November and February, has a varied program, and performances are held under the stars in an amphitheater at the Spier Wine Estate. You can catch the Spier steam train from the V & A Waterfront (the journey takes about an hour), wine and dine at one of the three restaurants or have a picnic dinner prepared by the estate, then enjoy the show and return to Cape Town on the train. As part of its program to introduce classical music to the general public, the philharmonic also stages a series of lunchtime concerts in the foyer of the Nico Malan complex. Far more exciting, though, is the summer program of open-air concerts at the Kirstenbosch National Botanic Gardens. The setting, in the shadow of Table Mountain, is unbeatable. The orchestra has hosted several guest conductors from Europe and the United States and has an active program, which includes a summer program of free concerts at the outdoor AGFA Amphitheatre at the waterfront.

Film

Ster-Kinekor and Nu Metro screen mainstream American and British movies at cinema complexes all over the city. The waterfront alone has 10 cinemas to choose from. The cinema complex closest to the center of town is in the Golden Acre on Adderley Street. Check newspaper listings for what's playing.

IMAX Cinema (⊠ BMW Pavilion, Waterfront, ☎ 021/21–4715 or 021/21–4743), with a giant, nearly hemispherical, five-story screen and six-channel wraparound sound, makes viewers feel as if they're participating in the filmed event. At press time, shows included a feature on whales. Another show on Serengeti takes viewers into the thundering middle of the legendary animal migrations in East Africa. For the best and most controversial Continental, British, and American films, visit the cinema complex at Cavendish Square.

The Labia (⊠ 68 Orange St., Gardens, ☎ 021/24–5927) is an independent art cinema that screens quality mainstream and alternative films, including the works of some of the best European filmmakers. A coffee bar serves snacks.

Theater

The **Baxter Theatre Complex** (⊠ Main Rd., Rondebosch, ☎ 021/685–7880) is part of the University of Cape Town and has a reputation for producing serious drama. Plays by Athol Fugard are often staged here. The complex features a 657-seat theater, a concert hall, a smaller studio, and a restaurant and bar.

Dock Road Theatre (⊠ Waterfront, ☎ 021/419–7722) stages some of Cape Town's most successful theater productions. The focus is on the works of South African writers, including Pieter-Dirk Uys, Paul Slabolepszy, Jenny Reznick, and Andrew Buckland. Most of the productions have mainstream appeal, but foreigners may not always be familiar with the subject matter.

Nightlife

The city's nightlife is concentrated in the revitalized harbor. You will always find something to do at the waterfront, when you consider that you have almost a dozen cinemas, 40 restaurants, and 10 bars from which to choose. The rest of the City Bowl, except for isolated restaurants and bars, empties out after business hours, and lone couples may not feel safe walking these deserted streets at night. The big exception is the few square blocks around the intersection of Long and Strand streets, which have become a cauldron of youth-oriented nightclubs, bars, and restaurants. Even here, though, exercise caution late at night. Sea Point, once a major after-dark scene, has lost much of its business, except for the hookers that trawl Main Road.

Bars and Pubs

The **Perseverance Tavern** (⊠ 83 Buitenkant St., Gardens, ☎ 021/461–1981), which dates to 1836, has a strong claim to be the oldest tavern in the city. The facade has been beautifully restored, but you may feel claustrophobic in the small, interconnected rooms. The wood-lined pub at **Mijlof Manor Hotel** (⊠ 5 Military Rd., ☎ 021/26–1476) in Tamboerskloof is a popular watering hole for the after-work crowd, including politicos. The **Stag's Head** (⊠ 71 Hope St., Gardens, ☎ 021/45–4918) in Gardens is a rowdy joint that attracts a big crowd of beer-chugging partyers. The **Firkin Brew Pub** (⊠ 22 Kloof St., ☎ 021/24–4222) brews its own beer; you can sit inside near the brewing vats or outside on the steps. If you're single and want to mingle, slip into something black and head for **Flute's Restaurant and Wine Bar** (⊠ 196 Loop St., ☎ 021/22–2378).

The **Sports Bar** (⊠ Victoria Wharf, Waterfront, ☎ 021/419–5558) is a huge place with large-screen TVs. The bar gets into the spirit of major foreign sporting events like the Super Bowl and the FA Cup (England's soccer championship). Final and is undoubtedly the best place to watch sports in the city. **Quay Four** (⊠ Quay 4, ☎ 021/419–2008), also at the waterfront, is big with the after-work suit-and-tie brigade, which clogs picnic tables on the wooden deck overlooking the harbor. Just outside the entrance to the waterfront is the **Fireman's Arms** (⊠ Buitengracht and Mechau Sts., ☎ 021/419–1513), a great old bar that serves pizzas cooked in a wood-fired oven. The frenetic **Brunswick Tavern** (⊠ 17 Bree St., ☎ 021/25–2739) attracts a mainly gay clientele with its loud pulsating music. The restrained but fairly funky gay crowd lean towards **Cafe Erte** (⊠ 265a Main Rd., Sea Point, ☎ 021/434–6624).

Dancing

Nightclubs open and close faster than you can find out where they are. Aside from the waterfront, the area bounded by Loop, Long, Strand, and Riebeeck streets is the best place to get a feeling for what's going on in town. Clubs and bars don't hit their stride until after 11. **The Fringe** (⊠ 46 Canterbury St., ☎ 021/461–9061) spins reggae and alternative music, and appeals to the 18-to-25-year-old crowd. **West End & Arena** (⊠ Port Rd., ☎ 021/21–5355), near the entrance to the waterfront, entertains disco-lovers on Friday and Saturday nights.

Jazz

Many of the mainstream jazz clubs in the city double as restaurants. Cover charges range from R6 to R15. If you're passionate about jazz, get hold of Captour's free brochure "Jazz in the Cape." The **Green Dolphin Jazz Restaurant** (⊠ Waterfront, ☎ 021/21–7471) attracts some of the best mainstream musicians in the country as well as a few from overseas. The cover charge is R10–R15 and there's a food and beverage minimum of R60 for a seat at a table (the kitchen specializes in pasta and seafood). **Dizzy's Jazz Cafe** (⊠ 41 The Drive, Camps Bay, ☎ 021/438–2686) is an intimate club in an old Cape Dutch building in Camps Bay. Come here to listen to small groups that won't completely dominate your dinner or drinks. If you want to explore the cutting edge of Cape jazz, you have to head to the townships. On Sunday after 4 PM **Club Ubuntu** in Guguletu (⊠ NY1, ☎ 021/419–4732) showcases the best of the township musicians, playing a mix of American and indigenous jazz. **Riffs Jazz Pub** (⊠ 39 Wetton Rd., Wetton, ☎ 021/73–2676) is a bare-bones joint that features live music Wednesday through Saturday. **West End & Arena** (⊠ Port Rd., ☎ 021/21–5355) is split into 2 levels: upstairs is jazz, Wednesday through Sunday; downstairs is a disco on the weekend.

OUTDOOR ACTIVITIES AND SPORTS

Participant Sports

Boating

If you enjoy sailing, visit the **Cape Royal Yacht Club** (⊠ Duncan Rd., Table Bay, Cape Town 8000, ☎ 021/21–1354, FAX 021/21–6028) to organize a jaunt on a private yacht. It's a great way to see Cape Town and Table Mountain. At the waterfront or Hout Bay you can charter a cruise from **Waterfront Charters** (☎ 021/25–3804, FAX 021/25–3816) who will take you cruising in Table Bay and around Robben Island (with no disembarkation). The trip is two hours and costs R80. At Hout Bay, **Hout Bay Passenger Launches at Hout Bay,** ☎ 021/790–1040, FAX 021/790–5722) takes you around Seal (Duiker) Island. The trip takes approximatley one hour and costs R17.50.

Canoeing and White-Water Rafting

Felixe Unite River Adventures (⊠ 141 Lansdown Rd., Claremont, ☏ 021/683–6433, FAX 021/683–6488) is the leader in the field and has run water adventures for years. The staff leads 1-day to 4-day trips (for R180–R880) of the best waters in the area.

Diving

Divers can explore several marine reserves, as well as the hundreds of wrecks that litter the waters around the Cape peninsula. Far more exciting is the chance to descend in a diving cage among great white sharks, which breed in the waters around the Cape. All the major diving companies offer PADI or NAUI scuba-diving courses for about R600. Contact **Aquasport** (⊠ Strand St., across from Cape Sun Hotel, ☏ 021/419–1835), **Blue Print Diving** (⊠ Quay 5, Waterfront, ☏ 021/418–5806), **Scuba Shack** (⊠ 14 Surrey St., Goodwood, ☏ 021/592–5698), or **Waterfront Scuba** (⊠ Hout Bay Harbor, behind NSRI, ☏ 021/790–1106).

Adventure Safaris & Sports Tours (⊠ Box 32176, Camps Bay, ☏ 021/438–5201, FAX 021/438–4807) organizes fishing, diving, hiking, bird-watching, canoeing, black-water tubing, river rafting, mountain biking, and great white shark diving adventures.

Fishing

Neptune Deep Sea Angling (☏ 021/782–3889) offers two types of fishing in its 24-foot ski boat: bottom fishing in Simon's Town Bay for kabeljou, snoek, yellowtail, and crayfish (in season); and deep-sea fishing for marlin and other big game fish. Think twice about going far out to sea in such a small boat if you suffer from motion sickness. A day's fishing costs about R1,000.

Golf

Most golf clubs in the Cape accept visitors, but prior booking is essential. Expect to pay R40–R80 for 18 holes. Most clubs offer equipment rental. The Winelands in particular has some spectacular courses (☞ Chapter 5).

Clovelley Country Club (☏ 021/782–6410) in Fish Hoek is a tight course that requires masterful shot placement from tee to green. **Durbanville Golf Club** (☏ 021/96–8121) may not be the most challenging course in the Cape but it has tremendous views and bird life. **King David Country Club** (☏ 021/934–0365) is famous for its layout, with undulating fairways and elevated tees; the 12th hole plays into the wind and is probably the toughest par-3 in the Cape. **Milnerton Golf Club** (☏ 021/52–1047), sandwiched between the sea and a lagoon, is the Cape's only links course and can be difficult when the wind blows. **Mowbray Golf Club** (☏ 021/685–3018), with its great views of Devil's Peak, is a magnificent parkland course that has hosted several major tournaments; there are a number of interesting water holes. Unfortunately, noise from the highway can spoil the atmosphere. **Rondebosch Golf Club** (☏ 021/689–4176), also in the shadow of Devil's Peak, is a gently undulating course that crosses the Black River several times. Founded in 1885, **Royal Cape Golf Club** (☏ 021/761–6551) in Wynberg is the oldest course in the country and has hosted the South African Open many times. Its beautiful setting and immaculate fairways and greens make a round here a must for visitors. The club does not rent equipment. **Westlake Golf Club** (☏ 021/788–2020) is laid out around a large lake in the shadow of rocky mountains; the 7th and 14th holes are extremely difficult.

Hiking and Garden Tours

Cape Town and surrounding areas offers some of the finest hiking in the world. There are beach and mountain hikes, walks through

winelands, gentle hikes inland through valleys along rivers, and spectacular gorges. **Footprints Adventures** (✉ Box 2822, Cape Town, ☎
021/461–1999, ⨳ 021/461–7068) offers some of the best hikes and
day walks in Cape Town and farther afield in the Transkei. Jonathan
Musikanth and Gal Zimerman, who lead the hikes are particularly
knowledgeable about their surrounding. Rates are reasonable beginning at R150 and vary depending on the hike.

Botanical Tours (✉ 19 Hofmeyer St., Welgemoed, ☎ 021/913–4580)
leads guided tours of Kirstenbosch and visits to some of the Cape's loveliest gardens. Wear comfortable walking shoes and keep an umbrella
handy in case the weather changes.

Horseback Riding

Sleepy Hollow Horse Riding (✉ Sleepy Hollow La., Noordhoek, 021/
789–2341) offers 1½ and 2-hour rides down Noordhoek Beach, a 6-
km (4-mi) expanse of sand that stretches from Noordhoek to Kommetjie. Experienced guides lead the rides, which are limited to six
people. Moonlight, champagne, and sunset rides are also offered.

Swimming Pools and Baths

Even on the hottest days, you have to be a seal to swim in the Cape's
frigid waters (☞ Beaches, *above*), and many Capetonians opt to cool
off in the city's municipal swimming pools instead. **Long Street Swimming Pool** (✉ Long St., Cape Town, ☎ 021/400–3302), in the center
of town, has a heated swimming pool and Turkish steam baths. In the
southern suburbs head for **Newlands Swimming Pool** (✉ Main and
Sans Souci Rds., Newlands, ☎ 021/64–4197). Head for the **Muizenberg Seawater Swimming Pool** (✉ Muizenberg Beach Front, ☎ 021/
788–7881) or **Sea Point Seawater Swimming Pool** (✉ Beach Rd., Sea
Point, ☎ 021/434–3341) if you want to swim in a pool and also at
the beach.

Spectator Sports

It's easy to get tickets for ordinary club matches and Inter-Provincial
tickets. An international test match is a challenge; however, there's always somebody selling tickets at a price, of course.

Cricket

The huge sporting complex off Boundary Road in Newlands is known
country-wide simply as Newlands (after the sponsors). It's the home
of the **Western Province Cricket Union** (☎ 021/64–4146), which competes in the annual Castle Cup against provincial sides from all over
South Africa. Newlands is also one of the major venues in the country for one- and five-day test matches, in which the South African team
takes on touring international competitors.

Rugby

Western Province Rugby Football Union (✉ Boundary Rd., Newlands,
☎ 021/689–4921) also calls the huge Newlands sports complex home,
playing in a brand-new stadium built for the Rugby World Cup in 1995.
During winter, Newlands is the site of annual Currie Cup matches against
other South African provincial teams, as well as test matches between
the Springboks (the South African team) and teams from other countries.

SHOPPING

A number of surprisingly good stores in Cape Town sell African art
and crafts. None of the work is local—much of it comes from Zulu-

land or neighboring countries—and you'll pay slightly more than you would pay where the goods are made. Street vendors, particularly on St. George's Mall and Greenmarket Square, often sell the same curios for half the price.

The Captour desk at the Tourist Rendezvous Travel Centre (☞ Contacts and Resources *in* Cape Town A to Z, *below*) has helpful brochures describing an Antique Route and an Arts and Crafts Route that cover the city and peninsula.

Markets

Greenmarket Square. Artisans and hawkers sell their wares in this open-air market. You can get good buys on clothing, T-shirts, hand-crafted silver jewelry, and locally made leather shoes and sandals. It's lively and fun whether or not you buy anything. ⊘ *Mon.–Sat. 9–4:30.*

Red Shed Craft Workshop. Here you can watch artisans blowing glass, knitting sweaters, and weaving rugs. All of the work is for sale. ⊠ *Victoria Wharf, Waterfront.* ⊘ *Mon.–Sat. 9–7, Sun. 10–6.*

Waterfront Art and Craft Market. In this indoor market, more than 140 artisans and artists show their work: an assortment of hand-crafted jewelry, rugs, glass, pottery, and leather shoes and sandals. ⊠ *Waterfront,* ☎ *021/418–2850.* ⊘ *Weekends 8:30–6.*

Specialty Stores

AFRICAN ART

African Heritage. This upscale shop specializes in jewelry from all over Africa, including Tuareg bangles and Ethiopian silver crosses strung on beaded necklaces. The store also carries works by local artists. ⊠ *Shop 102, Victoria Wharf, Waterfront,* ☎ *021/21–6610,* FAX *021/21–7413.* ⊘ *Mon.–Sat. 9–9, Sun. 10–9.*

African Image. Look here for traditional and contemporary African art and curios, colorful cloth from Nigeria and Ghana, plus West African masks, Malian blankets, and beaded designs from southern African tribes. A variety of Zulu baskets is also available at moderate prices. ⊠ *52 Burg St., 021/23–8385.* ⊘ *Weekdays 8:45–5, Sat. 9–1:30.*

The Collector. Serious buyers with unlimited spending power favor this museumlike shop, with its small, select assortment of works ranging from West African ornamental beads to hand-painted Tuareg leather pillows and Zairian Kuba knives. Tags describe the place of origin and uses of all pieces. It's an interesting place in which to learn about African artifacts. ⊠ *59 Church St.,* ☎ *021/23–1483.* ⊘ *Weekdays 10–1 and 2:15–4, Sat. 10–1.*

Third World Spectator. A large selection of traditional southern African artifacts—everything from from Zulu beer pots to wooden meat trays, Tonga stools, and wooden earplugs (used to stretch earlobes)—is carried here. The shop also carries an assortment of musical instruments. ⊠ *Shop 8, Protea Assurance Bldg., Greenmarket Sq., 021/24–2957.* ⊘ *Weekdays 9–5, Sat. 9–1.*

AFRICAN CLOTHING AND FABRICS

Mnandi. Here you'll find a range of African fabrics, including traditional West African prints and Dutch wax prints. The store sells ready-made African clothing for adults and children. You can also have clothing made to order. ⊠ *90 Station Rd., Observatory,* ☎ *021/47–6814,* FAX *021/47–7937.* ⊘ *Weekdays 9–5:30, Sat. 9–1.*

N.C.M. African Styles. This is the place to go for traditional West African clothing. One of the most striking outfits is the brightly colored bubu, a loose-fitting garment with a matching head wrap. You can buy off the rack or order a custom outfit from a wide selection of fabrics. ⊠ *150 Main Rd., Claremont,* ☎ *021/683–1022.* ⊙ *Weekdays 9–5:30, Sat. 9–1:30.*

BOOKS

Exclusive Books. This is one of the best all-around bookshops in the country. The chain carries a wide selection of local and international periodicals and coffee-table books on Africa. Be prepared, though, to pay at least twice as much for books as you would in the United States or Britain. ⊠ *Shop 225, Victoria Wharf, Waterfront,* ☎ *021/419–0905,* FAX *021/419–0909.* ⊙ *Mon.–Thur. 9 AM–10:30 PM, Fri.–Sat. 9–11 , Sun. 10–9.*

CRAFTS

The **Cape Heritage Shop.** You won't have to turn anything over here to look at the "Made in . . ." label: the hand-crafted goods sold here are all made in Cape Town. Choose from hand-painted pillowcases, tablecloths, wall hangings, T-shirts, cards, wire sculptures, pottery, glassware, toys, and jewelry. ⊠ *Burg and Church Sts.,* ☎ *021/24–9590,* FAX *021/24–3159.* ⊙ *Weekdays 9–5, Sat. 9–1.*

CAPE TOWN A TO Z

Arriving and Departing

By Bus

All intercity buses depart from the Captour office on Adderley Street. Ask about special fares, which are available for all destinations at various times of the year (☞ Contacts and Resources, *below*). **Greyhound** (⊠ 1 Adderley St., ☎ 021/418–4312) offers daily overnight service to Johannesburg and Pretoria; the one-way fare is about R250. **Intercape Mainliner** (⊠ Captour office, Adderley St., ☎ 021/386–4400) operates a far more extensive network of routes in the Western Cape than does Greyhound, with daily service up the West Coast to Springbok (R175) and along the Garden Route to George (R100) and Port Elizabeth (R140); a bus also travels daily to Johannesburg (R250). **Translux Express Bus** (⊠ Captour office, Adderley St., ☎ 021/405–3333) offers a similar network of routes at comparable prices.

The **Baz Bus** (☎ 021/439–2323, FAX 021/439–2343) calls itself the budget traveler's bus and is a fun alternative—and is much cheaper—than scheduled services. You might try this hop-on, hop-off option if you aren't on a strict timetable. Baz buses are popular with young travelers and usually stop at youth hostels. You can take around-the-country trips from Cape Town to everywhere, including Swaziland, the Drakensburg, and Zululand, for just over R1,000.

By Car

Parking in the city center can be a hassle. Parking spaces are so scarce that most hotels charge extra for the service, and even then you won't be guaranteed a space. If you don't mind leaving your car in the care of derelict youths (don't worry, everyone does it), you can usually find parking out on the lots on Buitengracht Street or on the Grand Parade. The Sanlam Golden Acre Parking Garage on Adderley Street offers covered parking.

The main arteries leading out of the city are the N1, which runs to Paarl and, ultimately, Johannesburg; and the N2, which heads to the Overberg and the Garden Route. The M3 leads to Constantia, Muizenberg, and the small towns of the peninsula; it splits from the N2 just after Groote Schuur Hospital, in the shadow of Devil's Peak.

CAR RENTAL

Most of the large car-rental agencies offer similar rates; expect to pay through the nose if you rent by the day. A Nissan Sentra or Toyota Corolla costs about R100 a day plus a whopping 80¢–R1 per kilometer. If you rent for three days or more, you get 200 km–300 km (124 mi–186 mi) free per day with a daily rate of about R200. You must take out insurance. Cape Town drivers are considered the worst in the country for disregarding traffic rules. There's also been an increase in car theft in the past years.

Among the major rental agencies in Cape Town proper are **Avis** (✉ 123 Strand St., ☎ 021/24–1177); **Budget** (✉ 63a Strand St., ☎ 021/23–4290); **Dolphin Car Hire** (✉ 345 Main Rd., Sea Point, ☎ 021/418–8621), Europcar's representative in the Cape; and **Alisa Car Rental** (✉ 139 Buitengracht St., , ☎ 021/22–1515), Hertz's South African subsidiary. You can obtain rates about a third lower at budget agencies like **Economy Car Hire** (✉ 3 Anchor Bay Rd., ☎ 021/434–8304), and **Wheelrent** (✉ 11 Portswood Rd., Waterfront, ☎ 021/419–7750), but these companies usually offer limited breakdown support.

By Plane

Cape Town International Airport, formerly known as D.F. Malan, lies 22½ km (14 mi) southeast of the city in the Cape Flats. For flight arrival and departure information call 021/934–0444. International airlines flying into Cape Town include **Air France** (☎ 021/934–8818), **Air Namibia** (☎ 021/934–0757), **British Airways** (☎ 021/25–2970), **KLM** (☎ 021/21–1870), **Lufthansa** (☎ 021/25–1490), **Singapore Airlines** (☎ 021/419–0495), **South African Airways** (☎ 021/25–4610), and **Swissair** (☎ 021/21–4938).

The major domestic carriers serving Cape Town are **British Airways/Comair** (☎ toll-free 0800/9611196), **Sabena/Nationwide** (☎ 021/936–2050/1/2), **South African Airways** (☎ 021/936–1111), and **Sun Air** (☎ 021/934–0918).

Cape Town International Airport is tiny: the domestic and international terminals are no more than 200 yards apart. In addition to a VAT refund office (☞ Money and Expenses *in* the Gold Guide), there is a Western Cape Tourism Board booth and an accommodations hot line, open daily 7–5, that provides information on guest houses around the city. Trust Bank exchanges money weekdays 9–3:30 and Saturday 8:30–10:30; it stays open later for international arrivals and departures.

BETWEEN THE AIRPORT AND CAPE TOWN

Intercape Shuttle (☎ 021/386–4414) operates a minibus service between the city and the airport for R20 per person. Buses drop passengers off at the Tourist Rendezvous Travel Centre in Adderley Street. Buy tickets at the Intercape Shuttle desk in the domestic arrivals terminal or, after hours, from the bus driver. Buses depart every half hour.

Taxis are available at ranks outside the terminals. Only those with airport licenses are allowed to pick up arriving passengers, and drivers must use the meter. Expect to pay about R110 for a trip to the city center.

Avis (☎ 0800/0021111 or 021/934–0330), **Budget** (☎ 0800/016622 or 021/934–0216), **Imperial** (☎ 0800/131000 or 021/934–0213), and **Tempest** (☎ 021/934–3845) have car-rental offices at the airport (☞ Arriving and Departing by Car, *above*).

By Train

Cape Town's **train station** is in the heart of the city, behind the Tourist Rendezvous Travel Centre. Mainline Passenger Services' *Trans-Karoo* runs daily between Cape Town and Johannesburg; the trip takes about 25 hours and costs R340 in first class. The *Southern Cross* makes the 24-hour trip to Port Elizabeth on Fridays (R159 in first class); it's a night ride, so forget about seeing the splendors of the Garden Route. The luxury *Blue Train* (☞ Rail Travel *in* the Gold Guide) makes the Cape Town–Johannesburg run three times per week in peak season and weekly in the low season; call 021/405–2672 for information and reservations. The *Rovos Rail Pride of Africa* (☎ 021/21–4020), another luxurious train, travels from Cape Town to Johannesburg and up the Garden Route. ✉ *Cape Town Station, Adderley St.,* ☎ *021/ 405–3871.* ☉ *Reservations office Mon.–Thurs. 8–4:30, Fri. 8–4, Sat. 8–noon. AE, DC, MC, V.*

Getting Around

If you confine yourself to the City Bowl you won't need a car—in fact, the shortage of parking spaces makes having a car in the city a nightmare. A rental car is your only feasible option, however, if you want to explore the peninsula or Winelands and are not on a guided tour.

By Bus

Apart from the bus to the Table Mountain cableway, the only other bus that visitors are likely to use is the waterfront shuttle. It runs every 10 minutes between the waterfront and the Tourist Rendezvous Travel Centre on Adderley Street; stops are posted along the way. Another shuttle runs through Green Point and along Beach Road to Sea Point every 15–20 minutes. The fare is about R3.

Golden Arrow (☎ 080/121–2111) operates an extensive network of local buses serving the City Bowl and outlying suburbs. Generally, service is infrequent and slow. Most buses leave from the Grand Parade, but some (including those going to the cable way and Hout Bay) leave from a bus stop in front of the OK Bazaars on Adderley Street. An information kiosk at the Grand Parade provides information as well as printed timetables for each bus route. Pay your fare as you enter the bus. Exact fare is preferable (fares vary according to the destination), but the driver will make change if he can. If you travel the same route frequently, consider a clipcard, available at the Grand Parade: The weekly clipcard is good for 10 rides on a designated route within a two-week period; the monthly card allows you 48 trips on a particular route within 37 days. Savings differ from route to route, but they're substantial.

By Taxi

Taxis are metered, reasonably priced, and offer an easy, quick way to get around a city where parking is such trouble. Don't expect to see the throngs of cabs you find in London or New York. You may be lucky enough to hail one on the street, but your best bet is to summon one by phone or head to a major taxi rank—Greenmarket Square, the Tourist Rendezvous Travel Centre, or the top of Adderley Street. **Sea Point Taxis** (☎ 021/434–4444), probably the most reliable of the companies, start the meter at R2 and charge R4.20 per kilometer. Other companies are **David's Taxis** (☎ 021/782–2097), **Yellow Taxi Hire** (☎ 082/444–8281), and the more expensive **Marine Taxis** (☎ 021/434–0434). Expect to pay R20 to R25 for a trip from the city center to the waterfront, and R35 to R45 to the hotels in Sea Point.

You will also see local **minibus taxis** tearing around town at high speed, stuffed to capacity with hapless commuters. These buses ply routes all over the city and suburbs, but you can flag them down anywhere along the way. The depot is on top of the train station. For the modest fare of R2, you'll have an opportunity to experience some local color.

By Train

Cape Metro (☎ 021/405–2991) is Cape Town's commuter line and offers regular service to the southern suburbs and the towns on the False Bay side of the peninsula, including Muizenberg, St. James, Kalk Bay, Fish Hoek, and Simon's Town.

All trains depart from Cape Town Station on Adderley Street. The trip to False Bay takes 45–60 minutes and costs about R10. Cape Metro also serves Paarl, Stellenbosch, and Somerset West in the Winelands (☞ Chapter 5). If you'll be in Cape Town for a while, consider buying a weekly or monthly pass. The weekly pass gives you a round-trip ticket each day on the same route; the monthly pass allows you to ride as many times as you like on one designated route.

Contacts and Resources

Changing Money

Don't even think about changing money at your hotel. The rates at most hotels are criminal, and the city center is swamped with banks and bureaux de change that give much better rates. **American Express**'s (⊠ Thibault Sq., ☎ 021/419–3085; ⊠ Shop 11A Alfred Mall, ☎ 021/21–6021) downtown office is open 8:30–5 weekdays and 9–12 Saturdays; at the Waterfront, 9–7 weekdays and 9–5 weekends. **Rennies Travel**'s (⊠ 2 St. George's Mall, ☎ 021/25–2370; ⊠ Upper Level, Victoria Wharf, ☎ 021/418–3744) downtown office is open weekdays 8:30–5 and Saturdays 9–noon. The Waterfront location is open until 9 daily.

Consulates

Australian High Commission. ⊠ *Thibault Sq., BP Centre, 14th floor,* ☎ *021/419–5425.*

Canadian High Commission. ⊠ *30 Hout St.,* ☎ *021/23–5240.*

U.K. Consulate. ⊠ *8 Riebeeck St.,* ☎ *021/25–3670.*

U.S. Consulate. ⊠ *Broadway Bldg., Heerengracht (bottom of Adderley),* ☎ *021/21–4280.*

Emergencies

Dial 10177 for an ambulance and 10111 for the police. The police also operate a **Tourist Assistance Unit** (⊠ Tulbagh Sq., ☎ 021/418–2853) for foreign visitors who are robbed or experience other trouble. The unit can provide translators and will help you contact your embassy or consulate if need be.

DOCTORS AND DENTISTS

Doctor and Dental Emergencies (☎ 021/61–3634 or 021/61–2924) is a 24-hour referral service. You can also consult the local telephone directory for names and numbers of doctors and dentists.

HOSPITAL EMERGENCY ROOMS

Groote Schuur Hospital. ⊠ *Anzio Rd., Observatory,* ☎ *021/404–9111.* ☉ *24 hrs.*

Red Cross Children's Hospital. ⊠ *Klipfontein Rd., Rondebosch,* ☎ *021/ 658–5111.* ☉ *24 hrs.*

Guided Tours

BOAT TOURS

Until the middle of this century most travelers' first glimpse of Cape Town was from the sea, and that's still the best way to get a feeling for the city, with its famous mountain as a backdrop. Several companies offer trips into the harbor in a variety of vessels. The tours, all of which leave from the waterfront, are essentially the same: a one-hour tour of Table Bay (about R30); a 90-minute sunset cruise (R45) with free sparkling wine; and a two- to three-hour cruise to Robben Island (R80), Nelson Mandela's erstwhile prison home. Wear flat shoes, and keep in mind that the weather can be fickle, so be sure to take a warm jacket. To book a tour call the motor yacht *Condor* (☎ 021/448–5612); **Sealink** (☎ 021/254480, FAX 021/419–7072); **The Spirit of Victoria** (☎ 021/25–4062, FAX 021/461–9733); or **Waterfront Charters** (☎ 021/25–3804, FAX 021/25–3816).

Drum Beat Charters (☎ 021/438–9208, FAX 021/438–9208) and **Circe** (☎ 021/790–1040) offer one-hour trips (R18) from Hout Bay marina to see the Cape fur seals in their natural habitat on Duiker Island. Unfortunately, you spend only 5–10 minutes with the seals; the rest of the time is spent cruising Hout Bay.

HELICOPTER TOURS

Court Helicopters (✉ Waterfront, ☎ 021/25–2966) and **Civair Helicopters** (✉ Waterfront, ☎ 021/419–5182) offer tours of the city and surrounding area ranging from 20 minutes to several hours. Custom tours can be arranged.

ORIENTATION

A host of companies offer guided tours of the city, the peninsula, the Winelands, and anyplace else in the Cape you might wish to visit. Among the most reliable operators are **Classic Cape Tours** (☎ 021/686–6310, FAX 021/686–9216), **Disa Tours** (☎ 021/797–3471, FAX 021/797–7637), **Hylton Ross Tours** (☎ 021/511–1784, FAX 021/511–2401), **Ideal Tours** (☎ 021/468–5415, FAX 021/685–4260), **Mother City Tours** (☎ 021/418–2580, FAX 021/418–2581), **Platinum Tours** (☎ 021/683–1590), **Springbok Atlas** (☎ 021/25–1271), and **Welcome Tours & Safaris** (☎ 021/26–2134, FAX 021/22–1816).

Most of these operators offer the same basic itineraries with small variations. Tours are usually in minivans or buses. The city tour lasts about a half day and stops at the major sights. Full-day peninsula tours, sometimes paired with a city tour or a trip up Table Mountain, head down the False Bay side of the peninsula to Cape Point and return via the Atlantic coast.

A cheaper and more casual way to see the sights is with **Topless Tours** (☎ 021/448–2888, FAX 021/448–1836), which runs seven-hour tours of the peninsula (R60) and two-hour tours of the city (R25) aboard topless double-decker buses. On city tours, passengers can hop off at designated points, then catch a later bus. In high season, buses leave hourly from the Tourist Rendezvous Travel Centre in Adderley Street (☞ Contacts and Resources, *below*) and the Dock Road Café at the waterfront. In off-season there are three tours per day, at 10, noon, and 2.

ROBBEN ISLAND TOURS

Boat trips to Robben Island (☞ Boat Tours, *above*) don't actually land on the famous island. If you want to tour the island where Nelson Mandela spent a good chunk of his life, you need to organize a tour through the **Robben Island Museum** (☞ Exploring, *above*).

TOWNSHIP TOURS

For R75, **One City Tours** (☎ 021/387–5351, FAX 021/387–1338) offers eye-opening tours of the Cape's black townships. Tours are perfectly safe, conducted in minivans, and led by a well-spoken, knowledgeable guide. Visitors are introduced to District Six, a colored neighborhood razed to satisfy the Group Areas Act, and to some of the country's most notorious townships and squatter camps, including Crossroads and Khayelitsha. You'll visit the cramped living quarters of a hostel, a spaza shop, and a *shebeen* (a makeshift bar). The three-hour tour is well worth the time and money: It reveals a side of the country that most white South Africans have never seen.

Legend Tours (☎ 021/697–4056, FAX 021/697–4090) offers Walk to Freedom Tours that cover District Six, Bo-Kaap, the townships, and Robben Island. The well-informed guides lead the tours, casting a strong historical and political emphasis.

WALKING TOURS

Ideal Tours (☎ 021/468–5415, FAX 021/685–4260) conducts a 2½-hour walking tour of Cape Town Monday–Saturday for R50 per person. The tour, which includes a light lunch and all entrance fees, stops at the Castle, the Company's Gardens, the historic buildings in the city center, the Bo-Kaap, and the Houses of Parliament.

Shereen Habib of **Tana-Baru Tours** (☎ 021/24–0719, FAX 021/23–5579) leads two-hour guided walks through the Bo-Kaap, otherwise known as the Malay Quarter. The tour, which costs about R50, winds through the quarter's cobbled streets to the Bo-Kaap Museum, the oldest mosque in the country, and the shrines of various saints. It ends with tea and traditional Malay cakes.

Travel Agencies

American Express Travel Service changes money, books trips and airline tickets, and offers a range of services to cardholders, including holding mail (☞ Changing Money, *above*).

Rennies Travel, which represents Thomas Cook in South Africa, has several branches throughout the city, but the main office is in the city center on St. George's Mall. In addition to providing the usual services of a travel agent, the office operates a bureau de change (☞ Changing Money, *above*).

Visitor Information

Captour is the city's official tourist body and by far the most helpful and informative of South Africa's regional promotional offices. Captour's Tourist Rendezvous Travel Centre is a huge complex that provides information on tours, tour guides, hotels, restaurants, rental cars, and shops in Cape Town and the Cape. The staff also makes hotel, tour, and travel bookings. The travel center houses information offices for SATOUR, the Western Cape Tourism Board, the National Parks Board, and Cape Nature Conservation. ⊠ *Adderley St. (Box 1403), Cape Town 8000,* ☎ *021/418–5214,* FAX *021/418–5227.* ⊙ *Weekdays 8–7, Sat. 8:30–5, Sun. 9–5.*

The **National Parks Board** office can give you information on all of South Africa's national parks and accepts reservations for park accommodations and wilderness trails. You can also make reservations here for entry to Kruger National Park. A Parks Board desk at the Tourist Rendezvous Travel Centre offers the same service. ⊠ *44 Long St.,* ☎ *021/22–2810.* ⊙ *Weekdays 8–4:45.*

5 The Western Cape

The wonders of the Western Cape are nearly endless. The jagged mountains, elegant estates, and delicious wines of the Winelands; the pristine, mountain-edged beaches and historic towns of the Overberg; and the glorious wildflowers, old fishing villages, and interior ranges of the West Coast provide some of South Africa's most memorable experiences.

ANCHORED BY CAPE TOWN in the southwest, the Western Cape is South Africa's most delightful province, a sweep of endless mountain ranges, empty beaches, and European history dating back more than three centuries. In less than two hours from Cape Town you can reach most of the province's highlights, making the city an ideal regional base.

The historic Winelands, in the city's backyard, produce fine wine amid the exquisite beauty of rocky mountains, serried vines, and elegant Cape Dutch estates. By South African standards this southwestern region of the Cape is a settled land, with a sense of tradition and continuity lacking in much of the rest of the country. Here, farms have been handed down from one generation to another for centuries, and old-name families like the Cloetes have become part of the fabric of the region.

Even first-time visitors may notice subtle differences between these Cape Afrikaners and their more conservative cousins in the hinterland. For the most part, they are descendants of the landed gentry and educated classes who stayed in the Cape after the British takeover in 1806 and the emancipation of slaves in 1834. Not for them the hard uncertainties of the Great Trek, when ruddy-faced Boers (farmers), outraged at British intervention, loaded their families into ox wagons and set off into the unknown, a rifle in one hand and a Bible in the other.

The genteel atmosphere of the southwestern Cape fades quickly the farther from Cape Town you go. The Overberg, separated from the city by the Hottentots Holland Mountains, presides over the rocky headland of Cape Agulhas, where the Indian and Atlantic oceans meet at the tip of the continent. Unspoiled beaches and coastal mountains are the lure of this remote area. North of Cape Town on the West Coast and Namaqualand, civilization drops away altogether, bar a few lonely fishing villages and mining towns. Each spring, though, the entire region explodes in a spectacular wildflower display that slowly spreads inland to the grassy Hantam Plateau and the Cedarberg mountains.

Wildflowers are one extraordinary element of a region truly blessed by nature. The Western Cape is famous for its *fynbos* (pronounced *feign*-boss), the hardy, thin-leafed vegetation that gives much of the province its distinctive look. Fynbos comprises a major part of the Cape floral kingdom, the smallest and richest of the world's six floral kingdoms. More than 8,500 plant species are found in the province, of which 5,000 grow nowhere else on earth. The region is dotted with nature reserves where you can hike through this profusion of flora, admiring the majesty of the king protea or the shimmering leaves of the silver tree. When the wind blows and mist trails across the mountainsides, the fynbos-covered landscape takes on the look of a Scottish heath.

Not surprisingly, people have taken full advantage of the Cape's natural bonanza. In the Overberg and along the West Coast, rolling wheat fields extend to the horizon, while farther inland jagged mountain ranges hide fertile valleys of apple orchards, orange groves, and vineyards. At sea, hardy fishermen battle icy swells to harvest succulent crayfish (clawless lobsters), delicate perlemoen (a type of abalone), and a variety of line fish, such as kabeljou, which make excellent eating.

For untold centuries, this fertile region supported the Khoikhoi and San, indigenous peoples who lived off the land as pastoralists and hunter-gatherers. With the arrival of European settlers, however, they were chased off, killed, or enslaved. In the remote recesses of the Cedarberg Mountains and along the West Coast, you can still see the fading rock paint-

The Western Cape and Namaqualand

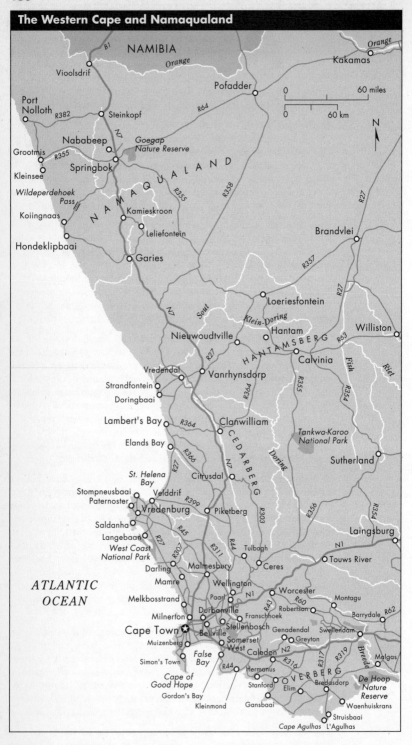

NAMIBIA

Orange

Kakamas

B1

Vioolsdrif

Port
Nolloth
R382

Pofadder

R64

0   60 miles

0   60 km

N

Steinkopf

Nababeep

*Goegap
Nature Reserve*

N A M A Q U A L A N D

Grootmis
R355

Springbok

Kleinsee

*Wildeperdehoek
Pass*

Koiingnaas

Kamieskroon

Leliefontein

R355

R358

Brandvlei

R27

N A M A Q U A L A N D

Hondeklipbaai

Garies

N7

Sout

R357

Loeriesfontein

R27

Williston

Klein-Doring

Hantam

H A N T A M S B E R G

R63

Nieuwoudtville

R27

Calvinia

Vredendal

Vanrhynsdorp

R355

Fish

Riet

R364

R354

Strandfontein

Doringbaai

Lambert's Bay

R364

Clanwilliam

C E D A R B E R G

*Tankwa-Karoo
National Park*

Sutherland

Elands Bay

R27

R366

Doring

*St. Helena
Bay*

Velddrif

Citrusdal

N7

R356

R354

Stompneusbaai

R399

Laingsburg

Paternoster

Vredenburg

Piketberg

R303

Saldanha

R45

Langebaan

R27

Tulbagh

N1

*West Coast
National Park*

R307

R311

R44

Ceres

Touws River

Darling

Malmesbury

*ATLANTIC
OCEAN*

Mamre

Wellington

Worcester

Montagu

Melkbosstrand

Paarl

N1

R43

R60

Robertson

Barrydale

R62

Milnerton

Durbanville

Franschhoek

Cape Town ✪

Bellville

Stellenbosch

Genadendal

Swellendam

Muizenberg

Somerset
West

Greyton

R319

Malgas

Simon's Town

*False
Bay*

Caledon

N2

R317

Breede

*Cape of
Good Hope*

R44

Hermanus

Elim

Bredasdorp

*De Hoop
Nature
Reserve*

Gordon's Bay

Stanford

O V E R B E R G

Kleinmond

Gansbaai

Waenhuiskrans

Struisbaai

Cape Agulhas   L'Agulhas

ings left by the San, whose few remaining clans have long since retreated into the Kalahari Desert. The population of the Western Cape today is largely "colored", a catchall term to describe South Africans of mixed race and descendants of imported slaves, the San, and the Khoikhoi.

Pleasures and Pastimes

Architecture

The most visible emblem of local culture is Cape Dutch architecture. As you travel from estate to estate, you will see a number of 18th- and 19th-century manor houses that share certain characteristics: thick white-washed walls, thatched roofs curving around elegant gables, and small-pane windows framed by wooden shutters. It's a classic look—a uniquely Cape look—ideally suited to a land that is hot in summer and cold in winter. The Cape Dutch style developed in the 18th century from traditional long houses: simple, rectangular sheds capped by thatch. As farmers became more prosperous, they added the ornate gables and other features. Several estates, most notably Vergelegen and Boschendal, have opened their manor houses as museums.

Art and Crafts

The well-respected galleries throughout this region could surprise you with anything from protest paintings from the apartheid era to high-quality ceramics and pewter work. Also keep an eye open for smaller local craft shops, which can provide you with unique souvenirs.

Dining

South African cuisine at its finest can be found in the Western Cape. If silver service is not your cup of tea, however, local laid-back country-style cooking can be just as satisfying. The area is home to some of the country's best Cape Malay cuisine, characterized by mild, slightly sweet curries and the use of aromatic spices. Be prepared for fluctuations in the level of service. Generally, South Africans are still trying to get this right, but there are some remarkable exceptions to what appears to be a general go-slow. For a description of South African culinary terms, *see* Pleasures and Pastimes *in* Chapter 1. For price ranges, *see* Chart 1 *in* On the Road with Fodor's.

Golf

Fourteen golf courses lie within a 45-minute drive of the center of the Winelands, and four are situated within the Winelands themselves. All accept foreign visitors and most rent clubs. Greens fees for 18 holes average R70–R195. You shouldn't have a problem finding a course to your liking, the very best being situated in Somerset West, where you will find the Gary Player–designed Erinvale.

Lodging

The Winelands are sufficiently compact that you can make one hotel your touring base for your entire stay. Stellenbosch and Paarl offer the most flexibility, situated close to dozens of wineries and restaurants, as well as the major highways to Cape Town. Franschhoek is comparatively isolated, which many visitors consider a blessing. Tourist offices (☞ Contacts and Resources *in* Winelands A to Z, *below*) have extensive information on bed-and-breakfasts and self-catering options, many of which are less expensive than hotels and often give you a more personal taste of life in the Winelands. For price ranges, *see* Chart 2 (A) *in* On the Road with Fodor's.

Scenery

Few places in the world can match the drama of the Winelands, where African mountains rise sheer above vine-covered valleys and 300-year-old homesteads snooze in the shade of giant oaks. It's a place of such enviable beauty that you catch yourself glancing through the local real-estate pages. In Namaqualand in spring, vast fields that seemed barren only a month before blush with blossoms of every conceivable color. Vygies and Namaqualand daisies brightly splash the hillsides and valleys like a crazy painter's easel.

Wine

Buried for years by sanctions, South African wines were largely unknown on the international scene. With the demise of the apartheid era, South African wine exports soared. No one could have expected such interest; as a result, the best are now in short supply in their country of origin and South African wine lovers are peeved at the price they have to pay for a bottle of good local vino. Armed with foreign currency and a favorable rate of exchange, you will, however, still be able to get value for money. While the quantity of South African wines remains a problem until the extensive new vine plantings come of age and the supply increases, the quality is improving with each vintage. Cape reds have recently won a slew of international awards. You must taste Pinotage, South Africa's own grape variety, a hybrid of Pinot Noir and Cinsaut (or Hermitage, as it was once called in the Cape). If you're really serious about wine, arm yourself with *John Platter's Wine Guide,* an annual pocket guide, or buy a copy of *WINE* magazine, a monthly publication that specializes in detailed features on local wineries. Keep in mind that many wineries close at lunchtime on Saturday and don't open at all on Sunday. For more information on shipping wine home, *see* Customs and Duties *in* the Gold Guide.

Exploring the Western Cape

Moving from Cape Town in the northwest to the southeast there are five major areas of interest for the visitor. North of Cape Town, the West Coast and the neighboring interior are renowned for seafood and wildflowers respectively. To the south are the important wine-producing centers of Paarl, Stellenbosch and Franschhoek, and to the east the historically significant and scenic Swellendam area. The southern tip of Africa, Cape Agulhas, can be reached by leaving the inland region and traveling south to the coast. The southern coastal area incorporates the small towns or villages of Gansbaai, Hermanus, Kleinmond, and Gordon's Bay.

Great Itineraries

Many people spend their entire vacations in the Western Cape after getting a big-game fix in Mpumalanga. Although it's possible to explore Cape Town and the Winelands in three or four days—the area is compact enough to allow it—you need six or seven to do it justice. You can get a good sense of the either Overberg or the West Coast on a three- or four-day jaunt, but set aside a week if you plan to tackle the vast distances of Namaqualand, in the Northern Cape. The most practical and enjoyable way to explore the region is by car.

Numbers in the text correspond to numbers in the margin and on the Winelands map.

IF YOU HAVE 3 DAYS

From Cape Town, take the N1 to **Paarl** ㉖, gliding off the highway at the ▣ **Franschhoek** ㉒ turnoff. Book in and off load your luggage at L'Auberge du Quartier Français, before setting off to the Cabriere estate, for a pre-arranged tour. Enjoy lunch at the **Haute Cabriere** ㉓ cellar or La Petite Ferme, both of which are on the Franschhoek pass and have great views. After lunch, visit **La Motte** ㉑, **Boschendal** ⑱, or **L'Ormarins** ⑲ estates. In the late afternoon explore the antiques shops and art galleries in the main street of Franschhoek or visit the Huguenot Museum. On the second day, head for Paarl on the R45. Along the way visit **Backsberg** ㉚, **Fairview** ㉙, **Nederburg** ㉔, the **KWV** ㉗, or **Rhebokskloof** ㉕. Stop for lunch at the Grande Roche Hotel. If you've had a surfeit of wine-tasting, take a walk up Paarl Mountain, wander down the main street for a spot of shopping, soak up some old Cape architecture, or spend the afternoon on the front veranda at the Grande Roche and enjoy the view. Overnight, really splash out and spend a night at the ☒ **Grande Roche Hotel.** Next morning head for **Stellenbosch** ⑥ via the N2 and the R44, en route back to Cape Town. Stop at **Vergelegen** ① for lunch, at the Lady Phillips Tea Garden. Allow plenty of time—it would be a shame to leave this vast estate without wandering around the gardens.

IF YOU HAVE 5 DAYS

Leaving Cape Town on the first day, take the N7 and head north to the ☒ **Bushmans Kloof** game lodge in the Cedarberg ("Cedar Mountains"). This drive will take you through Clanwilliam and the Swartland, the beginning of the wildflower route, which is best in spring. Try to reach the lodge by 3 PM, giving yourself time to unpack, enjoy a sumptuous tea, and be ready for the late afternoon game drive. Spend the second day here, taking in all that the lodge and its inspiring environment has to offer. On the third morning head west to ☒ **Lambert's Bay.** This coastal town certainly has charm and the Marine Protea Hotel on the harborside will be more than adequate as a base from which to explore. After breakfast and a stroll on the fourth morning, set off on the R27 (mostly good gravel) south to ☒ **Langebaan**'s lagoon and West Coast National Park. Overnight at the Farmhouse, on the hill overlooking the lagoon, and absorb the tranquil sights and sounds which make Langebaan famous. It is a comfortable, 90-minute drive back to Cape Town on the fifth day.

IF YOU HAVE 7 DAYS

The first two days of this tour follow the schedule described in either of the two itineraries above. The third day, however, takes you northeast towards the coast, your destination being ☒ **Bartholomeus Klip Game Lodge** and farm. From Clanwilliam take the N7 to Piketberg, and then the R44 to Wellington, passing through the hamlets of Riebeek West and Riebeek Kasteel (try the Village Taverna in the latter for lunch). Once again, try to get to the lodge in time for tea and the afternoon game drive or a walk around the farm. Spend the following day here, ample time to take it all in. On day five, travel over the Franschhoek Pass, join the R43 at Villiersdorp, circumnavigating the extensive Theewaterskloof Dam. Head on to ☒ **Grootbos** game lodge, where you'll spend the next day. On the seventh day retrace your route to the N2 and head back to the city.

When to Tour the Western Cape

The high season in the Western Cape is, of course, summer, and you will seldom visit major places of interest without the presence of busloads of fellow visitors. The weather is warm and dry, and although strong southeasterly winds can be a nuisance, they do keep the temperature bearable. If soaking up the sun is not of primary importance and you prefer to tour during quieter times, spring (September and October) and autumn–early winter (late March through May) are ideal. The weather is milder and the lines shorter. Spring also brings southern right whales close to the shores of the Western Cape to calve, and late August–October are the months to see the wildflowers explode across Namaqualand and the West Coast. If the Winelands are high on your list of must-dos, remember that the busiest time in the vineyards and cellars is January–March.

THE WINELANDS

Frank Prial, wine critic for the *New York Times,* wrote that he harbored "a nagging suspicion that great wines must be made in spectacular surroundings." If that's true, the French may as well rip up their vines and brew beer, because the Cape Winelands are absolutely stunning.

All of this lies only 45 minutes east of Cape Town in three historic towns and valleys. Founded in 1685, Stellenbosch is a gem; it's also a vibrant university community. Franschhoek, enclosed by towering mountains, is the original home of the Cape's French Huguenots, whose descendants have made a conscious effort to reassert their French heritage. Paarl lies beneath huge granite domes, its main street running 11 km (7 mi) along the Berg River past some of the country's most elegant historical monuments. Throughout the region you will find some of South Africa's best restaurants and hotels.

It's no longer entirely accurate to describe these three valleys as *the* Winelands. Today, they make up only 35% of all the land in the Cape under vine. This wine-growing region is now so vast that you can trek to the fringes of the Karoo Desert in the northeast and still find a grape. There are altogether more than 10 wine routes, as well as a newly established brandy route, in the Western Cape, ranging from the Olifants River in the north to the coastal mountains of the Overberg (☞ *below*).

Each of the wine-producing areas has its own wine route where member wineries throw open their estates to the public. They maintain tasting rooms where you can sample their vintages either gratis or for a nominal fee. Happily, no one expects you to be a connoisseur, or even to buy their wines. Just relax and enjoy yourself, and don't hesitate to ask tasting room staff which flavors to expect in what you're drinking. Some wineries have restaurants; at others, you can call ahead to reserve a picnic hamper to enjoy on the estate grounds.

The secret of touring the Winelands is not to hurry. Dally over lunch on a vine-shaded veranda at a 300-year-old estate; enjoy an afternoon nap under a spreading oak; or sip wine while savoring the impossible views. This may not be the Africa of *National Geographic,* but no one's complaining. Nowhere in South Africa is the living more civilized and the culture more self-assured.

The Winelands encompass scores of wineries and estates. The ones listed below are chosen for their great wine, their beauty, or their historic significance. It would be a mistake to try to cover them all in less than a week. You have nothing to gain from hightailing it around the Winelands other than a headache. The vineyards fan out around three major towns, Stellenbosch, Franschhoek, and Paarl. If your interest is more aesthetic and cultural than wine-driven, you would do well to focus on the historic estates of Stellenbosch and Franschhoek, after which you might head south into the Overberg (☞ *below*). Most of the Paarl wineries on this tour stand out more for the quality of their wine rather than their beauty.

Somerset West

40 km (25 mi) southeast of Cape Town on the N2.

Somerset West is on the edge of the Winelands. Just before you reach the center of town you'll see the turnoff to Lourensford Road, which
★ ❶ runs 3.2 km (2 mi) to **Vergelegen.** This first winery may well spoil you for the rest. It is one of the most gracious, peaceful, and beautiful places in the Cape. Wine-tasting is a major reason to visit here, but you would be mad to leave without touring the grounds.

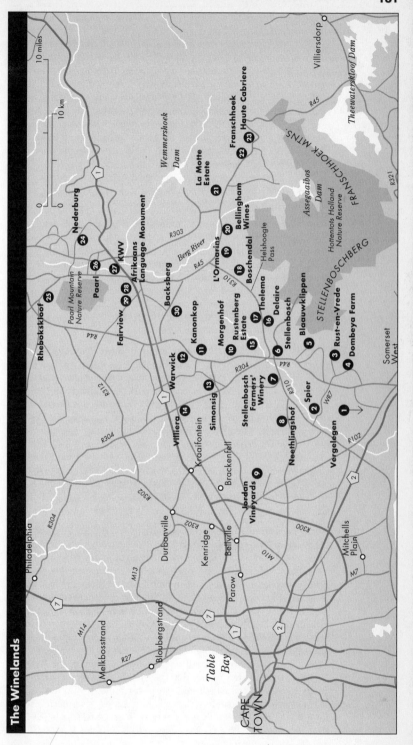

The Winelands

Vergelegen was established in 1700 by Willem Adriaan van der Stel, who succeeded his father as governor of the Cape. His classic Cape Dutch homestead, with thatch roof and gables, looks like something out of a fairy tale. An octagonal walled garden aflame with flowers surrounds it, and huge camphor trees, planted almost 300 years ago, stand as gnarled sentinels. The estate was purchased for Lady Phillips by her husband, Sir Lionel, in 1917 and she spent vast sums on the restoration of the homestead, library, and gardens. The homestead is now a museum and is furnished in period style. Other historic buildings include a magnificent library (⊘ Mon.–Sat. 11–3) and the old stables, now the reception area and interpretive center. Behind the house, Lady Phillips Tea Garden serves lunch and tea (☞ Dining, *below*), and the Rose Terrace café looks onto a formal rose garden. Much of the fresh produce is supplied by the Margaret Roberts Herb and Vegetable Garden, which is next to the reception area.

While Vergelegen still buys in grapes from neighboring farms, the vineyards that were planted in 1989, during what is described as the renaissance of the farm, are beginning to give an inkling of some very good wines to come. You really should taste the Merlot, with its ripe, plumy flavors. The Chardonnay has touches of wood fermentation and maturation. ⊠ *Lourensford Rd., Somerset West,* ☎ *021/847–1334,* FAX *021/847–1608.* ☜ *R7.50; tastings free.* ⊘ *Daily 9:30–4 (no tastings Sun.). Cellar tours: Mon.–Sat. 10:30, 11:30, and 2:30 (reservations essential).*

❷ Describing **Spier** as simply a wine estate is doing Spier Home Farms an enormous disservice. The vast new complex comprises a manor house, wine cellars, wine and farm shop, rose garden, restaurants, conference center, open air amphitheater, cheetah park, and equestrian facilities. It's all designed in Cape-country style, with whitewashed walls and thatch roofs, set along the verdant north bank of the Eerste River. You can even get to Spier's own little railway station by vintage locomotive from the V & A Waterfront in Cape Town. So, yes, it's seriously touristy, but still delightful. Try the Sauvignon Blanc (a local award winner), Chardonnay, and Cabernet Sauvignon from the 1996 vintage to get a feel of the type of wines to come from this vast estate. ⊠ *On the R310, Stellenbosch,* ☎ *800/220–282 or 021/881–3096,* FAX *021/881–3634.* ☜ *Free; tasting R10; train ride: R75.* ⊘ *Daily 9–5.*

Nestled against the base of the Helderberg and shaded by giant oaks, ❸ the peaceful **Rust-en-Vrede** winery looks over steep slopes of vines and roses. Owned by former Springbok rugby great Jannie Engelbrecht, it's a comparatively small estate that specializes entirely in red wine—and produces some of the very best in South Africa. Rust-en-Vrede Estate is the flagship wine, a blend of predominantly cabernet sauvignon, shiraz, and just over 10% merlot grapes. It has already won several awards both locally and abroad, but it would do well to mature in the bottle for another 10 years or more. Another interesting wine is the Shiraz, which has an inviting bouquet with the vanillin sweetness that American oak imparts; it will age for five to eight years. Rust-en-Vrede is one of the few estates that opens its historic winery and beautifully restored Cape Dutch homestead for tours. It also has a short birding trail that meanders through indigenous, riverine forest. ⊠ *R44, between Stellenbosch and Somerset West,* ☎ *021/881–3881,* FAX *021/881–3000.* ☜ *Free.* ⊘ *Weekdays 8:30–12:30 and 1:30–4:30, Sat. 9–1. Cellar tours on request.*

❹ Next door to Rust-en-Vrede is **Dombeya Farm,** one of the few places in the Western Cape to see spinning and handweaving. The farm makes jerseys, blankets, and wool rugs, all in the bright, feminine patterns that are Dombeya's hallmark. The shop also sells patterns and wool. A garden tearoom serves light lunches and snacks. ⊠ *Annandale Road, Stellenbosch,* ☎ FAX *021/881–3746.* ☉ *Daily 9–5.*

❺ Established in the late 17th century, **Blaauwklippen** sits at the foot of the Stellenboschberg, shaded by oaks. It's a large winery that is well equipped to handle tour buses and will keep even non-oenophiles entertained. From October to April, you can take carriage rides (R2) through the vineyards, and there is also a free museum of old coaches, furniture, and kitchen utensils. If you arrive between noon and two, consider settling down on the veranda for a Coachman's Lunch of cold meats, cheeses, and pâté. Blaauwklippen produces a good range of both red and white wines. Its Zinfandel is by far the best of the four produced in the Cape, and it has fared extremely well in competition with American Zinfandels. The Shiraz and Cabernet Sauvignon are also most commendable. For easy drinking right now, Red Landau, a blend of cabernet sauvignon and merlot grapes, is good value. A country shop sells souvenirs, as well as jams, Cape Malay chutneys, and *weinwurst* (a salami-like sausage). ⊠ *R44 between Stellenbosch and Somerset West,* ☎ *021/880–0133,* FAX *021/880–1250.* ▨ *R1.70 for booklet of 5 tasting tickets.* ☉ *Weekdays 9–5, Sat. 9–1. Cellar tours Dec.–Jan. on request; Feb.–Nov., weekdays 11 and 3, Sat. 11.*

Dining and Lodging

$$$ ✕ **L'Auberge du Paysan.** Come to this little cottage near Somerset West for classic French cuisine. Tall upholstered chairs, small brass table lamps, and snowy linen set the tone for dishes from several Gallic provinces. Specialties include snails Provençale, seafood casserole, and roast duck, but don't dismiss the excellent Cape mussel soup and East Coast sole with almonds. For dessert, local port enhances black cherries wrapped in a pancake flambéed in brandy, and the crème brulee is one of the Winelands' best. ⊠ *Raithby Rd., off R45, between Somerset West and Stellenbosch,* ☎ *011/842–2008. AE, DC, MC, V. Closed Sun. and 1 month in winter. No lunch Mon.*

$$ ✕ **Lady Phillips Tea Garden.** In summer you need to reserve a table three weeks in advance at this idyllic country restaurant on the Vergelegen estate. Whether dining inside or alfresco on the terrace, you will savor a luncheon of classy simplicity, but presented with panache. Start with grilled pear and Gorgonzola on bruschetta, follow with the chicken and prawn curry or pan-fried sole with shrimp and saffron sauce. The brandy snap basket filled with ice-cream and fresh fruit makes a perfect finale. If schedules do not permit reservations, head to the Rose Terrace during summer for light meals. ⊠ *Vergelegen Estate, Lourensford Rd., Somerset West,* ☎ *021/847–1334. Reservations essential Nov.–Apr. AE, DC, MC, V. No dinner.*

$$$ ▥ **Willowbrook Lodge.** This lodge makes a good base for exploring the entire southwestern Cape, including the peninsula, the Winelands, and the Overberg. The lodge lies hidden among beautiful gardens that extend down to the Lourens River; in the distance, the peaks of the Helderberg are visible. It's a very peaceful place, with no TVs in the rooms, which are large and comfortable with a sliding door opening onto the gardens. ⊠ *Morgenster Ave., Box 1892, Somerset West 7129,* ☎ *024/513–759,* FAX *024/514–152. 12 rooms with bath. Restaurant, bar, pool. No children under 12. AE, DC, MC, V.*

Golf

Somerset West Country Club (⊠ Rue de Jacqueline, ☎ 021/852–2925) is an easy course (R85 for 18 holes) with plenty of leeway for errant tee-shots. **Erinvale Golf Club** (⊠ Lourensford Rd., Somerset West ☎

021/847–1144) is a Gary Player–designed course (R250 for 18 holes) nestled beneath the Hottentots Holland Mountains.

Stellenbosch

★ ❻ *15 km (9½ mi) north of Somerset West.*

Stellenbosch may be the most delightful town in South Africa. It's small, sophisticated, and beautiful, and you could easily while away a week here. The second-oldest town after Cape Town, it actually *feels* old, unlike so many historic towns in South Africa. Wandering the oak-shaded streets, which still have open irrigation furrows, you'll see some of the finest examples of Cape Dutch, Georgian, Victorian, and Regency architecture in the country. The town was founded in 1679 by Simon van der Stel, first governor of the Cape, who recognized the agricultural potential of this fertile valley. Wheat was the major crop grown by the early settlers, but vineyards now blanket the surrounding hills. The town is also home to the University of Stellenbosch, the country's first and most prestigious Afrikaans university.

A brief walking tour of the town starts at the corner of Dorp Street and the R44, where you first enter Stellenbosch. The **Rembrandt van Rijn Art Museum** occupies the historic Libertas Parva manor house, which displays the H shape so typical of Cape Dutch architecture. Built in 1780, the house has hosted some of the biggest names in South African history, including Cecil Rhodes and Barry Herzog. Jan Smuts, who became prime minister and a major player on the world scene after the Great War, was married here. The art museum displays the work of some major South African artists, including Irma Stern, Willie Bester, and sculptor Anton van Wouw. ⊠ *31 Dorp St.,* ☎ *021/886–4340,* ℻ *021/887—1645.* ⊡ *Free.* ◷ *Weekdays 9–12:45 and 2–5, Sat. 10–1 and 2–5.*

The **Stellenryk Wine Museum** is housed in the 18th-century wine cellars behind Libertas Parva. The cellar setting is appropriate for the museum's collection of wine-related artifacts, including presses, vats, and an interesting collection of wine vessels ranging from antiquity to the 18th century. ⊠ *31 Dorp St.,* ☎ *021/888–3588.* ⊡ *Free.* ◷ *Weekdays 9–12:45 and 2–5, Sat. 10–1.*

Stroll up oak-lined Dorp Street, Stellenbosch's most historic avenue. Almost the entire street is a national monument, flanked by lovely, restored homes from every period of the town's history. Redolent with tobacco, dried fish, and spices, **Oom Samie Se Winkel** is a Victorian-style general store and one of Stellenbosch's most popular landmarks. In addition to the usual Cape kitsch, Oom Samie's sells some genuine *boere* (farmers') products, including *witblitz* and *mampoer,* the Afrikaner equivalent of moonshine. The shop operates a wine-export business and restaurant, too. ⊠ *82/84 Dorp St.,* ☎ *021/887–2612.* ℻ *021/883—-8621.* ◷ *Weekdays 8.30–5:30, Sat. 9–5.*

As you continue up Dorp Street, keep an eye out for **La Gratitude** (⊠ 95 Dorp St.); the all-seeing eye of God on its gable will be doing the same for you. **Voorgelegen** (⊠ 176 Dorp St.) and the houses on either side of it form one of the best-preserved Georgian ensembles in town.

When you reach Andringa Street, turn left and then right onto Kerk (Church) Street. On your left is **d'Ouwe Werf,** possibly the country's oldest boarding house (☞ Dining and Lodging, *below*), which first took in paying guests as long ago as 1802.

At the corner of Kerk and Ryneveld streets is the **Stellenbosch Village Museum,** which is well worth a visit. The museum comprises four dwellings scattered within a two-block radius. These houses date from different periods in Stellenbosch's history and have been furnished to reflect changing lifestyles and tastes. The oldest of them is the very basic Schreuderhuis, which dates from 1709. The others date from 1789, 1803, and 1850, respectively. ✉ *18 Ryneveld St.,* ☎ *021/887–2902.* ☞ *R10.* ☉ *Mon.–Sat. 9:30–5, Sun. 2–5.*

Continue down Ryneveld to Plein Street. Turn left and walk to the **Braak,** the grassy town square. Some of Stellenbosch's most historic buildings face the square, which is a national monument. At the southern end is the **Rhenish Church** (✉ Bloem St.), erected by the Missionary Society of Stellenbosch in 1823 as a training school for slaves and coloreds.

St. Mary's Church stands at the far end of the Braak. Built in 1852, it was consecrated by Bishop Robert Gray in 1854 and reflects the growing influence of the English in Stellenbosch. Across Bloem Street from St. Mary's is the **Burgher House,** built in 1797. Today, it houses the offices of Historical Homes in South Africa.

Next to the Burgher House, on an island in Market Street, stands the **V.O.C. Arsenal.** It took 91 years for the Political Council to hammer out the decision that Stellenbosch needed its own magazine. With the hard part behind them, it took just six months in 1777 to complete the structure. ✉ *Bloem St., no phone.* ☞ *R1.* ☉ *Aug.–May, weekdays 9:30–1:30 and 2–5.*

Walk down Market Street past the Tourist Information Bureau (☞ Winelands A to Z, *below*). On your left, facing a large lawn, is the **Rhenish Complex,** one of the most impressive restoration projects ever undertaken in South Africa. The complex consists of the old Cape Dutch Rhenish parsonage (1815); the Leipoldt House, which melds elements of English and Cape architecture; and a two-story building that is typically English.

Continue down Market and turn left on **Herte Street.** The whitewashed cottages along this street were built for freed slaves after the Emancipation Act of 1834. Although they were originally thatched, the houses are still evocative of 19th-century Stellenbosch. From here, follow Herte back to Dorp Street, where the walking tour began.

From Stellenbosch, wine routes fan out like spokes of a wheel, making excellent day trips if you're staying in town. Several excellent wineries lie nearby off the R310. To reach them, get back in your car, follow Dorp Street across the R44, and turn left at the Shell station.

Around Stellenbosch

❼ It's less than a mile from town to the **Stellenbosch Farmers' Winery** (SFW). Founded by a Kentuckian, William Charles Winshaw, SFW is the largest wholesale wine producer/merchant in South Africa and is responsible for almost 40% of the country's table wine. SFW also produces fortified wines, several brandies, and very good fruit juices and ciders. The SFW flagship is the Zonnebloem range of reds and whites, including among others a good Shiraz (particularly those from the early 1980s). The Lanzerac Pinotage was the first of the variety ever made in South Africa (back in 1961), and it's still a good wine.

The **Farmers' Winery Center,** where tours begin, stands directly opposite the winery above a vineyard of Cabernet Sauvignon grapes. Here you'll find the wine-tasting center and salesroom. Each summer, concerts ranging from African jazz to opera and ballet are staged at the **Oude Libertas Amphitheatre,** a delightful open-air venue. For program listings and reservations, contact Computicket or phone 021/808–7474. ✉ *Adam Tas Rd., off R310,* ☎ *021/808–7569,* 🖷 *021/887–2506.* 📧

Tastings R3.50; cellar tours R6. ☉ *Weekdays 8:30–5, Sat. 10–12:30: cellar tours, Mon.–Thur. 10–2:30; Fri. 10; Sat. on request only.*

⑧ A long avenue of pines and oaks leads to the lovely estate of **Neethlings-hof,** which traces its origins back to 1692. The magnificent 1814 Cape Dutch manor house looks out across formal rose gardens to the Stellenbosch Valley and the Hottentots Holland Mountains. The wines produced on this estate and those from its sister farm, Stellenzicht, are highly regarded both locally and abroad, and so be prepared for a rush of tour buses during the high season. The Gewürztraminer is an off-dry, very elegant wine with rose-petal and spice aromas, while the Weisser Riesling is a good example of the few virtually dry wines made from this grape variety. Neethlingshof also produces an excellent Noble Late Harvest sweet dessert wine. Do not, however, leave the tasting room, without trying the pièce de résistance, the Stellenzicht Syrah. ⊠ *R310,* ☎ *021/883–8988,* 𝗙𝗔𝗫 *021/883–8941.* ☞ *Tastings R20 for 8 wines of your choice.* ☉ *Weekdays 9–5, weekends 10–4. Cellar tours by appointment.*

There are number of established estates, such as Overgaauw and Uiterwyk, on Stellenbosch Kloof Road. They are certainly worth a visit, but **⑨** set your sights on **Jordan Vineyards,** a newer winery at the end of this road. Flanked by the hills of the Bottelaryberg and overlooking a vision of rolling vineyards and jagged mountains, it enjoys an enviable setting at the head of Stellenbosch Kloof. Gary and Cathy Jordan are a husband-and-wife team who studied at the University of California at Davis and worked at California's Iron Horse Winery. Although they produced their first vintage only in 1992, they have already established their reputation as producers of quality wines. The Sauvignon Blanc and Chardonnay are delicious in their own ways, the former with lots of gooseberry fruit, the latter elegant and toasty. Also look for a combination of the two in the versatile Chameleon dry white, a flavorful, well-priced buy. Wine critics are also keeping their eyes on the Jordans' spicy Cabernet Sauvignon. ⊠ *Stellenbosch Kloof Rd.,* ☎ *021/881–3441,* 𝗙𝗔𝗫 *021/881–3426.* ☞ *Tastings R5.* ☉ *Weekdays 10–4:30, Sat. 9:30–2:30. Cellar tours by appointment.*

Some of the Cape's most important wineries are on the stretch of the R44 that runs north from Stellenbosch. **Morgenhof** lies in the lee of a **⑩** steep hill covered with vines and great pine trees. It's a beautiful Cape Dutch estate, with a history stretching back 300 years. In 1993, Morgenhof was acquired by the Huchon-Cointreaus of Cognac, France. They have spared nothing to make this one of the jewels of the Winelands, and behind the glamour there is an extremely talented winemaker and distinguished wines. Jean Daneel's award-winning 1992 Merlot, for example, is a bold mouthful of a red wine, but his Morgenhof Chenin Blanc is the one currently making waves in the Cape. This workhorse wine tastes like a fine Chardonnay. Apart from these celebrity wines, try the Sauvignon Blanc, Chardonnay, and Pinotage. Morgenhof is an excellent place to stop for lunch. From October through April, you can reserve picnic hampers and dine on the lawns under a huge tree. The rest of the year, there are light lunches of homemade soup, freshly baked bread, cheese, and quiche. Reservations are advisable in summer. ⊠ *R44, between Paarl and Stellenbosch,* ☎ *021/889–5510,* 𝗙𝗔𝗫 *021/889–5266.* ☞ *Tastings R2.50.* ☉ *Weekdays 9–4:30, Sat. 10–3; Nov.–Apr., also Sun. 10–3. Cellar tours by appointment.*

In the days when ships of the Dutch East India Company used Cape Town as a revictualing station on the way to the East, they would fire a cannon as they entered the harbor to let farmers know they needed provisions. A relay cannon was then fired from a hill on this farm; **⑪** *Kanonkop* is Afrikaans for Cannon Hill. The beauty of **Kanonkop** is not in its history or its buildings but in its wine. Since the early 1980s, wine making has been in the hands of legendary Beyers Truter. In 1991 he won the "Winemaker of the Year" award and the Robert Mondavi Trophy at the International Wine & Spirit Competition in London. No one would argue that Kanonkop's Pinotage is the best new-style Pinotage produced in South Africa. It's more wooded than most and shows excellent complexity and fruit; it will age for 8 to 15 years. Paul Sauer is a very good blend of about 80% Cabernet Sauvignon with the balance made up of equal parts Merlot and Cabernet Franc. ⊠ *R44, between Paarl and Stellenbosch,* ☎ *021/884–4656,* ℻ *021/884–4719.* 🍷 *Tastings free.* ⊙ *Weekdays 9–5, Sat. 8:30–12:30. No cellar tours.*

⑫ **Warwick** is not a member of the Stellenbosch Wine Route, and you should visit this estate only if you're very keen to taste and buy wine; the tasting area is in a tiny cellar room cluttered with wine-making equipment (if possible, make an appointment first). Wine maker Norma Ratcliffe is very traditional in her approach to wine. She spent a couple of vintages in France perfecting her techniques and is now producing first-rate reds. Trilogy is one of the finest blended reds in the Cape, a stylish and complex wine made predominantly from Cabernet Sauvignon, with about 20% Merlot and 10% Cabernet Franc. The Cabernet Franc is undoubtedly the best wine made from this varietal in the Winelands. The 1992 vintage is a particularly fruity wine, a real standout. ⊠ *R44, between Paarl and Stellenbosch,* ☎ *021/884–4410,* ℻ *021/884–4025.* 🍷 *Tastings R5.* ⊙ *Weekdays 8:30–4:30, Sat. by appointment. Cellar tours by appointment.*

⑬ **Simonsig** sits in a sea of vines with tremendous views back toward Stellenbosch and the mountains. Its range of 15 white and red wines covers the whole taste and price spectrum. The Kaapse Vonkel is one of South Africa's best Méthode Cap Classique sparkling wines. Tiara is among the best cabernet blends in the Winelands, and the Pinotage is an excellent example of how well this varietal fares with no wood aging. You can bring your own picnic to enjoy at tables by the small playground. ⊠ *Kromme Rhee Rd.,* ☎ *021/882–2044,* ℻ *021/882–2545.* 🍷 *Tastings R3.50–R9 (depending on number of wines).* ⊙ *Weekdays 8:30–5, Sat. 8.30–4. Cellar tours weekdays 10 and 3, Sat. 10. Large groups should make an appointment.*

⑭ **Villiera** is actually part of the Paarl Wine Route, but its location in the open flats near the N1 motorway makes it just as close to Stellenbosch as to Paarl. In just over a decade of wine making, the Grier family has notched up numerous successes—such as Jeff Grier's late-1997 honor as the coveted Winemaker of the Year for his Bush Vine Sauvignon Blanc, the best in the Cape out of 72 entries. Jeff's Merlot also ranks among the top five in the country, with excellent depth of fruit. ⊠ *R101 and R304 (Old Paarl and Stellenbosch Rds), Koelenhof,* ☎ *021/882–2002,* ℻ *021/882–2314.* 🍷 *Tastings free.* ⊙ *Weekdays 8:30–5, Sat. 8:30–1. No cellar tours.*

A narrow lane runs through cattle pastures and groves of oak and birch ⑮ to **Rustenberg Estate,** a Cape Dutch homestead (1811) and vision of bucolic bliss. Unlike some of the more touristy wineries, Rustenberg feels like a working farm. The estate is known for red wine, its Rustenberg Cabernet Sauvignon having enjoyed an unblemished record since it was first bottled over 50 years ago. It's a lovely, unblended wine that will age for a decade or two. Try buying five bottles and drinking one every five years. ⊠ *Off R310 (Rustenberg Rd.), Ida's Valley,* ☎ *021/ 887–3153,* ℻ *021/887–8466.* 🍷 *Tastings free.* ⊙ *Weekdays 9–4:30, Sat. 9–12:30. Cellar tours by appointment.*

⓰ Perched high above the valley, **Delaire** enjoys one of the most spectacular settings of any winery in the country. Sit on the terrace of the tasting room or restaurant and look past a screen of oaks to the valley below and the majestic crags of the Groot Drakenstein and Simonsberg mountains. It's an ideal place to stop for lunch, or even a short breather. The restaurant (open Tues.–Sat. noon–2) serves light lunches and will provide picnic hampers to visitors who want to follow one of the scenic trails through the estate (open Sept. 15–Apr. 15). The tasting room is unpretentious and casual. ⊠ *R310, between Stellenbosch and Franschhoek (Helshoogte Rd.),* ☎ *021/885–1756,* ⓕⓐⓧ *021/885–1270.* 🖾 *Tastings R5.* ☉ *Mon.–Sat. 10–4. No cellar tours.*

⓱ On the slopes of the Simonsberg, **Thelema** is an excellent example of the exciting developments in the Cape Winelands since the early 1980s. When Gyles and Barbara Webb bought the farm in 1983, there was nothing here but very good soil and old fruit trees. It's a testament to their efforts that the winery has had regular prize-winners ever since. The 1992 Cabernet Sauvignon-Merlot blend won Gyles Webb the Diner's Club Winemaker of the Year title in 1994. Two years later he took the award again with the '94 Cabernet. Not say that his white wines do not win accolades—Thelema's Sauvignon Blanc and Chardonnay are certainly among the Cape's best. To cap it all off, the view of the Groot Drakenstein mountains from the tasting room is unforgettable. ⊠ *R310, between Stellenbosch and Franschhoek (Helshoogte Pass),* ☎ *021/885–1924,* ⓕⓐⓧ *021/885–1800.* 🖾 *Tastings free.* ☉ *Weekdays 9–5, Sat. 9–1. No cellar tours.*

Dining and Lodging

$$$$ ✕ **Jonkershuis.** The culinary influences that have contributed to traditional Cape cuisine—Cape Malay, Dutch, French, and German—are all celebrated here with a gargantuan buffet feast that you can savor under venerable oaks or inside the well-restored 18th-century homestead. Start with the soup of the day and farm breads or head for the cold table, laden with chicken satay in peanut sauce, lamb *frikkadels* (patties), excellent pickled fish, and well-dressed mussels. Cape chicken pie and roasts complete with a curry or two are among the main dishes. Look for the time-honored desserts *melktert* (a sweet milk tart sprinkled with cinnamon and sugar), *koeksisters* (a plaited doughnut served with a gingery syrup), and brandy pudding. For lighter fare, try the Spier Café and the Taphuis. ⊠ *Spier Estate, Lynedoch Rd., Stellenbosch* ☎ *021/881–3096. AE, DC, MC, V. No dinner Tue.–Sat.*

$$$ ✕ **Lord Neethling.** In an 18th-century Cape Dutch manor on the historic Neethlingshof estate, this lovely restaurant overlooks a patchwork of vineyards and the Stellenbosch Mountains. Despite the Cape setting, the Continental menu reflects German tastes. Diners can choose straightforward roasts, both ostrich and beef fillet, or less common dishes like Viennese-style chicken and beef in red-wine sauce served with chilies and spaetzle. A selection of fruity sorbets makes an agreeable summer dessert, but apple strudel and warm vanilla sauce are more likely to hit the spot on rainy winter days. ⊠ *Neethlingshof Estate, R310, Stellenbosch,* ☎ *021/883–8966. AE, DC, MC, V. No dinner Sun.*

$$ ✕ **De Volkskombuis.** Former laborers' dwellings now house the "People's Kitchen," on the banks of the Eerste River in Stellenbosch. Bare floorboards, low-beamed ceilings, and simple furnishings set the scene for a restaurant devoted to traditional Cape cooking. A good starter is a pâté of smoked *snoek* (a popular Cape fish) or *biltong*. Main courses include chicken or lamb pie and curried *sosaties* served with *geelrys* (rice with turmeric and raisins). You can always count on finding Malay *bredie* and *bobotie*, too. The Cape country sampler offers smaller portions of four traditional specialties. For dessert, try trifle, a slice of brandy tart, or *granadilla* (passion-fruit) cheesecake. ✉ *Old Strand Rd., Stellenbosch.* ☎ *021/887–2121. Reservations essential. AE, DC, MC, V. No dinner Sun.*

$ ✕ **Vinkel en Koljander.** This casual lunch spot occupies an elegant outbuilding on the 300-year-old Lanzerac estate on the outskirts of Stellenbosch. The à la carte menu is slanted toward traditional Cape fare like pickled cold fish and roasted *boerewors* skewered with onion and tomato and served with polenta. Vegetarians will enjoy a flavorful baked crepe with spinach, mozzarella, black mushrooms, aubergine, and tomato. For dessert, consider iced lemon meringue or the cheesecake. ✉ *Lanzerac Hotel, Jonkershoek Rd., Stellenbosch,* ☎ *021/887–1132. AE, DC, MC, V. No dinner.*

$$$ ⌂ **Lanzerac Manor.** For generations, this hotel was "home" to students from Stellenbosch University, who knew that the best cheese platter in the Winelands and a jolly good afternoon's respite could be enjoyed after a morning's serious wine tasting. In 1991, however, Lanzerac was acquired by a Cape businessman and his family, and since then some R30 million has gone into remodeling, renovation, and refurbishment. Now Lanzerac Manor and Winery boasts state-of-the-art facilities of all kinds, and the 40 guest rooms have been tastefully redecorated in a luxurious style. A sense of history, dating back to 1692, still remains, and the sheer beauty of the setting has been left untouched: a classic Cape Dutch manor house flanked by the rolling vineyards and mountains of the Jonkershoek Valley. ✉ *Jonkershoek Rd., 1 km (½ mi) from Stellenbosch (mailing address: Box 4, Stellenbosch 7599),* ☎ *021/ 887–1132,* ℻ *021/887–2310. 40 rooms with bath. 3 restaurants, bar, room service, pool. Breakfast included. AE, DC, MC, V.*

$$ ⌂ **De Goue Druif Guest House.** On Stellenbosch's most historic street, this tiny inn occupies an 1811 Georgian home that is also a national monument. Now settled in beautiful Stellenbosch, Belgian owners Catharina Cools and Yvan van Maercke go out of their way to make guests feel welcome in their gracious guest-house with its high ceilings, wooden floors, and collection of antiques. Since taking over the business in 1995, the Van Maercke's have upgraded the entire guest house, adding a swimming pool, a sauna, and gym facilities, overhauling the garden, and redecorating the guest rooms. Not surprisingly, the rejuvenated lodge was classified by Satour as the first three-star, silver classified guesthouse in Stellenbosch ✉ *110 Dorp St., Stellenbosch 7600,* ☎ ℻ *021/883–3555. 5 double rooms with bath. 1 cottage comprising 2 bedrooms, bath and lounge. Breakfast included. MC, V.*

$$ ⌂ **d'Ouwe Werf Country Inn.** A national monument, this attractive 1802 inn is thought to be the oldest in South Africa. From the street, guests enter the original living room, a beautiful space enlivened by wood floors, a lofty beamed ceiling, and elegant antiques. The hotel is divided into two parts: the old inn with luxury rooms on its Georgian second story and a new wing with more standard rooms. All luxury rooms are furnished with antiques, including four-poster beds, draped sash windows, and bronze bathroom fittings. The standard rooms have reproductions only. A lovely coffee garden in a brick courtyard shaded by trellised vines is opens for meals and drinks throughout the day. ✉ *30 Church St., Stellenbosch 7600,* ☎ *021/887–1608 or 021/887–4608,* ℻ *021/ 887–4626. 25 rooms with bath. Restaurant, room service, pool. Breakfast included. AE, DC, MC, V.*

Horseback Riding

Several riding outfits offer a range of rides for beginners and experts. Most lead standard one- and two-hour rides, as well as more interesting trips, including moonlight and sunset rides, wine-tasting trails, and even overnight camping. In Stellenbosch, contact **Amoi Riding Trails** (☎ 082/650–5794) or **Wine Valley Riding Club** (☎ 082/981–6331 or 083/226–8735).

Golf

Stellenbosch Golf Club (✉ Strand Rd., ☎ 021/880—-0103) has long, tree-lined fairways that will pose a problem if you don't hit the ball straight.

Franschhoek and the Franschhoek Valley

22 km (14 mi) northeast of Stellenbosch.

From Thelema, the road runs down Helshoogte Pass into the fruit orchards and vines that mark the beginning of the Franschhoek Valley. This is the most isolated and spectacular of the three wine routes, a long valley encircled by towering mountain ranges and fed by a single road. Franschhoek takes its name from its first white settlers, French Huguenots who fled to the Cape to escape Catholic persecution in France. By the early 18th century, 270 of them had settled in the Cape, but their descendants—with names like de Villiers, Malan, and Joubert—now number in the tens of thousands. With their experience in French vineyards, the early Huguenots were instrumental in nurturing a winemaking culture in South Africa. As spectacular as the valley is today, it must have been even more so in the late 17th century when it teemed with game. In calving season, herds of elephants would migrate to the valley via the precipitous Franschhoek Mountains. The last wild elephant in the valley died in the 1930s. Some leopards still survive.

⑱ **Boschendal** lies at the base of Helshoogte Pass. With a history dating back three centuries, this lovely estate competes with Groot Constantia as one of the Cape's major attractions; you could easily spend half a day here. Cradled between the Simonsberg and Groot Drakenstein mountains, the farm "Bossendaal" was originally granted to Jean le Long, one of the first French Huguenot settlers in the late 17th century.

Boschendal runs one of the most pleasant wine-tastings in the region: You can sit inside at the Taphuis, a Cape Dutch longhouse and the oldest building on the estate, or outside at wrought-iron tables under a spreading oak. In 1978, Boschendal was the first to pioneer a Cape Blanc de Noir, a pink wine made in a white-wine style from black grapes. The Boschendal Blanc de Noir remains the best-selling wine of this style. If you prefer sparkling wines, try the extremely popular Boschendal Brut, a blend of pinot noir and chardonnay made by the Méthode Cap Classique. From the Taphuis, it's a two-minute drive through vines and fruit trees to the main estate complex. The excellent Boschendal Restaurant (☞ Dining, *below*) serves a buffet of Cape specialties. Le Café serves light meals at tables under the oaks leading to the manor house. And Le Pique Nique (☉ Nov.–Apr.) provides picnic hampers for visitors to enjoy on the lawns. Calling ahead for the restaurant and the picnic is essential. A gift shop sells wine, locally made rugs, preserves, and other Cape kitsch. ✉ *R310, between Franschhoek and Stellenbosch (Pniel Rd., Groot Drakenstein),* ☎ *021/874–1252,* ℻ *021/874–2137.* 🎫 *Tastings R5; cellar tours R5.* ☉ *Dec. and Jan., Mon.–Sat. 8.30–4.30, Sun. 8.30–12.30. Feb.–Nov., Weekdays 8:30–4:30, Sat. 8:30–12:30. Cellar tours by appointment. Vineyard tours weekdays 10:30 and 11:30, Sat. 10:30.*

⑲ Even in a region where superlatives seem to fall short, **L'Ormarins** stands out as something special. The 1811 manor house, approached through a tunnel of oaks, is spellbinding: a classic Cape Dutch building festooned with flowers and framed by majestic peaks. The huge tasting room is modern and slick, in great contrast to the manor house—which indicates the modern winemaking style here. Using classic grape varieties, winemakers here are producing big, complex red wines, ready for early drinking but with excellent maturation potential. Optima is such a wine. A blend of predominantly cabernet sauvignon and merlot, it has great complexity that will improve in the bottle for 10 to 15 years. The straight cabernet is just as pleasing; among whites, try the Rhine Riesling. ⊠ *R45 (Franschhoek Rd., Groot Drakenstein),* ☎ *021/874–1026,* ℻ *021/874–1361.* ▨ *Tastings R5.* ☉ *Weekdays 9–4:30, Sat. 9–12:30. Cellar tours weekdays 10, 11:30, and 3; Sat. 11.*

㉑ **Bellingham Wines** lies deep in the shadows of old oaks, its Cape Dutch manor house almost completely hidden from view. The house is off-limits, but you can stroll unaccompanied through the vineyards, which run up the slope toward the craggy base of the mountains. From December to January, you can also order light luncheon platters to eat under the trees. There has been a renaissance here in recent years: Much money and oodles of talent have turned this estate's wines around. Ignore the also-ran range and head straight for the wines with the Premium and Vintage labels. Don't miss the Cabernet Franc, a big, rich, spicy wine, and the sweetish, fruity Pinotage, or the value-for-money Sauvenay (a blend Sauvgnon Blanc–Chardonnay blend) among the whites. ⊠ *R45,* ☎ *021/874–1011,* ℻ *021/874–1712.* ▨ *Tastings R5.* ▨ *Tastings R3.* ☉ *Weekdays 9–5, Sat. 10–12:30. No cellar tours.*

㉑ The R45 shares a narrow bridge over the Berg River with the railway line. Less than 2 km (1 mi) beyond the bridge is the **La Motte Estate,** owned by a branch of the same Rupert family that owns L'Ormarins. The elegant and rather formal tasting room looks into the cellars through a wall of smoked glass. Visitors sit at a long, marble-topped table and sample five to seven wines. The Shiraz is one of the biggest and boldest that you'll taste of this variety, full of rich flavors; it needs 4 to 8 years to reach its peak. The Millenium is a very good blend of just over 50% Cabernet Sauvignon with the balance consisting of Merlot and a little Cabernet Franc. This wine needs time to develop, coming into its own in 5 to 10 years. ⊠ *R45 (Huguenot Rd.),* ☎ *021/876–3119,* ℻ *021/876–3446.* ▨ *Tastings R2.60.* ☉ *Weekdays 9–4:30, Sat. 9–noon. No cellar tours.*

㉒ The village of **Franschhoek** lies at the base of the Franschhoek Mountains, which seal off the eastern end of the valley. It's a delightful village, with a pleasant, slow pace that belies the extraordinary number of restaurants, cafés, and small inns in town. It's makes a great stop for lunch or overnight.

The **Huguenot Memorial** (⊠ Lambrecht and Huguenot Sts.) stands at the end of the main road through Franschhoek. It was built in 1943 to commemorate the contribution of the Huguenots to South Africa's development. The three arches symbolize the Holy Trinity, the sun and cross form the Huguenots' emblem, and the female figure in front represents Freedom of Conscience.

Next to the memorial is the **Huguenot Memorial Museum.** Its main building is modeled after Thibault's 1791 Saasveld in Cape Town. The museum traces the causes of the Huguenots' flight from France and the life they carved out for themselves in the Cape. Wall displays profile some of the early Huguenot families. Exhibits also focus on other aspects of the region's history: One explains the development of Cape Dutch architecture; another explores the culture and life of the Khoikhoi, also known as Hottentots. ⊠ *Lambrecht St.,* ☎ *021/876–2532.* ▨ *R4.* ☉ *Weekdays 9–5, Sat. 9–1 and 2–5, Sun. 2–5.*

Built in 1994 on the lower slopes of the Franschhoek Mountains, **㉓** **Haute Cabrière** is the brainchild of Achim von Arnim, one of the Cape's most colorful wine makers. To avoid scarring the mountain, the complex hunkers into the hillside. In the restaurant, you can see the underground cellar through a large window—a very avant-garde touch for the Cape. Von Arnim makes five sparkling wines strictly according to the methods used in Champagne. It is said that his a fruity, mouth-filling '94 Pinot Noir set the standard by which Cape Pinot Noirs are judged. Also delicious is the Chardonnay/Pinot Noir blend, an ideal, extremely quaffable wine to enjoy at lunchtime. ⊠ *R45 to Villiersdorp,* ☎ *021/876–2630,* 𝔽𝔸𝕏 *021 876–3390.* ▣ *Tastings R5, cellar tours and tastings R10 (by appointment only).* ⊘ *Weekdays 8–5, Sat. 11–1.*

Dining and Lodging

$$$$ ✕ **La Maison de Chamonix.** No expense was spared when this run-down farmstead was transformed into a winery and upscale restaurant a couple of years ago. Today, it's one of the reasons why Franschhoek enjoys a reputation as the gourmet capital of the Cape. Local smoked salmon trout or chicken liver parfait with truffle oil make good preludes to loin of venison with red-wine sauce or a spinach and cheese roulade on tomato cream. Desserts range from light sorbets to crepes filled with caramelized pears and mascarpone. A buffet lunch is served Sunday. ⊠ *Uitkyk St., Franschhoek,* ☎ *021/876-2393. Reservations essential. AE, DC, MC, V. Closed Mon. in Aug. No dinner Sun.*

$$$$ ✕ **Le Quartier Français.** This restaurant in a 19th-century home has garnered impressive local and international awards. On summer nights, glass doors open onto a spotlighted garden; in winter, a log fire burns in the hearth. Chef Margot Janse's entrees include seaweed brioche with a ginger sabayon, or deep-fried tripe with cilantro-sparked maize meal and parmesan shavings. Her double-baked blue cheese souffle comes with watercress gnocchi and a red-pepper compote. *Snoek* is skewered on lemongrass and teamed with spiced couscous and fried banana. Creative desserts include lemon-scented meringue with brandied prunes and almonds and a berry gazpacho with fruity sorbet. ⊠ *16 Huguenot Rd., Franschhoek,* ☎ *021/876-2151. Reservations essential in season. AE, DC, MC, V. No dinner Sun.*

$$$ ✕ **Boschendal Restaurant.** Reserve well in advance for the buffet lunch here at one of the Cape's most beautiful and historic wineries. A wide selection of soups, quiches, and pâtés prefaces a bewildering array of cold and hot main dishes, including pickled fish, roasts, and imaginative salads; traditional Cape dishes are well prepared. End with a sampling of local cheeses and preserves or a classic Cape dessert like Malva pudding. ⊠ *R310, between Franschhoek and Stellenbosch,* ☎ *021/874-1252. Reservations essential. AE, DC, MC, V. Closed 3 wks mid-winter. No dinner.*

$$$ ✕ **Haute Cabriere.** Dine here atop a working winery built into the mountainside. Try to secure a window table for views across the vine-clad valley as you select from a mix-and-match menu created to complement the estate wines maturing in the cellar beneath you. Order half or full portions of the region's homegrown salmon trout, salad greens, and mushrooms. Sample the rack of lamb teamed with a sun-dried tomato and herb crust, potato rosti, and rosemary jus. Don't miss the warm chocolate tart with white chocolate sauce, or indulge in a savory finale of brie with fruit and green fig preserve. Brandy, coffee, and handmade chocolates complete the feast. ⊠ *Franschhoek Pass, Franschhoek,* ☎ *021/876-3688. Reservations essential in season. AE, DC, MC, V. No dinner Sun.–Tue.*

$$ ✕ **Le Ballon Rouge.** Diners come all the way from Cape Town to savor the food at this restaurant in a turn-of-the-century guest house in the center of Franschhoek. New owners Rory and Theresa Morgan are continuing the tradition of transforming the freshest ingredients into contemporary Cape-Gallic cuisine. Start with vibrant salads, such as grilled goat cheese dressed with balsamic or pesto vinaigrette, or Franschhoek salmon trout. Lamb is a main-course specialty, either a garlic-studded roasted leg or a grilled rack with mustard-herb crust. Desserts are equally appealing, whether fresh berries with warm sabayon or French lemon tart with seasonal fruit coulis. ✉ *12 Reservoir St., Franschhoek,* ☎ *021/876–2651. Reservations essential. AE, DC, MC, V.*

$$ ✕ **Polfyntjies.** The name means "souvenirs," and this restaurant on the outskirts of Franschhoek will leave you with lingering memories of Cape traditional fare. Sitting inside the 19th-century farmhouse or outside, with pleasant views of vines and forests against a mountain backdrop, you might choose to begin with sustaining *boontjiesop* (dried bean soup). For a main course, consider *bobotie* or *bredie*. The two most popular desserts are Malva pudding and milk tart. ✉ *R45, Franschhoek,* ☎ *021/876–3217. AE, DC, MC, V. Closed Mon. No dinner Sun.–Thurs. Closed one month mid-winter.* .

$$$ ▦ **L'Auberge du Quartier Français.** In the center of town, this classy guest house is a Winelands favorite. Separated from the village's main drag by a courtyard bistro and a superb restaurant, the guest house exudes privacy and peace. Rooms in two-story whitewashed cottages face a pool deck and central garden exploding with flowers. Decor is low-key, with rustic furniture, sponge-painted walls, and small fireplaces. Upstairs rooms have timber beams and mountain views, but they're hot in summer. Rooms have TVs and ceiling fans, but no air-conditioning. ✉ *Berg and Wilhelmina Sts. (mailing address: Box 237), Franschhoek 7690,* ☎ *02212/2151,* 𝔽𝔸𝕏 *02212/3105. 14 rooms with bath. 2 restaurants, bar, pool. AE, DC, MC, V.*

$ ▦ **Le Ballon Rouge Guest House.** In an old homestead in the center of Franschhoek village, this colonial-style guest house offers good value for money. Rooms open onto a veranda directly fronting the street—ideal for watching the world go by—and are small and feminine, with pretty floral fabrics, brass bedsteads, and country armoires. ✉ *12 Reservoir St., Box 344, Franschhoek 7690,* ☎ 𝔽𝔸𝕏 *02212/2651. 7 rooms with bath. Restaurant, room service, pool. Breakfast included. AE, DC, MC, V.*

Paarl

21 km (13 mi) northwest of Franschhoek.

Soon after you pass La Motte on the R45, turn right onto the R303, which runs into North Paarl. Cross under the N1 and continue for a couple of blocks. At the traffic lights, turn right onto Optenhorst Street and follow the signs to Nederburg, on the Paarl Wine Route.

㉔ **Nederburg** is the Cape's most established wine label; no restaurant's wine list would be complete without some of its wine. It's a vast estate, and it is easy to feel overwhelmed by the industrial white buildings. Fortunately, the tasting room is friendly and welcoming, and cellar tours lead visitors through the estate's fine Cape Dutch homestead, built in 1800. You can also reserve picnic hampers to enjoy on the estate's lawns (except during the build-up to the annual Nederburg Auction in March or April). The auction is one of the world's most glamorous wine events, when the very best wine from all over the Cape is sold to the highest bidders; nearly half to overseas buyers. Besides those produced specially for the auction, Nederburg produces about 20 wines under its regular label, covering the spectrum of reds and whites. The estate's Noble Late Harvest is exceptional. For an easy-drinking dry white wine, try Prelude, a successful blend of Sauvignon Blanc and Chardonnay. Paarl Cabernet Sauvignon is a traditional unblended cabernet with subtle wood tones. It ages extremely well for 5 to 10 years. ✉ *WR4 (Meaker Rd., Huguenot),* ☎ *021/862–3104,* ℻ *021/ 862–4887.* 🚋 *Tastings free.* ☉ *Weekdays 8.30–5, Sat. 9–1. Cellar tours (in English, Afrikaans, German, or French) by appointment.*

Drive back down Optenhorst and continue straight through the traffic lights. At the next light, turn right onto North Main Street and drive 5 km (3 mi) to **Rhebokskloof.** The winery sits at the head of a shallow valley, backed by hillsides covered with vines and fynbos. It's a lovely place for lunch on a sunny day. The Victorian Restaurant serves à la carte meals and teas on an oak-shaded terrace overlooking the gardens and mountains; in inclement weather, meals are served in the Cape Dutch Restaurant, as is a Sunday buffet lunch. The full-bodied Cabernet Sauvignon is the pick of the bunch, with good fruit, cassis, and cedar-box aromas that follow through to the palate. It will develop for four to six years. ✉ *WR8,* ☎ *02211/638386,* ℻ *02211/638504.* 🚋 *Tastings R5.* ☉ *Nov.–Apr., daily 9–5; May–Oct., daily 9–4:30. No cellar tours.*

Paarl takes its name from the granite domes of Paarl Mountain, which looms above the town—*paarl* is Afrikaans for "pearl." The first farmers settled here in 1687, two years after the founding of Stellenbosch. The town has its fair share of historic homes and estates, but it lacks the charm of its distinguished neighbor simply because it's so spread out. Main Street, the town's oak-lined thoroughfare, extends some 11 km (7 mi) along the western bank of the Berg River. You can gain a good sense of the town's history on a drive along this lovely street.

Main Street North doglegs to the right at Lady Grey Street before continuing as Main Street South. On your left, the **Paarl Museum** (formerly Oude Pastorie) occupies a gorgeous Cape Dutch home built as a parsonage in 1787. In fact, the building itself is of more interest than the collection, which includes odds and ends donated by local families, including silver, glass, and kitchen utensils. A pleasant café at the side of the museum serves tea and snacks at tables on the museum lawns. ✉ *303 Main St.,* ☎ *021/872–2651.* 🚋 *R2.* ☉ *Weekdays 8–5.*

From the Paarl Museum walk about 200 yards along Pastorie Street to the **Afrikaans Language Museum** (Afrikaanse Taalmuseum), in the Gideon Malherbe House. It was from here in 1875 that the Society of True Afrikaners launched their campaign to gain widespread acceptance for Afrikaans, hitherto considered a sort of inferior, kitchen Dutch. The museum will be of limited interest to many visitors, since the displays are entirely in Afrikaans. ✉ *Pastorie St.,* ☎ *021/872–3441.* 🚋 *R2.* ☉ *Weekdays 8–5.*

Continue along Main Street past the Paarl Publicity Office (☞ Winelands A to Z, *below*) to **Zeederberg Square,** a grassy park bordered by some excellent examples of Cape Dutch, Georgian, and Victorian homes. A little farther down Main Street on the left is the old **Dutch Reformed Church,** a thatched building dating back to 1805. The cemetery contains the tombstones of the Malherbe family, which was instrumental in the campaign to gain official recognition for Afrikaans.

Continue down Main Street until you see signs leading to KWV Cellars. **KWV** is short for *Ko-operatieve Wijnbouwers Vereniging* (Cooperative Winegrowers' Association), which for nearly 80 years has regulated and controlled the Cape wine industry. KWV sells wine and spirits in over 40 countries and more than 30 U.S. states, and its brandies, sherries, and fortified dessert wines regularly garner gold medals at the International Wine & Spirit Competition in London. It also offers one of the most popular and most crowded cellar tours in the Winelands. KWV's cellars are the largest in the world, covering some 55 acres. Among the highlights is the famous Cathedral Cellar, with a barrel-vaulted ceiling and giant vats carved with scenes from the history of Cape wine making. In an adjoining cellar, you can see under one roof the five largest vats in the world. The tour begins with a short audiovisual presentation and ends with a tasting of some of KWV's products. ⊠ *André du Toit Bldg., Kohler St.,* ☎ *021/807–3007,* ⅁⅍ *021/863–1942.* ⌸ *Cellar tours and tasting R10 (reservations essential). Tours Mon.–Sat. 9:30, 10:15, 11, 2:15.*

Return to Main Street and turn left. After the N1 bridge, a sign on your right points the way to the **Afrikaans Language Monument** (Afrikaanse Taalmonument), set high on a hill overlooking Paarl. Like the Voortrekker Monument in Pretoria, this concrete structure holds a special place in the hearts of Afrikaners, who struggled for years to gain acceptance for their language alongside English. The rising curve of the main pillar is supposed to represent the growth and potential of Afrikaans. When it was erected in 1973, the monument was as much a gesture of political victory as a paean to the Afrikaans language. Ironically, it may become the language's memorial. Under the new South Africa, Afrikaans has become just one of 11 official languages and is gradually losing its dominance. The view from the top of the hill is incredible, taking in Table Mountain, False Bay, Paarl Valley, and the various mountain ranges of the Winelands. A short, paved walking trail leads around the hillside past impressive fynbos specimens, particularly proteas. ⊠ *Afrikaans Taalmonument Rd.* ⌸ *R2.* ☉ *Daily 9–5.*

Halfway down the hill from the monument is a turnoff onto a dirt road and a sign for the Paarl Mountain Nature Reserve. The dirt road is **Jan Philips Drive,** which runs 11 km (7 mi) along the mountainside, offering tremendous views over the valley. Along the way, it passes the **Mill Water Wildflower Garden** and the starting points for myriad trails, including hikes up to the great, granite domes of Paarl Mountain. The dirt road rejoins Main Street at the far end of Paarl.

Fairview is one of the few wineries where visitors might feel comfortable taking their families. Children will get a kick out of seeing peacocks roaming the grounds and goats clambering a spiral staircase into a goat tower. Every afternoon at four the goats are milked. Fairview produces a superb line of goat cheeses, all of which you can taste gratis. If you want to put together a picnic for the lawn, a deli counter sells sausages and cold meats to complement the estate's wines and cheeses.

Don't let Fairview's sideshows color your judgment about the wines. Charles Back, a member of the family that sells Backsberg (☞ *below*), is one of the most successful and innovative wine makers in the Cape, and the estate's wines are excellent and often surprising. Back has produced a Shiraz-Merlot blend, a Shiraz-Gamay, a Crouchen-Chardonnay, a Sauvignon Blanc–Chenin Blanc, and an excellent Sauvignon Blanc–Semillon. ⊠ *WR3, off R101 (Suid-Agter-Paarl Rd.),* ☎ *021/863–2450,* ⅁⅍ *021/863–2591.* ⌸ *Tastings free.* ☉ *Weekdays 8:30–5, Sat. 8:30–1. Cellar tours by appointment.*

For 80 years **Backsberg** winery (framed by the mountains of the Simonsberg) has been run by the Back family, well known for producing award-winning wines of good value. An unusual feature of the winery is the self-conducted cellar tour. Visitors follow painted lines around the cellars, pausing to watch video monitors that explain the wine-making process. It's a low-pressure introduction to wine making and an ideal starting point for novices. Backsberg produces a comprehensive range of red and white wines, a Méthode Cap Classique sparkling wine, and a fine brandy made from Chenin Blanc. Their Chardonnay is consistently one of the best made, a rounded, fruity wine that develops well in the bottle for five or more years. Backsberg is the only producer of a Malbec, full of fruity berry flavors; it won a Veritas Gold award in 1994 and is very easy to drink. ✉ *WR1, between R44 and R45 (Simondium Rd.),* ☎ *021/875–5141,* ℻ *021/875–5144.* ☜ *Tastings R5; cellar tours free.* ⊙ *Weekdays 8:30–5, Sat. 8:30–1.*

Ballooning

Wineland Ballooning (☎ 021/863–3192) in Paarl makes one-hour flights over the Winelands every morning from mid-October until the end of April, weather permitting. The balloon holds a maximum of six people, and the trip costs R750 per person. After the flight, everyone returns to the Grand Roche Hotel for a champagne breakfast.

Dining and Lodging

$$$$ ✕ **Bosman's.** Set amid the heady opulence of the Grand Roche Hotel
★ in Paarl, this elegant restaurant ranks as one of the country's finest. It has won several awards both for its Continental cuisine and its extensive wine list. The level of service is extraordinary, commensurate with the finest European restaurants, although some diners may find the attention a little suffocating. Diners can choose from a three-course luncheon, a popular seasonal selection, a five or seven-course table d'hote gourmet dinner, a vegetarian and a low-cholesterol menu, and à la carte dinner choices. After a complementary amuse-bouche, first courses include quail with marinated asparagus and a foie gras roti with apple and balsamic beurre blanc. Linefish, baked sole with scallops and lime foam, or meaty items like poached beef fillet with chive butter sauce are regular main dishes. Beautifully plated desserts like timbales of peach and mascarpone on white coffee sauce, or a box of marbled chocolate filled with iced praline finish the meal in sophisticated style. ✉ *Grand Roche Hotel, Plantasie St., Paarl,* ☎ *021/863–2727. AE, DC, MC, V.*

$$$$ ✕ **Roggeland.** For an unforgettable Cape experience, make a beeline for this glorious Cape Dutch manor house on a farm outside Paarl. Meals are long, languid rituals, whether it's an al fresco lunch in the garden, or a four-course dinner in the 18th-century dining room. An evening might start with baby leeks sparked with fresh ginger and coriander, accompanied by sesame-coated oyster mushrooms. A second course of red radish soup with pink peppercorns may be followed by marinated eye of silverside beef, roasted with pickled green peppers and parsnip chips. Finish with a plum and almond meringue bake. A different wine, included in the price, accompanies each course. ✉ *Roggeland Rd., North Paarl,* ☎ *021/868–2501. Reservations essential. AE, DC, MC, V.*

$$$$ 🏨 **Grande Roche.** A member of the prestigious Relais & Chateaux chain,
★ this establishment can stake a claim as the best hotel in South Africa. In a gorgeous Cape Dutch manor house that dates from the mid-18th century, the hotel sits amid acres of vines beneath Paarl Mountain, overlooking the valley and the Drakenstein Mountains. Suites are housed either in the historical buildings—slave quarters, stables, and wine cellar—or in attractive, new terrace buildings constructed in traditional Cape Dutch style. Rooms are a tasteful mix of the modern and the old: Reed ceilings and thatch comfortably coexist with heated towel racks

and air-conditioning. The staff, many of whom trained in Europe, outnumber the guests two to one, and offer a level of service extremely rare in South Africa. ✉ *Plantasie St., Box 6038, Paarl, 7620,* ☎ *021/ 863–2727,* FAX *021/863–2220. 35 suites with bath. Restaurant, bar, room service, 2 pools, 2 tennis courts, exercise room. Breakfast included. No children under 7. AE, DC, MC, V.*

$$$$
★ 🏠 **Roggeland Country House.** Dating back to 1693, this historic farm is one of the most delightful lodgings in the Winelands. The setting in Dal Josaphat Valley is breathtaking, with stunning views of the craggy Drakenstein Mountains. Guest rooms in restored farm buildings have reed ceilings, country dressers, and mosquito nets (not just for effect). The 1779 manor house, which contains the dining room and lounge, is a masterpiece of Cape Dutch architecture. Dinner and breakfast in the fine restaurant (☞ Dining, *above*) are included in the rates. Be prepared for the slightly jarring sight of Fairyland, a shantytown a few minutes down the road from the inn, in case you happen upon it. ✉ *Roggeland Rd., Box 7210, Northern Paarl 7623,* ☎ *021/868–2501,* FAX *021/868–2113. 10 rooms with bath. Restaurant. AE, DC, MC, V.*

$$$$–$$$ 🏠 **Bartholomeus Klip Farmhouse.** For a break from a long bout of wine-tasting, head to this Victorian guest house near Wellington on a game reserve–cum–working farm. Its luxurious accommodations and excellent food come in the middle of 9,900 acres of rare *renosterveld* scrubland that is home to the endangered geometric tortoise. There are also plenty of eland (for which the farm is named), zebra, wildebeest, springbok, rhebok, bontebok, bat-eared fox, and birdlife in and around the mountains, streams, and plains. A wander around the farm, amid the barking of sheepdogs, is also amusing, and you can hike, mountain bike, or swim, as well. Rates include all meals, drinks, teas, and game drives. ✉ *Box 24, Hermon, 7308,* ☎ *022/448–1820,* FAX *022/ 448–1829. 3 rooms and 1 cottage with bath. AE, MC, V.*

$ 🏠 **Lemoenkloof Guesthouse.** In the heart of Paarl and a national monument, this house is decorated in sophisticated country style. While the modern accouterments such as television, air-conditioning, bar fridge, and tea/coffee-making facilities in each of the guest rooms make your stay comfortable, the swimming pool and art gallery add an element of fun. A full South African breakfast is included in the rate and dinner can be arranged. ✉ *396A Main St., Box 2726, Paarl 7620,* ☎ *021/ 872–7520 or 021/872–7532,* FAX *021/872–3782. 14 rooms with bath. Pool, art gallery. Breakfast included. MC, V.*

$ 🏠 **Rodeberg Lodge.** Right on Main Street in the heart of Paarl, this homey inn is one of the best examples of Victorian architecture in town. There's nothing flashy about the place—its main attraction is the personal attention of owners Karl and Antoinette Rode. Rooms are simply furnished, with rustic pine furniture, plain bedspreads, and hardwood floors. Downstairs rooms, with their high ceilings and large windows, are a better choice than those upstairs, which feel as if they're in an attic. If you're staying a few days, opt for the self-catering cottage in the pretty gardens at the back of the house. None of the rooms has TV. ✉ *74 Main St., Box 2611, Paarl 7620,* ☎ *021/863–3202,* FAX *021/ 863–3203. 6 rooms (two with bath, others with shower) and 1 cottage. Breakfast included. AE, DC, MC, V.*

Golf

Paarl Golf Club (✉ Wemmershoek Rd., ☎ 021/863–1140) is surrounded by mountains, covered with trees, and dotted with water hazards. The greens fee is R100 for 18 holes.

Winelands A to Z

Arriving and Departing

BY CAR

From Cape Town it shouldn't take more than 30 minutes to Somerset West, 45 minutes to Stellenbosch and Paarl, and an hour to Franschhoek. If you're heading to Paarl or Franschhoek, it's a straight shot up the N1 before the turnoff onto the R45. To reach Somerset West, take the N2 to the R44/Somerset West turnoff and then follow the signs onto Main Street, the town's main drag. If you continue straight up the R44 instead, you come to Stellenbosch. The quickest way to reach Stellenbosch, however, is to leave the N2 at the Eerste Rivier/Stellenbosch exit and follow the R310 straight into town.

BY TRAIN

Cape Metro trains run from Cape Town to Stellenbosch and Paarl, but locals complain about theft and muggings on the journey. Several trains run during the morning and evening commute, but otherwise you may wait for hours. Trains for the Winelands depart from Platforms 9 and 10 in Cape Town and take about an hour (☎ 021/405–2991 for information).

Getting Around

BY BICYCLE

As long as you stick to the valley floors, you shouldn't have too many problems touring the Winelands on a bike, although summers here are very, very hot. You can rent mountain bikes for R40–R50 a day. In Stellenbosch, contact **Village Cycles** (☎ 021/872–8909).

BY CAR

Traveling around the Winelands in your own car is a snap. The whole Winelands region is quite small, and it's almost impossible to get lost. To help you even further, most of the wineries, hotels, and major attractions are clearly signposted with large, brown road signs. If you've arrived in the Winelands without a car, call **Avis** (☎ 021/887–0492), **Budget** (☎ 021/887–6935), **Premier** (☎ 021/883—9103), or **Imperial** (☎ 021/883–8140) in Stellenbosch; in Paarl contact **Wine Route Rent-a-Car** (☎ 021/872–8513 or 083/225–7089).

BY TAXI

Roland's Tours and Taxis (☎ 021/887–7295, FAX 021/887–7293) in Stellenbosch will provide a minibus and driver for four to seven people to tour the Winelands for a half-day at R135 per person, or a full day at R165 per person. In Paarl, **Paarl Radio Taxis** (☎ 021/872–5671) will transport up to four people at R4 per km.

Contacts and Resources

EMERGENCIES

Dial 10111 for the **police,** 10177 for an **ambulance.**

GUIDED TOURS

Vineyard Ventures (⊠ 5 Hanover Rd., Fresnaye, Cape Town 8001, ☎ 021/434–8888) is the best of several companies offering tours of the Winelands. Sisters Gillian Stoltzman and Glen Christie are knowledgeable and passionate about wine, and will tailor tours to your interest. You can also opt for one of their standard one-day tours. All tours feature wine-tastings at top cellars and an excellent lunch.

If your interest in wine is limited, you're better off taking a general-interest tour of the Winelands that throws in only a couple of wine-tastings. In the Winelands, contact **Travelmark** (☎ 02211/21994) or

Vintage Cape Tours (☎ 02211/26092), both based in Paarl. Otherwise, call one of the big Cape Town operators like **Hylton Ross, Ideal Tours,** or **Mother City Tours** (☞ Cape Town A to Z *in* Chapter 4).

For about R500, **Cape Eco Safaris** (☎ 02211/63–8334) offers 30-minute flights over Paarl and the surrounding area for two to three adults. **Civair** (☎ 021/419–5182) offers 2½-hour helicopter tours of the Winelands and part of the Peninsula for R1480 per person, including lunch at a winery.

VISITOR INFORMATION

Franschhoek Vallée Tourismé. ⊠ Huguenot Rd., *Franschhoek,* ☎ 021/876–3603, 𝔽𝔸𝕏 021/876–2768. ☉ *Mon.–Sat. 10–5, Sun.10–1.*

Paarl Tourism Bureau. ⊠ *216 Main St., Paarl,* ☎ 021/872–3829 *or* 021/872–4842, 𝔽𝔸𝕏 021/872–9376. ☉ *Weekdays 9–5:30, Sat. 9–1, Sun. 10–1.*

Somerset West Tourist Information Bureau. ⊠ *11 Victoria St., Somerset West,* ☎ 021/851–4022, 𝔽𝔸𝕏 021/851–1497. ☉ *Weekdays 8:30–1 and 2–4:30, Sat. 9–noon.*

Stellenbosch Tourist Bureau. ⊠ *36 Market St., Stellenbosch,* ☎ 021/883–3584, 𝔽𝔸𝕏 021/883–8017. ☉ *Weekdays 8–5:30, Sat. 9–5, Sun. 9:30–4:30.*

THE OVERBERG

Overberg means "over the mountains" in Afrikaans, an apt name for this remote region at the bottom of the continent, separated from the rest of the Cape by mountains. Before 19th-century engineers blasted a route through the Hottentots Holland range, the Overberg developed in comparative isolation. To this day, it possesses a wild emptiness far removed from the settled valleys of the Winelands.

It's a land of immense contrasts, and if you're planning a trip along the Garden Route (☞ Chapter 6), you would be well advised to add the Overberg to your itinerary. The coastal drive from Gordon's Bay to Hermanus is as beautiful as anything in the Cape; an unfolding panorama of deserted beaches, pounding surf, and fractured granite mountains. Once you pass Hermanus and head out onto the windswept plains leading to Cape Agulhas, you have to search harder for the Overberg's riches. Towns are few and far between, the countryside comprising an expanse of wheat fields and sheep pastures. The occasional reward of the drive is a coastline of sublime beauty. Enormous stretches of dunes and unspoiled beaches extend for miles. Unfortunately, no roads parallel the ocean, and you must constantly divert inland before heading to another part of the coast.

Hermanus is the best place in South Africa to watch the annual migration of southern right whales, but you can spot the great creatures all along the coast between July and November, when they sometimes come within 100 ft of shore. Spring is also the best time to see the Overberg's wild flowers, although the region's profusion of coastal and montane fynbos is beautiful year-round.

The upper part of the Overberg, north of the N2 highway, is more like the Winelands, with 18th- and 19th-century towns sheltered in the lee of rocky mountains. Here the draws are apple orchards, inns, and hiking trails that wind through the mountains. The historic towns of Swellendam and Greyton make the most logical touring bases.

To tour the whole area would take three to four days. For a shorter trip, focus on the splendors of the coastal route from Gordon's Bay to Hermanus, then head north towards the Winelands.

Towns and sights are marked on the Western Cape and Namaqualand map.

Gordon's Bay

70 km (44 mi) southeast of Cape Town.

Gordon's Bay is an attractive resort built on a steep mountain slope overlooking the vast expanse of False Bay. You can often see whales and their calves in False Bay in October and November.

From Gordon's Bay, the road hugs the mountainside, slipping between the craggy peaks of the Hottentots Holland Mountains and the sea far below. The coastal drive between Gordon's Bay and Hermanus is one of the country's best, particularly if you take the time to follow some of the dirt roads leading down to the sea from the highway.

The road passes tiny Rooielsbaai (pronounced *roy*-els-buy) then cuts inland for a few kilometers. A turnoff leads to **Pringle Bay,** a collection of holiday homes sprinkled across the fynbos. The village has little to offer other than a beautiful wide beach (check out the sign warning of quicksand). If you continue through Pringle Bay, the tar road soon gives way to gravel. This road, badly corrugated in patches, runs around the looming pinnacle of **Hangklip** and along a deserted stretch of magnificent beach and dunes to Betty's Bay (☞ *below*).

If you don't fancy the gravel road, return to the R44 and continue 1.6 km (1 mi) to the turnoff to Stony Point, on the edge of Betty's Bay. Follow Porter Drive for 3.2 km (2 mi) until you reach a sign marked MOOI HAWENS and a smaller sign picturing a penguin. Follow the penguin signs to a **colony of jackass penguins,** one of only two mainland colonies in southern Africa. The colony lies about 600 yards from the parking area along a rocky coastal path. Along the way, you pass the concrete remains of tank stands, reminders of the days when Betty's Bay was a big whaling station. The jackass penguin is endangered, so the colony has been fenced off as protection against man, dogs, and other predators. This particular colony was once savaged by a leopard.

Return to Porter Drive and turn right to rejoin the R44. Back on the main road, go another mile to the **Harold Porter National Botanical Garden,** a 440-acre nature reserve in the heart of the coastal fynbos, where the Cape Floral Kingdom is at its richest. The profusion of plants supports 78 species of birds and a wide range of small mammals, including large troops of baboons. You couldn't ask for a more fantastic setting, cradled between the Atlantic and the towering peaks of the 3,000-ft Kogelberg range. Walking trails wind through the reserve and into the mountains via Disa and Leopard's kloofs, which echo with the sound of waterfalls and running streams. Back at the main buildings, a pleasant restaurant serves light meals and teas. ⊠ *Box 35, Betty's Bay 7141,* ☎ *028/272–9311,* FAX *028/272–9333.* ☞ *R2.* ☉ *Daily 8–6.*

Kleinmond

25 km (15½ mi) southeast of Gordon's Bay.

The small town of Kleinmond ("small mouth") is nothing special, it has a couple of restaurants and guest houses, but it presides over a magnificent stretch of shoreline, backed by the mountains of the Palmietberg. At press time, the **Kleinmond Coastal Nature Reserve,** a 990-acre area of fynbos that extends to the sea, was closed, but the beach and small lagoon that front the reserve are still accessible from the Palmiet Caravan Park. Even more impressive are the 10 km (6 mi) of sandy beach that fringe Sandown Bay, at the eastern edge of town. Much of the beach is nothing more than a sandbar, separating the Atlantic from the huge lagoon formed by the Bot River. Swift currents make bathing risky.

Dining and Lodging

$$$ ✕🏨 **Beach House on Sandown Bay.** In quiet seaside Kleinmond, this comfortable guest house overlooks a 10-km (6-mi) crescent of beach and a beautiful lagoon. It's another good base for whale-watching in October and November, as well as for walks in the surrounding nature reserves. The hotel itself is attractive and simple. Rooms aren't especially appealing, with white wicker furniture and floral draperies and bedspreads; in sea-facing rooms, sliding doors open onto small balconies with tremendous views of Sandown Bay. The restaurant specializes in seafood, bought fresh in the local harbor. ⊠ *Beach Rd, Kleinmond 7195,* ☎ *02823/3130,* 🖷 *02823/4022. 23 rooms with bath. Restaurant, bar, pool. Breakfast included. AE, DC, MC, V.*

En Route The R44 cuts inland to circumnavigate the Bot River lagoon. Ten km (6 mi) past Kleinmond, the road comes to a junction; turn right onto the R43 toward Hermanus and cross the Bot River. The R43 swings eastward around the mountains, past the small artists' colony of Onrus.

Less than 2 km (1 mi) farther is the turnoff to the R320, which leads through the vineyards and orchards of the scenic Hemel-en-Aarde (Heaven on Earth) Valley and over Shaw's Pass to Caledon. **Hamilton Russell Vineyards** lies a short way down this rutted road, in an attractive thatched building overlooking a small dam. This winery produces some of the best wine in South Africa. The Pinot Noir won loud acclaim from Frank Prial of the *New York Times,* and is one of the two best produced in the country. The Chardonnay comes closer to the French style of Chardonnay than any other Cape wine, with lovely fruit and a touch of lemon rind and toast. It will be at its best in one to two years. ⊠ *Off R320,* ☎ *0283/23595,* 🖷 *0283/21797.* 🍷 *Tastings free.* ☉ *Weekdays 9–5, Sat. 9–1.*

Return to the R43 and drive 3 km (2 mi) to Hermanus. On the outskirts of town, keep watch on your left side for a pair of white gateposts set well back from the road, painted with the words ROTARY WAY—if

★ you pass the turnoff to the New Harbour you've gone too far. The **Rotary Way** is a scenic drive that climbs along the spine of the mountains above Hermanus, affording incredible views of the town, Walker Bay, and Hemel-en-Aarde Valley, as well as some of the area's beautiful fynbos. It's a highlight of a trip to the Overberg and you shouldn't miss it. The Rotary Way turns to dirt after a few km and becomes impassable to all but four-wheel-drive vehicles about a mile after that. The entire mountainside is laced with wonderful walking trails, and many of the scenic lookouts have benches.

Hermanus

24 km (15 mi) southeast of Kleinmond on the R43.

Hermanus is a popular holiday resort and the major coastal town in the Overberg. If you're looking for a base from which to explore the region, Hermanus is your best bet. Restaurants and shops line the streets, and the town retains a pleasant holiday feel having been spared the worst excesses of developers with more money than taste. The town is packed during the Whale Festival in September-October and Christmas school holidays, though, so head elsewhere if you want solitude.

Just a few kilometers away, pristine beaches extend as far as the eye can see, and the Kleinriviersberg provides a breathtaking backdrop to the town. Hermanus sits atop a long line of cliffs, which makes it the best place in South Africa to watch the annual whale migration from shore. An 11-km (7-mi) **cliff walk** allows watchers to follow the whales, which often come within 100 ft of the cliffs as they move along the coastline. In addition, a whale-crier, complete with sandwich board and kelp horn, disseminates information on whale sightings.

Originally, Hermanus was a whaling center. The **Old Harbour Museum,** in a small building at the old stone fishing basin, displays some of the horrific harpoons used to lance the giants. There are also exhibits on fishing techniques, local marine life, and angling records. Photographs of old Hermanus and some of its legendary fishermen are also displayed at the PFV Old Harbour Museum Photographic Exhibition, in the white building next to the harbor parking lot. ⊠ *Old Harbour, Marine Drive, Hermanus,* ☎ *0283/21–475.* ⚐ *R2.* ☉ *Mon.–Sat. 9–1 and 2– 5, Sun. 12–4.*

From Hermanus the R43 continues eastward, hugging the strip of land between the mountains and the **Klein River Lagoon.** The lagoon is popular with waterskiers, boaters, and anglers. You can hire a variety of boats down at Prawn Flats, including motor boats, canoes, and board sailers; expect to pay R20–R40 an hour depending on the type of boat. It's also possible to take a boat up the Klein River into the bird sanctuary to watch the birds roost at sunset. Contact **The Boathouse** (⊠ Prawn Flats, off R43, ☎ 0283/770925).

Dining and Lodging

$$ ✕ **Burgundy.** This restaurant occupies a fisherman's cottage overlooking the old fishing harbor. Ask for a table on the veranda or the lawn, from where you can savor views of Walker Bay. The menu brings French flair to South African ingredients, with an emphasis on seafood. A good choice is the grilled fresh line fish with champagne beurre blanc, accompanied by a bottle of local wine. Ice-cream crepes are a popular dessert. ⊠ *Market Sq.,* ☎ *0283/22–800. AE, DC, MC, V. Closed Mon. No dinner Sun.*

$$ ✕ **Trattoria-Ouzeri.** Step off the vacation track and into this colorful eatery, where you can order from a Greek or an Italian menu. Look for everything from a tasty bean salad with olive oil, lemon, and herbs to fish cakes or lamb stew—and from pizzas to pasta with mussels, tomatoes, and herbs. The Greek menu is unavailable Sundays, the Italian Mondays. The restaurant is on a lane off of of the main road in the center of town. ⊠ *60 St. Peter's La.,* ☎ *0283/700–532. DC, MC, V. No lunch Mon.*

$$ ☖ **Marine.** In a sprawling white building on the cliffs overlooking Walker Bay, this elegant hotel is easily the best in Hermanus. The huge sea-facing bed-sitters have excellent views over the bay, and bleached wicker and white tile create a relaxed seaside feel. Public rooms, on the other hand, are formal to a fault, furnished with stiff armchairs, antiques, and heavy drapes; you might feel awkward wandering around in your swimsuit. ⊠ *Marine Dr., Box 9, Hermanus 7200,* ☎ *0283/ 701–000,* ℻ *0283/700–160. 55 rooms with bath. Restaurant, bar, room service, 2 pools, billiards. AE, DC, MC, V.*

$$ ☖ **Windsor.** If you come to Hermanus in October or November, stay at this hotel in the heart of town. While it doesn't compare with The Marine (☞ *above*), the hotel's position atop the cliffs makes it the best place to view the annual whale migration. Request one of the second-floor, sea-facing rooms, with their huge sliding-glass doors and unbeatable views. The hotel itself dates back more than 100 years, and some of the corridors and public rooms look a bit time-worn. ⊠ *Marine Dr., Box 3, Hermanus 7200,* ☎ *0283/23727,* 𝔽𝔸𝕏 *0283/22–181. 59 rooms with bath. Restaurant, 2 bars. Breakfast included. AE, DC, MC, V.*

$ 🖼 **Whale Cottage Guesthouse.** If whale-watching, local art, good service, and peace of mind keep a smile on your dial, try this little lodge. Run by public relations consultant Chris von Ulmenstein, Whale Cottage and its five en-suite bedrooms are best described as seriously cute. Continental and English breakfasts are served, and picnic lunches are available on request to accompany you on your search for the great whales. ⊠ *20 Main Rd., Box 200, Hermanus 7200,* ☎ 𝔽𝔸𝕏 *0283/700–929. 5 rooms with bath. Breakfast included. MC, V.*

Stanford

24 km (15 mi) east of Hermanus.

Stanford lies on the banks of the Klein River. It's a pleasant hamlet, with a decent hotel and some shops, but little else. Turn left at Stanford onto the R326 to Salmonsdam and Riviersonderend. The road runs through rolling sheep country and wheat lands cut by rocky gorges. Along the way is the turnoff to the **Salmonsdam Nature Reserve,** a mountainous area of forests, deep valleys, waterfalls, and fynbos. Continue on the R326 to a four-way junction; turn right onto the R316 and drive through the town of Napier to Bredasdorp.

Bredasdorp

60 km (37½ mi) east of Stanford.

Bredasdorp is a sleepy agricultural town that has a certain charm, as long as you don't catch it on a Sunday afternoon, when everything's closed and an air of ennui pervades the brassy, windswept streets.

Once a year, however, the usual lethargic atmosphere is abandoned, and a radical sense of purpose takes its place when Bredasdorp hosts The Foot of Africa Marathon in each spring. Don't be lulled by the small-town, country setting into thinking that this race is a breeze and that you might give it a go. Word has it that the undulating landscape has the fittest athletes doubting their perseverence.

Housed in a converted church and rectory, the **Bredasdorp Museum** has an extensive collection of items salvaged from the hundreds of ships that have gone down in the stormy waters of the Cape. In addition to usual cannons and figureheads, the museum displays a surprising array of undamaged household items rescued from the sea, including entire dining room sets, sideboards, china, and phonographs. ⊠ *Independent St.,* ☎ *02841/41–240.* 🎟 *R2.* � *Mon.–Thurs. 9–4:45, Fri. 9–3:45, Sat. 9–12:45; Sun. 11–12:30 (Sept.–Apr. only).*

OFF THE
BEATEN PATH
ELIM—About 45 km (32 mi) west of Bredasdorp and accessible only by dirt road, Elim is a Moravian mission village founded in 1824. Little has changed in the last hundred years: Simple whitewashed cottages line the few streets, and the settlement's colored residents all belong to the Moravian Church. The whole village has been declared a national monument. The easiest access is via the R317, off the R319 between Cape Agulhas and Bredasdorp.

De Hoop Nature Reserve (☎ 02922/700) is a huge conservation area covering 88,900 acres of isolated coastal terrain as well as a marine reserve extending 5 km (3 mi) out to sea. Massive white-sand dunes, mountains, and rare lowland fynbos are home to eland, bontebok, and

Cape mountain zebra, as well as over 250 bird species. Visitors can rent self-catering cottages. Access is via the dirt road between Bredasdorp and Malgas.

Pont Malgas, past De Hoop Nature Reserve on the dirt road from Bredasdorp, is the last hand-drawn car ferry in the country. Two operators use brute strength to pull the ferry across the Breede River. The setting is beautiful, and the ride is unusual. ✉ *R6 per vehicle.*

En Route   From Bredasdorp it's just 37 km (23 mi) through rolling farmland to Cape Agulhas. Although it's the southernmost tip of the African continent, it's less exciting in reality than in concept, so unless reaching the bottom of the continent has some great personal meaning, give it a miss, and skip down to Waenhuiskrans.

Struisbaai and Cape Agulhas

30 km (19 mi) south of Bredasdorp.

On the way to Agulhas you pass through Struisbaai (pronounced *strayce*-bye), a forgettable little town on an unforgettable bay. As far as the eye can see, rolling white dunes enfold turquoise waters polka-dotted with colorful fishing boats. Few places in the world can claim beaches this splendid, and generations of surfers have stories to tell of the wild times they have had there.

From Struisbaai drive 6½ km (4 mi) through the small settlement of L'Agulhas to the lighthouse that stands sentinel over the Cape. Modeled after the noted Pharos of classical Alexandria, the 1849 Agulhas lighthouse is the second-oldest in South Africa. It's home to the **Agulhas Lighthouse Museum,** which houses an interesting collection of lenses and bulbs, as well as photos and descriptions of famous lighthouses from around the world. You can climb steep stairs and ladders to the top of the lighthouse for a great view over the Cape. Downstairs, a pleasant tearoom dishes up breakfast and light meals. ☎ 02846/56078. ✉ *R5.* ⊘ *Tues.–Sat. 9:30–4.45, Sun. 10–1:15.*

Take the dirt road around the lighthouse and follow the signs to **Cape Agulhas.** A stone marker and flimsy sign mark the southernmost spot on the continent and the point where the Atlantic and Indian Oceans meet. Without the signs, you would never know you were perched at the very bottom of Africa. The peninsula is flat, rocky, and undistinguished. It possesses none of the scenic beauty or emphatic finality of Cape Point south of Cape Town (☞ Chapter 4). At Cape Point, you feel like you're at the end of the earth; at Cape Agulhas, you find yourself wondering where you can get a good cup of tea.

Waenhuiskrans

★   *24 km (15 mi) northeast of Struisbaai.*

Waenhuiskrans, an isolated holiday village, is set on another of South Africa's most awe-inspiring stretches of coastline. The village is known among English-speaking South Africans as Arniston, after a British ship of that name that was wrecked on the Agulhas reef in 1815. Beautiful beaches, water that assumes Caribbean shades of blue, and mile after mile of towering white dunes attract anglers and holiday-makers alike. Only the frequent southeasters that blow off the sea are likely to put a damper on your enjoyment. For 200 years, a community of Cape Malay fishermen and their families has eked out a living here, setting sail each day in small fishing boats. Today, their village has been named a national monument, and it's a pleasure to wander around the thatched cottages of this still-vibrant community. The village has expanded enormously in the last 10 years, thanks to the construction of a host of holiday homes. Fortunately, much of the new architecture blends effectively with the whitewashed simplicity of the original cottages.

Waenhuiskrans means "wagon-house cliff" in Afrikaans, and the village takes its name from a **vast cave** a mile south of town that is theoretically large enough to house several wagons and their spans of oxen. Signs point the way over the dunes to the cave, which is accessible only at low tide. You need shoes to protect your feet from the sharp rocks, but wear something you don't mind getting wet.

Again, retrace your way to Bredasdorp. This time, take the R319 toward Swellendam. The road runs through mile after mile of rolling farmland, populated by sheep, cattle, and an occasional ostrich. In the far distance loom the mountains of the Langeberg (Long Mountain). After 64 km (40 mi), turn right onto the N2 highway. Continue for another 15 km (9 mi) before turning right to the **Bontebok National Park.** Covering just 6,880 acres of coastal fynbos, this is one of the smallest of South Africa's national parks. Don't expect to see big game here—the park contains no elephant, lion, or rhino. What you will see are bontebok, a graceful white-faced antelope nearly exterminated by hunters earlier in the century, as well as red hartebeest, Cape grysbok, steenbok, duiker, and the endangered Cape mountain zebra. Two short walking trails start at the campsite next to the Breede River. ⊠ *Box 149, Swellendam 6740,* ☎ *0291/42735,* 𝔽𝔸𝕏 *0291/42–626.* ▣ *R14 per vehicle.* ⊙ *Oct.–Apr. daily 7–7, May–Sept. daily 8–6.*

Dining and Lodging

$$$ ✕🏨 **Arniston Hotel.** You could easily spend a week here and still need
★   to be dragged away. The setting, in a tiny fishing village on a crescent of white dunes, has a lot to do with its appeal, but the hotel has also struck a fine balance between elegance and beach-holiday comfort. Rooms have a true beach feel, thanks to the cheery use of turquoise wicker, bold fabrics, and colorful sea prints. Request a room with a sea view, so you can enjoy the ever-changing colors that make this part of the coast so memorable. On request, the hotel takes guests by four-wheel-drive into the dune field for sundowners—not to be missed. A four-course dinner menu changes daily, but expect plenty of fresh seafood. À la carte lunches on the patio feature light Mediterranean fare. ⊠ *Beach Rd., Waenhuiskrans (mailing address: Box 126, Bredasdorp 7280),* ☎ *02847/59–000,* 𝔽𝔸𝕏 *02847/59–633. 30 rooms with bath. 2 restaurants, 2 bars, room service, pool. Breakfast included. No children under 12. AE, DC, MC, V.*

Swellendam

★   *72 km (45 mi) north of Waenhuiskrans.*

Return to the junction with the N2 and cross the highway into beautiful Swellendam, lying in the shadow of the imposing Langeberg. Founded in 1745, it is the third-oldest town in South Africa and many of its historic buildings have been elegantly restored. Even on a casual drive along the main street, you'll see a number of lovely Cape Dutch homes, with their traditional whitewashed walls, gables, and thatched roofs.

★   The centerpiece of the town's historical past is the **Drostdy Museum,** a collection of buildings dating back to the town's earliest days. The Drostdy was built in 1747 by the Dutch East India Company to serve as the residence of the Landdrost, the magistrate who presided over the district. The building is furnished in a style that was common in the mid-19th century. A path leads through the Drostdy kitchen gardens to Mayville, an 1855 middle-class home that blends elements of Cape Dutch and Cape Georgian architecture. Across Swellengrebel Street stand the old jail and the Ambagswerf (closed Sun.), an outdoor exhibit of tools used by the town's blacksmiths, wainwrights, coopers, and tanners. ⊠ *18 Swellengrebel St.,* ☎ *0291/41138.* ⌸ *R5.* ☉ *Weekdays 9–4:45, weekends and holidays 10–3:45.*

Swellendam's **Dutch Reformed Church** is an imposing white edifice, built in 1911 in an eclectic style. The gables are baroque, the windows Gothic, the cupola vaguely eastern, and the steeple a replica of one in Belgium. Surprisingly, all the elements work together wonderfully. Inside is an interesting tiered amphitheater, with banks of curving wood pews facing the pulpit and organ. ⊠ *7 Voortrek St.,* ☎ *0291/41225. Services Feb.–Nov. at 10 and 6, Dec. and Jan. at 9 and 6.*

If you'd like to get your feet on the ground and breathe some clean local air, take a hike in the **Marloth Nature Reserve,** in the Langeberg above town. Five easy walks, ranging from one to four hours, explore some of the mountain gorges. An office at the entrance to the reserve has trail maps and hiking information.

Dining and Lodging

$$$ ✕⛊ **Klippe Rivier Homestead.** Amid rolling farmland 3 km (2 mi) outside Swellendam, this guest house occupies one of the Overberg's most gracious and historic country homes. It was built around 1825 in traditional Cape style, with thick white walls, thatched roof, and a distinctive gable. Guests stay in enormous rooms in the converted stables. The three downstairs rooms are furnished with antiques in Cape Dutch, Colonial, and Victorian styles. Upstairs, raw wood beams, cane ceilings, and white wicker furniture set the tone for less-expensive, country-style rooms. Some public rooms cannot support the sheer volume of antique collectibles, taking on a museumlike quality. Dinner is table d'hote, prepared with fresh herbs, vegetables, fruit, and cream from surrounding farms. ⊠ *On a dirt road off R60 to Ashton (Box 483, Swellendam 6740),* ☎ *0291/43–341,* ⌶ *0291/43–337. 6 rooms with bath. Restaurant, saltwater pool. Breakfast included. No children under 10. AE, DC, MC, V.*

$ ✕⛊ **Adin's and Sharon's Hideaway.** The Victorian homestead and its three luxury cottages are set in a peaceful garden that displays some 400 rosebushes and is home to varied bird life. While the setting and beautifully appointed cottages are excellent reasons to stay at this establishment, the level of hospitality sets this place above the rest. Adin and Sharon Greaves (former owners of Mimosa Lodge in Montagu) let the plaques and other awards in their home stand as testimony to their success and dedication. It's a perfect, value-for-money base from which to explore historic Swellendam and environs. ⊠ *10 Hermanus Steyn Rd.,* ☎ ⌶ *0291/43–316. 3 double cottages with bath and shower. Breakfast included. MC, V.*

En Route   From Swellendam return to the N2 and turn right toward Cape Town. The road sweeps through rich, rolling cropland that extends to the base of the Langeberg mountains. A few kilometers after the town of Riviersonderend (pronounced riff-*ears*-onder-ent), turn right onto the R406, a good gravel road that leads to the village of Greyton in the lee of the Riviersonderend Mountains.

Greyton

32 km (20 mi) west of Swellendam.

The charming village of Greyton, filled with white, thatched cottages and quiet lanes, is a popular weekend retreat for Capetonians as well as a permanent home for many retirees. The village offers almost nothing in the way of traditional sights, but it's a great base for walks into the surrounding mountains (☞ *below*), and a pleasant place to pause for lunch or tea (☞ Dining and Lodging, *below*).

After Greyton, the R406 becomes paved. Drive 5 km (3 mi) to the turnoff to **Genadendal,** a Moravian Mission station founded in 1737 to educate the Khoikhoi and convert them to Christianity. Seeing this impoverished hamlet today, it's difficult to comprehend the major role this mission played in the early history of South Africa. In the late 18th century it was the second-largest settlement after Cape Town, and its Khoikhoi craftsmen produced the finest silver cutlery and woodwork in the country. Some of the first written works in Afrikaans were printed here, and the colored community greatly influenced the development of Afrikaans as it is heard today. None of this went over well with the white population. By 1909, new legislation prohibited "colored" ownership of land, and in 1926 the Department of Public Education closed the settlement's teacher's training college, arguing that "coloreds" were better employed on neighboring farms. Genadendal began a long slide into obscurity until 1994, when President Nelson Mandela renamed his official residence Genadendal.

In town, you can walk the streets of the settlement and tour the historic buildings facing Church Square. Genadendal is still a mission station, and the German missionaries will often show interested visitors around. Of particular interest is the **Genadendal Mission Museum,** spread through 15 rooms in three buildings. The museum collection, the only one in South Africa to be named a national cultural treasure, includes unique household implements, books, tools, and musical instruments, among them the country's oldest pipe organ. Wall displays examine mission life in the Cape in the 18th and 19th centuries, focusing on the early missionaries' work with the Khoikhoi. Unfortunately, many of the displays are in Afrikaans. ⊠ *Off R406,* ☎ *02822/8582.* ▣ *R5.* ☉ *Mon.–Thurs. 9–1 and 2–5, Fri. 9–3:30, Sat. 9–noon.*

En Route   To head back toward Cape Town, follow the R406 to the N2. After the town of Bot River, the road leaves the wheat fields and climbs into the mountains. It's lovely country, full of rock and pine forest interspersed with orchards. **Sir Lowry's Pass** serves as the gateway to Cape Town and the Winelands, a magnificent breach in the mountains that opens to reveal the curving expanse of False Bay, the long ridge of the peninsula, and, in the distance, Table Mountain.

Dining and Lodging

$$ ✕▦ **Greyton Lodge.** Built in 1882 as a trading store, this comfortable guest house looks right at home amid the whitewashed Cape homes of historic Greyton. The focal point of the hotel is the tea garden, filled with roses and fruit trees, and dominated by the sheer walls of the Riviersonderend Mountains behind. The standard rooms are small; you're better off taking the pricier deluxe rooms decorated in country style with light floral draperies and brass or antique bedsteads. Only some rooms have phones and none have TVs. The lunch menu is inexpensive, and features tried-and-true dishes like ploughman's lunch, steak and chips, salads, and quiche. ⊠ *46 Main St., Box 50, Greyton 7233,* ☎ *028/254–9876,* 🖷 *028/254–9672. 17 rooms with bath. Restaurant, bar, room service, pool. Breakfast included. AE, DC, MC, V.*

$$ ✕▦ **Post House.** Once the village post office and now a national monument, this 136-year-old country inn has loads of charm. The rooms, all named after Beatrix Potter characters, face onto a lovely lawn where guests can relax over drinks or tea. The rooms themselves, furnished in Edwardian country style, are dark and in need of redecorating:

Rugs are torn, drains back up, and there is a general air of neglect. The inn's new owners face a hard task restoring this country gem, but the potential is enormous. Dinner is a traditional four-course menu that satisfies but rarely shines. ⊠ *Main Rd., Greyton, 7233,* ☎ *028/254–9995,* ℻ *028/254–9920. 18 rooms with bath. Restaurant, bar, pool. Breakfast included. No children under 12. AE, DC, MC, V.*

Hiking

Walking is one of the major attractions of the Overberg, and almost every town and nature reserve offers a host of trails ranging in length from a few minutes to an entire day. For detailed information about these trails, contact the local visitor information offices (☞ Contacts and Resources *in* Overberg A to Z, *below*).

A fabulous one-day hike is the **Boesmanskloof Trail,** 32 km (20 mi) through the Riviersonderend Mountains from Greyton to the exquisite hamlet of McGregor. McGregor has several charming guest houses and cottages where you can spend the night, but you need to make transport arrangements to get back. Serious hikers should also consider the **Genadendal Hiking Trail,** a two-day hike that wends 24 km (15 mi) through the Riviersonderend Mountains, beginning at the Moravian Mission Church, with one night spent on a farm. Permits are required for both trails. Contact the manager, Vrolijkheid Nature Conservation Station (⊠ Private Bag X614, Robertson 6705, ☎ 02353/621).

Horseback Riding

Greyton Scenic Horse Trails and Riding Center (⊠ 82 Main St., Greyton 7233, ☎ 028/254–9009) takes visitors, including novices, on 90-minute rides through the beautiful hills and mountains surrounding Greyton.

Overberg A to Z

Arriving and Departing

BY BUS

Intercape Ferreira Coaches (☎ 021/386–4400) and **Translux Express Bus** (☎ 021/405–3333) offer regular service from Cape Town along the N2, stopping at Swellendam before continuing on to the Garden Route. Once there, you're stuck unless you arrange for other transport. The ticket agent for both bus lines in Swellendam is **Milestone Tours,** (☎ 0291/42137).

BY CAR

Leave Cape Town via the N2 highway. If you're following the above tour, take the R44 turnoff to Gordon's Bay. Otherwise, stay on the N2 over Sir Lowry's Pass to reach Swellendam, 232 km (145 mi) distant.

Getting Around

BY CAR

Unless you're on a guided tour, you will need a car to explore the Overberg. Distances are long, towns are few, and public transport is infrequent, if it exists at all.

Contacts and Resources

EMERGENCIES

Dial 10177 for an **ambulance,** 10111 for the **police.**

GUIDED TOURS

In addition to the services listed below, all of the large tour operators in Cape Town offer whirlwind tours of the Overberg (☞ Guided Tours *in* Chapter 4).

Cape Town Tourism Association. ⊠ *3 Adderley St., Box 1403, Cape Town 8000,* ☎ *021/418–5214,* FAX *021/418–5227.* ⊙ *Weekdays 8–5, Sat. 8:30–1, Sun. 9–1.*

Hermanus Tourism Bureau. ⊠ *Main Rd., Hermanus 7200,* ☎ *0283/22–629,* FAX *0283/700–305.* ⊙ *Weekdays 9–5, Sat. 9–2, Sun. 10:30–noon.*

Suidpunt Publicity Association has information on Bredasdorp, Elim, Cape Agulhas, Struisbaai, and Waenhuiskrans. ⊠ *Dirkie Uys St., Bredasdorp 7280,* ☎ FAX *02841/42584.* ⊙ *Weekdays 8–1 and 2–4:30, Sat. 9–1.*

Swellendam Publicity Association. ⊠ *Oefeningshuis, Voortrek St.,* ☎ FAX *0291/42770.* ⊙ *Weekdays 8–1 and 2–5, Sat. 9–12:30.*

WEST COAST AND NAMAQUALAND

During much of the year, the West Coast is a featureless expanse of fynbos scrub stretching from Cape Town to Vanrhynsdorp (pronounced fan-*rainz*-dorp), 288 km (180 mi) to the north. Lonely fishing villages dot a coastline of endless beaches fringing a cold, harsh Atlantic. It's a stark, empty land that you either love or hate. But every spring the West Coast explodes in a fiesta of wildflowers that transforms the entire region. Even the most hardened urbanites make the pilgrimage to witness this Cinderella miracle, driving up from Cape Town just for the day or basing themselves in coastal towns, such as Langebaan and Lambert's Bay.

As spring warms to its task, the flower show spreads inland to the Hantam, a high plateau where Afrikaner farmers raise merino sheep and hardscrabble laborers still shear wool by hand. The quality of the morning and evening light—a silky caress of reds, blues, and gold—has long drawn artists, and the delightful farming town of Calvinia is an obvious overnight choice. Spreading south from Calvinia, the high plains of the Hantam collapse into the Cedarberg mountains, one of the great mountain wildernesses of South Africa. Bizarre rock formations hide delicate San (Bushmen) paintings and the last remnants of the enormous cedar forests that once blanketed the region. Hiking here is great, and you can disappear for days at a time into its remote recesses. The historic town of Clanwilliam, lying in the shadow of the Cedarberg, makes a great base for short walks and scenic drives.

Compared to the few days needed to take the West Coast–Cedarberg loop, you'll need to commit twice that to see what may be the greatest floral spectacle on earth, the wildflowers of Namaqualand. This huge semidesert region extends north from the West Coast to Namibia, hundreds of kilometers from Cape Town. It's a remote, unpopulated area, with few facilities and comforts. In spring, however, it puts on a spectacle that makes the West Coast flowers pale in comparison. Vast fields that seemed barren only a month before blush with blossoms. Vygies and Namaqualand daisies brightly splash the hillsides and valleys with color.

Unless it's flower season, think long and hard about venturing this far afield. As in parts of the American West, distances are vast and the landscape brown and sere, and in summer the wind blows as hot as a blast furnace.

It can be difficult to plan a holiday around the flowers in both the West Coast and Namaqualand, since it's impossible to tell exactly when they'll bloom. The season is notoriously fickle, dependent on wind, rain, and sun. The display begins on the coast around July, with cooler mountain areas coming to life as late as August and lasting into October. As you might expect, some years are not nearly as good as others.

Tourist offices in all the towns provide up-to-date-sometimes hourly-information on wildflower action in their areas. Day by day they'll tell you where the flowers are blooming and the best routes to follow. Call them before you head out, or your whole trip may be wasted.

The best time of day to see color is between 11 and 3, but flowers are unlikely to open if the weather is cold and windy. Plants move with the sun, so make an effort to drive with the sun at your back to get the full effect.

Traveling by car is the only way to tour the West Coast and Namaqualand properly. A rental car can easily handle the tours mapped out below, despite the fact that much of the driving is along gravel roads. These roads are all in good condition, but stones can damage the underside of your car, particularly if you drive with a heavy foot. If you venture into Namaqualand, be sure your car is in good shape, carry drinking water and a spare tire, and fill up with gas whenever you can; like everything else, service stations are few and far between.

Towns and sights on are marked on the Western Cape and Namaqualand map.

West Coast, Hantam, and Cedarberg

A loop around the West Coast, Hantam, and Cedarberg starting from Cape Town will take a minimum of three days. Allow more time if you plan to walk extensively or frolic in fields of flowers.

Darling
From Cape Town, take the N1 toward Paarl. After just under 2 km (1 mi), exit left onto the R27 (the sign reads PAARDEN EILAND *and* MILNERTON*) and drive 80 km (50 mi) through fynbos-covered dunes to the junction with the R315, and turn right.*

Darling is a sleepy village in the heart of wildflower country, but in mid-September the village presents an annual Wildflower and Orchid Show (☎ 02241/2–422) that's famous throughout the Western Cape. This part of the coast usually flowers about two months after the first rains, and fades out between mid-September and mid-October. Expect to see daisies, bluebells, arum lilies, vygies, and namesias.

Back on the R27, head north 11 km (7 mi) to **West Coast National Park.** Even if you don't spend time here, the road that runs through the park to Langebaan is far more scenic than the R27 and well worth taking. The park is a fabulous mix of lagoon wetlands, pounding surf, and coastal fynbos. For a beautiful detour, follow the rutted dirt track 16 km (10 mi) onto the narrow peninsula that separates the Atlantic from Langebaan Lagoon. On a sunny day, the lagoon assumes a magical color, made all the more impressive by blinding white beaches and the sheer emptiness of the place. Birders will have a field day identifying water birds, and the sandveld flowers are among the best along the West Coast. At the tip of the peninsula's Postberg Nature Reserve, you'll likely catch glimpses of zebra, wildebeest, and bat-eared foxes. ⊠ *Off the R27,* ☎ *02287/22144.* ☒ *R25 per vehicle during high season (Easter, Christmas, and flower season); half price at other times.* ☉ *Daily 9–5.*

Langebaan
50 km (31 mi) northwest of Darling.

The paved road emerges from the park near Langebaan. Turn left out of the park, then right onto Oostewal Street and drive into town. Whereas many of the communities along the West Coast are bleak and uninviting, Langebaan is charming, and it makes a good base for ex-

In case you want to see the world.

In case you want to be welcomed there.

We're here to see that you're always welcomed at establishments everywhere. That's why millions of people carry the American Express® Card – for peace of mind, confidence, and security, around the world or just around the corner.

do more

Cards

In case you're running low.

We're here to help with more than 118,000 Express Cash locations around the world. In order to enroll, just call American Express before you start your vacation.

do more

Express Cash

And just in case.

We're here with American Express® Travelers Cheques
and Cheques *for Two.*® They're the safest way to carry
money on your vacation and the surest way to get a
refund, practically anywhere, anytime.
Another way we help you...

do more

**Travelers
Cheques**

ploring the surrounding area. The town sits at the mouth of Lange-baan Lagoon, overlooking West Coast National Park and the vast expanse of Saldanha Bay. The beaches are excellent, and the lagoon water is warmer than the ocean—although that's not saying much. There are several restaurants, a yacht club, and even a shop renting sailboards and small boats.

Return to the R27 and continue north. After a few kilometers, turn left onto the R79, which ends at a T junction. From here, you can turn left to Saldanha or right to Vredenburg.

DINING AND LODGING

$$ ✕⛫ **Farmhouse.** Less than 90 minutes by car from Cape Town, this
★ lovely guest house sits on a hillside overlooking the turquoise waters of Langebaan Lagoon. It's a great base for exploring West Coast National Park and a popular retreat for bird-watchers. The guest house, in a restored farmstead built in the 1860s, features thick white walls, tile floors, and timber beams. The rooms, decorated with rustic pine furniture and bright floral fabrics, have their own fireplaces and views of the lagoon. The hotel's à la carte menu features a good selection of Cape cuisine, prepared fresh and served in the attractive dining room, notable for its Oregon-pine furniture, fireplace, and high ceiling. ⊠ *5 Egret St., Box 160, Langebaan 7357,* ☎ *02287/22062,* 𝖥𝖠𝖷 *02287/21980. 10 rooms with bath. Restaurant, bar, pool. Breakfast included. No children under 12. MC, V.*

Paternoster
50 km (31 mi) northwest of Vredenburg.

Paternoster remains a truly unspoiled village of whitewashed fishermen's cottages perched on a deserted stretch of coastline. The population here is consists mainly of fishermen and women who for generations have eked out a living harvesting crayfish and other seafood. Despite the overt poverty, the village has a character and sense of identity often lacking in larger towns.

Along the coast just south of Paternoster is the **Columbine Nature Reserve,** a great spot for spring wildflowers, coastal fynbos, and succulents. Seagulls, cormorants, and sacred ibis are common here. ☎ *02281/752–718.* ⛫ *R4.* ☺ *Daily 7–7.*

Stompneusbaai
1 km (1½ mi) northeast of Paternoster.

Like Paternoster, Stompneusbaai is home to a community that relies on the sea for its livelihood. The stench of fish from the local fish-processing factory detracts from the charm of the village's whitewashed cottages and their brightly colored roofs. An unimpressive monument just outside of town marks the spot where Vasco da Gama landed in 1497, after a three-month voyage from Europe.

Velddrif
26 km (16 mi) east of Stompneusbaai.

Velddrif sits at the mouth of the Berg River. Forming a long estuary as it nears the sea, the Berg is a haven for water birds, including flamingos, pelicans, and the rare blue heron and redshank. Velddrif is a fishing community, and you can still see fishermen hanging bunches of *bokkems* (fish biltong) to dry in sheds along the estuary.

After the Berg River bridge, turn left on Voortrekker Street, which leads into **Laaiplek,** Velddrif's sister town and the site of the fishing harbor and beach. Turn right on Jameson Street and head out of town. After 11 km (7 mi), the tar road reverts to good-quality gravel.

Elands Bay

60 km (37½ mi) north of Velddrif.

Compared with the barren flats of the sandveld, Elands Bay enjoys an incredible setting, backed by a lagoon fringed with reeds and dotted with flamingos and waterfowl. A line of rocky cliffs runs down one side of the lagoon, ending at Baboon Point and a crayfish-processing factory. Drive out to Baboon Point (the sign says JETTIES) and look back toward the town. Fishing boats ride at anchor on startlingly blue water and, in the distance, a great field of white-sand dunes slopes down to the water's edge. The beach fronting the town is superb and draws crowds of Cape Town surfers on weekends and holidays. Birders, too, flock here to see the 200 species of birds that frequent the lagoon. Several San rock-art sites are also hidden away in the region, but they're almost impossible to find on your own; ask around for guides in Elands Bay. Unfortunately, the town itself is completely forgettable, with a characterless hotel and a couple of shops.

En Route   Follow the gravel R366 out of town for 4 km (2½ mi), then turn left at the sign to Lambert's Bay. After 13 km (8 mi), turn left again at a T junction. This road passes high above the **Wadrif Salt Pan,** formed by the Langvlei River. After a rain, the pan fills with water and attracts thousands of flamingos and other water birds.

Lambert's Bay

30 km (19 mi) north of Elands Bay.

Lambert's Bay isn't some spruced-up version of dock life like Cape Town's Victoria & Alfred Waterfront but a working fishing town—you can smell the fish-processing plants, and the boats in the harbor look like they spend their days battling Atlantic swells. If you don't expect anything cute, the innate charm of the town will seduce you. One of its major attractions is **Bird Island,** accessible along a stone breakwater from the harbor. The island is home to a colony of 14,000 Cape gannets, aggressive seabirds that live packed tightly together, fighting and screaming. The odor and the noise are incredible, but the colony must rate as one of the best bird-watching spectacles in South Africa. If you can see beyond the blur of gannets, you can also sometimes spot jackass penguins and seals.

OFF THE
BEATEN TRACK   **DORINGBAAI**—From Lambert's Bay, take the R364 past the BP station toward Clanwilliam (to which you could proceed directly for a shorter tour; ☞ *below*). After 5 km (3 mi), turn left onto a dirt road leading to Doringbaai and Vredendal. The wildflowers along the coast usually bloom from mid-July to mid-August, and the ordinarily featureless sandveld explodes with violets, wild tulips, harpuis, and sporrie. After 32 km (20 mi), turn left again to reach Doringbaai, perched on a deserted coastline of rocky cliffs. It's a popular holiday retreat for farmers from the Karoo but of little interest to most other travelers. **Strandfontein,** a few kilometers farther north, is another isolated holiday resort, backed by steep hills but ruined by the unsightly brick houses so common in the region. The road becomes tar again at Strandfontein and runs north along the coast. After a few kilometers you descend into the Olifants River valley, an oasis of vineyards, fields, and orchards. Continue into Vredendal, a nondescript agricultural center, and then on to Vanrhynsdorp via the R27.

DINING AND LODGING

\$\$ ✕ **Muisbosskerm.** For the true flavor of West Coast life, come to this
★   open-air seafood restaurant on the beach south of town. It consists of nothing more than a circular *boma* (enclosure) of packed *muisbos* (mouse

bush), with benches and tables haphazardly arranged in the sandy enclosure. Cooking fires blaze and you watch food being prepared fresh before your eyes: Snoek is smoked in an old drum covered with burlap, bread bakes in a clay oven, and everywhere fish sizzles on grills and in giant pots. Bring your own drink, and prepare to eat as much as you can, using your hands or mussel shells as spoons. Be sure to try some of the Afrikaner specialties like *bokkoms* (dried fish) and *waterblommetjie* (water lily) stew. Unless you have an enormous appetite, don't order the half crayfish (it costs extra). The only drawback is high-season crowding: As many as 150 diners can overwhelm the experience. ⊠ *Elands Bay Rd., 5 km (3 mi) south of Lambert's Bay,* ☎ *027/ 432–1017. Reservations essential. V.*

$ ⊞ **Marine Protea.** Next to the harbor in the center of Lambert's Bay, this modern hotel offers conventional comfort but little charm. It's a good overnight choice, though, if you're dining at the nearby Muisbosskerm. Rooms are large, decorated in blue tones, and feature a sitting area with TV and phone. ⊠ *Voortrekker St., Box 249, Lambert's Bay 8130,* ☎ *027/432–1126,* FAX *027/432–1036. 46 rooms with bath. Restaurant, 2 bars, room service, pool. AE, DC, MC, V.*

Vanrhynsdorp
64 km (40 mi) northeast of Lambert's Bay.

At Vanrhynsdorp you have a choice. You can strike north on the N7 into the empty vastness of Namaqualand (☞ *below*) or cut eastward along the R27 toward the **Hantam,** a high plateau that marks the fringes of the Karoo Desert and the extreme range of the winter rainfall area. The wildflowers usually bloom here in mid-July and last through mid-September. Among the most common are vygies, daisies, katsterte, and pietsnotjies.

To reach the Hantam Plateau, you must first scale the looming wall of the Bokkeveld Escarpment, which rises almost vertically from the flat expanse of the sandveld. The road zigzags up Vanrhyns Pass, providing excellent views back over the Olifants River valley.

Nieuwoudtville
58 km (36 mi) northeast of Vanrhynsdorp.

On the cusp of the escarpment, Nieuwoudtville gets more rain than elsewhere in the Hantam, and its vegetation differs accordingly. The town is famous for its bulbs, including a mass display of more than half a million orange bulbinellas, which are endemic to the area.

Calvinia
72 km (45 mi) east of Nieuwoudtville.

Calvinia shelters under a looming mesa known as the Hantamsberg. Founded in 1851, it's a lovely farming town, with a relaxed feel and several beautifully restored historic homes. It makes a good base for exploring the **Akkerendam Nature Reserve** north of town. Two hiking trails of one and six hours traverse the slopes of the Hantamsberg and the plateau on top.

The **Calvinia Museum** is one of the best country museums in South Africa. Displays examine the fashions and furnishings that prevailed in this remote corner of South Africa over the past 150 years. Many of the exhibits reflect the town's agricultural focus, especially sheep farming. ⊠ *44 Church St.,* ☎ *0273/411–043.* ☜ *R1.* ⊙ *Weekdays 8–1 and 2– 5, Sat. 8–noon.*

NEED A
BREAK?

Die Hantam Huis, a lovely 1853 Cape Dutch homestead, is the oldest surviving building in Calvinia. It's now a delightful lunchroom and coffee shop. ⊠ *44, Hoop St.,* ☎ *0273/41–1606.* ⊙ *Daily 24-hrs during the flower season; rest of the year, weekdays 7:30–5, Sat. 7:30–2.*

En Route   Drive 37 km (21 mi) back along the R27 toward Nieuwoudtville, then turn left onto the gravel R364 to Clanwilliam. This is a magical 112-km (70-mi) drive, especially in the two to three hours after sunrise or before sunset, when the desert colors take on a glowing richness that is almost mystical. Thirty-two km (20 mi) before Clanwilliam you come to a farm called **Travellers Rest** (☎ 0274/82–1824). A host of San rock paintings lie within a two-hour walk of the farmhouse, but you must get permission before walking out to look for them. The gravel road descends to Clanwilliam through the beautiful **Cedarberg,** a mountain range known for its San paintings, bizarre rock formations, and, once upon a time, its cedars. Most of the ancient cedars have been cut down, but a few giant specimens still survive in the more remote regions. The Cedarberg is a hiking paradise for Capetonians—a wild, largely unspoiled area where you can disappear from civilization for days at a time. About 172,900 acres of this mountain range have been declared the Cedarberg Wilderness Area, and entry permits are required if you wish to hike or drive into this part of the range. It's advisable, if you intend exploring this protected area, to contact the Nature Conservation offices in Cape Town (☎ 021/483–4098) for permit details.

DINING AND LODGING

$$$$ ✕🖼 **Bushmans Kloof Game Lodge.** The most attractive, sophisticated, and comfortable base from which to explore this area is Bushmans Kloof and its surrounding 10,600 acres of reserve. It's advisable to arrive by 3 PM at the latest, which will give you time to unpack, restore your equilibrium after the bumpy ride, have a sumptuous cream tea, and set off on the late-afternoon's game drive. What makes the place so special? The stark beauty of the mountains, the prehistoric rock formations, the waterfalls, the 125 sites of ancient San (Bushman) rock paintings, five different botanical communities, the beasts (wildebeest, zebra, eland, mountain leopard, Cape hunting dog, aardwolf, genets, mongoose, Cape clawless otter, to name but a few) and the birds (from waterbird to raptor and everything in between). The freestanding, thatched, double cottages have every possible modern convenience, the food is of a high standard and in abundance, the hospitality is sincere and sophisticated, and the game rangers experts in their field. ⊠ *Box 267, Clanwilliam 8135,* ☎ *027/482—2627,* 𝖥𝖠𝖷 *027/482—1011. 10 double cottages with bath and shower. Meals and game drives included.*

$ 🖼 **Die Dorphuis.** In a restored Victorian house that is now a national
★   monument, this lovely bed-and-breakfast offers warm Afrikaner hospitality amid elegant period furnishings. Rooms have antique brass bedsteads and elaborate ceilings, and are hung with photos of old Calvinia. If you want something completely different, book the slave quarters: The room, lit only with candles and kerosene lanterns, features a reed floor and ceiling, and bedcovers made from animal skins. ⊠ *Water St., Box 34, Calvinia 8190,* ☎ 𝖥𝖠𝖷 *0273/411–606. 10 rooms with bath. Breakfast included. No credit cards.*

Clanwilliam
120 km (75 mi) southwest of Calvinia.

Clanwilliam serves as the base for hiking trails and drives into the Cedarberg. It's better geared for tourism than Calvinia, and it's equally charming, with tree-shaded streets and several restored 19th-century buildings. The town was founded around 1800 and has blossomed into the center of the rooibos-tea industry. Rooibos is a bush that grows wild in the Cedarberg and forms the foundation of many herbal teas sold worldwide.

Wildflowers hit their peak in Clanwilliam in the second and third weeks in August. One of the best places to see them is the **Ramskop Wildflower Garden,** less than a mile out of town. ⊠ *Ou Kaapseweg, Clanwilliam,* ☎ *027/482–2133.* ⊡ *R7.70.* ☉ *7:30–sunset.*

Return to the N7 and head south to the turnoff to **Algeria.** A scenic dirt road winds into the Cedarberg to this Cape Conservation outpost and campsite, set in an idyllic valley amid towering eucalyptus trees. Algeria is the starting point for several excellent hikes into the Cedarberg. No permit is needed for the short, one-hour hike to a waterfall, or a longer hike to a copse of cedars atop the mountains.

Continue down the N7 to **Citrusdal,** a fruit-growing town in the Olifants River valley surrounded by the peaks of the Cedarberg. From here, it's just 90 minutes back to Cape Town through the **Swartland** ("black land"), which takes its name from the dark renoster bush that grows in the area. Today, the Swartland is a rolling landscape of wheat fields and vineyards. From July until the end of October, you can see plenty of flowers from the highway, including lovely arum lilies. There are a number of commercial protea farms here, too.

DINING AND LODGING

$ ✕⊡ **Strassberger's Hotel Clanwilliam.** Right on the main street, this friendly, family-run hotel makes an excellent base for exploring the Cedarberg. Rooms are large, decorated with rustic cane furniture and plaid country fabrics. Pieter du Toit, a hotel employee, can arrange hikes and tours into the surrounding mountains. Dinner in the hotel restaurant is a traditional four-course affair that is satisfactory but lacks inspiration. Reinholds, the hotel's à la carte restaurant, serves more innovative fare, like crumbed pork chops with sweet-and-sour sauce. ⊠ *Main Rd., Box 4, Clanwilliam 8135,* ☎ *027/482–1101,* ⒻⒶⓍ *027/ 482–2678. 17 rooms with bath. 2 restaurants, bar, pool, squash. Breakfast included. AE, DC, MC, V.*

Namaqualand

Unless it's flower season, think twice about trekking into this vast desert wilderness. Hotels and restaurants are basic, and the distances are immense. It's 544 km (340 mi) from Cape Town to Springbok, the capital of Namaqualand and a major base for exploring the region's flowers, and a 4- to 5-hour drive just to reach Kamieskroon, the closest Namaqualand hamlet with a decent hotel. To do the area justice, you need to add three days to a West Coast itinerary or budget a minimum of five days if you're visiting Namaqualand only. Don't come up here looking for traditional tourist sights; aside from the flowers, this is empty, untamed country. The tour below simply maps out some of the most rewarding flower routes.

Namaqualand stretches north from Vanrhynsdorp, a small farming town at the northern limit of the West Coast tour (☞ *above*).

Garies

144 km (90 mi) north of Vanrhynsdorp on N7.

A one-horse town cradled amid sun-baked hills, one of the best flower routes runs 100 km (60 mi) from just north of Garies to Hondeklipbaai on the coast. The road winds through rocky hills before descending onto the flat coastal sandveld. Flowers in this region usually bloom at the end of July and early August. If you're lucky, fields along this route will be carpeted with purple vygies, but also look for Namaqualand daisies, aloes, and orchids. Another common plant is the quiver tree, a giant aloe whose bark was used by the San to make quivers for their poison arrows.

Hondeklipbaai
100 km (60 mi) northwest of Garies.

Hondeklipbaai itself is a depressing, windblown settlement perched on desolate flats by the sea. It's a diamond-mining area, and huge holes gouged out of the earth mar the terrain. From Hondeklipbaai, take the road toward Kooiingnaas, another diamond-mining settlement, and then northeast to Springbok. The road climbs steeply into the granite mountains to **Wildeperdehoek** (Wild Horses Pass), offering tremendous views back over the coastal plain and the sea. From here, the road winds back and forth through the hills, cresting Messelpad Pass before rejoining the N7 highway.

Springbok
85 km (53 mi) northeast of Hondeklipbaai.

Springbok is set in a bowl of rocky hills that form part of the Klipkoppe, a rocky escarpment that stretches from Steinkopf in the north to Bitterfontein in the south. The town owes its existence to the discovery of copper here in 1685. It's a pleasant enough place, especially after the emptiness of the desert, but it offers little more than a chance to fill your gas tank, pick up food and flower information, and spend the night.

Sixteen km (10 mi) outside town is the **Goegap Nature Reserve,** which is transformed each spring into a wildflower mosaic. There are two short walking trails from the information center as well as several longer ones. In season, the reserve conducts daily flower safaris (R25 per person, minimum of 10 persons, booking essential). Bicycles are available for hire (R27 per day). Goegap is also home to the Hester Malan Wildflower Garden, which displays an interesting collection of succulents, including the bizarre halfmens or "half man" (*Pachypodium namaquanum*), consisting of a long, slender trunk topped by a bushel of leaves. It looks somewhat like an armless person, hence the name. ⊠ *R355 from Springbok,* ☎ *0251/21880,* FAX *0251/81286.* ☎ *R5.* ☉ *Daily 7:45–4:30.*

En Route   Another excellent flower drive is a 320-km (200-mi) rectangular route that heads north on the N7 from Springbok to Steinkopf and then west on the paved R382 to Port Nolloth. From there a dirt road leads south through the sandveld to Grootmis, then east along the Buffels River before climbing the Spektakel Pass back to Springbok. If the rains have been good, the route offers some of the best flower viewing in the region. Try to time your return to Springbok to coincide with the sunset, when the entire Spektakel Mountain glows a deep orange-red.

DINING AND LODGING

$$$ ✕🏠 **Naries Guest House.** Twenty-four kilometers (15 miles) from Springbok along a dirt road, this Cape Dutch–style guest house looks out over the mountains of the Spektakelberg. The gracious owner makes guests feel comfortable, and will even lead hikes around the farm. Guest rooms are large, decorated in bold floral fabrics. Dinner, included in the room rate, is a four-course feast of robust Afrikaans home-cooking, including such dishes as venison stew, pumpkin fritters, and cabbage and beans. ⊠ *24 km (15 mi) west of Springbok on Kleinzee Rd.,* ☎ FAX *0251/22462. 5 rooms with bath, 1 self-catering cottage. Breakfast and dinner included. MC, V.*

$ ✕🏠 **Springbok Lodge.** Rooms at this lodge in the center of Springbok are clean, cheap, and basic; most have TVs, and kettles for making coffee and tea. The advantage of staying here is the owner, who runs his own information office and is a fount of knowledge about the area. He has established the Namib Mine Museum at the lodge, and its own hiking trail. A restaurant serves typical diner food, including English breakfasts and sandwiches. ⊠ *37 Voortrekker St., Box 26, Springbok 8240,* ☎ *0251/21321,* 𝔽𝔸𝕏 *0251/22718. 30 rooms with bath, 12 self-catering cottages. Restaurant. MC, V.*

Port Nolloth
110 km (69 mi) northwest of Springbok.

Take time from smelling the flowers to walk around Port Nolloth. It started life as a copper port, but today it's better known as a fishing and diamond center. Head over to the harbor to check out the diamond-vacuuming boats, with their distinctive hoses trailing astern. Divers use the hoses to vacuum under boulders on the seabed in search of the diamonds that washed into the sea from the Orange River ages ago. It's a highly lucrative endeavor, but not without its dangers; at least one diver has been sucked up the vacuum hose to his death.

LODGING

$ 🏠 **Bed Rock Lodge.** Across the street from the sea, this weathered old guest house looks as though it's seen better days. The interior, however, is delightful, decorated with an eclectic collection of Africana and antiques. Each room has its own bathroom, not always en suite, however. ⊠ *Coast Rd., Port Nolloth,* ☎ *0255/8865. 2 rooms with bath. 3 self-catering cottages. MC, V.*

Kamieskroon
72 km (45 mi) south of Springbok on the N7.

Kamieskroon is another base for exploring Namaqualand in spring. Although the town itself has nothing to recommend it, the Kamieskroon Hotel (☞ Dining and Lodging, *below*) is probably the best source of information on wildflowers in Namaqualand.

The 2,470-acre **Skilpad Wildflower Reserve,** 18 km (11 mi) west of Kamieskroon on the Wolwepoort Road, can usually be counted on for flower displays. ⊠ *Wolwepoort Rd.,* ☎ *027/672–1948.* 🎫 *R5 per person, R50 per bus and R5 per person.* ☉ *8–5.*

An interesting detour from Kamieskroon runs 29 km (18 mi) to **Leliefontein,** an old mission station at the top of the Kamiesberg with spectacular views across the desert to the sea. The wildflowers here bloom much later than those on the coast, often lasting as late as the end of October. Even if there are no flowers, it's a beautiful drive back down the Kamiesberg to Garies, 72 km (45 mi) away.

LODGING

$ 🏠 **Kamieskroon Hotel.** At first glance, this hotel offers little to distinguish it from every other one in Namaqualand. The newly renovated rooms are clean and comfortable, but certainly nothing to write home about. The reason to come is the hotel's world-renowned series of Namaqualand photographic workshops (☞ Guided Tours *in* West Coast and Namaqualand A to Z, *below*), which are conducted annually by the owners. Even if you don't participate in a workshop, you can still benefit from their tremendous knowledge of the area and of how to capture the annual floral miracle on film. They also provide day-to-day updates on where flowers are blooming. ⊠ *Off N7, Old National Rd., Box 19, Kamieskroon 8241,* ☎ *027/672–1614,* 𝔽𝔸𝕏 *027/672–1675. 20 rooms with bath. Restaurant, bar. DC, MC, V.*

West Coast and Namaqualand A to Z

Arriving and Departing

BY BUS

Intercape Mainliner (✉ Captour office, Adderley St., ☎ 021/386–4400) operates daily service up the West Coast to Springbok (✉ R165), stopping at Citrusdal, Clanwilliam, Vanrhynsdorp, Garies, and Kamieskroon.

BY CAR

The southernmost towns on the West Coast lie within 80 km (50 mi) of Cape Town. Namaqualand is over 320 km (200 mi) away.

Getting Around

BY CAR

With the great distances involved and the absence of any real public transport the only way to get around in a car.

Contacts and Resources

EMERGENCIES

Dial 10177 for an **ambulance,** 10111 for the **police.**

GUIDED TOURS

Lambert's Bay Travel and Exploration (✉ Waterfront, Lambert's Bay, ☎ 027/4321715) offers one-hour boat trips (R50) up the coast to see Benguela dolphins, seals, great white sharks, and jackass penguins. Evening trips head up the coast to a quiet bay, where guests feast on crayfish and wine. By advance arrangement, the company also conducts four-wheel-drive expeditions onto the Cedarberg, the Karoo Desert, and Botswana.

Namaqualand Photographic Workshops (✉ Kamieskroon Hotel, Old National Road, Kamieskroon, ☎ 027/672–1614, ℻ 027/672–1675) are world-famous photographic seminars led by professional photographers Freeman Patterson, Colla Swart, and J.J. van Heerden. Four week-long workshops are held during flower season, consisting of lectures and field trips to photograph the flowers and landscape. Two summer seminars, held outside flower season, include three days of camping.

VISITOR INFORMATION

The **Flowerline** is a central hot line that offers details about where the flowers are best seen each day. ☎ *082 990 5395/4 or 021/418–3705.* ☉ *June–Oct., daily 8–4.30*

Calvinia Tourist Office. ✉ *Calvinia Museum, 44 Church St., Calvinia,* ☎ *0273/411712,* ℻ *0273/411–2750.* ☉ *Weekdays 8–1 and 2–5, Sat. 8–noon.*

Clanwilliam Tourism Association. ✉ *Main Rd., Clanwilliam,* ☎ *027/482–2024,* ℻ *027/482–2361.* ☉ *Daily in flower season 8:30–6; rest of the year, weekdays 8.30–5, Saturday 8.30–12.30.*

Lambert's Bay Information Office. ✉ *Strandveld Museum, D.F. Malan St., Lambert's Bay,* ☎ *027/432–1000,* ℻ *027/432–2335.* ☉ *Mon.–Sat. 9–1 and 2–5. Open Sun. during flower season.*

Springbok. ✉ *Old Church, Luckhof St., Springbok,* ☎ *0251/22071,* ℻ *0251/81333.* ☉ *Weekdays 8:30–4.30, variable hrs on weekends in flower season.*

6 Garden Route and Little Karoo

The Garden Route takes its name from the region's riot of vegetation. Here, you'll find some of South Africa's most inspiring scenery: forest-cloaked mountains, myriad rivers, and golden beaches backed by thick bush. You'll also find Plettenberg Bay, South Africa's glitziest beach resort, and Knysna, a town built around an oyster-rich lagoon. The Little Karoo (pronounced ka-roo-ah), separated from the coast by a range of mountains, is famous for its turn-of-the-century "feather palaces" and the Cango Caves, one of the world's most impressive networks of underground caverns.

THE 208-KILOMETER (130-MILE) STRETCH of coastline from Mossel Bay to Storms River encompasses some of South Africa's most scenic country, but don't expect the jagged, dramatic beauty of the Western Cape. The Garden Route's appeal is softer—a land of lakes and rivers, of green mountains, thick forests, and beaches combed by the Indian Ocean. It's the kind of place where you'll have trouble deciding whether to lie on the beach or go on an invigorating hike.

The Garden Route owes its verdant mien to the Outeniqua and Tsitsikamma mountains, forested ranges that shadow the coastline, trapping the moist ocean breezes which then fall as rain. These same mountains are also responsible for robbing the interior of water, creating the semi-arid deserts of the Little and Great Karoo. A trip into this sere world of rock and scrub offers a glimpse of what much of South Africa's vast hinterland looks like. The Little Karoo, the narrow strip of land wedged between the Swartberg and Outeniqua ranges, is famous for its ostrich farms, as well as the subterranean splendors of the Cango Caves. Even if all of this leaves you cold, it is still worth the effort to explore some of the spectacular passes that claw through the mountains into the desert interior.

Until recently, anyone with limited time would have to choose between the Garden Route and the classic African game experience of Mpumalanga. This is no longer the case. Shamwari Game Reserve, an hour's drive from Port Elizabeth, has all the hallmarks of becoming a classic for big-game adventure. It also has the advantage of lying in a malaria-free zone.

Pleasures and Pastimes

Dining
Oysters, oysters, oysters—when you come to the Garden Route, don't miss 'em. It's only logical, too, that with all of this coastline, seafood in general is a highlight. The farms of the Little Karoo provide fresh ostrich meat, which will stand up to the South African red wine that you'll find on menus. You'll also find curries here and there, and even a vegetarian restaurant or two.

Lodging
The Garden Route wouldn't have such allure if it wasn't for its exclusive seaside getaways and colonial manor houses, or its more rustic inland farms and national-park log cabins. Breakfast is included in many lodges' rates, and if your guest house serves dinner, eating the evening meal in situ often has a welcome intimacy after a day of exploring. The flipside of that is self-catering cottages where you can prepare your own meals—pick up some local seafood and make yourself a feast.

Outdoor Activities and Sports
You can take in, or take on, the Garden Route's outdoors just about any way you'd like—from horseback riding to five-day hikes along the coast, and from the mountains that line the Little Karoo desert to the Robberg Peninsula with its whale- and dolphin-watching. The Garden Route is one of the most popular hiking regions in the country, and there are hundreds of trails from which to choose. We cover the most popular ones below; to find additional local favorites, tourist offices in all the towns have listings and maps of hikes in their areas (☞ Contacts and Resources *in* Garden Route A to Z, *below*). And keep Shamwari Game Reserve in mind if you want to get some wildlife-viewing in on this leg of your trip.

Exploring the Garden Route

For most travelers, the Garden Route remains very much a "route," a drive of several days from Cape Town to Port Elizabeth, or vice versa, with a flight out of Port Elizabeth to the next part of the trip. Increasingly, though, people are eschewing the standard driving tour in favor of a longer holiday, basing themselves in a central town like Knysna (pronounced *nize*-nuh) and exploring from there. This certainly has its advantages, not least because almost the entire Garden Route lies less than an hour from this busy town.

In addition, resorts like Plettenberg Bay offer the kind of classic beach vacation you fantasize about during interminable office meetings. The beaches are among the world's best, and you can take your pick of water sports. The ocean may not be as warm as in KwaZuluNatal, but the quality of the accommodations tends to be far superior.

Great Itineraries

Because of compactness of the Garden Route, you can see much of it even in three days, but there's plenty to occupy you for a week or more. The essential places to see are Mossel Bay, the Wilderness, Knysna, Plettenberg Bay, and Tsitsikamma—try to fit them into whichever itinerary you choose. They run in a line along the coast from Cape Town to Port Elizabeth, which makes them ever so easy to string together.

Numbers in the text correspond to numbers in the margin and on the Garden Route map.

IF YOU HAVE 3 DAYS

⚅ **Mossel Bay** ① and ⚅ **Wilderness National Park** ⑫ are a good one-day combination. Begin by exploring the small village of **Mossel Bay**, where you can take a short seal-sighting cruise from the harbor. A 40-minute drive west on the N2 will bring you past the resort town of ⚅ **Wilderness** ⑪ and into the wetlands paradise of **Wilderness National Park**. Spend the night either in Wilderness or the park itself if you plan to head inland to **Oudsthoorn's** ③ ostrich farms, the **Cango Caves** ④, and **Swartberg Pass** ⑤ on the second day. If you'd rather stay at a charming resort and explore the coastal headlands and Featherbed Nature Reserve, book a room in ⚅ **Knysna** ⑭. On the third day, pamper yourself in ⚅ **Plettenberg Bay** ⑱, where you can stretch out on the beaches alongside affluent, trendy Gautengers. There's also good shopping here for arts and crafts. Spend the night here or in Knysna, depending on whether you'll fly out of George or Port Elizabeth the next day.

IF YOU HAVE 5 DAYS

With five days, you can accomplish both the inland route and Knysna-area exploring described above. You'll also have time to spend your fifth day picnicking and walking through ⚅ **Tsitsikamma National Park** ⑳—one of the standouts of the Garden Route. The park has good accommodations if you want to overnight here, or you can return to ⚅ **Plettenburg Bay** ⑱ for your last night. If you're leaving (or entering) the Garden Route through Port Elizabeth, you might want to trek the 31 miles up to **Addo Elephant Park** ㉒.

IF YOU HAVE 8 DAYS

Bliss—you have eight days and plenty to keep you busy. Use ⚅ **Mossel Bay** ① or ⚅ **Wilderness** ⑪ as a base for the first two or three nights, and spend a full day on the edge of the Little Karoo desert to take in the contrasts of the region. For the next two or three days relax in the resorts of ⚅ **Knysna** ⑭ or ⚅ **Plettenberg Bay** ⑱, making sure to take a long walk on one of the beaches. Both towns have local markets to potter around—weaving, painting, woodwork, pottery are the featured

The Garden Route

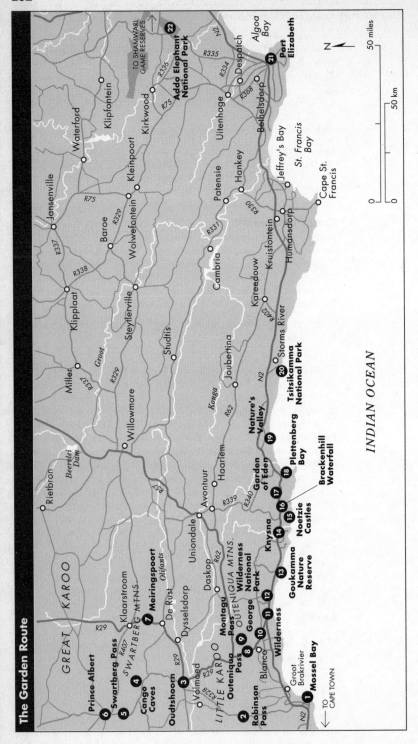

INDIAN OCEAN

N

50 miles

50 km

crafts. In ⚁ **Knysna,** take a trip on the vintage steam train **Outeniqua Choo-Tjoe** to George. Next, head east for several options. Spend a couple of days in and around **Tsitsikamma National Park** ⑳ where you can exercise with a canoe safari or a hike, or push on to ⚁ **Port Elizabeth** ㉑ and the **Addo Elephant National Park** ㉒ to ogle at elephants, rhino, eland, kudu, and buffalo. Or go all out and continue past Port Elizabeth to Shamwari Game Reserve, whose great wildlife includes lion, leopard, and other predators.

When to Tour the Garden Route

There's no best time to visit the Garden Route, although the water and weather are warmest from December through March. If saving money is an issue, stay away during this peak season when hotel prices soar, in some cases nearly doubling. Between May and September, winter gets wet and cold. But—and it's a big but—when you do get sunny winter weather, it makes all the more cozy the huge, blazing log fires and large bowls of steaming soup that hostelries along the coast provide. And, of course, there are fewer tourists. Even in these colder months, wildflowers bloom along the Garden Route from July to October, the same time as the annual whale migration along the coast.

Mossel Bay

❶ *384 km (240 mi) from Cape Town via the N2 highway.*

Mossel Bay, at the western end of the Garden Route, can't compete with Knysna or Plettenberg as a resort town, but it's pleasant nevertheless, built on a hillside overlooking the Bay of Mussels and the Outeniqua Mountains. Dolphins—as many as 100 at a time—frequently move through the bay in search of food, and whales swim past during their annual migration (July–October). In addition, boats cruise out to Seal Island, home to a breeding colony of more than 2,000 Cape fur seals (☞ Guided Tours *in* Garden Route A to Z, *below*). The town's main beach, Santos, offers protected bathing and much smaller waves than you will typically find along the Garden Route's coastline.

In 1488, Bartolemeu Dias landed on the site of present-day Mossel Bay after he was blown off course during his search for a route to the East Indies. After that, other Portuguese sailors—including Vasco da Gama—regularly called here to replenish their water supplies from a small spring near the coast.

You can still see this spring and numerous artifacts of this period at the excellent **Bartolomeu Dias Museum Complex.** The complex consists of three museums set amid lawns sloping down to the sea. **The Maritime Museum** has a full-scale replica of the caravel in which Dias journeyed to the Cape. **The Shell Museum** may sound hokey, but it's first-rate, with a fine collection of local shells as well as live mollusks and fish in aquariums. **The Local History Museum** (closed Sunday) traces the history and culture of Mossel Bay itself. Besides the museums, you can see an ancient milkwood tree that served as the first post office in South Africa. In 1500, a Portuguese sailor placed some mail in an old boot and set it under the tree in hopes that another passing ship would deliver it. The tree subsequently became a frequent drop site for letters, and you can still post letters in a mailbox shaped like an old boot. ⊠ *Church and Market Sts.,* ☎ *0444/91–1067.* 🔲 *Free.* ☉ *Weekdays 9–5, Sat. 10–4, Sun. 2–5.*

Leave Mossel Bay via the R328 and follow the signs 94 km (40 mi) north to Oudtshoorn in the **Little Karoo.** The Little Karoo is a semi-arid region whose landscape differs so radically from the verdant bush of the Garden Route it's difficult to believe they're separated by just a few kilometers. In summer the Little Karoo can be a blast furnace, while winter nights are bitterly cold. Little Karoo refers to the narrow plain between the Outeniqua and Swartberg mountains, and should not be confused with the Great Karoo, a vast scrub desert that starts on the other side of the Swartberg. The word *karoo* derives from the San (Bushman) word for thirst.

The highlight of the trip between Mossel Bay and Oudtshoorn is ❷ **Robinson Pass,** which cuts through the Outeniqua Mountains. Built in 1886 by Sir Thomas Bain, the road climbs through forests of exotic pine and hillsides covered with *fynbos* ("*feign*-boss"), the abundant native Cape flora. From May through July the proteas bloom, and their magnificent flowers are a stunning contrast to the fractured rock and deep gorges of these ancient mountains.

Dining and Lodging

$$ ✕ **Gannet.** Tour-bus crowds occasionally descend on this popular spot, but don't let that put you off. The emphasis here is solidly on seafood, whether it's freshly shucked oysters, grilled Mossel Bay sole, or prawntail kebabs. Stick to the simpler grilled dishes–some of the more ambitious choices, such as calamari risotto and seafood bisque, miss the mark. If you don't want seafood, you can order a pizza from the wood-burning oven. In summer, sit outside on the shaded terrace overlooking the bay, or, inside with the eclectic collection of country antiques. The restaurant also serves full breakfasts. ⊠ *Market and Church Sts.,* ☎ *0444/91–1885. AE, DC, MC, V.*

$$–$$$ 🏨 **Santos Protea Hotel.** Very popular with families, this comfortable three-star hotel has stunning sea views since it's right on the main bathing beach. The standard rooms do not face the sea; the 35 deluxe doubles do. The atmosphere is warm and friendly and staff go out of their way to make you feel welcome. There are tennis courts nearby for guests' use. ⊠ *Santos Rd., Box 203, Mossel Bay 6500,* ☎ *0444/91–7103,* 🖷 *0444/91–1945. 58 rooms. Restaurant, bar, pool, beach. AE, DC, MC, V.*

$$ 🏨 **Old Post Office Tree Manor.** This pleasant guest house—the third-oldest building in Mossel Bay—has the best location of any hotel in town, just meters from the town's museum complex and overlooking the beach and sea. You can take that in while relaxing at the Blue Oyster Cocktail Bar, a delightful pub and terrace with panoramic views of Munro's Bay. The bright rooms are simply furnished, but comfortable, and have excellent bay views. Breakfast is served at the nearby Gannet Restaurant (☞ *above*). ⊠ *Market St., Box 349, Mossel Bay 6500,* ☎ *0444/91–3738,* 🖷 *0444/91–3104. 30 rooms with bath. Restaurant, bar, room service, pool. Breakfast included. AE, DC, MC, V.*

Hiking and Walking

The **St. Blaize Trail** is a 13-km (8-mi) hike that starts at the cave below the St. Blaize lighthouse and runs along the coast to Dana Bay. The walk takes about five hours and has great views of cliffs, ocean, and numerous rocky bays and coves.

Oudtshoorn

❸ *65 km (40 mi) north of Mossel Bay*

For more than a century, Oudtshoorn has been famous for its ostriches. Nowhere else in the world do these huge birds thrive like they do in the Little Karoo. Farmers began raising them in Oudtshoorn around 1870 to satisfy the European demand for feathers to adorn women's hats and dresses. In the years leading up to World War I, ostrich feathers were almost worth their weight in gold, and Oudtshoorn experienced an incredible boom. Many of the beautiful sandstone buildings in town date back to that period, as do the "feather palaces," huge homes built by prosperous feather merchants and buyers. In the evening, after the heat of the day, it's fun to wander the streets to look at these old houses.

Most of the feather palaces are still private, but you can visit the sandstone **Town House,** built in 1909 and furnished in period style. ⊠ *High and Loop Sts.,* ☎ *044/272–7306.* ⊑ *Free.* ⊙ *Weekdays 9–5.*

The Town House is administered by the **C.P. Nel Museum,** one of the finest country museums in South Africa. Not surprisingly, it focuses on the ostrich and Oudtshoorn's boom period at the beginning of the century. Many of the exhibits are set up like shopfronts, including a pharmacy, a bank, and a department store. Others replicate the dining room, bedroom, and music room of a wealthy Oudtshoorn family. A fascinating exhibit traces the history of Oudtshoorn's once-large Jewish community. In the years prior to World War I, Oudtshoorn became known as Little Jerusalem, as nearly the entire feather trade was run by Jewish merchants, many of whom had emigrated to South Africa from Eastern Europe between 1880 and 1910. The exhibit is built around a synagogue that is still in use. ⊠ *Baron van Reede St.,* ☎ *044/272–7306.* ⊑ *Free.* ⊙ *Mon.–Sat. 9–1 and 2–5.*

These days, ostrich farms probably derive as much profit from visiting tourists as they do from the sale of ostrich feathers, meat, and leather. The entire town of Oudtshoorn has moved in that direction, offering a host of kitschy attractions that would make Nashville proud. Three farms compete for the tourist buck, offering almost identical tours. In summer, crowds can be horrendous.

Highgate Ostrich Show Farm was the first to turn ostrich farming into a major attraction. Knowledgeable guides take you through every step in the production of feathers, ostrich leather, and meat, and explain the bird's extraordinary social and physical characteristics. During the 90-minute tour, you'll get a chance to sit on a penned ostrich and even to ride one around a small enclosure. To cap it all off, three jockeys race the birds up and down a short course. A curio shop sells a variety of ostrich products and kitschy souvenirs. ⊠ *Off R328 to Mossel Bay,* ☎ *044/272–7115,* ℻ *044/272–7111.* ⊑ *R15.* ⊙ *Daily 8–5. Tours every 15 mins.*

★ ❹ From Oudtshoorn, follow the R328 for 32 km (20 mi) to reach the **Cango Caves,** deservedly one of the most popular attractions in the area. The caves are huge and stunningly beautiful, stretching for several kilometers through the mountains. Unfortunately, some of the grandeur is lost when you have to share the experience with as many as 200 people. The passage of so many people over the years has turned the rock formations from milky white to red and brown, due to a buildup of iron oxide and acid damage from human breath. The main part of the tour lasts about an hour and passes through three huge chambers notable for their giant stalagmites and stalactites. Some of the guides' commentary is trite, but it's much better and more informative than at Sudwala Caves in Mpumalanga. After the third chamber, you'll have the option to turn back or continue on the "adventure" portion of the tour. Think long and hard about pressing on if you're overweight, very tall, claustrophobic, or have knee or heart problems, because you end up shimmying up narrow chimneys on your belly and wriggling your way through tiny tunnels. It's exhilarating, but the temperature and humidity levels are high, and there's not much oxygen. If you plan to take the second part of the tour, wear shoes with a good tread and old clothes—you'll do a lot of sliding on your bum. ⊠ *Off R328 between Oudtshoorn and Prince Albert,* ☎ *044/272–7410.* 🖪 *R16.50.* ☉ *Daily 9–4. Tours hourly.*

Cango Wildlife Ranch. The ranch is on the way to Cango Caves and is home to 500 or so crocodiles as well as cheetahs, pumas, jaguars, and lions. You can spy on some of these creatures from an elevated catwalk. There's also a snake park, pygmy hippos, a small museum, and general game of the area, including antelope. ⊠ *Caves Road, Oudtshoorn 6620,* ☎ *044/272–5593.* 🖪 *R22* ☉ *Daily 8–5.*

Drive down the hill from the Cango Caves and turn right onto the R328 toward Prince Albert, on the other side of the mountains. On the way, ★ ❺ the road traverses **Swartberg Pass,** one of the scenic highlights of any trip to South Africa. This pass was also built, between 1881 and 1886, by the legendary engineer Sir Thomas Bain, who warned that the road would have to be steep. He wasn't exaggerating. Soon after it begins to climb, the tar gives way to gravel and becomes very narrow. At times, the road barely clings to the mountainside, held in place only by Bain's stone retaining walls. Cresting the pass at 5,230 ft, you look out toward the hot plains of the Great Karoo Desert and the distant mountains of the Nuweveldberg. Of more immediate note is the huge gorge that cuts through the mountains below you, revealing sheer walls of red, red rock. Descending, the road snakes back and forth across the mountain. At every bend the views seem to get better and better, until you're zig-zagging through narrow cuts in the vertical rock walls.

Dining and Lodging

$$$ ✕🖻 **Rozenhof Country Lodge.** In a restored Victorian farmhouse looking out at the Swartberg mountains, this lovely guest house is by far your best choice in Oudtshoorn. Antiques and works by South African artists complement the house's yellowwood beams and Spanish-tile floor. Rooms, in white cottages arranged around a central lawn and fountain, are bright and elegant, warmed by old-fashioned brass bedsteads and satinwood furniture. The restaurant serves an excellent five-course dinner, with an emphasis on regional cuisine given a *cordon bleu* twist. Look for such dishes as butternut soup enlivened with cream and nutmeg, phyllo parcels of mackerel, and ostrich paupiettes with port sauce. Nonguests can reserve a table if space allows. ⊠ *264 Baron van Reede St., Box 1190, Oudtshoorn 6620,* ☎ *044/272–2232,* 𝐅𝐀𝐗 *044/272–3021. 12 rooms with bath. Restaurant, bar, room service, pool. Breakfast included. AE, DC, MC, V.*

$$–$$$ ✕🖻 **Altes Landhaus.** Near Oudtshoorn in the tranquil Schoemanshoek Valley, Heinz and Helen Meyer welcome you to their working ostrich farm and old Cape Dutch farmstead. It is beautifully renovated and filled with authentic antiques; in three of the bedrooms, you'll enjoy authentic, but modernized Victorian baths and showers. The food is satisfying: breakfasts are large and homey, dinner is country cooking at its best, and there's a superb wine selection. Breakfast is included in the rate, other meals are extra. A unique touch is the saltwater swimming pool. ⊠ *Altes Landhaus, Box 1491, Oudtshoorn 6620,* ☎ *044/272–6112,* 𝐅𝐀𝐗 *044/279–2652. 3 rooms with bath; 1 room with shower; 1 suite with bath; 1 cottage with bath. Saltwater pool. DC, MC, V.*

Prince Albert

❻ *45 km (28 mi) northeast of Oudtshoorn.*

Prince Albert is a town time forgot, a classic Karoo town in the shadow of the Swartberg. It has retained some excellent examples of 19th-century architecture, and most of the homes have the corrugated-iron roofs and *stoeps* (porches) so typical of the Karoo. The town offers plenty of small hotels and bed-and-breakfasts, but there's nothing to keep you long except the chance to hike in the mountains or do nothing at all.

Prince Albert to George

❼ A good way back to Oudtshoorn is through the **Meiringspoort** via De Rust. The road runs along the bottom of a deep gorge created by the Groot River. It doesn't have the panoramic views of Swartberg Pass, but it's still incredible. The road leapfrogs the river 26 times as it cuts through the red cliffs of the gorge. Halfway through the Meiringspoort is a rest area from which a path leads to a 200-ft waterfall.

❽ From Oudtshoorn, take the R29 to George by way of **Outeniqua Pass,** yet another of the stunning passes that cuts through the region's moun-
❾ tains. A more historic route leads you over **Montagu Pass,** a narrow gravel road that has excellent views and some great picnic sites. The road was built in 1843 by Henry Fancourt White, and the old toll house still sits at the bottom of the pass. To get to the head of the pass, turn left onto the R62 at its junction with the R29.

George

❿ *45 km (28 mi) northeast of Mossel Bay and 50 km (31 mi) southeast of Oudtshoorn.*

George is the largest town and de facto capital of the Garden Route, but you won't find much to keep you here. The city lies 11 km (7 mi) from the sea and makes its money from timber rather than tourism. It's a pleasant place though, tucked beneath the peaks of the Outeniqua Mountains and graced with plenty of parks and gardens. Named after King George III, the city was laid out in 1811 as a base for logging operations in the surrounding forests.

The **George Museum** has extensive displays on the timber industry of the southern Cape, but it's most interesting for its collection of memorabilia associated with P. W. Botha, who served as prime minister from 1978 to 1989. Botha was the last of the hard-line Nationalist leaders, and the museum takes an unapologetic look at his rule during the country's darkest years. Displays include an AK47 rifle carved from ivory and presented to Botha as a gift by Jonas Savimbi, leader of the Angolan rebel movement, UNITA. It's believed that much of UNITA's military campaign was financed by the slaughter of Angola's elephant herds. ⊠ *Courtenay St.,* ☎ *044/873–5343.* ▣ *50¢.* ☉ *Weekdays 9–4:30, Sat. 9–12:30.*

A block down York Street from the museum is **St. Mark's Cathedral** (⊠ York and Cathedral Sts., no phone), a tiny Anglican church that gives George its city status. Consecrated in 1850, the stone cathedral is notable for its interesting memorials and large number of stained-glass windows.

Follow Courtenay Street back onto the N2. The road descends steeply to the sea through a heavily forested gorge formed by the Kaaiman's River. Look to your right to see a curved railway bridge spanning the river's mouth. This is one of the most photographed scenes on the Garden Route, especially when the Outeniqua Choo-Tjoe puffs by (☞ Getting Around *in* Garden Route A to Z, *below*). As the road rounds the point, a breathtaking view of mile upon mile of pounding surf and golden beaches unfolds before you.

Dining and Lodging

$$ ✕ **Copper Pot.** Pink walls, candlelit tables, and dark floral drapes set the tone for this elegant restaurant. The specialty is seafood, competently prepared—although many of the dishes could benefit from additional seasoning. An excellent starter is tender calamari sautéed in butter, lemon juice, garlic, and parsley. Other appetizers include spring rolls in phyllo pastry, smoked ostrich, and oysters. For the main course, choose from fish of the day, Mossel Bay sole, or a mild Mauritian curry of mussels, shrimp, calamari, and fish. ⊠ *12 Montagu St., Blanco, George 6530,* ☎ *044/870–7378. Reservations essential in season. AE, DC, MC, V. Closed Sun. May–September. No lunch weekends.*

$$$$ ✕▥ **Fancourt Hotel and Country Club Estate.** In the shadows of the Outeniqua Mountains, this luxury resort hotel has a country club feel—anyone who doesn't play golf may feel out of place. The showpiece is a 27-hole golf course, open to members and guests only, designed by Gary Player. At the heart of the hotel is an 1860 manor house, now occupied in part by an expensive restaurant. Elegant rooms are located either in the old manor house itself or in white villas scattered around the huge complex. ⊠ *Montagu St., Box 2266, George 6530,* ☎ *044/ 870–8282,* ⊞ *044/870–7605. 88 units with bath. 4 restaurants, 3 bars, 3 pools, 27-hole golf course, fitness center. Breakfast included. AE, DC, MC, V.*

$$$ ✕▥ **Bramble Lodge.** This elegant and gracious country house set in scenic farmlands has views of the Outeniqua Mountains and overlooks Fancourt Country Club. You'll have the choice of six luxurious and individually designed bedrooms. This small lodge has acquired a reputation for its very good small restaurant and guests will be delighted with the comprehensive wine list. You can prearrange to include dinner in your rate. ⊠ *Box 7221, Blanco 6531,* ☎ *044/870–8541,* ⊞ *044/ 870–8542. 6 rooms with bath. Restaurant, bar. AE, DC, MC, V.*

$$$ ▥ **Hoogekraal.** About 16 km (10 mi) outside George, this historic farm sits on a grassy hill with panoramic views of the Outeniqua Mountains and the Indian Ocean. The farm has been in the same family since the early 18th century, and the lodge is filled with antiques and precious heirlooms. Suites in the original 1760 wing have timber ceilings and antique country armoires and dressers. Other rooms are in a house dating back to 1820. Breakfast is included, and most guests choose to stay for the four-course dinner as well, served at a communal table in the magnificent dining room (*$$$$*, wine included). ⊠ *Glentana Rd., off N2 between George and Mossel Bay, Box 34, George 6530,* ☎ *044/ 879–1277,* ⊞ *044/879–1300. 4 rooms and 3 suites with bath. Restaurant. No children under 13. MC, V.*

Golf

The two best courses along the Garden Route are in George. Unfortunately, you have to stay at the **Fancourt Hotel and Country Club Estate** (☞ Dining and Lodging, *above*) to play its magnificent 36-hole, Gary Player–designed course. The same policy does not apply, however, at the 18-hole **George Golf Course** (☎ 044/873–6116).

Wilderness

⑪ *12 km (7 mi) southeast of George.*

Wilderness is a popular holiday resort for good reason. Backed by thickly forested hills and cliffs, the tiny town presides over a magical stretch of beach between the Kaaiman's and Touw rivers. These rivers constitute the western end of a whole system of beautiful waterways, lakes, and lagoons strung out along the coast, separated from the sea by towering overgrown dunes.

⑫ Much of the area now falls under the control of **Wilderness National Park,** a 6,500-acre reserve that stretches east along the coast for 31 km (19 mi). It's a wetlands paradise and draws birders from all over the country to its two bird hides. Walking trails wend through the park, including the circular 10 km (6 mi) Pied Kingfisher Trail, which covers the best of what Wilderness has to offer: beach, lagoon, marshes, and river. You can rent canoes (R10 for two) to explore the lagoon and channels. ⊠ *Off N2, Wilderness,* ☎ *044/877–1197.* ☟ *R8 per person.* ☉ *Daily 8–5.*

From Wilderness, the highway runs along a high ridge of vegetated dunes, with occasional glimpses of the ocean on your right and a string of lakes on your left. As beautiful as it is, the view from the road pales in comparison with the scenery down by the beach. It would be sheer folly to experience the Garden Route from the highway alone—at the end, you may wonder what all the fuss is about. Instead, take the time to follow some of the small roads (some of them dirt) that lead down to the shore. Road signs mark the turnoffs to beaches that are invariably
⑬ spectacular. One of the best is the beach separating the **Goukamma Nature Reserve** from the **Goukamma Marine Nature Reserve.** Backed by steep hills covered with dense bush, it's deserted except for a few fishermen. To get here, turn off the N2 at the Lake Pleasant and Groenvlei exit, drive past the Lake Pleasant Hotel, and follow the dirt road for 3.2 km (2 mi).

Dining and Lodging

\$\$\$ ✕▥ **Karos Wilderness Hotel.** Set amid attractive lawns and gardens, this huge resort hotel is just minutes from Wilderness Beach and the bird-rich Touws River lagoon. The hotel is especially popular with families for the wide range of outdoor activities available, including tennis, minigolf, and swimming. The hotel lacks a beach feel, however, and unless you look outside you could be in any luxury chain hotel anywhere. Rooms have been recently renovated and are conventional but comfortable, with plenty of blond wood and bold floral fabrics. The hotel's dinner buffet is one of the best you'll find along the coast. ⊠ *Off N2, Box 6, Wilderness 6560,* ☎ *044/877–1110,* 䘏 *044/877–0600. 158 rooms with bath. Restaurant, 2 bars, room service, 3 pools, sauna, 2 tennis courts, bowling, squash, bicycles. AE, DC, MC, V.*

\$\$\$ ✕▥ **Lake Pleasant Hotel.** This three-star hotel sits on the edge of a beautiful lake in the Goukamma Nature Reserve, and will appeal to anyone who wants to commune with nature. At the heart of the hotel stands a century-old hunting lodge, but today you can only watch the 200 species of birds that live in the area. All rooms have lake views, the best being the executive suites with large glass doors that open onto lawns spreading down to the water. By contrast, the standard suites feel bland and empty. The hotel is open to nonguests for pub lunches and Sunday lunch buffets, but the table d'hôte dinner is reserved for guests only. ⊠ *Off N2, Box 2, Sedgefield 6573,* ☎ *04455/3–1313,* 䘏 *04455/3–2040. 25 rooms with bath. Restaurant, bar, pool, boating, fishing. Breakfast included. No children under 6. AE, DC, MC, V.*

\$ ▥ **Wilderness National Park.** Wilderness Restcamp is the larger of two self-catering camps, offering a selection of four-bed log cabins and six-bed cottages. From the verandas of the log cabins, which are built on stilts, there are lovely views of the reeds and marshes of the Serpentine Channel, and the cabin interior is pleasantly decorated with cane furniture. The cottages, on the other hand, have no appeal, filled with old furniture and grotty carpets. The Ebb and Flow Restcamp, overlooking the river, is much more rustic, consisting of two-bed rondawels (round huts modeled after traditional African dwellings) without their own bathrooms; cooking facilities are limited to a fridge and a hot plate. ⊠ *Off N2, Wilderness,* ☏ *044/877–1197,* FAX *044/877–0111. Reservations: Box 787, Pretoria 0001,* ☏ *012/343–1991,* FAX *012/343–0905. 10 log cabins, 13 cottages, and 15 rondawels. AE, DC, MC, V.*

Knysna

⑭ *40 km (25 mi) east of Wilderness.*

Knysna is the most popular destination on the Garden Route. The focus of the town is the beautiful Knysna Lagoon, ringed by forested hills dotted with vacation homes. Towering buttresses of rock, known as the Heads, guard the entrance to the lagoon, funneling the ocean through a narrow channel. The sea approach is so hazardous that Knysna never developed into a major port, like Durban. Today, Knysna is very much a resort town, with a quaint charm that the Garden Route's other major drawing card, Plettenberg Bay, lacks (☞ *below*). However, that charm is being threatened by burgeoning development that is totally changing the character of this erstwhile sleepy and attractive resort. In season, traffic is a problem and the once unspoilt lakeside and surrounding area is being covered with not always aesthetic building developments. Walking is the best way to get around the town center, which is filled with arts-and-crafts shops, galleries, restaurants, and coffeehouses.

Not surprisingly, the town has become popular as a base for exploring the rest of the Garden Route. The only drawback is that the closest beaches are 20 minutes away by car—if you want a traditional beach holiday, you're probably better off in Plettenberg Bay. Whatever you do, don't leave town without trying some of Knysna's renowned oysters, harvested fresh from the enormous beds in the lagoon.

Besides tourism and oysters, Knysna makes its living from timber. Logging started in the hills in the early 19th century, when settlers harvested the ancient forests of stinkwood and yellowwood. Much of the indigenous forest has now been cleared and replanted with exotic pine and eucalyptus. Habitat loss is largely responsible for the decline of the famous Knysna elephants that still roam wild in the hills above the town. In 1876, as many as 500 elephants lived in the thick forests behind Knysna. Today, only seven remain, and they are seldom seen by anyone except forestry employees. Several walking trails and drives wind through Knysna's forests, many offering tremendous views back over the ocean. Even if you don't see elephants, you're likely to spot the Knysna lourie, a brilliantly plumed forest bird that is a common sight around town. Detailed maps of trails and forestry roads are available from the Knysna Publicity Association (☞ Contacts and Resources *in* Garden Route A to Z, *below*).

You can get a feel for the growth of the town and its industries at the **Knysna Museum,** a complex of minor museums housed in the Old Gaol, a structure that dates back to 1859. **The Maritime Museum** displays some interesting pictures of old sailing schooners entering the Knysna Heads, as well as trophies from the famous Cape Town–Rio yacht race. The highlight of the **Angling Museum** (▣ R2) is a 176-pound coelacanth, a prehistoric fish that was thought to have become extinct 65 million years ago; in 1938, however, a South African fisherman landed a specimen that was very much alive. **The Knysna Art Gallery,** also in the Old Gaol, is an unattractive exhibition space where local artists display their works. ⊠ *Queen and Main Sts.,* ☎ *0445/82–6138.* ⊠ *Free.* ⊙ *Weekdays 9:30–12:30 and 1:30–4:30, Sat. 9:30–1.*

The most interesting building in the area stands across the lagoon from Knysna, in the exclusive community of Belvidere. **Holy Trinity Church,** built in 1855 of local stone, is a lovely replica of a Norman church of the 11th century. Holy Trinity was erected by Thomas Duthie, a young ensign of the 72nd Highland Regiment who settled in Knysna in 1834. The interior is notable for its beautiful stinkwood and yellowwood timber and stained-glass windows. To reach the church, follow the N2 west out of Knysna and take the Belvidere turnoff just after the bridge. Follow signs from there.

NEED A BREAK?

If you do visit Belvidere, be sure to stop at **Crabs Creek** (⊠ Belvidere Rd., ☎ 0445/87–1043), a fun tavern that sits on the bank of the Knysna Lagoon. On a sunny day you may have to wait for an outside table, but it's worth it—the view across the water to Knysna is better than the food. Fried seafood is the focus—the pint of prawns is very popular—or you can order the usual pub fare.

You can't come to Knysna without making a trip out to the **Heads** at the mouth of the lagoon. These rock sentinels guard the narrow approach to the town and provide great views of both the sea and the lagoon. Only the developed, eastern side of the Heads is accessible by car, via George Rex Drive off the N2. You have two options: to park at the base of the head and follow the walking trails that snake around the rocky cliffs, just feet above the crashing surf; or to drive to the summit, with its panoramic views and easy parking.

Unlike its eastern counterpart, the western side of the Heads is completely unspoiled and part of **Featherbed Nature Reserve,** a private park that has been declared a National Heritage Site. In addition to a bizarre rock arch and a cave once inhabited by the indigenous Khoikhoi, the reserve is home to various small mammals, over 100 species of birds, and 1,000 plant species. It's well worth a visit. To get here, take one of the ferries that departs from the municipal jetty (☞ Guided Tours *in* Garden Route A to Z, *below*).

Six and a half kilometers (4 mi) east of Knysna along the N2 is the turnoff to Noetzie, a tiny holiday community with a difference. If you thought the presence of a Norman church in Belvidere was odd, then ⑮ brace yourself for the **Noetzie Castles,** vacation homes built to resemble European castles, crenellations and all. The castles are more a curiosity than anything else—evidence of people with more money than taste. From the parking lot, it's a steep hike down a hill to reach them, but it's worth the trek just to enjoy the magnificent beach.

⑯ **Brackenhill Waterfall** lies 5 km (3 mi) east of the Noetzie turnoff along the N2. A dirt road leads through a plantation of enormous eucalyptus trees to the falls, which plunge into a highsided gorge overgrown with indigenous forest. Picnic tables make this a good spot for lunch or a snack.

If you're not planning on hiking anywhere along the Garden Route, ⑰ consider a stop at the **Garden of Eden,** a small grove of indigenous trees next to the highway 5 km (3 mi) east of Brackenhill. Despite the traffic noise, the grove gives you a feel for the coastal forests that once blanketed the region. Short walking trails wind past towering Outeniqua yellowwoods, Cape plane trees, and Cape forest ferns. ⊠ *Off N2, no phone.* ⊠ *R2.* ⊙ *Sunrise–sunset.*

Dining and Lodging

$$ ✕ **La Loerie.** Run by a husband-and-wife team, this tiny restaurant serves some of the best fish on the Garden Route. No dinner in Knysna would be complete without fresh oysters from the lagoon. Beyond those, choose among starters like calamari rings, smoked salmon trout, or mussels. For the main course, you can't beat the sole meunière, pan-fried to perfection. If you don't want seafood, consider ostrich fillet in mushrooms or curried lamb. Amarula truffles are a heavenly final touch. Phone after 5:30 for reservations. ⊠ *57 Main St.,* ☎ *0445/2–1616. Reservations essential. DC, MC, V. Closed Sun. No lunch.*

$ ✕ **Knysna Oyster Company.** If you love oysters, make a beeline for this
★ tasting tavern, attached to one of the world's largest oyster-farming operations. Diners sit at picnic tables next to the lagoon, with great views of the Heads. Each tasting consists of 6–8 fresh oysters and a basket of brown bread. It's worth ordering a plate of mussels, too, to dunk your bread in the garlic-lemon butter. Chase the oysters with excellent local Mitchells beer—then do it all again. It's easy to spend an entire day like this. ⊠ *Long St., Thesens Island,* ☎ *0445/82–6942. Reservations not accepted. DC, MC, V.* ☉ *Mon.–Thurs. 8–5, Fri. 8–4, weekends 9–3.*

$ ✕ **Pink Umbrella.** On a sunny day, this is a great place for an alfresco lunch (and keep in mind that it closes every day at 5 PM). Chef June David serves only vegetarian and seafood dishes, but her food is good enough to keep even big meat-eaters happy. Her nutty dal topped with sweet chutney sauce is excellent, as is the corn and herb pie. Seafood dishes include a daily special and Mossel Bay sole. For many regulars the first courses are just a warm-up for the restaurant's desserts, huge concoctions guaranteed to add inches to any waistline. ⊠ *14 Kingsway, Leisure Island,* ☎ *0445/22409. Reservations essential. MC, V.*

$$$$ ✕⌂ **Belvidere Manor.** This is one of the most attractive and desirable
★ lodgings along the coast. White cottages face each other across a lawn that slopes down to Knysna Lagoon and a boat jetty. On the other side of the lagoon, some 6.5 km (4 mi) away, lies Knysna itself. Cottages are airy and bright, with a country feel. Choose from one and two-bedroom units, all with dining areas, sitting rooms with fireplaces, and fully equipped kitchens. The manor house, a lovely 1834 farmstead, has been converted into a restaurant and guest lounge. In summer, breakfast is served on a wooden deck looking over the lagoon. Sizable discounts are offered for long stays. ⊠ *Lower Duthie Dr., Belvidere Estate, Box 1195, Knysna 6570,* ☎ *0445/387–1055,* 𝖥𝖠𝖷 *0445/387–1059. 33 cottages with bath. Restaurant, room service, pool. Breakfast included. No children under 10. AE, DC, MC, V.*

$$$$ ⌂ **St. James of Knysna.** This elegant getaway is right on the edge of
★ Knysna Lagoon. A garden with tranquil koi pools and a magnificent aviary show off the plentiful bird-life of the area. Indoors, the decor emulates a posh club. Large suites are exquisitely furnished with white linen and pieces made with native woods. Each suite has a grand four-poster bed, a spacious and well-equipped bathroom, and a lounge, as well as uninterrupted views of the lagoon. Activities include boating picnics, sundown cruises, scuba diving, and waterskiing. ⊠ *The Point, Main Rd., Box 1242, Knysna 6570.* ☎ *0445/826–750,* 𝖥𝖠𝖷 *0445/826–756. 10 suites. Restaurant, bar, 2 pools, tennis court, croquet, fishing, billiards.*

$$$ ⌂ **Point Lodge.** This small bed-and-breakfast possesses an enviable site on a point jutting into Knysna Lagoon. The view from the pool deck and five of the rooms encompasses bird-rich wetlands, the lagoon, and the distant Heads. Rooms are decorated in Biggie Best style, South

Africa's equivalent of Laura Ashley—lots of floral and striped fabrics. In the evening, guests usually meet for drinks in the lounge and bar. ⊠ *Off N2, Box 767, Knysna 6570,* ☎ *0445/2–1944,* 🖷 *0445/2–3455. 7 rooms with bath. Bar, pool. Breakfast included. No children under 15. AE, DC, MC, V.*

$$$ 🏨 **Portland Manor.** This charming, historic stone manor may be
★ Knysna's best kept secret. It was built in 1864 in a vast estate of orchards, game park, and indigenous forests. It's beautiful antique furnishings are made of the area's yellowwood and stinkwood. Each bedroom is individually designed: the Sun and Field is done in shades of yellow, the Royal Beecham has a more formal decor. The atmosphere is leisurely and relaxed, and, weather permitting, you can breakfast on the patio overlooking a lagoon, a small game camp, and the Outeniqua mountains. Activities nearby are horseback riding, game walking, fishing, and boating. Candlelight dinners with home-style meals are pleasurable affairs, and cold winter nights are warmed by blazing log fires. ⊠ *Rheenendal Rd. between Knysna and Sedgefield, Box 2463, Knysna 6570,* ☎ *0445/4804,* 🖷 *0445/4863. 6 rooms, 4 with bath, 1 suite. Restaurant, bar, pool. Breakfast included. AE, DC, MC, V.*

$$ 🏨 **Wayside Inn.** This hotel in the center of Knysna is absolutely charm-
★ ing. The owners have achieved a colonial African feel through the use of black wrought-iron bedsteads topped with white cotton duvets, pale yellow walls hung with African art, overhead fans, and wall-to-wall sisal matting. All rooms have TVs and phones. Continental breakfasts are served in the rooms on white wicker trays, and picnic hampers are available for lunch. ⊠ *Pledge Sq., 48 Main Rd., Box 2369, Knysna 6570,* ☎ 🖷 *0445/82–6011. 15 rooms with bath. Breakfast included. AE, DC, MC, V.*

Fishing

In Knysna, **Kelsea Fishing Charters** (☎ 0445/825–577) offers deep-sea fishing trips in an 8-meter (26-ft) ski boat. The emphasis is on bottom-fishing for reef fish like steenbras, stumpnose, red roman, and cob. Bait and tackle are supplied.

Plettenberg Bay

18 *32 km (20 mi) east of Knysna.*

Plettenberg Bay is South Africa's premier beach resort. It attracts large numbers of the BMW crowd from the northern suburbs of Johannesburg—people who dress up for the beach and call each other "doll." Not surprisingly, hotels are expensive, and the place gets packed during school holidays. The town itself, sprawled across the side of a steep hill above the sea, can't compare with charming Knysna, but the beaches and views will astonish you. "Plet," as it is commonly known, presides over a stretch of coastline that has inspired rave reviews since the Portuguese first set eyes on it in 1497. Golden beaches beckon as far as the eye can see, curving round to form what the Portuguese called "Bahia Formosa" (Beautiful Bay). Three rivers debouch into the sea here, the most spectacular of which—the Keurbooms—backs up to form a large lagoon. For swimming, surfing, sailing, hiking, and fishing, you can't do much better than Plet, although the water is still colder than it is around Durban and in northern KwaZulu-Natal (☞ Chapter 7).

Whales and dolphins make frequent visits to the bay, and the **Robberg Peninsula,** a rocky spit that juts out into the sea, is a tremendous spot from which to watch whales and dolphins. Three circular walking trails, ranging in length from 45 minutes to four hours, run along the escarpment and through large areas of fynbos. The vegetation offers little shade, so think twice about venturing out here in midsummer.

From Plet take the N2 east. The road runs across a flat, coastal plain of fynbos, with the forested Tsitsikamma Mountains on your left. Just after the Crags, turn off the N2 onto the R102, a far more interesting and scenic route. The R102 passes through farmland before dropping suddenly to sea level through a steep gorge. It's a great descent, with the road worming back and forth through a tunnel of greenery, impenetrable bush pressing in on either side. At the bottom of the pass, ★ 19 turn right into **Nature's Valley,** a magnificent lagoon hemmed in by bush-cloaked cliffs and hills. Part of the Groot River, the lagoon empties into the sea past a wide, idyllic beach—a popular spot for canoeing and sailboarding. There are toilet and picnic facilities.

From Nature's Valley, the R102 climbs back into the mountains, breasting the Groot River and Bloukrans passes before finally rejoining the N2. It's another 24 km (15 mi) to the turnoff to Tsitsikamma National Park and the mouth of the Storms River.

Dining and Lodging

$$$$ ★ **Hunter's Country House.** Just 10 minutes from town, Hunter's is a sophisticated lodge that easily outshines the more famous and expensive guest lodges of Mpumalanga. It's one of those places you can't bear to leave. Perhaps it's the overwhelming sense of tranquility—of pure country silence that can be so difficult to find—or perhaps it's the setting amid gardens that fall away into a valley of indigenous forest. The heart of the lodge is an old farmstead, a lovely thatched building with low beams and large fireplaces. Guest rooms are in individual thatched white cottages, each with its own fireplace and veranda. Victorian antiques grace the rooms, and claw-foot tubs are the centerpiece of many of the gigantic bathrooms. And service is outstanding. Most guests eat at the hotel's excellent table d'hôte restaurant, which brings a French touch to local South African produce. Reservations are essential for nonguests. ✉ *Off N2, between Plettenberg and Knysna, Box 454, Plettenberg Bay 6600,* ☎ *04457/7818,* FAX *04457/7878. 21 cottages with bath. 2 restaurants, 3 bars, pool. Breakfast included. No children under 12. AE, DC, MC, V.*

$$$$ **Plettenberg.** High on a rocky point in Plettenberg Bay, this luxury hotel commands unbelievable views of Formosa Bay, the Tsitsikamma Mountains, Keurbooms Lagoon, and miles of magnificent beach. Built around an 1860 manor house, the hotel has two distinct parts: a summery, beachside wing and a more formal winter lounge in the old house. Rooms borrow elements from both aspects of the hotel and the result is bright and refreshing: Sponge-painted yellow walls, bold butterfly-motif fabrics, and original paintings by South African artists. Even if you don't stay here, treat yourself to lunch on the hotel terrace. Diners sit under large fabric umbrellas looking out over a pool that seems to extend right into the incredible views. The lunch menu is small, with a selection of salads and sandwiches, as well as a pasta dish and catch of the day. Dinner is a fancier affair, focusing on local meat and seafood. The hotel is a member of the exclusive Relais & Chateaux group. Nonguests must make reservations for dinner. ✉ *Look Out Rocks, Box 719, Plettenberg Bay 6600,* ☎ *04457/3–2030,* FAX *04457/3–2074. 40 rooms with bath. Restaurant, bar, 2 pools. No children under 14. AE, DC, MC, V.*

$$ **Bayview Hotel.** In the center of Plettenberg, this comfortable hotel enjoys good views out over Formosa Bay, particularly from the terrace café and bar. Rooms are decorated with rattan furniture and white walls, but the overall effect is rather spartan. Sea-facing rooms on the lower floors suffer from traffic noise; inner rooms are cheaper, cooler, and quieter, but lack that unbeatable view. All rooms have TVs and air-

conditioning. The beach is a 10-minute walk away. ✉ *Main Rd. and Gibb St., Box 1047, Plettenberg Bay 6600,* ☎ *04457/3–1961,* FAX *04457/3–2059. 35 rooms with bath. Bar, café. Breakfast included. AE, DC, MC, V.*

Horseback Riding
Equitrailing (☎ 04457/9718), 5 km (3 mi) outside Plettenberg, offers various guided horseback rides ranging from 1½ hours to all day, as well as moonlight and champagne rides.

Tsitsikamma National Park

★ ⑳ *56 km (35 mi) east of Plettenbert Bay.*

Tsitsikamma National Park is a narrow belt of coastline extending for 80 km (50 mi) from Oubosstrand to Nature's Valley and beyond. It encompasses some of the most spectacular coastal scenery in the country, including deep gorges, evergreen forests, tidal pools, and long, empty beaches. The best way to see the park is on the five-day Otter Trail, South Africa's most famous hike (☞ Walking and Hiking, *below*). A less strenuous highlight is the Storms River mouth, at the midpoint of the park. The river enters the sea through a narrow channel carved between sheer cliffs. Storms River was aptly named: When gale winds blow, as they often do, the sea flies into a pounding fury, hurling spray onto the rocks and whipping spume high up the cliffs. From the visitor center, a .8 km (½mi) trail descends through the forest (different tree species are all labeled) and over a narrow suspension bridge strung across the river mouth. It's a spectacular walk, a highlight of any trip to the Garden Route. On the other side of the bridge, a steep trail climbs to the top of a bluff overlooking the river and the sea. Other trails, ranging from .8 to 3.2 km (½ to 2 mi), lead either to a cave once inhabited by the Khoikhoi or through the coastal forest. A restaurant with great views of the river and the ocean serves breakfast, lunch, and dinner. ✉ *Off N2,* ☎ *04237/607.* 💲 *R5 per vehicle.* ◷ *Daily 5:30 AM–9:30 PM.*

Dining and Lodging
$ ✕🏠 **Tsitsikamma National Park–Storms River Mouth.** Parks Board lodging seldom gets rave reviews for its charm, but it will be clean and comfortable. An added bonus here is the setting, almost within soaking distance of the pounding surf at the mouth of the Storms River. Choose either a two-bed log cabin or a three-bed oceanette, all with fully equipped kitchens and bathrooms. An à la carte restaurant overlooking the river mouth serves food throughout the day. ✉ *Off N2, near Storms River,* ☎ *042/541–1607. Reservations: Box 787, Pretoria 0001,* ☎ *012/343–1991,* FAX *012/3430905 or National Parks Board, Box 7400, Roggebai 8012* ☎ *021/22–2810. Restaurant. AE, DC, MC, V.*

Walking and Hiking
Otter Trail is the king of South Africa's hiking trails. It runs along the coast from the mouth of Storms River to Nature's Valley, passing rocky cliffs, beaches, fynbos, rivers, and towering indigenous forest. The trail is only 42 km (25 mi) long, but it's billed as a five-day hike to give you time to swim and just hang out. Accommodation is in overnight huts equipped with sleeping bunks, braais (barbecues), and chemical toilets. You must carry in all food and carry out all trash. Only 12 people are allowed on this popular trail per day, making it vital to book at least a year in advance. *Reserve through National Parks Board,* ✉ *Box 787, Pretoria 0001,* ☎ *012/343–1991,* FAX *012/343–0905.*

Port Elizabeth

㉑ *160 km (100 mi) east of Tsitsikamma National Park.*

It's a long, uneventful drive from Storms River to Port Elizabeth, South Africa's fifth largest city and the center of the country's auto industry. When a place bills itself as the "Friendly City," you know it's having a hard time finding a reason for tourists to visit. Indeed, the city has little to hold you long, and most foreign travelers use Port Elizabeth only as an entry or exit point for the Garden Route. The city's beach-front area—its main appeal—is highly developed, both with industrial docklands and kitschy amusement parks. After the splendors of the Garden Route, it can leave a bad taste in your mouth. The old center of the town, however, has some interesting historical buildings, especially around Donkin Reserve and Market Square, with its grand 1858 City Hall.

If you do find yourself in Port Elizabeth for a day, you should head to **㉒** **Addo Elephant National Park,** 50 km (31 mi) to the northeast. This small park covers only 35,900 acres, but it's home to a population of over 200 elephants. The Addo bush is very thick, making it harder to find them than you might think. If and when you do come across them, the elephants are likely to be in herds of as many as 50. The park is also home to small populations of buffalo, kudu, black rhino, and red hartebeest. You can explore Addo in your own vehicle during the day or opt for a guided day or night drive with a game ranger (☎ R40 per person). An à la carte restaurant serves all three meals, and the park's rest camp offers accommodation in fully equipped, efficiency cottages. ⊠ *Access from P.E. via the R335,* ☎ *0464/40–0556. Lodging reservations: Box 787, Pretoria 0001,* ☎ *012/343–1991.* ☎ *R15 per vehicle (free if you stay overnight).* ☉ *Daily 7–7.*

Lodging

$$ 🏨 **Holiday Inn Garden Court–Kings Beach.** Opposite the beach and just five minutes from the airport, this high-rise hotel offers standard rooms, with all the amenities you'd expect from a major hotel chain, including air-conditioning, TVs, and tea- and coffeemakers. Request a sea-facing room on an upper floor—they don't cost any more and the views are great. The Oceanarium and a host of restaurants are within easy walking distance. ⊠ *La Roche Dr., Humewood, Box 13100, Port Elizabeth 6013,* ☎ *041/52–3720,* 🖷 *041/55–5754. 283 rooms with bath. Restaurant, bar, pool. AE, DC, MC, V.*

$ 🏨 **Edward.** The rooms look a bit ratty, but for sheer character and history you can't do better than this grand old hotel on Donkin Reserve in the city center. The building dates back to the turn of the century and retains an Edwardian feel—some of the rooms even have four-poster beds. If modern amenities are important to you, though, you're better off at the Holiday Inn. Most rooms at the Edward have neither air-conditioning nor showers (only bathtubs). ⊠ *Belmont Terr., Box 319, Port Elizabeth 6001,* ☎ *041/56–2056,* 🖷 *041/56–2056. 110 rooms with bath. 2 restaurants, 2 bars, room service. AE, DC, MC, V.*

Shamwari Game Reserve

The extraordinary Shamwari is the only major game lodge in the Eastern Cape, and it makes for an ideal jump-off from a tour of the Garden Route. And when it comes to game-viewing, the great advantage that the Cape has over Mpumalanga or KwaZulu-Natal is the absence of malaria. It's a comparatively new reserve, yet is one of the finest in the country and offers the full Big Five experience. Owner Adrian Gardiner has reintroduced large stocks of game once indigenous to the area and has a proactive black rhino program. Numbers of this endangered and magnificent species have increased only because of Shamwari's perseverance. Don't come here expecting the classic safari lodge experience of East Africa or Mpumalanga. Shamwari's showpiece lodge, an Edwardian mansion, would look right at home in the English countryside, and the reserve's mixed vegetation is about as far from thorn-tree savanna as you can get. But the setting is absolutely magnificent: rolling hills and mountains stretch as far as the eye can see, rived by forested valleys, gorges, and rivers. Shamwari has four lodges, including two smaller, inexpensive self-catering options. The reserve is an hour's drive northeast of Port Elizabeth on the Bushman's River. If you're traveling from Johannesburg, you could take the reserve's Shamwari Express, a beautifully refurbished version of a safari train, which delivers you right to Shamwari.

For a general introduction to wildlife-viewing, *see* the Big Game Adventures portrait *in* Chapter 11. Prices here range from R1,250 to R1,850 per person, per night, including all meals and activities, and vary according to the lodging you select. ✉ *Shamwari, Box 32017, Summerstrand, Port Elizabeth 6019,* ☎ *042/851–1196,* 𝔽𝔸𝕏 *042:851–1224. No children under 12 without prior arrangement. AE, DC, MC, V.*

Shamwari is marked on the South Africa map at the front of this guide.

Game Experience: The reserve was laid out on reclaimed farmland, and the game-restocking program still continues. Shamwari's lions are kept in a separate enclosure and probably won't be released into the reserve for another couple of years. You will see wonderful elephant here, and the grasslands are thick with game, especially antelope of all species. The park marks the convergence of five different biomes: semi-arid Karoo scrub, eastern grassland, savanna, thick coastal bushveld, and fynbos, a hardy heath that predominates in the Cape. This diversity of habitat translates into a wide diversity of animals, including species such as blesbok and springbok that you won't find in Mpumalanga, as well as 300 species of birds. Shamwari has a white rhino population in addition to the black one, and general game like leopard, buffalo, zebra, wildebeest, and giraffe. No more than 12 vehicles at a time traverse the reserve's 19,760 acres, and you'll never see more than one other Land Rover at a sighting.

$$$$ **Shamwari Lodge.** With its thatch roof, safari decor, and white guest cottages, this rustic, but luxurious lodge comes closest to the kind of accommodations offered by private game reserves in Mpumalanga. Hidden in the cleft of a steep valley, the lodge faces in on a circle of lawns and a swimming pool. Low wood beams, animal paintings, and a mounted buffalo head set the tone of the main lounge; the five luxury guest rooms have wall-to-wall carpeting, under-floor heating, and private patios. *12 guests. Bar, pool, steam room, private airstrip.*

$$$ **Carn Ingly.** Although this restored pioneer cottage also dates back to 1860, it feels more modern than Highfield (☞ *below*) and lacks the time-worn charm of that structure. Situated in the heart of the reserve, it operates on the same block-reservation, self-catering plan, including use of a four-wheel-drive vehicle and ranger (extra cost). Mounted eland heads adorn the walls and a giant fireplace dominates a living room furnished with art-deco sofas. *6 guests. Pool.*

$$$ **Highfield.** Don't be surprised to find rhinos grazing on the lawns of this charming farmhouse dating back to 1860. Overlooking a bush-cloaked valley, the old house now operates as a self-catering lodge and must be booked *en bloc* (six guests maximum). The interior is decorated in period style, with lovely antique dressers, old-fashioned bedsteads, and timber floors and ceilings. The cottage has a fully equipped kitchen and is serviced daily. Guests also have a ranger and four-wheel-drive vehicle at their disposal, although game drives do cost extra. Even so, this is one of the best deals in the country. *6 guests. Pool.*

$$$ **Long Lee Manor.** As long as you don't expect roaring campfires and bush living, this pink Edwardian mansion will knock your socks off. Tastefully restored, the elegant manor looks past manicured lawns, fountains, and white balustrades to grassy plains dotted with game. The interior is a rich spectacle of wood paneling, graceful staircases, and original art. Request one of the original en suite bedrooms upstairs, decorated with antique dressers and armoires, four-poster beds, and delicate floral fabrics. Standard rooms in an adjoining wing employ sisal matting, mosquito nets, and painted country wardrobes to create a welcoming, old-fashioned feel. Unlike those of most lodges in South Africa, all rooms have TVs and phones. Long Lee's only drawback is its location, on the very edge of the reserve with a plain view of neighboring farms and buildings. *34 guests. Bar, pool, steam room, tennis, exercise room, private airstrip.*

GARDEN ROUTE A TO Z

Arriving and Departing

By Bus

Both **Intercape Mainliner** (☎ 021/386–4400) and **Translux Express** (☎ 021/405–3333 in Cape Town, ☎ 041/507–3333 in Port Elizabeth) offer regular service along the Garden Route between Cape Town and Port Elizabeth, stopping at all major destinations; Translux buses also call at Oudtshoorn in the Little Karoo. Intercape offers a package known as the Boarding Pass that allows you to buy a single Cape Town–Port Elizabeth ticket but break your journey anywhere along the Garden Route and catch later buses; it costs R40 more than a regular ticket.

By Car

Mossel Bay, at the western end of the Garden Route, lies 384 km (240 mi) from Cape Town along the N2 highway. A trip up the Garden Route is a logical extension of a driving tour of the Overberg (☞ Chapter 4).

By Plane

If you're coming by plane, it's best to fly into either George, at the western end of the Garden Route, or Port Elizabeth, at the eastern end.

The **George Airport** (☎ 044/876–9310), 5 km (3 mi) outside of town, is served by **South African Airways** (☎ 044/876–9000) and **S.A. Express** (☎ 044/873–8448), the commuter branch of S.A.A and **Sabena/Nationwide** (☎ 044/873–8414).

Port Elizabeth Airport (☎ 041/51–2984) is served by **S.A. Express** (☎ 041/50–7111), **Airlink** (☎ 041/51–2311), and **British Airways/Comair** (☎ 080/961–1196). A taxi from the airport to the city center costs about R35.

By Train

Spoornet's **Southern Cross** (☎ 021/405–3871 in Cape Town, ☎ 041/507–2400 in Port Elizabeth) runs from Cape Town to Port Elizabeth on Friday and returns on Sunday, making stops at George and Oudtshoorn. The journey takes nearly 24 hours, and does not enjoy the same glorious views as the Outeniqua Choo-Tjoe (☞ *below*).

Getting Around

By Car

Avis (☎ 044/876–9314), **Budget** (☎ 044/876–9204), and **Imperial** (☎ 044/876–9017) all have car-rental offices at George Airport.

At Port Elizabeth Airport, you'll find rental desks for **Avis** (☎ 041/51–1306), **Budget** (☎ 041/51–2459), and **Imperial** (☎ 041/51–1268).

By Train

A highlight of any trip to the Garden Route is a ride aboard the **Outeniqua Choo-Tjoe** (☎ 044/873–8288 in George, ☎ 0445/21–361 in Knysna), a vintage steam train that runs between Knysna and George, offering stunning views of some of the Garden Route's most famous scenic landmarks. Two trains run in each direction daily, except on Sunday. The one-way trip takes 2½ hours, and advance reservations are advisable. **Sam's Tours** (☎ 0445/2–3522) offers a minibus shuttle service that handles pickups and dropoffs in Knysna and George.

Contacts and Resources

Emergencies

Dial 10111 for the **police**, 10177 for an **ambulance**.

Guided Tours

BOAT TOURS

Featherbed Ferries (☎ 0445/81–0590) runs trips to the Featherbed Nature Reserve, on the Western Head of the Knysna Lagoon. Boats leave from the municipal jetty daily at 10 and noon. Once in the reserve, passengers can follow the Bushbuck Trail, a 2.4 km (1½mi) guided hike through the reserve, and even opt for a fish braai at the reserve's restaurant.

For cruises of Knysna Lagoon, including a trip out to the Heads, contact **John Benn** (☎ 0445/2–1693), **Knysna Lagoon Cruises** (☎ 0445/2–3116) or **Lightley's Holiday Cruisers** (☎ 0445/87–1026). Cruises, which depart from the municipal jetty or the angling club next to the railway station, last about two hours and cost from R50 per person. Drinks and light meals are served.

In Mossel Bay, **Romonza** (☎ 0444/3101) and the **Infanté dom Henrique** (☎ 0444/95-0502), two wooden sailing vessels, offer regular one-hour trips to view the seals at Seal Island, as well as sunset cruises and fishing trips. Seal trips leave from the harbor and cost about R40.

An excellent way to see Wilderness National Park and its bird life is aboard the **Kingfisher Ferry** (✉ Freesia Rock, Freesia Rd., ☎ 044/877–1101), which cruises up the Touw River twice daily. Choose between a four-hour cruise and walk (💳 About R50), which ends at the Touw River Falls, or a simple two-hour cruise (💳 About R30).

NATURE AND ADVENTURE TRIPS

Odyssey Adventures (☎ 041/992–5749), based in Port Elizabeth, has stunning blackwater tubing tours down the Storms River in the Tsitsikamma Forest, an hour west Port Elizabeth.

Paradise Expeditions (☎ 041/55–1977), also in Port Elizabeth, has many hikes from day trips to longer and rents full kits of hiking gear. Graeme Lund leads hikes all over the Eastern Cape and Garden Route, including the Blindekloof in the Groendal Wilderness Area.

Goukamma Adventures (☎ 04455/3–1313), based in Sedgefield, has 3½-hour tours of the Goukamma Nature Reserve in open Land Rovers for a minimum of five people. The tour wends its way amid towering dunes and through coastal fynbos and Knysna Forest. It's particularly popular among birders—more than 250 species have been spotted in the area. Tours depart from the Lake Pleasant Hotel (☞ Wilderness, *above*) and include a short walk on the beach, a picnic lunch, and soft drinks.

Visitor Information

Mossel Bay Marketing Association. ⊠ *Church and Market Sts., Mossel Bay,* ☎ *0444/91–2202.* ⊙ *Weekdays 9–5, weekends 10–4.*

Klein Karoo Marketing Association. ⊠ *Voortrekker St., Oudtshoorn,* ☎ *0443/22–6643.* ⊙ *Weekdays 8–5:30, Sat. 8:30–1.*

George Tourism Information. ⊠ *124 York St., George,* ☎ *044/863–9295.* ⊙ *Weekdays 7:45–4:30, Sat. 9–noon.*

Regional Tourist Information Office. ⊠ *124 York St., George,* ☎ *044/873–6355.* ⊙ *Weekdays 7:45–4:30.*

Knysna Publicity Association. ⊠ *40 Main St., Knysna,* ☎ *0445/82–5510,* FAX *0445/21646.* ⊙ *Weekdays 8:30–5, Sat. 9–12:30.*

Plettenberg Bay/Tsitsikamma Tourist Information. ⊠ *Victoria Cottage, Kloof St., Plettenberg Bay,* ☎ *04457/3–4065,* FAX *04457/3–4066.* ⊙ *Weekdays 8–5, Sat. 8–1.*

Tourism Port Elizabeth. *Donkin St., Port Elizabeth.* ☎ *041/55–8884 or 041/582–1315* ⊙ *Weekdays 8.30–5.*

Port Elizabeth Publicity Association. ⊠ *Donkin Reserve,* ☎ *041/52–1315.* ⊙ *Weekdays 8–4:30.*

Wilderness Eco-tourism Association. ⊠ *Leila's La., Wilderness,* ☎ *044/877–0045.* ⊙ *Mon.–Sat. 8:30–5.*

7 Durban and KwaZulu-Natal

Steamy heat, the heady aroma of spices, and a polyglot of English, Indian, and Zulu give bustling Durban a tropical feel. Some of the country's most popular bathing beaches extend north and south of the city; inland you can tour the battlefields where Boer, Briton, and Zulu struggled for control of the country. The Drakensberg mountains are a breathtaking sanctuary of soaring beauty, crisp air, and phenomenal hiking. In the far north, Hluhluwe-Umfolozi and several private reserves offer a big-game experience rivaling that of the Mpumalanga.

By Andrew
Barbour

Updated by
Sue Derwent
and Tony
Pinchuck

FOR SOUTH AFRICANS, the comparatively small province of KwaZulu-Natal is one of the country's premier holiday areas. Here lie the highest and most beautiful mountains in southern Africa, some of the finest game reserves, and a landscape studded with memorials commemorating the great battles between Briton, Boer, and Zulu. The main draw, though, is the subtropical climate and the warm waters of the Indian Ocean. In fact, the entire 480-km (300-mi) coastline from the Wild Coast in the south to the border with Mozambique is essentially one long beach, attracting hordes of bathers, surfers, and anglers.

Durban, South Africa's third-largest city, is the busiest port in Africa. Its chief appeal to tourists is its long strip of high-rise hotels and popular promenade—known as the Golden Mile—fronting its beaches. To find beaches unmarred by commercial development, you need to travel northeast to Zululand. Much of the coastline here is protected, but this means that there are few decent places to rest your head. One notable exception is Rocktail Bay Lodge, an idyllic getaway in Maputaland, in the far north of the province. With no other buildings for miles, the lodge presides over deserted beaches, towering dunes, and virgin bush, making it a highlight of any visit to South Africa.

But you don't have to go all the way to Maputaland to experience the true African wilderness. Just a couple of hours west of Durban are the Drakensberg mountains, offering tremendous hiking amid some of the country's most spectacular, unspoiled scenery. And three hours northeast of Durban, in Zululand, lies a collection of game parks and nature reserves easily rivaling the Kruger National Park. One of these, Hluhluwe-Umfolozi Game Reserve, is the jewel in the crown of the Natal Parks Board and is responsible for bringing the white rhino back from the brink of extinction. It would be a mistake to visit Hluhluwe (pronounced shloo-*shloo*-ee) without also exploring the nearby St. Lucia Greater Wetland Park, an enormous estuary where crocodiles, hippos, and sharks all share the same waters.

Zululand, the region north of the Tugela River, is the traditional home of the Zulu tribe. In the early 19th century, Zulus established themselves under King Shaka as one of the preeminent military powers in the region. At the Battle of Isandlwana, Zulu *impis* (regiments) inflicted one of the most famous defeats on the British army in history, before being ultimately crushed in 1879. A visit to Zululand would be incomplete without learning something of the Zulus' fascinating culture, and a tour of the old battlefields will enthrall history buffs.

KwaZulu-Natal's two-part moniker is just one of the many changes introduced since the 1994 democratic elections. Previously, the province was known simply as Natal, a name bestowed by explorer Vasco da Gama, who sighted the coastline on Christmas Day, 1497. KwaZulu, "the place of the Zulu," was one of the nominally independent homelands created by the Nationalists (1948–94) to deprive blacks of their South African citizenship. The two are now one.

During the years of white rule, parts of Natal were seen as a bastion of English-speaking South Africans. Its first white settlers—a party of British officers seeking trade with the Zulu in ivory—established themselves in Port Natal (now Durban) in 1824. The colony of Natal was formally annexed by the British in 1843. Cities like Durban and Pietermaritzburg present strong reminders of the colonial past with their Victorian architecture and public monuments. The province's huge Indian population is another reminder of Britain's imperial legacy. In the

1860s the British brought thousands of Indians to South Africa to work as indentured laborers cutting sugarcane, which grows abundantly on the coastal hills. Today, the Indian population of Durban alone numbers 1 million, and they play a major part in the economic and cultural life of the province.

Warning: Visitors to the northern parts of the province, including Zululand, are advised to take antimalarial drugs, particularly during the wet summer months.

Pleasures and Pastimes

Dining

Durban's dining public is fickle by nature, and restaurants tend to change hands fairly often. This means that what is popular today may often be totally out tomorrow. However, there are a couple of old favorites whose food is consistent. Durban does have some superb dining, provided you eat to its strengths. Thanks to its huge Indian population, it has some of the best curry restaurants in the country. Durban's other great strength is its fresh seafood, especially prawns and langoustines, brought down the coast from Mozambique. LM prawns (LM stands for Lourenço Marques, the former Portuguese name for Maputo) are a revered delicacy in South Africa. Served with *peri-peri*—a spicy Portuguese marinade of chiles, olive oil, garlic, and sometimes tomato—they are a real taste sensation.

The growing international interest in Zululand, the battlefields, and the wilderness of the Drakensberg has encouraged the establishment of a number of outstanding restaurants in these areas. Most resorts include dinner and breakfast—a good option if you don't feel like going out after a day of hiking or sightseeing. At the same time, it's well worth the effort to take a short scenic drive to one of the many excellent, tucked-away restaurants, often run by the type of interesting and unusual people drawn to settle in beautiful rural places. Some of these dining spots have additional extras, such as champagne breakfasts as you watch the sun rise from the top of a mountain, or sunset picnic baskets of local cheeses and wines.

For a description of South African culinary terms, *see* Pleasures & Pastimes *in* Chapter 1. For price ranges, *see* Chart 1 *in* On the Road with Fodor's.

Fishing

The Drakensberg and its low-lying areas are not only famous for spectacular scenery; they are also popular with fly-fishermen. The crystal-clear Drakensberg streams are good for trout, and many farmers have stocked their dammed ponds to cater to fly-fishermen. With its long stretch of coastline, saltwater fly-fishing is growing as a sport, and an early morning or an evening on the long, empty beaches of the north coast can provide some wonderfully rewarding fishing. In winter, when huge shoals of sardines pass along the KwaZulu-Natal coast, rock and surf anglers are out following the flocks of sea birds and hoping to catch some of the accompanying game fish. Obtain permits from the Natal Parks Board.

Lodging

Apart from the Royal Hotel, most of Durban's main hotels lie along the Golden Mile, Durban's beachfront. Southern Sun, the giant chain that operates Sun and Holiday Inn hotels in South Africa, has a virtual monopoly on Durban accommodations. On the plus side, you can be assured of decent facilities and clean rooms; the minus is that few Durban hotels have character, and prices tend to be standardized. To

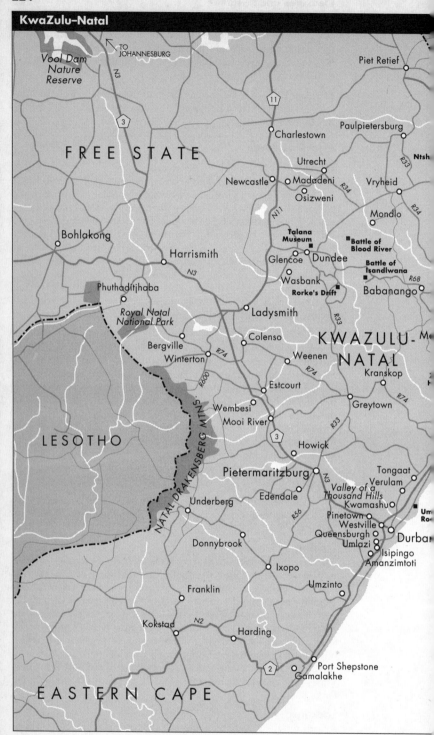

TO JOHANNESBURG

Vool Dam Nature Reserve

N3

3

FREE STATE

11

Charlestown

Piet Retief

Paulpietersburg

Utrecht

Ntsh

Newcastle
Madadeni
Osizweni

Vryheid

R34

R33

N11

Mondlo

Bohlakong

Talana Museum

Battle of Blood River

Harrismith

Glencoe
Dundee

Battle of Isandlwana

N3

Phuthaditjhaba

Wasbank
Rorke's Drift

Babanango

R68

R34

Royal Natal National Park

Ladysmith

KWAZULU-

M

Bergville
Winterton

R74

Colenso

Weenen

NATAL

R74

Kranskop

R600

Estcourt

R33

Greytown

R74

Wembesi
Mooi River

LESOTHO

Howick

Tongaat
Verulam

NATAL DRAKENSBERG MTNS

3

Pietermaritzburg

N3

Valley of a Thousand Hills

Kwamashu

Um Ro

Underberg

Edendale

R56

Pinetown
Westville
Queensburgh
Umlazi

Durban

Donnybrook

Isipingo
Amanzimtoti

Ixopo

Umzinto

Franklin

Kokstad

N2

Harding

Port Shepstone
Gamalakhe

2

EASTERN CAPE

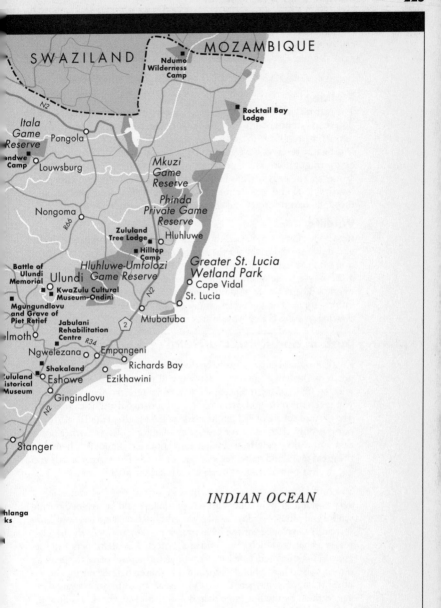

SWAZILAND

MOZAMBIQUE

Ndumo
Wilderness
Camp

N2

Rocktail Bay
Lodge

*Itala
Game
Reserve*

Pongola

ndwe
Camp

Louwsburg

*Mkuzi
Game
Reserve*

R66

Nongoma

*Phinda
Private Game
Reserve*

Zululand
Tree Lodge

Hluhluwe

Hilltop
Camp

Battle of
Ulundi
Memorial

*Hluhluwe–Umfolozi
Game Reserve*

Ulundi

KwaZulu Cultural
Museum–Ondini

*Greater St. Lucia
Wetland Park*

Cape Vidal

St. Lucia

Mgungundlovu
and Grave of
Piet Retief

N2

Jabulani
Rehabilitation
Centre

Imoth

R34

Mtubatuba

2

Ngwelezana

Empangeni

Richards Bay

Shakaland

Ezikhawini

ululand
istorical
Museum

Eshowe

Gingindlovu

N2

Stanger

INDIAN OCEAN

hlanga
ks

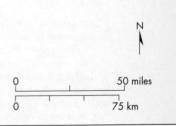

N

| 0 | | 50 miles |

| 0 | | 75 km |

opt instead for surf, sand, and sun, drive a half hour up the coast from Durban to the resort town Umhlanga Rocks. The beaches there are excellent, but just as busy as Durban. Umhlanga (pronounced M-*shlang*-gah) also has a host of decent restaurants, movie theaters, and shops.

For price ranges, *see* Chart 2 (A) *in* On the Road with Fodor's.

Walking

The warm climate and magnificent scenery of KwaZulu-Natal is conducive to just about any outdoor activity you can imagine, and the variety of environments allows for hikes and walks to suit nearly everyone. Most game reserves have guided day walks, if you don't have time for an overnight hike. The landscapes of the Drakensberg wilderness are fantastic. The province has literally hundreds of equally enjoyable, but less dramatic and less strenuous, hikes and walks along beaches and through coastal forests and the area's many nature reserves.

Wildlife

Big Game viewing in KwaZulu-Natal at Hluhluwe-Umfolozi, Phinda, and Itala reserves in the northeastern corner of the province is superb, if not on the scale of Kruger National Park. The experience of seeing a rhino or a pride of lion in their natural environment while walking in one of the few true wilderness areas left—with an armed guide—is unforgettable. For a complete rundown on Southern African wildlife-viewing, *see* Big Game Adventures *in* Chapter 11.

Exploring Durban and KwaZulu-Natal

KwaZulu-Natal can generally be divided into five areas. As you head north of Durban along the coast you will pass through small coastal villages, fields of sugarcane, and commercial forestry plantations until you reach the more industrial towns of Empangeni and Richards Bay. The greatest sphere of Zulu influence extended south to the Tugela River, but it is only after you have crossed the Umfolozi River farther north that you really begin to feel the magic of old Zululand; it is here that the great Zululand game reserves are situated. The farther north you go, the less populated and more traditional the area becomes.

South of Durban, the coastal strip is known as the Dolphin coast, a very popular local holiday destination that should be avoided during school and public holidays at all costs. Although the area has been commercially developed for the local tourist market, many of the beaches retain a charm of their own, and are protected by shark nets and lifeguards, making them safe for swimming and a good place to spend an out-of-season beach holiday. Swimming is often banned during the annual sardine season when the area's shark nets are lifted to prevent damage to them by the big game fish, dolphin, and sharks that follow the sardines up the coast. The angling at this time is generally very good.

Moving inland takes you to the Natal Midlands, which you will pass through either to or from the Drakensberg mountain range and the coast. The rolling green hills and lush pastures have given rise to a local joke that the region is not really part of Africa at all but rather a small piece of England. Racehorse stud farms and large dairy farms are found here; the area has also attracted numerous artists, bohemians, and those who make their living from leatherworking, farming herbs, weaving and knitting, making cheeses, and practicing ceramics and fine art. A wonderful way to experience this part of the province is to follow the "Midlands Meander" (a route set up by the local tourism board), which starts outside Pietermaritzburg and takes you around farms and farmstands. You can stop for coffee and cakes or lunch at some of the quaint hotels or restaurants along the way.

In the northwestern part of the province is the dramatic Drakensberg mountain range, a spectacular wilderness national park. Spread along the base of the range are small hotels, restaurants, B&Bs, guest houses, and lodges catering to all tastes. Sharing the lowlands areas on the approach to the Drakensberg are white farmers, some of whose families settled in the area more than a hundred years ago, and a number of sprawling villages and subsistence farms populated by Zulus, many of whom were displaced by the system of forced removals during the apartheid years.

The farther north you go in the province, the more conservative the population, whether traditional Zulu, obstinate Afrikaner, or staunch English-speaking folk. The local towns, dotted among the Zululand battlefields, tend to be a little ugly and dusty during the dry winter months, but this is an area to visit more for its historic than its scenic value, and for its opportunities to meet the salt-of-the-earth, rural people who have made the country what it is.

Great Itineraries

IF YOU HAVE 2 DAYS

Two days doesn't give you much time for an in-depth experience of all this province has to offer, but you can get a good idea of it by basing yourself on the ⚄ **Durban** beachfront on arrival. Take an early morning walk along the Golden Mile to watch the surfers and later wander around the Indian District. Spend the afternoon on a township tour. A 50-minute drive on the N3 the next morning will get you to **Pietermaritzburg,** with its Victorian architecture and maze of small shopping lanes. If you are not in a hurry, take the scenic route through the **Valley of a Thousand Hills** back to Durban.

IF YOU HAVE 5 DAYS

With five days at hand, you can do a round-trip of many of the main places of interest in KwaZulu-Natal. Pick one of two combinations: the **Drakensberg** and **Zululand,** or Zululand and the more northern section, which takes in the coastal strip and some of the northern game parks, such as **Hluhluwe-Umfolozi Game Reserve** and the private lodges around it. If you opt for the mountains, plan a day or two hiking and walking, overnighting in one of the reserves, then head toward the battlefield sites of **Isandlwana, Rorke's Drift,** and the **Talana Museum** at Dundee. Within two or three hours of the battlefields or the Berg (the Drakensberg), you can be in **Durban** and at the coast. Spend at least one day in Durban, wandering around the Indian market and the African Traditional Healers market, or going on a township tour. It will give you a good perspective of urban living, as opposed to the rural areas from which you have just come.

If you decide to head up the north coast, after a day or two in Durban, stop off at **Shakaland** or **Simunye** for a night to get the total Zulu cultural experience. Then continue to **Hluhluwe-Umfolozi Game Reserve, Greater St. Lucia Wetlands Park,** and **Phinda Private Game Reserve,** scheduling at least two days in the area to see some of the big game for which these reserves are well-known. A trip in **Greater St. Lucia Wetlands Park** to see hippo and crocodiles in the wild is another great experience. There is a crocodile farm and education center near by. Again, allow a day for Durban either at the beginning or the end of this part of your trip.

IF YOU HAVE 7 TO 10 DAYS

Don't pass **Durban** by altogether, but once you have spent a day or two, shake off the city and head up to **Hluhluwe-Umfolozi Game Reserve** for the incredible wildlife. A three-day trail in the wilderness of Umfolozi, or a two- or three-day hike or horse ride back in the **Drakensberg mountains** could be a high point in your trip. Although these hikes are not terribly strenuous, you may still prefer something more sedate, in which case the long drive to spend three days at **Rocktail Bay Lodge,** close to the Mozambique border, is every bit worth the effort, particularly during the turtle breeding season from September to March. Diving around the reefs off of **Greater St. Lucia Wetland Park**'s Sodwana Bay is some of the best in the country; inshore snorkeling to see the abundance of colorful little tropical fish is also sensational. Another distant park near the edge of the province is the delightfully less-visited **Itala Game Reserve.** You could encorporate it on a grand loop: Head from Durban to Zululand, through Greater St. Lucia Wetland Park and Hluhluwe-Umfolozi Game Reserve or Phinda Private Game Reserve, then on to Itala, finally turning back toward Durban and driving through the battlefields.

When to Tour Durban and KwaZulu-Natal

The best time to tour KwaZulu-Natal is definitely early autumn through winter and into the spring. Summer can be terribly hot and humid, and some facilities in the Zululand game reserves close because of the extreme and unpleasantly high temperatures in that area. The coast is particularly pleasant during winter, and it is at this time that the Ocean Action festival is held on Durban's Golden Mile. Centering around the world-famous Gunston 500 surfing championships, Ocean Action includes 10 days of exciting outdoor, watersport-related activities, including night surfing. An abundance of market stalls on the promenade are open until late.

Game viewing is better during winter (late June, July, August) when the grass is shorter, many trees have lost their leaves, and the animals tend to congregate around the water holes. Northern parts of the province are dry and dusty during winter, but the frosty mornings and crisp late afternoons make up for it. The cold weather does not deter the thousands of folk-music lovers of all ages who congregate in May every year, for the Splashy-Fen folk-music festival held at Splashy-Fen farm in the Drakensberg; during this four-day celebration, both local and international folk musicians perform.

DURBAN

No city in South Africa feels more African than Durban. Cape Town could be in the Mediterranean, and Johannesburg's endless suburbs could be anywhere in America. Durban alone has the pulse, the look, the complex face of Africa. It may have something to do with the summer heat, a clinging sauna that soaks you with sweat in minutes. You don't need to take a township tour here to see the emerging new South Africa. Hang out in Farewell Square in the city center and rub shoulders with Zulus, Indians, and whites. Wander into the Indian District or drive along Umgeni Road, and the *real* Africa rises up to meet you in a hundred ways: traditional healers touting animal organs, vegetable and spice vendors crowding the sidewalks, and the incessant hooting of minibus taxis trawling for business. It's by turns colorful, stimulating, and hypnotic.

By no means should you plan an entire holiday around Durban because there is so much more to see beyond the city. Nevertheless, it's definitely worth a stopover, perhaps between trips to the Drakensberg mountains or the game reserves in the north. To get the most from a stay in the city, explore the areas where Durban's residents live and work. Be sure to take a drive through the lovely neighborhoods of the Berea or a walk through the vibrant markets of the Indian District.

Durban is a large port city with all the negative baggage that this implies. Don't wander around the Central Business District (CBD) alone at night, and in general be sure to hold onto that expensive camera that you might have slung over your shoulder. Another type of hazard altogether is the school holidays. It's best to avoid Durban and the KwaZulu-Natal coast during summer vacation (mid-December to mid-January), when thousands of vacationers from the inland provinces descend on the beaches to cavort and carouse en masse.

The city breaks down easily into four parts: the city center around Farewell Square; the Indian District; the Durban beachfront; and outlying attractions. Apart from the outlying districts, all four can be followed on foot, but you may need a taxi or car to get between them.

Numbers in the text correspond to numbers in the margin and on the Durban map.

City Center

A Good Walk

This walk takes you past several of Durban's historic buildings. Start at the **Tourist Junction** ①, the city's main tourist information center, on Pine Street. Cross the street to the early 20th-century **St. Paul's Church** ② and follow the pedestrian thoroughfare to West Street. Cross the street to **Farewell Square** ③ in front of the imposing **City Hall** ④, also built in the early 20th century. Walk down the Smith Street side of City Hall to get to the steps up to the **Durban Natural Science Museum** ⑤ inside, and above it the **Durban Art Gallery** ⑥. Directly opposite is the entrance to the Playhouse Theatre, Durban's major cultural center. If you continue the short distance to the end of the Smith Street block, you will reach the **Local History Museum** ⑦. From outside the museum's front entrance on Aliwal Street, turn right and walk toward the bay. Cross the Esplanade, and pass through the walkway under the railway line and you'll reach the **Bartle Arts Trust (BAT) Center** ⑧ on the quayside. Wander around the center's small shops and through the working studios where all sorts of visual and performing artists are at work; you can also get a light bite to eat here while tugs and ships move in and out the harbor. If you end up here in the late afternoon you may catch local jazz musicians playing out on the deck.

TIMING

The center of the city can get horribly humid from December through February, so avoid town and avoid walking too much during the midday heat. This walk would be better to do a little later in the afternoon, having spent the morning on the beach or shopping. Remember to set aside enough time for browsing in the museums and galleries, most of which close at 4:30. A great way to end your afternoon would be on the balcony of the BAT centre, where in the early evenings, you can listen to local jazz musicians playing out on the deck.

Sights to See

★ ⑧ **Bartle Arts Trust (BAT) Centre.** To some, the Bartle Arts Trust Centre seen from across the bay resembles a giant flying bat. The vibrant arts center is always abuzz with Durban's trendy set—artists, musicians, and other hipsters. At any time of the day—and some nights—you can watch sculptors, dancers, musicians, and painters at work, and at night the BAT theater comes alive with plays, music, and African film or video festivals. A coffee bar overlooks the bay, Funkies restaurant has live music, and shops sell bric-a-brac and artwork, including African fabrics and ceramics. ⊠ *45 Maritime Pl., Small Craft Harbour,*☏ *031/332–0468.* ☺ *8:30–4:30.*

230

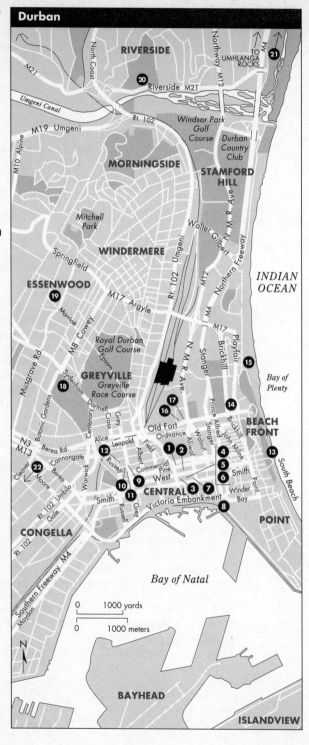

Durban

④ City Hall. Built in 1910 in Edwardian neobaroque style, the hall looks as if it has been shipped straight from London column by column. The main pediment carries sculptures representing Britannia, Unity, and Patriotism, and allegorical sculptures of the Arts, Music, and Literature adorn the exterior. Ask the guard to allow you inside to see the huge theater's ornate molding and grand parterre boxes, or join an official tour run by Durban Unlimited (☞ Guided Tours *in* Durban A to Z, *below*). ✉ *West and Church Sts.* ☎ *031/300–6911* ☉ *Daily 8–4.*

NEED A BREAK?   The **Royal Coffee Shoppe,** in the Royal Hotel, is a popular meeting place for Durban society and pre- and posttheater crowds. Crystal chandeliers, etched glass, and live piano music create a rich atmosphere of old-time Durban. The café serves a selection of coffees, teas, and cakes, as well as quiches, salads, and sandwiches. ✉ *267 Smith St.,* ☎ *031/ 304–0331.* ☉ *Daily 7 AM–11 PM.*

⑥ Durban Art Gallery. The museum features the work of local and international artists. Recent exhibits have included the FNB Vita Craft Now show, staged to highlight the cultural diversity of handicrafts in South Africa. Exhibits change every few months, so call ahead to find out what's being shown. ✉ *City Hall, Smith St. at Church St., 2nd Floor,* ☎ *031/300–6234.* 🎟 *Free.* ☉ *Mon.–Sat. 8:30–4, Sun. 11–4.*

⑤ Durban Natural Science Museum. Despite its small size, this museum provides an excellent introduction to African wildlife, birds, and insects. It's a great place to bring the kids, or to familiarize yourself with the animals before heading up to the game parks in northern KwaZulu-Natal. ✉ *City Hall, Smith St. at Church St.,* ☎ *031/300–6211.* 🎟 *Free.* ☉ *Mon.–Sat. 8:30–4, Sun. 11–4.*

③ Farewell Square. Right in the heart of Durban, the square is a lovely, shady plaza, bordered by some of the city's most historic buildings. Walkways lined with stately palms and flower beds crisscross the square and lead to monuments honoring Natal's important historic figures. The square stands on the site of the first European encampment in Natal, established by Francis Farewell and Henry Fynn in 1824 as a trading station to purchase ivory from the Zulus. A statue representing Peace honors the Durban volunteers who died during the Boer War (1899–1902); the Cenotaph commemorates the South African dead from the two world wars. The square is at its most pleasant in the morning, before office workers throng it during their lunch break. The square is bounded by Smith, West, and Gardiner streets and the Church Street pedestrian mall.

⑦ Local History Museum. Exhibits focus on Natal's colonial past, including a reconstruction of Henry Fynn's original 1824 wattle-and-daub hut, as well as simulated shopfronts of a turn-of-the-century apothecary and department store. The museum is in the old courthouse, built in 1866. During the Zulu War of 1879, when Durban was in danger of attack, the exterior of the building was temporarily provided with loopholes so defenders could fire their rifles from inside. ✉ *Smith and Aliwal Sts.,* ☎ *031/300–6241.* 🎟 *Free.* ☉ *Mon.–Sat. 8:30–4, Sun. 11–4.*

② St. Paul's Church. The current church, built in 1909 in Gothic Revival style, stands on the site of a previous church dating back to 1847. From the outside it's not much to look at, but the interior is beautiful: notice the lovely wood ceiling and the stained-glass chancel windows. ✉ *Church and Smith Sts.* ☎ *031/035–4666.*

① Tourist Junction. As the city's principal tourist information outlet, the office occupies Durban's old railway station, an attractive brick building constructed in 1894 in Flemish Revival style. The "NGR" above the main entrance stands for Natal Government Railways. Durban Unlimited, the city's tourist authority, is found here. ⊠ *160 Pine St., at Soldier's Way,* ☎ *031/304–4934.* ☻ *Weekdays 8–5, weekends 9–2.*

Around the Indian District

A Good Walk

One of the most fascinating parts of Durban is the **Indian District** ⑨. From the **Tourist Junction** walk west up Pine Street or Commercial Road, away from the direction of the beach front. About three or four blocks up, turn right on Grey Street, generally considered to be the heart of the district. A little further along, near the junction of Queen and Grey Streets, is the **Jumah Mosque** ⑩; right next door is the **Madressa Arcade** ⑪. At the corner of Queen and Russell Streets, you'll reach the most hyped part of the Indian District, the bustling **Victoria Street Market** ⑫. At the end of Victoria Street, turn right onto Russell Street past the bustling mini-bus and taxi rank. Under the bridges and along the road's shoulders, you will find the largest and most extensive *muthi* (traditional medicine) market in Southern Africa.

TIMING

The best time of day to do this is in the morning. Set off before just before nine, when it's still relatively cool. This also gives the street sellers time to set up their stalls. Their part of town can be quite grubby, and in the midday summer heat, it can get unpleasantly humid. The walk should take between two and three hours.

Sights to See

★ ❾ **Indian District.** The streets here are thronged with Zulus and Indians, producing an intoxicating mix of Africa and Asia. Narrow doorways lead into fascinating spice shops, and traders touting saris are squeezed in next to traditional herbalists, whose dark stores are hung with wizened claws, animal organs, and roots. Outside on the narrow sidewalks, vendors sell vegetables, hair weaves, and fake Rolexes. Head for Russell Street Extension to see hundreds of Zulu women selling muti, traditional medicines concocted from crushed roots, bark, and other natural products. The entire area is popular with pickpockets, so don't carry a lot of money or jewelry, and keep your valuables in a safe place.

❿ **Jumah Mosque.** Built in 1927 in a style that combines Islamic and colonial features, this is the largest mosque in the Southern Hemisphere. Its colonnaded verandas, gold-domed minaret, and turrets give the surrounding streets much of their character. As long as you take your shoes off, you can go into the mosque through a narrow entrance on Queen Street. Tours can be arranged through Durban Unlimited (☞ Guided Tours *in* Durban A to Z, *below*). ⊠ *Grey and Queen Sts.*

⓫ **Madressa Arcade.** The thoroughfare has a Kiplingesque quality recalling the bazaars of the East. Built in 1927, it's little more than a narrow, winding alley, perfumed by spices and thronged with traders. You can buy everything from plastic trinkets to household utensils and recordings of Indian music here. ⊠ *Entrances on both Queen and Cathedral Sts.*

NEED A
BREAK?
While you're in the Indian District, you should try one of Durban's specialties, the bunny chow at **Patel Vegetarian Refreshment** (⊠ Rama House, 202 Grey St., ☎ 031/306–1774); the dish consists of a hollowed-out loaf of bread filled with bean curry. Another excellent takeout store in the same district is **Angaans** (⊠ 86 Queen St., ☎ 031/307–1366), where you can get a range of both North and South Indian

foods. While waiting for your food to be prepared, ask to go into the kitchen to watch naan breads being baked in the clay oven.

★ ⑫ **Victoria Street Market.** Masses of enormous fish and prawns lie tightly packed on beds of ice, and vendors competing for your attention shout their respective prices. In the meat section, goat and sheep heads are stacked into neat piles, while butchers slice and dice every cut of meat imaginable. The noise is deafening. The place pulsates with life, and even if you have no kitchen in which to cook, it's tough to resist joining the fray. In an adjacent building—where all the tour buses pull up— you'll discover a number of curio shops whose proprietors are willing to bargain over wood and stone carvings, beadwork, and basketry. You'll also find shops selling spices, recordings of African music, and Indian fabrics. The current structures stand on the site of an original, much-loved market, a ramshackle collection of wooden shacks that burned down during the years of Nationalist rule. ⊠ *Queen and Russell Sts.,* ☎ *031/306–4021.* ☉ *Weekdays 6–6, Sat. 6–4:30, Sun. 9–3.*

Durban Beachfront

A Good Walk and Drive

Either you will hate the **Durban Beachfront** for its commercial glitz, or you'll love it for its endless activity; it stretches from South Beach to North Beach and the Bay of Plenty. Since it was turned into a pedestrians-only walkway, Durbanites have taken to this promenade in droves—strolling, jogging, rollerblading, cycling, or just sitting in the sun to watch the surfers and body-boarders. The beachfront is a bit of a hike from the city center; it's best to take a taxi or drive to the end of West Street or Commercial Road. A good place to start your tour is at South Beach's main attraction, **Sea World Durban** ⑬. Walk north along Marine Parade to reach the **Natal Museum of Military History** ⑭. A little further along, almost on the beach itself, is the **Fitzsimons Snake Park** ⑮.

TIMING
Unless you are fond of crowds, avoid the beach-front area on weekends, particularly when the weather is good. However, the beach front is busy most of the day, often even early in the mornings when people come to surf before going to work. Head off early, but try to time your walk so that you visit the Snake Park during feeding times or when there is a demonstation. At a leisurely pace, this walk should take two or three hours.

Sights to See
Durban Beachfront. The Golden Mile, as it is known, extends from South Beach, at the base of Durban Point, all the way to North Beach and the Bay of Plenty. Once past the Bay of Plenty, the shoreline is largely undeveloped and is used mostly by joggers and fishermen. (☞ *Beaches in* Outdoor Activities and Sports, *below*).

⑮ **Fitzsimons Snake Park.** The zoo houses a slithery collection of snakes from around the world. Live snake demonstrations are held in a small amphitheater; on weekends these shows are followed by a feeding. The park is also home to a few Nile crocodiles. ⊠ *Snell Parade,* ☎ *031/ 37–6456.* ▱ *R10.* ☉ *Daily 9–4:30. Snake demonstrations daily at 10, 11:30, 1, 2:30, and 3:30. Crocodile feedings daily at 2.*

⑭ **Natal Museum of Military History.** Housed in a huge warehouse on the beachfront, the museum displays a large collection of weapons and military equipment, much of it dating back to World War II. Exhibits from different periods tend to be jumbled together, but military buffs will get a kick out of climbing about on a U.S. Sherman tank, a French Mirage jet fighter plane, and an enormous helicopter. ⊠ *Snell Parade and Old Fort Rd.,* ☎ *031/332–5305.* ⊡ *R5.* ⊙ *Daily 9–5.*

⑬ Sea World Durban. Attached to the Oceanographic Research Institute, Sea World has an interesting collection of tropical fish, but the tanks holding sharks, sea turtles, and rays are unimpressive. There are daily dolphin and seal shows and shark feedings three times a week. ⊠ *South Beach,* ☎ *031/37–3536.* ⊡ *R25.* ⊙ *Daily 9–9. Dolphin and seal shows at 10, 11:30, 2, 3:30, and 4. Fish feeding daily at 11 and 3:30. Shark feeding Tues., Thurs., and Sun. at 12:30.*

Around Durban

★ ⑲ Campbell Collections. Now administered by the University of Natal, the collections include the Killie Campbell Africana Library, the William Campbell Furniture Museum, and the Mashu Museum of Ethnology. The museum is housed in Muckleneuk, a lovely Cape Dutch-inspired home built in 1914 for Sir Marshall Campbell, a wealthy sugar baron, and his family. The house is furnished much as it was when the Campbells lived here, and contains some excellent pieces of Cape furniture as well as an extensive collection of oil paintings by early settlers. The highlight, however, is the Mashu Museum of Ethnology, which displays perhaps the best collection of traditional beadwork in the country, as well as African utensils, weapons, carvings, masks, pottery, and musical instruments. Paintings of African tribesmen by artist Barbara Tyrrell add vitality to the collection. ⊠ *220 Marriott Rd., at Essenwood Rd. (take Field St. to Epsom Rd., which turns into Marriott),* ☎ *031/207–3432.* ⊡ *Free.* ⊙ *By appointment only.*

⑱ Durban Botanic Gardens. Opposite the Greyville Racecourse, these gardens can't compare with the Kirstenbosch National Botanic Gardens in Cape Town, but they are still a delightful oasis of greenery, interlaced with walking paths, fountains, and ponds. The site is renowned for its orchid house and collection of rare cycads. There is also a garden for the blind and a herb garden featuring many of the medicinal plants used by traditional African healers. The Tea Garden enjoys a sylvan setting far from the city's hustle and bustle. It's a great place to take the weight off your feet and settle back with a cup of hot tea and cakes. ⊠ *Sydenham Rd. (take Ordnance west to the M4, then the m13; turn right on the M8 to the gardens),* ☎ *031/22–3472.* ⊡ *Free.* ⊙ *Apr. 16–Sept. 15, daily 7:30–5:15; Sept. 16–Apr. 15, daily 7:30–5:45.*

★ ㉑ Natal Sharks Board. Durban's shark-research institute is probably the foremost one in the world. Most of the popular bathing beaches in KwaZulu-Natal are protected by shark nets maintained by the institute. Each day, crews in ski boats check the nets and collect any snared sharks. These are then brought back to the institute, dissected, and studied. The Natal Sharks Board offers regular one-hour tours that include a peek into the enormous freezer where shark carcasses are stored, a shark dissection, and a fascinating audiovisual presentation on sharks and shark nets. When you learn the principles on which shark nets work, you may think twice about ever entering the water again. ⊠ *M12, Umhlanga Rocks. Take the M4 (Northern Freeway) out of Durban for 16 km (10 mi) to reach Natal,* ☎ *031/561–1001.* ⊡ *R10.* ⊙ *Tours Tues., Wed., and Thurs. at 9 and 2.*

㉒ NSA Gallery. The National Society of the Arts' gallery complex houses not only a delightfully sophisticated open-air restaurant, but also three exhibition areas, a craft shop, and the Durban Centre for Photography. The center's clean architectural lines and leafy setting make this a popular venue with Durban's trendy set. It's a wonderful place to cool off after a hot morning in town. The gallery and craft shop support and promote local art, so once you have finished your cappuccino and cheesecake, it's worth wandering around the craft shop for tasteful souvenirs. Thursday evening is jazz night and there is always live music on weekends. The restaurant's food is tasty and artistically presented, but the service tends to be slow. ⊠ *166 Bulwer Rd., Glenwood (follow Ordnance Rd. to the M4, then the M13; turn south on the M8, which is first Cleaver Rd. then Bulwer Rd.),* ☎ *031/22–3686.* ⊙ *Tues.–Fri. 9–5; Sat. 9–4, Sun. 10–4, closed Mon.*

16 Old Fort. Opposite Kingsmead Cricket Ground, this is the site of a fortified camp where, in 1842, the 27th Regiment (Inniskilling Fusiliers) survived a Boer siege led by Andries Pretorius. A model of the fort—little more than a laager of wagons and trenches—stands inside the park. In 1858, the encampment was transformed into a proper military post, and served until 1897 as headquarters for successive regiments. Today, the Old Fort is a pleasant, overgrown park with a good collection of cycads. The fort's old magazine has been transformed into a chapel. It is a short drive out Ordnance Rd. to Aliwal Rd; turn right to get to Old Fort Place. ⊠ *Old Fort Rd. and Old Fort Pl., no phone.* ⊡ *Free.* ⊙ *Daily 7–4.30.*

Shree Ambalavaanar Alayam Temple. One of Durban's most spectacular Hindu shrines may be found in Umkumbaan, on the outskirts of town. The temple's facade is adorned with brightly painted representations of the Hindu gods, notably Ganesha, Shiva, and Vishnu. The magnificent doors leading to the cella were salvaged from a temple built in 1875 on the banks of the Umbilo River and subsequently destroyed by floods. During an important Hindu festival held around the same time as Easter, unshod fire-walkers cross beds of burning coals. ⊠ *Bellair Rd., Umkumbaan, no phone. Take M13 (from Leopold St.) out of the city; at major fork in road after Westridge Park and high school, veer left onto Bellair Rd.*

20 Umgeni River Bird Park. Despite the absence of raptors, this park is far bigger and better than the World of Birds near Cape Town. It is built under high cliffs next to the Umgeni River and features three huge walk-through aviaries, as well as a host of smaller, specialized ones. The variety of birds, both exotic and indigenous, is astonishing; the collection of extravagantly plumaged macaws is particularly outstanding. ⊠ *Riverside Rd. Head north out of Durban on Umgeni Rd. and cross the river to reach the park.* ☎ *031/579–4600.* ⊡ *R15.* ⊙ *Daily 9–4:30.*

17 Warrior's Gate and MOTH Museum. Built in 1937, the Warrior's Gate is a monument to those who died protecting their country. It is situated next to the ☞ **Old Fort.** The MOTH (Memorable Order of Tin Hats) Museum houses an interesting collection of weapons, military equipment, and regimental insignia, most dating from World War II. ⊠ *Old Fort Rd. and N.M.R. Ave.,* ☎ *031/307–3337.* ⊡ *Free.* ⊙ *Tues., Fri., and Sun. 11–3; Sat. 10–noon.*

Dining

$$$$ ✕ **Cafe Fish.** Right in the middle of Durban's yacht basin, this elegant restaurant almost floats on the water and has one of the best views in Durban. Starters of calamari or a deep-fried feta salad also make wonderful light lunches; the seafood platter main course is almost too much for one person. A little on the expensive side, the crayfish thermidor is otherwise highly recommended. An elegant upstairs bar opens in the late morning; it's a great place to while away a few hours drinking coffee and watching the yacht-owners at work. Upstairs there's an excellent bar lunch.⊠ *31, The Yacht Mole, Victoria Embankment,*☎ *031/305–5062. Reservations essential. AE, DC, MC, V.*

$$$$ ✕ **Colony.** Specialties in this elegant environment are typical South African game and seafood dishes. Ostrich, nyala, and guineafowl adorn the menu, along with a wide selection of seafood dishes. A favorite local temptation is warthog pie, served in a deep dish under a light, golden crust. Fresh fruit-flavored sorbet makes a refreshing finale to your meal. ⊠ *Windermere and Innes Rds.,* ☎ *031/23–8270. Reservations required. AE, DC, MC, V. Closed Sun. No lunch Sat.*

$$$$ ✕ **Royal Grill.** This restaurant in the Royal Hotel has one of Durban's
★   most grand dining settings. The dining room—all that remains of the original Royal Hotel—has the grace of an earlier age: silver and crystal reflect the light from chandeliers, burnished wood glows from decades of polishing, and a pianist or harpist plays unobtrusively in the background. The food is a nouvelle take on classic French cuisine and is usually (but not always) very fine. Spinach ravioli, served with crayfish medallions in a beurre blanc, is superb, as are sautéed shiitake mushrooms with a balsamic vinaigrette. Fillet of rock cod, sautéed in butter, is also excellent. The dessert trolley displays a selection of gâteaux and puddings; most are heavy on the whipped cream. ⊠ *Royal Hotel, 267 Smith St.,* ☎ *031/304–0331. Jacket and tie. AE, DC, MC, V. No dinner Sun.*

$$$$ ✕ **St. Geran.** Owner Robert Mauvis, who hails from the island of Mauritius, brings a touch of spice to an otherwise French menu at this restaurant in beautiful new premises. The popular menu has few changes. Head straight for calamari in a spicy Creole sauce. For a main course, consider octopus and prawn curry or the excellent *vindaye de poisson,* a mild curry of fresh fish with turmeric and small onions, served alongside black lentils and basmati rice. Grilled lamb and grilled rabbit with garlic and herbs are typical of the meat dishes offered. Crème brûlée is always popular for dessert, but don't overlook the soufflé au Grand Marnier or flambéed bananas. ⊠ *178 Florida Rd., Morningside,* ☎ *031/303–2630. AE, DC, MC, V. Closed Sun. No lunch Sat.*

$$$ ✕ **Eatceteras.** This cozy and eccentric restaurant serves Western-Asian fusion that turns up on Australian menues. The specialty is a Chinese-inspired sizzling platter—raw vegetables quickly sauteed then mixed with a choice of ostrich, chicken, prawns, calamari, or other seafood or meat. Choose a sauce to add, and the whole combination will arrive at your table sizzling. Lighter meals are also on the menu. For dessert, you can order one of the best lemon meringues in town. The sticky toffee dessert is to die for. ⊠ *45 Windermere Rd., Greyville,* ☎ *031/ 303–3078. AE, DC, MC, V.*

$$$ ✕ **The Gulzar.** Named after a traditional Indian musical instrument, this small restaurant serves food worth singing about. For many years most of the Indian food found in Durban was of South Indian origin, having been introduced to the city by the original indentured laborers who came predominantly from southern India. This is one of the few restaurants in town offering both the more subtle tastes of North Indian cuisine along with the more traditional hot southern curries. Southern Indian cuisine is well known for its strong, spicy foods, while Northern Indian cooking in comparison uses more yogurt, lemon juice, and sweeter spices such as cardamom, cumin, and coriander. Many of Durban's Indian elite can be found eating here, which is always a sure sign of a good Indian restaurant. A specialty is *rogan josh*—lamb cooked in an aromatic sauce. The chicken *tikka masala* is always good, and you can't go wrong with anything on the vegetarian menu.

Dining

Baanthai, **6**

Café Fish, **21**

The Colony, **5**

Eatceteras, **8**

Famous Fish Company, **17**

Gulzar, **7**

Pakistani Restaurant, **18**

The Royal Grill, **20**

St. Geran, **19**

Sea Belle's, **3**

Victoria Bar & Restaurant, **16**

Lodging

Beverly Hills Sun, **4**

Breakers Resort, **1**

Cabana Beach, **2**

City Lodge, **11**

The Edward, **14**

Holiday Inn Crowne Plaza, **10**

Holiday Inn Garden Court–Marine Parade, **13**

Holiday Inn Garden Court–North Beach, **9**

Holiday Inn Garden Court–South Beach, **15**

Palace Protea, **12**

Royal Hotel, **20**

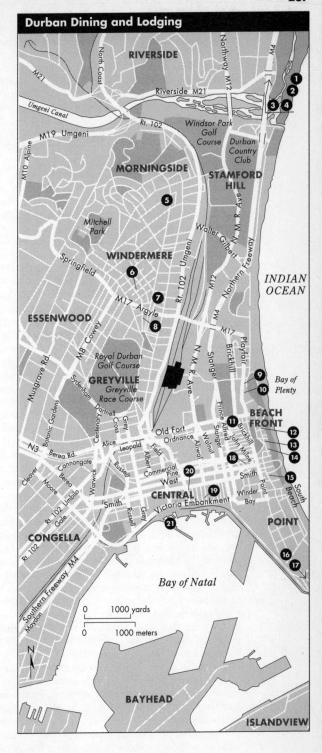

Durban Dining and Lodging

✉ *71 Stamford Hill Rd., Greyville,* ☎ *031/309–6379. AE, DC, MC, V. Closed Mon.*

$$ ✕ **Baanthai.** On the second floor of a converted town house, this Thai restaurant brings a refreshing flavor to Durban's dining scene. Thai chefs, working in an open kitchen, whip up authentic dishes that make heady use of lemongrass, coriander, and *galangal* (a type of ginger). Among the starters, the beef waterfall salad (thinly sliced grilled beef tossed with onions and coriander) is excellent, as are *pad thai* noodles. Other winners are chicken with garlic and pepper and Thai curries made with coconut milk. *Brinjal* (eggplant) with chiles is a delicious vegetarian option. ✉ *138 Florida Rd.,* ☎ *031/303–4270. BYOB. AE, DC, MC, V. Closed Sun.*

$$ ✕ **Famous Fish Company.** The setting of this busy restaurant right at the mouth of the harbor makes up for the mostly ordinary menu and mediocre service. Sitting out on the deck, you can watch the yachts and massive tankers move in and out of the harbor, and at night the spotlights draw dolphins, which come to feed in the harbor's narrow mouth. Downstairs is a lively, sometimes noisy, but friendly pub. A comprehensive selection of shellfish and fresh line fish are served. ✉ *King George VI Battery, North Pier, Point Rd.,* ☎ *031/368–1060. AE, DC, MC, V.*

$$ ✕ **Victoria Bar & Restaurant.** Adjoining the city's most charismatic and earthy bar, this unpretentious Portuguese restaurant on the docks serves good, no-frills seafood. Red tablecloths and tightly packed tables give it a cozy appeal. If you decide on a bar lunch or supper, the same food is slightly cheaper than in the restaurant, and you're likely to meet some fairly colorful characters. Depending on the mood of the chefs, your meal could be excellent or merely mediocre. Prawn curry is a solid favorite, as is the chicken-calamari mix. Excellent main courses are grilled or baked sole, line fish topped with a tomato and onion sauce, peri-peri chicken, and grilled langoustines. A less expensive alternative to langoustines is prawns à la Victoria, done with garlic and peri-peri. Dessert is limited to ice cream and mousses. ✉ *Point and Bell Sts.,* ☎ *031/37–4645. DC, MC, V. Closed Sun.*

$ ✕ **Pakistani Restaurant.** Wander into this tiny Pakistani restaurant near
★ the beachfront, and your first impulse is to flee. Shielded from the street by a green curtain, the restaurant comprises a mere six tables in a bare room. Don't be deterred, for you'll find some of the best Indian food in the city here. The husband-and-wife owners travel to Karachi or Lahore each year just to find new recipes. They buy their meats fresh every day, and their spices, too, are laden with flavor. The painstaking care taken in the kitchen is immediately obvious—the curries are notable for their flavor and subtlety. A real taste sensation is *atchar ghosh,* a slightly sweet curry dish made with boneless chicken and served with roti. Another popular choice is chicken *boti,* cubes of chicken marinated in herbs and spices, then cooked over an open fire. For something lighter, try a *seekh kebab,* skewers of pure ground beef marinated in a green-chile spice and grilled. ✉ *92 West St.,* ☎ *031/32–6883. No alcohol allowed. MC, V. Closed Mon.*

$ ✕ **Sea Belle's.** The superb curries at this Indian restaurant in La Mercy—a half hour's drive north of the city—draw crowds of Durbanites at lunch. You certainly wouldn't go for the decor, best described as disco industrial (the restaurant doubles as a nightclub). Order the bean curry, not only the cheapest but also the tastiest of the curries on the menu. The prawn curry is excellent, too. Accompanied by rice and rotis, an order of three curries is ample for four persons. ✉ *Sea Belle's Hotel, Beach Rd., La Mercy,* ☎ *0322/91–5551. AE, DC, MC, V.*

Lodging

Durban

$$$$ 🏨 **The Edward.** One of Durban's oldest hotels, originally built in 1939 in a classic colonial style, the Edward has recently been restored to its former elegance. Stylish cut-glass chandeliers, molded ceilings, and subtle art deco details bring to mind echoes of Durban's older, more refined past. Rooms are tastefully furnished with plenty of oak; 10 have balconies overlooking the sea, and the others have bay windows with sea views. The hotel faces South Beach, just a 10-minute walk from the CBD. ✉ *Marine Parade (mailing address: Box 105), Durban 4000,* ☎ *031/37–3681,* FAX *031/32–1692. 100 rooms. 3 restaurants, 2 bars, room service, pool, beauty salon. AE, DC, MC, V.*

$$$$
★ 🏨 **Royal Hotel.** The city's best hotel and a cherished Durban institution, the Royal stands in the heart of the CBD. The hotel caters mainly to businesspeople, but it's also an excellent option for tourists who don't insist on a beachfront location. It dates back to 1842—the city's infancy—and has frequently hosted visits by British royals. Sadly, the original Royal was replaced in 1978 by a high-rise, and all that remains of the old building is the grand Royal Grill (☞ Dining, *above*). Nevertheless, the hotel maintains some appealing old-fashioned touches. An army of liveried staff provides a level of service rare in South Africa today. Rooms, too, are slightly dated, with two-tone yellowwood furnishings and antique bird prints on the walls. Deluxe-class rooms are larger, featuring separate bath and shower, and have spectacular views of Durban harbor (request a room on an upper floor). The hotel's location, right on bustling Farewell Square, is great during the day, but a liability at night, when the CBD shuts down and the streets become unsafe. ✉ *267 Smith St. (mailing address: Box 1041), Durban 4000,* ☎ *031/304–0331,* FAX *031/304–5055. 272 rooms. 4 restaurants, 3 bars, room service, pool, health club, squash. AE, DC, MC, V.*

$$$ 🏨 **Holiday Inn Crowne Plaza.** Formerly known as the Elangeni, this is the best hotel on the Durban beachfront, at least until the reopening of the Edward. The 21-story high-rise overlooks North Beach, a two-minute drive from the CBD, and attracts a mix of business, conference, and holiday guests. All rooms have views of the water, but request a room on an upper floor with a full-on ocean view. Rooms are small and narrow, with a beachlike, seaside feel at odds with the formality of the marbled lobby and public rooms. ✉ *63 Snell Parade (mailing address: Box 4094), Durban 4000,* ☎ *031/37–1321,* FAX *031/32–5527. 446 rooms. 3 restaurants, 2 bars, room service, 2 pools, beauty salon, health club. AE, DC, MC, V.*

$$ 🏨 **Holiday Inn Garden Court—Marine Parade.** If you don't need room service, porters, or a concierge, choose this hotel over the more expensive Crowne Plaza, for the rooms are just as pleasant. You can't beat the location either, midway between South and North beaches, and the CBD is just a 10-minute walk away. Rooms are attractive and modern, with textured wallpaper, bold floral bedspreads, and a small sitting area. All face the sea, but request one on an upper floor. Views from the pool deck on the 30th floor are superb. ✉ *167 Marine Parade (mailing address: Box 10809), Durban 4056,* ☎ FAX *031/37–3341. 344 rooms. Restaurant, bar, indoor pool. AE, DC, MC, V.*

$$ 🏨 **Holiday Inn Garden Court—North Beach.** Overlooking a relatively quiet stretch of beachfront, this is the most upscale of the Garden Court hotels. It occupies the old five-star Maharani, and although the current hotel is a no-frills affair, some of the Maharani's former elegance shines through in rich wood doors, molded ceilings, and a wood-paneled residents bar. Rooms are large, each with its own sitting area, and decorated in delicate blues and rusts. All have excellent sea views.

⊠ *83/91 Snell Parade (mailing address: Box 10592), Durban 4056,* ☎ *031/32–7361,* FAX *031/37–4058. 270 rooms. Restaurant, breakfast room, bar, pool, beauty salon. AE, DC, MC, V.*

$$ ☷ **Palace Protea.** Facing right onto North Beach, this self-catering hotel is a good option for families; couples can probably do better at one of the nearby Holiday Inns. For groups of up to six, the large deluxe suites are ideal and incredibly cheap. Suites feature fully equipped kitchens, living rooms, two bedrooms, and outstanding sea views. Standard rooms, on the other hand, are small and basic. ⊠ *Marine Parade and Foster Pl. (mailing address: Box 10539), Durban 4056,* ☎ *031/32–8351,* FAX *031/32–8307. 76 rooms. Restaurant, bar, 2 pools, steam room. AE, DC, MC, V.*

$ ☷ **City Lodge.** This is a less expensive and convenient alternative to the Holiday Inns, set a couple of blocks farther inland but still within walking distance of the beach. The rooms are welcoming and comfortable, but rather characterless as hotel chains tend to be. The restaurant serves standard family fare. ⊠ *Old Fort and Brickhill Rd.,* ☎ *031/332–1447,* FAX *031/332–1483. 161 rooms. Restaurant, bar, breakfast room, pool. AE, DC, MC, V.*

$ ☷ **Holiday Inn Garden Court—South Beach.** This is the cheapest of the Garden Courts on the beachfront, and attracts a lot of budget-minded South African families. Its position, facing the carnival of South Beach and close to the CBD, is ideal if you want to be in the thick of the party action. Rooms are small, with utilitarian furnishings and tiny bathrooms, but the views from the sea-facing rooms are wonderful. ⊠ *73 Marine Parade (mailing address: Box 10199), Durban 4056,* ☎ *031/37–2231,* FAX *031/37–4640. 400 rooms. Restaurant, 2 bars, breakfast room, pool. AE, DC, MC, V.*

Umhlanga Rocks

$$$$ ☷ **Beverly Hills Sun.** In a high-rise building right on the beach, this up-market hotel is popular with both vacationers and businesspeople. The service is excellent and the facilities are superb. However, if you're the sort of beachgoer who likes to loll about in a bathing suit, you may find this hotel too formal. The public lounge, festooned with huge floral arrangements and yards of gathered drapes, serves a full silver-service tea in the afternoon, and a pianist plays in the evening. Guest rooms are fairly small, but all have terrific sea views, particularly those on the upper floors. The decor makes extensive use of bleached-wood furniture and bold floral fabrics. For a more open, beachlike feel, take one of the cabanas, large duplex rooms that open onto a lovely pool deck. ⊠ *Lighthouse Rd. (mailing address: Box 71), Umhlanga Rocks 4320,* ☎ *031/561–2211,* FAX *031/561–3711. 95 rooms. 2 restaurants, 2 bars, room service, pool, beauty salon. Breakfast included. AE, DC, MC, V.*

$$$ ☷ **Breakers Resort.** This resort enjoys an enviable position at the northern tip of Umhlanga, surrounded by the wilds of the Hawaan Forest and overlooking the unspoiled wetlands of Umhlanga Lagoon. Of all the resorts in Umhlanga, this one suffers the least from crowds—amble north along the beach and you will see scarcely another soul and no buildings. The disadvantage is that you probably need a car to get into town, and you can't swim directly in front of the resort because the surf's too dangerous. The building is unattractive, with long, depressing corridors, but the rooms themselves are fine, with fully equipped kitchens and great views of the beach and lagoon. ⊠ *88 Lagoon Dr. (mailing address: Box 75), Umhlanga Rocks 4320,* ☎ *031/561–2271,* FAX *031/561–2722. 80 rooms. 2 restaurants, bar, pool, tennis court, playground. Breakfast included. AE, DC, MC, V.*

$$$ ⊞ **Cabana Beach.** For families wanting a traditional beach holiday, you
★ can't do better than this large resort in Umhlanga. Children under 18
stay free, the bathing beach lies directly in front of the hotel, and there
are tons of activities to keep kids happy. Considering its huge size, the
Cabana is one of the most attractive hotels on the beach: a whitewashed,
Spanish-style structure that steps down to the sea in a series of terraces.
The room decor is simple, comfortable, and absolutely appropriate for
a beach holiday. Each cabana comes with a fully equipped kitchen, din-
ing/living area, and a veranda with great sea views. Request a tower
or beachfront apartment for the most attractive and practical space con-
figuration. ⊠ *10 Lagoon Dr. (mailing address: Box 10), Umhlanga Rocks
4320,* ☎ *031/561–2371,* FAX *031/561–3522. 217 rooms. 3 restaurants,
bar, 2 pools, tennis court, health club, squash. Breakfast included. AE,
DC, MC, V.*

Nightlife and the Arts

What's on in Durban, a free monthly publication put out by the tourism
office, lists a diary of upcoming events. The entertainment section of
the *Natal Mercury,* Durban's principal newspaper, is a good informa-
tion source. Tickets for shows, movies, concerts, and other events can
be obtained through **Computicket** (☎ 031/304–2753), which has out-
lets throughout the city.

The Arts

The **Playhouse** (⊠ Smith St., across from City Hall, ☎ 031/304–
3631) stands at the heart of Durban's cultural life. The complex en-
compasses five performing arts venues, and the Playhouse Company
stages productions of music, ballet, drama, opera, and cabaret. The
Playhouse is also home to the Natal Philharmonic Orchestra.

Nightlife

BARS AND PUBS

The beachfront area is lined with bars catering to holiday crowds. **Joe
Kool's** (⊠ 137 Lower Marine Parade, ☎ 031/32–9697), a California-
style bar and restaurant, packs hordes of young partying singles onto
its outdoor terrace. **Cattleman** (⊠ 139 Lower Marine Parade, ☎ 031/
37–0382), a stone's throw down the beach, attracts a slightly older
crowd. At the harbor entrance is **Thirsty's** (⊠ Point waterfront, ☎ 031/
37–9212), an upscale two-pub complex where you can eat lunch on
the deck and watch enormous tankers, tugs, and yachts moving in and
out of the harbor. Further along the quayside on the old Wilson's
Wharf is **Charlie's Croft,** (⊠ 18 Boatmans Rd., ☎ 031/307–2935), a
restaurant and pub with an outdoor dockyard atmosphere. Perhaps the
biggest meet-market in the city is the **Queens Tavern** (⊠ 16 Stamford
Hill Rd., Greyville, ☎ 031/309–4017), a bar-cum-Indian restaurant
that is regularly mobbed, particularly on Friday nights. If you're look-
ing for something less frenetic, head to Morningside and the **Keg and
Thistle** (⊠ Florida Rd., ☎ 031/23–5315), the first in a blossoming chain
of pubs across the country, or **Woodcutters** (⊠ Windermere Rd., ☎
031/303–1026). The most charismatic bar in the city is the gritty **Vic-
toria Bar** (⊠ Point Rd., ☎ 031/37–4645), down in the docks on Dur-
ban Point. Attached to a Portuguese restaurant, it attracts a crowd of
weird and wonderful regulars.

NIGHTCLUBS AND LIVE MUSIC

The best places to hear live **African music and jazz** are Tekweni Junc-
tion (⊠ Umgeni Rd., ☎ 031/309–1282) and the **Moon Hotel** (⊠ 522
S. Coast Rd., Rossborough, ☎ 031/465–1711). If you want to get down
and groove, **Sand Pebbles** (⊠ South Beach Ave., ☎ 031/368–2447) is
a long-standing beachfront favorite, a multilevel entertainment com-

plex that draws all kinds of people. In the CBD, **The Aliwal Lighthouse Grill**, (⊠ 51 Aliwal St.,☎ 031/304–3965), directly around the corner from the Playhouse, serves light snacks and a good cappuccino to late-night live music. **Funkey's** (⊠ The BAT Centre, ☎ 031/368–2029) promotes local bands and serves good, light meals. On Durban Point, **330** (⊠ 330 Point Rd., ☎ 031/37–7172) attracts hip crowds of models, glitterati, and wannabes with loud techno music. Over in Morningside, the club of choice among Durban's see-and-be-seen crowd is **Bonkers** (⊠ Florida Rd., ☎ 031/303–1146).

Outdoor Activities and Sports

Beaches

The sea near **Durban,** unlike that around the Cape, is comfortably warm year-round: in summer, the water temperature can top 80°F, whereas in winter 65°F is considered cold. All of KwaZulu-Natal's main beaches are protected by shark nets and staffed with lifeguards, and there are usually boards stating the wind direction, water temperature, and whether there are any dangerous swimming conditions. **The Golden Mile,** stretching from South Beach all the way to the Bay of Plenty, is packed with people, who enjoy the water slides, singles bars, and fast-food joints. A little further north are the **Umhlanga Rocks beaches,** and on the opposite side of the bay are the less commercialized beaches on Durban's Bluff. A visit to the Wildlife Society of South Africa's coastal reserve and environmental education center, at **Treasure Beach on the Bluff,** will give you an idea of what this section of the coast looked like before it was commercially developed. Another pretty beach and coastal walk, just north of the **Umhlanga Lagoon,** leads to miles of near-empty beaches backed by virgin bush.

Participant Sports

FISHING

Lynski Charters (☎ 031/561–2031) takes up to six people deep-sea fishing for barracuda, sailfish, sharks, and reef fish. Trips, in a 35-ft game-fish boat, cost R1,600 for up to six people fishing, although the boat can take nine people altogether. The price includes equipment, tackle, bait, and cold drinks. In Umhlanga Rocks, **Mike Plotz** (☎ 031/561–3259) launches his small ski boat right off the beach through the waves. His fishing trips cost about R190 per person. Equipment, tackle, bait, and refreshments supplied.

GOLF

As long as you tee off between 7 AM and 9 AM on weekdays, you can play on two of the country's best courses while in town. **Durban Country Club** (⊠ W. Gilbert Rd., ☎ 031/23–8282) has hosted more South African Opens than any other course and is regularly rated the best in South Africa. Tees and greens sit atop large sand dunes, and trees add an additional hazard to a course that plays like a links. **Royal Durban Golf Club** (⊠ 16 Mitchell Crescent, Greyville, ☎ 031/309–1373), situated inside the Greyville race course, offers no protection from the wind and makes hitting the narrow fairways very difficult. Both courses rent clubs. **Roger Manning Golf Shop** (⊠ Windsor Park Golf Course, N.M.R. Ave., ☎ 031/303–1728) also rents out clubs for R50–R150 per day.

Spectator Sports

CRICKET

Kingsmead Cricket Ground (⊠ 2 Kingsmead Close, ☎ 031/32–9703) is home to the Natal provincial team and a frequent venue for international test matches between South Africa and touring teams from abroad.

HORSE RACING

The **main season** extends from May to August. Meets are usually held Tuesday, Wednesday, or Thursday, and every Saturday, and usually consist of 9 or 10 races. The area's three **racecourses** take turns holding meets: **Greyville** (⊠ Avondale Rd., ☎ 031/309–4545), almost in the city center; **Clairwood Park** (⊠ Exit 7 or 8 off Southern Fwy., ☎ 031/42–5332), 11 km (7 mi) out of town; and **Scottsville** (⊠ New England Rd. exit off N3, ☎ 0331/45–3405), in Pietermaritzburg. The **Durban July** at Greyville—probably the country's most famous horse-racing event—is a day when the outrageous fashions worn by female racing fans attract almost as much attention as the horses themselves.

RUGBY

KwaZulu-Natal's team, known as the Sharks, plays at **Kings Park Rugby Ground** (⊠ West Gilbert Rd., ☎ 031/23–6368). Natal is a strong contender in the annual round-robin Bankfin Currie Cup competition.

SURFING

Surfing commands a fanatical following in Durban, and several international tournaments are staged on the city's beaches or at nearby Umhlanga Rocks. Crowds of more than 10,000 are not unusual for night surfing competitions or the annual Gunston 500 surfing championship event. The most popular surfing beach is probably the Bay of Plenty, on Durban's Golden Mile; for more experienced surfers, there's Cave Rock on the Bluff.

Shopping

African Art Centre. This nonprofit center acts as a sales outlet for the work of rural artisans. It carries an excellent selection of original African arts and crafts, including Zulu beadwork, ceramics, wood sculptures, and beautifully crafted wire baskets. The store will ship purchases overseas. ⊠ *8 Guild Hall Arcade,* ☎ *031/304–7915.* ☉ *Mon.-Thurs. 8:30–5, Fri. 7:30–4, Sat. 8–12:30.*

Africa Art Gallery. Tucked away in a shopping plaza, this small gallery sells an interesting collection of paintings, hand-blown glass, and wood and stone sculpture. This is an excellent place to buy top-quality works by prominent South African artists, both white and black. ⊠ *5 Granada Centre, Chartwell Dr., Umhlanga Rocks,* ☎ *031/561–2661.* ☉ *Weekdays 9–5, Sat. 9–1, Sun. 10:30–12:30.*

NSA Gallery. This small, trendy complex supports and promotes both local and international artists and craftsmen, whose creations are sold in the craft shop. ⊠ *166 Bulwer Rd., Glenwood,* ☎ *031/22–3686* ☉ *Tues.-Fri. 9–5, Sat. 9–4, Sun. 10–4.*

The most exciting market in the city is the **Victoria Street Market** (☞ Exploring Durban, *above*), where you can buy everything from recordings of African music to curios and curry spices. If you don't want to go all the way to the Indian district for your spices, stop in at the **Spice Emporium** (⊠ 31 Pine St., ☎ 031/32–6662), near the beachfront. You can select from a tantalizing array of fresh spices, as well as hand-mixed curry powders. The shop also sells mixes for creating your own vegetable *atchars* (Indian relishes), tea masala, and chili bites.

One of the best **shopping malls** in Durban is The Workshop (⊠ 99 Aliwal St., ☎ 031/304–9894), a slick renovation of the city's cavernous old railway workshops. You'll find everything from expensive clothing stores to curio shops, cinemas, and fast-food restaurants. Other major malls in the city are The Wheel (⊠ 55 Gillespie St., ☎ 031/32–4324) and **Musgrave Centre** (⊠ Musgrave Rd., Berea, ☎ 031/21–5129). Two giant malls in the suburbs are **The Pavilion** (⊠ Jack Martens Dr., Westville, ☎ 031/265–0558) and **La Lucia Mall** (⊠ 90 William Campbell Dr., ☎ 031/562–8420).

Side Trips from Durban

Pietermaritzburg

Pietermaritzburg lies in a bowl of hills in the Natal Midlands, 80 km (50 mi) inland from Durban. The city is the current cocapital of KwaZulu-Natal along with Ulundi in Zululand. It's a pleasant town, with wide, tree-lined streets and a temperate climate that escapes the worst of the coastal heat and humidity. Its redbrick colonial architecture offers tangible reminders of Natal's and South Africa's British past; dozens of late-19th-century buildings line the streets in the center of town. It's worth visiting just to see this slice of Victorian England.

The town is often referred to as "The Last British Outpost," even though it was first settled in 1838 by Voortrekkers escaping British rule in the Cape. The city takes its name from Pieter Mauritz Retief, commonly known as Piet Retief, the famous Voortrekker leader who was murdered by the Zulu king, Dingane.

Numbers in the text correspond to numbers in the margin and on the Pietermaritzburg map.

A GOOD WALK

Pietermaritzburg's city center is small and most of the places worth visiting are within easy access of each other. Start your tour of Pietermaritzburg at the **Pietermaritzburg Publicity Association** ㉓ on Commercial Road before crossing the street to the **Tatham Art Gallery** ㉔, which was formerly the old Supreme Court. The **Supreme Court Gardens** ㉕ are right next to the gallery. Across Commercial Road from the gardens stands the imposing **City Hall** ㉖. From here, head down Church Street to reach the **Voortrekker Museum** ㉗. Walk back up Church Street, cross Commercial Road, and stroll along the Maritzburg Mall, a quasi-pedestrian thoroughfare lined with some superb examples of Victorian architecture. Fronting the Colonial Building is a **statue of Gandhi** ㉘. Next, turn left down Greys Inn Lane to reach **Harwin's Arcade** ㉙. From the arcade stroll down Theatre Lane until you reach Longmarket Street and then turn left. The street runs past the **Old Natal Parliament** ㉚. Back on Commercial Road, turn right and then right again onto Loop Street to reach the eclectic **Natal Museum** ㉛. To visit the **Macrorie House Museum** ㉜, a little more than 1 km (.6 mi) southwest of Commercial Road on Loop Street (at the corner of Pine Street), you probably need a car. For a good view of Pietermaritzburg, drive back down Loop Street, turn left on Commercial Road, which after a while, becomes Old Howick Road. Follow the signs to **World's View** ㉝.

Timing: Even though many of the sidewalks are shaded and the Mall is quite leafy, it is wise to get any serious walking done with either in the cooler earlier morning hours or in late afternoon, particularly in summer. Set aside a few hours in the morning to do this walk, and when the heat begins to settle in, take a drive out to World's View for a good view of town.

SIGHTS TO SEE

㉖ **City Hall.** Built in 1900, this grand edifice is the largest all-brick structure in the Southern Hemisphere. It's a classic Victorian edifice, notable for its stained-glass windows, soaring clock tower, and ornate gables and domes. ⊠ *Church St. and Commercial Rd.*

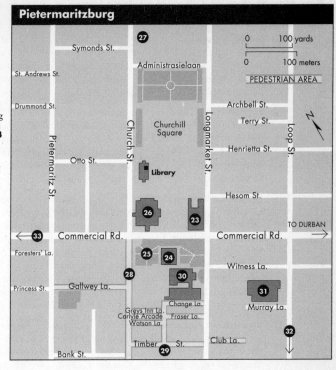

Pietermaritzburg

Harwin's Arcade. Perhaps Pietermaritzburg's most popular attraction, this warren of charming pedestrian lanes and alleys is lined with shops, cafés, and small businesses. It extends between Timber Street and Theatre Lane through an Edwardian building constructed in Renaissance Revival style. A skylight runs the entire length of the two-story arcade, which houses a bookstore and other small shops.

Macrorie House Museum. This lovely residence with a corrugated-iron roof and ornate ironwork is typical of old Pietermaritzburg. Bishop Macrorie lived in the house from 1870 to 1892, and it's been furnished to reflect that period. ⊠ *Loop and Pine Sts.,* ☎ *0331/94–2161.* ⌸ *R2.* ⏾ *Tues.-Thurs. 9–1, Sun. 11–4.*

Natal Museum. One of five national museums in the country, the exhibition building contains a little of everything: a natural science hall displays dinosaurs, African animals, sea life, and Natal birds; a history section recreates an 1880s Pietermaritzburg street complete with a settler's cottage, shops, a pharmacy, and a smithy; the display on sub-Saharan cultures is by far the most interesting, highlighting religious, ceremonial, military, and household artifacts from across the continent. Several San (Bushman) rock paintings are on display, too. ⊠ *237 Loop St.,* ☎ *0331/45–1404.* ⌸ *R2.* ⏾ *Mon.-Sat. 9–4:30, Sun. 2–5.*

Old Natal Parliament. The building once housed the twin-chamber colonial parliament. A statue of Queen Victoria stands in front of the red-brick building, which was erected in 1889. ⊠ *Longmarket St. and Commercial Rd.*

Pietermaritzburg Publicity Association. The office distributes detailed pamphlets and maps of the town; it is found in a classic redbrick building erected in 1884 to house the Borough Police. In those days, the bell tower signaled a curfew for blacks at 9 each night. ⊠ *177 Commercial Rd.,* ☎ *0331/45–1348.* ⊙ *Weekdays 8:30–4:30, Sat. 8:30–12:30.*

㉘ Statue of Gandhi. The statue marks the centenary of the day in 1893 when Gandhi, an Indian who had come to South Africa as a lawyer, was thrown off a train at Pietermaritzburg station because he was riding in a whites-only carriage. He later stated: "My active nonviolence began from that date." ⊠ *Church St. Mall.*

㉕ Supreme Court Gardens. The gardens are the city's memorial park. Several monuments commemorate those who died in wars that raged in this country and abroad: the Zulu War of 1879, the Boer War (1899–1902), and World War I. The monuments all have a very English feel, emphasized by the legends on the commemorative stones extolling Queen, Country, and Empire. ⊠ *Commercial Rd. at Church St.*

㉔ Tatham Art Gallery. Completed in 1871 and housed in the old Supreme Court, the gallery is yet another of Pietermaritzburg's fine redbrick colonial structures. The museum is first-rate, with a solid collection of 19th-century English and French paintings. Of keenest interest, though, is the South African Collection, which displays works by contemporary black and white artists, including linocuts and such traditional crafts as beadwork, baskets, and tribal ear plugs. The museum also presents changing exhibits. ⊠ *Commercial Rd. at Church St., across from Publicity Assoc.,* ☎ *0331/42–1804.* ⊠ *Free.* ⊙ *Tues.-Sun. 10–6.*

㉗ Voortrekker Museum. The museum occupies the Church of the Vow, an immensely important monument in the eyes of many Afrikaners. After the murder of Voortrekker leader Piet Retief in 1838, the Voortrekkers sought revenge on the Zulus and their king, Dingane. A Boer commando under the leadership of Andries Pretorius vowed to build a church if God granted them victory. The result was the Battle of Blood River (☞ Zululand and the Battlefields, *below*), in which 3,000 Zulus died and the Boers managed to emerge without a single casualty. Constructed in 1841 in typical Cape Dutch style, the church now houses a variety of Voortrekker artifacts, including an old wagon, flintlock rifles, and Piet Retief's prayer book. Next door, the thatched home of Andries Pretorius is also open to the public. ⊠ *Longmarket St.,* ☎ *0331/94–6834.* ⊠ *R2.* ⊙ *Weekdays 9–4, Sat. 8–noon.*

㉝ World's View. The spectacular outlook commands panoramic views of the city and miles of surrounding countryside. The viewpoint lies on the route used by the Voortrekkers on their long migration from the Cape in the 19th century. A large diagram traces their route, and labels the major landscape features. From town, follow Commercial Road northwest until it turns into Howick Road, then follow signs to the overlook.

DINING

$ ✕ Botanic Gardens Tea Shop. One of the more pleasant places to spend a lunch hour in town is the tea shop in the Botanic Gardens. You can relax over breakfast or a light lunch on a shady patio overlooking the enormous old trees and gardens. The shop has a great selection of tea-time cakes. ⊠ *Botanic Gardens, Mayors Walk, Prestbury,* ☎ *0331/442–207.* ⊙ *Mon.–Sat 8:30–4:30, Sun 8:30–5. MC, V.*

$ ✕ Tatham Coffee Shop. On the second floor of the Tatham Art Gallery, this pleasant café serves a wonderful selection of teas and coffees, as well as light meals and desserts. Among the heartier dishes are cottage pie, chicken curry, quiche, and lasagna. If the weather's fine, sit outside on the narrow veranda overlooking Commercial Road. ⊠ *Commercial Rd. at Church St.,* ☎ *0331/42–8327. No credit cards. Closed Mon.*

By Bus. Greyhound (☎ 031/361–7774) and **Translux** (☎ 031/361–7461) buses stop at the Pietermaritzburg Publicity Association on their runs between Johannesburg and Durban. **Cheetah** (☎ 0331/422–673) runs a minibus service twice daily between Durban and Pietermaritzburg and is probably the most convenient way to travel between the two cities.

By Car. The easiest way to reach Pietermaritzburg from Durban is along the N3, a direct 80-km (50-mi) run. Far more interesting and scenic, however, is the route that follows Old Main Road (R103) through the Valley of a Thousand Hills (☞ *below*) and rejoins the N3 east of Pietermaritzburg.

By Train. Spoornet (☎ 031/361–3388) runs between Johannesburg and Durban and stops daily in Pietermaritzburg.

Valley of a Thousand Hills

Only 45 km (28 mi) inland from Durban, the Valley of a Thousand Hills makes a beautiful half-day excursion from the city. The name is an apt description of this area of plunging gorges and bush-covered hills. The Old Main Road (R103) from Durban to Pietermaritzburg runs along the crest of the hills, offering some tremendous views. This is the route taken by runners during the annual Comrades Marathon, South Africa's most famous road race. Each year, thousands of masochistic participants sign up for the 80-km (50-mi) event, which is run "uphill" to Pietermaritzburg one year and "downhill" to Durban the next. It may be wiser, however, to come in a car instead. In fact, for generations, Durbanites have driven up to the Valley of a Thousand Hills on weekends for lunch or tea. In addition to several tearooms and small restaurants, the route is dotted with craft shops and farm stands. To get here, follow the M13 out of Durban. Stay on this road through the suburbs of Kloof and Gillitts until you see the turnoff to Old Main Road (R103) and the Valley of a Thousand Hills.

DINING
$$ ✕ **Raven's Croft.** This is one of those places you come back to again
★ and again. The restaurant couldn't be better situated—in an old trading store with breathtaking views over the Valley of a Thousand Hills. Choose between sitting inside near a cozy fire during cold weather or outdoors on the lawn when the weather is fine. There are two menus from which to choose. One a more classic French-style menu, the other has lighter meals, which include a Greek lamb pie in a delicate phyllo pastry, quiche, and a sublime sandwich made with sun-dried tomatoes, parmesan, olive oil, salami, and salad greens. The deep fried ice-cream dessert is a must. On weekends make lunch reservations to avoid wait that can run to an hour or more. ⊠ *Old Main Rd., Drummond,* ☎ *0325/3–4598. Reservations required. AE, DC, MC, V.* ☻ *Closed Mon. No dinner Sun.*

Durban A to Z

Arriving and Departing

BY BUS
Greyhound (☎ 031/309–7830) and **Translux Express** (☎ 031/361–8333) offer long-distance bus service to cities all over South Africa. A cheaper company, **Golden Wheels** (☎ 031/29–9229), offers frequent service to Johannesburg only. All intercity buses leave from **New Durban Station** (⊠ off N.M.R. Ave., between Old Fort Ave. and Argyle Rd.)

BY CAR
Rental Cars. The cheapest rental car costs about R85 per day plus 85¢ per km. Prices fall dramatically if you rent for three days or more and

plan to drive long distances. The major **car rental agencies** are **Avis** (✉ Ulundi Pl., City Center, ☎ 031/304–1741), **Berea Car & Bakkie Hire** (✉ Tourist Junction, 160 Pine St., ☎ 031/22–3333), **Dolphin Car Hire** (✉ 36 Broad St., ☎ 031/304–7924), **Imperial Car Rental** (✉ 34 Aliwal St., ☎ 031/37–3731), and **Tempest Car Hire** (✉ Victoria Embankment, Esplanade, ☎ 031/368–5231).

BY PLANE

Durban International Airport (☎ 031/42–6156), formerly known as Louis Botha Airport, lies 16 km (10 mi) south of town along the Southern Freeway. **International airlines** serving the area include **South African Airways** (☎ 031/450–2209), which flies direct between Durban and London twice a week, and **SAA** and **British Airways** (☎ 031/304–4741), which offer flights to London via Johannesburg. **Domestic airlines** serving Durban include **SAA, BA/Comair** (☎ 031/42–6022), **Airlink** (☎ 031/42–2136), and **Sunair** (☎ 031/469–3444).

Avis (☎ 031/42–3282), **Budget** (☎ 031/42–3809), **Dolphin** (☎ 031/469–0667), **Imperial** (☎ 031/42–4648), and **Tempest** (☎ 031/368–5231) all have **car-rental** desks in the domestic terminal.

Between the Airport and City Center. The airport company operates a **shuttle bus** from outside the domestic terminal to the City Air Terminal (✉ Smith and Aliwal Sts., ☎ 031/465–5573) in the center of town. Buses run about every hour and the trip takes 20 minutes; the fare is R20 per person. **Airport Shuttle Bus** (☎ 031/469–0309) offers 24-hour minibus service between the airport and any address in Durban. Fares to the city center and beachfront are about R70 for 1–2 people, and R10 for every extra adult in the party thereafter. Taxis aren't much more expensive, about R80.

BY TRAIN

New Durban Station (✉ N.M.R. Ave., ☎ 031/361–7621) is a huge, ghastly place that is difficult to find your way around. Spoornet's **Trans-Natal** train runs daily between Durban and Johannesburg, stopping at Pietermaritzburg, Estcourt, and Ladysmith. The trip takes 13 hours and costs about R140, one-way.

Getting Around

BY BUS

Durban Transport operates two types of bus service, but you need concern yourself only with the **Mynah buses.** These small buses operate frequently on set routes through the city and along the beachfront, and cost R2 a ride. Bus stops are marked by the symbol of a mynah bird. The main bus depot is Pine Street, between Aliwal and Gardiner. You pay as you board; exact change is not required. Route information is also available at an information office at the corner of Aliwal and Pine Streets (☎ 031/307–3503).

Umhlanga Express Shuttle Service (☎ 031/561–2860) operates a weekday minibus service between Durban (across from Tourist Junction) and all the major hotels in Umhlanga Rocks. Buses leave every two hours or so and the trip takes 20 minutes. Saturday service is extremely limited.

BY TAXI

Taxis are metered and expensive. The meter starts at R2.50, and clocks the fare at about R5 per km. Expect to pay about R20 from City Hall to North Beach, and R80 to the airport. The most convenient taxi stands are around City Hall and in front of the beach hotels. Some of the major taxi companies are **Aussie's Radio Taxis** (☎ 031/37–2345), **Bunny Cabs** (☎ 031/32–2914), **Checker Radio Taxis** (☎ 031/21–1133), **Deluxe**

Radio Taxis (031/37–1661), and **Morris Radio Taxis** (031/37–2711).
Eagle Radio Taxis (☎ 031/38–8333) charge about R1 more per km
than other companies.

BY TUK TUK

Tuk tuks are three-wheel, open cabs powered by a motorcycle engine.
They cruise the beachfront area and are cheaper than taxis for short
trips. Negotiate the fare before you set off.

Contacts and Resources

CONSULATES

United Kingdom: ✉ *320 Smith St., City Center,* ☎ *031/305–2929.* **United
States:** ✉ *Durban Bay House, 333 Smith St., City Center,* ☎ *031/304–
4737.*

EMERGENCIES

Dial 10177 for an **ambulance,** 10111 for the **police,** and 031/361–0000
for the **fire brigade.**

GUIDED TOURS

Sarie Marais Pleasure Cruises (☎ 031/305–4022) and **Isle of Capri** (☎
031/37–7751) both offer **pleasure cruises** around Durban Bay. Tours,
which last about 90 minutes and cost R20 per person, depart from the
jetties next to the Natal Maritime Museum (✉ Victoria Embankment
at Aliwal St.).

Strelitzia Tours (☎ 031/86–1904) offers daily minibus tours of Durban for about R80. The three-hour tours touch on all the major historic and scenic points in the city, including the beachfront and harbor,
exclusive residential areas like Morningside, the Botanic Gardens, and
the Indian District.

Hamba Kahle Tours (☎ 031/7070–1509) takes you to see the other side
of South Africa, in the poverty stricken townships surrounding Durban. Township Fever is a three-hour tour of the northern townships,
including stops in Kwa-Mashu, Bhambayi, and the Gandhi Museum
in Phoenix. Get to Grips is a four-hour tour that takes you into hostels and squatter camps, and includes dancing, dinner, and drinks.
Shebeen Crawling is a pub crawl through several township bars; the
tour includes dinner and drinks. Tours cost approximately R130.

Zulwini Safaris (☎ 031/307–1567) provide standard tours (including
Drakensberg, the Battlefields, Game Parks and Adventure travel) and
design custom tours anywhere in the province; they also do small
groups. Their specialties are unusual, adventure, or out-of-the-way trips.

Durban Unlimited (✉ Tourist Junction, 160 Pine St., ☎ 031/304–
4934) has a series of city walking tours during the week for R25 per
person. Tours depart from the Tourist Junction weekdays at 9:45 and
return at 12:30. The Oriental Walkabout explores the Indian District,
including Victoria Market and several mosques. The Historical Walkabout covers the major historic monuments in the city, while the Feel
of Durban Walkabout explores some of the city's military past, including
the Old Fort, Warrior's Gate, and the original armory.

HOSPITALS

Addington Hospital (✉ Erskine Terr., South Beach, ☎ 031/32–2111)
operates a 24-hour emergency ward.

LATE-NIGHT PHARMACIES

Daynite Pharmacy (✉ West St. and Point Rd., ☎ 031/368–3666) is
open daily until 10:30.

Rennies is the South African representative of Thomas Cook, and also operates a foreign-exchange desk. ⊠ *320 West St., at Smith St.,* ☎ *031/ 304–1511.* ⊘ *Weekdays 8:30–4:30, Sat. 8:30–noon.*

American Express has a full range of client services (no client mail pick-up on Saturday). The Amex foreign-exchange bureau (⊠ 350 Smith St., ☎ 031/301–5562) is in a separate office, just 200 yards away. ⊠ *2 Durban Club Pl., off Smith St.,* ☎ *031/301–5541.* ⊘ *Weekdays 8– 5, Sat. 8:30–noon.*

The **Tourist Junction,** in the restored old station building, houses a number of tourist-oriented companies and services, where you can find information on almost everything that's happening in Durban and KwaZulu-Natal. Among the companies represented are Durban Unlimited, the city's tourism authority; an accommodation service; an intercity train reservations office; a Natal Parks Board booking desk; regional KwaZulu-Natal tourist offices; and various bus and transport companies. ⊠ *160 Pine St.,* ☎ *031/304–4934.* ⊘ *Weekdays 8–5, weekends 9–2.*

Umhlanga Publicity Association. ⊠ *Chartwell Dr., off Lighthouse Rd., Umhlanga Rocks,* ☎ *031/561–4257.* ⊘ *Weekdays 8:30–4:30, Sat. 9– 12:30.*

THE DRAKENSBERG

Afrikaners call them the Drakensberg: the Dragon Mountains. To Zulus, they are *uKhalamba*—the Barrier of Spears. Both are apt designations for this wall of rock that rises from the Natal grasslands, forming a natural fortress protecting the mountain kingdom of Lesotho. The Drakensberg is the highest range in southern Africa and possesses some of the most spectacular scenery in the country. It's a hiker's dream, and you could easily pass several days here just soaking up the awesome views.

The blue-tinted mountains seem to stain the landscape, cooling the "champagne air"—as the natives refer to the heady, sparkling breezes that blow around the precipices and pinnacles. The mountains, with names like Giant's Castle, Cathedral Peak, and the Sentinel, seem to have a special atmosphere, as well as unique topography. It's no surprise that South African-born J.R.R. Tolkien—legendary author of the cult classic *Lord of the Rings*—was inspired by the fantastic shapes of the Drakensberg massif when he created the phantasmagorical settings of his Middle Earth.

The Drakensberg is not a typical mountain range-it's actually an escarpment separating a high interior plateau from the coastal lowlands of Natal. It's a continuation of the same escarpment that divides the Transvaal highveld from the hot malarial zones of the lowveld (☞ Chapter 3). However, the Natal Drakensberg, or Berg as it is commonly known, is far wilder and more spectacular than its Transvaal counterpart. Many of the peaks—some of which top 10,000 ft—are the source of sparkling streams and mighty rivers that have carved out myriad valleys and dramatic gorges. You can hike for days and not meet a soul, and the mountains retain an untamed majesty missing in the commercially forested peaks of Mpumalanga.

The Berg has a range of places to stay, including expensive hotels, lodges, and guest houses, camping, self-catering cottages, and B&Bs. The older Berg resorts tend to be more family-oriented establishments, by and large, that encourage guests to participate in outdoor activities and sports, including daily guided hikes, horseback rides, tennis, lawn bowls, even golf. However, never to be left out, many farmers in the area have opened B&Bs that range from quaint and cute, warm and welcoming, to just plain mediocre.

Besides hiking and drinking in the sheer beauty of the mountains, the other great attraction of the Berg is the San (Bushman) paintings. The San are a hunter-gatherer people who once roamed the entire country. More than 5,000 of their paintings are sprinkled in scores of caves and on rock overhangs throughout the Berg—probably the finest collection of rock paintings in the country. They tell the stories of bygone hunts, dances, and battles, and touch on the almost mystical relationship of the San with the animals they hunted. With the arrival of the Nguni peoples from the north and white settlers from the southwest, the San were driven out of their traditional hunting lands, and they retreated into the remote fastnesses of the Drakensberg and the Kalahari Desert. San attacks in Natal in the late-19th century occasioned harsh punitive raids by white settlers, and by 1880 the last San had disappeared from the Berg. Today, only a few clans remain in the very heart of the Kalahari Desert.

The best times to visit the Berg are spring (September–October) and autumn (March–April). Summer sees the Berg at its greenest and the weather at its warmest, but vicious afternoon thunderstorms, which can put a severe damper on long hikes, are an almost daily occurrence. In winter, the mountains lose their lush overcoat and turn brown and sere. Winter days in the valleys, where most of the resorts are located, are usually sunny and pleasant, with only occasional cold snaps (don't be put off by alarmist reports of frigid weather). Nights are chilly, however, and you should pack plenty of warm clothing if you plan to hike high up into the mountains or camp overnight. Snow is common at higher elevations. Hikers heading above the 10,000-ft level are advised to sign the mountain register at the nearest Natal Parks Board office in case of emergency.

The Natal Drakensberg is not conducive to traditional touring. The nature of the attractions and the limited road system make a connect-the-dots tour impractical and unrewarding. Check into a resort for two or three days instead and use it as a base for hiking and exploring the immediate area.

Numbers in the margin correspond to points of interest on the Drakensberg map.

❶ A good place to start your Berg exploration is the **Winterton Museum,** which gives you a good overview of the area. Most of the exhibits in this delightful and informative museum were donated, made, or built by people from the Winterton and nearby communities. If you are planning to hike to see any of the San (Bushman) paintings in the Berg later in the day, first take a look at the musuem's San Art Gallery, the most extensive photographic record of Berg San paintings, consisting of 10 panels of 180 photographs. The last San were seen by honeymooners in the area at the end of the last century. On a more contemporary note, a small but poignant display depicts Winterton residents casting their votes during the historic 1994 democratic elections. If you are planning a tour of the battlefields, pop into the private reading room where an outstanding private collection of books on the Boer War is available for perusal. These volumes are used as reference sources by many of the professional battlefields tour guides. ✉ *Winterton Village,* ☎ *036/488–1620.* ▣ *Free.* ☉ *Mon.–Thurs. and Sat. 9–noon, Fri. 1–4.*

The Drakensberg

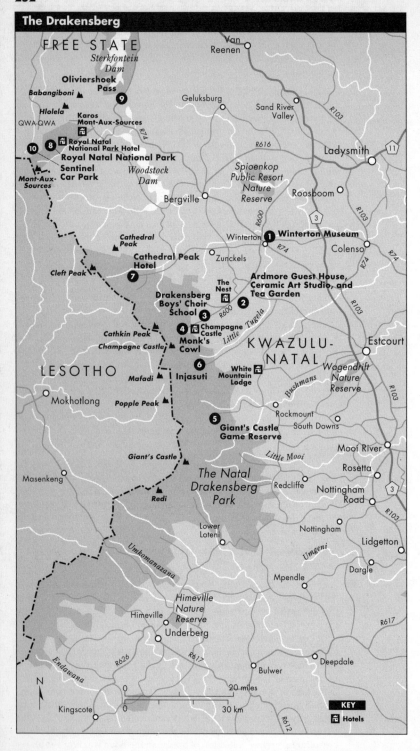

FREE STATE

Van Reenen

Sterkfontein Dam

Oliviershoek Pass 9

Babangiboni

Geluksburg

Sand River Valley

R103

Hlolela

QWA-QWA

Karos Mont-Aux-Sources

R74

R616

Ladysmith

11

10 8 **Royal Natal National Park Hotel**

Royal Natal National Park

Sentinel Car Park

Mont-Aux-Sources

Woodstock Dam

R600

Spioenkop Public Resort Nature Reserve

Roosboom

Colenso

R74

R74

R103

Bergville

Winterton 1 **Winterton Museum**

R74

Zunckels

Ardmore Guest House, Ceramic Art Studio, and Tea Garden

Cathedral Peak

Cathedral Peak Hotel 7

Cleft Peak

The Nest

Drakensberg Boys' Choir School 3

R600

2

Little Tugela

KWAZULU-NATAL

Estcourt

Cathkin Peak

4 **Champagne Castle**

Champagne Castle

Monk's Cowl

6

Injasuti

White Mountain Lodge

Wagendrift Nature Reserve

Bushmans

R103

Mafadi

Popple Peak

Mokhotlong

LESOTHO

5 **Giant's Castle Game Reserve**

Rockmount

South Downs

Little Mooi

Mooi River

Rosetta

Giant's Castle

Masenkeng

The Natal Drakensberg Park

Redcliffe

Nottingham Road

3

R103

Umkomanazana

Lower Loteni

Nottingham

Lidgetton

Umgeni

Dargle

Redi

Mpendle

Himeville Nature Reserve

Himeville

Underberg

R617

R626

R617

Bulwer

Deepdale

Endawana

N

Kingscote

0   20 miles

0   30 km

R612

KEY

Hotels

The R600, accessible from the N3 via Winterton, leads to many of the resorts and attractions in the Central Berg. Twenty-seven kilometers **②** (17 mi) down the R600 from Winterton is the turnoff to the **Ardmore Guest House, Ceramic Art Studio, and Tea Garden.** Started on a farm by artist Fée Berning in 1985, the studio is now home to nearly 40 Zulu and Sotho artists, each pursuing their own artistic visions in clay. Their ceramics have won national and international awards and are displayed in galleries around the world. The work is colorful and very African, with zebras and giraffes serving as handles on teapots, bowls, and platters. You can watch artists at work or just browse through the collection, in a converted farm shed. The studio ships purchases overseas. Have tea and scones in the tea garden or stay a night in the old farm house, now a unique guest house. ⊠ *D275, off R600, Central Berg,* ☎ *036/468–1314.* ◷ *8–4:30.*

★ **③** A few kilometers farther down the R600 is the turnoff to the **Drakensberg Boys' Choir School** Mentioned in the same breath as the Vienna and Harlem boys' choirs, this is one of the most famous choirs in the world. It performs in the school's auditorium on Wednesdays at 4 and sometimes on Saturdays. Performances run the musical gamut from the classics to ethnic songs. Reservations are essential. There are no performances during school holidays. ⊠ *Off R600,* ☎ *036/468–1012,* FAX *036/468–1709.*

④ The R600 runs directly into the mountains, ending at **Monk's Cowl,** a Natal Parks Board station and the gateway to several amazing day and overnight hikes into the high Drakensberg. Among the highlights are a one-hour walk to Sterkspruit Falls, the largest waterfall in the area, and a 3½-hour walk to the top of the Little Berg. On this walk you pass the Sphinx—a formation that looks like the famous Egyptian monument—and Breakfast Falls before joining the contour trail for panoramic views of Champagne Castle, Cathkin Peak, Dragon's Back, and Sterkhorn. Hikers who wish to camp out in the mountains must sign the mountain register and pay R6 per person per night. ⊠ *Private Bag X2, Winterton 3340,* ☎ *036/468–1103.* ▣ *R6.50* ◷ *Oct.–Mar. daily 5 AM–7 PM, Apr.–Sept. daily 6–6.*

⑤ South of Monk's Cowl, **Giant's Castle Game Reserve** is an 85,500-acre reserve in the Central Berg region, encompasses rolling grasslands as well as some of the highest peaks in the Drakensberg. A host of trails, ranging in length from two hours to overnight, start at the main visitor center. The most popular tourist attraction is the Main Caves, which have the finest collection of San paintings in the Drakensberg. More than 500 paintings, some now barely discernible, adorn the faces of two huge rock overhangs just a 30-minute walk from the camp. Many of the paintings depict eland hunts, for the huge antelope holds a special religious significance for the San. Guided tours (▣ R7 per person) of the caves are conducted 9–3 daily, on the hour.

Another fascinating attraction is the Lammergeyer Hide, set high on a cliff, where bird-watchers can observe the endangered lammergeyer, or bearded vulture. On weekend mornings between May and September, rangers put out meat and bones for these birds below the hide (blind). Besides giving birders a close-up view of the vultures, the feeding program is intended to draw the birds away from nearby farmland, where they might feed on poisoned carcasses. Afrikaner farmers erroneously believe that the birds kill their young livestock, hence the name *lammergeyer,* "lamb-killer." The hide accommodates a maximum of six people. The hide tours are extremely popular and are sometimes fully booked six months in advance, so if you would like the experience, make sure you book before leaving home or the minute

you arrive in the country. (✉ R50 per person, with a minimum charge
of R200). (✉ Hide Bookings, Giant's Castle Game Reserve, Private
Bag X7055, Estcourt 3310, ☎ 0363/2–4616). A ranger drives you up
to the blind at 7:30 AM, and you're on your own for the walk back.
From Monk's Cowl, head back along the R600 towards Winterton.
At the big T-junction follow signs to Loskop, and along that road there
are large signs for Giant's Castle. ✉ *Mooi River toll plaza exit off N3
or Central Berg/Giant's Castle exit near Estcourt,* ☎ *0363/2–4718.
✉ R6.50.* ☉ *Oct.–Mar. daily 5 AM–7 PM, Apr.–Sept. daily 6–6.*

❻ Injasuti, 32 km (20 mi) down a dirt road off the Central Berg/Loskop
Road, is a collection of huts (☞ Dining and Lodging, *below*) set in the
northern section of the Giant's Castle Game Reserve. A number of spectacular hikes start from here, including a guided 5-km (3-mi) walk (✉
R25) up the Injasuti Valley to Battle Cave, which holds one of the most
fascinating collections of San paintings in the country. Some 750 paintings cover the rock walls of the cave, but it's the subject matter that is
most enthralling: one vignette clearly depicts two Bushman clans at war
with one another. Tours of Battle Cave leave daily from the camp office at 8:30, and reservations are essential. ✉ *Private Bag X7010, Estcourt 3310,* ☎ *036/488–1050.* ✉ *R6.50.* ☉ *Oct.–Mar. daily 5 AM–7
PM, Apr.–Sept. daily 6–6.*

Another tremendous base for hikes—and drives—into the mountains
❼ is the **Cathedral Peak Hotel** (☞ Dining and Lodging, *below*), accessible from Winterton or via dirt roads off the R600. Although the Natal
Parks Board levies R6.50 per person to enter the area, the hotel acts
as the de facto center for hikers heading into the surrounding mountains. It publishes an excellent hiking booklet that describes all the trails,
indicating their length and level of difficulty. A scale model of the area
in the hotel lobby gives hikers a sense of the lay of the land before they
set off. Cathedral Peak (9,900 ft) is the easiest of the major peaks to
scale. Anyone who is fit and accustomed to long hikes can make the
19-km (12-mi) round-trip journey from the hotel to the summit; only
the last portion is difficult. Budget 9–10 hours to get up and down, allowing plenty of time to drink in the view from the top—surely one
of the highlights of the region. ✉ *Cathedral Peak Rd. from Winterton
(mailing address: P.O. Winterton 3340),* ☎ FAX *036/488–1888.*

❽ Access to **Royal Natal National Park** is via the R74, north of Bergville.
The park contains some of the most stunning mountain scenery in the
Drakensberg. The highlight is the Amphitheatre, a sheer rock wall mea-
suring an unbelievable 5 km (3 mi) across and more than 1,500 ft high.
Another showstopper is the Tugela River, which flows off Mont-
aux-Sources (10,836 ft) and plunges nearly 3,000 ft over the plateau
in a series of five spectacular falls. The park's most popular and scenic
walk winds up the Tugela Gorge, a six-hour hike that crosses the river
several times and passes through a tunnel before emerging into the Amphitheatre. Hikers often turn back at the first fording of the river; but
persevere, for the scenery gets better and better. ✉ *North Berg Rd.,
off R74,* ☎ *036/438–6303.* ✉ *R6.50* ☉ *Oct.–Mar. daily 5 AM–7 PM,
Apr.–Sept. daily 6–6.*

Just past the turnoff to Royal Natal National Park, the northbound
❾ R74 begins a twisty ascent up the **Oliviershoek Pass** (6,912 ft), offering tremendous views back over the plains and hills. If these views don't
satiate you, continue on the R74 past the Sterkfontein Dam until the
road ends at a T junction. Turn left onto the R712 and head into Qwa
Qwa, also known as Phuthaditjhaba. Follow signs to the Witsieshoek
Mountain Resort. Just before the resort, the road splits and continues
❿ for about 13 km (8 mi) to the **Sentinel Car Park** (8,580 ft), where you

can follow a path some 450 ft to the very edge of the Drakensberg escarpment. The views from here are breathtaking—the entire Royal Natal National Park lies below you, and you can see all the way to Estcourt. The car park is also the starting point for a strenuous hike to the top of Mont-aux-Sources. From the car park, it's an easy drive back down the R712 to Harrismith and the N3 highway to Johannesburg and Durban.

Dining and Lodging

$$–$$$ ✕ **St. Antons.** Six generations of the Zunkel family have lived in the central Berg district, and their five-star restaurant, close to the Drakensberg Boys' Choir School, with outstanding views of Champagne Castle and Cathedral Peak, has the most friendly service and wonderfully warm mountain atmosphere. Start your meal with Thai pumpkin soup with lemongrass, or the most popular mushrooms St. Anton, button mushrooms in a creamy garlic cheese sauce with flaked almonds. Seafood creole and the Drakensberg trout are excellent main courses, and the chicken and prawn curry and oxtail are also highly recommended. Monday night is pizza night and weekends there is a buffet. Another part of the family business is **St. Antons Gourton Hall.** In an old restored farmers hall, 17 km (11 mi) from the restaurant, the Zunckels have opened a night club and sports bar with the latest sound systems, pool tables, and giant TVs. Locals travel up from the coast to watch the big games and dance until the wee hours. ⊠ *Off R600, Winterton,* ☎ *036/468–1218. MC, V.*

$$$ ✕▥ **Karos Mont-Aux-Sources.** Although this hotel is more than 8 km (5 mi) from the hiking trails of Royal Natal National Park, it more than compensates with its views—stunning panoramas of the Drakensberg that take in the Amphitheatre, the Eastern Buttress, and miles of the escarpment. They are the hotel's greatest asset, so be sure to request a front-facing room. The rooms themselves are no great shakes, being reminiscent of chain hotels around the world. Likewise, the public rooms lack warmth, seeming more suited to the hotel's midweek conference business. Breakfast and dinner are served buffet-style, with extensive selections ranging from roasts to vegetarian curries. ⊠ *Northern Berg Rd., off R74 (mailing address: Private Bag X1670, Bergville 3350),* ☎ ℻ *036/438–6230. 73 rooms. Restaurant, bar, room service, 2 pools, miniature golf, tennis court, horseback riding, squash, volleyball. Breakfast and dinner included. AE, DC, MC, V.*

$$ ✕▥ **The Nest.** Most of the guests at this well-run resort seem content to park themselves on the sun-drenched lawns, soak in the dazzling mountain views, and await the next round of tea, drinks, or meals. Few manage to muster the energy to drive the 8 km (5 mi) to the trailheads at Monk's Cowl. The hotel, built by Italian prisoners of war, is one of the most attractive and appealing of the Berg resorts. Rooms are very pleasant, with pine ceilings, simple cane furniture, heated towel racks, and under-floor heating (there are no TVs). Be sure to request a mountain-facing room. All meals are table d'hôte, with an emphasis on traditional South African cuisine, including home-cooked specialties like roasts, oxtail, and cottage pie. The quality of the food is much higher than at any of the other Berg resorts. ⊠ *R600, Central Berg (mailing address: Private Bag X14, Winterton 3340),* ☎ *036/468–1068,* ℻ *036/468–1390. 53 rooms. Restaurant, bar, pool, tennis court, croquet, horseback riding, mountain bikes, playground. Breakfast, lunch, and dinner included. AE, DC, MC, V.*

$$ ✕⚎ **Royal Natal National Park Hotel.** The "Royal" in this hotel's name refers to the visit of King George VI in 1947, and the place retains an old-fashioned colonial charm. Situated within the boundaries of Royal Natal National Park, it's an ideal stopover for hikers and walkers—fall out of bed and you're likely to find yourself at the start of a trail. Indeed, the hotel's setting is magnificent, encircled as it is by mountains, including the towering cliffs of the Amphitheatre and the Eastern Buttress. For some reason, though, the hotel was designed with an almost obsessive desire to shield its guests from the surrounding beauty—neither the public areas nor the rooms have views worth mentioning. Thankfully, the hotel gardens provide a lovely substitute. Rooms are clean and simple, with white walls and light floral patterns; there's no TV. ⊠ *Northern Berg Rd., off R74 (mailing address: Private Bag 4, Mont-aux-Sources 3353),* ☏ *036/438–6200,* ☏ *036/438–6101. 64 rooms. Restaurant, bar, pool, horseback riding, tennis court. Breakfast and dinner included. AE, DC, MC, V.*

$$ ⚎ **Cathedral Peak Hotel.** Few hotels in South Africa can rival the
★ exquisite setting of this large resort, high above the Ulamboza River and ringed by towering peaks. Hiking trails start right from the hotel and wend their way through a dozen mountains and valleys. No buildings obscure the incredible views, and you won't be running into guests from other hotels since there are none. Opt for a luxury room—they cost just a few rand more and are far more pleasant than the standard rooms or thatched bungalows. French doors open onto private verandas overlooking the gardens or the mountains, and pine furnishings give the rooms a pleasant, rustic feel. Besides its tremendous location, the hotel's other big advantages are a nine-hole golf course and daily helicopter sightseeing trips. The major drawback is the food, which can paralyze your taste buds with boredom—insipid roasts and cream-covered cakes and parfaits. ⊠ *Cathedral Peak Rd. from Winterton (mailing address: P.O. Winterton 3340),* ☏ ☏ *036/488–1888. 90 rooms. Restaurant, 2 bars, room service, pool, 9-hole golf course, tennis court, croquet, exercise room, horseback riding, squash. Breakfast and dinner included. AE, DC, MC, V.*

$$ ⚎ **Champagne Castle.** Along with Cathedral Peak, this old family-style hotel enjoys one of the best settings of any of the Berg resorts. It lies right in the mountains, with magnificent views down Champagne Valley to the towering Champagne Castle and Cathkin Peak. A host of hiking trails begin practically on the hotel's doorstep, and the trailheads at Monk's Cowl lie just minutes away. There's nothing remotely fancy about the hotel itself, but it's a peaceful haven where genteel traditions linger—gentlemen are still required to wear ties to dinner. Rooms, in thatched *rondawels* (traditional round huts) and bungalows scattered through the pleasant gardens, are unexceptional but comfortable. Meals are served buffet-style, with an emphasis on traditional South African roasts and vegetables. Unfortunately, the food's very ordinary, far below the standards set by the Nest (☞ *below*). ⊠ *R600, Central Berg (mailing address: Private Bag X8, Winterton 3340),* ☏ *036/468–1063,* ☏ *036/468–1306. 45 rooms. Restaurant, 2 bars, pool, putting green, tennis court, horseback riding, volleyball. Breakfast, lunch, and dinner included. AE, DC, MC, V.*

Self-Catering Lodging

$ ⚎ **Giant's Castle.** This camp offers comfortable but basic accommodation in Giant's Castle Game Reserve. Hidden away in a beautiful valley close to the sheer face of the High Drakensberg, it is an ideal base for viewing the San paintings in the Main Caves and bearded vultures from the Lammergeyer Hide (☞ Exploring the Drakensberg, *above*). Accommodations are either in bungalows, which share communal kitchens, or in self-contained cottages. You must provide your own food, which is then cooked by camp staff. A store in the main office sells staples like milk, bread, charcoal, and packs of meat. Giant's Castle also manages three mountain huts, situated at the 7,260-ft level and a 4- to 5-hour walk from the main camp. The huts are rudimentary, furnished only with bunk beds and mattresses. Hikers must provide all their own cooking facilities, food, and bedding. ⊠ *Reserve through Natal Parks Board, Box 1750, Pietermaritzburg 3200, ☎ 0331/47–1981, ℻ 0331/47–1980. 13 bungalows and 4 cottages, 3 mountain huts. AE, DC, MC, V.*

$ 🔝 **Injasuti.** In the northern section of the Giant's Castle Game Reserve, this camp lies at the head of the Injasuti Valley, with great views of Cathkin Peak, Monk's Cowl, and Champagne Castle. The camp operates much like the one at Giant's Castle, except that you do your own cooking and washing. Cabins sleep up to six people and all feature kitchens and a dining room/living room. Electricity is available only from 5:30 until 10 each night. Injasuti also manages three caves in the mountains where hikers can sleep overnight. The caves feature only basic toilet facilities and hikers must bring everything else with them, including bedding and food. Reservations for caves must be made through the camp manager (⊠ Private Bag X7010, Estcourt 3310, ☎ 036/488–1050). ⊠ *Reserve through Natal Parks Board Reservations, Box 1750, Pietermaritzburg 3200, ☎ 0331/47–1981, ℻ 0331/47–1980. 17 cabins, 3 caves. AE, DC, MC, V.*

$ 🔝 **Tendele Hutted Camp.** Smack in the middle of Royal Natal National Park, this camp makes a great base for long hikes into the mountains. Accommodations are in a variety of bungalows, cottages, and chalets, each with excellent views of the sheer rock face of the Amphitheatre. You must bring all your own food, although you can purchase staples and frozen meat at the main visitor center and at the Royal Natal National Park Hotel. In the bungalows and cottages, all food is prepared by the camp staff, but the chalets are self-catering. If you don't fancy providing for yourself, you can always walk to the hotel for your meals, although you should make reservations first. ⊠ *Natal Parks Board Reservations, Box 1750, Pietermaritzburg 3200, ☎ 0331/47–1981, ℻ 0331/47–1980. 28 bungalows, chalets, and cottages. AE, DC, MC, V.*

Horseback Riding

Many resorts in the Berg offer **horseback rides** through the mountains for everyone from beginners to experts. Most of these rides last two to three hours. **Rugged Glen** (☎ 036/438–6303) in Royal Natal National Park, and **Hillside** (☎ 0363/24–4350), a campsite in the Giant's Castle Game Reserve, also conduct morning and afternoon guided rides through their respective parks. No experience is necessary, and rides cost R30 per hour. Hillside also offers more adventurous two- and three-day pony trails that take riders through some of the most breathtaking scenery in the Drakensberg. Riders sleep in caves or huts in the mountains, and the Natal Parks Board provides everything you need except food. Bookings for these rides, which cost about R210 per day, must be made with the reservations officer (⊠ Natal Parks Board, Box 662, Pietermaritzburg 3200, ☎ 0331/47–1981).

Drakensberg A to Z

Arriving and Departing

The main resort area of the Drakensberg lies 380 km (250 mi) from Johannesburg and 240 km (150 mi) from Durban—an almost direct shot along the N3 motorway. A car is not strictly necessary for a trip to the Berg, although it is certainly a convenience. On request, most resorts will pick up guests at the **Greyhound** (☎ 011/333–2130 or 031/309–7839) or **Translux** (☎ 031/361–7461) terminals in Estcourt (✉ Municipal Library, Victoria St.), Ladysmith (Ted's Service Station), or Swinburne (Montrose Service Area). Buses from both lines stop at these towns at least once a day on their runs between Durban and Johannesburg. Once at the resort—particularly those situated right in the mountains—most guests are content to hike or enjoy the hotel facilities. If you do want to see some of the surrounding area, you can usually arrange for guided tours and transport.

Contacts and Resources

GUIDED TOURS

Also part of the family operation is **Bush and Berg Tours,** which cater a maximum of seven guests for mountain cocktails, or full-day trips in a luxury air-conditioned Land Rover. This is a most civilized and comfortable way to see the nearby game reserves or go up into the little Berg to otherwise inaccessible places.

Mount Aire (✉ Box 229, Winterton 3340, ☎ 036/468–1141), near the main resorts in the Central Berg, offers 20-minute scenic flights over the mountains. For two or three passengers, expect to pay about R120 per person.

VISITOR INFORMATION

Drakensberg Publicity Association. ✉ *Tatham St., Bergville,* ☎ *036/448–1557.* ◷ *Weekdays 9–4.*

Ietz Nietz Info and Coffee Shop. ✉ *Main St., Winterton,* ☎ *036/488–1180.* ◷ *Closed Sun.*

ZULULAND AND THE BATTLEFIELDS

Zululand stretches north from the Tugela River all the way to the border of Mozambique. It's a region of rolling grasslands, gorgeous beaches, and classic African bush. It has also seen more than its share of bloodshed and death. Modern South Africa was forged in the fiery crucible of Zululand and northern Natal. Here, Boers battled Zulus, Zulus battled British, and British battled Boers. The most interesting historic sites, however, involve the battles against the Zulus. Names like Isandlwana, Rorke's Drift, and Blood River have taken their place in the roll of legendary military encounters.

Indeed, no African tribe has captured the Western imagination quite like the Zulus. A host of books and movies have explored their warrior culture and extolled their martial valor. Until the early 19th century, the Zulus were a small, unheralded group, part of the Nguni peoples who migrated to southern Africa from the north. King Shaka (1787–1828), the illegitimate son of a Zulu chief, changed all that. Before Shaka, warfare among the Nguni had been a desultory affair in which small bands of warriors would hurl spears at one another from a distance and then retire. Shaka introduced the short stabbing spear (*assegai*), teaching his warriors to close with the enemy in hand-to-hand combat. He also developed the famous chest-and-horns formation, a cattle analogy for a classic maneuver in which you outflank and encircle your enemy. In less than a decade, Shaka created a military machine unrivaled in black Africa. By the time of his assassination in 1828, Shaka had destroyed 300 tribes and extended Zulu power for 800 km (500 mi) through the north, south, and west.

Fifty years after Shaka's death, the British still considered the Zulus a major threat to their planned federation of white states in South Africa.

The British solution, in 1879, was to instigate a war to destroy the Zulu kingdom. They employed a similar tactic 20 years later to bring the Boer republics to heel and the rich goldfields of the Witwatersrand into their own hands.

The best way to tour the battlefields is with an expert guide who can bring the history to life (☞ Guided Tours *in* Zululand and the Battle-fields A to Z, *below*). Unless you've done extensive research or have a vivid imagination, you may find it difficult to conjure up the furious events of a century ago. Many of the battle sites are little more than open grassland, graced with the occasional memorial stone. If you're not a history buff, it's better to head straight to the game reserves and natural wonders of northern Zululand (☞ Chapter 9).

Towns and sights on this tour appear on the KwaZulu-Natal map.

Stanger

75 km(47 mi) north of Durban on the N2.

Today, Zululand starts on the other side of the Tugela River. In Shaka's day, the Zulu empire was much larger, encompassing much of present-day KwaZulu-Natal. Shaka himself had his military kraal at Dukuza, the site of present-day Stanger, on the north coast. The KwaZulu Monuments Council (☎ 0358/79–1854) is currently erecting an interpretive center in Stanger that will focus on the Shaka period, as well as dispense information on sites in the area.

Eshowe

45 km (28 mi) northwest of Stanger; leave the N2 at Gingindlovu and follow the R68.

Eshowe is a pleasant town, high up in the hills and with great views of the Dhlinza Forest and fields of sugarcane. It is the site of **Fort Nongqayi**, which houses the **Zululand Historical Museum.** The fort was built in 1883 and served as the headquarters of the Nongqai Police, a black police contingent under British command. Museum displays trace the role of the fort in the Bambata Rebellion of 1906, when Chief Bambata took up arms to protest a £1 poll tax on every African male. A particularly interesting exhibit deals with John Dunn (1834–95), the son of settler parents, who was fluent in Zulu, Afrikaans, and English. He became Chief Cetshwayo's political adviser in 1856 and was given the status of a Zulu chief. Dunn observed Zulu customs and laws, going so far as to marry 49 Zulu wives, by whom he had 117 children. Periodically, the descendants of John Dunn stage reunions. ✉ *Nongqai Rd., Eshowe,* ☎ *0354/4–1141,* ℻ *0354/7–4733.* ⊞ *Free.* ☻ *Daily 9–4.*

Thirteen kilometers (eight miles) north of Eshowe on the R68, you'll see the turnoff to **Shakaland,** a living museum of Zulu culture and one of the most popular tourist stops in the region. Originally the movie set for *Shaka Zulu,* Shakaland consists of a traditional Zulu kraal, with thatched beehive huts arranged in a circle around a central cattle enclosure. The emphasis here is on Zulu culture as it existed under King Shaka in the 19th century. You can watch Zulus, dressed in animal skins or beaded aprons, engaged in everyday tasks: making beer, forging spears, and crafting beadwork. Opt for a three-hour day tour or spend the night (☞ Dining and Lodging, *below*). A Zulu cultural advisor leads you through the kraal, explaining the significance of the layout and the roles played by men and women in traditional Zulu society. A highlight of the visit is a half-hour dance performance, featuring a variety of Zulu and other traditional dances. The whole setup is touristy and some critics have labeled it a Zulu Disneyland, but you learn a great deal about Zulu culture nevertheless. A buffet lunch of Zulu specialties and Western food is included in the tour. ⊠ *Off R68, 13 km (8 mi) north of Eshowe,* ☎ *03546/912,* ⠟ *03546/824,* ⊠ *R85 (includes lunch). Daily tours at 11 and 12:30.*

Dining and Lodging

$$$ ✕⊞ Shakaland. Shakaland is best known as a living museum of traditional Zulu culture (☞ *above*), but it's also possible to stay overnight at the complex, an experience that is far more rewarding than the three-hour daytime tour. Overnight guests see a more extensive program of cultural events than day visitors (the program begins at 4 PM and concludes at 11 AM the next day), and get to experience a night in a quasi-traditional Zulu dwelling. The rooms here are among the most attractive and luxurious of all the African-inspired accommodations in the country: enormous beehive thatch huts supported by rope-wrapped struts are decorated with African bedspreads, reed matting, and interesting African art that create an appealing ethnic elegance. Modern bathrooms are attached to all but three huts. All meals are included in the price, and feature a selection of Western-style dishes as well as some Zulu specialties. ⊠ *Off R68, 13 km (8 mi) north of Eshowe (mailing address: Box 103, Eshowe 3815),* ☎ *03546/912,* ⠟ *03546/824. 40 rooms, 37 with bath. Restaurant, bar, pool, shop. Breakfast, dinner, and cultural tour included. AE, DC, MC, V.*

Melmoth

30 km (19 mi) north of Eshowe.

Return to the R68 and turn left. After a few kilometers you come to the tiny settlement of Nkwalini. Turn right onto the R34 toward Empangeni to reach the **Jabulani Rehabilitation Centre.** Run by the Natal Cripples' Care Association, the center is home to more than 100 Zulus with disabilities, many of whom have been victims of polio. The residents learn a variety of crafts, from beadwork to spear- and shield-making, and much of their work is used and sold at tourist centers like Shakaland. The center has its own crafts outlet; prices here are often much lower than at the major curio shops, and you can watch the artisans at work. A small museum houses some antique spears and *knobkerries* (wooden fighting sticks). ⊠ *R34, between Nkwalini and Empangeni,* ☎ *0351/92–8144.* ⊠ *Free.* ☉ *Daily 8–5.*

Return to the R68 and turn right. The road snakes up and over the beautiful **Nkwalini Pass,** where you'll have knockout views of valleys and hills dotted with Zulu kraals. Stay on the R34 through the town of Melmoth and then continue for another 32 km (20 mi) to the turnoff for the R66 and **Ulundi.** Ulundi is currently the joint capital—with Pietermaritzberg—of KwaZulu-Natal. Except for a huge legislative complex, however, it's an empty, ghastly place, full of blowing trash and ramshackle buildings.

Lodging

$$$ ⊞ Simunye Pioneer Settlement. If Shakaland is too commercial for your
★ tastes, consider this small settlement tucked away in a remote valley of Zululand. Like Shakaland, Simunye attempts to introduce you to traditional Zulu culture, but the emphasis here extends to contemporary Zulu lifestyles, too. You'll reach the camp on horseback or ox-wagon, and the one-hour ride into the valley is one of the highlights of a visit. During a stay, you'll watch Zulu dancing and visit a working kraal, complete with traditional beehive huts, where you'll learn

about Zulu culture and meet the kraal's residents. You can opt to sleep overnight in one of the beehive huts; otherwise, stay in the more luxurious main camp, built into the side of a hill overlooking the Mfule River. Rooms, built of stone and thatch, are a classy mix of Zulu and pioneer cultures. There's no electricity—light is provided by candles and hurricane lanterns. Unfortunately, the stone bathrooms were designed more for their aesthetic value than any practical purposes: awkward steps lead to a hand-filled stone bath, and just getting in and out requires balance and agility. For this reason alone, Simunye would be difficult for the elderly or anyone with disabilities. Most people stay only one night, but try to book for two days over a weekend and arrange to attend a wedding or coming-out ceremony in a neighboring village. These ceremonies are purely local affairs, and you won't experience a more authentic celebration of rural Zulu culture. ✉ *D256, off the R34, 6 km (4 mi) south of Melmoth (mailing address: Box 103, Eshowe 3815),* ☎ *03546/912,* ℻ *03546/824. 6 rooms. Breakfast, lunch, and dinner included. AE, MC, V.*

Ulundi

35 km (22 mi) north of Melmoth.

A mile before you reach Ulundi you'll see the turnoff to the **Battle of Ulundi Memorial** (✉ Cetshwayo Hwy., no phone). A stone temple with a silver dome marks the site of the battle on the sun-baked uplands surrounding Ulundi. The Battle of Ulundi marked the culmination of the Zulu War of 1879. Lord Chelmsford, smarting from his defeat at Isandlwana (☞ *below*), personally led the march on Ulundi and King Cetshwayo's royal kraal, Ondini. Cetshwayo, already disheartened by heavy losses at Kambula and Gingindlovu, sent messengers to the British seeking peace. In reply, Chelmsford demanded the disbandment of the Zulu regiment system and the surrender of the royal cattle herd. For the Zulu, to whom cattle represent the very thread of the social fabric, such terms were unacceptable.

On July 4, 1879, a British force of 5,317 crossed the White Mfolozi River, marched onto the open plain near Ondini, and formed an infantry square. Mounted troops then harassed the 15,000-strong Zulu force into making an undisciplined attack. None of the Zulu warriors got within 100 ft of the British square before being cut down by rifle and artillery fire. Within 45 minutes, the Zulus were in flight and the British 17th Lancers and a flying column gave pursuit, spearing the fleeing Zulus from horseback. The Zulu dead numbered 1,500. British losses amounted to a mere 13.

The British burned Ondini to the ground, and King Cetshwayo fled into the Ngome Forest. He was captured two months later and exiled to Cape Town and, finally, to England. Although he was restored to the throne as a puppet in 1883, the Zulu empire had been shattered.

Continue down the dirt road to the **KwaZulu Cultural Museum—Ondini,** the original site of King Cetshwayo's royal kraal. Ondini was modeled after Dingane's kraal at Mgungundlovu (☞ *below*). At the time of its destruction in 1879, the kraal consisted of 1,500 huts and was home to some 5,000 people. Today, only the royal enclosure has been restored, but a stroll among the deserted beehive huts gives you a feel for the kraal's size and scope. An interesting site museum at the entrance traces the history of the Zulu kings and displays the silver mug and bible presented to King Cetshwayo by Queen Victoria in 1882. The Cultural Museum, in a separate building, is excellent and well worth a visit. It houses a superb collection of beadwork from various tribes, plus detailed exhibits on Zulu life, including some of the changes in Zulu customs in modern times. ⊠ *Cetshwayo Hwy.,* ☎ *0358/79–1854.* 🎫 *R5.* ☉ *Daily 8–4.*

En Route From Ulundi, retrace your route back down the R66 and turn right onto the R34 toward Vryheid. The turnoff to **Mgungundlovu** and the **Grave of Piet Retief** lies just a few kilometers farther on. Mgungundlovu was the site of Dingane's royal kraal and home to his 500 wives. Dingane (ruled 1828–40) was Shaka's younger brother; he killed Shaka in 1828 to seize power for himself. During Dingane's rule, the Zulu came under increasing pressure from white settlers moving into the area. In 1837, Piet Retief and a party of Voortrekkers petitioned Dingane for land. The king agreed on condition that Retief retrieve some Zulu cattle stolen by a rival chief. Retief duly recovered the cattle and returned to Mgungundlovu with nearly 100 men. Dingane welcomed the Voortrekkers into the royal kraal, instructing them to leave their guns and horses outside. Once they were inside, Dingane shouted "Kill the wizards!" and 8 to 10 warriors seized each of the unarmed men. The Voortrekkers were dragged to Execution Hill and murdered. A monument now stands on the hill where Piet Retief and his men are buried. Retaliation from the Voortrekkers was slow in coming but ultimately terrible. At the Battle of Blood River (☞ *below*), in December 1838, Dingane's army was completely destroyed. Dingane burned Mgungundlovu to the ground and fled to the north. He met his end in 1840 at the hands of another brother, Mpande, who succeeded him as king. Today, the beehive huts of the royal enclosure have been reconstructed on their original foundations and a guide leads short tours of the kraal. A site museum has also opened, but as yet it contains little of interest. ⊠ *R34,* ☎ *03545/2254.* 🎫 *R5.* ☉ *Daily 8–4.*

Babanango

6.4 km (4 mi) from the Grave of Piet Retief turnoff on the R34, turn left (west) onto a good-quality dirt road for the 32-km (20-mi) run to to Babanango.

A dirt road connecting the R34 to Babanango passes through some of the most beautiful countryside in Zululand, with seemingly endless views over rolling grasslands. The road ends at the tarred R68. Turn right and drive less than 2 km (1 mi) into the pleasant hamlet of Babanango.

From Babanango, follow the R68 for 48 km (30 mi) to the turnoff to Isandlwana. The **Battle of Isandlwana,** on January 22, 1879, was a major defeat for the British army. Coming as it did at the very beginning of the Zulu War, the defeat sent shudders of apprehension through the corridors of Whitehall and ultimately cost Lord Chelmsford his command. Chelmsford was in personal charge of one of three invasion columns that were supposed to sweep into Zululand and converge on Cetshwayo's capital at Ulundi. On January 20, Chelmsford crossed the Buffalo River into Zululand, leaving behind a small force at Rorke's Drift to guard the column's supplies. He encamped at Isandlwana. Two days later, believing there was no danger of attack, he led a large portion of his troops on a mission in support of another commander, leaving the camp woefully unprepared to defend itself. Unknown to Chelmsford, the heart of the Zulu army—20,000 men—had taken up a position just 5 km (3 mi) away. Despite their obvious advantage, the Zulus stayed their attack, persuaded by a *sangoma* (diviner) that the moment was not propitious. When a British patrol stumbled on the hidden army, however, it rose up and charged. Using Shaka's classic chest-and-horns formation, the Zulus swept toward the British positions arrayed beneath the distinctive peak of Isandlwana. The battle hung in the balance until the

Zulus' left horn outflanked the British. The fighting continued for two hours before the British fled the field, with the Zulus in triumphant pursuit. About 1,000 Zulus perished in the attack, as did 1,329 British troops, including 52 officers. A further 300–400 British soldiers fled by various routes back toward Rorke's Drift and Natal. Today, the battlefield is dotted with whitewashed stone cairns and memorials marking the resting places of fallen soldiers. Even now, as you stand on the hillside overlooking the vast plain, the thought of 20,000 warriors rushing forward with their short stabbing spears is enough to make you shudder. The visitor center houses a small museum of mementos and artifacts. ⊠ *Off R68, no phone.* ▦ *R5.* ☉ *Daily 8–4.*

Dining and Lodging

$ ✕ **Stan's Pub.** In the five-room Babanango Hotel, you can relax in one of the country's most famous watering holes. It's a tiny place crammed full of bric-a-brac, pictures of naked women, rude bar sayings, and uniforms used in the filming of *Zulu Dawn*. The owner, Stan, is a genial fellow, a former Royal Marine who served in Burma during World War II. The pub serves light lunches, including good pies with curry gravy and fries. It's worth a stop if you don't mind the bare-bums-and-boobs decor. ⊠ *16 Justice St.,* ☎ *0358/35-0029. MC, V.*

$$$ ▦ **Babanango Valley Lodge.** This tiny guest lodge lies at the end of a rutted, 15-km (9-mi) dirt road on a 5,000-acre cattle farm. Obviously, it's not the sort of place where you constantly pop in and out, but that's okay—you probably won't want to leave anyway. The lodge sits at the head of a steep valley, far from any other buildings and with tremendous views of acacia-studded grasslands and hills. John and Meryn Turner, the charming young hosts, go out of their way to make guests feel at home. John is a registered guide (☞ Contacts and Resources *in* Zululand and the Battlefields A to Z, *below*), and many people stay at the lodge as part of his battlefields tour. Rooms are decorated with rustic armoires and dressers, white fluffy duvets, and frilly lamp shades—simple, comfortable country stuff. The four-course table d'hôte dinner focuses on traditional South African fare, including fresh farm produce. ⊠ *15 km (9 mi) off R68, near Babanango (mailing address: Box 10, Babanango 3850),* ☎ ℻ *0358/35–0062. 6 rooms. Pool. Breakfast and dinner included. MC, V.*

Rorke's Drift

35 km (22 mi) east of Isandlwana; turn left when you get back to the R68, and continue to the turnoff to Rorke's Drift.

★ Rorke's Drift is by far the best of the Zulu War battlefields to see without a guide. An excellent museum and orientation center superbly retell the story of the battle, with electronic diagrams, battle sounds, and dioramas. From the British perspective, this was the most glorious battle of the Zulu War, the more so since it took place just hours after the disaster at Isandlwana. The British force at Rorke's Drift consisted of just 141 men, of whom 35 were ailing. They occupied a Swedish mission church and house, which had been converted into a storehouse and hospital. The Zulu forces numbered some 3,000–4,000 men, comprised of the reserve regiments from Isandlwana. When a survivor from Isandlwana sounded the warning at 3:15 PM, the tiny British force hastily erected a stockade of flour bags and biscuit boxes around the mission. The Zulus attacked 75 minutes later and the fighting raged for 12 hours before the Zulus faltered. When the smoke cleared, 500 Zulus and 17 Britons lay dead. More Victoria Crosses, 11 in all, were won at Rorke's Drift than at any other battle in British history.

The staunch resilience of the British defenders has been immortalized in the classic 1964 movie *Zulu*. ⊠ *Rorke's Drift Rd., off R68*, ☎ 03425/ 627. ☞ *R5*. ☉ *Daily 8–4*.

Rorke's Drift is still a mission station, run by the Evangelical Lutheran Church. The **Rorke's Drift ELC Art and Craft Centre** at the mission sells super pottery, hand-woven rugs, and linocuts, all created by mission artists. ⊠ *Rorke's Drift Rd., off R68, no phone*. ☉ *Weekdays 8–4:30, weekends 10–3*.

Retrace your steps to the R68 and turn left. After 24 km (15 mi), the road intersects with the R33. Turn right and drive 21 km (13 mi) to the turnoff to the site of the **Battle of Blood River,** one of the most important events in the history of South Africa. This battle, fought between the Boers and the Zulus in 1838, predates the Anglo-Zulu War by more than 40 years. After the murder of Piet Retief and his men at Mgungundlovu in February 1838 (☞ *above*), Dingane dispatched Zulu impis to kill all the white settlers in Natal. The Voortrekkers bore the brunt of the Zulu assault. For the next 10 months, their future hung in the balance: entire settlements were wiped out and a Boer commando was smashed at the Battle of Italeni. By November, a new commando of 464 men and 64 wagons under Andries Pretorius had moved out to challenge the Zulus. On Sunday, November 9, the Boers took a vow that should God grant them victory they would forever remember that day as a Sabbath and build a church in commemoration. They repeated the vow every night for the next five weeks. On December 16, an enormous Zulu force attacked the Boers, who had circled their wagons in a strategic position backed by the Blood River and a deep *donga*, or gully. Armed with only spears, the Zulus were no match for the Boer riflemen. At the end of the battle, 3,000 Zulus lay dead, but not a single Boer had fallen. The immediate effect of the victory was to open Natal to white settlement, but the long-term effects were far more dramatic. The intensely religious Voortrekkers saw their great victory as a confirmation of their role as God's chosen people. This deeply held conviction lay at the spiritual heart of the apartheid system that surfaced more than a century later, in 1948. Indeed, when you see the monument, there's no mistaking the gravity and importance that the Nationalist Government ascribed to its erection. The laager of 64 wagons has been reconstructed in exacting detail, made from a mix of cast steel and bronze that is expected to last at least 200 years. It's a truly haunting monument, made even more poignant by its position on empty grasslands that seem to stretch for eternity. ⊠ *Off R33, between Dundee and Vryheid*, ☎ 03424/695. ☞ *R5*. ☉ *Daily 8–4*.

Lodging

$$$$ 🏨 **Fugitives' Drift Lodge.** Set on a 4,000-acre game farm, this attractive lodge is a Zulu battlefields favorite. It lies just a few kilometers from the site of the famous engagement at Rorke's Drift and overlooks the drift where survivors of the British defeat at Isandlwana fled across the Buffalo River. Even more important, the owner is Dave Rattray, the best battlefield guide in the country (☞ Guided Tours *in* Zululand and the Battlefields A to Z, *below*). From its position high above the river, the lodge presides over a panorama of classic Zululand—thorn trees, savanna, and, in the distance, the distinctive peak of Isandlwana. Rooms, in individual cottages that open onto lovely lawns and gardens, feature fireplaces, antique dressers, and wicker furniture. The focal point of the lodge is the lounge and dining room, a stone-floored hall decorated with old rifles, British regimental flags, Zulu spears, and antique military prints. All meals are included in the price, and guests eat

together at a communal table. The lodge has no electricity. ⊠ *On Rorke's Drift Rd. (mailing address: P.O. Rorke's Drift 3016),* ☎ FAX *034/6421–843. 8 chalets. Dining room, bar. Breakfast, lunch, and dinner included. DC, MC, V.*

Dundee

35 km (22 mi) north of Rorke's Drift.

The first-rate **Talana Museum,** on the outskirts of Dundee, encompasses nine separate buildings and is well worth a visit. Fascinating exhibits trace the history of the area from the early San hunter-gatherers to the rise of the Zulu nation, the extermination of the cannibal tribes of the Biggarsberg, and finally the vicious battles of the Boer War (1899–1902). The museum itself stands on the site of the Battle of Talana (October 10, 1899), the opening battle in the Boer War. Two of the museum buildings were used by the British as dressing stations during the battle, which was won by the British. The Miners Rest Tea Shop in a delightfully restored miner's cottage on the grounds of the Talana Museum serves refreshments as well as more substantial dishes like peri-peri chicken livers or spinach, feta, and chicken pie in phyllo pastry. The food is good, and the atmosphere most welcoming. ⊠ *2 km (1 mi) outside Dundee on R33 to Vryheid,* ☎ *0341/2–2654.* 🖼 *R3.* ☺ *Weekdays 8–4, Sat. 10–4, Sun. noon–4.*

Ladysmith

60 km (37 mi) southwest of Dundee.

Ladysmith became famous around the world during the Boer War, when it outlasted a Boer siege of 118 days. Nearly 20,000 people were caught in the town when the Boers attacked on November 2, 1899. During the next four months, there was little fighting around Ladysmith itself—the Boers seemed content to shell the town with their Long Tom siege guns—but the town's food supply steadily dwindled. By the end of the siege, the desperate residents were slaughtering half-starved horses to supplement their diets, and 28 people died each day of sickness and malnutrition.

Much of the early part of the war revolved around British attempts to raise the siege. The incompetence of the British general, Sir Redvers Buller, became apparent during repeated attempts to smash the Boer lines, resulting in heavy British losses at Spioenkop, Vaalkrans, and Colenso. Finally, sheer weight of numbers saw the British defeat the Boers in the epic 10-day Battle of Tugela Heights, and raise the siege of Ladysmith on February 28, 1900.

The **Ladysmith Siege Museum** brings the period of the siege skillfully to life, with the use of electronic mapping, artifacts from the period, and black-and-white photos. The museum can arrange guided tours, but it also sells two self-guiding pamphlets: the "Siege Town Walkabout" and the "Siege Town Drive-about." ⊠ *Murchison St., next to Town Hall,* ☎ *0361/2–2231.* 🖼 *R2.* ☺ *Weekdays 8–4, Sat. 10–noon.*

Next to the Siege Museum, directly in front of Town Hall, stands a replica of a **Long Tom,** the 6-inch Creusot gun used by the Boers during the siege. Also in front of Town Hall are two howitzers used by the British and christened Castor and Pollux.

Dining and Lodging

$ ✕🖼 **Royal Hotel.** This three-star hotel will suffice if you find yourself in Ladysmith at the end of the day. It's a typical South African country hotel that has seen more glorious days. Expect small, run-down rooms and ancient furniture, although TVs and air-conditioning are standard features. The hotel was built in 1880, just 19 years before the town was attacked by the Boers during the Boer War. During the siege, a shell from a Long Tom gun exploded on the hotel veranda, killing a doctor. The hotel offers several dining options, from a family-style Italian restaurant to expensive Continental cuisine in Swainsons. ✉ *140 Murchison St., Ladysmith 3370,* ☎ FAX *0361/2–2176. 71 rooms. 3 restaurants, 3 bars, room service. Breakfast included. AE, DC, MC, V.*

Zululand and the Battlefields A to Z

Getting Around
Unless you're on a tour, it's almost impossible to see this part of the country without your own car. Your best bet is to rent a car in Durban, and perhaps combine a trip to the battlefields with a self-drive tour of KwaZulu-Natal's game reserves. Roads are in excellent condition, although some of the access roads to the battlefields are of gravel.

Contacts and Resources
GUIDED TOURS

The visitor information offices in Dundee (at the Talana Museum) and Ladysmith (☞ *below*) have lists of registered battlefield guides. At the Talana Museum in Dundee you can also rent or buy cassette tapes describing the events at Rorke's Drift and Isandlwana.

Of all the battlefields guides in the region, **David Rattray** (☎ FAX 0341/2–3319) is widely considered to be the finest. His accounts of the action at Rorke's Drift, Isandlwana, and Fugitives' Drift sometimes move listeners to tears. Many combine one of David's tours with a stay at his lodge, just a few kilometers from Rorke's Drift. David is slowly losing his voice, so part of the tour now consists of David's taped narrative.

Another reputable guide to the Zulu battlefields is **John Turner** of the Babanago Valley Lodge (☎ FAX 0358/35–0062). For more information about battlefields guides, contact any of the information centers.

VISITOR INFORMATION

Eshowe Information Centre. ✉ *Main St.,* ☎ *0354/4–1141, ext. 155.* ☉ *Weekdays 8–4.*

Ladysmith Information Bureau. ✉ *Town Hall, Murchison St.,* ☎ *0361/2–2992.* ☉ *Weekdays 8–4, Sat. 8–noon.*

Talana Museum. ✉ *R33, 3 km (2 mi) outside Dundee,* ☎ *0341/2–2654,* FAX *0341/2–2376.* ☉ *Weekdays 8–4, Sat. 10–4, Sun. noon–4.*

HLUHLUWE-UMFOLOZI GAME RESERVE

Hluhluwe-Umfolozi ("shloo-*shloo*-ee uhm-fuh-*low*-zee") lies in Zululand, 264 km (165 mi) up the north coast from Durban. In an area of just 906 square km (325 square mi), Hluhluwe delivers the Big Five plus all the plains game, as well as species like nyala and red duiker that are rare in other parts of the country. Equally important, it boasts one of the most biologically diverse habitats on the planet, a unique mix of forest, woodland, savanna, and grassland. You will find about 1,250 different species of plants and trees here—more than in some entire countries.

The park is administered by the highly regarded Natal Parks Board, the wildlife arm of KwaZulu-Natal province. Thanks to its conservation efforts, the park can take credit for saving the white rhino from extinction. So successful was the park at increasing white rhino numbers that in 1960 it established its now famous Rhino Capture Unit to relocate rhinos to other reserves in Africa. The park is now trying to do for the black rhino what it did for its white cousins. Poaching has decimated Africa's black rhino population from 14,000 a decade ago to a saddening 2,250. Twenty percent of Africa's remaining black rhinos live in this reserve, and you won't get a better chance than this of seeing them in the wild.

Until 1989, the reserve consisted of two separate parks, Hluhluwe in the north and Umfolozi in the south, separated by a fenced corridor. Although a road (R618) still runs through this corridor, the fences have been removed and the parks now operate as a single entity. Hluhluwe and the corridor are the most scenic areas of the park, notable for their bush-covered hills and knockout views, whereas Umfolozi is better known for its broad plains.

Compared with Kruger, Hluhluwe-Umfolozi is tiny—less than six percent of Kruger's size—but such comparisons can be misleading. You can spend days driving around this park and still not see everything, or feel like you're going in circles. Probably the biggest advantage Hluhluwe has over Kruger is that game-viewing is good year-round, whereas Kruger has seasonal peaks and valleys. Another bonus is its proximity to Mkuzi Game Reserve and the spectacular coastal reserves of Greater St. Lucia Wetland Park (☞ Excursions from Hluhluwe-Umfolozi, *below*). The park is also close enough to Durban to make it a worthwhile one- or two-day excursion.

Parks and lodges in this section appear on the KwaZulu-Natal map.

Park Activities

See Hluhluwe-Umfolozi A to Z, *below,* for information about reservations and fees.

Bush Walks
Armed rangers lead groups of eight on two- to three-hour bush walks departing from Hilltop Camp. You rarely see much game on these walks, but you do learn a great deal about the area's ecology and how to recognize the signs of the bush, including animal spoor. Walks leave daily at 5:30 AM and 3:30 PM (6 and 3 in winter), and cost about R25; reserve a few days in advance at Hilltop Camp reception.

Game Drives
A great way to see the park is on game drives led by rangers. These drives (about R60 per person) hold several advantages over driving yourself around the park: you sit high up in an open-air vehicle, with a good view and the wind in your face; a ranger explains the finer points of animal behavior and ecology; and your guide has a good idea where to find animals like leopard, cheetah, and lion. Game drives leave daily (except Sunday) at 5:30 AM in summer, 6:30 AM in winter. The park also offers three-hour night drives, during which you search for nocturnal animals with powerful spotlights. These three-hour drives depart at 7, and you should make advance reservations at the Hilltop reception desk.

Wilderness Trails
The park's wilderness trails are every bit as popular as Kruger's, but they tend to be tougher and more rustic. Led by an armed ranger, you must be able to walk 16 km (10 mi) a day for a period of three days and four nights. All equipment, food, and baggage are carried by donkeys. The first and last nights are spent at Mndindini, a permanent tented camp. The other two are spent under canvas in the bush. While in the

bush, hikers bathe in the Mfolozi River or have a hot bucket shower; toilet facilities consist of a spade and toilet-paper roll. Trails, open March–November, are limited to eight people, and should be reserved a year in advance. Expect to pay about R900 per person.

If that sounds too easy, you can always opt for the **Umfolozi Primitive Trail.** On this trek hikers carry all their own kit and sleep out under the stars. A campfire burns all night to scare off animals, and each participant is expected to sit a 90-minute watch. A ranger acts as guide.

A more genteel wilderness experience is **Weekend Trails,** based out of the tented Dengezi Wilderness Camp, where you're guaranteed a bed and some creature comforts. The idea behind these trails is to instill in the participants an appreciation for the beauty of the untamed bush. The weekend begins on Friday at 2:30 and ends on Sunday at 3. Participation is limited to eight people, and costs about R500 per person.

Lodging

Like Kruger, Hluhluwe-Umfolozi offers a range of accommodations in government-run rest camps, with an emphasis on self-catering (only Hilltop has a restaurant). Unfortunately, most foreign visitors can't avail themselves of the park's secluded bush lodges and camps, as each of them must be reserved en bloc, and the smallest accommodates at least eight people. At Hilltop you can expect to pay R80 per person for a rondawel and R165 for an en suite, self-catering chalet.

$ ☷ **Hilltop Camp.** It may be a government-run camp, but this delightful lodge in the Hluhluwe half of the park beats anything you'll find in Kruger. Perched on the crest of a hill, it commands panoramic views over the park, the Hlaza and Nkwakwa hills, and Zululand. Thatch and ocher-color walls give it an appropriately African feel. Scattered across the crown of the hill, self-contained chalets have high thatched ceilings, rattan furniture, and small verandas. If you plan to eat all your meals in the restaurant, forgo the more expensive chalets with fully equipped kitchens. If you're on a tight budget, opt for a basic rondawel with two beds, a basin, and a refrigerator; toilet facilities are communal. ✉ *Natal Parks Board, Box 1750, Pietermaritzburg 3200,* ☎ *0331/47–1981,* ℻ *0331/47–1980. Restaurant, bar, shop, gas station. AE, DC, MC, V.*

Near Hluhluwe-Umfolozi

$$$$ ☷ **Zululand Tree Lodge.** Eight miles from the park, this classy lodge
★ lies in a forest of fever trees on the 3,700-acre Ubizane Game Reserve, a small park stocked with white rhino and plains game. It's by far the most luxurious accommodation in the area, and makes a great base from which to explore Hluhluwe, Mkuzi, and St. Lucia. Built of thatch and wood, the open-sided lodge sits on stilts overlooking the Mzinene River. Rooms are in separate cottages, also on stilts, along the riverbank. The rooms themselves are small, but among the most tastefully decorated you will find: mosquito nets cover old-fashioned iron bedsteads made up with fluffy white duvets, and African-print cushions, wicker, and reed matting add a real *Out of Africa* feel. If you want the experience of sleeping alfresco, fold back the huge wood shutters dividing the bedroom from the open deck. Game rangers lead bush walks and game drives through the small reserve. ✉ *Hluhluwe Rd. (mailing address: Box 116, Hluhluwe 3960),* ☎ *035/562–1020,* ℻ *035/562–1032. 20 rooms. Restaurant, bar, pool. Breakfast, dinner, and game drives included. AE, DC, MC, V.*

Excursions from Hluhluwe-Umfolozi

Mkuzi Game Reserve. Forty-eight kilometers (30 mi) north of Hluhluwe-Umfolozi, this 88,900-acre reserve lies in the shadow of the Ubombo Mountains, between the Mkuze and Msunduze Rivers. The park is famous for its birds and rhinos. More than 400 bird species have been spotted here, including myriad waterfowl drawn to the park's shallow pans in summer. Several blinds, particularly those overlooking Nsumo Pan, offer superb views. Along with Hluhluwe, Mkuzi is probably the best place in Africa to see rhino in the wild. With an area only a fraction of the size of Kruger, the park supports a population of some 70 black and 120 white rhino. You won't find any lion, buffalo, or elephant, but the low-lying thornveld supports healthy populations of general game, including zebra, giraffe, kudu, and nyala. The park also features a spectacular forest of towering sycamore figs. ⊠ *Follow N2 north from Hluhluwe for 37 km (23 mi) and follow signs,* ☎ *0331/47–1961 for general information.* ⊡ *R25 per vehicle, R6 per person.* ⊘ *Daily 6–6.*

Greater St. Lucia Wetland Park. This huge park is one of the most important coastal and wetland areas in the world. The focal point is Lake St. Lucia, a broad, 95,545-acre lake dotted with islands and populated by hundreds of crocodiles and hippos. Bird-watchers rave about the avian life, too—at times, the lake is pink with flamingos. The Natal Parks Board offers guided trips up the estuary aboard the *Santa Lucia,* an 80-seat motor launch that makes the 90-minute voyage three times daily (reservations are essential). The Parks Board maintains an office and self-catering camp in the small but fast-expanding fishing resort of St. Lucia, near the mouth of the estuary. The village is also the access point to the thin strip of land that runs up the coast between Lake St. Lucia and the Indian Ocean, with some of the country's best beaches as well as the highest vegetated dunes in the world. The small Natal Parks Board camp of Cape Vidal, 20 km (12 mi) north of St. Lucia, has whale-watching towers and is one of the world's best places for shore-based sightings of southern right whales and humpbacks, which drift south on the warm Aghulas current around October each year. The area is also a magnet for beer-swilling fishermen with more horsepower than sense and real cowboy mentalities. ⊠ *24 km (15 mi) east of the Mtubatuba exit off the N2. Mailing address: Natal Parks Board, Private Bag, St. Lucia 3936,* ☎ *035/590–1340,* ⅏ *035/590–1343.* ⊡ *Boat tours R35.* ⊘ *Tours daily at 8, 10:30, and 2:30 with an additional trip on Fridays and Saturdays at 4.*

Hluhluwe-Umfolozi A to Z

Arriving and Departing

BY CAR

From Durban, drive north on the N2 highway to Mtubatuba, then cut west on the R618 to Mambeni Gate; otherwise, continue up the N2 to the Hluhluwe exit and follow the signs to the park and Memorial Gate. The whole trip takes about three hours.

BY PLANE

The closest airport to the park is at Richards Bay, about 100 km (60 mi) south of Hluhluwe-Umfolozi, which is served by **British Airways/Comair** (☎ 0351/4–1361) flights at least once daily from Johannesburg. **Avis** (☎ 0351/98–6555) and **Imperial** (☎ 0351/4–1414) have **car rental offices** at the Richards Bay airport.

Reservations and Fees

Admission to the park costs R25 per vehicle plus an additional R6 per person. The park is open October–March from 5 AM to 7 PM and April–September 6–6. Reservations for all accommodations and wilderness trails must be made through the **Natal Parks Board** (✉ Box 1750, Pietermaritzburg 3200, ☎ 0331/47–1981, FAX 0331/47–1980).

Safari Operators

Zululand Safaris (✉ Box 79, Hluhluwe 3960, ☎ 035/562–0144, FAX 035/562–0205) is by far the largest tour operator in Zululand and offers a full range of half- and full-day game drives in Hluhluwe-Umfolozi, as well as night drives and bush walks. The company also leads game drives into the nearby Mkuzi Game Reserve, and guided tours to the bird-rich wetlands and beaches of St. Lucia (☞ *above*).

ITALA GAME RESERVE

Itala is in the north of KwaZulu-Natal, 221 km (138 mi) from Hluhluwe-Umfolozi, close to the southern Swaziland border. At 296 square km (107 square mi) it is small even compared with the relatively compact Hluhluwe-Umfolozi. Its size and the fact that there are no lions is probably why this delightful park is usually bypassed even by South Africans—but they clearly don't know what they're missing. The other four of the Big Five are here—it's excellent for black and white rhinos—and the park is stocked with cheetah, hyenas, giraffe, and an array of antelope among its 80 mammal species. The stunning landscapes and the relaxed game-viewing make this area a breath of fresh air after the Big Five melee of Mpumalanga.

Founded in 1972, the reserve, run by the Natal Parks Board, is a rugged region that drops 3,290 ft in just 15 km (9 mi) through sandstone cliffs, multicolored rocks, granite hills, ironstone outcrops, and quartz formations. Watered by nine small rivers rising in its vicinity and covered with rich soils, Itala supports a varied cross-section of vegetation, encompassing riverine thicket, wetland, open savanna, and acacia woodland. Arrival at its Ntshondwe Camp is nothing short of dramatic. The meandering road climbs from open plains to the top of a plateau dotted with granite formations, which at the last minute magically yield the rest camp at the foot of pink and russet cliffs.

Park Activities

See Itala A to Z, *below,* for information about reservations and fees.

Game Drives

Guided day and night drives (costing about R50) in an open vehicle are a highly recommended way of getting the most from your stay. The open vehicles are high off the ground, giving you a better angle of vision; at the same time, you benefit from the expertise of your ranger who knows where to find game and shares interesting tips about the ecology of the park. Because you aren't allowed to drive yourself around after dark, night drives, in which powerful spotlights are used, are the only way you'll get to see the entirely different cast of nocturnal animals that patrols the park after sunset.

Self-Guided Trails

An unusual feature of Itala is its self-guided walking trails in the mountainside above Ntshondwe camp. It gives you a chance to stretch your limbs if you've just spent hours cooped up in a car. It also has the advantage of giving you the chance to get really close to the euphorbias, acacias, and other fascinating indigenous vegetation that festoon the hills. Ask at the camp reception for further information.

Lodging

Although Itala has several exclusive bush camps, these are booked up en bloc months ahead by South Africans, making the chalets at its main camp the only practical place for foreign visitors to stay. Two people sharing a two-bed unit at Ntshondwe will pay R270.

$$ ▣ **Ntshondwe Camp.** In terms of architecture, landscaping, and style,
★ this beautiful government-run rest camp, comes closer than any other in the country to matching the expensive private lodges. Built around granite boulders and vegetation that is lush with acacias, wild figs, and giant cactuslike euphorbias, the 39 airy chalets with steep thatched roofs blend perfectly with the surroundings. Its two-, four-, and six-bed units can accommodate a total of 200 guests. Each chalet has a spacious lounge simply furnished with cane chairs, a fully equipped kitchen, and a large veranda surrounded by indigenous bush. If you're cooking yourself, buy supplies in Durban or one of the larger towns, such as Vryheid, before you come, because the camp shop is poorly stocked and Louwsburg is a one-horse town. Ntshondwe's à la carte licensed restaurant is better than you'd expect in a government game park, and dishes range from escargot to steaks. Outside, a magnificent game-viewing deck jetties out over a steep decline to provide views of the water hole and extensive panoramas of the surrounding valleys. ✉ *Natal Parks Board, Box 1750, Pietermaritzburg 3200,* ☎ *0331/47–1981,* ℻ *0331/47–1980. Restaurant, bar, pool, shop, gas station, private airstrip. AE, DC, MC, V.*

Itala A to Z

Arriving and Departing
BY CAR
From Durban, drive north on the N2 highway to Empangeni, then head west on the R34 to Vryheid. From here, cut east on the R69 to Louwsburg. The reserve is immediately northwest of the village, from which there are clear signposts. The journey from Durban takes around five hours and about 2½ hours from Hluhluwe-Umfolozi.

BY PLANE
The closest airport to the park is at Richards Bay, about 224 km (140 mi) south of Itala, which is served by **British Airways/Comair** (☎ 0351/4–1361) flights at least once daily from Johannesburg. **Avis** (☎ 0351/98–6555) and **Imperial** (☎ 0351/4–1414) have **car rental offices** at the Richards Bay airport.

Reservations and Fees
Admission to the park costs R25 per vehicle plus an additional R6 per person. The park is open October–March from 5 AM to 7 PM and April–September 6–6. Reservations for accommodations must be made through the **Natal Parks Board** (✉ Box 1750, Pietermaritzburg 3200, ☎ 0331/47–1981, ℻ 0331/47–1980).

PRIVATE GAME RESERVES AND LODGES

KwaZulu-Natal's best private lodges lie in northern Zululand and Maputaland, a remote region close to Mozambique. With one exception, the lodges reviewed here do not offer the Big Five. However, they are sufficiently close to one another and Hluhluwe-Umfolozi Game Reserve to allow you to put together a bush experience that delivers the

Big Five and a great deal more, including superb bird-watching and an unrivaled beach paradise. Malaria does pose a problem, however, and summers are hot, hot, hot.

For information about arriving and departing, contact the individual lodges listed *below*; *see also* Hluhluwe-Umfolozi Game Reserve, *above*.

CATEGORY	COST*
$$$$	over R1,600
$$$	R1,200–R1,600
$$	R800–R1,200
$	under R800

*All prices are per person sharing a double room, including all meals, bush walks, and game drives.

Ndumo Wilderness Camp

$$ This bush camp lies in Ndumo Game Reserve in Maputaland, a remote northern region of KwaZulu-Natal, near the Mozambique border. The 24,700-acre park does not have the Big Five, and visitors wanting to see big game should head elsewhere. What makes Ndumo famous is its birds. Along with Mkuzi (☞ National Parks and Game Reserves, *above*), the park is probably the premier bird-watching locale in the country. More than 400 species of birds—60% of all the birds in South Africa—have been spotted here, including the gorgeous purple-crested lourie, the green coucal, and the elusive trogon. Myriad waterfowl also flock to the reserve's Nyamiti and Banzi pans, and summer migrants take up residence from October until April.

Ndumo Wilderness Camp is a small tented lodge raised on stilts in a fig forest abutting Banzi Pan. Wooden walkways connect the camp's luxurious East African safari-style tents, each with its own bathroom and veranda overlooking the pan. The pan is home to scores of crocodiles, and the stillness of the night is often shattered by the sound of their splashes or the panicked screams of a doomed bush pig. The main lodge is an open-sided thatch shelter with broad decks extending over the water. Armed with a pair of binoculars, you could sit here for hours and never get bored.

Game Experience: Ndumo has no lion or elephant, but it supports a healthy population of black and white rhino, rare suni antelope, and red duiker, as well as the usual plains animals. And even though it may not have the Big Five, it is one of the most beautiful reserves in the country. Forests of yellow fever trees are mirrored in glassy lakes, and giant sycamore figs provide shelter for crowned eagles and owls. Crocodiles numbering in the hundreds bask on the grassy banks, while hippos honk and blow in deep pools. In addition to the usual game drives, rangers often take guests on extended bush walks. The best time to visit is October, when migrant birds return and antelope start bearing their young. ✉ *Box 651171, Benmore 2010,* ☎ *011/884–1458,* ℻ *011/883–6255. 16 guests. Bar, pool. AE, DC, MC, V.*

Phinda Private Game Reserve

Established in 1991, this flagship Conservation Corporation reserve is a heartening example of tourism serving the environment with panache. Phinda (*pin*-duh) is Zulu for "return," referring to the restoration of 42,000 acres of overgrazed ranchland in northern Zululand to bushveld. But there's no hiding the fact that it's still a work in progress, and even its exceptional accommodation and the excellence of its rangers can't make up for its limited quantity of mammals. If, as is planned, it manages to join up with neighboring government reserves, this shortcoming will instantly be dispelled and Phinda will take its place among the great game experiences of Africa.

You have a choice of four lodges at Phinda, each evoking some aspect of the environment. The two newest, Vlei and Rock Lodge, were scheduled to open at press time. Vlei, which has six suites similar to the ones at Forest Lodge, is on the edge of the reserve's sand forest overlooking a water hole. In a different vein, Rock Lodge houses 12 people in stone and glass chalets suspended from a cliff face.

$$$$ **Forest Lodge.** Hidden in one of the last remaining sand forests in the ★ world, this fabulous lodge overlooks a small water hole where nyalas, warthog, and baboons frequently come to drink. The lodge is a real departure from the traditional thatched structures so common in South Africa. It's very modern, with a vaguely Japanese feel thanks to glass-panel walls, light woods, and a deliberately spare, clean look. The effect is stylish and very elegant, softened by modern African art and sculpture. Guest suites use the same architectural concepts as the lodge, where walls have become windows, and rely on the dense forest (or curtains) for their privacy. As a result, guests feel very close to their surroundings, and it's possible to lie in bed or shower while watching delicate nyalas grazing just feet away. This lodge is a winner. *32 guests. Bar, pool, private airstrip.*

$$$$ **Mountain Lodge.** This attractive thatched lodge sits on a rocky hill overlooking kilometers of bushveld plains and the Ubombo Mountains. Wide verandas lead into the lounge and bar, graced with high ceilings, dark beams, and cool tile floors. In winter, guests can snuggle into cushioned wicker chairs next to a blazing log fire. Brick pathways wind down the hillside from the lodge to elegant split-level suites with mosquito nets, thatched roofs, and large decks overlooking the reserve. African baskets, beadwork, and grass matting beautifully complement the bush atmosphere. *42 guests. Bar, pool, private airstrip.*

Game Experience: Phinda can deliver the Big Five, although not as consistently or in such numbers as its competition in Mpumalanga. Its sheer diversity of habitats—ranging from savanna and mountain woodland to broad-leaved woodland, sand forest, palm veld, wetland, and riverine forest—is some compensation. The bird life here is extraordinary, too. But somehow, the drama of life and death in the African bush is missing. This may have something to do with the fact that parts of the ecological puzzle are missing. For a start, there are no scavengers to clean up after the predators have eaten their fill. Where Phinda does score top grades is in the superb quality of its rangers, who can provide a fascinating commentary on local birds, insects, trees, or frogs—you name it. Phinda also has adventure trips, including boat or canoe trips down the Mzinene River for a close-up look at crocodiles, hippos, and birds; big-game fishing or scuba-diving off the deserted Maputaland coast; and sightseeing flights over Phinda and the highest vegetated dunes in the world. Depending on whether you choose Phinda's resort or safari plan, these trips may or may not be included in the general rate. ⊠ *Private Bag X27, Benmore 2010,* ☎ *011/784–7077,* FAX *011/784–7667. AE, DC, MC, V.*

Rocktail Bay Lodge

$$ If Robinson Crusoe had washed ashore on the pristine coastline of Ma-★ putaland, he wouldn't have found anybody to call Friday—and he certainly wouldn't have cared what day of the week it was. It's that empty and that magnificent. No other buildings lie within 16 km (10 mi) of Rocktail Bay Lodge, tucked away in Maputaland Coastal Reserve, a narrow strip of wilderness that stretches from St. Lucia all the way to Mozambique. If you love untouched beaches, fishing, snorkeling, and walking, coming here will be one of the highlights of a visit to South Africa. Rocktail Bay is not a game lodge—the only animals you're likely to see are loggerhead and leatherback turtles. It is included in this chapter because it lies far from any other major tourist destination and operates much like a game lodge. In fact, unless you have a four-wheel-drive vehicle, the lodge must collect you for the final 11-km (7-mi) journey along deep sand tracks carved through coastal dune forest.

The lodge lies in a swale formed by enormous dunes fronting the ocean. Walkways tunnel through the dune forest to a golden beach that sweeps in a gentle arc to Black Rock, several miles to the north. There are no lifeguards or shark nets, but the swimming and snorkeling are fabulous. The lodge consists of 10 simple A-frame chalets raised on wood platforms above the forest floor. Wood and thatch create a rustic ambience, complemented by solar lighting and basic furnishings. A large veranda and adjoining thatched bar provide the backdrop for alfresco meals under a giant Natal mahogany tree. These are interrupted only by Gremlin, a tame thick-tailed bushbaby with a sweet tooth.

From a weather standpoint, the best times to come are probably spring (September–October) and autumn (March–May). In summer, the temperature regularly soars past 100°F, and swimming during winter is a brisk proposition. August is the windiest month.

Game Experience: Rocktail Bay *does not offer traditional game-viewing,* although many guests combine a visit here with a trip to Phinda (☞ *above*), about 95 km (60 mi) to the south. Besides glorious beaches, its major attraction is the annual arrival of giant loggerhead and leatherback turtles to lay their eggs. The beaches here are one of the few known laying areas of these endangered animals, and the season extends from the end of October through February. During these months, rangers lead after-dinner walks down the beach to look for turtles, and guests can expect to cover as much as 16 km (10 mi) in a night. Other activities include great surf fishing (tackle provided), snorkeling, and long beach walks. Rangers also lead excursions to see hippo pools, the rich birdlife of Lake Sibaya, and Kosi Bay, where the local Tembe people catch fish using an age-old method of basket-netting. For many people, though, a trip to Rocktail Bay is a chance to kick back and just soak in the atmosphere of an unspoiled coastal wilderness. ✉ *Box 651171, Benmore 2010,* ☎ *011/884–1458,* FAX *011/ 883–6255. 20 guests. Bar, pool. AE, DC, MC, V.*

8 Swaziland

From the rolling hills in the northwest to the purple Lubombo Mountains in the east, Swaziland has the look of an African paradise, where you can explore craft markets, ride horses through Ezulwini Valley, and raft the mighty Usutu River.

By Bronwyn
Howard

COVERING A MERE 17,000 square km (6,570 square mi), Swaziland is one of the smallest African countries. Surrounded by the giants of South Africa and Mozambique, this tiny, land-locked kingdom has somehow retained its ancient Swazi culture.

The same prehistoric upheaval that created the Drakensberg Mountains in South Africa also formed the Swazi Highveld, a spectacular escarpment cut by deep gorges, lush valleys, and fast-flowing rivers and waterfalls. The Highveld is also home to Swaziland's main game areas, where you can watch crocodiles and hippos at a waterhole, surprise antelope on foot, see Goliath herons take flight, and raft the country's fastest river. The Middleveld, a densely populated grassland plateau, links the west with the Lowveld, where sugar cane plantations briefly tame the African bush, and "fever trees," acacias with greenish bark, mark this as a malarial area. Against the Lowveld sky are the spectacular, inaccessible Lubombo Mountains, a lofty, blue divide.

The picturesque Swaziland region has been inhabited since the Stone Age, first by nomadic bushmen, then by the Sotho and Nguni tribes, as part of a vast human migration from east and central Africa. In 1750, King Ngwane III led a band of Nguni to settle among the hills overlooking the Pongola River, where he became a fierce custodian of his domain. Perhaps as tribute, the tribe came to call themselves the Ngwane.

Despite fierce opposition from the Zulus, the next king, Sobhuza, gained control of southern Swaziland. But the Zulus continued to cause trouble until the king requested assistance from traders at Lorenço Marques (Maputo). From this encounter with westerners the Ngwane first discovered maize, a food which was to become the staple of southern African peoples. Swaziland acquired its name from Sobhuza's son, Mswati II.

During the mid-1800s, white adventurers began arriving in numbers, attracted by rumors of gold. In 1880 King Mbandzeni began selling land concessions and, by the time King Sobhuza II inherited the throne, most of the country belonged to the concessionaires. Sobhuza II embarked on an extensive campaign to return land to his people. Even today, no Swazi owns his land outright, it remains the property of the nation.

After World War II, a sizable cash injection from the British fostered economic development. In 1967 Swaziland became independent of Britain, with Sobhuza as the new nation's official leader. In April 1986 his successor, King Mswati III, was crowned.

Today's Swazis mix age-old traditions with modern Western influences. While many have converted to Christianity and wear Western dress, you will still find locals in colorful, traditional costume. Rites, rituals, and customs passed down through generations still govern every aspect of a person's life. Ancestors are respected, and their spirits play a part in family affairs; chastity is valued, as are strict courtship rituals; marriage requires the payment of lobola—a dowry, usually in the form of cattle, a sign of wealth in Africa; and a young bride adopts the youngest child from her husband's family until she has children of her own. Even the king is not exempt from tradition: His eldest son is not necessarily the one who inherits the crown; the Royal Council chooses a new king who must be unmarried.

Pleasures and Pastimes

Arts and Crafts

Swaziland never really had an industrial revolution, and many people still obtain their livelihood from cottage industries, making everything from pottery and leather ware to candles and batiks. Swaziland has some unique arts and crafts routes in the Ezulwini and Malkerns Valleys which shouldn't be missed. You will be welcomed into many of the workshops at craft outlets to see the master craftsmen and women perform their ancient tasks. As you examine the lines of curios at roadside stalls, keep your eyes open for wooden bowls (usually unadorned), baskets woven from banana leaves, dolls dressed in traditional Swazi garb, and hand-dyed bolts of cloth.

Festivals

Despite Westernization, Swazi traditions are still strongly upheld. The main ceremony is the Ncwala (Festival of First Fruits) in December or January, a six-day event celebrating the dawn of a new year. The colorful celebration involves singing, dancing, and sacred rituals performed by the king. Another important ceremony is the Umhlanga (Reed Dance) in late August and early September. Marriageable Swazi maidens gather at the Queen Mother's residence and are sent to gather reeds to repair a windbreak. After spending the fifth day preparing their elaborate dresses, the girls sing and dance on the sixth and seventh days. The men have their own counterpart to the Umhlanga, the Tingoma Temabhaca.

Hiking

Although the weather can be extremely rainy at times, Swaziland is great hiking country, particularly in the Highveld towards Piggs Peak. Reserves such as Malolotja are a great favorite with backpackers and day walkers, with a wide network of stunningly scenic routes. Almost every country hotel has nature trails, and you can go on guided or self-guided walks at many game reserves.

Horse Riding

Most Swazis are keen riders, and there are stables everywhere. You can make arrangements to ride wherever you stay: If the establishment doesn't have its own horses, it's sure to be able to refer you to a stable in the vicinity. You don't have to be an accomplished horse person either; novices are always welcome. It's a wonderful way to see the countryside—the Mlilwane Game Reserve even features horseback riding as a way of getting up close to wildlife.

Wildlife

Although it's not often thought of in conjunction with big game, Swaziland has its fair share. Poaching activities were a major problem in Swaziland's reserves during the early 1990's, but vigilant antipoaching measures and strict wildlife laws have effectively controlled the problem. Swaziland's four game areas offer different wildlife experiences. You can see antelope and smaller game at Malolotja while on a hiking trail. Mlilwane was the first area to be declared a reserve, but the largest animals you're likely to see there are hippos basking in a waterhole. There is also unique accommodation in a Swazi beehive hut. Mkhaya *is* big game country, where you can see everything except lions. The tented camp here is set in pristine bushveld and is unfenced. Hlane Game Reserve is similar to Mkhaya but has all the Big Five and two marvelous waterholes. For a complete rundown on Southern African wildlife-viewing, *see* Big Game Adventures *in* Chapter 11.

Exploring Swaziland

The main geographic units of Swaziland are the very distinct Highveld, Middleveld, and Lowveld. The four main game reserves are Malolotja, Mlilwane, Mkhaya, and Hlane.

Great Itineraries

Swaziland makes a good side trip from South Africa. You will need a minimum of two days to see the highlights, but there's easily enough to do for five days. Wildlife experiences are more hands-on than in many places in South Africa: Most rest camps are unfenced and you could conceivably be chased by a blue crane or surprise antelope outside the door of your cottage.

If you've a little longer, spend more time in the tranquil mountain areas before taking in the major tourist route in Ezulwini and Malkerns.

Numbers in the text correspond to numbers in the margin and on the Swaziland map.

IF YOU HAVE 2 DAYS

If you enter Swaziland at Jeppes Reef/Matsamo, travel down the scenic route through the beautiful Ngwenya Hills to **Mbabane** ①. If you enter at Oshoek/Ngwenya, pause en route to Mbabane to see the Ngwenya Glass Factory. In Mbabane, have something to eat at the Swazi Mall before seeing the Mbabane Craft Market. Take the route towards Manzini through the **Ezulwini Valley** ②, exploring craft markets along the road to Malkerns. At Malkerns, see the cottage industries, specializing in batiks and candle making before returning to the Ezulwini Valley. Stay overnight at one of the hotels or **Mlilwane Game Reserve** ④. Then take the main route from Manzini to Siteki and follow the signs to Lomahasha, the route to **Hlane Game Reserve** ⑦. The main road goes through the Reserve; look out for the signs to Ndlovu Rest Camp where you'll check in.

IF YOU HAVE 5 DAYS

Enter Swaziland and drive through spectacular scenery to Piggs Peak; stay overnight at **Phophonyane Lodge** ⑤. Move on to the **Malolotja Nature Reserve** ③, where you can enjoy self-guided auto trails, bird watching, and hiking. Drive to Mbabane and spend a few hours viewing the city. Spend the night outside town en route to the Valley. If you wish, enjoy a morning horse ride at your accommodation before spending the rest of the day exploring craft markets and cottage industries in Ezulwini and Malkerns. Spend the night at Mlilwane Game Reserve and in the morning enjoy one of the many activities at Mlilwane. Afterwards, drive to Manzini where you can obtain provisions if you're self-catering. Move on to **Mkhaya Game Reserve** ⑥ for an afternoon game drive. Spend the day at the game reserve, enjoying bush walks and game drives. Leave the reserve and drive back to Siphofaneni to stock up with provisions before driving on to Hlane Game Reserve where'll you'll spend the night.

When to Tour Swaziland

As in South Africa, the hottest time of year is November–February. Visit in autumn (March–May) and spring (September –October) for the best weather. The Swazi Highveld has a climate similar to Johannesburg; hot rainy summers and cool frosty winters. Chill winds blow during late winter and early spring. Heavy fog may occur in the hill country near Piggs Peak when it rains. In winter, smoke from grass fires can blur those magnificent scenic panoramas. To the east, the climate becomes considerably hotter and more humid, being almost subtropical close to the Lubombo Mountains. This can make life very unpleasant

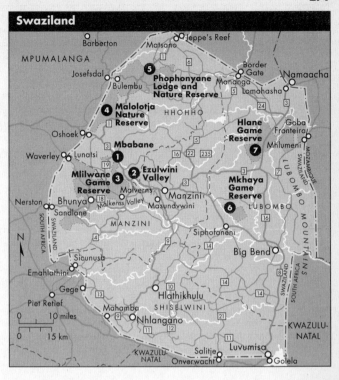

Swaziland

(Map locations shown: Barberton, Matsano, Jeppe's Reef, MPUMALANGA, Josefsdal, Bulembu, Phophonyane Lodge and Nature Reserve ⑤, Border Gate, Mananga, Namaacha, Lomahasha, Malolotja Nature Reserve ④, HHOHHO, Oshoek, Mbabane ①, Goba, Hlane Game Reserve ⑦, Fronteira, Mhlumeni, Waverley, Lunatsi, Ezulwini Valley ②, Mlilwane Game Reserve ③, Malverns, Manzini, Mkhaya Game Reserve ⑥, Bhunya, Malkerns Valley, Masundvwini, LUBOMBO, Nerston, Sandlane, MANZINI, Siphofaneni, LUBOMBO MOUNTAINS, Sicunusa, Big Bend, Emahlathini, Gege, Hlathikhulu, SHISELWINI, Piet Retief, Mahamba, Nhlangano, Salitje, Luvumisa, KWAZULU-NATAL, Onverwacht, Golela)

during summer. Winter is definitely the time to tour eastern Swaziland; malaria is less prevalent then.

Mbabane

① Mbabane is the capital and largest city of Swaziland. By South African standards, it's dusty, small, and laid back. Traffic tends to be confusing; once you leave the main routes, you're likely to find yourself in a warren of unmarked streets.

En route to Mbabane you will pass the **Ngwenya Glass Factory.** Recycled glass is used to create beautiful African animals as well as tableware and glasses. Go inside to see the glass blowers at work and stop at the shop to make a purchase or go upstairs to the coffee shop, which has a glorious view on three sides. ⊠ *5 km (3 mi) from Oshoek/Ngwenya border post, follow the yellow signposts,* ☎ FAX *268/24–053 or 268/24–151.* ☎ *Free.* ⊙ *Daily, 9–3:30, factory closed on weekends.*

Located in a house in town, the **Indingilizi Gallery** contains treasures from all over southern Africa. The walls are lined with colorful artwork, beadwork, and wall-hangings. The rooms are a potpourri of pottery, masks, cloth, batiks, and candlesticks. Most of the articles are produced in Swaziland. Behind the house is an informal restaurant area serving light lunches with an ethnic flavor. ⊠ *112 Johnson St., Mbabane,* ☎ *09268/46–213.* ☎ *Free.* ⊙ *Weekdays 8:30–5; Sat. 8:30–1.*

Dining and Lodging

$$ ✕ **La Casserole.** Light wooden paneling and pale green and apricot decor create a relaxed atmosphere at Mbabane's best restaurant. Enormous picture windows make the place light and airy and on warm days and evenings visitors may venture out onto the patio—corrugated iron roofs, alas, mar the view, but the cool air is welcome. Starters include soups and crepes; main courses include steaks, fish dishes, schnitzels, and other German specialties. The restaurant is fully licensed, and all wine comes from South Africa. On a practical note, there's plenty of safe underground parking. ⊠ *Omni Centre, Allister Miller St., Mbabane,* ☎ *268/46–426. AE, DC, MC, V.*

$$ 🏨 **Foresters Arms Hotel.** You'll find this delightful, family-run establishment high in the mountains near Mhlambanyatsi, 27 km (17 mi) from Mbabane. Rooms are furnished in bright floral prints and have en suite bathrooms, heaters, and televisions. Verandahs equipped with chairs command sweeping views across pine forests. Relax in the comfortable lounge, library, and bar reminiscent of old England, with armchairs, old-fashioned wallpaper, and enormous log fires. You can also dine by candlelight and savor delicious country cuisine. The hotel offers nature trails, horseback riding, trout and bass fishing, golf, and tennis. Nearby you can tour a genuine Swazi homestead, visit a sacred place, or see a practicing Inyanga (witch doctor) throwing the bones. ⊠ *Box 14, Mhlambanyatsi,* ☎ *268/74–144 or 268/74–377,* 𝖥𝖠𝖷 *268/ 74–051. 23 rooms with bath. Pool, sauna. AE, DC, MC, V*

$$ 🏨 **Mountain Inn.** This airy, Mediterranean-style hotel commands stunning views of the Ezulwini Valley from its prime location 4 km (2½ mi) from Mbabane. There are glorious vistas from every attractively furnished room, where wooden furniture and pastel shades predominate. Each has a television and phone. The pastel theme continues through the public areas, creating a fresh, breezy atmosphere. The pool area takes full advantage of the view but is not very private. The bar downstairs is a disappointment: It has a neglected air of faded grandeur. ⊠ *Box 223, Mbabane,* ☎ *268/42–781 or 268/42–773,* 𝖥𝖠𝖷 *268/45–393. 60 rooms with bath. Pool, room service. AE, DC, MC, V.*

Shopping

The pleasant **Mbabane Craft Market** (⊠ *Bypass Rd. and main road to Manzini, no phone)* is worth seeing and the local women selling the crafts are very friendly. You'll find row upon row of the ubiquitous African masks, malachite bracelets, and wildlife carvings. But among the rows, you'll find quality Swazi drums, locally-woven cloth, unusual marula tree carvings, basketware, and wooden bowls. Prices are reasonable.

Omni Centre deserves a mention as it houses the city's one and only internet café, which offers an e-mail service. It also has Mbabane's best restaurant. ⊠ *Allister Miller St., Mbabane. No phone.*

Swazi Mall has the most up-market South African shops, such as Woolworths and Spar, and numerous smaller establishments. Enjoy an ice cream or coffee and cake out on the terrace. ⊠ *Bypass Rd. (opposite Swazi Plaza), Mbabane. No phone.*

Ezulwini Valley and Malkerns

Ezulwini is 9 km (6 mi) from Mbabane; Malkerns is 19 km (12 mi) beyond Ezulwini.

2 The Ezulwini Valley is a delightful enclave on the way to Manzini. It's home to some of Swaziland's most exclusive hotels, a casino, a world-standard, 18-hole golf course, horse-riding stables, and numerous cottage industries. It's also known for some of the country's finest restaurants.

About the only thing to recommend the **National Museum** is the enormous, pristine signboard off the main Ezulwini/Manzini road. It's filled with unexciting exhibits which are poorly displayed and there are few explanatory notes about anything. There is a reasonable collection of Swazi clothing and domestic utensils as well as a photographic display on the role of Europeans in Swazi history, but it's nothing to write home about. Next to the museum is a traditional Swazi homestead; guided tours are advertised, but finding the guide could be a problem. Nearby is the King Sobhuza II Memorial Park, usually closed to visitors. ⊠ *Off the main route between Ezulwini and Manzini.* ⊒ *E10.* ⊘ *Weekdays 8:30–4:30.*

Continue down the road toward Manzini and take the second turn to Bunya to get onto the **circular crafts route,** set among pineapple fields.

Baobab Batik. Batik lovers will be in their element with this vast collection of batiks ranging from wall-hangings to clothing. Go behind the scenes in the workshop and see how it's done. ⊠ *Box 35, Malkerns,* ☎ *268/83–177.* ⊘ *Daily 9–5, factory closed on weekends.*

Gone Rural is the first craft place you'll find on the Malkerns road. Upstairs, the shop sells a selection of place mats, coasters, baskets, and rugs, all created from grass. Gone Rural employs a score of local women to collect grass and make items for the shop. The grass is dyed in enormous vats, weighed, and tied into bundles; go behind the house to see it all happening. ⊠ *Box 446, Malkerns,* ☎ *268/83–439.* ⊘ *Daily 8–4:45.*

The **Swazi Candle Factory** is where you'll find the famed regional candles in every shape and size. You can purchase candles shaped like mushrooms, birds, wildebeest, and so on, and you also get the chance to observe the unique candle making process. ⊠ *Box 172, Malkerns,* ☎ *268/83–219.* ⊘ *Daily 9–5, factory closed on weekends.*

Dining and Lodging

$$ ✕ **Calabash International Restaurant.** Plush maroon decor, fresh flowers, and bird prints combine to make this restaurant one of the more stylish in the Ezulwini Valley. Airy luncheon rooms are perfect for groups and the attractive bar area tempts you to have that pre-dinner drink. A Swiss chef ensures a very continental menu: Choose from dishes originating in Austria, France, Germany, Italy, Portugal, and Switzerland. Eisbein is very popular, followed closely by seafood. ⊠ *Box 85, Ezulwini,* ☎ *268/61–187. AE, DC, MC, V.*

$$ ✕ **Malandela's Farm House Restaurant.** If you're on the Ezulwini/Malkerns craft route, this is the spot for lunch; it's right next to Gone Rural and Tshweshwe Crafts. The design is based on a Dutch barn, combining burnt-umber walls, thatched roof, and heavy timber ceiling beams. Dine indoors or el fresco on the wide, shady porch and admire the wonderful view across the farms. The food is excellent, with a varied, changing menu chalked up daily on a blackboard. Only fresh, homegrown produce is used, together with farm cream and milk produced in the area. South African wines are served. There is an attractive bar off the main dining area. ⊠ *Box 39, Malkerns,* ☎ *268/83–115.* ⊘ *Tues.–Sun. 9–11, Closed Mon. AE, DC, MC, V.*

$$$ ⌂ **Ezulwini Sun Hotel.** Part of the Sun International group, this hotel was recently refurbished with an open, airy look. Decor is predominantly blue, pink, and white. Pineapple motifs on the doors, tiled floors, and light furnishings create a relaxed, Caribbean feel. Rooms are simply furnished, continuing the pink and blue theme. Every room overlooks the gardens and has a TV. The hotel restaurant serves buffet breakfasts and à la carte lunches and dinners. Complimentary casino vouchers for the Royal Swazi Sun Casino and a shuttle bus service to other Sun International hotels in the valley are available. ⊠ *Private Bag, Ezulwini,* ☎ *268/61–201 or 268/61–650,* ℻ *268/61–782. 120 rooms with bath. Restaurant, lounge, pool, horseback riding.*

$$$ 🏨 **Royal Swazi Sun Hotel & Casino.** Established 31 years ago, this Sun International hotel is perhaps the most exclusive in Swaziland. Five-star luxury surrounds you from the moment you enter its cavernous reception area. Comfortable, tastefully furnished rooms face the pool area or golf course, both set against the magnificent backdrop of the surrounding hills. Luxury rooms upstairs have private balconies. All public areas are immaculate and you'll notice fresh flowers everywhere. The lounge is furnished in Sanderson prints and international newspapers are provided. The outdoor terrace, pool, and bar are a focal point where people gather. Children's entertainment is available during the day. ⊠ *Private Bag, Ezulwini,* ☎ *268/61–001 or 268/61–450,* ⅨⅩ *268/61–859. 202 rooms with bath. 3 restaurants, lounge, bar, pool, room service, Jacuzzi, 18-hole golf course, tennis, squash, casino, parking, shuttle bus.*

$$ 🏨 **Mantenga Lodge.** If you've no desire to stay in a chain hotel, try this quaint place close to the Ezulwini/Malkerns arts and crafts route. In the heart of a beautiful riverine forest, the lodge offers standard rooms, pool rooms, and chalets. Outside the rooms are painted apricot with pale-green doors. Inside they're furnished with white cane furniture and more of the apricot and green theme. The bathrooms are a little on the small side, with either showers or baths. Chalet verandas overlook the forest. Meals are taken in a separate dining area where a Mauritian chef ensures the menu has a definite French flavor. There's not much to do on the premises, so it's best to use the lodge as a one-night stopover.⊠ *Box 68, Ezulwini,* ☎ *268/61–049 or 268/62–168,* ⅨⅩ *268/61–049. 32 rooms with bath. Restaurant, bar, pool, nature trails. AE, DC, MC, V.*

Shopping

Mantenga Craft Centre. A group of shops in a rustic "shopping center" off the main road, Mantenga specializes in crafts made by rural groups. **Country Leather** has handmade leatherware of all kinds. If angora's your pleasure, you'll love **Carol of Swaziland's** selection of woolens. **Fluidesign Studio Shop** offers colorful, handmade caps and shorts and tie-dyed cotton cloth. **The Silver Shop** is a fine jewelry shop stocked with beautifully crafted items. Hand-woven cotton rugs and tapestries are the province of **Shiba Rugs. Hawu** features clay pots and bowls, some batiks, and beadwork. Next door you'll find **Akekho,** an unusual pottery shop. ⊠ *Box A5, Swazi Plaza,* ☎ *268/61–136.* ☉ *Daily 8–4:30.*

Tshweshwe Crafts. This kitsch curio shop is rather disappointing with its run-of-the-mill handcarved animals, gemstone trees, African masks, and baskets. You may find something a little different, though, like a handmade Swazi chess set with the pieces straight from Swaziland villages. Prices are very high. ⊠ *Box 376, Malkerns,* ☎ *268/83–336.* ☉ *Daily, 8–4:45.*

Mlilwane Game Reserve

20 km (12 mi) from Ezulwini Valley and Malkerns

❸   Mlilwane Game Reserve was the first region set aside for conservation in Swaziland by renowned Swazi conservationist, Ted Reilly. The 4,500-hectare sanctuary was once the Reilly family farm. It's a beautiful, secluded area where rolling grassland sweeps to the foot of craggy mountains.

The reserve offers a range of activities, with something for everyone. Enjoy a morning, sunset, or evening game drive (E50–E150), take a guided walk through the reserve (E10/person), or go horseback riding (E35/hr), a unique way of getting really close to game. You can also take a guided mountain bike trail (E25/hr). Alternatively, walk the **Ma-**

cobane Mountain Trail, a three-hour, self-guided route through the Nyonyane Mountains.

The only big game you'll see here are the hippos in the **waterhole** at the main camp. (Don't miss feeding time daily at 3PM.) View giraffe, zebra, wildebeest, bontebok, impala, nyala, and warthog. The main camp is unfenced, so you can surprise impala early in the morning, and watch out for the resident blue crane, which has quite a temper!

Dining and Lodging

Book all lodgings listed below through the **Big Game Parks Central Reservations** (⊠ Box 234, Mbabane, ☎ 268/44–541, ℻ 268/40–957. AE, DC, MC, V).

$$ ✕⛿ Lodge. A new lodge, perched on a hill above the reserve, is scheduled to open in late August 1997. The lodge will accommodate eight couples in four rooms with bathrooms en suite or nearby. An attractive stone house, the lodge promises to be romantic, with wooden floors, colonial light fittings, brass beds, floral wallpaper, and broiderie anglaise linen. A terraced garden filled with arbors and nature trails is presently being landscaped. *4 rooms with bath. Main Camp facilities available.*

$ ✕⛿ Main Camp. Accommodation at main camp consists of six log cabins and two beehive huts, accommodating two–five people. Each cabin has a bathroom (shower only) en suite, wardrobe, and honor bar. A communal kitchen, dining room, and lounge are housed in a separate building. The lounge has a vast picture window suspended over the waterhole, so you can watch game and birds in comfort. The restaurant offers a limited menu specializing in game-based dishes. Main Camp also has an open-air dining area and fireplace over which a barbecue grid is placed. A summer house and ablution block are available for day visitors and there is a viewing area beside the waterhole. A small shop sells wine, beer, soft drinks and some tinned goods and toiletries. *6 cabins with bath. Pool, lounge, dining room.*

$$ ⛿ Shonalanga. This is a self-contained, fully-equipped cottage accommodating six. The cottage comprises a lounge, dining room, kitchen with refrigerator, bathroom, and two bedrooms. An open-air barbecue area affords attractive views over the reserve. *1 cottage with bath. Main Camp facilities available.*

$ ⛿ Beehive Village. Each beehive hut accommodates two–three people and contains only beds. Communal bathroom facilities are shared with campers. *8 huts. Main Camp facilities available.*

Malolotja Nature Reserve

32 km (20 mi) from Mbabane

❹ Set in the Ngwenya Hills, this pristine nature reserve is well worth visiting, either en route from Piggs Peak or as a side trip from Mbabane. Malolotja is a hiker's paradise and the best way to experience it's natural wonders is on your own two feet. At the gate, ask for the comprehensive map and a list of walks. Self-drive dirt roads lead to the start of walks or to picturesque view points. Some of the longer and more interesting walks are the **Gold Mine Walk**, the **Malolotja Falls Walk**—these falls are the highest in Swaziland, accessible only on foot—and walks along the **Majolomba River**. Numerous shorter routes are also available.

Most routes descend, and the return journey entails a lot of uphill effort. On longer routes, allow sufficient time by starting as early as possible. Wear sturdy footwear and carry a minimum of 2 liters of water as it can be very hot and dry. Some roads may be fairly rough in places. Look out for routes marked "4x4" and avoid them. The roads are not all-weather roads and may be closed in wet conditions. Take note of any "Road Closed" signs you may encounter. There are no shops in the reserve so remember to take your own lunch and refreshments, purchasing them at Mbabane or Piggs Peak.

Walk quietly in single file and you'll probably see a variety of animals. It's worth asking at the gate which areas have been burned recently as blue wildebeest, blesbuck, zebra, and red hartebeest will concentrate there. Also look out for black wildebeest, a variety of different antelope, warthogs, bush pigs, baboons, vervet monkeys, and black-backed jackal. The Cape clawless otter lives near streams and rivers. The birdlife is also magnificent, with over 280 recorded species. Finally you'll find an incredible diversity of plants and flowers. ⊠ *On the road to Piggs Peak; take the Piggs Peak/Matsamo turn-off from the main Ngwenya/Mbabane road (Box 1797, Mbabane)*, ☎ *268/24–241.* ☞ *E10.* ☺ *Winter, daily 6:30 AM–6 PM; summer, daily 6 AM–6 PM.*

Phophonyane Lodge and Nature Reserve

42 km (26 mi) from Malolotja Nature Reserve

❺ You'll find this picturesque lodge and reserve high in the hills among the pine forests near Piggs Peak. The grounds resemble a green, tropical paradise, with the **Phophonyane Falls** as a focal point, tumbling down a series of steep drops.

Nature trails wind through the cool, green beauty of the forest to spectacular view sites. Excursions to bushman paintings further afield are arranged on request. Small game abound at Phophonyane: Look out in particular for bushbuck, the Cape clawless otter, and the rare red duiker. The reserve is a birdwatcher's paradise and the prize sighting here is the colorful narina trogan.

Dining and Lodging

$–$$ ✕🔯 **Phophonyane Lodge.** The reference to a lodge is a misnomer: Accommodation is in romantic self-contained cottages, each set in its own private garden. There are four thatched cottages, one of which (Cottage 4) is a luxury dwelling commanding a stunning view across the Hhohho Valley. All cottages are open-plan with spacious bathrooms, African prints, wooden furniture, and fully-equipped kitchens. At the edge of the Phophonyane River is a tented camp where comfortably furnished safari tents face the river. Meals and drinks are delivered to most cottages (depending on their proximity to the kitchen), and you can also eat in an open-air dining hut or the attractive Leadwood Bar. Cottage 4 is the only one with a television; Phophonyane is definitely a get-away-from-it-all type of place! ⊠ *20 km (12½ mi) from Piggs Peak, on the road to Matsamo (Box 199, Piggs Peak)*, ☎ *268/71–319 or 268/71–429,* 🖷 *268/71–319. 4 cottages sleeping 2–5 people each with bath; 2 safari tents sleeping 6. Bar, pool, hiking. AE, DC, MC, V.*

Mhkaya Game Reserve

95 km (59 mi) from Mbabane

❻ Mkhaya Game Reserve is designated as a refuge for endangered species. Covering over 6,250 hectares, the reserve lies off the Big Bend/Lavumisa road. Strict antipoaching measures have been adopted and entry to the reserve is carefully controlled: You cannot enter the park on your own; a ranger will meet you at the turn-off and escort you from there to a central point with secure parking. Arrival and departure times are 10 AM and 4 PM respectively. You will be taken the rest of the way by landrover.

The chief activity at Mkhaya are game drives, of which there are two: a morning drive at 6 AM and a sunset drive at 4 PM. In addition, you can arrange for a 3-hour guided walking safari with your ranger. If you're an adrenaline-junkie, you might enjoy white-water rafting on the **Great Usutu,** Swaziland's mightiest waterway. Rafters ride the wild river through the rugged **Bulunga Gorge** in inflatable rafts.

At Mkhaya it's possible to get really close to big game. It's not unusual to experience elephants patting the Land Rover with their trunks or to have rhinos stare at you from a few meters away. Animals you might see include elephants (the herd at present numbers 16), black and white rhinos, water buffalo, giraffes, and hippos. Usually seldom seen, the majestic male nyala is plentiful in the reserve. Expect to also see impala, kudu, waterbuck, eland, roan and sable antelope, zebra, and wildebeest. After good rains, it's possible to see several animals with their young. The birding is fabulous, too, so don't forget your binoculars!

Dining and Lodging

$$–$$$ ✕🖾 **Stone Camp.** This glorious camp is set in a leafy indigenous forest. Accommodation is in standard or luxury safari tents, or you can stay at the more comfortable Swallows Nest Cottage (accommodates six). All tents have a river frontage where it's possible to watch wildlife at close quarters. Luxury tents have en suite showers and "loos with a view," while standard tents have shared bathrooms nearby. Bedding and towels are provided. The main communal area, comprising a thatched lounge, bar, and outdoor dining section is a little way from the tents. There is no electricity; paraffin lamps and candles contribute to the *Out of Africa* atmosphere. All meals, drives, and walks are included in the cost. ✉ *Big Game Parks Central Reservations, Box 234, Mbabane,* ☎ *268/44–541,* 𝔽𝔸𝕏 *268/40–957. 10 tents accommodating 4–5 people each; cottage accommodating 6. Lounge, bar. AE, DC, MC, V*

Hlane Game Reserve

105 km (66 mi) from Mbabane

❼ On the eastern side of Swaziland in the heart of sugar cane country, Hlane offers a relaxed wildlife experience. You won't find any signposts to Hlane: Follow signs to Lomahasha on the MR3, approximately 12 km (7½ mi) from the Lonhlupheko junction you will see a signboard to Ndlovu Rest Camp. The access road is dirt but in good condition. You will need to call here and pay your entrance fee before proceeding to Bubesi Camp. Rangers at the gate will direct you to Bubesi as the road through the park is not always accessible during the rainy season.

Take your own vehicle and enjoy a self-driving tour along the vast network of roads through the park. While here, visit the enormous main **waterhole** where hippo yawn in the water, waterbirds bask on the shore, and countless wildlife come to drink in the mornings. Alternatively, plan to spend dusk here, where the sunsets are spectacular. You can also take a guided walks with a Swazi ranger (E10/hr). Visitors can arrange to see the lion or cheetah breeding enclosure (E10/person), a unique opportunity to get fairly close to these wonderful creatures.

Hlane has all of the Big Five—lion, elephant, rhino, buffalo, and leopard. Besides this, you may see a wide range of antelope, zebra, wildebeest, warthog, giraffe, crocodile, ostrich, baboon, and vervet monkeys. In the late afternoon, look out for hyena. Hlane has one of the densest bird populations in any of Swaziland's game areas, including several birds of prey.

Lodging

Accommodation at Hlane Game Reserve is self-catering. There are two camps, both of which provide fully equipped accommodation, including refrigerator and stoves. There is no shop in the reserve so stock up with provisions at Manzini, where the shops at Manzini Mall should satisfy all your requirements. Alternatively, if you're going on to Hlane from Mkhaya, return to Siphofaneni which has an excellent general dealer who has most of what you'll need.

$ 🎮 **Bubesi Camp.** Accommodation here consists of two delightful, two-bedroom stone cottages. As at Ndlovu, these come fully-equipped and accommodate four people each. They are modern and spacious and there is electricity. Staff will cook for you on request. The cottages face onto the river and there is a great view from their back porches. A short trail along the river starts at the cottages. ⊠ *Big Game Parks Central Reservations, Box 234, Mbabane,* ☎ *268/44–541, ℻ 268/40–957. 2 cottages accommodating 4 people each. AE, DC, MC, V*

$ 🎮 **Ndlovu Rest Camp.** This is the main camp. Accommodation is in five thatched rondavels comprising a living room, upstairs bedroom, kitchen, and bathroom (with shower). The rondavels tend to be cluttered with heavy wooden furniture. Each comes fully equipped with cutlery, crockery, pots and pans, basic kitchen utensils, bedding and towels, dish washing liquid, and dishcloths and drying cloths. Other facilities at the camp include two bomas where firewood is provided, a covered boma, and an ablution block. There is also a waterhole, but no electricity: lighting is by means of candles and paraffin lamps which are brought to your rondavel at dusk. The geyser, refrigerator, and stove are all gas. ⊠ *Big Game Parks Central Reservations, Box 234, Mbabane,* ☎ *268/44–541, ℻ 268/40–957. 5 rondavels accommodating up to 5 people each. AE, DC, MC, V.*

SWAZILAND A TO Z

Arriving and Departing

By Car

The major border post between Swaziland and South Africa is Oshoek/Ngwenya, open from 7 AM to 11 PM. On weekends or public holidays, expect to wait in long queues behind busloads of Swazi nationals coming in from South Africa to visit their families. If you can, it's recommended that you use one of the other border posts at such times.

Traveling to Swaziland from Mpumalanga, enter at Jeppe's Reef/Matsamo, open 8 AM to 6 PM. If you're entering from the KwaZulu-Natal side, the nearest border posts are either Golela/Lavumisa (near Jozini), open 7 AM to 11 PM, or Mahlamba (near Piet Retief), open 7 AM to 11 PM.

A road toll levy (E5) is payable at the border and a receipt is issued. Keep the receipt with you. As in South Africa, drive on the left. Unlike South Africa, distances are much shorter, particularly if you're doing most of your traveling on the western side of the country. There are no highways: the major through routes tend to be the tarred roads. There are presently extensive roadworks between Mbabane and Manzini as the road is being widened to create a dual carriage way. Exercise patience and caution and allow for delay.

By Plane

Swaziland has only one airport, **Matsapha** (⊠ Box 487, Manzini, ☎ 268/8–4372) 8 km (5 mi) from Manzini. An airport departure tax of E20 is levied. Although the airport has sophisticated equipment, there are times when it is not functioning properly and certain airlines may refuse to fly to Swaziland on occasions, particularly during inclement weather. Bear this in mind and make allowances for delays. There is also some controversy as to whether Royal Swazi Airways airplanes are air-worthy although there have been no unfortunate incidents.

The national carrier is **Royal Swazi National Airways** (☎ 268/86–155 in Swaziland or 011/616–7323 in Johannesburg, FAX 011/616–7757). Other airlines flying into Swaziland are **British Airways** (operating as Comair: ☎ 011/921–0111) and **S.A.Airlink** (☎ 011/973–2941).

BETWEEN THE AIRPORT AND TOWN

Taxis operate from the airport to hotels and main towns. Be very careful of the condition of the taxi: Make sure it's road worthy. Approximate costs: Airport to Ezulwini E60; to Mbabane E70; to Manzini E50. **Courtesy Buses** are offered by Sun International Hotels.

Getting Around

By Car

Logistically, the easiest way to get around Swaziland is by car, even though it's not without its pitfalls. Roads are extremely narrow (one lane each way) and invariably have solid white barrier lines, allowing no passing for long stretches. Road shoulders are often nonexistent or unpaved. Although tarred roads are in reasonable condition, you won't find the super-highways of the sort you experience in South Africa. Official speed limits are 60 km/hour in town and 80 km/hour on the open road, but you'll quickly find that you need to travel at slower speeds. Off the beaten track, you'll more than likely need four-wheel-drive. Check when making bookings as to whether places are accessible, particularly during the rainy season.

Swazi drivers have little regard for other road users. Be careful on blind rises in particular: it's not unusual to reach the crest of a hill or round a series of bends to find yourself facing an oncoming vehicle on your side of the road. Logging trucks negotiating winding mountain roads are particularly bad at staying on their side (watch out for logs slipping off too). You will need to be patient as many people drive slowly or suddenly turn off the road without signaling. It is recommended that you do not drive at night as even major routes are not lit and, with the unpredictability of most of Swaziland's driving population, it's simply not worth the trouble.

Licenses from most countries are recognized provided they are printed in English or accompanied by an English translation. But international driving permits are still recommended for simplicity. If you intend taking a hired car from South Africa into Swaziland, ensure that the car rental company provides you with a letter authorizing you to take the vehicle across the border.

GAS

Gas (or petrol as it is known in southern Africa) is easily available in main centres such as Mbabane, Manzini, Piggs Peak, and the Ezulwini Valley, where garages are numerous and many offer 24-hour service. Gas is cheaper in Swaziland than in South Africa, so plan to fill up when you arrive and before you leave. Unleaded petrol is not always available. When travelling to outlying areas, bear in mind that the petrol supply can be erratic: there may be garages but the fuel reservoirs will not necessarily be full.

Contacts and Resources

Car Rental
Avis Rent-A-Car (✉ Box 31, Manzini, ☎ 268/86–350) and **Imperial Car Hire** (✉ Box 1825, Manzini, ☎ 268/41–384). You can arrange for cars to be delivered or collected at your hotel.

Currency
The monetary unit in Swaziland is the Emalangeni (E), equivalent to the South African Rand. The Emalangeni is divided into 100 Lilangeni (cents). Strictly speaking, South African currency is no longer legal tender in Swaziland. However, you can use South African rand at most hotels and tourist facilities but will receive Swazi currency as change. You can ask to receive rand as change and most people will endeavor to oblige. Change your Emalangeni into rand before you leave; it's not possible to do it after you return to South Africa.

Customs and Duties
Swaziland lies in the Southern Africa Common Customs Union. Any visitor entering Swaziland from South Africa is not liable for any customs duties. You will, however, need to complete a statistical form listing items imported.

If you are entering Swaziland directly, you may import goods to the value of E50 duty free. Further goods to the value of E50 are subject to 20% duty. Personal effects and sporting and recreational equipment are exempt.

Emergencies
Ambulance, fire brigade, and **police** call 999.

DOCTORS
It is not recommended that you go to any of the public hospitals in Swaziland. Clinics in out-lying areas are usually not a good bet either. Ask your hotel to refer you to a reliable private practitioner.

Embassies and High Commissions
British High Commission. ✉ *Private Bag, Allister Miller St., Mbabane,* ☎ *268/42–581,* FAX *268/42–585.*

U.S. Embassy. ✉ *Central Bank Bldg., Warner St., Mbabane (Box 199, Mbabane),* ☎ *268/46–442,* FAX *268/45–959.*

Guided Tours
Swazi Trails (✉ Box 2197, Mbabane, ☎ and FAX 268/62–180) offers full- and half-day tours including history and culture tours, Swazi art and craft trails, wildlife trails (at Mlilwane, Hlane, and Mkhaya Game Reserves), and adventure trails taking in hiking, horseback riding, river rafting, absailing, paragliding, and 4x4 excursions. Specialist, incentive, and conference group tours are also arranged. They offer airport to hotel transfers and accommodation booking services.

Go Africa Tours (✉ Box 93064, Yeoville, 2143, ☎ 011/487–1254, FAX 011/487–2769.) This Johannesburg-based operator offers arts and crafts tours of Swaziland, concentrating on the Ezulwini Valley and Malkerns.

Health and Safety
As in South Africa, all water is drinkable. Bilharzia exists in rivers and dams; don't swim in sluggish or still water. Precautions against tetanus, cholera, typhoid, and polio are recommended. If you intend visiting the low-lying areas in the vicinity of the Lubombo Mountains, take antimalarial precautions, much the same as you would if you were visiting Mpumalanga or KwaZulu Natal in South Africa. Larium is gen-

erally recommended but can have unpleasant side-effects, so check with your doctor before leaving home.

Swaziland is, on the whole, a very safe country; certainly far safer than South Africa. However, petty pilfering does occur, so watch your valuables and do not leave them in your car where they might be seen. A few incidents of carjacking have occurred in Mbabane and Manzini but these are rare.

Language
English and Seswati are the official languages. Most Swazi people speak and understand English very well.

Mail
Post offices in Swaziland are open from 8:30–4 on weekdays and from 8:30–11 AM Saturday mornings. All the usual postal services are available. Postage stamps may also be purchased at hotels.

Opening and Closing Times
Offices and shops are open from 8:30–5 on weekdays and from 8:30–1 on Saturdays. Most establishments are closed on Sundays. Lunch hour is 1–2. Banks all open at 8:30 but many close at as early as 2:30. All banks are open until 11 AM Saturdays.

Packing
Packing for Swaziland is not much different from packing for South Africa. Casual clothes such as shorts, t-shirts, sundresses, and jeans are recommended for daytime wear. Remember to pack comfortable shoes and sturdy walking boots and sandals. The western part of the country can be extremely cold in winter, particularly in the mountainous areas towards Piggs Peak, so pack warm clothing if you intend travelling during the winter months. A warm jersey or jacket is always a good idea. Take a good raincoat, particularly during summer. The eastern part of Swaziland is subtropical, so take light, cool clothing, and try to wear khaki and olive green when visiting game reserves. If you intend staying at any of the smarter hotels, remember that a jacket and tie may be required after 6 PM. Pack binoculars for game viewing and bird watching. A torch, insect repellent, roll of toilet paper, basic first aid kit, and Swiss army knife (or similar utility knife) are usually good ideas. Mbabane and Manzini are the best places to shop if you find you have forgotten something.

Passports and Visas
At present, nationals of the United States, United Kingdom, and Canada do not need visas; a valid passport is sufficient.

Travel Agencies
The main travel agency in Swaziland is **Swazi Trails** (☞ Guided Tours, *above*).

Big Game Parks (⊠ Box 234, Mbabane, ☎ 268/44–541, ℻ 268/40–957) offers packages and information for the active and adventurous traveler. Activities center on the game reserves at Mlilwane, Mkhaya, and Hlane. Enjoy game viewing, bird watching, game drives, horseback riding, mountain biking, river rafting, and absailing. Big Game Parks will also arrange and take bookings for accommodation in the parks.

Visitor Information
Department of Tourism. ⊠ *Ministry of Tourism and Communication, Swazi Plaza, Mbabane (Box 2652, Mbabane),* ☎ *268/44–556 or 268/46–420,* ℻ *268/46–438.* ⊘ *8:30–5.*

9 Zimbabwe

In contrast to South Africa, with its mix of peoples and races, Zimbabwe is black Africa. Zimbabwean friendliness is well-known, and even in cities, the pace of life is slower. And then there are the country's landscapes and wildlife: from hippos snorting in the Zambezi River to elfin klipspringer antelope bounding around the granite hills of Matobo National Park. In between are the stone ruins of Great Zimbabwe, more national parks, and the world's best white-water rafting.

ZIMBABWE HAS ITS FEET FIRMLY planted in two Africas: the modern and the traditional. The younger generation listens to rap and watches American television, and you can hop on line at a Harare internet café. And while Bulawayo, the country's second city to the west, looks like it's still trying to emerge from the 1970s, there's no doubt that the pulse of Harare, the capital, is quickening toward the end of the century.

By Michael
McKeown
and June
Muchemenyi

Outside of the cities, all of this changes. Much of the population depends on farming for its living, and cattle ownership is a sign of wealth in rural areas. Driving around the country you will frequently pass communal lands, where local people live in mud-walled, thatch-roof huts, many of them beautifully painted and immaculately kept. To make a trip to Zimbabwe—or even to Africa—complete, a communal land visit is a must.

What so many people come to Zimbabwe for, of course, is the fantastic numbers of wildlife: from the lion, elephant, and wild dogs of Hwange National Park to the hippos and stealthy crocodiles of Mana Pools—and all kinds of birds and beasts in between. The country prides itself on its largely successful game management policies, and the fact that a good 13% of Zimbabwe is dedicated wildlife country or protected nature reserves is a source of pride. Such wildlife management policies as CAMPFIRE—the Communal Areas Management Programme for Indigenous Resources—has effectively reduced the incidence of poaching by engaging local communities to foster the wildlife with which they share their land and profit from fees charged for access to their herds. The country's sound game management practices have also been responsible for the successful reintroduction of endangered species, such as rhinoceros, into national parks.

You might argue that game is game anywhere. But how one is introduced to the wild makes the difference between an African safari and an intimate and educational African wildlife experience. In Zimbabwe all professional guides must pass rigorous proficiency tests administered by the Department of National Parks and Wildlife Management. A practical minimum of three years' experience in the bush is required before a guide qualifies to take this test, and only licenced guides are allowed to take you out on foot among elephants, lions, buffalo, leopard, and rhinoceros—the Big Five of hunters' lore, deemed the most dangerous of animals in the African bush. Zimbabwe's game rangers are superbly qualified to teach you about animals, birds, and the minutest details of the country's ecosystems—so much so that Zimbabwe has become the standard by which neighboring countries measure their own guides.

Zimbabwe is Africa, and it has its share of exotic associations in the bargain. In major cities you'll see hand-pushed carts weaving in and out of the busy city-center traffic, vendors peddling stone, wood and wire curios, and cars—still running—of makes now long forgotten in the First World. And there are markets abuzz with secondhand clothes business, vegetables, curios, traditional African medical concoctions and even paraphernalia for the attendant *n'anga* (traditional healer).

Note: All areas of Zimbabwe covered in this chapter are malarial, and you are advised to take antimalarial drugs.

Pleasures and Pastimes

Arts and Local Crafts

Harare and Bulawayo are Zimbabwe's cultural centers, and community theatre plays depict concerns from AIDS to international politics

Zimbabwe

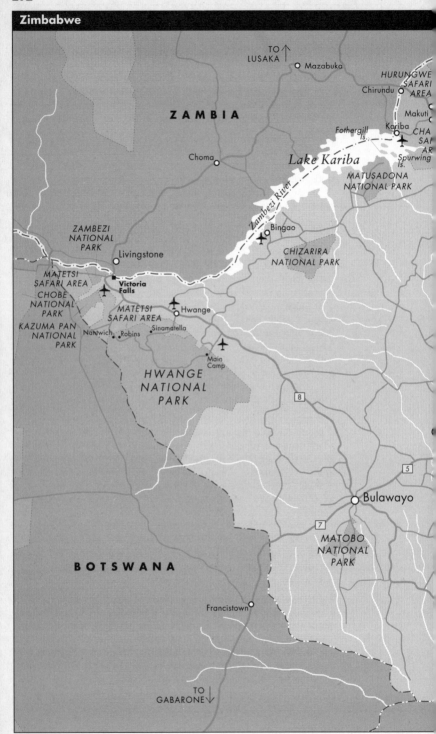

TO LUSAKA ↑

ZAMBIA

Mazabuka

HURUNGWE SAFARI AREA

Chirundu

Makuti

Choma

Fothergill Is.

Kariba

CHA SAI AR

Lake Kariba

Spurwing Is.

MATUSADONA NATIONAL PARK

Zambezi River

ZAMBEZI NATIONAL PARK

Livingstone

Bingao

CHIZARIRA NATIONAL PARK

MATETSI SAFARI AREA

Victoria Falls

CHOBE NATIONAL PARK

MATETSI SAFARI AREA

Hwange

KAZUMA PAN NATIONAL PARK

Nantwich

Robins

Sinamatella

Main Camp

HWANGE NATIONAL PARK

8

5

Bulawayo

7

MATOBO NATIONAL PARK

BOTSWANA

Francistown

TO GABARONE ↓

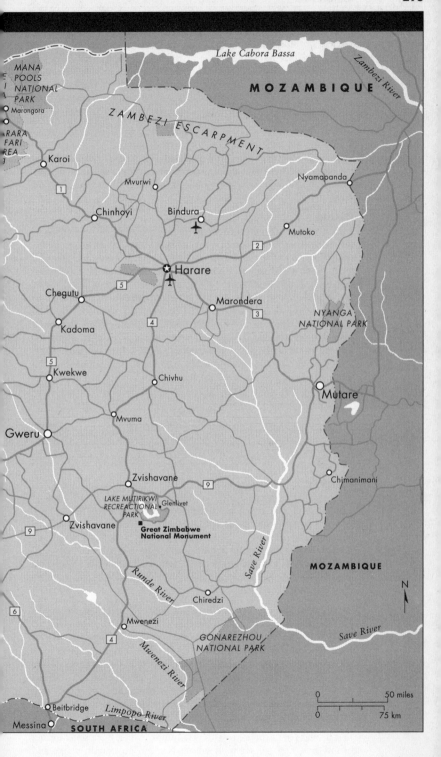

to gender issues. Even if you are not a contemporary art freak, you'll find the myths and legends depicted in Zimbabwean stone sculpture fascinating. You'll find plenty of roadside curio vendors and another local craft: lacemaking, although the cotton material used doesn't make lace work as beautifully as it would in linen or silk. The most promising work is the fabric printing both outside of Harare and in the studios behind the National Gallery in Bulawayo. If you are buying wooden items, check their quality—you may pick an item carved before the wood dried properly, and this in time will start cracking and splitting.

Be prepared for the typical selling style of Zimbabwe's vendors: Many insistently accost or pursue you, trying to take you to the finest of their items, whether you show interest or not. If you decide to buy, bargain away!

Dining

Don't come to Zimbabwe for the food: It's neither exotic nor exciting. So thoroughly colonized was this small state that it took on everything English at the expense of its own cuisine. It's only recently that the trendsetting larger hotels have rediscovered traditional Zimbabwean cuisine, and this is by far the most interesting fare you'll eat: *sadza,* the staple thick porridge, usually made of maize flour, often accompanied by *nyama* (a stew) and green vegetables. They also serve such delicacies as *madora* or *macimbi*—sun-dried caterpillars harvested from mopane trees and cooked with peanut butter or seasoned and served as a snack. And there's always *biltong*—dried beef or game jerky, sometimes cooked in a peanut sauce. You'll also find game meats like kudu, which can be fairly tough, and warthog, which is quite tender.

CATEGORY	COST*
$$$$	over Z$500
$$$	Z$350–Z$500
$$	Z$200–Z$350
$	under Z$200

Prices are per person, excluding drinks and service.

Lodging

Although conventional hotels are found in the major resort areas of Zimbabwe, lodges are often a friendlier and more attractive option. Lodges come in both the safari camp variety—in the midst of the bush in everything from a zip-up tent with a shower in the back to the currently fashionable stone-and-thatch, African-inspired dream-hut—and in the suburban bed-and-breakfast variety, again at all price levels and in styles from Cape Dutch to African. Typically, lodges take no more than 20 guests at a time.

At private game lodges, all meals are included in the rates. Usually, drinks are as well (you might want to ask this when you make a reservation). Professional guides are on staff to take you on drives and, those who are fully-licensed, walks. These guides and the camp managers look after your needs throughout the day and dine with you at meals. Game lodges also provide laundry service: If you're spending two weeks going from safari camp to safari camp, it would be cruel if they didn't. Consider spending three days at one of the lodges on your trip to be sure to allow enough time for your clothes to dry.

In national parks there are also rest camps, which have self-catering cabins and park guides with whom you can go out on walks and drives. National park rest camps are completely affordable: Z$250 per couple per night as opposed to US$250 and up per person per night at private lodges. You'll have to fend for yourself at meals at rest camps, and the guides aren't at your disposal, but the animals are out there just the same.

CATEGORY	COST*
$$$$	over Z$6,000
$$$	Z$3,000–Z$6,000
$$	Z$1,500–Z$3,000
$	under Z$1,500

Prices charged may be in U.S. or Zimbabwe dollars; price categories in this chapter reflect Zimbabwe dollar equivalents and refer to a standard double room, including tax.

People

Zimbabwean people are known in Africa for their friendliness. You'll certainly find that hotel and lodge staff are sunny and sincere—it's their job—but you're likely to find that the same is largely true if you want to encounter "real" people in townships (high-density areas formerly reserved for black workers in the cities) and rural communal lands. In Harare, the Mbare Musika market area is one exciting place to see local life up close, but it's also a hotspot for pickpockets. Several companies offer rural and township tours, which will show you the bare bones of Zimbabwean lifestyle and living. If you're looking for more than this, there are such experiences as "home-stays"—you can spend from hours to nights with local folk, participate in their day-to-day activities and experience first-hand a little of what it means to be an ordinary Zimbabwean.

Wildlife and National Parks

Apart from the thundering spectacle of Victoria Falls, Zimbabwe is best known for its wildlife. The big-name parks and some of the most notable animal species you'll see are as follows: **Hwange National Park** is in the western part of the country below Vic Falls. Elephant herds here are huge; buffalo, lions, giraffe, zebra, wildebeest, and antelope are plentiful. You might also see bat-eared foxes, and wild dogs are making a real comeback. Most of the park is wilderness that knows little human presence. **Matusadona National Park** is at the northeastern end of vast Lake Kariba. Its waterside greenery and parched interior make for stunning contrasts. Here you can add hippopotamus to the roster and waterbuck in the antelope category, and the numbers of cheetah are on the rise. Bird life is tremendous, and it is a superb place for tiger fishing. At **Mana Pools National Park,** with the Zambezi River flowing quietly past—again, the presence of water brings a variety of animals—time seems to run backwards. You might see lions, buffalo, crocodiles, hippos, waterbuck, leopard, hyena, possibly even the timid nyala antelope. Being on the Zambezi, the sabre-toothed tiger fish are abudant here, too.

Turning south, below Bulawayo, **Matobo National Park** is yet another world of its own. Granite formations have eroded away over eons to take on nearly human forms. In and around the hills on which they stand, there are zebra, giraffe, sable, warthog, and white rhino (with a square mouth, as opposed to the black rhino's pointed snout). There are leopard as well, and the small, enchanted-looking klipspringer antelope that bound up and down the rocky hills.

For a complete rundown on Southern African wildlife-viewing, *see* Big Game Adventures *in* Chapter 11.

Exploring Zimbabwe

From the ever-changing watercourse of the Zambezi River to Hwange National Park's open country to the granite hills of the Matobos, Zimbabwe's landscapes and the people and animals that live in them provide a fascinating variety of nature and culture. The best way to see the country is to alternate between cities and rural areas. Start in Victoria Falls: While it is almost a must if you're coming to southern Africa, there is something of a desperate air about the place—like nowhere else in Zimbabwe, it seems, people are singly motivated by making money. Get it behind you in order to move on to parts that will give you an accurate picture of the country. By contrast, both Harare and Bulawayo are pleasant cities; their wide, spacious avenues have an African dignity, even if the shops look somewhat dated to Western eyes.

Trip planning gets difficult when it comes time to choose which national parks to visit, especially if you've set your sights on seeing wildlife in South Africa and Botswana. Don't forget that the professionalism of Zimbabwe's guides makes the county a stand-out in terms of game experience. If you won't make it to Botswana's Okavango Delta, don't miss out on the beautiful waterways of Mana Pools or the Lake Kariba shoreline at Matusadona National Park. The entry points to Zimbabwe by plane are Victoria Falls and Harare.

Great Itineraries

If you're going to include Zimbabwe as a component of a larger African trip and time allows, put aside at least a week for getting to know Zimbabwe. Any less would give you neither a realistic impression nor a reasonable appreciation of the country. Although geographically small, the variety of things to do and places to see will keep you more than interested. In Zimbabwe, ten days is sufficient time to gain a reasonable and holistic impression; a week if you undertake a whirlwind trip to see just the highlights; half a week to whiz over the Falls and catch a glimpse of an elephant herd at Hwange.

Don't worry about organizing your day if you're intending to stay at the more exclusive private game lodges—timetables are arranged for game walks and drives and meals, all of which you can join or skip as you wish.

IF YOU HAVE 3 DAYS

If your itinerary begins with ⊞ **Victoria Falls,** take the first day to visit the falls, **Big Tree,** and rain forest—no need to contain your curiosity once you've arrived. This could take up two to three hours—the better part of an afternoon or morning. Then visit the **Falls Craft Village** for some bargaining for curios and Falls memorabilia if the spirit moves you. In the evening go dining, perhaps even dancing—your hotel will probably have a marimba band or traditional dance troupe performing nightly, so you needn't go away from your hotel if you don't feel so inclined. If you don't go for a morning rafting trip, head to ⊞ **Hwange National Park,** a great, nearby opportunity for some of the country's best animal viewing. Arrive in time for the afternoon game walk or drive. Evening meals are taken together in a central *boma* (traditional thatched dining structure) if you have chosen a private game lodge, and are often prefaced by drinks under open star-studded skies. If you went for a game drive the day before, start the day with an early morning game walk accompanied by your professional guide—walks can often reveal detail that you miss from a vehicle, like spoor, droppings, birds small plants, and tiny insects. And at dawn, chances of viewing animals are best, as it's still cool, and they congregate at watering points. On the morning of your departure, get up for that final game walk or drive before breakfast, then go catch your plane.

IF YOU HAVE 6 DAYS

With six days you need to decide whether to add time in ⊞ **Harare** or ⊞ **Bulawayo,** for a taste of Zimbabwean city life, or go all-wilderness.

In the first category, you could spend the first day in ⚅ **Victoria Falls,** leaving town first thing in the morning for **Kariba,** the connection on the way to ⚅ **Matusadona National Park** or ⚅ **Mana Pools National Park.** After two or three days, transit back to civilization for a day or two in Harare and another at the tremendous stone ruins of ⚅ **Great Zimbabwe.** The wilderness option would be to combine Victoria Falls with Hwange National Park and then either Matusadona and Mana Pools. The variety of both animals and environments would be remarkable.

IF YOU HAVE 10 OR MORE DAYS

If you plan to focus on Zimbabwe in a Southern African trip, allot 12 days minimum and choose four major parts of the country to tackle. Start in ⚅ **Victoria Falls** to get it out of the way first. If you arrive in the afternoon, head straight for the falls itself after checking into your hotel, then drop into town to sign up for a morning of rafting on the Zambezi. If you want to avoid a night in the area and don't feel like getting wet, take in the falls and head straight for the luxurious ⚅ **Matetsi Game Reserve** or to ⚅ **Hwange National Park** for two or three days of superb wildlife viewing. Spend the following four days in ⚅ **Bulawayo**—this thoroughly African city makes a great break from the wilds of Matetsi or Hwange—and the haunting ⚅ **Matobo National Park.** Two days in each place will give you a good taste of life in Matabeleland. Then move on to part of the Zambezi watershed: the wilds of ⚅ **Matusadona National Park** across the lake from Kariba town, or the downriver delights of ⚅ **Mana Pools.** One fantastic way to go downriver is a three-or-more day canoe safari past Zambian villages on the northern shore, hippos and crocs in the water, and a variety of other animals on the Zimbabwe side of the Zambezi. Then go by boat, car, and plane (the only way to do it) to ⚅ **Harare,** where you can pick up those Zimbawean fabrics, tapes, or CDs, and whatever other souvenirs you plan to take home with you.

When to Tour Zimbabwe

Zimbabwe has two distinct seasons—the wet summer, October through March, and the dry winter, from April through September. Generally June and July are the coolest months, with night temperatures hovering around and sometimes dropping below 0°C (32°F). Summer highs can reach 36°C (97°F), or even exceed 40°C (104°F) in the low-lying areas around the Zambezi and Lake Kariba—avoid the Zambezi Valley at this time. During the rainy season, the vegetation is thick and tall, which reduces wildlife visibility. Water is abundant, and animals are scattered over large areas because there is no need to gather at watering holes, where they are easier to spot. Summer, too, is when malaria-carrying mosquitoes—and in the middle Zambezi Valley the tsetse fly, which causes trypanosomiasis, or sleeping sickness—are most active.

Winter is a good time for everything. The Falls are at their highest level because waters from the Zambezi's catchment areas north in Angola are flowing into the river. Drier, shorter vegetation makes game-viewing easier all over the country. And cooler temperatures allow for more comfortable walking, riding, canoeing, and hiking. In winter, Kariba is where the locals and neighboring South Africans head to escape the cold, as it's always the warmest part of the country.

Time your city stays so that you're not in town on Sundays, when most or all of what you'll want to see and do will be closed.

HARARE

Harare as a city is now a century old. Before colonial settlement at the end of the last century, the area was believed to have been the domain of the Shona chief Haarari, "the one who never sleeps," whose influence extended over much of the area now occupied by the present-day city. The first white settlers arrived in ox- and horse-driven wagons, in what became known as the Pioneer Column, and in 1896 hoisted the Union Jack atop the rocky hilltop known as the Kopje (pronounced *kop*-ee). The history of Harare is closely linked with the establishment of farms and mines in areas now outlying the city, and tobacco still plays an influential role in the life of the city.

Although after independence there was a "free for all" policy in terms of housing and social amenities, evidence of past racial segregation is still evident: The city's expensive northern suburbs continue to house the wealthier, mostly white section of the population, while the densely populated former townships are almost 100% black-populated. Mbare, where the famous Musika (market) is found, is probably an extreme example of this, but it does reflect the housing conditions of a majority of Harare's urban population. Apart from Mbare, with its appeal for the adventurous, these areas don't feature on any tourist itinerary yet, but will be of interest to anyone wanting to see more than just the pretty face of Zimbabwe.

Harare's population is estimated at about 1½ million, but it is growing as a result of rural–urban migration. Repeated droughts and rural poverty have driven people out of their homes in search of better living standards in the city. That these dreams have largely come to nought has resulted in squatter camps sprouting on the outskirts of the city, and an increasingly worrying number of "street people."

That said, Harare is a clean city, fairly well managed and attracting investment. Insurance companies and pension funds yearly develop highrise office complexes, and the city is dotted with construction sites. There is also a drift away from the central business district to the quieter suburbs, where corporate parks are a current trend.

Besides nightclubs and restaurants, nightlife in Harare is somewhat limited—but by African standards it beats all other centers above South Africa. By day, you can visit shops and markets, art and sculpture galleries, and walk around the business district to check the pulse of this African city.

Exploring Harare

It's a good idea to rent a car if you wish to get out of city and explore the surrounds. If don't plan on wandering too far from your hotel, the city is small enough to allow for easy walking from one end to another, and taxis are cheap.

City Center

The relatively compact downtown, where streets are arranged in a grid, makes it easy to see all in a day. Harare's profusion of jacaranda blossoms festoon the avenues in summer, when the city is green. Parks in the center include the African Unity Square, just north of the Meikles Hotel on Jason Moyo Avenue. Fashioned on the Union Jack, it was formerly known as Cecil Square after Cecil John Rhodes. The other park is the Harare Gardens, overlooked by the crecent-shape Holiday Inn Crowne Plaza. Both parks have peddlers selling curios, souvenirs, handicrafts, and crochet works. The area between these parks and over to Fourth Street is the central business district. The First Street pedes-

trian mall runs between Samora Machel Avenue on the north end and
Speke Avenue to the south.

Anglican Cathedral. Across from the northwest corner of African Unity
Square and next to the House of Parliament, the cathedral is a Harare
landmark. Step inside for a look at the stations of the cross murals,
and maybe you'll catch a women's choir practice in session. ⊠ *Nelson Mandela Ave. at Second St.*

The Kopje. This hilltop site west of the city center is where the early
British pioneers raised the Union Jack. It overlooks the central business disctrict and is the site of present-day Zimbabwe's eternal Independence Flame. The character of the city changes as you approach
the Kopje area from the city center, and on the far side of the hill, Harare's
high-density suburbs begin.

National Gallery. On the ground floor, stonework from the prodigious
output of Zimbabwe's own artists predominates. Upstairs there is a
fine collection of objects from around the African continent: ritual and
domestic objects and some weapons. The gallery also has special exhibits. Next door at the Gallery Market, you can buy stone sculpture
and local crafts, from baskets and jewellery to printed fabrics. ⊠
Julius Nyerere Way at Park La., ☎ *14/704–666 or 14/724–391.* 🖾
Z$5; free Sun. ⊙ *Daily 9–5.*

National Museum of Human Sciences. Also known as the Queen Victoria Museum, this institution has displays of life from earlier ages in the
southern African region. Like other museums in the country, it won't be
like what you're used to back home, and if you're going on to Bulawayo,
the natural history musuem there is Zimbabwe's best. The museum is
on the west end of the city; you'll need a car or taxi to get here. ⊠ *Rotten Row at Raleigh St.,* ☎ *14/751–797.* 🖾 *US$2.* ⊙ *Mon.–Sat. 9–5.*

Parliament of Zimbabwe. In this stately monument to the colonial years,
Zimbabwe's lawmakers still carry on the traditions of a British-style
House of Commons. The street on which it stands was officially named
after South African President Nelson Mandela in September of 1997
while he was here on a state visit. It was formerly Baker Avenue,
named for the cathedral's architect, Sir Herbert Baker. ⊠ *Nelson Mandela Ave.,* ☎ *14/700–181. Admission by prior arrangement.*

Around Harare

Mbare Musika (market). This is a typical, bustling African megamarket, where you'll find everything from traditional handcrafted kitchen
utensils and musical instruments to medicinal herbs and concoctions—
maybe even a practicing n'anga. It is also the site of the country's largest
bus terminal, where hundreds of "chicken buses" (so called for their
frequent nonhuman passengers) take on and disgorge thousands of travelers daily. Mbare is a place where hordes of unemployed people try
to eke out a living in differnt ways, including pickpocketing. So be on
guard: Take no valuables, only limited cash, and a camera for catching the scene on film. To get here, take Rotten Row on the west side
of the city past the Pioneer Cemetery flyover. Taking a taxi is advisable, as a rental car is likely to be tampered with or end up minus a
few "spare" parts on your return. Arrange with the taxi driver to return at an appointed time, or to wait, as it may be difficult to find decent transport back into town. Otherwise take a local guide who'll show
you around and help you bargain for good prices on artifacts you may
wish to buy.

Chapungu Kraal. This expansive sculpture garden contains some of the best known names in Zimbabwean art. There is a tea garden and shop, and on request you can see the artists at work at the back of the landscaped gardens. There is explosive traditional music and dance in the amphitheatre on weekends starting around 1 PM and continuing throughout the afternoon. ⊠ *1 Harrow Rd. (off the road to Mutare about 6 km, or 4 mi, from town), Msasa.* ☎ *14/486–648.* ⊠ *Z$5.* ☉ *Daily 8–6.*

Ewanrigg Botanical Gardens. Best known for its fantastic displays of aloes, this is the one stop where most of the country's flora can be found in peaceful and scenic surroundings. As there is no restaurant on site, put together a picnic to take along. Follow Enterprise Road out of the city, then turn off half way onto the Shamva-Bindura Road. The gardens are about 30 km (19 mi) from the city center. ⊠ *US$1.20.* ☉ *9–6.*

Dining

$$$$ ✕ **22 Victoria Drive.** Arguably the best Italian restaurant in in the area, this suburban eatery serves four-course set menues that include choices of antipasti, pasta dishes, main courses, desserts, and grappa or sambucca to finish. Sample dishes include prawns with white beans and onions, carpaccio, and chicken with a white wine and mushroom sauce. ⊠ *22 Victoria Dr., Newlands, (5 mins from the city center by car off Enterprise Rd.),* ☎ *14/776–429. Reservations essential. MC, V. No lunch, closed Sun.*

$$$ ✕ **Bagatelle.** In Meikles Hotel, this is one of the city's classiest restaurants, with fine service and an international menu. Steak and seafood are the specialties; try grilled prawns in periperi sauce for a local twist. ⊠ *Meikles Hotel, Jason Moyo Ave. and 3rd St.,* ☎ *14/79–5655. Reservations essential. AE, DC, MC, V. Closed Mon. No lunch weekends.*

$$ ✕ **Gee Gees.** This tastefully fitted restaurant—with marbled walls, plenty of fresh flowers, and candlelit tables—serves some of Harare's tastiest food. Examples from the frequently changing menu include a deep-fried sesame seed–crusted camembert starter and chicken breast grilled with sesame seeds and served with a chick pea and garlic sauce. For dessert there is the ever-popular chocolate mousse. ⊠ *Borrowdale Race Course, off the Borrowdale Rd.* ☎ *14/883–632. Reservations essential weekends. MC, V. No dinner Sun.; lunch Sun. only.*

$ ✕ **Kombahari.** For a taste of African cuisine in decidedly cosmopolitan African surrounds, this is where you'll find delicacies such as pumpkin leaves, kapenta, mopane worms, and sadza, all done with a touch of international hotel panache. ⊠ *Sheraton Harare Hotel, Pennefather Ave.,* ☎ *14//729–771. AE, DC, MC, V.*

Lodging

$$$$ ☷ **Meikles Hotel.** With its 1960s International Style lobby and efficient air, Harare's best known hotel has a pleasant dignity about it, as well as conveniences like voice mail and fax modems. Rooms are tastefully decorated in greens and peaches, with English country prints on walls. Housekeeping standards are refreshingly high. Bathrooms in deluxe suites have black marble and brass fittings. The newer west wing of the hotel commands views of Africa Unity Square and the Anglican Cathedral. ⊠ *Jason Moyo Ave., Third St., Box 594,* ☎ *14/795–655,* FAX *14/707–753. 318 rooms. 5 restaurants, pool, beauty salon, sauna, excercise room, concierge. AE, DC, MC, V.*

$$$ ☷ **Imba Matombo.** The distiction of being Zimbabwe's only Relais & Chateaux member comes with a certain cachet. The lodge is in a prestigious Harare suburb, and most guests make this the starting or end-

ing point of a Zimbawe adventure—a bit of luxury and creature comforts are welcome after endless flights and bush camps. Thatch roof guests lodges have wicker and heavy teak furnishings and native craft work. Three of the standard lodges have verandas. The lodge has car service for city sightseeing and airport transfers at high rates. A rental car will be cheaper. ⊠ *3 Albert Glen Close, Glen Lorne (Box HG 800 Highlands), Harare,* ☎ *14/499–013,* ℻ *14/499–071. 5 lodges, 3 suites. Restaurant, pool, tennis court. AE, MC, V.*

$$–$$$ 🏨 **Best Western Jameson Hotel.** A convenient city center location makes this ideal if you don't plan to rent a car while you're in the city. The best known room at the Jameson is the honeymoon suite, with its circular bed and complimentary large round mirror above it, and a jacuzzi. As with other suites, it has its own lounge and seating area, furnished with a couple of armchairs and sofa. One of Harare's top restaurants, Tiffany's, is in the hotel. ⊠ *21 Samora Machel Ave., Box 2833, Harare,* ☎ *14/794–641* ℻ *14/794–655. 123 rooms, 7 suites. 2 restaurants, 3 bars, pool, concierge. AE, DC, MC, V.*

$ 🏨 **Bronte Hotel.** Superbly maintained gardens give this the feel of a country hotel in the city center. With immaculately-kept lawns and Cape Dutch–style buildings, it is the most affordable of the city's best lodgings. All rooms are decorated simply in natural woods, with floral soft furnishings. Rooms accomodating families are also available. Request a garden facing room. Service is warm and personal. ⊠ *132 Baines St.,* ☎ *14/796–631 or 14/796–635,* ℻ *14/721–429. 80 rooms, 8 family suites. Restaurant, pool. Breakfast included. AE, DC, MC, V.*

Nightlife and the Arts

Harare has rather limited evening entertainment options—live music, discos, pubs, and theater are in short supply. It is generally safe to be out at night, but don't wear valuables and carry credit cards or only as much cash as you'll need. If possible, be in the company of someone who knows his or her way around. If you're visiting an establishment outside of a hotel, you will need Zimbabwean cash.

The Arts

Alliance Francaise (⊠ 328 Herbert Chitepo Ave., ☎ 14/720–777). This cosy venue hosts plays and musicals. An on-site cafe serves excellent light meals at very reasonable prices. Check local papers for what's playing. Bookings not normally necessary.

Nightlife

Harpers (⊠ 124 Nelson Mandela Ave., behind Best Western Oasis Hotel). Also known as Harpers at the Sphinx, this is a decent club where some of Zimbabwe's top names, like reggae-mbira fusion maestro Andy Brown and jazz band Z-Brass perform weekly. It isn't great for food, but light snacks are served. It is sometimes closed for private functions, so check the entertainment page of the daily *Herald*. The club closes around midnight.

Sandro's (⊠ Union Ave. and Julius Nyerere Way). Popular with locals, this spot is ideal if you want to get a feel of a typical Harare night out on the town. Live band play, sometimes there is rhumba-theme disco music. Sandro's has good pub grub.

Keg & Sable. This suburban sports bar has wholesome pub food and a good choice of local and imported beers. Satellite sports coverage on large TV monitors adds to the lively atmosphere. ⊠ *Sam Levy's Village, Borrowdale Rd.,* ☎ *14/884445.*

Shopping

Here, too, suburban shopping centers have become the convenience—minus street-kids and parking hassles. But your most interesting shopping will be in the city. The quietest times will be midweek, month-end Saturday mornings are particularly busy. Most shops are closed Saturday afternoons and Sundays.

Malls

Eastgate. This modern office and shopping complex occupies its own block and is the pride of Harare residents. A network of ground floor shops cater for just about all your requirements, with a QV pharmacy, music shop, local designer shops, and a food court. ⊠ *Between Third and Second Sts., Speke Ave. and Robert Mugabe Way.*

Sam Levy's Village, Borrowdale. An upmarket village-style complex with banks, boutiques, restaurants, takeaways and cafés, supermarkets, pharmacies, jewellers, bookshops, sports shops, and other specialist shops. There are outdoor Sunday markets as well, but the items for sale aren't terribly appealing. ⊠ *Borrowdale Rd., about 17 km (11 mi) from city center.*

Markets

Besides Mbare Musika (☞ Around Harare, *above*), there are no markets in Harare, unless you're interested in exploring a flea market. Visit the **Union Avenue flea market,** open daily from about 9 to 5. At both you'll find an assortment of cheap goodies, mostly imported from South Africa, including clothing, trinkets, and ornaments at giveaway prices, but the quality is not especially high.

Specialty Stores

Kudhinda Fabrics sells a colorful variety of ethnic print fabrics, some of the ideas borrowed from other parts of Africa, that display the skill and pattern-making talent of the Zimbabwean women who make them. The shop also sells tastefully made pottery, curios, and cane furniture. ⊠ *1 Harrow Rd., Doon Estate, Msasa, very near Chapungu Sculpture Park,* ☎ *14/486–683 or 487–103.* ⊘ *Weekdays 8–5, 8–noon Sat.,*

The Trading Company is the place to go for high-quality African-made outdoor casual wear, Zairean Kuba cloth, other artefacts, and locally-make paper products. If you are looking for one place to shop on a quick trip through Harare, this is your best bet. There are locations downtown and in the suburbs of Avondale and Newlands. ⊠ *AT&T House, 1st St. and Samora Machel Ave.,* ☎ *14/746–666; and Southampton Life Centre (near the Miekles Hotel), 2nd St. and Jason Moyo Ave.,* ☎ *14/704–499.*

Grassroots Books, a small, Pan-African bookstore, is probably the best stop for locally published books and works by other African authors. Famous Zimbabwean names include Noma award-winner Chenjerai Hove and internationally acclaimed Charles Mungoshi, Yvonne Vera, and Tsitsi Dangarembga. A great selection of anthologies, biographies and fiction are available at very good prices. ⊠ *Africa House, 100 Jason Moyo Ave.,* ☎ *14/792–551.*

Kingston's (⊠ Jason Moyo Ave. and 2nd St.) stocks stationery and a good selection of coffee-table books on Zimbabwean people and sights, as well as work of local writers and a somewhat limited choice of academic and special interest titles. It's a good one-stop shop for picking up curios, leather and copper souvenirs, and postcards, etcetera.

Spinalong (✉ Eastgate Shopping Mall, 2nd St. between Robert Mugabe Way and Jason Moyo Ave.) stocks a good range of tapes, CDs, and vinyl records. Expect to pay in the region of Z$200 for a CD. If you've heard of and like Zimbabwe's musicians and other African artists, this is the place to pick up a few cassettes or disks. They'll happily play it for you to test the sound quality of the tape, which is a smart thing to do in Zimbabwe.

CNA (✉ Robert Mugabe Way, near the corner of 1st St.) carries stationery items and gifts—although not necessarily African—and international magazines and books. Being part of the reputable South African chain, CNA will likely have a more up-to-date selection of music and magazines than most other shops in Harare.

Harare A to Z

Arriving and Departing

BY BUS

Luxury buses are the slowest way to get around Zimbabwe. Fares are are based on distance—the six-hour Harare–Bulawayo trip is about Z$350 one way. Top of the range coaches serve biscuits and soft drinks, so bring a sandwich if you'll travel through lunch. Stops are made at selected hotels en route. **Blue Arrow Luxury Coaches** (☎ 14/729–514) runs from Speke Avenue, a block east of the Miekles Hotel downtown.

BY CAR

Harare is 440 km (275 mi) from Bulawayo, 300 km (190 mi) from Masvingo (close to Great Zimbabwe), and 880 km (550 mi) from Victoria Falls by car. Generally, main roads are named by the towns they link: From Harare to Bulawayo, look for the Harare–Bulawayo Road, and from Bulawayo to Victoria Falls, the Bulawayo–Vic Falls Road. There is no direct route by road to Victoria Falls from Harare: You must go via Bulawayo and Hwange or through slow secondary roads from Kariba. Zimbabwean roads are well maintained and often policed, so watch your speed unless you're prepared to part with substantial amounts of Zim dollars.

BY PLANE

Flying within Zimbabwe can be alternately humorous and exasperating. On an Air Zimbabwe flight, you might actually board an Air Zambia plane; or your flight just might be cancelled for no apparent reason. On-time records are not stellar, either. That said, safety records are quite good, and flight attendants are polite and pleasant in true Zimbabwean form. Routing around the country can be inflexible, as well. In order to get to Hwange from Bulawayo—only 260 km (160 mi)—you might have to fly to Harare, Kariba, and Vic Falls en route.

Harare International Airport (☎ 14/575–528), lies about 15 km (9 mi) south of the city center.

Air Zimbabwe (☎ 14/575–111) flies to Bulawayo daily, to Victoria Falls and Hwange and Kariba and other regional centers such as Johannesburg and Cape Town. Schedules often change at short notice, so call to check flights and routes. **Zimbabwe Express** (☎ 14/705–266, 14/705–923) flies to Johannesburg, and can connect to Cape Town. Domestic routes take in Bulawayo, Victoria Falls, and Hwange.

Other airline contacts are **Air Botswana** (✉ Southampton House, 5th Floor, First St. and Union Ave., ☎ 14/733–836) and **South African Airways** (✉ Takura House, 2nd Floor, 69–71 Union Ave., ☎ 14/738–922).

Between the Airport and City. The **taxi** fare between the airport and the city is about Z$80.

Departure Tax. All foreigners leaving the country by air must pay a US$20 departure tax, or the equivalent, whether from Harare or Victoria Falls. If you don't have exact change, Zimbank on Livingstone Way (☞ Money Matters, *above*) sells departure stamps, and you may pay in Zimbabwe dollars providing you can produce a Zimbabwean receipt for your foreign-exchange transaction. Zimbank also operates an agency at the airport, but its hours change frequently.

Getting Around

BY BUS

Generally, public transport Zupco buses are unreliable for time, although cheap. So-called emergency taxis—minibuses—are the cheapest, but they are also the riskiest. They are not a recommended mode of transport.

BY CAR

This is your best bet for convenience and safety. Driving around Harare is still relatively tame, if you are used to driving on the left-hand side of the road. Drivers are normally courteous, except at peak hours when some may rush through an amber traffic light without a thouught. Avoid driving alone, especially at night, to the high density suburbs or around Mbare market, as you risk losing hub caps and other parts, if not the car itself, to thieves.

BY TAXI

When hailing a cab, select newer-looking cars. The recommended companies are **Rixi** (✉ Harare St. and Samora Machel Ave., or Union Ave. between Julis Nyerere and Angwa St., ☎ 14/753–080) and **A1** (☎ 14/703–334 or 14/706–996). Avoid others—they tend to have overactive meters. Also, it may be difficult to trace property if you lose it on other companies' taxis. You can summon taxis by phone or hire them from ranks.

Contacts and Resources

CAR RENTALS

Recommended car hire companies are **Hertz** (☎ 14/727–209), **Europcar** (☎ 14/750–622/4) and **Avis Rent-a-Car** (☎ 575–431). Rates range from Z$315 for an economy class car to Z$850 for a Mercedes Benz per day, with a sliding surcharge per kilometer. If you intend to hire the car for five or more days, you get about 250 km (155 mi) free per day. You can also hire off-road 4x4s, vans, and minibuses. Unfortunately, most companies do have drop-off charges for one-way rentals.

Another travel/accommodation option is to hire a **Campervan**—a pickup truck fitted out as a caravan that takes up to three passengers—from **VFR** (✉ 35 Samora Machel Ave., 5th floor, ☎ 14/774–740) for about US$80 per day with the first 100 km (62 mi) free, and a charge of US$.35 thereafter.

DOCTORS

The Avenues Clinic is a large, well-equipped private hospital. ✉ *Baines Ave. and Mazowe St.,* ☎ *14/732–055.*

Montagu Clinic. ✉ *135 Jason Chinamano Ave. and 5th St.,* ☎ *14/700–216, or 14/727–194/6.*

Parirenyatwa Hospital is the country's largest referral center and government hospital. ✉ *Mazowe St.,* ☎ *14/794–411.*

EMBASSIES AND HIGH COMMISSIONS

British Embassy. ✉ *Corner House, Samora Machel Ave. and Leopold Takawira St., 7th floor,* ☎ *14/772–990/774–700,* FAX *14/774–617.*

Canadian High Commission. ✉ *45 Baines Ave., Box 1430,* ☎ *14/733881/5,* FAX *14/735–400.*

U.S. Embassy. ⊠ *172 Herbert Chitepo Ave., Box 3340,* ☎ *14/794–521.*

EMERGENCIES
Ambulance (☎ 994), **fire brigade** (☎ 993), and **police** (☎ 995).

GUIDED TOURS
A number of companies offer rather exciting tours to the high density suburbs, nearby rural villages, national parks, and to other parts of Zimbabwe starting in Harare.

African Portfolio, a Harare- and New York–based tour operator, can arrange all aspects of a Zimbabwean itinerary, whatever your interests and budget, whether from the moment you leave your home or for smaller local segments—for example arranging transportation and lodging for a Harare–Great Zimbabwe jaunt or for a three-plus day canoe safari down the Zambezi River to Mana Pools. ⊠ *160 Enterprise Rd., Highlands,* ☎ *14/481–117,* FAX *14/495–704.*

Connemara Tours and Safaris has day tours to rural areas on the outskirts of Harare. Small groups of up eight are taken to sample typical rural life—pay a courtesy call on the chief or headman of the village, witness cattle herding, food preparation, or if you're lucky a traditional ceremony or ritual in progress. ⊠ *Suite 1, Katherine Ct., 103 Nelson Mandela Ave.,* ☎ FAX *14/704–866.*

Nyati Travel takes groups of two to eight people on 6-day tours of Zimbabwe's communal lands, which are ideal for seeing Zimbabwean life in its most typical and unaffected forms, as well as the subtle similarities and differences in lifestyle between Zimbabwe's ethnic groups. The cost is US$485 per person, and tours depart the first Saturday of each month. ⊠ *Box GD887, Greendale, Harare,* ☎ *492556,* FAX *492509.*

UTc has a city tour that takes in historic buildings, Mbare Market, the National Gallery, the Natural History Museum, the hilltop Kopje for a panoramic view of Harare, and the world's largest tobacco auction floors (in season). The tour starts at 9 AM and lasts about three and a half hours; the cost is about US$20. UTc also has day-trips to Great Zimbabwe, as well as numerous other tours throughout the country. ⊠ *Beverly Ct. and Nelson Mandela Ave.,* ☎ *14/703–821.*

TELEPHONE NUMBERS
Zimbabwean phone numbers in this chapter are printed as they should be dialed within Zimbabwe. When dialing from outside of the country, drop the initial *1* after you dial the 263 country code.

TRAVEL AGENCIES
American Express Travel/Manica Travel Services. ⊠ *Bluebridge, Eastgate Mall, 2nd floor, 2nd St. at Jason Moyo Ave.,* ☎ *14/703–421 or 14/708–441.*

Thomas Cook. ⊠ *Vanguard Centre, Jason Moyo Ave.,* ☎ *14/704–181-8.*

The Travel Company. ⊠ *Travel Centre, 2nd floor, Third St. at Jason Moyo Ave.,* ☎ *14/731–771.*

VISITOR INFORMATION
Your hotel concierge or guest relations desk may be useful for information, as will the **Info Carde** box, which is full of all kinds of tourist services, at hotel front desks.

The **Harare Publicity Association** might be useful for some information, but it is usually short of brochures and uninformed of new developments. It does publish a regular Harare diary with current goings-on and places to visit. ⊠ *Africa Unity Sq., Jason Moyo Ave. and 2nd St.,* ☏ *14/705–085.* ⊙ *Weekdays 8*AM *to 4*PM *(closed noon– 1*PM*), Sat. 8 to 12*AM.

The **Zimbabwe Tourism Authority** will field questions and take complaints and comments. ⊠ *3 Anchor House, 7th floor, Fourth St. and Jason Moyo Ave.,* ☏ *14/793–666 or 14/763–765.* ⊙ *Weekdays 8–5.*

GREAT ZIMBABWE NATIONAL MONUMENT

The granite ruins of Great Zimbabwe, the largest ancient stone building south of the Sahara, sprawl across two and a half square miles of a wide, grassy valley surrounded by hills. Developing from a small settlement in the 8th century it evolved into a wealthy and powerful city state which flourished between AD 1250 and 1450 and at its zenith contained nearly 20,000 people. Now a World Heritage site, the ruins stand some 20 km (12½ mi) from the provincial capital Masvingo in southeastern Zimbabwe.

The site comprises the Great Enclosure, the Hill Complex, and the Valley ruins. Of these the Hill Complex is the oldest. Built at the top of an almost sheer granite cliffs, it is a labyrinth of stairways, narrow winding passages, and interlocking walls. As both a citadel and a holy place, Hill Complex access was originally limited to a single route known as the Ancient Way. At a later time, the Watergate Path was opened up for domestic servants.

The massive, curving walls of the Great Enclosure, 36 ft high and over 800 ft in circumference, consist of nearly one million hand-cut granite blocks. Even today, the sheer size and symmetry of this monumental structure, with its open courtyards, narrow passages, and chevron wall patterns, is remarkable. The exact function of the Great Enclosure is still debated, but it was almost certainly used by the royal court and by priests and prophets conducting religious rites.

Scattered along the length of the rolling grasslands are the lichen covered stone walls that once were the homes and workshops of ordinary citizens.

Although cattle was almost certainly crucial to its wealth, Great Zimbabwe prospered as the result of its trade in gold and ivory with the Swahili and Arab traders from the coast. By the 16th century the kingdom had fallen into irreversible decline. Creepers, lichen, and grass covered the graceful, curving walls, long abandoned to sun and solitude, until an impoverished German hunter, Adam Renders, stumbled across them in 1867. Long before Renders, however, the ruins had attracted rumours and speculation by early Portuguese traders and missionaries who spoke of "a great city of stone" made powerful by gold. Many believed it to be the site of the biblical Ophir, known to Solomon and Sheba and built by some unknown Mediterranean race.

Such theories appealed to Victorians who were busily engaged in expanding the British Empire into Africa. The idea that such an intricate architectural complex might have been built by the very people they were preparing to subjugate in the name of Christianity was clearly unthinkable. And so they eagerly supported claims that the ruins were built by Phoenicians, Egyptians, and—even more implausibly, given the huge disparity in the time scale—the ancient Minoan Greeks.

Great Zimbabwe has lasted for over 700 years, a remarkable duration considering that the walls were constructed using the dry-stone technique by which blocks were laid one on the other without mortar.

The best way to explore Great Zimbabwe is with one of the many expert guides who are able to bring the splendours and mysteries of past vividly back to life. In addition to exploring the grounds, there is a small but informative museum. ⊙ *Daily 8–5:30.* ✉ *US$5; museum US$2 extra.*

Dining and Lodging

Both of the following lodges are adjacent to Great Zimbabwe and have guided trips to a local game park, to nearby Bushmen paintings, or to the ruins themselves.

$$$ ✕⊡ **Great Zimbabwe Hotel.** Ideally situated within walking distance of the ruins, this hotel makes a good base for exploring the area. The hotel itself is rather simple; rooms have modern funiture with African prints, but none of the inspiration of the Lodge of the Ancient City. Meals are served on a pleasant patio surrounded by gardens. ✉ *Mailing address: Box 9082, Masvingo,* ☎ *139/62–274 or* ☎ *139/62–449,* FAX *139/64–884. 47 rooms and 6 self-catering lodges. Restaurant, bar, pool, 4 tennis courts. AE, DC, MC.*

$$$ ✕⊡ **Lodge at the Ancient City.** Graceful reminders of Great Zimbabwe
★ will strike you at every turn in this elegantly designed lodge on a wooded granite *kopje* (outcrop) near the ancient city, overlooking the Great Enclosure. Giant rounded boulders, a feature of the local landscape, form an integral part of the architecture, with dry-stone walls arching gracefully over them. Public spaces are attractively fitted with African objects, and accommodation is in 20 thatched, traditionally ochred cottages scattered about the wooded property. Guided trips to Great Zimbabwe, to local villages, or to nearby Lake Mutirikwi are available. Full- or partboard rates and rates that include all activities are available. ✉ *Mailing address: Box 6, Hillside, Bulawayo,* ☎ *19/74–589,* FAX *19/229–088. 20 cottages. Restaurant, bar, pool. AE, DC, MC, V.*

Great Zimbabwe A to Z

Arriving and Departing

BY BUS

Blue Arrow Luxury Coaches (☎ 14/729–514, FAX 14/729–572) runs three times a week to Great Zimbabwe from Harare's Chester House terminal (✉ Steke Ave. between 3rd and 4th Sts.) and Bulawayo's Unifreight House terminal (✉ 73A 5th St). A one-way trip costs Z$240 and takes six hours from either city.

BY CAR

Harare is 300 km (190 mi) north of Masvingo; Bulawayo is 270 km (170 mi) west. Masvingo is 27 km (17 mi) north of Great Zimbabwe.

BY PLANE

Expedition Airways (☎ 14/781–517) flies to Masvingo from Harare and Bulawayo.

Contacts and Resources

GUIDED TOURS

Tourism Services Zimbabwe (☎ 14/733–771, FAX 14/733–770) have tours to Great Zimbabwe and Lake Mutirikwi.

VISITOR INFORMATION

Maps to the monument are available at the entrance gate.

Travelworld (✉ Robert Mugabe St., Masvingo, ☎ 139/62–131) is the local agent for Air Zimbabwe and major car-rental companies. Other contacts include the **Automobile Association** (✉ 5 Robert Mugabe Way, Masvingo, ☎ 139/62–563) and the **Masvingo Publicity Association** (✉ Robert Mugabe Way (across from the Chevron Hotel, Masvingo, ☎ 139/62–643), which have local maps and information. Offices are closed Saturday afternoons and Sundays.

BULAWAYO

The center of a vast regional ranching industry, Bulawayo is Zimbabwe's second largest city, formerly the seat of the legendary Ndebele kings. With its laid back tempo and distinctly *déjà vu* ambience, Bulawayo can be a thoroughly enjoyable place to while away a day or two. Adjust yourself to the leisurely pace and, like others before you, you may end up spending longer than you intended.

A short stroll through the city center quickly reveals how much it has so far largely escaped the commercial realities of demolition, high rise buildings, and slick renovation. Covered ox-wagons have long since rolled out of town, but the wide, tree-lined streets—which were designed to allow a team of 16-oxen to turn full circle—have remained and are still lined with many of the original handsome colonial buildings.

Bulawayo, which means "place of slaughter" in the Ndebele language, evolved from the kraal of King Lobengula (1836–1894), son of the great Mzilikazi. A former commander in the army of the legendary Zulu general, Shaka (1787–1828), Mzilikazi led his people northward across the Limpopo River into the towering granite outcrops and grassy valleys of the Matobo hills south of Bulawayo.

Much of modern Zimbabwe's history was shaped here, and formidable ghosts still haunt the stage: Lobengula himself; the British Leander Starr Jameson, leader of the infamous Jameson Raid that sparked the Anglo-Boer War; and none other than Cecil John Rhodes, the brilliant but ultimately flawed imperialist whose Borgia-like web of deceptions and intrigue finally trapped and tricked Lobengula into signing away the rights to his own kingdom. Rhodes' grave, in fact, is on a promomtory in nearby Matobo National Park.

At the height of his powers Lobengula ruled over some of Africa's richest and most coveted lands. He commanded a superbly disciplined army modelled on the tactics of the great King Shaka, and but for the arrival of the Europeans in Africa his dynasty might have continued unbroken to this day. In a memorable description of a person irreversibly caught up in the web of fate, novelist Evelyn Waugh likened the Ndebele king to a deeply tragic figure from Shakespeare, combining, as he did, elements from Lear, Macbeth, and Richard II.

Exploring Bulawayo

The city, which is laid on a grid pattern, can easily be explored on foot. The Publicity Association, Art Gallery, Public Library, Jairos Jiri Craft Shop, and Main Post Office for instance are all on or between Leopold Takawira Way and Eighth Avenue. A ten minute walk down the latter will bring you to the spacious and well tended Centenary Park and the Museum of National History, regarded as one of the finest in central and southern Africa—bearing in mind that southern African museums are generally not terribly polished. At the other end of Leopold Takawira is the imposing City Hall. Nearby on Eighth Avenue the City Hall Bus

Terminus. Head south down Lobengula through the busy African shopping quarter for the Railway Station and nearby Railway Museum.

Sights to See

Bulawayo Home Industries Centre. If you are looking for local craft items, this is one of a few venues in Bulawayo to go. The range of batiks, weaving, and embroidery are all produced on site. ⊠ *Taylor Ave. (near Mzilikazi Art and Craft Center),* ☎ *19/65–376.* ⊙ *Mon.–Fri. 8–4:30.*

Mzilikazi Art and Craft Center. Mzilikazi is one of the city's oldest townships, and there is a permanently up-beat mood to the Art and Craft Center, where you can watch a young generation of artists producing hand-made pottery and sculpture. Proceeds go toward subsidising an art school and training others to work with ceramics. The center is close to Mpilo Hospital in Mzilikazi Square, off of Old Falls Rd; the route is well signposted. ☎ *19/67–245.* ⊙ *Weekdays 8–12:30 and 2–4.*

★ **Museum of National History.** If you see nothing else, visit the Museum of National History. The dioramas of Zimbabwean mammals are superb, and the collection includes the second largest mounted elephant in the world, its ivories weighing 40 and 41 kilos respectively. As a quick guide to everything you ever wanted to know about the bush before heading off into it, this is ideal preparation. ⊠ *Centenary Park, Leopold Takawira Ave.,* ☎ *19/60–045.* ⊠ *US$2.* ⊙ *Daily 9–5.*

★ **The National Gallery.** Located in a fine old colonial house, the gallery maintains a permanent collection of local artists' work and mounts exhibitions on subjects such as the art and culture of the Ndebele. Artifacts from Matabeleland such as woven baskets, mats, and other household products are well represented. The musuem shop sells craft items, books, and Zimbabwean music. On site there is also a studio building where local artists work and sell their work: Look for the potato-printed fabrics. ⊠ *Douslin House, Main St. at Leopold Takawira Ave.,* ☎ *19/70–721.* ⊙ *Tues.–Sun. 9–5.* ⊠ *Z$5; free Sun.*

★ **Township Square Cultural Center.** This forum for the arts, local culture, and community activities grew out of the success of the local Amakhosi Theatre group, and you'll find everything from theater to kid's soccer games going on here. Concerts with major Zimbabwean musicians or local bands, traditional dancing, and demonstrations of traditional Zimbabwean food-making—such as brewing sorghum beer or cooking up sadza—are among the other things you'll come across. There is also a restaurant and a beer hall popular among locals. ⊠ *Old Falls Rd. at Basch St.* ☎ *19/76–673 or 19/79–397.* ⊠ *Free.* ⊙ *7–5:30.*

Zimbabwe National Railways Museum. Steam train enthusiasts from the world over visit this museum, near the main station, which houses a display of locomotives and rolling stock—some in fine shape, some on the rusty side—dating back to the end of the last century. Among them is Cecil John Rhodes's private 1896 Pullman coach—a lavish creation entirely in keeping with his own lofty, egocentric dreams. ⊠ *Prospect Ave. off J. Chinamano Rd.,* ⊙ *Tues., Wed., and Fri., 9:30–noon and 2–4.* ⊠ *Z$1.*

Dining

$$–$$$ ✕ **Olav Bistro.** This deservedly popular restaurant in the Selborne Hotel has an imaginative menu that successfully combines French and Scandinavian cookery. Look for Norwegian smoked salmon or escargot appetizers, and steak or seafood main dishes. The wine list includes estate-bottled South African and Zimbabwean vintages. ⊠ *Selborne*

Hotel, Leopold Takawira Ave. and George Silikunde St., ☎ *19/76–335. MC, V. Closed Mon; no lunch weekends.*

$ ✕ **Township Square Cultural Center.** For a taste of Zimbabwean fare, this home-grown forum for local traditions also serves lunch. Watch food being made, then have a taste of sadza and stew, some barbecue, or *matumbu* (offal) if you're feeling more adventurous. Don't miss out on a glass of traditional sorghum beer, which is also made at the center. ⊠ *Old Falls Rd. at Basch St.* ☎ *19/76–673 or 19/79–397. No credit cards. Lunch only.*

Lodging

$$–$$$$ 🏨 **Induna Lodge.** This homey lodge in suburban Bulawayo is owned by sincere and affable hosts Rob and Edwina MacDonald. Rob's grandfather came from Scotland to help build Cecil Rhodes's African railroad dream, which makes Rob able to share a personal history of three generations of Zimbabwean life. Guest rooms are a bit spare and could use sprucing up, but they're immaculate. Meals are taken with the hosts, and food is simple and generally good home-cooking. Rates are available for bed and breakfast or breakfast and dinner (generously poured drinks included). ⊠ *16 Fortunes Gate Rd., Matsheumhlope, Bulawayo,* ☎ *19/45–684,* 𝔽𝔸𝕏 *19/45–627. Pool. 4 double rooms with bath, 2 single rooms with shared bath. Breakfast included. MC, V.*

$$–$$$ 🏨 **Nesbitt Castle.** Set in 14-acres of woodland and gardens, this improbable Scottish castle, built by an eccentric former mayor, is a cherished Bulawayo institution. The spacious high-ceilinged rooms furnished with antiques, and the balustrades, and the long echoing corridors are a perfect setting for Lady Macbeth or Banquo's ghost. The Coach House Restaurant is highly regarded by local residents, particularly for its five course menu. Nesbitt Castle is 6 km (4 mi) from the center of town. ⊠ *4 Percy Ave., Hillside, Bulawayo,* ☎ *19/42–735 or 19/42–726,* 𝔽𝔸𝕏 *19/41–864. 9 rooms. Bar, pool. Breakfast included. AE, DC, MC, V.*

$$ 🏨 **Bulawayo Rainbow Hotel.** This convenient central business district hotel has a kind of faded '60s charm, and it is clearly a mainstay in Bulawayo. Formerly the Bulawayo Sun, it lacks any real character, but the rooms are attractive enough and have with appropriate modern conveniences. The Homestead Restaurant serves home cooked meals; the Bistro provides an up-market à la carte menu. The Alabama bar is a good place to hear a little jazz. ⊠ *Joshia Tongogara St. at 10th Ave., Box 1876, Bulawayo,* ☎ *19/60–101,* 𝔽𝔸𝕏 *19/61–739. 172 rooms. 2 restaurants, 2 bars, room service. Breakfast included. AE, DC, MC, V.*

$$ 🏨 **Churchill Arms.** Located eight km from the city Center on the road to the Matopos and only 2 km from Tshabalal Wildlife Sanctuary, this mock-Tudor building with mullioned windows and paneled walls radiates an olde worlde charm and sense of plenitude. Rooms are decorated to reflect Tudor style. The Inglenook restaurant serves both a la carte and set menus. ⊠ *Matopos Rd. at Moffat Ave, Box 9140, Hillside, Bulawayo,* ☎ *19/44–243 or 19/46–956,* 𝔽𝔸𝕏 *19/46–551. 50 rooms. 2 bars, pool, room service. Breakfast included. AE, DC, MC, V.*

Nightlife

If you're determined to hear Zimbabwean music, you'll have little difficulty in Bulawayo. Look in the *Chronicle* or at posters displayed on walls and trees around town. Smanje Manje music, with its distinctive South African rhythm, is one popular form in Bulawayo. Check out the **Cecil Hotel** (⊠ Fife St. and Third Ave., ☎ 19/60–295), **Eland Royal Hotel** (⊠ George Silukinda and Sixth Ave., ☎ 14/540–318), **Waver-**

ley Hotel (⊠ 134 Lobengula St., ☎ 19/60–033), and **Subterrania** (⊠ Monte Carlo Center, Fife St. and Twelfth Ave., ☎ no phone).

Shopping

Most Bulawayo shops are within a five minute walk of City Hall. Apart from the ubiquitous wood carvings, look for good buys in baskets, ethnic prints, Batonka stools from the Kariba area, and safari clothing, including the ultimate bundu-bashing (bushwhacking) gear—a pair of Courtenay boots, named for the famous Victorian explorer Frederick Courtenay Selous. **Jairos Jiri** (⊠ Robert Mugabe Way, behind City Hall) has a fine selection of baskets and other handicrafts by disabled craft-workers. **Tsaka's Den** (⊠ Ninth Ave. and Fife St.) has a wide selection of wooden carvings, jewellery, batiks, and prints. The **National Gallery** (☞ *above*) and the artists' studios behind it are also worth visiting. Shops are open 8–5 weekdays, 8:30–12:30 weekends.

Markets

Street vendors cluster and clamour the length of Lobengula Street. For the most lively and authentic market, take a taxi (Z$10) five minutes out to **Makokoba Market,** in Makokoba township on the west end of town. Here you will be able to taste such local gourmet delicacies as dried mopane worms, as well as purchase herbal remedies for every disorder you've ever heard about—plus a great many you never dreamed existed. Look out for the various baskets and beads that are popular with locals.

Side Trips from Bulawayo

Made famous by the TV series *Orphans of the Wild*, **Chipangali Orphanage** (☎ 19/70–764) was originally a sanctuary for orphaned and abandoned animals. While caring for the needs of these animals, the refuge is now an internationally famous center for the research and conservation of endangered species. Chipangali is 23 km (14 mi) east of Bulawayo on Masvingo Road; take Leopold Takawira Avenue out of town. It is open Tuesday–Sunday 10–4:30; admission is Z$20. Eleven kilometers (7 mi) south of town on the Matobo road, the **Tshabalala Wildlife Sanctuary** has a varied selection of wildlife—wildebeest, zebra, giraffe, among others—but no predators—and offers walking, cycling, and horse-riding inside the reserve. The best opportunities for seeing animals are early morning and late afternoon. Tshabalala is open daily 6–6; admission is $Z50.

Matobo National Park

Of all the short trips to take from Bulawayo, one to Matobo National Park is the most rewarding. A large chunk of Zimbabwe's past lies buried here amidst the compelling grandeur of the ancient Matobo Hills. Massive granite boulders and wind-sculpted kopies climb chaotically one upon the other like the discarded playthings of some capricious god. It was here, some twenty thousand years ago, that the San first began to decorate the caves and overhangs with their unique, highly stylistic art, using pigments and natural minerals which have survived for millennia.

The brooding splendour of the hills made a lasting impact on three key figures of the last century, whose destinies were interwoven in the making of modern Zimbabwe—King Mzilikazi, his son Lobengula, and Cecil John Rhodes. Rhodes in particular regarded the Matobo with considerable awe. It was here that he held his peace *indaba* with the Ndebele chiefs a little over a hundred years ago and about the same time came across the great granite dome of Malindidzuma—Matabele for "Place of Benevolent Spirits." Impressed by the grandeur of the setting, he named it World's View. Today, **World's View** is a favorite excursion for its marvellous views—sunsets here are a must—and as the site of Rhodes's grave. As requested in his will, he lies buried here, quite close to the tomb of King Mzilikazi, in the hills that became the last citadel of Lobengula's *impis* (warriors) in his fight against Britain's scramble to colonise his lands.

Besides visiting rock art sites—**Silozwane** at the southern end of the park in the communal lands is particularly striking—hiking, and enjoying the uniquely stunning landscape, there is the chance to see white rhino in the **Whovi Wilderness Area** game reserve, along with zebra, giraffe, sable, the rock-hopping klipspringer, and other antelope throughout. The hills are also home to the largest concentration of Black Eagles in the world.

Unless you have your own car, in which case the hour-plus drive to the park from Bulawayo allows for easy day trips, the best way of seeing the Matopos is to take a day or half day tour with one of the many guided tour companies (see Guide Tours, *below*). Entrance to the park is US$2. In order to get into the adjacent game reserve to see the rhinos, you will have to go with a licensed guide from a tour company or from a private lodge.

LODGING

$$$–$$$$ ▣ **Matobo Hills Lodge.** Set in the mysterious splendor of the Matobo Hills, this lodge is an excellent base from which to explore the area. The camp itself is one of the more permanent looking around, with large, stone huts, tended gardens, raised pathways, enormous lounges, and a small pool. The guest huts are very spacious and attractive, with a curious blend of French doors and thatch roofs. Meals are served buffet-style under a large covered, patio. The food is very good and will accomodate vegetarians, whom the rest of Southern Africa has left hungry. Staff and guests mix comfortably at tables. The sore point at the lodge is constant drink charges, even for bottled water in the middle of hot days—a glaring glitch in an otherwise flawless presentation. **Park and Game Experience:** Matobo Hills Lodge, along with other members of the Touch the Wild group, were the first camps in Zimbabwe to employ black Africans in higher than junior staff positions. And there is a great sense of relief when the lodge experience is free from vestiges of the racist past, and guides can tell you about Zimbabwe's past and present culture, not just about flora and fauna. Visits to nearby communal lands with a guide who speaks Ndebele is a highlight, as are trips to caves with Bushman paintings and sunsets at World's View, where Rhodes is buried. As for animals, the Matobo Hills are known for their rhinos (in the Whovi Wild Area only), sable antelope, numerous but elusive leopard, and the rock-loving delicate klipspringer. The densest concentration of black eagles in the world is found here. Horseback safaris can be arranged; they are a great way to explore the area. ⊠ *Private Bag 6, Hillside, Bulawayo,* ☎ *19/74-589 or 19/44–566,* ꜰᴀX *19/229-088. Restaurant, bar, pool. 12 lodges. MC, V.*

Bulawayo A to Z

Arriving and Departing

BY BUS

Blue Arrow Luxury Coach Services (⊠ Fife St., opposite Central Police Station ☎ 19/65–548, ꜰᴀX 14/729–572) runs regular air-conditioned buses to Harare via Chivu (6 hrs) and to Victoria Falls via Hwange (6 hrs).

Bulawayo Airport (☎ 19/226–423) is 22 km (14 mi) north of the city. **Air Zimbabwe** (☎ 19/72–051), **Zimbabwe Express** (☎ 14/229-797), **South African Airways** (☎ 19/71–337). An Air Zimbabwe bus meets all flights at the airport.

Between the Airport and Bulawayo. Taxi fare between the airport and the center of town at press time was Z$110. **DFK Tours** (☎ 19/75–742 and 19/77–380) and Moomba Safari Adventures ☎ 19/79–478 and 19/78–576) also run transfers to the city as well as to hotels and lodges.

BY TRAIN
National Railways of Zimbabwe (☎ 14/322–284) has passenger service from Bulawayo to Victoria Falls, Harare and Johannesburg. There is also a daily train to Botswana. The central railway station is on Anthony Taylor Avenue, off the south end of Lobengula Street. A luxury steam train runs between Bulawayo and Victoria Falls, its lavish 1920s-style coaches evoking memories of a more elegant and leisurely age.

Getting Around
BY CAR
If you plan to see any of the sights around Bulawayo, a car is almost essential.

BY TAXI
Taxi. ☎ *19/60–666 or 19/61–933.*

Contacts and Resources
CAR RENTAL
The following have offices in town and at the airport: **Avis** (☎ 19/68–571 and 19/61–306), **Europcar Interrent** (☎ 19/67–925), **Hertz** (☎ 19/74–701 and 19/61–402) **Transit Car and Truck Hire** (☎ 19/76–495).

EMERGENCIES
Central Hospital (☎ 19/72–111). **Police** (☎ 19/72–515).

GUIDED TOURS
Moomba Safari Adventures (☎ 19/79–478 and 19/78–576) takes small groups to Matobo National Park to see San (Bushman) cave paintings and a cultural tour of the Matabele village of Silozwani. Other companies with tours to major sights in the area include **Africa Dawn** (☎ 19/74–941), **Black Rhino Safaris** (☎ 19/41–662), **Matopo Tours** (☎ 19/72–748), **Gemsbok Safaris** (☎ 19/63–906), and **UTc** (☎ 19/61–402).

VISITOR INFORMATION
Automobile Association. ✉ *Fanum House, Leopold Takawira Ave. at Josiah Tongogara St.,* ☎ 19/70–063.

HWANGE NATIONAL PARK

Almost the same size as Belgium, Hwange National Park is Zimbabwe's premier wildlife showcase, a moveable feast to satisfy even the most impassioned game viewer. The largest protected wilderness area in southern Africa, it is also one of the continent's last remaining great elephant sanctuaries.

Hwange—the name means peace in the local Nambia dialect—lies in the extreme northwest of the country and covers an area of over 14,600 square km (5,800 square mi). Elephants are the park's recurring image, a transient population of 22,000 backed by a supporting cast of virtually all the country's wildlife species. Current estimates figure on 17,000 buffalo, 6,000 impala, 5,000 sable, 5,000 kudu, and 3,000 each of giraffe and zebra.

Along with its zoological treasures, Hwange boasts a marvellously varied habitat ranging from woodland, open grasslands, granite *kopjes* (hillocks) and ancient riverbeds. Indeed, with 107 different mammals, over 400 species of birds, some 260 varieties of trees and shrubs, and 1,100 plants, the park can claim a species diversity unsurpassed in southern Africa.

There are two main ecological zones. The well-drained northern Zambezi watershed region consists predominantly of mopane and commiphora woodlands interspersed with broken and occasionally hilly country merging into open grasslands. To the south are the Kalahari scrublands with scattered woodlands of teak which drain into the great Makgadikgadi Depression of Botswana.

Access to visitors is mainly confined to the northern regions of the park divided into three main areas with national park rest camps—Main Camp, Sinamatella, Robins, and Nantwich—all of which are linked by nearly 500 km (300 mi) of well-maintained roads. A number of luxury private lodges and camps in private concessions border the park's eastern and northern boundaries. The vast southern section of the park is a wilderness area accessible only to a few specialist safari and photographic operators.

Due to its position on the edge of the Kalahari, temperatures in Hwange are extreme. During the rainy season, usually November to February, it is hot but not uncomfortably so. Nights generally are cool, and in winter (May to August) the mean minimum temperature drops to 3.5°C (25°F), and frost is frequent. Bring warm jackets and wool sweaters for winter nights.

From May to October, local vegetation becomes progressively sparser, and animals begin to congregate at the pans (waterholes, many of them manmade). Most of the park's accommodation is open throughout the year, but some roads, especially those in the Robins-Nantwich area, are closed in the rainy season—when animals tend to be harder to spot—between November and April.

Game Experience. There are animals wherever you go in Hwange, and the park is an avian paradise. Often you see a dozen species or more in the space of a ten minute drive—elephant, buffalo, giraffe, zebra, wildebeest, hyena, black-backed jackal, warthog, baboon, kudu, impala, eland, sable, and maybe the odd pride of lions or a cheetah for good measure. Apart from the better known species there is a good chance of seeing such rare animals as gemsbok, tsessebe, pangolin (a primitive, scaly anteater) and a pack of wild dogs, for which Hwange is becoming well-known.

Dining

All private lodges serve substantial meals accompanied by local and imported wines. In the national park, Main Camp, Sinamatella, and Robins camps have restaurants, as does the Baobab Hotel in Hwange Town. Main Camp also has a store with basic supplies. The Game Reserve Hotel at Dete has rooms as well as a limited menu and a bar if you arrive by the late night train from Bulawayo or Victoria Falls.

Lodging

Rest Camps

Zimbabwe's National Park accommodations include lodges and chalets, as well as camping and caravan sites. Lodges have indoor cooking facilities; those of the chalets are outdoors and often shared. Together, these provide accommodation for about 1,000 visitors per day at a fraction of what it would cost you to stay in any of the exclusive private lodges or camps. Expect to pay around Z$225 for a one-bedroom self-contained lodge with two beds, and Z$100 for a two-bedroom chalet with four beds. The National Parks Department does not accept credit cards, so be prepared to pay cash for lodgings and game walks and drives.

Wildlife-viewing options include open-air-vehicle game drives and walking trails with a professional guide, which puts the feeling of the African bush in your boots. Moonlight game walks from Main Camp to observation platforms are one of the musts of any visit to Hwange. Main Camp is on the eastern end of the park, near the airport. Sinamatella, Robins, and Nantwich are in the northwest part of the park, nearer the Botswana border.

You can make arrangements for game walks and drives with guides when you arrive at the park. You should reserve a lodge or chalet at least six months in advance. There are no walking trails offered in the rainy season, November through March. ⊠ *Mailing address: National Parks, Box CY 140, Harare. In Harare:* ☎ *14/706–077 or 14/706–078,* ₣ᴀX *14/726–089 or 14/724–914. In Bulawayo:* ☎ *19/63–646,* ₣ᴀX *19/71–080.*

$ ⊞ **Main Camp.** For many visitors the entry point to Hwange is Main Camp, the administrative headquarters of the park. Facilities here are generally good, although water pressure in bathrooms noticeably wanes when the camp is full. There is a wide choice of self-contained lodges, as well as chalets with outdoor cooking facilities. Wildlife, especially around Nyamandhlovu and Dopi Pan, is all you could hope for, and even if you miss out on lion, those perennial heavyweights, elephant and buffalo, are plentiful. Bird life in this area is superb, including the acrobatic lilac-breasted roller, surely one of the loveliest of all the African birds. It was a favorite of the great Ndebele King Mzilikazi (1795–1868), who decreed that only he could wear its brilliant lilac, blue, and green feathers.

$ ⊞ **Nantwich.** More like a private lodge in its comforts than the other rest camps, remote Nantwich is beautifully sited on a rise, shaded by trees and aloes. The attractive three-bedroom thatch cottages are better equipped than their counterparts and all overlook a dam—with a constantly changing parade of passing wildlife. Part of Nantwich's Old World charm derives from the original Dover woodstoves still used in the kitchen, and its crockery, some of which bears the stamp "Federation of Rhodesia and Nyasaland." *3 lodges.*

$ ⊞ **Sinamatella.** This rest camp is on a plateau that has stunning views over an immense, ancient floodplain often favored by large herds of buffalo. Fever trees and grassy plains studded with outcrops of rock are typical of this area, which contains a good cross-section of the park's wildlife—among other species the small, doe-eyed klipspringer and the yellow-backed dassie. The camp has luxury chalets, cottages, and lodges, a restaurant, and guided walking trails between April and October. *20 chalets.*

$ ⊞ **Robins Camp.** This in many ways is the least appealing of the camps, both for its setting and its facilities, although it is noted for its frequent sightings of lion and hyena. Apart from this, however, it lacks the breadth and density of game elsewhere, and while the chalets contain the basic necessities, the camp's generator and its swimming pool are often indisposed. *3 lodges, 22 chalets.*

Private Lodges

The private lodges, on the east end of the park, suffer from one setback that makes the local bush a bit noisier: the rail line that runs along the park's eastern boundary. It isn't dreadfully loud, but you will hear trains passing by occasionally throughout the day and night.

$$$$ 🏨 **Hide Safari Camp.** On the eastern boundary of the national park, this friendly lodge is on the grassy banks of a loarge waterhole. You can view animals in privacy from the veranda of simple tented rooms, from the huge thatched A-frame main lodge, or in the namesake hide, a modest (if claustrophobic) underground bunker at water's edge with a narrow window for a front-row, hoof-level experience. Camp managers are warm and gracious, quickly putting guests at ease. Drinks are generously offered and refilled. Meals are served at one enormous teak dinner table, where the food unfortunately is less than impressive. Here guests are joined by the bantering, youthful guides who nevertheless prove themselves ably in the field. They are extremely knowledgeable and passionate about the flora and fauna of Hwange. ⊠ *Mailing address: Box 5615, Harare,* ☎ *14/707–438,* FAX *14/723–230. Bar. MC, V.*

$$$$ 🏨 **Ivory Lodge.** Tree houses have an undeniable appeal, evoking childhood dreams and memories, and Ivory lodge does exacltly that. Set on private land on the northern edge of the park at the edge of the Zingweni Vlei, the lodge is in the heart of the bush. The 10 twin-bed, thatched tree houses constructed from local teak are built into the spreading branches of teak trees. Rooms have high, thatched ceilings and are beautifully decorated with colorful African prints and artifacts. Wooden verandas provide panoramic views across the bush, and earlier this year guests sat riveted as a pack of wild dogs chased and killed an impala in the vicinity of the lodge. Ivory Lodge also has a game-viewing platform. ⊠ *Mailing address: Block Hotels, Box 2914 Harare.* ☎ *14/796–982 or 14/796–984,* FAX *14/796–989. 20 guests. Bar, dining room, pool. MC, V.*

$$$ 🏨 **Simba Lodge.** Set deep in the bush country of the Gwaai Valley and close to the national park this small rustic lodge lies in a grove of Brachystesia trees with commanding views across a wide, grassy *vlei* (open, usually flat grassland). The en-suite accommodations are generously sized and the rooms, tastefully decorated in African fabrics, all have their own balconies overlooking the vlei. Guests eat together in an informal atmosphere at a long, mukwa-wood table in the main boma. A large, open fireplace casts its spell during winter, inevitably calling for late nights and tall tales. Simba prides itself on personal attention and friendliness and as result enjoys a great deal of repeat business. ⊠ *Mailing address: 167 Enterprise Rd, Chisipite, Harare.* ☎ *14/495–057,* FAX *14/481–794 . 12 guests. Bar, pool. MC, V.*

Hwange A to Z

Arriving and Departing

BY BUS

Blue Arrow Luxury Coaches (Harare: ☎ 14/729–514, FAX 14/729–572) runs from Victoria Falls to Hwange for Z$125 one-way (2½ hours) and from Bulawayo to Hwange for Z$160 one-way (3½ hours). Buses are fully air-conditioned and have on-board toilets, light refreshments, and video/CD entertainment.

BY CAR

The turn-off to Main Camp is 261 km (162 mi) northwest of Bulawayo, a journey of approximately three hours. The distance from Victoria Falls is 160 km (100 mi), which takes just under two hours. Drive to the park during the day, as night brings animals rather unpredictably onto the roads.

Air Zimbabwe (☎ 14/575–021 or in Hwange 118/393) and **Zimbabwe Express** (Victoria Falls: ☎ 13/5992) run daily flights between Hwange, Harare, Victoria Falls, and Bulawayo. There is an airstrip at Main Camp for chartered planes.

BY TRAIN
National Railways (☎ 119/322-210) trains run from Bulawayo and Victoria Falls to the small railway staion of Dete on the eastern edge of the park. First class tickets cost Z$65 one-way.

Getting Around
All private lodges and camps arrange transfers from and to the airport. If you do not have your own transport and are not staying at one of the private lodges, take one of the many **UTc** (☎ 118/217 or 118/287) bus tours, which run within the park.

Contacts and Resources
CAR RENTAL
Hertz (☎ 118/393 or 118/217) has a rental desk at Hwange Safari Lodge.

HOURS AND FEES
Depending on the month, rest camp gates close between 5 and 6 PM and open at 6–6:30 AM. Admission to the park is US$5.00 per person. Pick up maps of the park at park entrances.

VICTORIA FALLS

Victoria Falls, which plunge 300 ft into a gorge permanently hidden by a veil of roaring spray, span the entire 2-km (1-mi) width of the Zambezi River. In the Kololo language, they're known as Mosi-Oa-Tunya—the "Smoke that Thunders." On a clear day, the falls' white spray is visible from 81 km (50 mi) away, a writhing mist rising above the woodland savannah like the smoke from a bush fire. To call the falls the Eighth Wonder of the World does little to suggest the blockbuster drama, the majesty, and the exquisite beauty of this quintessentially African sight.

Picture a Niagara Falls twice as tall and twice as wide and you still won't be prepared for the spectacle of Victoria Falls. Here, elephants come to bathe in the river, crocodiles patrol the deep pools, and hippos feed on upstream islands. At any moment you expect Humphrey Bogart and Katharine Hepburn to chug into view on the *African Queen*. Despite the growing influx of tourists, there is still the overwhelming sense that the untamed African bush lies all around you.

Victoria Falls lie in the southeastern corner of Zimbabwe, a part of the country that is still mostly wild. They're like a violent hiccup in the 3,200-km (2,000-mi) course of the Zambezi from its source in the northern Lunda highlands to the Indian Ocean in the east. The river serves as the border between Zambia and Zimbabwe, with each country competing for tourist dollars. Most visitors opt to stay on the Zimbabwean side, in the town of Victoria Falls, crossing over to visit the Zambian side for a highly recommended side trip.

In the late 1940s, when the town served as a refueling stop for Imperial Airways' seaplane route between South Africa and Britain, pilots referred to the small settlement as "jungle junction." Today, Victoria Falls is a burgeoning town totally given over to the pursuit of tourist business—which amounts to a rather reckless pursuit of money the likes of which you won't see elsewhere in Zimbabwe.

Yet there is still a whiff of the old jungle junction. Unlike the parks in South Africa, national parks here are unfenced, and elephants could parade down the town's main street if they felt so inclined. As it is, they usually don't cross the belt of woodland that encircles the town—venture into this bush fringe at your own risk—leaving the cultivated hotel lawns to troops of baboons and monkeys.

Victoria Falls has more to offer than just a view of the falls. Some of southern Africa's greatest game parks lie within easy driving distance of the town. And it is a center for adventure sports, whether it's bungee-jumping, microlighting (motorized hang gliding), or white-water rafting down the Zambezi, in certain months one of the most thrilling one-day trips in the world.

To see the falls at their roaring best, go during the April–June high-water peak, when more than 2 million gallons of water hurtle down every second. The weather in these months tends to be sunny and pleasant. In September–October, when it is brutally hot, the water level is at its lowest and large sections of the falls dry up, although white-water rafting is then at its best. November through March is the rainy season, when the climate turns muggy and even hotter, and malaria-carrying mosquitos pose their greatest threat.

Exploring Victoria Falls

Numbers in the text correspond to numbers in the margin and on the Victoria Falls map.

A Good Walk

The town of Victoria Falls is tiny and easily explored on foot. Most of the shops and safari operators are clustered around the intersection of Park Way and Livingstone Way. Head down Livingstone Way and turn left before the Post Office to reach the **Falls Craft Village** ①. Return to Livingstone Way, cross the street, and head down Mallet Drive to the **Victoria Falls Hotel** ②. On the Zimbabwean side the **Victoria Falls National Park** ③ is the main attraction. Exit from the National Park and turn left to reach the **Victoria Falls Bridge** ④. It's about a one-mile walk to the Zambian border post from Zimbabwe. Zambian taxis will carry you there if it's too hot or you don't feel up to the trek. Zambian immigration charges US$30, or its equivalent, for an entry permit. (Check the cost of a permit in rand, as it's sometimes cheaper than paying in dollars.) The Zambian equivalent of Zimbabwe's Victoria Falls National Park is **Mosi-Oa-Tunya National Park** ⑤, whose entrance lies just beyond the immigration control area. Back on the Zimbabwean side, an interesting drive, walk, or bike ride is **Zambezi Drive** ⑥. Midway along Zambezi Drive stands the **Big Tree** ⑦. From the Big Tree, Zambezi Drive heads back south and joins Park Way. Turn left and continue less than 1 km (½ mi) to return to town. If you turn right on Park Way and continue for 6.4 km (4 mi), you come to **Zambezi Nature Sanctuary** ⑧. Another hundred yards up the road is the entrance to **Zambezi National Park** ⑨.

Sights to See

⑦ **Big Tree.** This giant baobab is said to be 1,500 years old—the tree measures 80 ft in circumference and about the same in height. Early pioneers on their way north into Zambia used to camp under its massive branches. The baobab is known as the upside-down tree for obvious reasons, and several African legends offer explanations for the phenomenon. According to Khoisan (Bushman) lore, in the beginning of time the Creator handed each of the animals a tree to plant. The hyena was the last in line, and when his turn came all the beautiful trees had already been given to other animals. In fact, the only tree left was an almost leafless specimen as fat as it was tall. The hyena was so angry

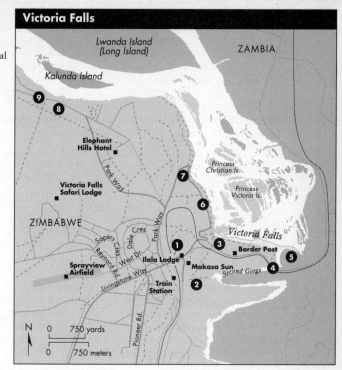

with God for giving him such an ugly tree that he deliberately planted
it upside down. ⊠ *Zambezi Dr.*

❶ Falls Craft Village. The "village" consists of life-size model homes typical of five different Zimbabwean tribes, as well as a San (Bushman)
dwelling. A pamphlet and on-site guides explain the living arrangements,
various crafts, and the uses of different tools. If you've an hour to spare,
it's probably worthwhile. At the back of the village you can watch artisans carving the stone and wood sculptures that are sold in the adjoining shop. For Z$20 you can have a n'anga or witch doctor throw
the bones to tell your fortune. ⊠ *Stand 206, Sopers Crescent,* ☎ *13/
4309.* ☞ *Z$25.* ☉ *Daily 8:30–1, 2–5.*

Curios. Several touristy curio and craft shops lie just beyond the Falls
Craft Village. Here you can buy everything from an 8-ft-tall wooden
giraffe to soapstone carvings and brightly colored Zimbabwean batiks.
For a true African market experience, however, walk into either of the
large white buildings on the left. Inside, seated on the floor and on carved
wooden stools, dozens of local women sell crocheted tablecloths,
woven baskets, carvings, and charms. The women bargain hard, but
they are more than willing to trade their wares for the shoes on your
feet, the T-shirts off your back, and other articles of clothing. If you're
concerned about how to get a near–life-size giraffe or a 50-pound carving back home, there's an international shipping agent sandwiched between the curio shops.

★ ❺ Mosi-Oa-Tunya National Park. During high water (April–June), the Zambian side of the falls provides a far more spectacular vantage point than
the Zimbabwean one, for the simple reason that the view is less ob-
scured by spray. Regardless of the time of year, it would be a mistake
not to arrange to see the falls from the Zambian side as well. The most
impressive views are from the trail leading to the Knife's Edge and East-

ern Cataract. The trail runs through dense rain forest, with side paths leading to several viewpoints overlooking the Eastern Cataract. This section of the falls dries up when the water is low, leaving an eerie stone face; in high water, when it's a thundering torrent, be prepared to get completely doused with spray. After a few hundred yards, the trail takes you across a narrow bridge over a gorge to a high, thin outcrop—the Knife's Edge—with unrivaled views of the Victoria Falls Bridge and Danger Point. If you don't fancy getting soaked, you can still get a panoramic view of the falls from a spot near the curio market. ✉ *Livingstone Rd., no phone.* 🎫 *Free.* ☽ *Daily 6–6.*

❹ Victoria Falls Bridge. This graceful structure spans the gorge formed by the Zambezi River, 360 ft below. Built in 1905, it's a monument to Cecil Rhodes's dream of completing a Cape-to-Cairo rail line. It would have been far easier and less expensive to build the bridge upstream from the Falls, but Rhodes was captivated by the romance of a railway bridge passing over this natural wonder. Miraculously, only two people were killed during construction of the bridge. Steam-powered trains continue to chug across the span, their billowing black smoke in stark contrast to the ever-present veil of mist created by the pounding cataracts. To get onto the bridge, you first have to pass through Zimbabwean immigration and customs controls. Depending on crowds, the simple procedure can take from five minutes to a half hour. The border posts are open daily 6–6. From the bridge you get a knockout view of the **Boiling Pot**—a churning cauldron of water—as well as a section of the falls. An added bonus is watching lunatics hurling themselves off the bridge in the sport's highest bungee-jump (☞ Outdoor Activities and Sports, *below*).

❷ Victoria Falls Hotel. Much of the town's history revolves around this monument to colonial nostalgia. It was built in 1904 by the railway company, which had extended the line to the falls earlier that same year. The original hotel, built right next to the railway line, was a simple wood and corrugated-iron structure that accommodated only 20 guests. It wasn't nearly large enough, and many early guests had to remain on the train to sleep and only take their meals in the hotel. In 1920 the hotel instituted its famous trolley service, a narrow-gauge railway that carried guests between the hotel and the falls. No engines were used; gravity was enough to carry the guests down, but it took two men to push each trolley back up. The service was discontinued in 1957, but one of these early trolleys is on view in the central courtyard of the hotel.

A respite on the terrace of the Victoria Falls Hotel remains one of the highlights of a visit to the falls. Under the shade of a giant Zimbabwe mahogany tree, guests can take in the view over the Zambezi River gorge, the Victoria Falls bridge, and a rising curtain of spray from the falls. It's an ideal place to sip a drink or have some tea before continuing to the falls themselves.

A walking trail leads from the bottom of the hotel gardens to the falls. It's a 10-minute walk through virgin bush. A second, 30-minute trail descends steeply into the gorge to the river itself (☞ Dining and Lodging, *below*.) ✉ *Mallet Dr.,* ☎ *113/4751.*

★ ❸ Victoria Falls National Park. Plan to spend at least two hours soaking in the splendors of this park. If you visit the falls during the high-water peak in April–June, you'll do well to carry a raincoat or umbrella (you can rent them at the entrance), and to protect your camera in a waterproof bag, because the spray from the falls creates a permanent downpour. Indeed, during high water the spray is so dense that it obscures much of the view from the Zimbabwe side and you should make an effort to see the falls from the Zambian side as well (☞ Mosi-Oa-Tunya National Park, *below*). The constant drizzle has created a unique rain forest that extends in a narrow band along the edge of the falls. A trail running through this dripping green world is overgrown with African ebony, Cape fig, Natal mahogany, wild date palms, ferns, and flame lilies. Side trails lead to viewpoints overlooking the falls. The most spectacular is Danger Point, a slippery rock outcropping that overlooks the narrow gorge through which the Zambezi River funnels out of Vic Falls. In low-water months (September–November), most of the water goes over the falls through the Devil's Cataract, a narrow passage separated from the main expanse of the falls by Cataract Island. A statue of David Livingstone stands on a terrace next to one of the Devil's Cataract viewpoints. During the full moon, the park stays open late so you can see the lunar rainbow formed by the spray—one of the most beautiful sights in Africa. ☒ *US$5.* ☉ *Daily 6–6, later during full moon.*

❻ Zambezi Drive. This 4-kilometer (2½-mile) loop road turns off Livingstone Way just before the entrance to Victoria Falls National Park (as you come from town). The road passes through pristine bush, so it's not uncommon to encounter elephants and other animals as they head down to the river. Keep a sharp lookout if you're not in a vehicle, and remember that you're venturing here at your own risk. Even more scenic than the tarred loop road is a walking path that runs for several miles along the river; to reach the beginning of the path, follow Zambezi Drive almost to the river's edge. The fence of Victoria Falls National Park will be on your right.

❾ Zambezi National Park. The park covers a 138,000-acre strip of land that runs alongside the Zambezi River. Game-viewing here is generally good, particularly in the dry season (September–October), when various species converge on the river to drink and bathe. A few of the park roads are negotiable in a standard rental car, but a four-wheel-drive vehicle is recommended. Vehicle entry into national park is US$5 and US$10 for small vehicles and minibuses respectively. Accommodations in the park range from self-catering lodges that sleep four to eight (About Z$300 to Z$600) to rustic fishing and bush camps (About Z$160) where you must provide everything except the toilet and shower. Entry into the **Rain Forest** is US$10. Reservations must be made through the Central Booking Office (☒ Box 8151, Causeway, Harare, ☎ 4/70–6077). ☒ *Park Way, no phone.* ☒ *Z$20 per day.*

❽ Zambezi Nature Sanctuary. It's a grandiose name for a run-of-the-mill tourist trap. It's a small zoo with several wild cats in cages and a crocodile farm displaying hundreds of Nile crocodiles. Feeding time for these prehistoric-looking beasts is 11 AM. ☒ *Park Way,* ☎ *113/4567.* ☒ *US$10.* ☉ *Daily 8–4:30.*

Dining and Lodging

Foreigners have to settle hotel bills in foreign currency, either with cash, credit cards, or traveler's checks. Hotel rooms in Victoria Falls are expensive, and the high prices are often unjustified. It's not necessary to stay close to the falls and town: You'll probably only visit the falls once, and the town itself has little to offer. Furthermore, the outlying hotels tend to offer better value and facilities, and they all operate free shuttles to and from town.

Victoria Falls is a culinary wasteland. In town you'll find a couple of nondescript pizza joints, a steak house, and a Wimpy's, but otherwise you're reliant on hotel restaurant fare. Several of the hotels offer a nightly barbecue accompanied by marimba music. If you're looking for something a little different, try **The Boma** Restaurant at the Victoria Falls Safari Lodge (☞ *below*), where you sit in a traditional African enclosure around a fire and sample various game meats; traditional dancers perform twice nightly. It costs about Z$250 per person for a three course meal including drinks. **Saddles** is a steak house with cowboy-theme interiors, on Parkway Drive. There are generous helpings for meat freaks, dessert lovers, but besides the portion sizes, food is not too recommendable. The **Oriental Restaurant** at the Rainbow Hotel (on Park Way) is an alternative night out, but again don't expect culinary heaven.

$$$$ ✕▥ **Victoria Falls Hotel.** For many years, this hotel *was* Victoria Falls. Built in 1904, only months after the railway reached the falls, the hotel stood for decades as a colonial outpost in the African wilds, attracting some of the continent's most colorful characters as well as the occasional visiting royal. Today, the hotel offers visitors—many of them elderly—a reprise of the days when gin-and-tonic was taken as the cure for malaria and Britain was considered home. The hotel still holds a nightly dinner-dance (jacket and tie suggested). Wide corridors hung with brass chandeliers are decorated with black-and-white photos of bygone days. However, the image of colonial Africa cannot withstand the constant influx of tour groups. You now have to be a real old-timer or highly imaginative to conjure up the colonial past. The hotel's famed service and aura of luxury are history, too. The suites are still elegant, but the regular rooms are faded and drab. What has not changed are the hotel's superb setting and gardens. The garden terrace, beneath a towering Zimbabwe mahogany, overlooks the Zambezi bridge and the whirling spray from the falls. Light meals and drinks are served here during the day, and at night there's a barbecue. ✉ *Mallet Dr., Box 10, Victoria Falls*, ☎ *113/4751*, ℻ *113/4586. 141 rooms with bath. 2 restaurants, 2 bars, room service, pool, hair salon, tennis, playground. Breakfast included. AE, DC, MC, V.*

$$$$ ✕▥ **Victoria Falls Safari Lodge.** This is by far the best hotel in Victo-
★ ria Falls, and it costs less than the Victoria Falls Hotel. A little more than 6 km (4 mi) outside town, the hotel sits on a hilltop overlooking the Zambezi River and miles of bush in Zambezi National Park. A water hole below the lodge attracts herds of game, including buffalo and elephant. The lodge itself draws its inspiration from colorful Ndebele culture. Soaring thatch roofs, huge wooden beams, reed ceilings, and very tasteful decorative items envelop you in a luxurious African atmosphere. The sides of the lodge are completely open to admit cooling breezes (air-conditioning in some rooms is insignificant). In rooms you can fold back the glass-and-wood screens leading to your private veranda if you want to sleep alfresco—just remember to put the mosquito net down. All rooms have scenic views, but request one overlooking the water hole. There is a courtesy shuttle to and from town and Victoria Falls. As a guest, you can go out on the lodge's five-hour night drives in open vehicles with spotlights. Night drives offer the chance to see nocturnal creatures like bushbabies, spring hares, and, if you're lucky, lions and leopards on the prowl. The trip costs about Z$300 and includes drinks and a light dinner. ✉ *Off Park Way, 6 km (4 mi) from Victoria Falls (mailing address: Box 29, Victoria Falls)*, ☎ *113/3202*, ℻ *113/3205. 72 rooms with bath. 2 restaurants, 2 bars, room service, 2 pools, travel services. Breakfast included. AE, MC, V.*

$$$ ✕▥ **Elephant Hills Intercontinental Resort and Conference Centre.** Also 6.4 kilometers (4 miles) from town, this large hotel sits high on a hill above the Zambezi. It's a resort and conference hotel, but don't let that drive you away. The service, rooms, and facilities are far superior to those of the more expensive Victoria Falls Hotel. The extensive use of thatch and African sculpture, masks, and batiks helps to minimize the hotel's size and business emphasis. Rooms, too, have an understated African flair: Rough gray walls are the neutral background for wicker furniture, modern African art, and Ndebele rugs. All rooms have air-conditioning and overhead fans. Request a front-facing room—for a few dollars more you get memorable views of the Zambezi River, miles of virgin bush, and clouds of spray from the distant falls. From the open-air Mapopoma bar and Kasibi restaurant, there is a similar knockout view. A shuttle bus runs hourly to town. ⊠ *Park Way, 6.4 km (4 mi) from Victoria Falls (mailing address: Box 300, Victoria Falls),* ☎ *113/4793,* 𝔽𝔸𝕏 *113/4655. 276 rooms with bath. 3 restaurants, 3 bars, room service, pool, hair salon, golf, tennis, exercise room, squash, casino, business services. Breakfast included. AE, DC, MC, V.*

$$$ ✕⌂ **Ilala Lodge.** Often overlooked in the stampede to stay in Victoria
★ Falls's mediocre large hotels, this small hotel is a gem. It lies right near the center of town, opposite the Makasa Sun and just 10 minutes from the falls on foot. Thatched roofs give the lodge a pleasant, African look. The dining room, with its curving thatched shelter, raw beams, and outdoor seating, is particularly attractive. Rooms are hung with African paintings and tapestries and filled with delicately caned chairs and tables and with dressers made from old railway sleepers. French doors open onto a narrow strip of lawn backed by thick bush. Unlike most hotels in town, Ilala Lodge has no fence around it, so at night it's not uncommon to find elephants browsing outside your window or antelopes grazing on the lawn. None of the rooms has air-conditioning, but they do have overhead fans. ⊠ *411 Livingstone Way, Box 18, Victoria Falls,* ☎ *113/4737,* 𝔽𝔸𝕏 *113/4417. 16 rooms with bath. Restaurant, 3 bars, room service, pool, casino, nightclub. Breakfast included. DC, MC, V.*

Matetsi Game Lodges

$$$$ When Matetsi opened late in 1997, a new standard for luxury arrived
★ in Zimbabwe. Belonging to the South Africa–based Conservation Corporation, Matetsi has high levels of service, design aesthetics, and culinary finesse not found elsewhere in the country. Forty km (25 mi) upriver from Victoria Falls, this private reserve is comprised of two separate camps. Cuisine is some of the best in the country, with fine service and attention to individual needs. Rates include all activities, but not imported liquor. There is a complimentary shuttle into Victoria Falls for mid-day sightseeing. ⊠ *Private Bag X27, Benmore 2010, South Africa,* ☎ *South Africa 11/784–7077,* 𝔽𝔸𝕏 *11/784–7667. AE, MC, V.*

Game Experience: Matetsi's 73,500 acres of former hunting concessions with access to neighboring Zambezi National Park assures fine game-viewing of elephant, buffalo, lion, leopard, sable, spotted hyena, kudu, hippopotamus, and other wildlife. But what sets these camps apart from others is the guides' attention to the interests of guests. Flexibility in allowing guests to customize their viewing is an indication of exceptional treatment. To answer questions, guides often turn off land rovers to deliver audible and thoroughly interesting talks with no sense that their agendas have been disturbed. And because there is a good number of indigenous guides, you will learn much about local culture and traditional relationships with the animals. All Matetsi guests can participate in two daily game drives, river cruises, canoeing, fishing, and guided walks.

Matetsi Water Lodge. On the banks of the Zambezi, this camp is divided into three sections of six suites each. The stunning lodges have king-size beds, enormous bathrooms, indoor and outdoor showers, and individual plunge pools. Emphasis here is on the river more than on tracking wildlife, making it more of a resort environment than the safari camp. *36 guests, 18 plunge pools.*

Matetsi Safari Camp. The inland setting of this camp on the edge of a swath of grassland allows great visibility of the vlei (former river bed) and parade of wildlife that the twelve luxury tents overlook. The large tents, made of canvas and teak, have an almost Asian elegance, with well-appointed baths and air-conditioning. Public areas are a style-book on the outdoor uses of teak. *24 guests, 2 pools.*

Nightlife

CASINOS

The **Makasa Sun Casino** (⊠ Livingstone Way, ☎ 113/4275) attracts a hard-eyed crowd of locals as well as the blue-rinse brigade, all furiously feeding slot machines day and night. You can also play blackjack and roulette. The **Elephant Hills Casino** (⊠ Park Way, ☎ 113/4793) is more upmarket and operates only in the evenings, from 8 PM until late. Games include blackjack, roulette, Zambezi poker, and punto banco, as well as a wide variety of Vegas-style slot machines. As with all casinos in Zimbabwe, no one under 18 is admitted.

Cheaper gaming tables and slot machines are now open at Ilala Lodge (☞ Lodging, *above*).

PUBS AND NIGHTCLUBS

Explorers (⊠ Soper's Arcade, Park Way, ☎ 113/4298) is the big watering hole in town for young locals and disheveled overland tourists traveling on the big commercial trucks. It's dark, crowded, and rowdy. Z$5 cover charge. **Downtime,** in the Ilala Lodge (⊠ Livingstone Way, ☎ 113/4737), is the town's only nightclub. Ilala Lodge also operates a large, open-air bar where the most of the rafting companies replay the day's videos of the white-water action and display photos shot along the river.

TRADITIONAL DANCING

The Victoria Falls Hotel stages a nightly **Africa Spectacular,** a one-hour display of costumed Makishi, Shangaan, and other tribal performers dancing to the beat of a half dozen drummers. Spectators sit around a roaring fire in a traditional boma. The show is worth seeing just for the fantastic costumes and masks of the Makishi dancers and stilt-walkers. You can purchase masks, drums, dolls, and other crafts from two craft shops adjoining the boma. ⊠: *Victoria Falls Hotel, Mallet Dr.,* ☎ *113/4751.* ☞ *Z$40. Shows daily at 7.*

Falls Craft Village is a not-so-atmospheric spot to see traditional dancing. ⊠ *Stand 206, Soper's Crescent,* ☎ *113/4309.* ☞ *Z$60. Shows daily at 6:30.*

Outdoor Activities and Sports

Bungee-Jumping

If the idea of white-water rafting doesn't start your pulse throbbing, take heart: You can always bungee-jump off the Victoria Falls bridge, a 110-meter (360-ft) freefall that is the highest in the world. The folks who run this masochistic operation are from **African Extreme,** an offshoot of Kiwi Extreme, the company that pioneered commercial jumping. A jump costs US$90, and all participants must sign a waiver form. Book through Shearwater Safaris or head out to the registration office at the Zambian end of the bridge. Jumps take place Tuesday–Sunday, 8–12:45. The bridge lies in the no-man's-land between Zimbabwe and Zambia. Jumpers should request a gate pass from Zimbabwe immigration; bring your passport as well.

Canoeing

Canoeing on the Zambezi River above the falls is a relaxing, fun alternative (or supplement) to white-water rafting. The river here is wide and sluggish, winding through islands of vegetation, splitting into myriad channels, and then suddenly debouching into broad stretches of open water. Occasionally, small rapids—nothing to worry about—propel you through narrows. Along the way, you are likely to spot crocodiles, hippos, and elephants. The one-hour game drive through Zambezi National Park to reach the launching point for the canoes is an added bonus. Most trips provide a bush breakfast before you start, a brief coffee or tea break, and a slap-up lunch on an island in the river. You can select either a half- or full-day trip, or even longer expeditions lasting two to three days, with nights at primitive tented camps along the river. Previous experience and a high degree of physical fitness are not required. Expect to pay about US$65 for a half day, and US$90 for a full day. The main operators are **Kandahar Safaris** (⊠ Soper's Arcade, ☎ 113/4502), **Safari Par Excellence** (⊠ Shop 4, Pumula Centre, ☎ 113/4424, FAX 113/4510), and **Zambezi Canoe Company** (⊠ Shop 14, Soper's Arcade, ☎ 113/2058).

Golf

Elephant Hills Golf Course (⊠ Park Way, ☎ 113/4793, ext. 1742 for caddy master, ext. 1893 for pro shop), 6.4 kilometers (4 miles) out of town, is a full 18-hole course laid out in a bulge formed by the Zambezi River. The course is fairly flat, with manicured fairways wending through woodland savannah. Although the course is fenced, you will probably have to share the fairways with warthogs, baboons, waterbuck, and impala. It might pay to hit the ball straight—recently a pride of lions was sighted lounging in the rough. If you are staying at one of the Zimbabwe Sun hotels (Elephant Hills, Victoria Falls or Makasa Sun), 18 holes will cost Z$150, nine holes Z$100. Nonguests pay Z$250, regardless. Rental clubs are available.

Horseback Riding

Safari Par Excellence (⊠ Shop 4, Pumula Centre, ☎ 113/4424, FAX 113/4510) conducts horseback game-viewing safaris for experienced riders that range anywhere from 2½ hours to one, two, or three days. Novice riders can go out for 1½ hours but will not be allowed close to animals such as elephants and lions. Expect to pay about US$40 for a short ride and US$100 for a full day.

White-Water Rafting

The Zambezi has the best one-day white-water rafting in the world—on all classes of rapids—and a trip down the river is one of the highlights of a stay in Vic Falls. Rafting takes place in the deep gorges that extend more than 24 km (15 mi) from the base of the falls. In peak season the majority of the 23-odd rapids along the river are classified as Grade 4 or 5, Grade 5 being the most difficult rapids commercially runnable. Despite this, you don't need prior rafting experience and shouldn't let inexperience deter you. Prime season is mid-August to mid-December, with the best rafting usually in September–October, when the water is at its lowest and the rapids at their most spectacular. In January-February and June–July, high water resulting from the rainy season softens many of the rapids but creates dangerous currents and whirlpools; during these months some operators offer only half-day trips. In April and May, the water is usually too high to permit rafting at all.

You can choose between oar boats and paddle boats. In an oar boat, your job is simply to hang on and use your body weight to help keep the boat upright; a professional oarsman does the rest. On a paddle boat, you are given a paddle and expected to use it, since the boat is likely to flip in rapids if it loses steering momentum. As it's much easier to fall out of a paddle boat, first-timers and older rafters should probably opt for an oar boat. You will wear helmets and life jackets, and each trip is preceded by a safety talk and practice sessions in calm water. The sport is not without danger, and the river has claimed a few lives and caused a number of injuries; which means that you'll have to sign an indemnity form. And you're likely to gulp a Zambezi cocktail—the inevitable mouthful of water that you'll take in if you end up in the water after a rapid.

Surely the most treacherous part of the trip, is the horrendously steep trek into the gorge down muddy trails and rail ladders—it's an almost sheer 229-meter (750-ft) drop. For this phase it's best to be physically fit; if you're going to have a heart attack, it'll be here. The climb out is steep, but far less fearsome.

The major operator on the river is **Shearwater Adventures** (⊠ Soper's Arcade, Park Way, Victoria Falls, ☎ 113/4471, 𝔽𝔸𝕏 113/4341), an outfit capable of putting 26 boats in the water on a single day. **Sobek** (⊠ 309 Park Way, Victoria Falls, ☎ 113/2069), an American company, was the first to start commercial rafting down the Zambezi, back in 1981. It has an excellent safety record and a reputation for having the best guides on the river. Sobek operates from the Zambian side of the river, which allows them to launch their boats at the Boiling Pot, right next to the falls. Because of this, they run the river from Rapid No. 1, whereas the Zimbabwe operators can only put their boats in the water above Rapid No. 4. **Safari Par Excellence** (⊠ Shop 4, Pumula Centre, ☎ 113/4424, 𝔽𝔸𝕏 113/4510) is the only company that offers a choice of rafting from Zambia or Zimbabwe. The fourth major operator, **Frontiers White Water Rafting** (⊠ Shop 1, Park Way, Victoria Falls, ☎ 113/5800, 𝔽𝔸𝕏 011/4417), is based on the Zimbabwe side of the river. Costs are the same regardless of which company you use: Half-day rafting costs about US$75, a full-day run about US$90. Lunch and drinks are included. Most of these companies also offer extended 3-, 5-, and 7-day rafting trips.

Victoria Falls A to Z

Arriving and Departing

BY BUS

The bus ride from Harare (Z$510) is a gruelling 12 hours; it's half of that from Bulawayo (Z$270). Drinks and light snacks are served on board. Contact **Blue Arrow** (Harare: ☎ 14/729–514 or 14/729–518) or **Translux** (Harare: ☎ 14/725–132; Bulawayo: ☎ 19/66-528).

BY PLANE

Victoria Falls Airport (☎ 113/4250) lies 22 km (14 mi) south of town. **South African Airways** has direct flights between Johannesburg and Victoria Falls on Tuesday, Saturday, and Sunday. **Air Zimbabwe** (☎ 113/4316 in Victoria Falls) flies direct between Johannesburg and Victoria Falls on Monday and Thursday. Otherwise, you can fly through Harare and catch a connecting flight on to Victoria Falls. **Zimbabwe Express Airlines** (☎ 13/5992) also flies into Vic Falls from Harare (daily), Bulawayo (Monday) and Hwange (daily) and Johannesburg (Wednesday, Friday, and Sunday).

Between the Airport and Town. Be prepared to have any number of local drivers accost you offering rides into town: This is the first sign that Vic Falls is after your wallet in a way that the rest of the country won't be. Most hotels send free shuttle buses to meet incoming Air Zimbabwe and South African Airways flights and provide free airport transfers for departing guests: Arrange this in advance with your hotel so that you don't get stranded. An **Air Zimbabwe** bus also meets incoming South African Airways and Air Zimbabwe flights to take passengers to the airport in good time for departures. The bus stops at the Rainbow Hotel, the Makasa Sun, Victoria Falls Hotel, and the Sprayview Hotel. Tickets cost Z$30. Taxis between town and the airport cost about Z$120.

BY TRAIN

South Africa's most luxurious trains, the **Blue Train** and **Rovos Rail** (☞ Train Travel *in* the Gold Guide), periodically run north from Pretoria to Zimbabwe, calling at Bulawayo and Victoria Falls on the two-night journey. Rovos Rail usually makes the trip twice a month, the *Blue Train* only once. If you have the time and inclination, Zimbabwe's own *Rail Safaris Train de Luxe* (National Railways, Bulawayo: ☎ 19/332-284) steam locomotive runs the Zambezi Special Safari from Bulawayo to Victoria Falls, stopping at Hwange en route for a game drive into the famed national park. The fare is approximately US$300, which includes three- to four-course silver service meals but does not cover drinks.

Getting Around

BY BICYCLE

Biking is a great way to get around town or over to Zambia. With a mountain bike you can also explore some of the roads and trails that wind through the bush around Victoria Falls. Remember, though, that there is no fence between you and the wildlife, so proceed in the bush at your own risk. **Bush Trackers** (✉ Stand 258A, Adam Standers Dr., ☎ 113/2024), next to the Falls Traditional Village, rents mountain bikes for about Z$30 an hour. You'll need to leave your passport details and a Z$100 deposit.

BY BUS

Most of the outlying hotels operate shuttle buses that run hourly to town. Inquire at your hotel in advance.

BY CAR

Most of the attractions in town are within walking distance or just a short taxi ride away. As a result, it's probably not worth renting a car. You can take rental cars on some roads in the nearby national parks, but to explore these parks properly you really need a four-wheel-drive vehicle. An even better option is to go game-viewing in an open Land Rover with a local safari operator (☞ *below*). **Avis** (✉ Livingstone Way and Mallet Dr., ☎ 113/4532) no longer has a desk at the airport, but if you have a confirmed reservation they will deliver the vehicle to the airport. **Hertz** (✉ Bata Bldg., Park Way, ☎ 113/4267, FAX 113/4225) has desks in town and at the airport (☎ 113/432–522). For a midsize car expect to pay about Z$390 per day plus Z$4.50 per kilometer. If you rent for more than five days, it will cost about Z$700 a day with 250 free km (150 mi) per day.

BY TAXI

Taxis are a cheap and convenient way to get around town. Hotels can summon them quickly or you can find them at the falls. Taxis are metered; expect to pay about Z$10 from town to the falls, and Z$40 from town to Elephant Hills. Zambian taxis will pick you up at the Zimbabwean border post, drive you the 1.6 kilometers (1 mile) to the Zambian control post, and from there continue into Livingstone.

Contacts and Resources

GUIDED TOURS

Victoria Falls is practically sinking under the weight of all the safari operators that have sprung up in the last few years. Most offer a few special tours of their own design, but survive by selling the same trips as everyone else. You can book your rafting, bungee-jumping, scenic flights, and game drives at almost all of the safari companies listed below. The major operators in Victoria Falls are **Dabula Safaris** (⌧ 309 Park Way, ☎ 113/4453), **Safari Par Excellence** (⌧ Shop 4, Pumula Centre, Park Way, ☎ 113/4424, ⨳ 113/4510), **Shearwater Adventures** (⌧ Soper's Arcade, ☎ 113/4471, ⨳ 113/4341), **Touch the Wild** (⌧ Victoria Falls Hotel, Mallet Dr., ☎ 113/4694), **United Touring Company (UTc)** ⌧ Zimbank Bldg., Livingstone Way, ☎ 113/4267), and **Zambezi Wilderness Safaris** (⌧ Ilala Lodge, Livingstone Way, ☎ 113/4637, ⨳ 113/4417).

Boat Trips: A host of operators run on the Zambezi River above the falls, usually in large, twin-deck boats or in smaller pontoon boats. During these trips, you're likely to see hippos, crocodiles, and often elephants. The most popular trip is a two-hour sundowner cruise (expect to pay about Z$250), essentially a booze cruise with great views of the sunset from the water. Breakfast, lunch, and bird-watching cruises are also available. Most boat trips depart from the jetties near the A'Zambezi Hotel, about 8 km (5 mi) north of town. Major operators include **Dabula Safaris, Mosi Oa Tunya Cruises** (⌧ 299 Rumsey Rd., ☎ 113/4780, ⨳ 113/4780), **Shearwater Adventures, UTc,** and **Zambezi Wilderness Safaris.** Perhaps the least expensive of them all is **Kalambeza Safaris** (⌧ Park Way, ☎ 113/4480, ⨳ 113/4644). If you're looking for a less touristy version of a booze cruise, consider the Wine Route offered by **Zambezi Canoe Company** (☞ Canoeing *in* Outdoor Activities and Sports, *above*), a three-hour sunset canoe trip featuring sundowners.

Game Drives: Zambezi National Park. Dabula Safaris, UTc, and **Zambezi Wilderness Safaris** all have half-day (about Z$580 per person) and full-day (US$50) game drives through Zambezi National Park. The full-day excursion includes lunch, sometimes on a boat on the Zambezi River.

Game Walks: Dabula Safaris and **Backpackers Africa** (book through Safari Par Excellence or ☎ 113/4510) both have half- and full-day walking safaris in Zambezi National Park. Walks are led by an armed guide. Half-day walks include drinks and cost about US$50; full-day trips (about US$90) also include mid-morning teas and a cold lunch.

Microlight Flights: Batoka Sky (book through Shearwater Adventures) takes you over the falls in two-person microlight aircraft. The flight over the falls (about US$80) lasts 15 minutes, but you can also take a 30-minute flight that heads upriver from the falls in search of game. Make no mistake, this is a more dangerous way to see the falls than in a helicopter or fixed-wing plane—it's also probably the most exciting. Batoka Sky operates out of Zambia. The company meets interested clients on the Victoria Falls bridge at 7 AM and 8:30 AM and in the afternoon at 3 and 4:15; you need to clear Zimbabwe immigration first. Budget about three hours from pick-up to drop-off.

Scenic Flights: Flying over the falls in a plane or helicopter is an exhilarating experience. Helicopter flights tend to be briefer and more expensive, but they offer better views—and photo opportunities—than planes do. **Southern Cross Aviation** (⌧ Elephant Hills Intercontinental Hotel, ☎ 113/4618, ⨳ 113/4609) has 25-minute plane flights over the falls and some Zambezi River gorges for about US$40—book at Shearwater; a 40-minute flight (☏ US$60) also includes game-spotting over Zambezi National Park. Similar flights in a helicopter last 12 (☏ US$65) or 30 minutes (☏ US$100). **United Air** (☎ 113/4530 or 113/4220) has 12-minute helicopter (☏ US$65) and 15-minute plane

(☎ US$40) flights over the falls, and 30-minute flights that combine a trip over the falls with game-spotting nearby.

Village Tours: Touch the Wild offers a Meet the People tour, on which tourists travel to communal tribal lands near Victoria Falls to talk to Ndebele villagers and visit a school. The tour lasts two hours and costs about US$37 and includes pick-up and drop-off from your hotel.

MONEY MATTERS

In Victoria Falls you must settle your Zimbabwean hotel bills in foreign currency, either with cash, credit cards, or traveler's checks, and if you are leaving by air pay an airport departure tax of US$20 (☞ Coming and Going, *below*).

If you limit your Zimbabwe visit to Vic Falls, it's not absolutely necessary to change money into Zimbabwe dollars, since everyone from taxi drivers to curio vendors accepts foreign currency (the same applies on the Zambian side of the falls). And the prices for most Victoria Falls activities are usually quoted in U.S. dollars (this unfortunate and insulting practice stems from the view that the U.S. dollar is more stable than the Zimbabwe dollar). If you want Zimbabwe dollars for tips and small purchases, you can get decent rates at **Zimbank, Barclays,** and **Standard Chartered,** all of which have branches next to one another on Livingstone Way. Bank hours are Monday–Tuesday and Thursday–Friday 8–3, Wednesday 8–1, and Saturday 8–11:30. A Zimbank airport branch keeps sporadic hours. Numerous bureaux de change have sprouted in town, but most offer similar rates as the banks and some are not well established enough to be recommended. Avoid black-market money dealings—it's a sign of the money-hungry attitude in Vic Falls that you're likely to be accosted any time anywhere in town, particularly around the Craft Village.

VISAS FOR VISITING ZAMBIA

Zambian visas are required of citizens of all non-Commonwealth countries; the Zambian authorities issue visas at the border for US$10 or the equivalent.

VISITOR INFORMATION

The **Victoria Falls Publicity Association** is fairly well stocked with brochures, but because of the proliferation of new operators and services, can't always keep up with news around town. It is best to seek advice from the many safari companies in town. ⊠ *412 Park Way,* ☎ *113/4202.*☉ *Weekdays 8–12:30 and 2–4, Sat. 8–noon.*

LAKE KARIBA AND THE MIDDLE ZAMBEZI RIVER

The Zambezi, which forms Zimbabwe's northern border with Zambia, is Africa's fourth largest river system after the Nile, the Zaire, and the Niger. Its basin includes most of central and southern Africa, an area slightly larger than the Sahara. Long stretches of its banks enjoy special protection status, and much of it, passing through the Zimbabwe's wildest and least populated region, has never been fully explored.

For centuries the Zambezi has attracted traders, missionaries and explorers. The most famous of these, David Livingstone, believed he could open a navigable route to the east coast, but he was defeated by the rapids at Cabora Bassa. Today, the still magnificent reaches of this river—its forests, wetlands, and extravagant parade of wildlife—and vast Lake Kariba draw people from all over the world to such wilderness sanctuaries as Matusadona National Park and Mana Pools.

Lake Kariba was formed in 1958 with the damming of the Zambezi River at a narrow, almost vertical gorge 620 km (390 mi) downstream from Victoria Falls to provide hydroelectric power for Zimbabwe and Zambia. At the time of its construction the dam was the largest in the world, and its slender arching design—over half a kilometer (⅓-mi) long and 128 m (4,200 ft) high—still remains a miracle of its kind.

For the Ba-Tonga tribe, who had lived in the valley for centuries, the construction of the dam meant a traumatic break with their roots. The Rhodesian government of the time ordered them to leave their ancestral riverside homes and resettle on higher lands. Before doing so, tribal elders warned that *Nyaminyami,* their half-serpent, half-fish god, and guardian of the Zambezi, would punish the white man for disturbing the river and with it their ancestral spirits.

Like oracles in an ancient Greek tragedy, their sybilline warnings proved correct. Dry-season weather saw temperatures climb murderously into the high 40°C range—nearly 120° F—and tools had to be carried in buckets of water. Subsequently, in unprecedented storms the river rose by more than 30 m (100 ft), bursting through the coffer dam, destroying cables and bridges, and sweeping workmen to their death as 13 million liters (3½ million gallons) of water hurtled through the gorge every second. In the last of the incidents, early in 1958, a platform holding 17 men collapsed, flinging them into wet concrete, their bodies entombed to this day in the dam wall.

The fate of the area's wildlife was no less perilous. As the waters slowly rose over the wild, hot Zambezi Valley, thousands of animals became trapped on rapidly disappearing islands, which gave rise to one of the most dramatic animal rescue feats ever mounted. Led by game warden Rupert Fothergill and his team of African and European rangers, Operation Noah captured the imagination of the world. By the spring of 1963 at the completion of the operation, Fothergill and his teams had rescued over 5,000 animals, including monkeys, baboons, antelope, lion, and rhino.

After the valley was flooded the tops of mopane and other trees remained above the water where they stand today like fossilised relics from an earlier age, providing perches for cormorants, kingfishers, and fish eagles. More than anything else perhaps it is these ghostly trees and their black, skeletal branches framed against one of Kariba's molten sunsets that form the lake's most enduring image.

Winter—the end of May through July—has the coolest months, but the Lake Kariba area is always hot, especially in October, when the mercury can climb to 40°C (95°F). Evenings and nights are tempered by lake breezes. After the rains come in November, lasting through February, animals become harder to find as they disperse into the bush.

Lake Kariba Outdoor Activities and Sports

Kariba town isn't something to fly half way around the world for, but activities that leave from this side of the lake are. Canoe trips down the Zambezi begin on the other side of the dam in Kariba Gorge, tiger fishing is superb, and sailing trips on the lake, from which you'll see great wildlife, begin near town.

Canoe Safaris

Three-, four-, or more-day canoe safaris from Kariba Gorge—paddling down the Zambezi toward Mana Pools by day among crocodiles and hippos and with elephants occasionally coming to the shoreline, then camping by the river at night—make for an unparalleled river-and-wildlife experience. **Zambezi Travel & Safari Co.** (⊠ Box 158, Kariba, ☎ 161/2532, ℻ 161/2291) has superb guided trips. A three-day trip costs around US$560 per person, including meals and transportation back to Kariba.

Fishing

Angling is taken seriously at Kariba, where the tigerfishing is regarded as the best in the world. An annual international tournament is held in October for this sabre-toothed gamefish, which can strike with such a lightening combination of strength and speed that many an unwary angler has lost his rod. Your hotel will arrange a boat for you from its dock.

For a serious fishing holiday, **Kuteya Tours** (Contact: Ron Armstrong, ⊠ Box GD 292 Greendale, Harare, ☎ 14/481–515) is a local specialist fishing camp. Kuteya's camp, consisting of stone-and-thatch cottages—choose either self-catering or with meals cooked and included in the price—are close to the edge of a large bay. Guides here will take you out for BIG fish. Prices start at Z$700 per night and include unlimited boating, fishing, and bird- and animal-viewing.

Sailing

Kariba Yachts (☎ 161/2983, ℻ 161/2575) runs six-day sails on the lake for two to three people, putting in in the evenings at creek mouths and in bays. Game sightings are frequent in the evening. Trips start at the Cutty Sark lodge and cost Z$3,000 all inclusive for six days.

Matusadona National Park

Part of the reason for Matusadona's magic is its remoteness—20 km (12 mi) across the water, Kariba town is almost worlds away. Even today, the park remains wonderfully untouched by anything more threatening than thousands of buffalo who share the succulent lakeside torpedo grasses (*panicum repens*) with Kariba's other heavyweights. Indeed, there can be few other places in Africa where you can watch elephants swimming, frolicking and occasionally wrestling in the water at such close quarters as here. The name Matusadona, in the local dialect, means something like "the dung rolls" or "constant dripping of dung"—evidence of all the wildlife around you.

Many of the animals here are descendants of survivors rescued by Rupert Fothergill and his team that were relocated here during Operation Noah in the late' 50s and early '60s. Faithful to the biblical injunction, they dutifully went forth and multiplied. What you'll see fluctuates seasonally, but as the animals gather in increasing quantities during the dry season, you'll never be far from enormous herds of buffalo or elephants ambling nonchalantly. Lions are permanent fixtures and, following a relocation program from the lowveld into the park some five years ago, the numbers of cheetah are increasing.

Matusadona lies between the Ume River and the deep, mountainous Sanyati Gorge. Two thirds of the park is virtually inaccessible to vehicles. The southern boundary is studded with bays and inlets, many of which are drowned valleys, and you normally get to it by power boat from Kariba, or more quickly by light aircraft. There is also a notorious boulder-strewn 80-km (50-mi) track, navigable only by four-wheel-drive vehicles, to the park off the Karoi to Mbilizi road—better just hop on a plane.

Luxury safari lodges—with all kinds of game-viewing by boat, vehicle, or on foot, as well as fishing—stand along the park's secluded bays and off-shore islands. Bird life is prolific and "twitchers" (the Queen's slang for birders) will have a literal field day with the various storks, duck, geese, egrets, herons, and cormorants that patrol the shallows together with that most striking of raptors, the fish eagle, a proud sight sitting sentinel on half-submerged trees.

Private Lodges

$$$ 🏨 **Spurwing Island.** Magical Spurwing Island is just off the edge of Matusadona National Park. The island is named after the lovely spurwing goose, a regular visitor to these parts. Accommodations are in 11 walk-in tents under thatch, all of which have uninterrupted views over the lake, as do the camp's six twin-bedded cabins and three chalets. An ongoing refurbishment program ensures that the camp maintains its high reputation. The wide open expanses between the lake and the campsite support a high density of wildlife, which includes elephant, buffalo, lion, zebra, waterbuck, and other antelope. Spurwing's three professional guides are highly knowledgeable, and on bush walks in particular they will teach you a great deal about animal and bird behavior, as well as the ecology of the area. Spurwing has a wildlife viewing platform, game drives by vehicle and boat, and there are two- to three-day walking safaris and fishing trips available as well. The lodge is a 45-minute powerboat ride from Kariba. ✉ *Box 101, Kariba.* ☎ *161/2466 or 161/2269,* FAX *161/2301. Restaurant, bar, pool. AE, MC, V.*

$$ 🏨 **Fothergill Island Safari Lodge.** Across the lake from Kariba and set against the magnificent Matusadona Mountains this highly regarded lodge is named after game warden Rupert Fothergill, mastermind of Operation Noah. The lodge's wide variety of natural habitat, from mopane (pronounced mo-*pah*-nee) woodland to open grassland and the succulent green swards of lakeside torpedo grass, ensures a diverse mix of animal and bird life. The fourteen Tonga-style lodges—open, thatched cottages in the style of the Ba-tonga tribe—are equipped with fans and four-posters with mosquito nets. An unobtrusive electrical fence prevents you from bumping into the occasional elephant or ill-tempered buffalo. For taking in the areas superb wildlife, the lodge has viewing platforms, game drives by vehicle and boat, bush walks, boat trips into Sanyati gorge, and fishing trips. ✉ *Fothergill Island. Mailing address: Private Bag 2081, Kariba,* ☎ *161/2253,* FAX *161/2240. Central reservations in Harare:* ☎ *14/737–944 or 14/735–681,* FAX *14/734–739. 14 cottages. Restaurant, bar, pool. AE, MC, V.*

Kariba and Matusadona A to Z

ARRIVING AND DEPARTING

By Bus. Blue Arrow Luxury Coaches (Harare: ☎ 14/729–514, FAX 14/729–572) has direct service three times a day between Harare and Kariba. All buses are fully air-conditioned and have reading lights, on-board toilets, light refreshments, and video and CD entertainment. The fare is Z$230 one-way; the trip takes 5 hours.

By Car. To get to Kariba from Harare, take Highway A1 300 km (190 mi) to Makuti, then turn southwest down the rolling escarpment for the final 75 km (47 mi) to Kariba. On the last stretch there is a good chance that you'll find elephant and other wildlife sharing the road.

By Plane. Air Zimbabwe (☎ 161/2913) and **Zimbabwe Express Airlines** (Harare: ☎ 14/705–266) have daily flights from Harare, Victoria Falls, and Hwange to Kariba Airport (☎ 161/2913 or 161/2914).

Mana Pools

The middle stretch of the Zambezi—below Lake Kariba to the Mozambique border—is arguably the wildest and most beautiful part of Zimbabwe. In the midst of this pristine wilderness, between the Sapi and

Ruckomechi rivers, lies Mana Pools, a World Heritage Site widely regarded as the loveliest of Zimbabwe's national parks.

Here, the Zambezi flows slowly northward. In the course of its wanderings over the centuries, it has left in its wake a number of game-rich pools and sandbanks along alluvial flood plains and abandoned river channels. On its fertile terraces and open park-like expanses, giant acacias, Natal mahoganies, and tamarind trees spread back to where the bush turns into mopane woodlands. All of this lies under the gaunt, blue-green escarpment.

The rich forests of winter-thorn acacia, which dominate the riverbank areas, are relished by elephants. With a deftness belying their enormous size, they stand on their hind legs to pluck their gourmet crescent pods. All part of nature's rich tapestry, the seeds from this haute cuisine are later re-cycled through the elephants' dung to renew the vegetation. Interestingly enough, elephants also swim well, and give every appearance of enjoying it. At Mana Pools whole herds commute back and forward across the Zambezi, a distance in some cases of up to five miles. And back on Lake Kariba, young and old migrate happily between the mainland and off-shore islands.

Heat-hazed escarpments and the wide, timeless river—its lush green banks crowded with game during the dry season—are the enduring images of this immensely beautiful area. Buffalo and elephant are prolific, and there is every prospect of encountering lion. Raucous, grunting hippos warm themselves on the sandbanks, sharing them with those last remaining links from the time of the dinosaur, the Nile crocodile. These crocs are horror-movie monsters indeed—they have been known to drag a full-grown buffalo into the river by its muzzle and hold it under water until the luckless animal drowns.

Bird life at Mana is also sensational, with more than 380 species recorded. Among them are the brilliant carmine bee-eaters, Nyasa lovebirds, turkey-sized hornbills, huge saddle-billed storks, ibises, jacanas, orioles, herons, and Bateleur eagles.

Even the approach to Mana Pools, by water, is a world apart from the rest of Zimbabwe. As you follow the river from Chirundu, whether by canoe or by speedboat, you pass parkland on the Zimbabwean side, and waterside villages on the Zambian shore. It could be Sunday or it could be Wednesday; it could be this year or it could be 100 years ago or even farther back. Men paddle dugout canoes and women and children work and play. Banana groves spring up here and there. Compared to the circles we run around in, this part of the river feels timeless.

At Mana you are free to walk through the park unaccompanied—strictly at your own risk—and this is risky business to be sure. The resultant close encounters with animals can be thrilling, but unless you have bush experience, it is best to share the wilds with one of the many experienced game scouts.

Mana Pools National Park itself, but not the private lodges, closes during the rainy season, from the end of October to the end of April.

Game Experience

Mana Pools is famous for the richness and diversity of its wildlife. Game rangers refer to this stretch of the Zambezi as "hippo city," and the park is renowned for its elephant and enormous herds of riverside buffalo. Here to you will have the chance to see lion, leopard, hyena, side-striped jackal, wild dog, warthog, kudu, sable, waterbuck, grysbok and the tiny, shy nyala antelope. There are mongoose, honey badgers, civets, genets, and turtles. The river is noted for its tiger fish, bream, nkupe, and vundu.

Private Lodges

$$$$ ⛺ **Ruckomechi Camp.** Situated on the banks of Zambezi under enormous stands of mahogany and winter thorn trees, Ruckomechi is frequently voted the best safari lodge in the country. Accommodations consist of 10 thatched cottages, and the camp has tremendous views over a broad swathe of the river and the Zambian escarpment beyond. An open, thatched bar above the river allows you to sit mesmerised by the flow of the water and birds flying past: kingfishers, ibises, and carmine bee-eaters among others. There is also a marvellous open-air bath on the river bank with one side completely open to the water. The camp has game drives, bush walks with professional guides, and afternoon canoe trips down the Zambezi, with cocktails served midway if the crocs and hippos permit. Food is better than average bush-camp fare, and the staff is particularly amiable. ⊠ *Box 3961, Harare,* ☎ *14/757–831,* FAX *14/757–836. 10 lodges. Restaurant, bar.*

Arriving and Departing

Private lodges usually arrange transfers by van for the 90-minute ride from Kariba to Chirundu, from which you take a speedboat another hour or more down the Zambezi.

By Car. Drive from Harare to Makuti (300 km; 190 mi), where you'll have the last chance to refuel. From there it is another 63 km (39 mi) to Chirundu, where you connect with speedboat transfers to the private lodges.

By Plane. There are small airstrips at Mana Pools National Park, Chikwenya, and Chewore.

10 Botswana

Botswana itself is a natural wonder. Its variety of terrains, from vast salt pans to the waterways of the Okavango Delta to the Kalahari Desert, have diversity seldom found in such a small area. And because there is so little industry, you may have never seen stars as bright as this. The Kalahari Bushmen say that you can hear the stars sing—listen.

ONCE UPON A TIME—a mere 20 years ago—Botswana was a Cinderella among nations, one of the world's poorest countries. Then the Fairy Godmother visited and bestowed her gift: diamonds. The resulting economic boom transformed Botswana into one of Africa's richest countries in terms of national per capita income.

By Kate
Turkington

The sixties were a decade of self-determination all over Africa, led by Uganda, Ghana, and Nigeria. The British Protectorate of Bechuanaland was granted independence in 1966 and renamed Botswana. Where other nations' celebrations quickly turned sour, Botswana's independence brought an enduring tide of optimism. The country sidestepped the scourge of tribalism and faction fighting that cursed much of the continent—including bordering South Africa and Zimbabwe—and is considered one of Africa's most stable democracies. The Batswana (singular: Motswana) are renowned for their courteousness and dignity.

Roughly the size of France or Texas, Botswana is relatively unknown on the tourist map. While cities such as Gaborone ("*ha*-bo-rone"), the capital, have been modernized, Botswana has little in the way of urban excitement. Outside the cities it's a land of amazing variety: The Kalahari Desert is in stark contrast to the lush beauty of the Okavango Delta, one of Botswana's most magnificent and best-known regions. A vast area of tangled waterways and aquatic, bird, and animal life, it's sometimes referred to as "the Swamps," but this gives a totally false impression. There are no murky mangroves here, no sinister everglades, just open tranquil waters of breathtaking beauty leading into narrow, papyrus-fringed channels.

Nearly 18% of this very flat country's total land area is proclaimed for conservation and tourism. The Moremi Wildlife Reserve, the first such reserve in Southern Africa to have been created by an African community (the Tawana people) on its own tribal lands, is a major draw. Here, as in other parts of northern and southeastern Botswana, you'll see elephant, lion, buffalo, wild dog, cheetah, leopard, giraffe, kudu, wildebeest, hippo, and hundreds of awesome birds.

Pleasures and Pastimes

Boating and Bird-Watching

In the Okavango you can glide in a mokoro boat through papyrus channels among reeds and waterlilies and past palm-fringed islands on some of the purest water in the world as your guide and poler avoids bumping crocs and hippos. Bird watching from these boats is a special thrill: The annual return of thousands of gorgeous carmine bee-eaters to the Swamps in August and September is a dazzling sight, as is a glimpse of the huge ginger-colored Pel's Fishing Owl, the world's only fish-eating owl and one of its rarest birds.

Dining

Don't come to Botswana expecting a profound gastronomic experience. There is little or no local cuisine, so the food in the camps and lodges is basically designed to appeal to a wide variety of international visitors—soups, roasts, pies, quiches, curries, vegetables, and fruits. Some places have excellent home-baked bread, muffins, and cakes, and often desserts such as meringues, eclairs, and homemade ice-cream. And you'll find plenty of tasty South African wine and beer.

Fishing

If you're an experienced angler, you can pit your skills, wits, and rod against the savage fighting Tiger Fish (three out of five hooked get away).

If you're a novice, or have always wanted to try fishing, then go for it now—the Delta in season is full of fish, particularly Bream. Cast a spinner or trawl your line behind a small, chugging boat and get both dinner and a picture to amaze your friends.

Lodging

There are first-class private camps or game lodges all over Botswana, most in spectacular settings with stunning views, comfortable accommodations, and superb personal service. "Land camps" are in one of the game reserves or contiguous concessions with two daily game drives, morning and evening. If you're not in a National Park you'll be able to go out for night drives off road with a powerful spotlight to pick out many nocturnal animals. "Water camps" are deep in the Okavango and often only accessible by air or water. The average price per person per night a private lodges is US$400. And each camp will arrange transfers for you from the nearest airport.

Hotels in Maun and Gaborone are reasonably priced, but quality varies, and it's better to check them out first unless they belong to a well-known chain.

CATEGORY	COST*
$$$$	over P400
$$$	P300–P400
$$	P200–P300
$	under P200

All prices are in pula and refer to a standard double room, including tax. At private lodges, prices include all meals and activities.

Wilderness and Wildlife

Superlatives are unavoidable. Botswana has some of the last great wilderness areas left in the world, all remarkable in their diversity. A short plane ride can whisk you from scorching desert to water wonderlands, from great salt pans to fertile floodplains. There are limitless horizons, deafening silence, and few people. Northern Botswana and the Moremi Wildlife Reserve are teeming with game. For photographers, Chobe sunsets are priceless.

For a complete rundown on Southern African wildlife-viewing, *see* Big Game Adventures *in* Chapter 11.

Exploring Botswana

The country is basically a flat, sand-filled basin. The Kalahari Desert covers the center and south of the country and extends into in to Angola, South Africa, and Namibia. The northwest of the country is the unique watershed produced by the Okavango River (Southern Africa's third largest watercourse) which rises in the highlands of Angola and then flows south, west, and south again into Botswana's interior. Here, as it fans out over the Kalahari sandveld, it creates an immense inland delta, a fragile and perfectly balanced ecosystem which is one of the wonders of the natural world.

Great Itineraries

You'll have to decide which is first on your list of priorities—the certainty of seeing wall-to-wall wildlife in Chobe, the peace of the Okavango Delta, the salt-pan moonscapes of the Makgadikgadi Pans, or the charms of the cities.

IF YOU HAVE 3 DAYS

Arrive in **Maun** and catch an air charter to one of camps in the **Moremi Game Reserve.** Take your first thrilling game drive in an open vehicle with a knowledgeable local guide. After your early morning game drive, hop another plane to one of the true water camps deep in the **Okavango Delta.** Next day, marvel at its beauty from a mokoro and watch the sun set on the tranquil waters. On the third day fly reluctantly back to Maun and the real world.

IF YOU HAVE 8 DAYS

Spend your first three days as outlined above. On the forth day fly to Jack's Camp in the **Makgadikgadi Pans.** After a good rest get up the next morning and roam the vast expanses of the largest salt pans in the world. On your sixth day head to Chobe and the best wild game in the country. Next day head to the capital, **Gaborone,** to take in a small African city in action. Leave from Gaborone on your last day.

When to Tour Botswana

The best time is in the southern hemisphere's autumn and winter months, April through September. In the Delta the water has come in from the Angola highlands, and elsewhere, as it's the dry season, the grass and vegetation is sparse and it's much easier to see game, which often has no choice but to drink at available waterholes or rivers. But be warned, it can be bitterly cold, particularly early in the morning and at night. Dress in layers which you can discard or add on as the sun goes up or down. From October onwards it gets very hot, so unless you're a tropical blossom or a keen bird watcher—for it's then the migrants return—stick with winter.

THE OKAVANGO DELTA

The Okavango Delta is in Ngamiland, the tribal land of the BaTawana tribe. It's the legendary hunting area that fueled the 19th-century European imagination with Dr. David Livingstone's accounts of his explorations. The delta is formed by the Okavango River, which descends from the Angola highlands and flows south and then fans out over north-west Botswana. It's made up of an intricate network of channels and crystal-pure quiet lagoons, papyrus-and-reed-lined backwaters, and a myriad of animal, bird, plant, and aquatic life. The mokoro boat, synonymous with the Okavango, was introduced to the area in the mid-18th century when the Bayei tribe moved down from the Zambezi. Today, because of the need to protect the great jackalberry, morula, and sausage trees from which the craft are fashioned, you may find yourself in the modern equivalent: a fiberglass canoe. Your skilled poler—who would put any tightrope walker to shame—is always on the alert for the ubiquitous hippos, but quite laid-back about the mighty crocs lying smiling in the sun. This is a water wilderness experience above all others, and don't miss the chance to go on a guided walk on one of the many islands.

There is big game but it's more elusive and difficult to approach than in the game reserves. You'll almost certainly see elephant, hippo, crocs, red lechwe (a beautiful antelope endemic to the swamps), and may catch a glimpse of the rare, aquatic sitatunga antelope. You'll probably hear lion but may not always see them. But you're not in the Delta for the big game—you'll see plenty of that elsewhere in Botswana. You're here for the unforgettable beauty of the world's greatest wilderness areas.

Camp Okavango

An electric fence around the camp keeps the elephants out of Okavango, but hippos and whatever is in the area at the time stroll around at night; you're quite safe within your canvas walls. The major experience here is the water. In season, fishing is good; and because the camp is so well-established the bird-life is prolific. There's no dawn chorus like it.

Dining and Lodging

$$$$ ✕🏠 **Camp Okavango.** Most people involuntarily draw a breath when they walk from the airstrip into the sprawling campsite. Situated on remote Nxaragha Island in the heart of the permanent delta, it's only accessible by plane or water. Built by an eccentric American million-aire many years ago (she used to jet off to L.A. to get her hair done) it combines style, comfort, and a year-round water wilderness experience. Huge old trees arch over the outdoor dining area with its worn flagstones, carved elephant stools, and cane furniture. Wooden masks and a display of baskets made by the women in the camp decorate the adjacent bar. Eleven comfortable tents dimly lit by solar power with Rhodesian Teak furniture and en-suite facilities are so well separated that you might believe yours is the only one in camp. There's also a stunning private honeymoon cottage. In hot weather take a dip in the plunge pool and watch the waterways from a cool, high observation deck. The silver service dinner with gleaming candelabra and excel-lent food and wine served under the stars is legendary. If you're going to the sister camp, Camp Moremi, go by water transfer, a three-hour trip with an island coffee stop on the way. ✉ *Desert & Delta Safaris, Box 1200, Paulshof 2056, South Africa,* ☎ *27/11/807–3720,* 🖷 *27/11/807–3480. 11 double tents. Bar, pool. MC, V.*

Xugana Island

Situated on a big, permanent waterway, Xugana (pronounced *Kug*-na) lets you do all the things the Okavango Delta does best: lap up tran-quillity as you glide in a mokoro through the papyrus; get the adrenaline going as you fight a tiger fish; listen to an elephant midnight-snacking next to your *mosasa* (the Setswana word for dwellings), walk on a lovely island searching for a Pel's Fishing Owl, and watch tiny jewel-like sunbirds sip nectar from flowering trees. The Island also has the Mokoro Trail, a three-night accompanied camping excursion by canoe which slowly follows the river and on to the next camping site (not offered in January, February, and March).

Dining and Lodging

$$$$ ✕🏠 **Xugana Island Lodge.** The lodge consists of eight, stylish reed-and-thatch mosasa perched high on stilts, under massive ebony and jackalberry trees overlooking the wide Xugana lagoon. In fact, in this camp everything is on the very edge of the lagoon. Each mosasa has en-suite shower and toilet. They're spacious, with wooden-floors, high roofs, colorful blinds, sturdy wooden furniture, and a ceiling fan for those very hot days. Huge mosquito-proof windows provide one of the best views in the Delta. Early morning tea and coffee is brought to your own personal wooden deck where you can sit and watch a wading elephant or listen to the tumultuous birdsong. Enjoy a drink at the cozy thatched bar that overlooks the lagoon, then dine on excellent food al fresco under the stars. This is a classy, well-established, gracious camp with a wonderfully intimate atmosphere; the result of years of experience and professionalism. ✉ *Hartley's Safaris, Box 69859, Bryanston, Johannesburg 2021, South Africa,* ☎ *27/11/708–1893,* 🖷 *27/11/708–1569 (3 Bailgate, Lincoln, LN13AE, United Kingdom,* ☎ *0522/511–577,* 🖷 *0522/511–372). 18 mosasas. Bar, pool. MC, V.*

Delta Camp

Activities from the camp include guided mokoro trails into the maze of waterways and game walks on adjacent islands with a professional licensed guide. Your walks will teach you about the African environment ranging from the habits of dung beetles and warthogs, to superb bird-spotting, to how to dodge a charging elephant. A major conservation plus for Delta Camp is that motorboats are not used, as the emphasis is on preserving the pristine purity of the environment, which adds immeasurably to the relaxed, peaceful atmosphere that pervades this lovely camp. The Sitatunga Trail can be arranged exclusively for select groups of a minimum of four who wish to further explore this wondrous place for six nights or more. You may meet big and little game; in the Delta there's no way of knowing.

Dining and Lodging

$$$$ ✕🏠 **Delta Camp.** This is an enchanting traditional camp set deep in the Okavango. Seven reed chalets each with en-suite facilities are furnished with wooden furniture and upturned mokoros; they look like something straight out of *The Swiss Family Robinson*. Look below your windows on to shallow pools, with deeper waterways only paces away from your front door. Family-owned for many years, the camp has an intimate relaxed atmosphere. Sit under the stars at mealtimes and sip tea and coffee round a blazing log fire. ✉ *Okavango Tours & Safaris, Box 52900, Saxonwold, Johannesburg 2132, South Africa,* ☎ *27/11/788–5549,* 🖷 *27/11/788–6575. 7 chalets. MC V.*

Chitabe Camp

An enthusiastic young staff runs Chitabe which is bordered by the Moremi Game Reserve to the north. The concession's boundary in the east is the Gomoti Channel and the Santantadibe River in the west. Elephant, buffalo, lion, leopard, and cheetah are among the main attractions of this area as well as a host of small nocturnal game such as porcupine, civet, and bush babies. Chitabe lies within a study area of the Botswana Wild Dog Research Project which has up to 160 dogs in 10–12 packs, so you're almost certain to see these fascinating "painted wolves". The area has a good variety of habitats, although the water around the immediate camp is low, so only a limited mokoro ride is possible; power boats are out because it takes a few hours to reach a large permanent waterway. The camp is new, so there's not the variety or quantity of birds found in older, more established camps.

Dining and Lodging

$$$$ ✕⛺ **Chitabe Camp.** This is a new attractive camp of eight luxurious, twin-bedded, East African–style tents with wooden floors, woven lala palm furniture, wrought-iron washstands, a tiny wooden deck, and en-suite facilities with hot and cold running water. Tents are reached by walking along raised wooden walkways which wind their way through palms and mopane trees—it's a bit like being in the middle of a Tarzan movie set. A separate thatched dining room, bar, and lounge area, also linked by wooden walkways, look out over a floodplain. However, the shallow water which surrounds the camp is hidden by the long grass so it's difficult to believe that you're actually in the Okavango Delta; there are no vistas of water. For groups who would like a camp to themselves, Chitabe Trails Camp, often used by visitors on overland safaris, accommodates eight guests in similar tents built on the ground with en-suite bathrooms, private dining room, bar, and lounge area. ✉ *Wilderness Safaris, Box 651171, Benmore 2010, South Africa,* ☎ *27/11/884–1458,* 🖷 *27/11/883-6255 or 27/11/884–6684. 8 tents at Main Camp, 4 at Trails Camp. Bar, pool. MC, V.*

Xakanaxa Camp

Xanakaxa's (pronounced Kak-an-*a*-ka) compelling attraction is that it's within the borders of the Moremi Game Reserve as well as on a large permanent waterway, so you can enjoy a game or a water experience, the best of two worlds. This is why many guests (often repeat visitors) come for several days at a time. You'll see masses of game including elephant, sable antelope, hyena, side-striped jackals, and lots of predators. However, because there is so much game to see in the Moremi, the guides tend to take you to the lions, cheetah, or whatever, and then sit back as if their job were now finished. More information on the grasses, trees, birds, and general topography would be welcome. In season it can sometimes seem as if there are too many vehicles in the reserve. No mokoro rides are offered—the water is too deep—but you can take scenic powerboat rides through truly classic Okavango waterscapes, go fishing, or take an all-day ride with a picnic.

Dining and Lodging

$$$$ ✕⛺ **Xakanaxa Camp.** This well-established camp comprises 12 tents situated in scrubland overlooking the Xakanaxa Lagoon. The tents have wooden floors, wooden decks with loungers, sturdy rustic furniture, and a spacious shower room with flush toilet and basin. The camp maintains its back-to-nature atmosphere by eschewing electricity, so all lighting is from candles and oil-filled hurricane lamps. The tents are very close to one another (some guests maintain this gives them a feeling of security), and others are cheek-by-jowl with the staff quarters which can be very noisy. You'll eat tasty, well-cooked meals by candlelight in a gracious thatched and reed dining area on an enormous burnished dining table made of railway sleepers, and take your tea and coffee (which is constantly on tap together with excellent homemade cookies) on comfortable canvas armchairs circling an open fire. ✉ *Xakanaxa Moremi Safaris, Box 2757 Cramerview, Johannesburg 2060, South Africa,* ☎ *27/11/465–3842,* 🖷 *27/11/465–3779. 12 tents. Bar. MC, V.*

Moremi Game Reserve

In the northeastern sector of the Okavango lies the spectacular Moremi Game Reserve. In 1963 Chief Moremi III and the local BaTawana people proclaimed 1800 sq. km of pristine wilderness— ancient mopane forests, lagoons, islands, seasonal floodplains, and open grassland— as a game sanctuary, a first in Southern African conservation history. Here, where the life-giving waters of the Okavango meet the vast Kalahari, lies one of Africa's greatest parks teeming with game and birds, and, unlike the Masai Mara or Kruger Park, with hardly any people. You'll love the Garden of Eden atmosphere even if you do encounter the odd snake or two.

As there are no fences, the big game—and there's lots of it— can migrate to and from the Chobe park in the north. Sometimes it seems as if a large proportion of Botswana's 70,000 elephants have made their way here, particularly in the dry season. Check off on your game list lion, cheetah, leopard, hyena, wild dog, buffalo, hippo, dozens of different antelope, zebra, giraffe, monkeys, baboons, and over 400 different kinds of birds. Although in the South African school holidays (around July) there are more vehicles than normal, traffic is mostly light and unlike many of Africa's other great reserves you'll often be the only ones watching the game.

There are two main camp areas in the reserve. **Camp Moremi** is situated so you get the best of both water and land. The early morning and evening game drives with excellent rangers (one is aptly named "Relax") will pretty much ensure that you see lions galore, elephants, giraffe, zebra, all kinds of antelope and often the elusive leopard, cheetah, and wild dog. The rare Pel's Fishing Owl regularly plummets down to the shallow pool below Tree Lodge to snag a fish and carry it away to the only spotlit tree. Bird watching is excellent throughout the year; maribou and yellow-billed storks, pelicans, and cormorants nest here in the summer months. You can take a powerboat to the heronries on Gadikwe and Xakanaxa Lagoons.

Mombo Camp is strictly a land activity camp. Although there is plenty of surface water in the area (marshes and floodplains), it's not deep enough for water activities. Mombo is situated deep within the Moremi and has exclusive use of a large area of the reserve, so privacy is assured. Because of its great wildlife, including all of the large predators, several award-winning documentaries have been filmed here. On one morning's drive, a well-traveled guest remarked that out of 1,000 game drives he had done all over Africa, this was one of the top 25. On that one drive he reported seeing a pride of 19 lions, ranging from tiny cubs to full-grown adults; two nomadic lions who were searching for a new territory; a train of hundreds of buffalo in single file which stretched from horizon to horizon and then stampeded spectacularly; cheetah cubs playing (one came and climbed up onto the bonnet of his open-sided vehicle); and a sleeping leopard up a tree.

Dining and Lodging

$$$$ ✕🏨 **Camp Moremi.** This is the luxurious sister camp to the Delta's Camp Okavango (☞ *above*), so expect the same high levels of service, food, and accommodation. Huge old African ebony trees, home to two-legged, four-legged, winged, and earthbound creatures, dominate the campsite situated on the edge of a lovely lagoon. From the high viewing platform in the trees you can look out on a limitless horizon as the sun sets orange and gold over the smooth, calm waters. Eleven tastefully decorated, comfortable tents with en-suite facilities sleep 22 guests, all well spaced so as to ensure privacy. Camp Moremi's attractive, tim-

ber-and-thatch tree lodge has a dining area, bar, main lounge, small library, and sun deck with great views of Xakanaxa Lagoon. There's a swimming pool for those really hot days (swimming in the natural waterways is not advisable because of hippos and crocodiles). ✉ *Desert & Delta Safaris, Box 1200, Paulshof 2056, South Africa,* ☎ *27/11/ 807–3720,* ℻ *27/11/807–3480. 11 tents. Bar, pool, curio shop, airstrip. DC, MC, V.*

$$$$ ✕▣ **Mombo Camp.** Situated on Mombo island, off the north-west tip of Chief's Island, this delightful camp is sometimes linked to Chief's Island, it depends on the ebb and fall of the Delta. Compared to some of the newer camps, its 10 walk-through tents with reed-enclosed, private, en-suite toilet and shower facilities are comfortable but a little shabby. Each tent has its own tiny verandah with chairs and table and looks out over rolling grassy plains. Solar-powered lights will let you get undressed without difficulty but don't try to read by them. The dining room, lounge, and pub are on big wooden decks also overlooking the magnificent savanna landscape dotted with animals and birds. The atmosphere is ultra-friendly, the attention to personal service great, the food excellent, and the guides top class. The camp isn't fenced so make sure you get escorted back to your tent after dinner, zip it securely up, and then just lie back and listen to the sounds of the African night: lions roaring, hyenas yipping, a solitary leopard coughing, and owls and nightjars calling. ✉ *Wilderness Safaris, Box 651171, Benmore 2010, South Africa,* ☎ *27/11/884–1458,* ℻ *27/11/883– 6255 or 27/11/884–6684. 10 tents. Bar, pool. MC V.*

The Okavango Delta A to Z

Arriving and Departing

BY CAR

Only the western and eastern sides of the Delta panhandle and the Moremi Game Reserve are accessible by car; but it's wisest to always take a four-by-four vehicle. Maun, the starting point for the panhandle, is easy to reach from all sides, including South Africa, Namibia, and Zimbabwe, but the distances are long and not very scenic. The road from Maun to Moremi North Gate is tarred for the first 47 km (29 mi) up to Sherobe when it becomes gravel for 11 km (7 mi) and then a dirt road.

BY PLANE

Gaborone and Kasane International airports and the northern safari capital of Maun are the gateways to the Okavango. There are regular flights to Kasane from Zimbabwe and Namibia. ☞ Arriving and Departing *in* Botswana A to Z for airline contact information.

Getting Around

Once you get into camp, staff will take you where you need to go. The age-old way to get around the delta is by mokoro boat, made from the trunks of the great jackalberry, morula, and sausage trees. A skilled poler will guide the craft at some speed through the narrow channels. In deeper waters, power boats are an option.

Much of the Delta, especially its game, can only be enjoyed on foot. A good guide and a good pair of boots are required at all times.

Contacts and Resources

GUIDED TOURS

None of the operators below will commit themselves to a fixed price for a safari. Most charge a per diem rate of around $400.

Wilderness Safaris (✉ Box 651171, Benmore 2010, South Africa, ☎ 27/11/884–1458/9, ℻ 27/11/883–6255) offers planned, detailed tours between their many camps, both fly-in safaris and overland. Itineraries include a four-night, five-day safari combining the Okavango and Moremi Game Reserve, or a longer trip continuing on to Savuti/Linyanti and the Central Kalahari. Advance booking essential.

Desert & Delta Safaris (⊠ Box 1200, Paulshof 2056, South Africa, ☎ 27/11/807–3720, FAX 27/11/807–3480) offers inclusive fly-in safari packages to Camp Moremi, Camp Okavango, and Nxabega Okavango Safari Camp with daily departures from Maun, Kasane, and Victoria Falls. Advance booking essential.

Hartley's Safaris (⊠ Box 69859, Bryanston 2021, South Africa, ☎ 27/11/708–1893, FAX 27/11/708–1569) has planned safaris to their Xugana (Okavango) and Tsaro (Moremi) Camps. Advance booking essential.

MAUN

Maun is the gateway to the Delta for everyone from well-heeled oldies to young broke backpackers. It's grown from a tiny pioneering outpost 100 years ago, to a population of 60,000 today. The government has poured in millions of pula over the last few years and the infrastructure is developing fast. It's also the tribal capital of the BaTawana people, who live in large traditional villages within the town's boundaries. African mud and grass huts, unchanged for centuries, happily rub shoulders with modern brick structures. There's a great spirit in Maun and always has been. It's also a place of exceptional, hard-living, hardworking, warm, and generous people who are bound in a spirit of sharing and friendship that is less common elsewhere in Africa. From the city it's possible to organize all your trips to the Delta.

Exploring Maun

A Good Drive

A block from Maun Airport is the **Nhabe Museum**—you can even catch it between planes if you're not staying. Turn right out of the airport and drive 200 yards along the airport road to the legendary **Duck Inn.** Just south of the Delta, only a 90-minute drive from Maun via Toteng, is **Lake Ngami.**

Sights to See

Duck Inn. This legendary meeting place/community center/watering hole/pub/restaurant for hunters, game guides, travelers, and tourists, is run with Swiss precision and discipline by Bernadette—known locally as Mother Duck—and Emerita, two indomitable frontierswomen. The infamous social institution keeps up Maun's reputation as the toughest, hardest-living, hardest-loving town in the north. ⊠ *Box 40, Maun,* ☎ *267/660–253.*

Lake Ngami. When flooded (December–March), Ngami is one of the greatest bird-viewing areas of Africa. You'll see thousands of flamingoes, huge flocks of pelican, heron, stork, ducks and geese, and many other migrants. Traditional Herero and Yei villages cluster round the lake. There's no accommodation, so take a picnic and make it a day trip.

Nhabe Museum. Designed by an experienced Australian museum designer who signed on as director/curator through a volunteer organization, the museum exhibits the work of local Batswana painters, printmakers, sculptors, wood-workers, and weavers. If you're in Maun for a couple of days, try catch a show at the outdoor performance Annex behind the main building. ⊠ *Airport Rd, opposite Safari South, Private Bag 268, Maun,* ☎ *267/661–346.* ⊙ *Weekdays 8:30–5, Sat. 9–4:30.*

Dining and Lodging

For cheap fast food there's a **Steers Steakhouse** (⊠ New Mall, ☎ 267/660–907) two blocks from the Airport, or try what's on offer at **The Duck Inn** (☞ Sights to See, *above*). Neither offers a memorable gastronomic experience but will keep your motor going.

$$ ✕🏨 **Riley's Hotel.** Another Maun institution, the comfortable modern hotel (a member of the Best Western Chain) you see today is a far cry from the seven dusty rooms built by the legendary Harry Riley in the mid-'30s. In those days, government officers, traders, hunters, and the rest of Harry's Crew took board and lodging at Riley's for months at a time. It's still one of the main gathering places in Maun, although planes no longer taxi straight up to the bar as in the good old days. With luxurious rooms and good eating at Riley's Grill, it's a top choice for discerning travelers. In the popular Harry's Bar, if you listen carefully enough, you might just hear the raucous merriment of the original Riley's Crew. ⊠ *Central Reservations, Gaborone,* ☎ *267/312–431,* FAX *267/375–376. 51 rooms. Restaurant, bar. MC, V.*

$ ✕🏨 **Island Safari Lodge.** On the way to the Moremi Game Reserve and only 12 km (7½ mi) outside of Maun, this lodge will give you your first taste of the Delta. You'll sleep in simple but comfortable chalets all with private bathrooms, three of which nestle on the banks of the Thamalakane River under the shade of big trees. You can make your own barbecue, have a bar snack, or eat in the decent restaurant. The atmosphere is very friendly and informal, with lots of partying at the weekends. The Lodge will also arrange Okavango trips by boat or mokoro, houseboat trips on the river, and vehicle trips with licensed guides throughout northern Botswana. ⊠ *Box 116, Maun,* ☎ *and* FAX *267/660–300. 8 chalets and a camping site. Restaurant, bar, restaurant. MC, V.*

Maun A to Z

Arriving and Departing

BY CAR

Gaborone to Maun is 915 km (572 mi) on a good tar road. To get to Maun from the Victoria Falls one would first have to drive to Chobe and then to Maun from there, not really a practical option.

BY PLANE

Air Botswana flies once daily to Maun from Johannesburg and Gaborone. Air charter companies serve the Kasane/Maun connection. ☞ Arriving and Departing *in* Botswana A to Z for airline contact information.

Between the Airport and City Center: You can leave your bags at the airport and walk into town (about a 30-minute walk), which is very hot in summer, or try to hitch a ride. There are no taxis at the airport. The hotels will provide transport on request.

Getting Around

BY CAR

You'll probably need a car to get around Maun. Roads are mostly tarred or good sand roads and driving is safe and easy. **Avis Safari Hire** (☎ 267/660–039); **Holiday Car Rentals** (☎ 267/660–820).

ON FOOT

You'll share the streets with lots of colorfully dressed locals and *kamikaze* goats. Find out in advance how long each walk will be, heat exhaustion can be a problem.

CHOBE NATIONAL PARK AND THE LINYANTI AND KWANDO RESERVES

Chobe National Park

A hundred kilometers (62 miles) west of Victoria Falls in Botswana's northeast corner is Chobe National Park, another of Africa's finest game sanctuaries. The 12,000 square km reserve is home to some 35,000 elephants. The wide and tranquil Chobe River is surrounded by a natural wilderness of floodplain, dead lakebed, sandridges, and forest. Upstream it is known as the Linyanti and forms the border between Botswana and Namibia, downstream it joins the mighty Zambezi on its journey through Zimbabwe and Mozambique to the Indian Ocean. The north of the park comprises riverine bush, so devastated by the hordes of elephants coming down to the perennial Chobe to drink, that in winter it looks like a First World War battlefield. Fortunately, the wide sweep of the Caprivi floodplains, where hundreds of buffalo and elephant graze silhouetted against almost psychedelic sunsets, softens this harsh, featureless landscape where it faces neighboring Namibia. Unlike the rest of Botswana, Chobe can become "crowded" in terms of tourists; there are too many vehicles on too few roads, particularly in season. However, the Ngwezumba River area of forests and pans in the more remote middle of the park is quieter, though the game is harder to find. In the southwest, the wide grassy sweep of the Savuti channel, dry now for over 15 years, is renowned for its abundant game, particularly the legendary carnivores.

As well as Chobe's great elephant herds, you should see lion, leopard, hyena, possibly wild dog, and impala, waterbuck, kudu, zebra, wildebeest (gnu), giraffe, warthogs, and much more. Watch closely at the waterholes when prey species come down to drink and are most vulnerable—they are so palpably nervous that you'll feel jumpy too. Lions in this area are often specialized killers with one pride targeting giraffe, another zebra, another buffalo, or even young elephant. But lions are opportunistic killers and you could see them pounce on anything from a porcupine to a lowly scrub hare. Birdlife along the river is awesome: Rarely seen birds will get the twitchers frenetic, including slaty egrets, rock pratincoles, pinkthroated longclaws, and lesser gallinules.

Dining and Lodging

$$$$ ✕🏨 **Chobe Chilwero Lodge.** If you enjoy an intimate atmosphere, then this tiny camp, nestled among green lawns and big shady trees a stone's throw from Chobe Park's main gates, fits the bill. Set on a hill above the Chobe floodplains, with panoramic views of the elephant and buffalo herds below, there are eight, twin-bed, thatched, A-frame wooden chalets with hot shower, hand basin, and flush toilet en-suite. Oil lamps (there is solar lighting but no electricity) and mosquito nets will remind you of the days when Dr. Livingstone was hereabouts, although the accommodations and food have come a long way since then. The thatched two-tier lounge overlooks a magnificent panorama of river and wildlife. Downstairs a huge dining table seats 16 guests and staff, and upstairs there's a small viewing platform with comfortable chairs. Coffee by full moon round the campfire will keep your memory banks in credit for years. There's a little gem of a curio shop (well worth a visit on its own) stocking local African crafts, batiks, jewelry, and some fascinating bushmen artifacts. There are three game drives daily at dawn, mid-morning, and afternoon in seven-seater, open-sided, four-by-four vehicles. Chobe Chilwero's guides have the reputation of

being among the best in the area. Morning and afternoon river cruises in eight-seater boats will take you as near to the huge flocks of birds as you want. ✉ *Mailing address: Box 782607, Sandton 2146, South Africa,* ☎ *27/11/781–1497,* 🖷 *27/11/781–0733. 8 chalets. Bar, curio shop. DC, MC, V.*

$$$$ ✕🖬 **Chobe Game Lodge.** The Lodge must have something; Liz Taylor and Richard Burton got married for the second time here in the '70s. The only permanent lodge set in Chobe National Park, this grand old lady still offers one of Botswana's most sophisticated stays. Terra-cotta tiles, Rhodesian teak furniture, African artifacts, the ubiquitous, beautiful handwoven Botswana baskets, give the feel of the dark continent. The solid Moorish-style buildings—with their graceful high arches and barrel-vaulted ceilings—insulate the not-so-intrepid traveler from too-close encounters of the animal kind: Baboon mothers have been known to teach their young how to turn a door knob! The gorgeous gardens are a riot of color and attract lots of small fauna. There's a well-stocked curio shop with great clothes and wildlife books. Don't miss out on the well-run daily activities from game drives to river cruises. An early morning canoe ride is also a must. ✉ *Chobe Game Lodge Reservations, Box 130555, Bryanston 2021, South Africa,* ☎ *27/11/706–0861,* 🖷 *27/11/706–0863. 88 guests. Bar, pool, billiards. DC. MC. V.*

Linyanti Reserve

This reserve, which borders Chobe National Park, is one of the huge concession areas leased to different companies for up to 15 years by the Department of Wildlife and National Parks and the Tawana Land Board. It's a spectacular wildlife area comprising the Linyanti marshes, open floodplains, rolling savanna, and the famed Savuti Channel. Only three photo safari camps have been built in this area: Kings Pool, Savuti, and DumaTau. Because it's a private concession, open vehicles can drive where and when they like, which means superb game viewing and thrilling night drives with spotlights.

At Linyanti your basic choices for viewing wildlife are on a game drive (including night drives), on a boat, or going for a walk with a friendly and knowledgeable Motswana guide. Even in peak season there are only a maximum of six game vehicles driving around at one time, allowing you to see Africa as the early hunters and explorers might have. The Savuti Channel has starred in several National Geographic movies and it's not hard to see why—stock up on film and for once you won't bore your friends with the results: hundreds of elephants drinking from pools at sunset, hippos and hyenas nonchalantly strolling past a pride of lions preparing to hunt under moonlight, and thousands of water and land birds everywhere.

Lodging

$$$$ 🖬 **DumaTau.** It comes as no surprise to learn that the old general manager of South Africa's prestigious Mala Mala Game Lodge is running this classy show. This spanking new camp, imaginatively decorated and furnished with raised tent chalets under thatch and overlooking the water, lies at the very heart of the concession. The eight spacious chalets have African fabrics; clever cane furniture decorated with plaited reeds, brass, and local beadwork; wooden floors with handwoven rugs; an all-glass shower (and another one on your outside deck so you can wash as you view); a green pottery sink; and personal touches such as a guinea fowl feather or dried seed pod placed artistically amongst your towels. The lounge and dining area of the main lodge are open on all sides (a bit cold in winter); the toilet at the end of the deck must have the best view of any in the world. The food is simple but superb. Before

you set out on your early morning game drive try a plate of piping hot porridge, a Danish straight from the oven, or a freshly cooked muffin. ⊠ *Wilderness Safaris, Box 651171, Benmore 2010, South Africa,* ☎ *27/11/884–1458,* ℻ *27/11/883–6255. 8 chalets. Restaurant, pool, bar, library. MC, V.*

Kwando Reserve

Like the Okavango, the Kwando River, lifeblood of the Linyanti, Savuti, and Chobe systems, comes down from the wet Angola highlands then meanders through a few hundred kilometers of wilderness. The 2,300-square-km (900-square-mi) private Kwando concession, newly opened to tourists, has more than 80 km (50 mi) of river frontage. It stretches south from the banks of the river, through huge open plains and mopane forests to the Okavango Delta. It's an area crisscrossed by thousands of ancient game trails—migratory trails of elephant, buffalo, zebra, and wildebeest which move freely between the Okavango Delta, Chobe, and the open Namibian wilderness to the north.

As you fly in you'll see a web of thousands of interlacing natural game trails—from hippo highways to the tiny paths of smaller animals. This should clue you to the area's wildlife diversity; wall-to-wall elephants, crowds of buffalo, antelope of all kinds including roan and sable, wild dogs, and lion. The experienced rangers—who learned their animal ethics at South Africa's Londolozi and Phinda camps—and their Bushman trackers have already managed to habituate what is truly wild game to vehicles and cameras. One famed night drive came upon a running battle between a pack of 14 dogs and two hyena who had stolen the dogs' freshly made kill. The noisy battle ended when a loudly trumpeting elephant, fed up with the commotion, charged the wild dogs and drove them off. There's a sheer joy in knowing that you are one of only two vehicles in half a million acres of wilderness.

Lodging

$$$$ 🏠 **Kwando Lagoon Camp.** The camp perches on the banks of the fast-flowing Kwando River, quite literally in the middle of nowhere. Six comfortable walk-through tents with en-suite facilities and private verandas nestle on grassy slopes under the shade of giant, hundreds-of-years-old Jackalberry trees. After a night spent next to one of these mighty trees, a major source of natural energy, people say you wake up rejuvenated, your body buzzing with new life. From the thatched dining and bar area you can watch herds of elephants only meters away as they come to drink and bathe, or hippos snoozing in the sun. You might also spot a Malachite kingfisher darting like a bejeweled minijet over the water. Go for a morning or evening game drive, drift along the river in a small boat, or go spinner or fly fishing for tiger and bream. The emphasis in the camp (run by two of South Africa's former top rangers and film-makers) is on informality, simplicity, and soaking up the unique wilderness experience. ⊠ *Kwando Wildlife Experience, Box 1264, Parklands 2121, South Africa,* ☎ *27/11/886–138 or 27/11/886–059,* ℻ *27/11/880–1393. 6 tents Restaurant, bar. AE, DC, MC, V.*

Chobe-Linyanti-Kwando A to Z

Arriving and Departing

This is not a practical way to travel unless you have plenty of time and don't mind driving very long distances. The drive from Victoria Falls to Chobe takes about an hour and a half on a good tarred road.

BY PLANE

Kasane International Airport (☎ 267/650–598) is 3 km (2 mi) from the entrance to Chobe National Park. ☞ Arriving and Departing *in* Botswana A to Z for airline contact information.

Getting Around

BY CAR

A four-by-four vehicle is essential in the park itself. The roads are sandy and/or very muddy, depending on the season.

THE MAKGADIKGADI PANS

These immense salt pans in the eastern Kalahari—once the bed of an African superlake—provide some of Botswana's most dramatic scenery. Two of these pans, Ntetwe and Sowa, the largest of their kind in the world, have a flaky, pastrylike surface that might be the nearest thing on earth to the surface of the moon. In winter, these huge bone-dry surfaces, punctuated by islands of grass and lines of fantastic palm trees, dazzle and shimmer into hundreds of mirages under the beating sun. In the summer months the last great migration in southern Africa takes place here: Over 50,000 zebra and wildebeest with predators in their wake come seeking the fresh young grass of the flooded pans. Waterbirds also flock here from all over the continent; the flamingoes are particularly spectacular.

But game (although not in these numbers) you can see elsewhere in Botswana, so visit May through September to find out why this place is unique. You can see stars as never before, maybe as the Bushmen say, even hear them sing. You might also ride four-by-four quad bikes into an always vanishing horizon; close your eyes and listen as an ancient Bushmen hunter tells stories of how the world began in his strange language of clicks; and just wander over the pie-crust, pristine surface of the pans.

Lodging

$$$$ 🏨 **Jack's Camp.** If you're bold-spirited, reasonably fit, and have kept your childlike sense of wonder, then make Jack's a definite stop on your itinerary. Situated in the Kalahari Desert on the edge of the great salt pans, it's a cross between a Fellini movie, a Salvador Dali painting, and *Alice Adventures Through the Looking Glass*. There are East African safari tents, ancient Persian rugs, brass-hinged boxes to store your things in, teak and canvas furniture, unending views over endless plains, copper jugs full of water to wash in, a flush toilet of your own, and a hot or cold bucket shower on demand. You'll eat your meals under a spreading acacia tree and drink tea and coffee in a large, open-sided, pagodalike tent, sprawled on more antique rugs and propped against venerable embroidered cushions. The rangers—zoologists and biologists every one—are known throughout Botswana and beyond for their love and knowledge of this unforgettable area. Remember though, this is the Kalahari Desert, very hot in summer and very cold in winter. ✉ *Uncharted Africa Safari Co., Box 173, Francistown, Botswana,* ☎ *267/212–277,* FAX *267/213–458. 8 tents. MC, V.*

Makgadikgadi A to Z

Arriving and Departing

BY CAR

There's a tar road to Gweta from Gaborone via Francistown and Nata, but the trip is 1,162 km (726 mi).

Synergy Seating (☎ 267/661–703) have air transfers from Maun.

GABORONE

Gaborone is not one of the world's tourist Meccas: There are no beaches, quaint inns, or nightlife to speak of (other than a couple of casinos); no performing arts, one pretty featureless golf course, no nearby scenic wonders, no public transport, and little in the way of craftwork. At best, Gaborone is a staging post for tourists traveling post haste to and from the Okavango Delta, Moremi Game Reserve, Chobe, and the Kalahari Desert. The city does have quite an interesting history. Gaborone was declared the capital of the new, independent Botswana in 1966, although it was little more than a village with a population of a few thousand. Even after 30 years of urbanization, Gaborone's population is still well under 200,000. It's big enough to have a decent infrastructure, embassies and consulates, a small stock exchange, travel agents, an international airport only 15 km (9 mi) from the city center, good roads, and hospitals and medical services. But Gaborone has retained its small town personality, where time moves at a different pace to that of more dynamic cities and you can observe southern African people going about the routines of their daily lives.

Exploring Gaborone

The best time in Gaborone is late afternoon when the sun has lost its fierceness, and citizens and office workers stroll round the broad square of the Mall—the main business and commercial area—pausing to pass the time of day with friends. It's a colorful scene, too, with its mixture of traditional and European dress and splashes of primary colors on the sidewalk stalls.

A Good Tour

Begin at the Mall and take a short walk to the **National Museum and Art Gallery.** Then hop in your rental car and take the Lobatse road for 14 km (9 mi) to the **Mokolodi Nature Reserve,** or go the 40 km (25 mi) north of the city to scenic **Mochudi** village. Twenty-two km (14 mi) along the Kanye road, past Kumakwane village and over the Kolobeng River, you'll come to the **Livingstone Memorial.**

Sights to See

Livingstone's Memorial. The name of Scots missionary Dr. David Livingstone is synonymous with the early exploration of this part of Africa. Drive 22 km (14 mi) along the Kanye road, past Kumakwane village and over the Kolobeng River and you'll come to Livingstone's house and two graves, one of which is said to belong to his son.

Mochudi. This large scenic Batswana village (a real one not a tourist trap) will give you a good idea of how traditional life still goes on. Beautifully painted courtyards front buildings with huge thatched roofs where people go about their daily lives. Mochudi has its own museum and arts and craft center—the **Phuthadikobo Museum** (☉ Weekdays 8–5, weekends 2–5).

Mokolodi Nature Reserve. You'll see game here, including lions, but the reserve is small and fenced and therefore won't be of great interest to you if you've recently seen game in the true wilderness or intend doing so. But the Park is worth visiting for a taste of the bush and its great bird spotting opportunities. ⊠ *Plot 183 Queens Rd., Box 170, Gaborone,* ☎ *267/353–959,* ℻ *267/313–973.* ☜ *10P per person, 10P per vehicle.* ☉ *Daily 7–6.*

National Museum and Art Gallery. It isn't a big museum and your visit won't take long, but you'll get a fascinating glimpse of a culture that is fast disappearing. There are displays of Botswana's early history, its wildlife, and traditional and modern arts and crafts. The museum booklet, "A Guide to Places of Historic and Natural Interest in and around Gaborone," will give you plenty of suggestions if you do have more time. ⊠ *Independence Ave., Gaborone,* ☎ *267/374–616.* ◷ *Tue.–Fri. 9–6, weekends 9–5.*

Dining

The following restaurants will average about P75 (US$25) for a three-course meal excluding drinks.

$$$ ✕ **Mokolodi Restaurant.** For a truly African feel, try this excellent restaurant on the edge of the Mokolodi Nature Reserve where the buildings and ambiance reflect the bush setting. The open-sided dining area is a large, high-ceilinged, thatched rondavel. The menu emphasizes southern African food with venison a specialty, although there's plenty more to choose from. ⊠ *Mokolodi Nature Reserve,* ☎ *267/328–396. Reservations essential. D, DC, MC, V.*

$$$ ✕ **Swiss Chalet.** Here you can choose from a motley jumble of different size rooms decorated in styles ranging from a large Bushman wooden frieze to Swiss style wooden paneling. The international menu is comprehensive and excellent, as is the wine cellar. There's always a festive atmosphere because the place attracts whatever international visitors are around, plus a fair smattering of locals. There's a tapas bar open every day except Monday. ⊠ *Tlokeng Rd., Gaborone,* ☎ *267/ 325–172. Reservations essential. DC, MC, V. Closed Sun.*

Lodging

$$$ 🏨 **Gaborone Sun.** Attractively situated by a golf course 2 km (1 mi) from the city center, this is a first-class, modern hotel with extensive conference facilities. Fully equipped rooms include suites, luxury, and standard rooms and all are air-conditioned. They have two excellent restaurants, Savuti for buffet and Giovanni's for a la carte, both with live entertainment. ⊠ *Private Bag 0016, Gaborone,* ☎ *267/351–111,* FAX *267/322–727 ext. 2522. 196 rooms. 2 restaurants, pool, 2 tennis courts, squash, casino. D, DC, MC, V.*

$$$ 🏨 **Grand Palm.** Four kilometers (2½ miles) outside of Gaborone, this luxurious complex is surrounded by lush gardens, walking trails, and a much-frequented bird pond. The rooms are nothing special, but they're clean and functional. ⊠ *Box 2025, Gaborone,* ☎ *267/312– 999,* FAX *267/312–989. 199 rooms, 10 suites. 2 restaurants, 3 bars, sauna, tennis court, squash, casino. D, DC, MC, V.*

$$ 🏨 **Cresta Lodge.** This lodge is centrally situated and built to international standards. The rooms are straightforward but comfortable. The landscaped gardens offer a shady retreat; you can even go on a short nature trail.⊠ *Private Bag 00126, Gaborone,* ☎ *267/375–375,* FAX *267/ 375–376. 80 rooms. Restaurant, bar, air conditioning, pool, courtesy transport. D, DC, MC, V.*

Shopping

The few smart shops are in the **Mall,** and at a newer center, **Broadhurst,** a few kilometers north of the city center. This informal trading sector is also home to street vendors offering beads, leather work, basketry, and carvings. Some of the carvings—often Zambian or Zimbabwean because Botswana doesn't have a strong tradition of this kind of handicraft—are beautifully fashioned and merit some of your precious baggage space. The best local craftwork is basketry—a skilled tradition handed down from mother to daughter—and woven wall hangings. A recent development is diamond and gold jewelry which marries the sophisticated brilliance of the gems to traditionally African themes. You'll be able to find silver acacia-thorn brooches studded with diamonds, and combretum leaf earrings in gold and silver, all beautifully fashioned by local craftspeople.

Curio shops around town are a good source of traditional Bushman crafts and artifacts, which range from bracelets made from tiny ostrich-egg beads, to bows and arrows, pipes, and handmade traditional women's aprons. Curio shops in larger hotels often have interesting things but are more expensive. A variety of handwoven articles, from rugs and tapestries to bedspreads and table mats, are available from the well-signposted **Oodi Weavers** (☎ 267/392–268, ⊘ Weekdays 8–4:30, weekends 10–4:30), 20 km (12½ mi) north of Gaborone on the Francistown Road, where you can watch the weavers at work.

Gaborone A to Z

Arriving and Departing

BY CAR

Gaborone is 915 km (571 mi) from Maun on a good (though very boring) tar road.

BY PLANE

Sir Seretse Khama Airport (☎ 267/314–518), 15 km (9½ mi) from the city center, has flights to and from Maun, Kasane, Francistown, and Selibi-Phikwe, and international flights to Johannesburg, Victoria Falls and Harare in Zimbabwe, and Windhoek in Namibia. ☞ Arriving and Departing *in* Botswana A to Z for airline information.

Between the Airport and City Center. Most hotels provide courtesy transport. **Taxis** are available at the airport for about 30 pula. This, however, is strictly negotiable, so make sure you agree a price with the driver before you get in the taxi.

Getting Around

Public transport is nonexistent so you will need to take a taxi or hire a car.

BY CAR

Generally speaking, drivers are careful and courteous, but keep a sharp lookout for the ubiquitous African taxis (minivans) which may often be overloaded and unsafe. Avoid rush hour traffic. Drive on the left, of course; the speed limit is 120 kmph (75 mph) on major routes, 60 km (40 mph) in built-up areas. It's not a good idea to venture out of the town at night as the roads are unlit, strewn with domestic animals (and the occasional antelope), and you could well get lost.

BY TAXI

Taxis are available, your hotel concierge will help or you can look for a blue number plate which indicates that the vehicle is a licensed taxi. Always negotiate your fare before taking off and expect to share with others; taxis stop and start at will to pick up passengers.

Contacts and Resources

CAR RENTAL

The main car rental firms in Botswana are **Avis** (✉ Gaborone, ☎ 267/375–469), **Imperial** (✉ Gaborone, ☎ 267/307–233), and **Holiday Safaris** (✉ Gaborone, ☎ 267/312–280).

EMERGENCIES
Ambulance ☎ 997. **Fire Brigade** ☎ 998. **Police** ☎ 999.

DOCTORS
If you need to see a doctor, consult your hotel, look in the pink pages of the telephone directory, or go to the local hospital as an out-patient. Avoid government hospitals unless you have hours and hours to spend waiting. **Gaborone Private Hospital** (☎ 267/301–601) is a good one to use. **Medical Rescue International** (☎ 267/301–601) offers 24-hour emergency help.

EMBASSIES AND HIGH COMMISSIONS
British High Commission (✉ 1079 Queen's Rd., Gaborone, ☎ 267/352–841, FAX 267/356–105). **U.S. Embassy** (✉ Government Enclave, Embassy Dr., Gaborone, ☎ 267/353–982, FAX 267/356–947).

BOTSWANA A TO Z

Arriving and Departing

By Car
All the main access roads from neighboring countries are tarred, and cross-border formalities are user-friendly. Maun is easy to reach from South Africa, Namibia, and Zimbabwe, but the distances are long and not very scenic. Gaborone is 360 km (225 mi) from Johannesburg via Rustenburg, Zeerust, and the Tlokweng Border Post.

By Plane
AIRPORTS
Sir Seretse Khama Airport (☎ 267/314–518) in Gaborone is Botswana's main point of entry.

Kasane International Airport, near the entrance to Chobe National Park, has flights to Namibia and Zimbabwe.

INTERNATIONAL CARRIERS
Air Botswana (Gaborone: ☎ 267/351–921; Kasane: ☎ 267/650–161; Maun: ☎ 267/660–391) has scheduled flights from Johannesburg to Gaborone and Maun on a daily basis. There are also regular scheduled flights from Harare and Victoria Falls in Zimbabwe, and Windhoek in Namibia. **British Airways** (☎ 267/372–594) also has daily flights from Johannesburg.

Getting Around

By Car
Forget about a car in the Delta, the water makes it more trouble than it's worth. In the game parks a four-by-four vehicle is essential. The roads within the parks tend to be sandy and/or very muddy, depending on the season. You'll need a car in Maun and Gaborone, as public transport doesn't exist. The "Shell Tourist Map of Botswana" is the best available map.

By Plane
In this huge, often inaccessible country, air travel is the easiest way to get around. Your starting points will be Gaborone, the capital, or Maun, gateway to the Delta. Air charter companies operate small planes from Kasane and Maun to all the camps. Flown by some of the youngest-looking pilots in the world, these flights, which your travel agent will arrange, are reliable, reasonably cheap, and average between 25 and 50 minutes. Maximum baggage allowance is 12 kg in a soft, squashy sports/duffel bag (no hard cases allowed), excluding reason-

able camera equipment. Because of the thermals, flights can sometimes be very bumpy—take air-sickness pills if you're not a good traveler, then sit back and enjoy the fabulous, bird's-eye views.

DOMESTIC CARRIERS
Chobe Air (⊠ Box 32, Kasane, ☎ 267/650–340, FAX 267/650–280) and **Quicksilver Enterprises** (⊠ Box 280, Kasane, ☎ 267/650–532, FAX 267/650–223) both fly into Kasane. **Mac Air** (⊠ Private Bag 329, Maun, ☎ 267/660–675, FAX 267/660–675), **Northern Air** (⊠ Box 40, Maun, ☎ 267/660–385, FAX 267/660–379), **Swamp Air** (⊠ Private Bag 33, Maun, ☎ 267/660–569, FAX 267/660–040), and **Synergy Seating** (⊠ Box 39, Maun, ☎ 267)/660–044, FAX 267/661–703) fly directly between Johannesburg's Grand Central Airport and Maun.

The Booking Company (⊠ Private Bag 198, Maun, ☎ 267/660–022) can coordinate all internal flights.

Contacts and Resources

Emergencies
In the case of mechanical breakdown, contact your car hire company in Botswana. Most safari companies include medical insurance in their tariffs. **Medical Rescue International** (☎ 267/301–601) offers 24-hour emergency help.

Guided Tours
There are many smaller specialist safari companies including **Bird Safaris** (⊠ Box 15, Maun, ☎ 267/660–614, FAX 267/660–925); **Des Pretorius Photographic Safaris** (⊠ Box 236, Maun, ☎ FAX 267/660–493); **Friedkin Adventure Companies** (⊠ Box 40, Maun, ☎ 267/660–211, FAX 267/660–379); **Ker & Downey Elephant Safaris** (⊠ Box 40, Maun, ☎ 267/660–211, FAX 267/660–379); **Mike Watson Fishing Safaris** (⊠ Box 448, Maun, ☎ and FAX 267/660–364); **Okavango Horse Safaris** (⊠ Private Bag 23, Maun, ☎ 267/660–822, FAX 267/660–493).

African Portfolio, a Harare- and New York–based tour operator, can arrange all aspects of a Botswana itinerary, for an entire trip or for smaller local segments. ⊠ *160 Enterprise Rd., Highlands, Zimbabwe,* ☎ *263/4/481–117,* FAX *263/4/495–704.*

Language
Although the national language is Setswana, English is the official one, and it is spoken nearly everywhere.

Telephone Numbers
Both Botswana and South African telephone numbers appear in this chapter. Botswana numbers begin with the 267 country code, which you shouldn't dial within the country (there are no area codes for Botswana). South African numbers begin with that country code (27) and are followed by the Johannesburg area code (11).

Travel Agencies
Kudu Travel (⊠ Box 00130, Gaborone, ☎ 267/372–224, FAX 267/374–224). **Manica Travel Services** (⊠ Box 1188, Gaborone, ☎ 267/352–021, FAX 267/305–552). **The Travel Center** (⊠ Box 1950, Gaborone, ☎ 267/304–360, FAX 267/305–840). **Travelwise** (⊠ Box 2482, Gaborone, ☎ 267/303–244).

Visitor Information
The **Department of Tourism** (⊠ Private Bag 0047, Main Mall, Gaborone, ☎ 267/353–024).

Tourist Information Centers (⊠ Maun: ☎ 267/660–492, FAX 267/661–676; Kasane: ☎ 267/650–357, FAX 267/650–841).

11 Portraits of South Africa

Big Game Adventures

The Long Road Home

Zimbabwe: A Brief History

Books and Videos

BIG GAME ADVENTURES

MENTION AFRICA and most of us conjure up visions of wildlife—lions roaring in the gathering dusk, antelope skittering across the savanna, a leopard silhouetted by the setting sun. The images never fail to fascinate and draw us in, and once you experience them in the flesh you're hooked. The look, the feel—the dusty smell—of the African bush seep into your soul, and long after you've gone you find yourself missing it with an almost physical longing. The wildlife experience in South Africa rivals the very best on the continent, and a trip to the bush should be a major part of your vacation.

Do everyone a favor, though, and pass up the impulse to rush out and buy khakis and a pith helmet. The classic safari is dead. Hemingway and the great white hunters took it to their graves, along with thousands upon thousands of equally dead animals. The closest you'll come to a real safari today is if you spend an ungodly sum of money to trek into the wastes of Selous National Park in Tanzania to nail some unfortunate lion.

Indeed, too many wildlife documentaries have conditioned foreign visitors into thinking that Africa is overrun with animals, and they half expect to be greeted by a lion in the airport's arrival terminal. The truth is far less romantic—and much safer—especially in South Africa, where fences or rivers enclose all major reserves. The rest of the country is farmland, towns, and suburbs.

South Africa has 17 national parks and a host of provincial reserves, but only a few contain all the indigenous species that once roamed the veld in vast herds. The crown jewel of South Africa's reserves is Kruger National Park, the second-largest game reserve in Africa. It's a magnificent tract of pristine wilderness that is home to an astonishing number of animals. Like all of South Africa's parks, it's completely open to the public, and you can tour and view game from the comfort of your own car. Good roads, plentiful and cheap accommodations, and excellent facilities are what differentiate South African parks from their East African counterparts.

The other, much more expensive option is to stay in a lodge on a private game reserve. If you can afford it, don't miss out, because these exclusive lodges offer a wildlife experience without parallel. You could spend a month bumping fenders with tourist minibuses in East Africa and never get as close to game as in these lodges. Bouncing over dirt tracks in an open Land Rover, you *know* you're in Africa. These luxury lodges give you a taste of the bush and the experience of living out in the wilds. Sure, you get comfortable beds, flush toilets, running water, hot showers—even air-conditioning—but the bush lies right outside your door, and nothing stops an elephant from joining you for dinner.

Talk to travel agents about private lodges and sooner or later they will start babbling about the Big Five. This was originally a hunting term referring to those animals that posed the greatest risk to hunters on foot—elephant, black rhino, leopard, lion, and buffalo—yet it has now become the single most important criterion used in evaluating a lodge or reserve. Although the Big Five label may have helped engender tourist interest in African wildlife, it can also demean the entire bush experience, turning it into a treasure hunt. You will be amazed how many visitors ignore a gorgeous animal that doesn't "rank" in the Big Five, or lose interest in a species once they've checked it off their list. After you've spent a few days in the bush, you will also recognize the idiocy of racing around in search of five animals when there are another 150 equally fascinating species all around you. It's up to you to tell your ranger exactly what kind of wildlife you want to see.

It's no coincidence that old game-watching hands find their thrills in the smaller, rarer animals—and in birds. South Africans are maniacal bird-watchers for very good reason: it's one of the best birding regions in the world. More than 500 species of birds have been recorded in Kruger alone, and their beauty and diversity are extraordinary. Don't overlook them just because they're small and harmless—your trip will be poorer for it.

Whether you're searching for elephant or the arrow-marked babbler, a sturdy pair of binoculars is essential, as is a camera. Use a point-and-shoot camera only if you want pictures of you and your companions out in the bush; forget about it if you want good wildlife shots. Ideally, you should use a 35mm camera with at least a 300mm lens and a sand bag to act as a rest, since you can't set up a regular tripod on a vehicle. The best all-purpose film is ASA100, but ASA400 is great for action photography, like a cheetah hunt. Light readings in the African glare can be tricky, so be sure to bracket your shots. No matter what camera or film you use, you're bound to take an embarrassing number of bum shots—animals caught fleeing—so it pays to shoot bucket loads of film.

When you go on safari, take precautions against malaria. The disease is no joking matter, and it claims its share of victims in South Africa every year. Summer is the height of malaria season, when the annual rains provide plentiful breeding grounds for mosquitoes. With a couple of notable exceptions, every reserve and lodge in this chapter lies in a malarial zone, and it's imperative that you take prophylactics. At press time, Lariam (mefloquine) was the preferred drug, but it has possible side effects. See your doctor at least a month before you depart—and don't put all your faith in pills. Even the most powerful medications don't always work and the only absolute protection against the disease is to avoid getting bitten in the first place. Cover up between dusk and dawn (when the mosquitoes are active) and apply a repellent to exposed skin. In your room at night sleep under a net if possible and use an electric mosquito destroyer, which takes a vaporizing pad, or burn coils. Leave that mosquito "zapper" at home as it's totally useless.

Game viewing can't be rushed. To make the most of your trip, plan on no less than two nights at any one place—be it a private lodge or a rest camp. Racing around from camp to camp on safari is a waste of time and money—give yourself the pleasure of slowing down, appreciating your surroundings, and taking in the sights and sounds of the bush, which are as much a part of the whole experience as the Big Five.

Timing

No two people can agree on the best time to visit the bush. Summer (December–March) is hellishly hot, with afternoon rain a good possibility, but the bush is green, the animals sleek and glossy, and the bird-life prolific. Unfortunately, it's the worst time of year to spot game. All of the foliage makes finding game harder, and animals tend to disperse over a wide area because they are no longer reliant on water holes and rivers. Winter, on the other hand, is a superb time for game-viewing, because trees are bare and animals congregate around the few remaining water sources. Because the weather's cooler, you may also see lions and leopards hunting by day. Most lodges drop their rates dramatically during winter months, often lopping as much as 30%–40% off their peak season prices. The drawback to a winter visit is the cold, and the fact that the bush looks dead and the animals thin and out of condition.

A happy compromise may be the shoulder seasons. In October and November the weather is pleasant, the trees have blossoms, and migrant birds are arriving—even better, the antelope herds begin to drop their young. In April the temperature is also fine, many of the migrant birds are still around, and the annual rutting season has begun, when males compete for the right to mate with females.

What to Pack

Just because you're going to Africa, don't think you can pack light cottons and nothing else. If you're heading to a private lodge, be sure to take a warm jacket, even in midsummer (December–March), since it can get mighty cold on an exposed Land Rover at 8 PM. All lodges provide blankets on their vehicles, but that's often not enough. In winter, consider bringing along an industrial heater, too, or you'll freeze in the early morning air.

National Parks and Game Reserves

If you picture yourself bouncing across the golden plains of Africa in an old Land Rover in pursuit of big game, South Africa's national parks will disappoint you. They bear less resemblance to the Serengeti than to America's national parks: they are superbly managed, frequently overcrowded, and a little too civilized. You could tour Kruger National Park in a Porsche if you so desired. Many of the park roads are paved, and rangers even set up speed traps to nail overzealous game-watchers (take your car off-road and the dung will really hit the fan). Signposts throughout the park direct visitors to everything from scenic viewpoints to picnic sites and rest areas selling soft drinks and snacks.

It's no wonder, then, that foreign visitors sometimes act like they're in a giant petting zoo. In recent years an Asian tourist was eaten when he left his car to hug some cuddly lions, and a European's rental car was turned into Swiss cheese when he drove too close to an elephant and her calf. South Africa's game reserves may impose a veneer of domesticity on the wilderness, but underneath it's the same raw, violent Africa you see on National Geographic specials.

The national parks look the way they do for good reason: They are the country's natural heritage, set up for the use and enjoyment of its citizens, which until recently meant whites only. For white South African families, a trip to a game reserve is an annual rite, as certain as death and taxes. We're talking load up the station wagon, cram the kids into the back, and drive, baby, drive. On December weekends, Kruger's rest camps look like they're on fire because of all the barbecue smoke. One reason for this popularity is their affordability: a couple probably won't pay more than R300 per night to stay in a rest camp.

Until recently, foreign tourists comprised an insignificant minority of visitors to the national parks, and if they didn't like what they found they could just lump it. That attitude is changing, but South Africa's game parks are still not geared to foreign tourists and their needs. Accommodations in the park rest camps are cheap, comfortable, and numbingly institutional. In Kruger, the National Parks Board symbol—the head of a kudu bull—is plastered over everything from your towel to the sheets to the bathroom walls. All the camps are fenced against the animals, and some have better facilities than small towns: gas stations, mechanics, grocery stores, launderette, cafeterias, restaurants—even a car wash. And the restaurants' food tends to be mediocre. Not surprisingly, many foreign tourists shy away from the rest camps in favor of luxury hotels on the park fringes.

It would be the biggest mistake of your trip, though, to write off the public parks. Few people can afford to stay in the exclusive private lodges more than a few days, and the game reserves offer visitors a chance to explore some of Africa's richest and most beautiful country at a fraction of the cost, especially if you drive yourself. Armed with a good field guide to wildlife, you can learn an enormous amount about African game from the driver's seat of a rental car.

It does take time to develop your ability to find motionless game in thick bush. On the first day you're less likely to spot an animal than to run it over. All those fancy stripes and tawny colors really do work. Slowly, though, you learn to recognize the small clues that give away an animal in the bush: the flick of a tail, the toss of a horn, even fresh dung. To see any of this, you have to drive *slowly*, 15–25 kph (10–15 mph). Fight the urge to pin back your ears and tear around a park at 50 kph (30 mph) hoping to find something big. The only way to spot game at that speed is if it's standing in the road or if you come upon a scrum of cars already at a sighting. But remember that being the 10th car at a game-sighting is less exciting than finding the animal yourself. Not only do the other cars detract from the experience, but you feel like a scavenger—a sort of voyeuristic vulture.

The best time to find game is in the early morning and early evening, when the animals are most active. During the heat of the day most of the game retreats into thick bush to find shade. So should you. Rest camp gates open around 5 AM in summer, and you should hit the road soon after that.

An indispensable aid is a good park map, showing not only the roads but also the location of watering holes, different ecozones, and the types of animals you can expect to find in each. It's no good driving around open grassland searching for black rhino when the lumbering browsers are miles away in a woodland region. You can buy these maps when you enter a park or at rest camp shops, and it would be a foolish economy to pass them up.

When planning your day's game drive, plot your route around as many water holes and rivers as possible. Except during the height of the summer rains, most game must come to permanent water sources to drink. In winter, when the land is at its most parched, a tour of water holes is bound to reap great rewards. Even better, take a picnic lunch along and park at the same watering hole for several hours. Not only will you see plenty of animals, but you'll find yourself slipping into the drama of the bush. Has that kudu seen the huge crocodile? What's making the impala nervous? What's that sitting on my car?

In South Africa, Kruger, Hluhluwe-Umfolozi, and Pilanesberg are the only national parks that have the Big Five. In Zimbabwe and Botswana, the national parks in which all five of these most threatening animals are most readily viewable are Hwange and Chobe.

Private Game Reserves and Lodges

You never forget your first kill. Mine was at night with three other tourists. We were trailing a pride of 13 lions padding single-file through thick bush. We battled to keep up in an open Land Rover, picking our way around rocks and flattening scrub that blocked our advance. Murderous thorns scraped the side of the vehicle, forcing us to duck again and again. Ahead, another Land Rover's spotlight caught the reflected glow of impala eyes and the rangers immediately doused their lights to avoid blinding the jittery antelope. We edged forward in the weak moonlight, tracing the outline of the lead lioness as she slunk closer and closer to the herd. When she charged, we all heard the thump of contact, the cry of a panicked impala, then silence. The arrival of the rest of the pride set off a free-for-all of slashing claws, snarling, and ripping flesh. The impala was devoured in seconds. It was cruel, it was thrilling—it was Africa. And it's the kind of experience that only a private lodge can offer.

No lodge can *guarantee* you a kill, but nowhere are your chances of seeing one better. And even if you don't witness this elemental spectacle, you will come within spitting distance of more animals than you imagined possible: hyenas in a den, an elephant herd, wild dogs on the prowl,

even a leopard with her cubs. Most lodges will show you the Big Five in three days or less.

These game lodges are not zoos or a Disney Africa. Most reviewed here are either in a national park or abutting one with no fence in between. You can get close to the animals only because, after many years of exposure, they no longer see the game vehicles as a threat. That doesn't mean they don't sometimes object to your presence: an elephant charge will clear out more than your sinuses.

The quality of the game-viewing is obviously the major attraction of a private game lodge, but the appeal goes far beyond that. These lodges also sell exclusivity, and many of them go out of their way to unite shameless luxury and bush living—the sense that you really are living in the African wilds. Camps are all unfenced, so animals (including lion and elephant) can and do wander through the camp. Thatch roofs, mosquito nets, and mounted trophies add to the ambience, although more and more lodges are now opting for luxury East African safari tents to provide that extra bush touch. Dinners are served in an open-air boma (traditional thatched dining hut). On game drives the ranger will stop at a scenic viewpoint so you can enjoy a gin and tonic with the sunset. If you stay more than two days, most lodges will also serve a bush *braai*, a full barbecue spread out in the veld, with hurricane lanterns hanging in the thorn trees, a crackling fire, and the sounds of Africa all around you. Under a full moon, it's incredibly romantic.

Make no mistake, you pay for all this pampering. Expect to spend anywhere from R2,300–R6,500 (US$500 to US$1,400) per couple per night. All meals and game drives are included (although for that kind of money they should probably throw in a buffalo as well). A visit to one of these lodges will be your single biggest expense on a trip to southern Africa. If you can afford it, a three-night stay is ideal, but two nights are usually sufficient to see the big game.

The time you spend at a private lodge is tightly structured. With some exceptions, the lodges offer almost identical programs of events. An early morning game drive is followed by breakfast and a short bush walk. After lunch, many people sleep or swim until tea before heading out for the evening or nighttime game drive. Dinner is usually served around 9.

During the four-hour game drives, you'll sit on tiered benches in open, four-wheel-drive vehicles. Depending on the lodge, the vehicle will seat anywhere from 6 to 10 guests. The rear bench has the best view, but it's tough to hear the ranger from the back, and you spend a lot of time ducking thorn branches. You're better off on the first bench where you can talk easily with the ranger.

On game drives, rangers at bigger camps stay in contact with one another via radio. If one finds a rhino, for example, he relays its location to the others so they can bring their guests to have a look. It's a double-edged sword. The more vehicles you have in the field, the more wildlife everyone is likely to see. At the same time, too many vehicles create a rush-hour effect that can destroy the whole atmosphere—and the environment. In choosing a game lodge, remember to check how much land a lodge can traverse and how many vehicles they use.

The low-traffic alternative to drives is bushwalks with armed guides.

For better or worse, the quality of your bush experience depends most heavily on your guide or game ranger. He is your host for your entire stay: taking you on game drives, often eating meals with you, taking responsibility for both finding the animals and explaining their habits and behavior—and if you're on foot keeping you alive in the presence of excitable elephant, buffalo, hippopotamus, and lion. A good guide will have you lauding the glories of Africa; a bad one just makes the bill look bigger.

The vast majority of rangers are white and male. Many have degrees in wildlife management, but they are just as often hired for their looks and charm. The image of the great white hunter with a deep tan and khaki uniform is still a major crowd-pleaser. Unfortunately, some of them believe in their own press. Being driven around the bush by a pair of testicles with a rifle gets old very quickly, so don't hesitate to request another ranger. Thankfully, most rangers are personable, knowledgeable, and devoted to conservation. The turnover rate is so high, however, that it's impossible in this book to recommend a particular ranger at a specific lodge. The best you can do is select a lodge that has a proven ranger-training program.

If you are lucky enough to get a black guide or ranger, you'll find that in addition to seeing and learning about animals and plants, you will hear about local native cultures and their traditional relationships with the land and its creatures—don't hesitate to ask if this is your interest. This link with traditional cultures adds immeasurably to an experience of Africa. In some parks, where local villages are nearby—Zimbabwe's Matobo for example—guides can take you to settlements where people are living much as they have for centuries.

At the end of your stay, you are expected to tip both the ranger and the tracker, who monitors the animal spoor from a seat mounted on the front of the vehicle. These trackers are invariably blacks who grew up in the area and know the bush intimately. Some of them become rangers, but few speak English well enough to communicate the extraordinary wealth of their knowledge. Tipping guidelines vary from lodge to lodge, but plan to give the local equivalents of about US$6 per person per day to the ranger and not much less to the tracker; an additional tip of US$25 for the general staff would be sufficient for a couple staying two days.

All lodges arrange transfers from nearby airports, train stations, or dropoff points, as the case may be. In more remote areas, most have their own private airstrips carved out of the bush and fly guests in on chartered aircraft at extra cost. If you're driving yourself, the lodge will send you detailed instructions, since many dirt back roads don't appear on maps and lack names.

–By Andrew Barbour

THE LONG ROAD HOME

I TOOK THE LONG WAY HOME, stealing a year with my wife to drive from Britain to South Africa in an old Land Rover. It was a lifelong dream, a chance to see what lay between Kipling's "great grey-green, greasy Limpopo" and the shifting sands of the Sahara.

When we finally crossed Beit Bridge, the border post between Zimbabwe and South Africa, we felt like we had driven out of Africa into the United States. A smartly dressed immigration official used a computer and bar code to register our entry, and a Kentucky Fried Chicken—the first in a strip of fast-food franchises and gas stations—greeted our arrival in the town of Messina.

As a South African, I shouldn't have been surprised, but months of traveling had altered my perceptions and expectations. This was not the Africa I had recently come to know—of drunk soldiers, officials on the take, and a decaying colonial infrastructure. Yet it *was* undeniably Africa, the stubby tail of a continent linked by history, geography, and blood. And therein lies the great riddle of this country. South Africa occupies a bizarre middle ground, caught between the First World modernity of the West and Africa—poor, addled Africa. And no one's quite sure which way it will go.

At first glance, South Africa seems to be a developed country. Its cities are forests of glass towers, the roads are all immaculately paved; you'll see more cellular phones in Johannesburg than in New York, and its number of BMWs and Mercedeses is probably second only to Germany's.

Yet just a few kilometers from where chlorinated, fluoridated water sparkles out of hotel faucets, black women and children queue for hours at a community's sole tap, waiting their turn to fill large buckets, hoist them onto their heads, and begin the long trek home. The juxtaposition of wealth and poverty is mind-blowing. The majority of South Africa's 31 million blacks live in pockets of poverty where electricity and basic sanitation are luxuries, and entire communities are constructed from corrugated iron, cardboard, and old tires.

Unless you actively seek it, you might not see this side of South Africa, hidden from view by the old Nationalist government. Occasionally, from the windows of a speeding car, you may glimpse a blur of blowing trash, mangy dogs, and ramshackle hovels. You can even take a tour to see black townships like Soweto and Crossroads, once-familiar names from the nightly news. But for the most part, your experience in South Africa will be a white one. Despite a black majority of nearly six to one, the people you meet, the food you eat, and the hotels where you sleep are likely to be products of European culture. Most blacks you encounter will be waiters, porters, game trackers, and bus drivers.

The April 1994 elections were supposed to change all that and to usher in a new era of democracy in South Africa, of black political power and freedom. And as far as the foreign press and most outside observers were concerned, it did. For them, the election was the climax—and the resolution—of the South African problem. They patted themselves on the back for a job well done, packed their bags, and left. Chalk one up for the good guys. The truth is that the election represented only the end of the beginning. While the rest of the world celebrated its good deed, the citizens of South Africa were left grappling with a whole new set of political realities.

For me, nothing captured the nuances of the new political landscape better than a small plate I bought while traveling in the Drakensberg mountains. Crafted by a semiliterate black artist, the plate depicts a group of whites and blacks standing together, but in the corner a large dog is shown attacking an approaching black. The painted caption reads: "Yes, we know that the apartheid is gone between whites and black people, but white people's dogs are still on, because when they see a black man, they want to bite him. I don't know why."

In five heady years, decades of apartheid legislation were scrapped: Gone are the hated pass laws that regulated the movement of blacks; gone is the Group Areas Act that governed where everyone could live; and, with the victory of the African National Congress (ANC) in the 1994 elections, gone is a political system that denied a voice to the country's majority. But no amount of legislation can change the savage bite of three centuries of cultural, social, and economic apartheid—a visceral reaction made up of equal parts habit and fear. You cannot change attitudes overnight.

FOR NELSON MANDELA, president of the new South Africa, the task ahead is Herculean: Bring that dog to heel, and try to dissuade aggrieved blacks from lashing out in retaliation. Whites control the lion's share of the economy, yet they make up only 12% of the population. They own the nicest homes and most of the land, drive the finest cars, and pull down the biggest salaries. Ironically, considering his 27 years of incarceration at their hands, Mandela needs the whites as much as they need him: They look to him to safeguard their interests, while he looks to them to keep Africa's most sophisticated economy humming, creating jobs and attracting foreign investment.

The pressure from blacks, who have had their noses pressed to the shop window for so long, may prove irresistible, however. Before the election, interviews showed that many blacks expected to receive a large house, a car, and good job after an ANC victory. The Reconstruction and Development Program (RDP), the government's project for rebuilding the infrastructure in black communities, did promise to build a million homes in five years, but the program is already far behind schedule. Black unemployment is at a staggering 45%–50%, and millions more make only a minimum wage. In a country where 50% of blacks are illiterate and men and women are routinely burned as witches as part of traditional beliefs, holding up pie charts of foreign investment doesn't do much good. How long before the country must face the ticklish issues of land allocation, of resources, and jobs on a mass scale?

However, the challenges facing the new South Africa cannot be boiled down to a simple issue of rich and poor, black and white. If we learned anything from the country's long years of anguish, it's that *nothing* in South Africa is ever black and white. South Africa is a mosaic of over a dozen black tribes, dominated by the Zulu, Xhosa, and Sotho peoples, each with their own proud, sometimes militaristic, traditions and culture. Throw in 3 million Afrikaners (Dutch descendants also known as Boers), 2 million English-speaking South Africans, 3 million coloreds (people of mixed descent), and a million Indians, and the former Yugoslavia begins to look positively homogeneous.

In KwaZulu-Natal Province, the competing Zulu-dominated Inkatha Freedom Party (IFP) and the ANC have already eschewed the ballot box in favor of spears, knives, and automatic weapons, and hundreds of people have died since the election. You don't have to look far to see the results of such freelance politicking. Africa is littered with the failed examples of countries that started out on the road to democracy, only to end up blindsided by tribalism, ignorance, and greed.

Only a rapid rise in the standard of living can head off an increase in such strife and curb a spiraling crime rate. For better or worse, the government is looking to America for examples of how to integrate blacks into the upper strata of the work force. And, as in America, the solutions have opened a can of worms that seethes with issues of injustice, entitlement, and merit. Affirmative action is the program du jour, and the English-language newspapers are filled with familiar stories of underqualified blacks taking jobs from whites, and of lowering admission standards at elite universities. Among young whites, many of whom voted for democracy, there is a growing sense of despair that no jobs are open to them, and renewed talk of emigration.

Where South Africa differs from America, however, is in its willingness to confront these issues head-on. Race is not the minefield that it is in the United States. There are no sacred cows or sugarcoated code words. South Africans—white, black, Indian, and colored—have lived with issues of race for so long that they speak of it with a candor that makes Americans squirm.

This is, after all, a country that has made a cottage industry out of racial discord. South Africa's entire world of arts and letters has drawn its inspiration from the cauldron of conflict. Writers like Mark Mathabane, Alan Paton, Nadine Gordimer, André Brink, and Athol Fugard all won international recognition with their stories of South Africa's racially warped society.

Ironically, the ANC victory in 1994 punctured this high-flying balloon, and South Africa's politically charged culture has lost much of its air. South Africans, so long denied a window on the outside world, have increasingly turned abroad for their cultural fix. Today, the worst exports of American and Australian TV clutter the screens, and you're as likely to see NBA basketball highlights as cricket, the national summer sport. In the townships, blacks espouse black American styles of dress, and one of the largest gangs in the townships around Cape Town is known as the Americans. Chicago Bulls caps are hot items, and American accents flood the airwaves, even when they're pushing South African products. The influx of imports threatens to smother post-apartheid culture in its infancy.

Although its present scale is unprecedented, American cultural influence is nothing new in South Africa. In the 1940s and '50s, my mother would religiously head to the cinema each week to see the latest Hollywood offering. The English-speaking population, in particular, has long looked to America and Britain for its cultural connections, never quite prepared to sever its ties in favor of an identity rooted in Africa alone. The Afrikaners, descendants of the first Dutch settlers who arrived in South Africa in 1652, called us *soutpiels,* literally "salt dicks," an obscene pejorative referring to settlers with one foot in Africa and the other in Britain, straddling the sea.

MY FAMILY GOES BACK eight generations in South Africa. I am African as much as any white in the United States is American. Yet there is no denying that Afrikaners have a stronger tie to the country than most English South Africans. They have shed more blood for it, and their history is tied to the land. Theirs is the stuff of pioneer legend—of guiding ox-drawn wagons over treacherous mountain passes, of forging a place for themselves out of the hot sands. The Afrikaners are often called the White Tribe of Africa, a hard, resilient people who give no quarter and expect none in return. On an African scale, they are modern-day Zulu who vanquished all the tribes around them, just as Shaka's warriors had done a century before.

The English, by contrast, were traditionally traders and businessmen, out of touch—like any urban dweller—with the rhythms of the land. Perhaps that is why so many English-speaking South Africans emigrated when the heat was on, when South Africa seemed to melt before our very eyes. Our departure stemmed not from some failed sense of belonging but a lack of connectedness. The Boers were tied to the land—they could not, would not leave. We were tied only to our trades.

My family left South Africa—twice. The first time, the ache of homesickness brought us back only to have the country's political woes drive us out again. For thousands of South Africans, the decision to leave was one of the most gut-wrenching of their lives. Even today, we return from visits to South Africa laden with specialties like fish paste and *biltong* (jerky), not just for the taste but its sheer familiarity, its link to a past that we sloughed off only reluctantly. The former head of the South African Tourism Office in New York confided that she used to run for cover whenever an expatriate wandered in seeking a familiar accent and shared memories.

It *is* hard for South African expatriates to close the door on the past. A few times each year, a day will dawn in New York or London that possesses the clarity of crystal, as if the day had been struck on a tuning fork. In that clarion perfection, the trucks and cars sound different, even the bark of a dog is amplified, and we're pulled back to Johannesburg, a mile high and a million miles away, and the memory of it is almost painful.

During my latest trip back, everyone asked the same question: "Are you going to move back?" I wanted to say yes, that I would return tomorrow. But I am now an American citizen, have an American wife, and have forged too many ties to the United States. If I were to go back, I would find myself toting jars of salsa and brownie mixes with the same religious fervor with which I now carry fish paste. Like so many South Africans, I'm caught in limbo, the *soutpiel* of the '90s, one leg in the New World and the other in the new South Africa.

For black South African emigrés, the circumstances of their departure were far more dire: Face prison or death, or flee. In Lusaka and Gaborone, thousands of black exiles—members of the ANC—found temporary refuge from the long arm of the South African government. Theirs was not an emigration, but a strategic retreat—a fallback from where they all vowed to return. And return they did, pouring back in the early '90s, their exultant faces telling the story as they emerged blinking from the hold of the aircraft.

I have often wondered what brings us all, white and black, back to this troubled land. It's a beautiful country for sure, "lovely beyond any singing of it," as Alan Paton wrote. But it wasn't for the scenery in the townships that the black exiles returned. What it was, and continues to be, is home, a collective experience we all share. It's strange how so much of what we remember has to do with smells: pap (maize meal) cooking in cast-iron pots, grass fires on the highveld, even the distinctive tang of the dust.

We are all bound up in these memories, and our futures are intertwined whether we like it or not. That is why the radical political fringes seem so frightening: the Pan African Congress with its previous motto of "One settler, one bullet," and the neo-Nazi AWB (Afrikaner Weerstandsbeweging) with its call for a separate white state.

The 1994 elections in South Africa were nothing less than a miracle, a second chance at redemption. And the architect of that redemption has been Nelson Mandela. Twenty-seven years of prison have left Mandela with the same burning idealism that he displayed at his trial in 1964. "I have fought against black domination and I have fought against white domination," he told the courtroom. "I have cherished the ideal of a democratic and free society in which all persons live together in harmony and with equal opportunities. It is an ideal which I hope to live for and achieve. But if needs be, it is an ideal for which I am prepared to die."

He is a true statesman, perhaps the most imposing leader on the planet. And, ominously, the future of the country rides on shoulders visibly weakened by advancing years and a life of deprivation. No one in South Africa commands the respect and affection of South Africans like Mandela, and what will happen when he is gone is anyone's guess.

Nothing illustrated Mandela's power better than the 1995 Rugby World Cup final between South Africa and New Zealand in Johannesburg. Rugby is a religion among South Africa's whites, and the new government had hinted that the Springbok, the symbol of white rugby, would be replaced after the tournament. So when President Mandela appeared at the final in the green and gold jersey of the Springboks, the crowd went berserk. His was a simple gesture, yet it spoke volumes to the predominantly white fans that packed the stadium. In turn, they responded by singing a Zulu work song and furiously waving the new South African flag. The words of the song welled up from 62,000 voices, the rich, deep sounds resounding through the stadium. It was a particularly African sound, sung by Africans who happened to be white, in appreciation of an African leader who happened to be black. Listening and watching, you could feel the nation shiver at the possibilities.

—By Andrew Barbour

ZIMBABWE: A BRIEF HISTORY

GREAT ZIMBABWE, a 13th-century stone city from which the country derives its name, holds secrets of past kingdoms and the legendary empire of the Rozvi people who ruled the area before the infiltration of external influences. There are numerous other such remnants of *madzimbabwe* (stone structures) scattered around the country, but this national monument and UNESCO World Heritage Site is the largest, and the best known.

The Rozvi rulers of the Munhumutapa empire (AD 1400–1500) are believed to have conquered and subjugated the peoples in areas extending outside of Zimbabwe's present-day borders. They traded iron implements for cloth and beads with early Portuguese explorers. Centuries later they were weakened and eventually defeated by the fleeing generals of the great Zulu king Tshaka. These people from the south intermarried with the locals—hence the influence of South African languages in the southern parts of Zimbabwe.

Shiploads of British settlers pouring into South Africa's Cape in the mid-19th century led to inevitable clashes with Afrikaner settlers of Dutch origin who had been in South Africa since the 17th century. The ensuing scramble for gold and diamonds saw the creation of Cecil John Rhodes' British South Africa Company, which became so powerful that it sponsored the occupation of Rhodesia (Zimbabwe) on behalf of the British government at the end of the 19th century. The last king of the southern Ndebele people, Lobengula—his father Mzilikazi fled from Tshaka and conquered what is still known as Matabeleland—is credited with having "sold" his country to Rhodes through the notorious Rudd Concession. Many modern historians believe that Lobengula was hoodwinked into signing an agreement that was intentionally mistranslated for him, and that he would have surely rejected had he known its contents. The result was a restless British occupation that lasted almost a century, with suspicion and racial tension culminating in a bitter and bloody revolution in the 1970s, and political independence for blacks in 1980.

Initial native uprisings, led by spiritual leaders Ambuya Nehanda and Sekuru Kaguvi at the end of the 19th century, offered stiff resistance to colonial settlement in the northern Mashonaland area. But after the British arrested and executed them in 1897 for inspiring what became known as the First Chimurenga, or war of liberation, resistance lost strength for a couple of decades.

The rise of African nationalism beginning in the 1920s came in the wake of land laws that displaced the natives onto poor, unproductive "reserves," which made way for commercial farm settlements for white settlers who bought them cheaply—or in the case of the first pioneers, claimed whatever land they could stake out after riding for a day. Landlessness, by the country's new laws, also meant that blacks were without the right to vote.

Rhodesia soon became the wealthiest country in central Africa, and soon a federation of British colonies in central Africa was mooted. This brought together Northern Rhodesia (Zambia), and Southern Rhodesia and Nyasaland (Malawi), and in 1953, the Federation of Rhodesia and Nyasaland under the jurisdiction of a British governor was born.

Ten years later, this arrangement was proving unprofitable for the Southern Rhodesians, and under Prime Minister Ian Smith they broke away from British rule and declared themselves independent. International pressure against Rhodesia's unilateral Declaration of Independence only spurred on the groups of African nationalists, who took the opportunity to press for political equality for blacks.

By the 1970s the Second Chimurenga had intensified, and come 1979, a settlement with the more moderate Methodist Bishop Abel Muzorewa brought about the short-lived Zimbabwe-Rhodesia—a transitional puppet government. After independence from Britain and black rule returned in 1980, an internal crisis arose in the southern Ndebele-speaking parts of the country and lasted through the decade. This divided Zimbabwe along tribal-political lines that sprang from long-standing differences between Shona and Ndebele peoples. The Unity Accord was finally brokered in 1989, bringing together the two main rival parties, the Shona-dominated ZANU PF (Zimbabwe African National Union Patriotic Front) and the Ndebele ZAPU (Zimbabwe African People's Union). Veteran nationalist and ZAPU leader Joshua Nkomo was made state vice-president together with former deputy prime minister Simon Muzenda under the still-incumbent president and war hero, Robert Mugabe. Since then, the new united ZANU PF has maintained a strong hold on Zimbabwean life.

Despite the rocky '70s and '80s, the country's agro-based economy—tobacco and maize being the principal crops—has continued to expand. And education policy has been very successful; so much so that there are more high school and college graduates than the job market can absorb. This is why economic planners are beating the tourism drum with such enthusiasm—they believe that a labor-intensive industry such as tourism could alleviate some of the country's unemployment woes. The potential is great indeed: Zimbabwe has some of Africa's best attractions within its borders, yet the world knows little about it.

Because the tourism industry has to report to a government ministry, there is real pressure to assist black entry into what is perceived to be a lucrative and at the moment fashionable industry. This is a good thing. And now more than at any other time in the history of the country's tourism, black Zimbabweans are involved in tourism projects, sometimes on their own, and sometimes as joint partners with whites. The benefit of this is a more racially representative experience of Zimbabwe for travelers in the wild, where safari companies used to be primarily white-run.

–By June Muchemenyi

BOOKS AND VIDEOS

Books

History and Politics

For 45 years, South Africa's political and historical writing focused on the issues of apartheid. With the democratic elections of 1994, much of that writing lost its relevance or, at the very least, became badly dated. Since then, a stream of hastily compiled histories has appeared, as have some long-awaited autobiographies and personal accounts. Foremost among these is *Long Walk to Freedom,* by Nelson Mandela. An inspiring account of the triumph of idealism, the book looks back over Mandela's life and also takes a pragmatic view of the difficult political road ahead—it should be required reading for South Africans and visitors alike. *Rainbow People of God* tells the story of another of the heroes of the anti-apartheid movement, Archbishop Desmond Tutu, through his speeches, sermons, and letters from 1976 to 1994.

One pre-apartheid book that survived the transition to democracy is *My Traitor's Heart,* by Rian Malan, an Afrikaner journalist who worked as a crime reporter for a South African newspaper. Notable for its searing honesty, the book apportions blame for South Africa's problems on everyone. Disgusted with the simplistic portrayal of South Africa's agony in black and white terms, Malan reveals the infinite shades of gray that color almost every issue-shades that the election has not washed away.

A classic and very readable study of the San (Bushmen), Elizabeth Marshall Thomas's *The Harmless People* describes the traditional ways of this culture endangered by the intrusion of industrial civilization. *Frontiers: The Epic of South Africa's Creation and the Tragedy of the Xhosa People,* by Noël Mostert, is an immense book covering an immense range of time. It tells of an important, little known chapter in the transition from the old world to modernity hinging as so often it did on a clash of races.

Fiction

South African writers have drawn steadily from the well of racial injustice to produce some of the finest literature of the 20th century. One of the first such novels may also be the best: Alan Paton's *Cry the Beloved Country* (1948). The story of a black father who heads to the city to save his son from execution for murder, the book contains writing of such breathtaking beauty and emotion that you find yourself reading passages again and again. In *Kaffir Boy,* Mark Mathabane paints a stark picture of life under apartheid from a black perspective. The title of the book itself is intended to shock-in South African vernacular, "kaffir" is the stinging equivalent of "nigger." Nadine Gordimer, who won the Nobel Prize for Literature in 1991, is known both for her short stories and her novels, including *July's People,* an account of a black servant who shelters his white employers when South Africa is consumed by civil war. Other major writers include J.M. Coetzee (*The Life and Times of Michael K, Waiting for the Barbarians,* and other books), winner of the Booker Prize; Athol Fugard (*Master Harold . . . and the boys, Boesman and Lena*), South Africa's most famous playwright and, for many years, a voice of sanity in the wilderness of apartheid; and André Brink (*An Act of Terror*).

South African writing has far more to offer than the carcass of apartheid, however. Until the turn of the century, South Africa was a wild frontier of marauding animals, gold rushes, and exotic diseases. No book captures this pioneer excitement better than *Jock of the Bushveld,* by Sir Percy Fitzpatrick. Set in the late 19th century, this classic of South African literature follows the exploits of Jock, a fearless Staffordshire terrier, in the untamed bush of the Eastern Transvaal.

A short-story writer who captured the slow, measured life of Afrikaner farmers and early settlers is Herman Charles Bosman. Laced with humor and irony, Bosman's stories recapture a time in South Africa's history when survival was a triumph and religion a necessary crutch.

Bosman's stories are now available in a variety of anthologies.

Lost World of the Kalahari, by Laurens van der Post, mentor to Britain's Prince Charles, is a fascinating mix of fact and fantasy, recalling the author's expedition into the Kalahari Desert after World War II to study the Bushmen (San). The book has a mystical, religious quality befitting a people who live in complete harmony with nature.

Videos

Most movies about South Africa focus on the tragedy of apartheid. In the latest offering, James Earl Jones follows in the footsteps of Sidney Poitier in a remake of Alan Paton's classic *Cry the Beloved Country. Cry Freedom,* starring Denzel Washington and Kevin Kline, follows the story of journalist Donald Woods and Steve Biko, a prominent black activist who was murdered in police custody in Port Elizabeth. *A Dry White Season,* with a cameo appearance by Marlon Brando, is another heavy-hitting apartheid drama. *Breaker Morant,* a superbly crafted Australian movie about the Boer War (1899–1902), looks at British military hypocrisy through the eyes of three Australian soldiers on trial for shooting Boer prisoners. *Zulu,* starring Michael Caine, is a jingoistic but gripping retelling of the Battle of Rorke's Drift, during the Zulu War of 1879. The movie spawned several other Zulu movies, among them *Zulu Dawn* and *Shaka Zulu.* The South African movie industry, although in its infancy, has produced one major hit, *The Gods Must be Crazy,* the enchanting story of a San (Bushman) clan in the Kalahari Desert.

INDEX

NOTES

NOTES

NOTES

NOTES

Fodor's Travel Publications

Available at bookstores everywhere, or call 1–800–533–6478, 24 hours a day.

Gold Guides

U.S.

Alaska	Florida	New Orleans	Seattle & Vancouver
Arizona	Hawai'i	New York City	The South
Boston	Las Vegas, Reno, Tahoe	Pacific North Coast	U.S. & British Virgin Islands
California		Philadelphia & the Pennsylvania Dutch Country	
Cape Cod, Martha's Vineyard, Nantucket	Los Angeles		USA
	Maine, Vermont, New Hampshire	The Rockies	Virginia & Maryland
The Carolinas & Georgia	Maui & Lāna'i	San Diego	Walt Disney World, Universal Studios and Orlando
Chicago	Miami & the Keys	San Francisco	
Colorado	New England	Santa Fe, Taos, Albuquerque	Washington, D.C.

Foreign

Australia	Europe	Montréal & Québec City	Scotland
Austria	Florence, Tuscany & Umbria	Moscow, St. Petersburg, Kiev	Singapore
The Bahamas			South Africa
Belize & Guatemala	France	The Netherlands, Belgium & Luxembourg	South America
Bermuda	Germany		Southeast Asia
Canada	Great Britain		Spain
Cancún, Cozumel, Yucatán Peninsula	Greece	New Zealand	Sweden
	Hong Kong	Norway	Switzerland
Caribbean	India	Nova Scotia, New Brunswick, Prince Edward Island	Thailand
China	Ireland		Toronto
Costa Rica	Israel	Paris	Turkey
Cuba	Italy	Portugal	Vienna & the Danube Valley
The Czech Republic & Slovakia	Japan	Provence & the Riviera	
	London		
Eastern & Central Europe	Madrid & Barcelona	Scandinavia	
	Mexico		

Special-Interest Guides

Adventures to Imagine	Fodor's Gay Guide to the USA	Halliday's New Orleans Food Explorer	Rock & Roll Traveler USA
Alaska Ports of Call	Fodor's How to Pack	Healthy Escapes	Sunday in San Francisco
Ballpark Vacations	Great American Learning Vacations	Kodak Guide to Shooting Great Travel Pictures	Walt Disney World for Adults
Caribbean Ports of Call			
The Complete Guide to America's National Parks	Great American Sports & Adventure Vacations	National Parks and Seashores of the East	Weekends in New York
Disney Like a Pro	Great American Vacations	National Parks of the West	Wendy Perrin's Secrets Every Smart Traveler Should Know
Europe Ports of Call	Great American Vacations for Travelers with Disabilities	Nights to Imagine	
Family Adventures		Rock & Roll Traveler Great Britain and Ireland	Worldwide Cruises and Ports of Call

Fodor's Special Series

Fodor's Best Bed & Breakfasts

America

California

The Mid-Atlantic

New England

The Pacific Northwest

The South

The Southwest

The Upper Great Lakes

Compass American Guides

Alaska

Arizona

Boston

Chicago

Colorado

Hawaii

Idaho

Hollywood

Las Vegas

Maine

Manhattan

Minnesota

Montana

New Mexico

New Orleans

Oregon

Pacific Northwest

San Francisco

Santa Fe

South Carolina

South Dakota

Southwest

Texas

Utah

Virginia

Washington

Wine Country

Wisconsin

Wyoming

Citypacks

Amsterdam

Atlanta

Berlin

Chicago

Florence

Hong Kong

London

Los Angeles

Montréal

New York City

Paris

Prague

Rome

San Francisco

Tokyo

Venice

Washington, D.C.

Exploring Guides

Australia

Boston & New England

Britain

California

Canada

Caribbean

China

Costa Rica

Egypt

Florence & Tuscany

Florida

France

Germany

Greek Islands

Hawaii

Ireland

Israel

Italy

Japan

London

Mexico

Moscow & St. Petersburg

New York City

Paris

Prague

Provence

Rome

San Francisco

Scotland

Singapore & Malaysia

South Africa

Spain

Thailand

Turkey

Venice

Flashmaps

Boston

New York

San Francisco

Washington, D.C.

Fodor's Gay Guides

Los Angeles & Southern California

New York City

Pacific Northwest

San Francisco and the Bay Area

South Florida

USA

Pocket Guides

Acapulco

Aruba

Atlanta

Barbados

Budapest

Jamaica

London

New York City

Paris

Prague

Puerto Rico

Rome

San Francisco

Washington, D.C.

Languages for Travelers (Cassette & Phrasebook)

French

German

Italian

Spanish

Mobil Travel Guides

America's Best Hotels & Restaurants

California and the West

Major Cities

Great Lakes

Mid-Atlantic

Northeast

Northwest and Great Plains

Southeast

Southwest and South Central

Rivages Guides

Bed and Breakfasts of Character and Charm in France

Hotels and Country Inns of Character and Charm in France

Hotels and Country Inns of Character and Charm in Italy

Hotels and Country Inns of Character and Charm in Paris

Hotels and Country Inns of Character and Charm in Portugal

Hotels and Country Inns of Character and Charm in Spain

Short Escapes

Britain

France

New England

Near New York City

Fodor's Sports

Golf Digest's Places to Play

Skiing USA

USA Today The Complete Four Sport Stadium Guide

WHEREVER YOU TRAVEL, *H*ELP IS NEVER FAR AWAY.

From planning your trip to providing travel assistance
along the way, American Express® Travel Service Offices
are always there to help you do more.

South Africa

American Express Travel Service
Thibault House, Thibault Square
6761 Roggebaai
Cape Town
21/215-586

American Express Travel Service
2 Durban Club Place
Durban
31/301-5541

American Express Travel Service Office
Everite House
20 DeKorte Street
Johannesburg
11/339-4881

American Express Travel Service Office
Shop U20, Upper Level 6
Sandton Sun Shopping Mall
Johannesburg
11/883-1316

American Express Travel Service Office
Shop 2, Penny Lane Centre
Corner Penny Lane & Old Pretoria Road
Midrand
11/315-8330

American Express Travel Service
Pamela Arcade, 2nd Avenue
Newton Park
Port Elizabeth
41/351-225

American Express Travel Service
Shop 129, 1st Floor, Tram Shed
288 Van Der Walt Street
Pretoria
12/322-2620

American Express Travel Service Office
Suite 1, Medprax Centre
Haiti Parking Lot No. 5
Richards Bay
351/41326

do more · AMERICAN EXPRESS

Travel

http://www.americanexpress.com/travel

**American Express Travel Service Offices are
located throughout South Africa.**